THE JOHN CARROLL PAPERS

VOLUME 1•1755-1791

John Carroll (1735-1815)

THE

John Carroll

PAPERS

VOLUME 1 • 1755–1791

Thomas O'Brien Hanley, S.J.

EDITOR

UNDER THE AUSPICES OF
The American Catholic Historical Association

ENDORSED BY THE
National Historical Publications and Records Commission

UNIVERSITY OF NOTRE DAME PRESS
NOTRE DAME   LONDON

280.092
C 319
V. 1

Library of Congress Cataloging in Publication Data

Carroll, John, Abp., 1735-1815.
  The John Carroll papers.
  Bibliography: p.
  Includes index.
  1. Carroll, John, Abp., 1735-1815. 2. Catholic
Church in the United States—Collected works. 3. United
States—Politics and government—Revolution, 1775-1783—
Collected works. I. Hanley, Thomas O'Brien.
BX4705.C33A34   282'.092'4 [B]   75-19879
ISBN 0-268-01186-9

TO THE MEMORY OF

The Reverend Charles H. Metzger, S.J.

(1890–1972) JOHN CARROLL UNIVERSITY

Editorial Staff

Contents

Illustrations

Acknowledgments

EDITING

Auspices: American Catholic Historical Association.

Collaborators: The John Carroll Committee of the American Catholic Historical Association: Harry J. Browne, William D. Hoyt, Jr., Annabelle M. Melville, and Charles H. Metzger.

Assistants: Elizabeth King McKeown (1969–70); Dianne Francesconi Lyon (1970); Frances Panchok-Berry (1971); Frances Dowling (1972, 1975).

Patronage: The Society of Jesus (Wisconsin Province, for the Editor's contributed services); The Raskob Foundation (Helena Springer Green, Cofounder); The Catholic University of America; American Catholic Historical Association.

Their Eminences: John Joseph Cardinal Carberry, Archbishop of St. Louis; John Cardinal Cody, Archbishop of Chicago; Terence Cardinal Cooke, Archbishop of New York; John Cardinal Dearden, Archbishop of Detroit; John Cardinal Krol, Archbishop of Philadelphia; Timothy Cardinal Manning, Archbishop of Los Angeles; Humberto Cardinal Medeiros, Archbishop of Boston; Patrick Cardinal O'Boyle, Former Archbishop of Washington, D.C.; Lawrence Cardinal Shehan, Former Archbishop of Baltimore.

The Jesuit Communities of Loyola College (Baltimore), John Carroll and Georgetown universities; The John Carroll Society of Washington, D.C., and Loyola College (Baltimore).

PUBLICATION

Auspices: National Conference of Catholic Bishops' Committee on the Bicentennial, John Cardinal Dearden, Chairman.

Patronage: The Archdiocese of Baltimore, William D. Borders, Archbishop, and Lawrence Cardinal Shehan, Former Archbishop through the generosity of Ralph and Dorothy DeChiaro Foundation; Knott Foundation; Henry and Marion Knott Catholic Community Fund; The Thomas F. and Clementine L. Mullan Foundation; John J. Raskob Foundation for Catholic Activities, Inc.; The Archdiocese of Baltimore: Annunciation, St. Clement, St. Francis of Assisi, Holy Trinity Monastery, Immaculate Conception, Immaculate Heart of Mary, St. Joseph Monastery, St. Mark, Maryland Chapter I.F.C.A., St. Michael, Most Precious Blood, Our Lady of Hope, St. Pius X, Sisters of St. Joseph (Chestnut Hill), St. Ursula, (all of Baltimore); St. Mary (Annapolis), St. Stephen (Bradshaw), Sacred Heart (Glyndon), St. Ignatius (Hickory), Our Lady of the Fields (Millersville), St. Jane Frances de Chantal (Riviera Beach), St. John the Evangelist (Severna Park), and St. Mary Magdalen (Maitland Park, Fla.).

LIBRARIANS, ARCHIVISTS, SCHOLARS AND OTHERS

The Mullan Library of the Catholic University of America provided constant service, particularly by the assistance of Moreau B. C. Chambers, former Archivist and Carolyn P. Lee, Head of the Theology and Philosophy Division. Gratitude is expressed to Joseph E. Jeffs, Librarian of Georgetown University, George M. Barringer, Director of Special Collections, and Jon K. Reynolds, Archivist; Rev. Thomas E. Blantz, C.S.C., Archivist and Lawrence J. Bradley, Assistant Archivist, of the University of Notre Dame; Rev. Armand Gagné, Archivist of the Archdiocesan Archives of Quebec; Rev. Edmund Halsey, Archivist, the Theological College of St. Charles Borromeo; Sister John Mary, Archivist, St. Joseph's Provincial House; Rev. Michael Roach, Archivist, St. Mary's Seminary, Baltimore; Rev. John G. Reckert, Assistant Archivist and

Rev. Hugo A. Kennedy, former Archivist of the Maryland Province Archives of the Society of Jesus; and Monsignor John Tracy Ellis. The Editor is also grateful for the assistance of Rev. Peter Huizing, S.J., Rene Soudeé, Rev. Vincent T. Tanzola, S.J., Joan Mazan, Pamela Galligan, and W. Joseph Spliedt.

Special gratitude is expressed to Rev. Robert Trisco, Secretary of the American Catholic Historical Association for his counsel and support in addition to helping with manuscripts in Italian. Very Reverend Bruce F. Biever, S.J., Provincial of the Wisconsin Province of the Society of Jesus and his predecessor, Rev. Joseph D. Sheehan, S.J. continually encouraged the efforts of the Editor, for which he is grateful. The Editor also wishes to thank his friend, Rev. Joseph P. Donnelly, S.J., for his invaluable advice and fraternal support. He expresses his thanks to Oliver W. Holmes, Director Emeritus of the National Historical Publications Commission, Rev. John J. Tierney, Archivist of the Archdiocesan Archives of Baltimore and to His Eminence Lawrence Cardinal Shehan, Former Archbishop of Baltimore, for their friendly assistance and encouragement in so many ways.

The John Carroll Manuscripts

John Gilmary Shea, the pioneer historian of the Catholic Church in the United States, was the first to use the manuscripts of John Carroll in an extensive and scholarly fashion. While his published history of the Church and biography of Carroll embody many extended citations of the originals, it is now clear that he had access to only a fraction of what is presented here. The case is much the same with his successor in this role, Peter Guilday, who wrote a biography. Although primarily concerned with their published studies, both men contributed significantly to the search and ordering of John Carroll writings and those received from his correspondents. John Carroll's own care in preserving his records made possible the nucleus from which both men worked, and which is now a part of the Archdiocesan Archives of Baltimore.

Because John Carroll was identified with two institutions that have fostered the preservation of historical records, his writings have fortunately been preserved in places other than the Baltimore archive. Letters and documents related to his role as a Church official and a member of the Society of Jesus have been found in Europe and North America. The records of the Congregation of the Propagation of the Faith and of the Stonyhurst College of the Society of Jesus in England possess numerous materials, a great amount of them not available in the Baltimore drafts. The Archdiocesan Archives of Quebec, the Maryland Province Archives of the Society of Jesus, and several other Catholic institutional archives retain many items. Because of his correspondence with civic and private individuals, the National Archives and several state and local historical societies hold Carroll writings.

Several scholars, as well as Guilday, have written since Shea on various phases of Carroll's episcopate and life, using manuscripts from sources other than Baltimore, often giving extended citations from them. These in a way called attention to the need of having a published edition at hand if any fulness would be given to a presentation of Catholic life in the eighteenth and early nineteenth century. At the present time these studies indicate major problems that yet remain to be explored, and conflicting interpretations challenge resolution. The most recent biography brings many of these into focus as well as remaining problems of his life and career. There is thus a pressing need for a comprehensive presentation of all known Carroll writings.

With the growing importance assigned to religion by historians concerned with the whole of American history, the John Carroll papers have taken on additional importance. The Editor has recently shown how this is true in the case of the American Revolution.

ORIGIN OF THIS EDITION

The first half of this century saw an extensive use of manuscript materials in publications of high quality. Many of these established important, new factual knowledge which considerably enlarged standard studies on major topics of American history. Others recast and even reversed previous interpretations. After World War II learned societies of historians increasingly found their annual meetings to be platforms of heated debate about long-standing interpretations. Often the need for further manuscript exploration by more scholars was evident.

In the face of this challenge, the President of the United States entered the picture. Encouraged by officials of historical societies, he called attention to the need of a dramatic new effort at providing letterpress and other forms of publication which would make manuscripts of the past and restricted printed records more easily available to scholars and the public generally. By executive order Dwight D. Eisenhower established the National Historical Publications Commission to foster such a growth in our knowledge of America's past. The President named John Carroll among distinguished Americans of historical importance whose papers should receive this attention.

Encouraged by these developments, the American Catholic Historical Association appointed the John Carroll Committee to initiate a program to publish the writings of John Carroll. Except for the search and photoduplication of manuscripts, the members worked without financial assistance. Henry J. Browne did the initial search, acquisition of manuscript copies, and indexing; Annabelle M. Melville prepared many French texts and translations; Charles H. Metzger transcribed and translated a large number of Latin manuscripts; William D. Hoyt, Jr. transcribed many of the more important letters written before 1790. Preliminary editing was done in some cases. In 1969, when some funding was provided, the Editor was appointed and an office established at the Catholic University of America.

At this last phase it was possible to enlarge the original program, which had anticipated publishing only the more important letters of Carroll. A new search was made for manuscripts in all categories and materials prepared for their publication. A microfilm edition of recipient letters for public distribution is being prepared.

Budgets inevitably affected many of these editorial decisions. The emphasis has been upon the text of Carroll's own writings, in locating and accurately presenting them. The time and financial resources remaining after this could have been more favorable to other elements in the edition. In view of criticisms made of over-edited series and disporportionate costs, however, the practices of this edition seemed reasonable in its restrictions. For it is the text of the subject which is destined to be the matrix of the enlarged history editing envisages.

Editorial Objectives

Manuscript and other texts will be presented literally except for instances later indicated. Final manuscript versions will be preferred to drafts, but the latter will be described in any cases where they significantly add to or clarify the former. Copies, transcriptions, or printed versions will be used where an autograph source is not available. In autograph drafts only the more important deletions will be given. Photoduplicates of these manuscripts will be in the microfilm edition, and those of all material in this edition will be at Mullen Library, The Catholic University of America (Department of Archives and Manuscripts, The American Catholic Historical Association, John Carroll Papers). Foreign language texts will be in literal form (retaining errors, abbreviations, accent omissions, etc.).

Given the limitations of financial and other resources, it has seemed best to focus editorial notes on historical circumstances and persons immediately and importantly related to Carroll's life and career. Very many of these have been drawn from unpublished recipient letters and special studies not readily available, while others are from biographies of Carroll. Proper names and historical topics will be given comment only where they first appear, for the most part, the index providing a means to further inquiry in given cases. The page where name identification is made is indicated by boldface type in the index. An introduction to each volume will give additional aid to understanding the context of individual items. The chronology and genealogical chart will serve a similar purpose. Scholars and others making detailed inquiry will be assisted by the microfilm edition of recipient letters and other materials.

Editorial Practices

The position of the title, introduction and conclusion to letters will be a modification of the alignment found in the original. The title will follow a consistent form which gives the complete name and correct spelling of the addressee. Topics have been assigned to most sermons, memoranda, and documents. Carroll's own form will be stated in the manuscript description if significant.

Date and place of origin will be in the form of the original. Although these are often at the end of the letter or document, they will be placed at the beginning and to the right of the title. Where different dates are assigned to appended passages, they will occur as they do in the original.

Where "Sir," and other salutations are alone on the first line, they will be placed on the first line of the text in this edition. Polite conclusions to letters will be run continuously from the period at the end of the main body of the text. Short postscript remarks will follow them immediately except in special cases.

Misspellings that are obvious and not misleading will not have an editorial *sic,* but stand as they are. Most abbreviations by Carroll are readily understood; in the case of opening and closing remarks to letters they will become so upon reading the earliest entries where they are completed by the editor. Elsewhere they will be completed where they first occur in early items.

Manuscript descriptions will be placed immediately following the text, giving in code (see Symbols below) what kind it is and where it is located. Reasoning for assigning addressees and dates, and comments on deletions, etc., will follow.

Footnotes will make reference to related text items of the edition by date only, unless more than one item appears under the date.

Where dashes (−) clearly stand for periods ending a sentence, a period will be placed. Raised letters will be lowered, and periods under them will be placed after them. The circumflex mark indicating abbreviations in Latin and English, and occasionally in other languages, will be omitted as well as the telde. The cross before his signature is omitted.

Where paragraphs are indicated in the original by a space between sentences without indentation on a new line, a new line with indentation will be made.

Capitalizations in the text will be carried as found in the original, and underscorings as italicized type.

Short foreign-language phrases will be translated within editorial brackets in the text. Longer passages will be placed in translation in the footnotes. In a few cases the translation alone will occur in the text with the original in the footnote.

Parentheses in the text indicate that they were in the original except in a few cases where this practice is changed and explained.

Titles have been adapted for sermons, which had none in any of the original manuscripts. Because of deletions in all of them they have been designated autograph drafts (ADf) in the manuscript description.

Abbreviations and Symbols

MANUSCRIPT DESCRIPTION

ACS   Autograph copy signed
AD   Autograph document
ADf   Autograph draft
ADfS Autograph draft signed
ADS   Autograph document signed
AL   Autograph letter
ALS   Autograph letter signed
AM   Autograph memorandum
C   Contemporary manuscript copy in another hand
CS   Contemporary manuscript copy in another hand signed
D   Manuscript document in another hand of the time
DS   Manuscript document in another hand signed
LS   Letter in another hand signed
L   Letterpress version of Carroll writing
S   Summary of an item's content by another as indicated
T   Noncontemporary transcription

MANUSCRIPT DEPOSITORIES

AAB   Archdiocesan Archives of Baltimore
AAQ   Archdiocesan Archives of Quebec
AAW   Archives of the Archbishop of Washington, D.C.
ACHS American Catholic Historical Society of Philadelphia
AIPSJ Archives of the Irish Province of the Society of Jesus

ASJCH Archives of St. Joseph's Central House, Emmitsburg, Maryland
BSSP Bibliothèque des S. Sulpice, Paris
CHS Chicago Historical Society
CMB Carmelite Monastery, Baltimore
CU G Catholic University of America–Guilday Collection
GU SC Georgetown University–Shea Collection
HSP Historical Society of Pennsylvania
HU Harvard University
JCHS John Carroll High School, Washington, D.C.
JCP John Carroll Papers Committee
LC Library of Congress
LCP Library Company of Philadelphia
LP Lee Family Papers (private collection)
MC Marygrove College
MHS Maryland Historical Society
MoHS Missouri State Historical Society
MPA Maryland Province Archive of the Society of Jesus
NA National Archives
NEHGS New England Historical and Genealogical Society
NYPL New York Public Library
PF Archives of the Congregation of the Propagation of the Faith
SB Societé des Bollandistes, Holland
SMS St. Mary's Seminary Archives, Baltimore
St Stonyhurst College Archives, England
UI Indiana University
UND University of Notre Dame

SYMBOLS

[ ] Editor's interpretation and remarks.
[Jan. 1, 1800] Estimated date assigned to item.
[Addressee] Estimate of Editor.

[?]	Addressee or date unknown and cannot be estimated.
[. . .]	Missing portion of a sentence.
[. . . .]	Incomplete paragraph; when at end of text, remainder of item is missing.
[*ind.*]	Indecipherable (arrangement of letters makes no intelligible word).
[*illeg.*]	Illegible (enough letters cannot be read to make word or words intelligible).
[*blank*]	Word or words are called for, but space has no writing on it.
[*torn*]	Manuscript has missing portion of paper at this point, which is assumed to have a word or words on it.
[*fold*]	Binding or other similar condition makes portion unreadable.

COMMON TEXT ABBREVIATIONS

affte.	affectionate
Baltre.	Baltimore, Md.
Bn	brethren
Bp.	Bishop
Congn.	Congregation
Dr.	dear and Doctor
Excy	Excellency
Fr.	Father - parent or clergyman
Genl.	General
Gn	gentleman
hble.	humble
J.C.	Jesus Christ
Jts.	Jesuits
Ld.	Lord
Ldps.	Lordships
Mons.	Monsignor

Mr.	Mister or mother
Mrs.	Misses and mother superior
obdt.	obedient
Philada.	Philadelphia, Pa.
Prpgda	Propaganda (Congregation of the Propagation of the Faith)
R.C and	
R. Cats.	Roman Catholics
Scmts.	Sacraments
Sp.	spiritual
Sr.	sister (of a family)
St.	servant
V.A.	Vicar Apostolic (Plural—V.V.A.A.)
Xt. and	
Xtians.	Christian and Christians
YMOS.	Your most obedient servant
Yr.	Your

GENEALOGY

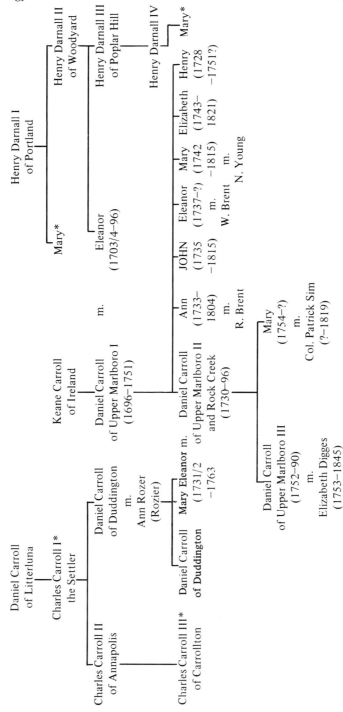

*Marriages of Darnalls into the Charles Carroll of Carrollton line.

Chronological Table

1735 Jan. 8		Birth in Upper Marlboro, Maryland, of Daniel and Eleanor (Darnall) Carroll
1746–48		At Bohemia Manor Academy, Maryland
1748 July		To St. Omer College in French Flanders
1753		To Jesuit novitiate at Watten, Flanders
1755		First vows of religion as a Jesuit
1756–57		Literary studies at Watten
1757–60		Philosophical studies at the Jesuit College in Liège
1761–65		Instructor in philosophy at Liège
1765–69		Theological studies at Liège
1769		Ordination to the priesthood
1770		Instructor at Jesuit College in Bruges
1771		Final vows as a Jesuit
		Tour of Europe to 1773 as tutor of Lord Stourton's son
1773		Prefect of the sodality at Jesuit College in Bruges
	July 21	Papal bull suppressing the Jesuits
	Oct.	Closing of college at Bruges
	Nov.	Chaplain to Lord Arundel of Wardour Castle, England
	Dec.(?)	On committee to seek indemnity for English Jesuit colleges on the continent
1774		To Rock Creek Manor, Maryland
1776 Apr.		Accompanied commission to Canada for the Continental Congress
	June	Return from Canada
		Ministry at St. John's Chapel, Forest Glen, Maryland
1782		Drafts plan for a clergy constitution

1783		Appointed to Board of Directors of Washington College, Chestertown, Maryland
1784		*Address to the Roman Catholics of the United States*
		Petition to Rome for a vicar-general
		"Form of Government, Rules for the Select Body of the Clergy, and Regulations for the Management of Plantations"
		Appointed to Board of Directors of St. John's College, Annapolis
	June 9	Made head of the missions of the United States
1785		Honorary degree from Washington College
	Mar. 1	Formal Report to Rome
1787	Dec.	Letter to *Columbian Magazine*
1788		Founding of Georgetown College
		President of the Board of Directors of St. John's College
	Sep. 7	Bull of Pius VI creating U.S. a diocese and naming Carroll first bishop
1789	Jan. 10	"Pacificus" letter by Carroll to the *United States Gazette*
	Dec.	*Address to Roman Catholics* on the presidency of George Washington
1790		Carmelite nuns organized at Port Tobacco, Maryland
	Aug. 15	Episcopal consecration by Bishop Charles Walmesley in Lulworth Castle, Dorset, England
1791	Nov.	First diocesan synod
1794		Office of coadjutor to Carroll authorized by Rome
1796		Augustinians established in Philadelphia
1798		Acquitted in courts of Pennsylvania of Holy Trinity and Westmoreland County parish trustee charges
1799		Acquitted of court charges by St. John's, Baltimore, trustee
		Founding of St. Mary's Seminary, Baltimore, and Visitation Academy, Georgetown, Maryland

1800 Feb. 2	Eulogy of George Washington at St. Peter's Church, Baltimore
Dec.	Consecration of Leonard Neale as coadjutor bishop
1801	Board director of the Female Humane Association Charity School of Baltimore
1803	President of the Board of Trustees of Baltimore College
1804	The Dominican Order of men arrives in his diocese
1805 June 21	Appoints Robert Molyneux superior of the restored (*viva voce*) Jesuits
1806 May 25	Administers the sacrament of confirmation to Elizabeth Bayley Seton
July 7	Lays cornerstone of the Cathedral of the Assumption, Baltimore
1808	St. Mary's College, Emmitsburg, Md., founded
Apr. 8	Archbishop over the sees of Philadelphia, New York, Boston and Bardstown
1809	St. Joseph's Academy, Emmitsburg, founded
1810	Consecrations as bishops of Michael Egan (Philadelphia), John Cheverus (Boston), and Benedict Flaget (Bardstown)
Nov. 15	Law of Church in the United States codified
1811 Aug. 18	Official reception of pallium of archbishop
1812	Provost of the University of Maryland position declined
	Louis Dubourg appointed apostolic administrator of Louisiana
Jan. 17	Confirmation of the Institute of the Sisters of Charity of St. Joseph's under Mother Seton
1814 Dec. 7	Papal bull restoring the Jesuits is received
1815	Louis Dubourg consecrated bishop of Louisiana
Nov. 23	Last sacraments received
Dec. 3	Death
1824	Remains placed in the Cathedral (later Basilica) of the Assumption, Baltimore

Introduction to Volume One

John Carroll is best known as the first Catholic bishop of the United States, first archbishop and the founder of the American Catholic hierarchy.

From the very beginning Carroll initiated the action which led to the formation of the first diocese of the United States. In the disordered conditions following the Revolutionary War he coordinated what clergy there were and recruited others from Europe to enlarge their ministry in the growing new nation. He led the movement in America which brought the Church its first bishop, so necessary for consolidating its life at that time. As bishop he established basic ecclesiastical law and saw to its implementation, forming the pattern upon which the Church grew thereafter. He was eminently successful in resolving problems which arose at the parish and regional level, while he established seminaries, colleges and religious communities to secure the spiritual well-being of American Catholics through those who ministered to them. When the growth and spread of the American Church to western territories took place, Carroll succeeded in creating in 1810 the independent dioceses of Philadelphia, New York, Boston and Kentucky. As archbishop and metropolitan he continued to guide the whole American Church until his death in 1815.

John Carroll was also honored with a prominent role in civil life. As a cousin of Charles Carroll of Carrollton, the only Catholic signer of the Declaration of Independence and the last of all the signers to die, he had additional entrée to the public life of the new nation. John Carroll's brother, Daniel, was prominent in the political life of those times, serving in the Continental Congress, the federal Constitutional Convention and as commissioner for the District of Columbia. But more in recognition of his own growing power of leadership, civil and cultural officials looked to John Carroll to play an important part in establishing American independence and in the founding and guiding of educational and philanthropic institutions. In the years before his death he was frequently called upon to honor patriotic occasions with his presence.

John Carroll was born of Daniel Carroll and Eleanor Darnall at Upper Marlboro, Maryland, January 8, 1735. His father was an emigrant from Ireland, where his family inheritance as well as his Catholic faith was attacked by British policy. Henry Darnall of England, the important agent of Lord Baltimore from whom Carroll's mother was descended, established a family of landed wealth through the Maryland proprietor's patronage. Charles Carroll of Carrollton later married into this same family. Catholic families originally came to Maryland for the benefits of religious freedom, but the establishment of the Church of England at the beginning of the eighteenth century deprived them of the right to vote, hold public office, and conduct public worship and their own schools.

An exception to this last discrimination was the tolerance of Bohemia Manor, in Kent County on the Eastern Shore of Maryland, where the Society of Jesus, a Catholic religious order of men known as the Jesuits, conducted a school. Here John went at the age of eleven. After two years he went to a higher Jesuit school in French Flanders, St. Omers, where he pursued the study of grammar and began his literary formation. He very soon entered the Jesuit novitiate at nearby Watten, having decided to join the religious order. He concluded his literary studies in the next few years and went to Liège in 1757 for an extended preparation for the priesthood, his ordination taking place in 1769.

The opening correspondence of John Carroll tells of the crucial situation of the Jesuits, among whom John had become a permanent member. Its continuance was in question at the time that he took his first appointment as an instructor at the College of Bruges in French Flanders. One of his duties in 1773 was to take Lord Stourton's son on a grand tour of western Europe. For his charge's instruction he composed a journal as he passed through France, Germany and into Italy, where the piece concluded. In many places it reflected the intellectual awakening in Europe known as the Enlightment, under whose influence the French Jesuit schools and Carroll himself had come. He criticized royal taxation in France and the state religions of Germany. The polite gentleman's knowledge was reflected in reference to James Addison and other literary figures. During his stay in Rome he became more aware of the gathering storm that threatened to destroy the Society of Jesus. The highly politicized papacy under the new pope, Clement XIV, was already preparing the bull of suppression. His fears and bitterness were revealed to his Jesuit colleague Ellerker and to his mother. He returned to Bruges to find the tragedy acted out in the closing of his college and in his own imprisonment.

Lord Arundell of Wardour Castle, England, rescued Carroll and provided a residence. Here John wrote an account of the closing of Bruges College in order to help English Catholic gentlemen win indemnities for the colleges they had sponsored on the continent. No longer a member of a religious order, he returned in 1774 to his mother's manor at Rock Creek near the site of the future Washington, D.C. Uncertain of his juridical status as a priest, he nevertheless ministered to those in the area and nearby Virginia. While awaiting a settlement of this problem, his cousin Charles Carroll of Carrollton encouraged him in January 1776 to join the cause of armed resistence to England and serve on a mission to Canada for the Continental Congress. John Carroll was an unofficial member of the commission, which included his cousin, Benjamin Franklin, and Samuel Chase. John Adams hoped that John Carroll would be able to minister to those French Canadians who had joined the American cause. The commission strove to win the support of the Canadian province and to improve the condition of the army there. While the long-range effect of the mission strengthened the American position, the immediate one ended in a retreat to central New York. Hostility to monarchical government had been instilled by the role of Bourbon monarchs in the suppression of the Jesuits and now brought Carroll to this full support of American resistance to the King of England and a Declaration of Independence.

Before the end of the war Carroll took the lead in creating freedom for the American Church. He feared that the Congregation of the Propagation of the Faith would rule even more directly than it had before the war. Carroll drafted a Constitution of the Clergy to secure the property of the American Church to itself rather than to the Roman congregation. He also initiated procedures to assure that Americans selected their ecclesiastical superiors in the United States. On this foundation and after delicate negotiations with authorities in Rome, Carroll was elected by a convention of the American clergy the superior of the American mission.

John Carroll again established his position of leadership of the American Catholic community by challenging an attack on it by Charles Wharton, a former Jesuit who had conformed to the Church of England and in 1784 was serving as a clergyman of the recently formed Protestant Episcopal Church, after the war the successor to that church in America. When Wharton charged that Catholics believed Protestants were damned, he threatened to be disruptive of the good relations with Protestants which Catholics had won during the war and in the new state constitutions which gave religious freedom to them. Carroll affirmed the primacy of personal conscience in religion. One who was faithful to this must be honored by every Catholic, whatever religious group one chose. In the course of the next few years he had occasion to express solidarity with all American people on the grounds of religious pluralism and freedom, notably as "Pacificus" in the *Gazette of the United States* and in an address to the first president of the United States. Carroll privately discussed the problem regarding the nature of the priesthood and episcopal office with Episcopalians. He served on the board of visitors of Washington College, established by interdenominational support. Through Georgetown College, which he founded, and lesser educational and philanthropic endeavors he contributed significantly to building up the cultural and social life of the young Republic.

While his first reports to the Congregation of the Propagation of the Faith in Rome told of the happy progress of the American Church, he had to appraise realistically the inadequacy of his means of leadership. He had not the powers of a bishop, and this lack inclined some in many quarters to challenge his decisions as well as his office. The Constitution of the Clergy created several districts with committees presiding over them, and his debate with these committees over several matters yielded his own valuable commentary on Church government for the enlightenment of others. But a continuing tension would be found among some former Jesuits who disagreed with Carroll over their status, appointments, and the landed estates of the order as now a part of the corporation of all of the clergy. Yet Carroll dealt with them respectfully and prevented alienation.

This was not the case with a more radical problem in Church life in the parish. John Carroll's power to settle which priest should be the pastor was at times frustrated by lay trustees in Boston, New York and especially in Holy Trinity Church, Philadelphia. The last case was complicated by the fact that it was a dominantly German congregation created for the benefit of having sermons in their native language. The tradition which they brought from their native land regarding parish trustees was alien to Carroll's understanding of this matter. Since the German laity largely accounted for funds which built the church, they claimed the right of presentation, as they explained, whereby they alone had the decisive voice in settling on a priest as pastor, one possibly claiming powers from a German bishop. Not being a bishop himself, Carroll was hard pressed to prove his authority to accept or reject the priest they presented for a pastorship.

The reports to the Congregation of the Propagation of the Faith by 1788 made it clear that this condition of the leader of the American Church could not continue. Not without some reluctance, the Roman authorities finally granted America a bishop with full powers of an ordinary, who would train and ordain American priests and himself directly control the exercise of ministerial powers of all priests. There was the danger, however, that an ecclesiastic from Europe would be appointed, the Roman Congregation having insufficient appreciation of the maturity of Carroll and his colleagues to govern American affairs. Carroll saw this as a danger to the whole situation of the Catholic community in a country with a dominantly Protestant population which feared any allegiance to a foreign power. At this point the Constitution of the Clergy served as a precedent where it provided for a choice of the American Church leader by a convention of the clergy in the United States. Carroll's genial companion on the mission to Canada in 1776, Benjamin Franklin, after some gauche gestures, succeeded in impressing the authorities in Rome through French prelates that Carroll was a most desirable appointee as bishop of the United States. When the convention of the clergy acted independently to this effect, Rome agreed to Carroll as a bishop elected by them. Sir Thomas Weld, an old friend of Carroll, provided his Lulworth Castle as a suitable place for his consecration by an English bishop in Dorset County, England.

While Carroll was in England, he contacted the superior of the

Society of St. Sulpice (Sulpicians), who had as one of their main apostolates the education of the clergy. Because of the persecution of the clergy in France during the French Revolution at this time, many of this order were contemplating emigration. Carroll hoped that they would establish a seminary in the United States to meet what he considered a major objective, the education of a native Catholic clergy. It was out of this that later developed the foundation of St. Mary's Seminary in Baltimore. The role of Georgetown College, already founded by 1790, was uncertain regarding the education of the clergy. More immediately, there was a great need for priests to minister to the French-speaking population, particularly in the Western territories. The French Sulpicians Stephen Badin and Benedict Flaget soon came to Kentucky and Gabriel Richard to the Michigan Territory. Pierre Gibault, a Canadian, ministered in the Indiana and Illinois territories. The continuation of the French Canadian ministry in Maine was another problem which Carroll had to deal with. He sought to involve the congregation of Boston in this. In these difficult circumstances Carroll continued to welcome clergymen from Ireland and Germany and sought to recruit other priests from Europe, awaiting the time when his own seminaries would supply this important need of the American Church.

Toward the end of 1791 Bishop Carroll succeeded in calling a synod of the American clergy. From this resulted the formulation of more specific ecclesiastical law for the American Church, which he hoped would remedy many of the disorders which had prevailed before his consecration as bishop. Only a beginning was made, however, and the rapid growth of the country and the Catholic population presented a formidable challenge to his leadership.

Throughout this period, as well as in those that follow, was a sustained series of writings which summarized Carroll's view of the American Church. His frequent reports to the Roman Congregation of the Propagation of the Faith described pastoral development and its accompanying problems. A more revealing kind of writing were his letters to Charles Plowden, who more than anyone else was John Carroll's confidant. A colleague of Carroll's during most of his life as a Jesuit, Plowden was at the College of Bruges when he and Carroll were expelled with the suppression of the Jesuits. Having returned to England, Plowden and his two brothers were prominent in Catholic life and the effort that led to Parliament's Relief Acts in favor of the toleration of Catholics. Carroll's own theological and social thought developed against this influence from English Catholics. He in turn wrote several times a year to Charles Plowden to tell of events in the American Church with the greatest candor. He spoke his mind freely regarding the tensions in the American-Roman relations. His letters to others in England supplement the Plowden correspondence.

THE JOHN CARROLL PAPERS

VOLUME 1●1775-1791

THE
John Carroll
PAPERS

TO CHARLES CARROLL OF CARROLLTON[1] [1755]

Dr. Cousin.   Fr. Jenison, who is now at the villa, sends me a commission to scold you for not sending us the directions to you. Pray how must I go about it? I believe you will mind very little, what I say to you, if I say it in a serious way. I never in my life remember to have been obligd to study so long to find out, what to write, as to day. I have neither political, domestic, or news of any other denomination to send you. Not one thought occurs to entertain you with, & I would absolutely differ writing for some days, when I am to send a letter to your Papa from Mr. Niset, who tells me he saw you at Rheims, if F. Jenison had not desird me to send of this as soon as possible, he having one of F. Thorpe[2] to be inclosed in the same packet with this for Fr. Crookshanks, to whom your inadvertency obliges me to trust this letter. I am D[ea]r. Charles   Your affectionate Cousin &c   John Carroll   The other side is for your Papa.

ALS   MHS 215-16   On date see Hanley, *Charles Carroll,* p. 31.
   [1] A distant cousin, last living signer of the Declaration of Independence, who went with Carroll to St. Omers College, France, in 1748. He then went to another Jesuit college at Rheims in 1754, while John was at the Jesuit Novitiate in Watten. John then had studies at Liège, where he was at this time.
   [2] John Thorpe, S.J., a close friend from these days, would later be Carroll's important contact at Rome for American affairs.

TO DANIEL CARROLL[1] Liège May 24th 1764

Dear Brother   Upon notice that our Cousin Charles Carroll is upon the point of setting out from London, I cannot fail profiting by this opportunity, tho' upon a supposition that he would have sailed last month, I inclosed a letter to you dated the end of march, which I hope he has forwarded, as I directed him to do. You will easily conceive, I am under a good deal of uneasiness, when I tell you I have not heard from Maryland for above this twelvemonth; & I should be at a loss to know whether my friends there were alive or dead, if my uncle's letters had not mentioned them. I am sorry that the return of peace, which, I hoped, would greatly facilitate our correspondence, has not hitherto afforded me that advantage. My uncle is advised by

3

his daughters that you design to come to Europe this spring, & to see us in Flanders. If this proves true, I shall receive abundant compensation from the pleasure of your conversation. My uncle boards at the English nuns of this town, & his conduct gives as general satisfaction as his company does entertainment.

It will not be necessary for me to write this time separately to our dearest Mother,[2] as this will be delivered into her hands, if you are out of the country, & if not, you will communicate it to her.

The death of the famous Marchioness of Pompadour will, it is generally believed by our French Brethren, occasion soon some great change in their circumstances; so far is certain, that they are delivered by this event from their greatest enemy, I mean the most powerful one, & who by her interest & influence over the King of France could more easily than any one else prevail upon him to view tamely the proceedings against the Jesuits, which she underhand encouraged by all the arts, which cunning & power could put into her hands. The Jesuits [*blank*—put] their hopes upon the declared attachment of all the royal family to their interests, upon the intimate connection & intelligence persisting between the King, & his Queen & children since the great ladie's death, upon the zealous intercessions of the Bishops, all the prime nobility, & every order of magistrates in the different cities & towns, where the Jesuits were heretofore established. If we add to this the general discontent, that has ensued upon the appointment & conduct both in morals, & literary pursuits of the newly installed masters for the education of youth we cannot absolutely pronounce these hopes to have an object merely chimerical; but I will own to you that the irresolute behaviour, which has appeared so much in the french government on many late occasions, makes me apprehend that vigour will be wanting to bring about so desirable a revolution, as it is likely to meet with great opposition from several parliaments, whose principles are very incompatible with those the Jesuits would endeavour to maintain & propagate in case of their restoration.[3] Thus you see the prospect before us, gives little cause to be content with this world, whilst past sufferings have served to strengthen, if possible, our belief in another better & more equitable than this. And indeed to a man lying under the publick imputation of crimes, from which his own conscience clears him, & who is persuaded of the existence of a Deity, I know no proof of an immortality more sensible & comfortable, than this reflection, that an all powerful & infinitely just being cannot, consistently with those attributes, refuse him in another life that justice, which passion & iniquity have denied him in this. To pretend, as some ancient & modern unbelievers have done, that virtue & a good conscience is its own reward, argues very little knowledge of the human heart: for many a hardy villain, from a natural alacrity & cheerfulness of mind, & possessed of worldly enjoyments, seldom finds, at least for any long time, his remorses to prey much upon him, or disturb his pleasures, whilst several good men on the contrary from an unhappy temper or sickly constitution but rarely feel any even intellectual enjoyments. I cannot otherwise account for my having fallen into this train of philosophizing, which I hope you will excuse, than because I have habituated myself to it, as the best relief amidst so many affecting & melancholy scenes. My uncle desires his love to you all, & especially to our dearest Mother, whose blessing I ask for myself, & whom I hope this will find well. Let my Sisters[4] know I always bear them in mind; assure Messrs Brent[5] of my love, & other friends of my best well wishes, not forgetting above all my Uncle John Darnall. I know not whether your next letters will find me at Liege, as I am uncertain what destination I may have after having finished my course of philosophy, which will be now in two months. But at all events forward your letters to Mr. Pyntz with Mr. Wright Banker in Henrietta Street Covent Gardens & they will reach me. I am at a loss for want of letters from you, who to apply to for money this year. Write as soon as possible, & believe me to be   Dr Br[other]   Your most affectionate Brother   John Carroll

ALS   MPA
[1] Older brother (1730-96), at this time at their father's estate in Upper Marlborough, Md. He later became distinguished as a member of the Constitutional Convention and the Congress of the U.S.
[2] Eleanor Darnall Carroll (1706-96), daughter of Henry Darnall (1682-1759) and Anne Digges (1685-1750).
[3] While the Society of Jesus was not officially suppressed by the Pope until 1773, France began repression at this time in imitation of Spain and Portugal.
[4] Anne, Eleanor, Mary, and Elizabeth Carroll.
[5] Eleanor Carroll married William Brent (1733-72) of Virginia.

ON THE SACRAMENTS IN GENERAL AND SOME IN PARTICULAR
[1769-70]

Part One: On the Sacraments in General. Part Two: On Some of the Sacraments In particular: 1. On Baptism; 2. On the Sacrament of Confirmation. 3. On the Sacrament of the Most Holy Eucharist.

AD   GU   In Latin. While bound with a MS on the Sacrament of Penance in a volume of 414 pp., the latter constitutes a separate work and MS and is nearly of equal length as the above. These very clearly are student notes and summations in the traditional form of the Catholic theological schools of the day; and therefore would seem to possess a minimum of originality. Especially Part Two follows the formula of state of the question, thesis, objection, and response. There are lengthy citations of authors (who are identified), paraphrases and summations of them individually or in sythesis. The date assumes that Carroll studied this matter in his fourth year of theology.

ON THE SACRAMENT OF PENANCE   [1769-70]

Questions: 1. On the Existence and Institution of the Sacrament of Penance. 2. On the Necessity of the Sacrament of Penance. 3. On the Instrinsic Constitution of the Sacrament of Penance. 4. On the First Part of Penance or on Contrition. 5. On the second part of the Sacrament of Penance or on Confession.

AD   GU   In Latin. See previous entry for description, date. etc.

TO DANIEL CARROLL   [February 1769]

Before you receive this letter you will have heard of the Pope's[1] death: in human appearance, nothing could have happened more unfortunate to us, especially in the critical moment when an answer was to have been given to the memorials of three united courts of the family compact, France, Spain, and Naples, requiring the immediate dissolution of the society. His Holiness had himself minuted the heads of the answer he intended to make in a few days, and had delivered it to his ministers to be put into the due form. The substance of it was, that no worldly consideration, no loss of temporalities, should ever force him into any measure which he could not justify to his own conscience: that the more he saw and knew of the Jesuits, the more he was convinced of their eminent services to religion, and of the falsehood of the imputations charged upon them: that he could not therefore acquiesce in the proposal made him by the allied courts. The answer entered into a much larger detail than I here mention, and would have been a glorious testimony of his Holiness' esteem and affection for the society. How matters will go on in the conclave, and after the election of the new Pope,[2] Heaven knows. Humanly speaking, we have every thing to dread from the combination formed against us: yet when I reflect on the atrocious falsehoods, injustices, cruelties, and mean artifices employed against us, I greatly confide that God's providence will not permit our dissolution to be effected by such wicked means. I know his kingdom is not of this world, and that they who seek to do his divine will, and promote his glory, are not to expect a visible interposition in their favor on every occasion, or to receive in this life an apparent testimony of innocence and divine approbation.

L. Brent, pp. 27-29.   On date estimate, see footnote 1 below.
   [1] Clement XIII died Feb. 2, 1769.
   [2] Lorenzo Ganganelli, Conventual Franciscan, elected Clement XIV, May 18, 1769, ultimately decreed the universal suppression of the Jesuits in 1773.

JOURNAL OF EUROPEAN TOUR   [1771-72]

The province of Alsace, one of the most fertile in Europe, after having been for many years in the possession of the house of Austria, was ceded to France by the treaty of Munster, in the year 1648. As the government exercised by the Austrian family was subject to several restrictions, on account of the privileges claimed by the inhabitants, so the cession of it to

France met with many difficulties. Besides Strasbourg, which was not comprehended in the treaty of cession, there were ten imperial towns governed by their own magistrates, and immediately subject to the empire. One of these was Colmar. These towns, as well as the dukes of Wurtenberg, Deux Ponts, and others, who had fiefs or possessions in Alsace, immediately relevant of the empire, insisted that the house of Austria could not transfer the sovereignty of the whole province, since it had itself never been possessed of it. They demanded that the imperial towns, their districts, and the above mentioned fiefs should retain their privileges and relevancy of the empire. The matter was left in a kind of ambiguity at the conclusion of the peace; but France being put in possession of the province, would not allow any favor to these pretensions, not admit there was any ambiguity in the treaty; and Strasbourg being surrendered to France in 1681, the full and entire sovereignty was confirmed to that crown by the treaty of Reswick. It still however retains some of its former usages. The Roman law is followed in the courts of judicature; even where it is contrary to the ordinances of the kings of France, if you expect some few which existed since the cession of Alsace and registered in the provincial court of judicature.

The court held at Colmar is called, *le Conseil Souverain d'Alsace,* and differs from the different parliaments of the kingdom. It consists of a first and second president, and of twenty-four judges, called conseillers. They are divided into two chambers, each presided by a president. There are besides an attorney and two advocates general. The attorney general (procureur general) has very great authority in the province. He has an inspection over every part, is charged to prosecute all breaches of the peace, to inform of all abuses, to receive and lay before the conseil all complaints, to discharge the king's trust of guardianship of orphans, &c.

The counsellors sit in the first and second chambers, by rotation; but the first president and dean of the council always remain, the former in the first chamber and the latter in the other. They sit every day, Sundays and holidays excepted. Three days in the week, each chamber gives audience, that is, hears and determines causes by the pleadings of the lawyers, whilst the other judges those matters which are discussed in writing. In all causes, which any wise affect the king, or where minors, corporations, &c. are concerned, after hearing the arguments of the respective lawyers, one of the advocates general resumes what has been urged on each side, delivers and enforces his opinion on the matter, and proposes it to be adopted by the court. When the advocate general is a man of much experience or considerable abilities, his opinion has great weight, but at present neither of them, any more than the attorney general, enjoys much reputation for knowledge.

This may appear extraordinary to an Englishman, since with us it is a certain mark of great eminence in the law to be raised to the rank of king's council. But this surprise will vanish, when it is considered that the charges of judicature in France are considered saleable; and that they are transmitted as an inheritance from father to son, dependently on some trifling duty on their passing from one to another. The money delivered for a charge is not so properly alienated, as placed out at interest; originally the king paid four or five percent, but at present the charges are very irregular. When the charges were fixed, those of judge or counsellor were rated at ten or twelve thousand livres, and the king received no more for them. But at present they are valued at twenty-four thousand livres, and sometimes sold for more. They are considered as a patrimonial fund, may be mortgaged, or given in fortune to a daughter. It is said that many of those in Alsace are loaned to the Jews, who swarm throughout the province.

An inconvenience arising from the sale of offices is, that the judges in general are not the most proper to determine matters of law and equity. A young man, who has fortune enough, need but spend a few months at the university of Strasbourg, take his degree of licentiate, which is granted without difficulty, present himself at the bar of Colmar, to be admitted advocate, and he is instantly qualified to be a counsellor. The venality introduced by Louis XII., Francis I., and the succeeding kings of France, occasioned this great abuse, which calls aloud for redress.

When the king sends to the council for any new ordinance to be published, or when any regulation of police concerning the province is to be made, the two chambers are assembled together, and every thing is determined by the majority of votes.

Strasbourg retained many privileges, when it submitted to France. The magistracy can determine finally and without appeal, all suits not exceeding a certain value, and is, I am told, the only town under the crown of France, where the intervention of the royal judges is not necessary to condemn a criminal to death. The free exercise of religion is allowed to Lutherans in the greatest part of the Province. The town magistracy and all municipal employments in Strasbourg, Colmar, &c., are divided between them and the Catholics. But the latter only are admitted to exercise any function whatever in the supreme council, and in general all the king's officers are of the reigning religion. The number of Lutherans has increased considerably since their subjection to France, though they enjoyed great credit during the administration of the Duke of Choisel, and in contested points had generally more influence than the Catholics. They are said to be secretly very averse to the French government, and firmly attached to the house of Austria, or rather to the empire. If they do not reconcile themselves with the Church, it does not proceed from any great zeal of their own tenets; they are mostly latitudinarians in religion, but bred up in a strong aversion to Catholicity.

The inhabitants are industrious and generally live comfortably. Property is very much diffused, children inheriting of their parents in equal shares. There is scarce a fortune in Alsace exceeding thirty thousand livres per annum, except the great estates possessed by the Bishop of Strasbourg, and some sovereign princes of Germany, who have fiefs in this province. Most of the counsellors of Colmar are poor, and he is thought to be in good circumstances, who has four or five thousand livres per annum, which few of them are possessed of. Notwithstanding this, and the low birth of many amongst them, they affect to be haughty and supercilious. The general character of the people is want of courtesy and affability. The men and women of fashion dress after the French mode; but the women of inferior rank, and most of the Lutherans plait their hair in ringlets upon their heads.

The entire province is amazingly fertile, and one of the most agreeable a spectator can behold. It is separated in its whole length from Lorraine by a chain of mountains, which are covered with firs. A beautiful plain about five leagues broad extends quite to the Rhine. The plain is watered by several rivers springing from the mountains; it produces amazing crops of all kinds of grain, and the sides of the mountains, as well as some parts of the plain, are covered with vineyards, which yield an agreeable table wine. The taste of it resembles that of Moselle. Grain and wine are the chief articles of exportation, great quantities of both being sent into Switzerland. We were in Colmar after two different crops, and three or four very bad vintages, and too large a quantity of corn had been exported. The price of wheat at a medium was twenty-six livres the sack, weighing one hundred and seventy pounds, and of the middle sort of wine, six sous the bottle. The roads through the whole province are excellent, and kept in perfect repair. The inspection over them belongs to the intendant, who resides at Strasbourg, and has great authority. He is properly the person of confidence of the court; the detail and levy of taxes is committed to his care; the municipal officers of the towns must be approved, and in effect, appointed by him; all secret orders of the court are transmitted to him, and he is entrusted with their execution. The method of keeping the roads in repair is this: Each town and village, through which they pass, has a certain number of roads allotted to its care, and the inhabitants choose the season in which they are least employed in agriculture to make the necessary reparations. This dispenses them from the necessity of turnpikes.

There are no manufactures of consequence in the province; great quantities of cloth are imported from Abbeville, Sedan and England. These latter are landed at Ostend, and sent from thence to Brussels, whence they are transported in wagons through the Ardennes and Lorraine. I was told likewise that considerable imports of other English manufactures were made clandestinely from Geneva, Switzerland, and the other side of the Rhine, as well into this as the neighboring provinces of Lorraine and Franche Comté. Perhaps our political writers do not know this, when they make the balance of our trade with France so much against us. The country is full of large and well peopled villages, besides the many populous towns; Strasbourg is the chief. The noble Cathedral and its remarkable high tower is famous through Europe. The bishop has a grand palace, built by Cardinal Rohan, the first of that family who enjoyed this see. Nothing pleased me more than the admirable gilding of the stucco work of the ceilings. The bishop has another still more magnificent palace, though not entirely built, at Taverne, about nine leagues from Strasbourg. Adjoining to it are large gardens finely planted, and in front of the palace a canal of two leagues long, terminated by a well built village. It has a fine effect to the eye though it would in my opinion be more agreeable, if it were serpentine. On both sides of the canal is a fine walk shaded with trees.

The military government of the province is under a marshal of France, who resides at Strasbourg, where there is generally a garrison of ten thousand men. There are many strong places in the province; in Upper Alsace, Belfort, Huninghen and New Brisach, on the Rhine; Schlestat near the centre of the province, Strasbourg, Landan and Fort Louis in Lower Alsace.

The increase of population is so great, that I heard from the rector of a parish, that there had been an augmentation of forty families in his village within twenty-five years. I do not suppose this enormous increase to be general throughout the province, and in the above mentioned village it must have been owing to some accidental circumstance which drew strangers thither. But I found in general, on the best information I could obtain, that in time of peace, the inhabitants multiply very fast. When France is at war, the province furnishes an immense number of recruits for the army. It is supposed, that during the last war they amounted to twenty thousand men.

I find however, in the remonstrances presented to the king in the year 1764, by the supreme council of Colmar, heavy complaints of the visible depopulation of the country, and of the bad state of agriculture, which they attribute to enormous taxes, and still more to the abuse committed in levying them. I am inclined to believe there is great exaggeration in these remonstrances; the counsellor, who was charged to draw them up, is said to have had some particular resentments to gratify; and certainly the flourishing state of agriculture in 1770 and 1771, is a proof that it was far from the deplorable condition in which it was represented in 1764. Much is left to the arbitrary determination of a commissary appointed to fix the quotas of the taxable. For instance, the tax of the vingtieme, or twentieth penny, is raised in such a manner, that it really becomes a fifth or sixth. Innumerable other abuses in raising the king's revenues, are placed in a strong light in the remonstrances, and certainly deserve redress, the more so, as they tend to the king's manifest prejudice. For instance, during the years 1760, 1761, 1762 and 1763, (I could find no materials of a more ancient date) the king's exchequer did not receive two thirds of the revenue raised in Alsace.

The different impositions under the names of *subvention, epis du Rhin, capitation, supplement aux gages, abonnement de Courtiers,* &c., *solde de milice, pepiniere, milices, gardes cotes: 1st, 2d* and *troisieme vingtieme, fourrages, fraix communs, comptes de communautes et villes, dons gratuits, impots sur les cuirs, les tabacs,* &c., yielded in 1764, *liv.* 3,899,540.12.8¼, and the king's coffers received no more than 2,177,15.17.0.

I cannot be so particular with regard to the province of Lorraine, though we saw a great part of it. It is much larger than Alsace, I believe nearly double, but not so generally fertile. Great part of it is not fit to bear wheat, but produces oats in plenty. This province for a long series of years enjoyed its own princes, separate in government, and mostly in politics and inclination, from France. In the wars, which for so many years raged between that kingdom and the house of Austria, Lorraine almost always took part with the latter, and when it did not openly, was still viewed with a jealous eye by the former. After the cession of Alsace to Louis XIV., the situation of Lorraine became more critical, as its communication with the empire was rendered extremely difficult. From that time, it was apparent that sooner or later it would fall under the dominion of France. This event took place in the year 1737. Francis, Duke of Lorraine, having married Mary Teresa, daughter of the Emperor Charles, and heiress to the Austrian dominions, found himself under the necessity of making over his paternal duchy to France: he received as an indemnification the grand duchy of Tuscany in Italy, which is now possessed by his second son, Archduke Leopold.

This cession was a terrible heart breaking to the Lorrainers. They had enjoyed a long series of benevolent princes, and especially Leopold, the immediate predecessor of Francis, had been rather the father than a sovereign of his subjects. Indeed, the passage from the dominion of their national princes to that of France, was softened by their first becoming subject to Stanislaus, king of Poland. For it was stipulated in the peace of 1737, that Lorraine should be ceded to this prince during his life, and afterwards devolve to France. Stanislaus undoubtedly had so many benevolent qualities, so much zeal for the interest and happiness of his subjects, that he would have made them entirely easy under his government, if he could have removed the prospect of their future devolution to France, or if any compensation could be made to men of liberal understandings, for transferring them without their consent or concurrence, like so many salves, from dominion to dominion. He beautified Nancy, their capital, making it one of the finest towns in Europe; he instituted noble foundations for the relief of his subjects, without any detriment to their industry; he encouraged all the fine arts; he propagated by his example and authority, a true spirit of religion, which he knew to be the best foundation of political as well as future happiness. He maintained at the same time a splendid court; and what is most remarkable, performed so many great things with a revenue, which would hardly suffice for the hunting parties of many sovereign princes. As far as he was above meanness, (no prince ever carried into his expenses nobler or more extensive views of public good,) with so strict an economy did he administer his little revenues; and he ought in every age to be held out to princes, as the *Man of Ross* is by our

great poet, to private fortune, for an example of what great things may be
done by small sums, by a prudent and an active zeal.

This amiable and beneficent prince would have done still more for the
prosperity of his subjects, had he been full master of his own actions. But a
few years after the cession made to him of Lorraine, he was constrained
through his dependence on France, to the levying and imposing of taxes, and
consented to receive a determined amount; I have not now by me some
memorials I had on the subject, and do not remember the precise sum; but
the consequence of this transaction was that Lorraine became taxed much
heavier than it had ever been under its own princes, which circumstance
constributed to render their memory dearer. If we may credit those who
remember the former government, the difference between the present and
past way of life of the farmer and laborer, is enormous; his clothing, his food,
every necessary of life, is infinitely worse than heretofore. But these complaints are so much the style of every country, and particularly of elderly
people, that I cannot tell what credit they deserve. In some respects, I cannot
help thinking the circumstances of this country greatly bettered by its
becoming subject to France. As long as it was governed by its own princes,
they generally took part with the Austrians, as was intimated before. By this
means, Lorraine was almost always exposed to the incursions of the French
armies, and their enormous contributions. It was surrounded by provinces
subject to other princes, and thus its imports and exports were liable to
impositions which necessarily prevented all growth or extension of trade. The
natural productions of the country, particularly the wine-growing in the
dutchy of Bar, must necessarily have been a very uncertain revenue, since the
vent of it abroad was so precarious, and dependent on the good pleasure of
the neighboring states. Whereas, at present, Lorraine having become a French
province, is under no other restraint than the rest of the kingdom. The
produce of its vines and fields enjoys a free circulation: the ingenuity and
industry of its inhabitants find an easy vent for their commodities; and the
strong frontiers, with which France is on every side secured against hostile
invasions, leave the Lorrainer no other rapine to fear, than that of the
merciless publican.

Justice is administered in this province, as in the others of France, by a
sovereign court, consisting of a first and another or more presidents, and a
number of judges called conseillers. The court or parliament of Lorraine is
different, however, in its constitution from the rest in this respect, that the
places are not saleable, but gratuitously bestowed by the governor, as was
practised under the ancient dukes of Lorraine. And it may not be improper to
inform the reader, of a great amelioration effected in the whole kingdom of
France since the above observations were made, namely, the abolition of
venality in the offices of judicature. Private animosities between the Dukes of
Arguillon and Choiseul, gave occasion to this salutary operation; the latter of

these noblemen, to oppress his competitor, drew on him the whole weight of parliamentary persecution, and was not very solicitous of its insulting the royal authority, provided the Duke of Arguillon was made to suffer. But he miscarried in his attempt. The king's patience was at length overcome. Choiseul was disgraced and Monsieur de Maupeon, chancellor of France, had the courage to plan, propose, and with the king's entire concurrence, to suppress all the parliaments of France, and re-establish them, but on a different footing. The sale of places was abolished. When a vacation happens, the parliament is to propose three subjects, who are recommended to be taken from amongst experienced barristers, and the king is to appoint one of them. The parliament of Metz having been suppressed with the others, it was not replaced by a new creation, but the jurisdiction of the ancient one was united to that of Lorraine, by which means the parliament of Nancy acquired a large addition of business and consequently of influence.

I cannot leave Lorraine without recording some particular institutions of the benevolent Stanislaus. For the encouragement of the arts, he erected an academy, to which were aggregated men of the best taste in the different branches of literature and the sciences. He founded annual premiums to be bestowed on those who excelled in sculpture, painting, architecture, &c., which besides the certainty of being employed and well paid, enkindled emulation amongst his subjects, and greatly contributed to the perfection of the noble buildings and public monuments which adorn Nancy, viz: the town house, the governor's palace, the brazen statue of Louis XV., the public fountains, the town gates, &c. He provided the academy with noble apartments and an excellent library in the town house. His attention was given to the smallest as well as the greatest things, and many of the numerous buildings which surround the square of Louis XV., particularly the iron work of the balconies, are finished with a taste and perfection, which the encouragement and understanding of a great prince is used to diffuse throughout all his undertakings.

The mission, as it is called, was another admirable institution of Stanislaus, calculated for the instruction, chiefly, of the country people, the preservation of manners, and consequently of industry amongst them, and for the relief of helpless indigence. With this view, he erected a noble house in one of the suburbs, and endowed it with sufficient revenues for the maintenance of a certain number of Jesuits, who were to be employed during the greatest part of the year, and particularly in the winter months, as being more convenient for the country people, in instructing them and enforcing the obligation and practice of the great christian duties. It was appointed that they should divide the province of Lorraine amongst them, going two and two together, and that no part might be left uninstructed, half the missioners were German, half French, each allotting to themselves, those districts respectively in which French or German was the ordinary language. It is incredible what advantages accrued from this institution; what abuses, arising greatly from ignorance, extirpated; what good practices introduced, and even what political improvement arose from the amendment and preservation of manners. The royal founder had this establishment so much at heart, that he forgot nothing to insure its success. That the missioners might be no grievance to the parish priests or others, during their excursions, he provided abundantly for the expenses of their journeys and maintenance. Wherever they went they were attended (and this, likewise, was owing to the provident care and princely foundation of Stanislaus) by a physician and apothecary with drugs to be administered gratis amongst the poor people, whom they should find in want of such assistance; and moreover a certain sum was allowed to the missioners to be dispensed in alms in each mission. It may be truly said of this excellent prince, that his mind enjoyed that rare quality of forming great and mature plans without losing sight of the minute details in carrying them into execution. He used every precaution which human prudence could direct, to perpetuate to future ages this monument of his love for his subjects. But he was scarce in his grave, when the court of Versailles ordered the missioners to evacuate their houses, the revenues were applied to other uses, or at least remained under sequestration, and so noble a foundation was at once wholly overturned.

Indeed, the fate, which immediately after Stanislaus' death attended many others of his establishments, is sufficient to convince princes, that the surest way to future remembrance, is to deserve the love of their subjects. The Lorrainers recall to mind their late sovereign with hearts full of gratitude and even tenderness, though the Duke of Choiseul during his ministry ordered many monuments of Stanislaus' magnificence to be destroyed. He gave instructions to this purpose with no much precipitation, that one is apt to think he was actuated by virulence, if the deceased prince could have raised these sentiments in any breast. Count Stainville, the duke's brother, was charged with the execution of these orders, and was not deficient in his trust. Malgrange, a palace near Nancy, and its fine gardens, were entirely destroyed, and the public was the more offended at the latter, as the old king had established in them some very edifying and popular practices of religion. Two or three other country seats were ruined; and what excited particular indignation, was, that many pictures painted by Stanislaus himself in his hours of relaxation, (for he was a stranger to none of the polite arts,) were allowed to be bought and carried off by a company of Jews. Though father-in-law to the king of France, and so munificent a benefactor of his subjects, no monument is erected to his memory. It cannot be doubted, but the province of Lorraine would gladly contribute to any public testimony of their gratitude, but the leading man who should set such a design in motion, knew the temper of the minister, and were too good courtiers to suggest a measure which they had reason to think would be interpreted as a condemnation of his proceedings.

The omission of a mausoleum was the more to be censured, as the spot for erecting it seemed to be particularly marked out. In the beautiful chapel of Bonsecours, just out of the gates of Nancy, Stanislaus had raised a noble monument to the memory of the queen his consort, and on the opposite side of the chapel a space was left, which was designed for the ashes and mausoleum of the kings. In that of the queen, the connoisseurs in statuary admire a noble medallion in white marble of charity. She is represented in an attitude of the greatest beneficence, accompanied by three children, one of whom lies asleep by her side, appearing to have been just relieved by her milk: she is actually giving suck to another, and the third is crying, that his turn is not yet come to get his nourishment.

If on the one hand, the Count de Stainville carried into execution his brother's instructions for destroying many of Stanislaus' works, it must be added, likewise, that with the concurrence of the same person he erected several others for the establishment of Nancy. The barracks for the soldiery deserve particular mention. They form an immense building of a noble, though unadorned style of architecture. The conveniences for health, cleanliness and all other purposes, are admirable. The foundations of another grand edifice, designed for the university, were just laid, when I was in Lorraine. The count undertook to fill up the town ditches, and lay them out into grand walks, Nancy for the future not being to be kept as a town of war. The prodigious depth and breadth of the ditches, renders this undertaking truly immense. It was not carried on during my abode there with the same spirit it was begun, and probably the decline of Count Stainville's credit, by the disgrace of his brother, may put it wholly at an end.

From Lorraine and Alsace, we proceeded across the Rhine into the empire. We passed over this river, by the wooden bridge, about three miles distant from Strasbourg. The bridge was formerly defended on the side of the empire by Fort Kehl, which is now quite gone to ruin. France has an easy entrance into Germany, whenever she wishes it. The first state one comes into on this side of the empire is the principality of Baden Baden. The capital town of his dominions is Baden, but the residence of the Count is at Rastadt, where there is a noble palace, with large gardens laid out in the taste of the country. In my journey from Strasbourg to this place, I was taken ill with a fever and ague, which put it out of my power to get the information of the country which I wished. I observed that part of it which lies toward the Rhine, to be chiefly fit for pasturage and Indian corn; the other side produces a good deal of wheat. The wine growing here, called *vin du marepusat,* is more esteemed than that of Alsace. From Rastadt we proceeded to Carlsruhe, the residence of the Prince of Baden Dourlach. The States of this prince were formerly united with those of Baden Baden, under one sovereign, who was called prince of Baden. But one of the branches of the family becoming Protestant, it was supported by that interest during the long thirty years' war of the empire in the last century; and it was settled in the treaty of Westphalia, that the principality should be so divided, that Baden Baden remain to the Catholic, and Baden Dourlach to the Protestant branch, with a provision, that if either become extinct, the survivor should inherit the other's dominions. This event took place about two months after my passage through these states, the prince of Baden Baden dying without issue. He was son to the famous General Prince Lewis, of Baden.

My illness continuing upon me, I found myself unable to see or learn the particular state of the Prince of Dourlach's government. I was the more concerned at it, as I was informed that he promoted with indefatigable application the welfare and happiness of his subjects, and that he very well deserved the accession to his fortune which he has now received. I heard in particular, that he provided every parish with an able schoolmaster, who taught the children reading, writing, arithmetic and surveying, without being any charge to the parents. All the children are obliged to frequent the school; and whilst employing their hands in forming the alphabet, they are taught to read and write on such subjects as may ever occur to them. At certain times of the year, their performances are sent to the prince, who with unparalleled zeal and patience examines their improvement in writing or orthography, arithmetic, &c., and rewards them accordingly; other schools are appointed for instructing girls in things proper for their sex. The prince is repaid for this gratuitous education in the following manner: He keeps about one thousand four hundred soldiers; the young men from eighteen to twenty-four years must be content to serve, if they be judged proper, for a certain term of years, during which they were very well kept and regularly paid. I was just able to walk through the palace of Carlsruhe, which is the prince's chief residence. It is a new and very large building, and some apartments, especially that of the princess, are fitted up with great elegance. The gardens are very large, and some beginnings appear of good taste in laying them out. If the prince continue to make this his principal sojourn, I doubt not but he will improve them much, as his abilities at present are so much greater. Following the course of the Rhine, we came next to Bruchsal, where the bishop and prince of Spire keeps his court. My companion went to see the palace, while my illness kept me abed: he told me it exceeded in the elegance of its taste and furniture those we had already met with on our road. The situation appeared very advantageous. I observed, in coming into the town, a salt refinery. I imagine there can be a few manufactures in these petty states. The consumption would never answer the expense. As they have a constant jealousy, one of the other, they naturally would lay heavy duties upon articles of importation from their neighbors. The people in general in this, as well as in both the principalities of Baden, have a heavy and awkward appearance, to which their dress contributes not a little.

Leaving Bruchsal, we soon entered into the states of the Elector Palatine, and came through Heidelberg to Manheim. The elector keeps a splendid court in this last town, which is seated at the confluence of the Rhine and the Neckar, and strongly fortified. The last elector having received some discontent from the citizens of Heidelberg, removed his court from that city to Manheim, and entirely rebuilt this latter place in a very regular form. The streets are all straight, and most of them terminate at one extremity at the elector's palace. This is an immense and regular building, but not formed on any grand style of architecture, though there are very rich apartments in it. The furniture of most is extremely costly and elegant. But the chief objects of curiosity are: 1. The gallery of pictures, which comprehends six rooms, though the two first contain nothing remarkable: 2. The collection of natural history, and antiquities: 3. A noble library of about forty thousand volumes: 4. A very magnificent theatre.

The elector is a prince of remarkable good parts, and very well versed in literature. He reads much, and speaks with fluency, besides his own language, Italian, French and English. Being learned himself, he encourages literary merit in others: he has erected an academy of arts and sciences, which, however, is not likely to be of much advantage to the state. The members employed to form the plan and regulations proceeded upon narrow and selfish principles of interest and envy; and under pretence of allowing entire liberty, and excluding all partiality, introduced a system of by-laws, which may prove very detrimental to revealed religion, as well as exclude from the academy the most learned men of the elector's dominions.

Those who were most distinguished for learning and merit, at the time of our passage through the electorate, were Fathers Desbillons, Meyer, and another Jesuit, whose name I do not remember, professor of philosophy at the university of Heidelberg, and Messrs. Maillot and Tchoflin, librarians to the elector. Father Desbillons has applied himself particularly to the study of the Latin classics and the Latin tongue, and is perhaps the most versed in the knowlege of both of any man in Europe. His elegant Latin fables, formed on the model and style of Phoedrus, are a proof of extraordinary improvement in his favorite study. It is a pity that the notes he has added, carry with them an air of pedantry. I heard he was employed in a great work which was eagerly expected by the learned Germans, and was to be entitled the History of the Latin Language. Father Desbillons is a Frenchman, and after the dissolution of the Jesuits in France, was graciously received and protected at Manheim by the elector. The particular library which he has collected, of about eight thousand volumes is remarkable for the judicious choice and rareness of the books and editions.

Father Meyer's studies are turned wholly on astronomy, of which he is a public electoral professor in the University of Heidelberg. He is a fellow of the Royal Society and several other academies. His mensuration of a degree of the meridian is esteemed among the learned. He was called to St. Petersburg, by the Empress of Russia, to observe the last transit of Venus, and had good success. The elector has caused an observatory to be erected at one of his country palaces, and furnished it with the best instruments from England. It is here that Father Meyer makes his observations.

Many schemes have been adopted for improving the natural richness of this state, by the establishment of different manufactures, and some have proved successful, particularly the China manufacture at Frankendahl. I saw several pieces of furniture executed there, which would do honor to Dresden. There are likewise some establishments for cloth, and linen manufactures. The advantages arising from these institutions, and chiefly a well regulated tax on the country, which is very fertile, would yield a sufficient revenue to the elector, if like most other German princes, he did not keep a court much too splendid for the extent of his states, and, perhaps, a too great number of soldiers. Another large expense to the elector is the public theatre of his palace. He pays the whole charges of actors, music, decorations, wardrobe, &c.; and those who are acquainted with theatrical entertainments, will easily form an idea of the immense sums, that are required to maintain them with splendor and dignity. Particulars pay nothing for going to see them. The consequence of the elector's magnificence is, that the subject is most enormously taxed.

The palatinate very early embraced the reformed religion, which during a long course of years, greatly prevailed in number and power over the Catholics, as the sovereigns espoused the new doctrines. Sometimes Lutheranism had the lead, sometimes Calvanism. But the eldest branch of the palatine line becoming extinct, the electorate devolved to the Duke of Newbourg, a Roman Catholic prince, and he brought an accession to his new state of the dutchy of Berg. Since that time, the Catholics have become nearly equal, if not superior in number and interest, to either the Lutherans or Calvinists, and their growth will probably continue to be still more considerable. The present elector has no successor, so that his states devolve to the Duke of Deux-Ponts, who likewise, will inherit the electorate of Bavaria, in default of issue from that and the palatine family.

From Manheim, we continued following the course of the Rhine to Cologne, passing through the bishopric of Worms, the electorates of Mentz, Trevers, and Cologne.

I shall say nothing of these countries, except that they produce great quantities of corn and wine. The government is absolute in these, as well as most other states in Germany. Mentz is the first electorate. It is likewise, as well as the two others, an archbishopric; and the archbishop is legate of the holy see throughout Germany. His revenues, however, are not in proportion to his dignity. Those of Trevers are still considerable, and neither they, nor the elector of Cologne, would be able to maintain such splendid courts, if they did not hold other bishoprics. Thus the present elector of Mentz, is likewise Bishop of Worms; that of Trevers, Bishop of Augsbourg, and that of Cologne, Bishop of Munster.

Having returned back to Manheim, we proceeded from thence, through Swabia to Augsbourg. Though Swabia be in general a plentiful country, chiefly in corn, yet the generality of the inhabitants appear to be extremely wretched. Whether it be owing to the weight of their taxes and abject dependence on their princes, or to the inland situation of the country, which leaves them no opportunity of carrying on foreign trade, I will not pretend to determine. One observation, however, the traveller through this country cannot avoid making, which is the strange contrast between the magnificence and politeness of the court of the Duke of Wurtemberg, which lies on the road, and the uncouthness of the other inhabitants. The dress and manners of the people, are the coarsest and most unseemly one can well imagine; that of the women in particular does not seem to have received the smallest degree of refinement. Their houses are so contrived, that the ground floor serves for a stable for their cattle; a ladder leads up to that in which the family abides. The filth and stench arising from such a distribution are to be conceived; had the people any ideas of cleanliness, it would be easy to keep their houses sweet and clean. I scarcely passed through a village in Swabia, where the streets were not plentifully watered by a constant stream. There is indeed to be observed in every country, a great difference between the gentry and lower class of people; but in none does this difference strike one so much, as in many parts of Germany; and it is natural to imagine, that it arises there chiefly from the nature of the feudal government. The generality of the inhabitants are under so slavish a dependence, and they are so much accustomed to consider their lords as beings of a superior class, that it is very probable much the greatest part never conceive an idea of the original equality, or of the common rights of mankind. Their sentiments in all likelihood might become more elevated, if the uniform equality of the subjects, one with another, did not stifle all the seeds of mutual emulation. In most other countries there is a regular gradation of ranks from the prince down to the peasant; but here there seem to be no intermediate condition; and in the whole course of our travels through Swabia, I do not remember to have seen on the road, the house of one subject which bespoke a master elevated above the condition of his fellow-subjects; at least, not till we came into the neighborhood and jurisdiction of the imperial city of Augsbourg.

That part of Swabia which belongs to the Duke of Wurtemberg is almost entirely Protestant, though the reigning duke himself professes the Catholic religion. His brothers are likewise Protestants. As the duke himself has no children, and being separated from his wife, probably never will, his estates devolve to his next brother, Prince Eugenius. The duke is very profuse, and has involved his finances in the utmost confusion. This has been to him a source of much mortification, as his subjects are greatly discontented with his administration; for, notwithstanding his difficult circumstances, he cannot refrain from extravagant expenses in building, hunting, keeping great bands of musicians and all the innumerable supports of an Italian theatre.

Augsbourg is a large, well built town; it was formerly one of the first trading cities in the world, when Venice was mistress of the entire communications with the Levant and East Indies. The effects brought to Venice were conveyed, by land carriage, to Augsbourg, and from thence spread throughout the whole empire. Even at present, there are great remains of its ancient wealth and industry. Manufactures of goods, silver, steel, and the art of engraving, are still in much credit here. The government is a mixture of democracy and aristocracy. As the religion is partially Catholic and partly Evangelical, the magistracy are equally chosen out of the two professions. The town house is a remarkable building, furnished with some very fine paintings of the Dutch school. The great hall, appropriated to the most solemn occasions, such as the entertainment of the emperor, is one of the finest, both its size and finishing, in Europe. There are other rooms designed for the assemblies of the magistracy, the different trading companies, &c. My stay was too short to inform myself of the state of letters.

The road from Augsbourg to Munich, in in general disagreeable, the greatest part of it is through forests of firs, and the land is incapable of improvement by cultivation. One proceeds but a little way from Augsbourg, before entering into the Duke of Bavaria's dominions. The harvest of 1771 was just gotten in, and the inhabitants were beginning to recover themselves from the dreadful famine of the preceding year. Yet still, wretchedness and want were painted in every object; provisions continued to bear a great price, much above the abilities of the poorer class of people. The roads were covered with miserable supplicants; instead of gratifying curiosity with the sight and observation of new countries, it was impossible not to have one's thoughts wholly occupied with the distress of so many fellow-creatures. Even Munich itself, though the capital of the country, and usual residence of a splendid court, appeared sad and gloomy, from the terrible circumstances of the times. The accidental scarcity was aggravated by the load of taxes laid on the subjects. I found the elector beloved by his people, but his ministers most heartily detested, particularly the Count de Baumgarten, who had the chief direction of affairs, a man of inflexible rigidity, who having gained an ascendant over his sovereign during his youth, continued still to overrule his judgment. This was a real misfortune to the people, as the elector himself is a prince of great goodness, and more than ordinarily humane. The taxes, though weighty of themselves, became still more grievous by the manner in which they were levied. All the duties of exportation and importation were farmed out; and the publicans harassed the people beyond measure, by searches, vexations, law-suits, and other such odious methods. It is indeed true, that the elector is under some kind of necessity of burdening his subjects with a heavy load. His ancestors were remarkable during several generations, for their magnificence and generosity, which perhaps sometimes degenerated into prodigality. Hence they contracted heavy debts, and the present sovereign entertains sentiments of known equity too strict not to consider himself bound to pay the creditors. His father, the Emperor Charles VII.'s misfortunes contributed to distress still more the public finances. These disorders however, are already greatly remedied by the prudent economy of the reigning prince. He is a lover of the arts and sciences; he has instituted an academy, and given it much public encouragement. He himself cultivates music and some other arts, with great success. His court was not at Munich, when we passed, and circumstances did not allow us to go to the country palace, where it then resided. The town palace is very large, but not a regular building. One of the apartments, consisting of seven or eight large rooms, and called the *green apartment,* is the most elegantly and completely furnished of any I have ever seen. Besides the richness and fine taste of the hangings, gilding, chairs, sofas, stoves, &c., it is adorned with a choice and magnificent collection of the best Italian and Flemish paintings. The theatre, likewise, belonging to the palace, though not very large, is however, finished with the greatest taste, and the machinery for shifting the scenes, &c. is admirable. The electoral treasury, consisting of gold and silver plate, curiously wrought arms, and curiosities of all kinds, is likewise well worth the observation of a traveller, and hardly to be equalled by any other repository of the same kind. Another object deserving to be seen is the Jesuits' church. The inside architecture in particular, is of the most noble and manly style; the builder was one of those children of genius, who are formed without a painful study of the rules of art. He was a common mason, and yet Italy, perhaps, cannot show so bold a vault as that from end to end, which forms the whole breadth of the church. It was erected by the generosity and piety of William, Duke of Bavaria. This prince, eminent for his prudence in government, as well as his chirstian virtues, ruled his states with great success, in very difficult times, about the middle of the sixteenth century. He thought himself greatly indebted to the zeal and learning of the Jesuits, for preserving his subjects from the contagion of the spreading religious errors, and through gratitude, as well as in order to perpetuate the same advantage to his people, he built and founded a college of Jesuits at Munich. After a most prosperous reign, he resigned his government to his son, several years before his death, and retired to a private life which he spent in the constant exercise of christian virtues. He passed several hours a day in the church he had built, and in his last will, ordered his body to be deposited in it, under a plain stone, without even the inscription of his name, in lieu of which, he directed these words, taken out of the book of Job, to be engraved: *Commissa mea pavesco et ante te erubesco, dum veneris judicare; noli me condemnare.* It is but doing justice to the Jesuits of this country to add, that they have perfectly corresponded with the views of their munificent benefactor. Indefatigable in the service of religion, their labors have greatly contributed to preserve it in Bavaria, not only uncorrupted with the pernicious tenets of the neighboring provinces, but moreover, to render the practical duties of it more generally, and more constantly attended to, than perhaps, in any other country in Europe. The belles lettres, likewise, and sciences are much cultivated by them, especially the study of physics, history, and mathematics.

I could get no clear state of the elector's revenues, which are considerable. His predecessors used to maintain a much larger body of troops than he has on foot at present. I was told there are not above eight thousand men. It would be well, probably, for the different states of Germany if the other princes followed this example.

Following the road from Munich to Inspruch, we very soon entered into the mountains which communicate with the Alps, and may properly be said to be a part of them. We passed by several lakes, formed at the foot of these mountains. This water is the finest one can see, and they are stocked with great quantities of excellent fish, and some of a peculiar species, to be met with no where else. The pleasing prospect these lakes afford, relieve the traveller, and form an agreeable contrast with the awful sight of impending mountains. The roads from Munich to Tyrol, are kept in bad repair, and in no degree comparable to those, which are made over the Alps. throughout this latter province. The entrance into it on the side of Bavaria, is defended by fortresses, impregnable more from their situation, than the work of art: the house of Austria, to whom the country of Tyrol belongs, makes it a capital point of politics, to preserve this passage into Italy, in its own hands. Indeed the country appears to be of little other importance to the court of Vienna, besides its serving to connect together its German and Italian states: the barren mountains, which form the whole province, can yield but a small revenue to the sovereign. But the undisputed communication with Italy, of which Austria is hereby possessed, must always give the latter great weight in all transactions relative to the former, or an advantage over France, especially when the latter chances not to be allied with the King of Sardinia. Inspruch, the capital of Tyrol, affords few things remarkable. There is a large palace with gardens much out of repair contiguous to it. The palace used to be the residence of the archduke, governor of the province: it was here the late Emperor Francis I., father of the present, and husband of the empress queen, died suddenly in 1765. He had come with the whole court of Vienna, to solemnize the marriage of his second son Archduke Leopold, with the Infanta of Spain, and to transfer to him the grand dutchy of Tuscany. The diversions on so solemn an occasion, were scarce begun, when the instantaneous death of the emperor put them to an end. A monument is erected at a small distance out of the town gates, to mark the spot where the Infanta was met by her future consort, and the whole court. On the other side of the town another monument is erected in the form of a triumphal arch, with an inscription, importing that the emperor, empress, &c., made their entrance that way. In the great church of the Franciscans, there is nothing remarkable, besides the monument erected to the memory of the Emperor Maximilian I., on which are engraven bas reliefs, and distributed in different panels, all around the monument.

Continuing to travel through the mountains, we met little remarkable, before we came to Trent. There appears to be a great trade carried on between Germany and the nearest Italian states, as we met immense quantities of wagons, which transport from Lombardy and the Venetian territory, corn and merchandise into Tyrol. Trent is a small town, of which the bishop is the prince. But his authority is much restrained by the court of Vienna, and must at all times be subservient to its interests. The bishop is chosen by the chapter of the Cathedral: the chapter, however, is generally forced to conform its choice to the dictation of Vienna.

Here the Italian language begins to be spoken. This town is famous for the holding of the last general council. As it was called chiefly to stop the progress of the errors which took their rise in Germany before the middle of the sixteenth century, its situation was judged most convenient for the German and Italian bishops. The great advantage, which the church derived from this assembly, is well known, though it was not so fortunate, as to put an end to the new heresies. The church of St. Mary Major, in which it was held, has nothing particular besides a remarkable fine organ. But the remembrance of that august assembly, which met in it so often, and procured so great services to christianity, made me view it as one of the most awful [awesome] sanctuaries in the world, and I could not refrain from expressing my gratitude to the Author of all good.

The mountains now began to decline apace: and proceeding along the Adige, which we had followed from its very source, we passed through Roveredo, a small lively town belonging to Austria, we came at last to Verona. We had now fairly emerged into Italy. It is impossible for the most saturnine constitution not to feel some of that enthusiasm, which the remembrance of great men, and great actions, the remains of arts and sciences, the monuments of sway and magnificence, are apt to excite in every cultivated mind.

As at our first entrance into Italy, I could speak but very little Italian, without which the traveller must be much at a loss for proper information, I could not get all those lights which I wished concerning Verona, Mantua and Modena, which lay in our road to Bolonia. I shall therefore reserve what occurs to be said of those places, till I return to visit them.

Bolonia is esteemed the second city of the pope's states; is the residence of a cardinal legate, and was erected into an archbishopric by Gregory XIII. a native of this town. Till that time, it was suffragan to the see of Ravenna. The archbishop is always a cardinal, and has the title of Prince of the Holy Empire. The city has undergone various revolutions: after the dismembering of the Roman empire, it formed sometimes a separate republic, and sometimes was subject to one or other of the petty princes, who tore Italy to pieces; when their tyranny became intolerable, it called the pope to its assistance, and made him a surrender of sovereignty: afterwards reassumed its independency, and finally submitted again to the holy see, retaining however, several privileges.

It is situated in the fertile and immense plain of Lombardy immediately under the Appenines, which separate that plain from Tuscany. This position renders Bolonia a very agreeable place to dwell in. The hills, which lie on one side, are covered with villas, which command a noble prospect over the populous and cultivated plains, and on the other side, the view of the mountains, one rising over the other, all thickly peopled and full of vineyards, cornfields, &c., afford on expressible pleasure to the eye. When one beholds the environs of Bolonia, as well as the throng of inhabitants in the town itself, the declamations of many English writers, on the wretched condition of the pope's states, the thinness of the population, the wretched condition of agriculture, appear as false as they are fulsome and tedious. I believe indeed, and may have occasion hereafter to remark, that they respect, chiefly that part of the ecclesiastical states, which is called the campania of Rome; but they use general expressions with so much confidence, that I cannot forbear observing how little credit ought to be given to them. Mr. Addison in particular, after a long enumeration of the perfections, which it were natural to imagine in the pope's government, concludes with saying that it is in fact the most imperfect of all, and the inhabitants infinitely more wretched than in the other states. This is undoubtedly a strange misrepresentation. Without question the pope's subjects are under some disadvantages peculiar to the nature of their government; as their sovereign is generally advanced in years, before he begins to reign, it is seldom he has that spirit which is necessary to enter upon any vigorous plan for the encouragement of industry and improvement of the natural richness of his dominions, and if now and then, some happy scheme is adopted, it runs great risk of not meeting with the same approbation in a succeeding reign. Thus many advantages proper to republics or hereditary states, are lost to this. Notwithstanding which, it is a truth most obvious to the traveller's observation, that the pope's subjects, (those at least, who inhabit the Bolognese, Ferrarese, the Romagna, the dutchy of Urbino, and the Marche of Ancona,) appear infinitely more happy, and at their ease, than those of Parma, Modena, and many other parts of Italy, to say nothing of several provinces of France and Germany. If trade do not flourish, (which is often owing to other causes besides want of the prince's encouragement,) at least private property is not exposed to arbitrary encroachments, as elsewhere; and if agriculture be not so improved as in England, much must be imputed to the natural fertility of the country, which makes the farmer more indifferent in cultivating his fields; and much to that invincible indolence which the violent heats produce in the inhabitants. However wise the legislator may be, he cannot always fully counteract the influence of the climate and seasons on the dispositions of the people. It appears to me that the great error of most travellers, in discoursing of the pope's states, arises from a comparative view of their former and present condition. When they behold the remains of ancient magnificence, and reflect on the immense population of former times, their imagination takes fire, and they give way to the popular declamations against priestly government, a monastical life, and the tyranny of Rome. These topics favor their prejudices; their trite and common-place reflections are esteemed profound philosophy; and they give themselves no farther trouble to find out other more general causes of the present decay. These the man of plain sense, without an extraordinary depth of observation, will easily be able to discover. When all the fine arts were carried to so great a perfection in Rome, when the city and its neighborhood swarmed so thick with inhabitants, is all this to be attributed merely to the superior excellency of the ancient, over the present government, and to the wiser political maxims of heathen Rome? Must its former splendor be owing entirely to former liberty, and the present decay to actual slavery, as superficial or passionate writers and poets often repeat? To overthrow this ungrounded supposition, let it be considered, that the noblest monuments and most perfect works of art, were performed during the reign of the first emperors, that is, during a period of infinitely more unrelenting tyranny, than was ever exercised by the worst of popes: that the population of Rome, its neighborhood, and of Italy in general, was the largest in the reign of Tiberius, and his inhuman successors, when not only private property, but the lives of the best men, were constantly exposed to the arbitrary dictates of a capricious tyrant.

The superiority, therefore, of ancient over modern Rome arose from the same cause, which, though in a much less degree, produces such a difference between London and Paris, and the adjacent country on one hand, and the remote provinces of the respective kingdoms on the other. If the conflux of inhabitants of a single kingdom, is able to spread such an air of magnificence and amazing population round the capital, can we be surprised at the different appearance of Rome and its environs, at the period when she gave laws to the whole world, and that, when she does not extend her empire over half Italy.

I might mention many other causes of the present decay more prevalent than the indolence of government; not that I deny this latter to have no part in producing the downfall. Abuses there are in every government, and perhaps they are the greatest where the government is mildest.

L Brent, pp. 223-76.   Carroll's letters to Ellerker, Oct. 26, 1772, and to his mother, Sep. 11, 1773, indicate the approximate date assigned here. Brent possibly implies (pp. 32-33) that this journal, like Carroll's History of England, was an instruction for Charles Philip, son of Lord Stourton, who was under his tutelage at this time.

HISTORY OF ENGLAND   1771-72

Not found. "While engaged in this tour [see Journal, 1771-72] he likewise wrote a succinct history of England, for the use of his pupil, in the form of a dialogue, principally to guard his young mind against the general irreligious tendency of soul, and the particularly hostile tendency of other writings, upon the same subject, against the Catholic faith."

See Brent, pp. 32-33.

TO THOMAS ELLERKER[1]   Rome Oct. 26—1772

My dear Sr.   I suppose this will find you returned from England, tho you have not yet given me any account of it. We are just arrived at Rome, viz: the 22d. of this month. My intention was to proceed the next day for Naples before any suspicion could be formed of my character here; but certain accidents will detain us here till the 27th. I keep a close incog[nito]. during this time, not going to any of our houses. I called privately to see Thorpe & Hothersall; but they were both in yr. country: so that having had no manner of communication with any Jt [Jesuit], I can send you no news concerning the affairs of ye Socty. I heared it said in some company, that such Sp [Spanish]: Jts, as being Europeans would not secularize themselves, would be obliged to settle in Majorca: the natives of America to be fixed in the Canaries. This will be a saving to Spain of a great sum of money, which is every year sent out of the country. I heared on the same occasion, that the *Luoghi di monte,* that is, the publick funds of this town have orders to issue no money to the soidisant, tho' they are concerned for great sums in them, several colleges having great part of their foundations lying there. But this, as well as other points I have not been able to clear up for the reasons above mentioned. The immediate cause of the suppression of the Irish College was a petition presented by the alumni to return to the Jts Schools. Cardl Marefoschi foamed with wrath, & violently insisted on the popes taking the step, which ensued.

We were much entertained on our road from Bolonia hither. The fine road along side of the Adriatick from Rimini to Loretto is most delightful. But of this and my other travelling observations you shall hear more at my return. A thousand Comp[limen]ts to Plowden,[2] who got, I hope, my letter from Milan: he shall hear from me likewise, either from Naples or at my return. I am in debt likewise to Ch. Wharton.[3] I cannot yet tell where my lodging will be when we come back: but a letter to Monsr Carroll Seigneur Anglois at Rome, or inclosed to the English College[4] will find me. Remember to pray for me; I did most earnestly for you at Loretto. Complts. to all my friend as usual. Ask Plowden if he remembers all the curious sepulchral inscriptions in the Church of S. Maria del Popolo. If he does not, I will send him a couple,

one of which is the most singular I believe anywhere extant.   Dr. Fr.   Ever
afftely Yrs   J. Carroll

ALS   St
   [1] Jesuit friend from County Durham, England and colleague at Liege.
   [2] Charles Plowden, S.J., friend from Carroll's days at Bruges and a principal correspondent.
   [3] Charles Wharton, S.J. (1748-1833), native of St. Mary's County, Maryland, he later left the ministry and the Catholic Church and published an attack on Carroll, who was a distant kinsman. See *Address to Roman Catholics of the United States,* 1784 below, which was a response.
   [4] Founded by Gregory XIII in Rome and entrusted to the Jesuits in 1578.

TO THOMAS ELLERKER   Jan 23–1772 [1773]

My dear Sir   Our catastrophe is near at hand, if we must trust to present appearances, & talk of Rome. The intelligence, which was talked of some time ago, importing that Spain had acceded at length to the Pope's plan, is greatly confirmed by universal persuasion at present; and I am assured that some of our best friends in the Sacred College, tho' not admitted to state secrets, yet now look upon the determination of our fate as entirely certain. All this notwithstanding, I am far from regarding this intelligence as infallible: to be sure, we have great reason to fear it to be true; but we have been alarmed so often during the present Pontificate with like reports, and the date of our destruction has been fixed so often without anything coming of it, that I hope this will have the same issue. Our friends however hope in nothing but the interposition of providence: and indeed by the attack made against the sacred heart,[1] & so much encouraged here, the cause of J[esus] . C[hrist] . has been so closely connected with ours, that this cannot fail of giving much confidence under the present dreadful appearances. Another very late fact may corroborate the idea you have probably formed of the spirit of the times here. On the feast of the chair of S. Peter, it is customary for a graduate of ye Sapeinza to make a discourse before the pope. The young man, who made it this year, proved the truth of ye. doctrine of the Rom: See from the constant succession of its pastors, & having occasion to introduce the mention of heresies springing from the poisoned minds of their founders, he said Ante Nestorium non fuere Nestoriani, ante Lutherum, Lutherani &c, nec *ante Jansenium fuere Jansenistae.*[2] You will not believe that at Rome this was looked upon as highly blameable, & I was astonished beyond measure, when I heared the poor ignorant Child Gastaldi, who hears all the Cardl York's[3] family discourse, wondering how the orator came to rank Jansenius amongst the sectaries, or Jansenism amongst the heresies. I am assured likewise that when printed copies of the discourse were afterwards carried to the Cardls according to custom, Marefoschi refused taking his, saying he would not have it because Jansenius made in it the figure of an archheretik. You have probably heared that this Cardl has begun a visit of a college left under the administration of the Gen[era]l, called from its founder Fucili College. He has Alfani for his cooperator, & no doubt between them, they will make fine work of it.

My situation at Rome affords me many opportunities of hearing the sentiments of the uninterested publick on the present situation of affairs. You may be assured that discontents against the Government are very high, particularly on account of the omnipotence of Fr. Bontempi, & one Bischi & his wife. The scandalous chronicle says the Lady in particular is a great favourite of Bontempi: it is certain that the pope is entirely governed by this junto, & that not one Gentleman of Rome has any interest with them. Their hatred against the favourites is great of course; perhaps it extends in some measure to the master, whom they seldom go near. I have inclosed to Ld Stourton a copy of the map printed and circulated here by Almada: you will receive it from his Ldsp, after which I desire you to forward it to Ch. Plowden at Bruges. That Almada should get such a thing printed, is not surprizing to those, who know what a fool, or madman rather, he is: but that so horrid a profanation of the Church prayers & its most august sacrifice should pass unnoticed in the very center of Catholicity, is astonishing, & gives a strange idea of the toleration allowed here to every thing done or said against us, while oppressed innocence is not allowed to urge the least defence in its favour. The Dominican Fr. Mamachi, of whom Zacheria often makes honourable mention, & who had gained much reputation by former works, has been gained over to Spain, & to serve certain ambitious views, has just published a work in favour of Palafoxe's orthodoxy. But when I see you, I will let you into some anecdotes concerning that prelates cause, which will convince you of its being lost beyond recovery. In the mean time, with complts as usual, I remain,   Dr Fr   Ever Yrs   J. C.

ALS   St   Contents in reference to previous letter show the date intended was 1773.
    [1] Devotion to the Sacred Heart of Jesus.
    [2] "Before Jansenius, there were no Jansenists," etc. Court enemies of the Jesuits now had occasion to be mild with the adversaries of the Jesuits in France—the Jansenists.
    [3] Henry Benedict, Duke of York (1725-1807), known to Jacobites as Henry IX, last of the Stuarts, often became a source of embarrassment to English Catholics.

TO THOMAS ELLERKER   Feb. 3–1773

My dear Fr   You Liegois are sad correspondents. I dare say you are curious to hear news, and yet give no encouragement to your friends to write. Yet you have many particularities to communicate to us at this distance, which would give some relief to the gloom, which overspreads us here at Rome. The report of an agreement being at length settled with Spain has subsisted now so long, that it gains very much credibility. The articles of it are said to be, 1o., depriving the Jesuits of their general. 2o. subjecting them to ye ordinaries, as a congregation of priests. 3o. Forbidding them (I suppose those of the Ecclesiastical State) to admit any supplies into their body. 4. Avignon to be restored. 5. The town of Aquila with its dependencies to be ceded to the pope in lieu of Benevento. 6. Castro & Ronciglione to be recognised formally as belonging to the Holy See. This agreement with Spain will be published, 'tis said, about Easter. It is likewise stipulated (tho not expressed in the paper which circulates about Rome) that the Jesuits are all to be sent at least 20 miles from hence, that they may not keep up a spirit of fanaticism and blind zeal amongst the cardinals and prelates.

While the Irish College was under the Jesuits, a vineyard belonging to it was sold to the novitiate of S. Andrew. A commission is now made out for Cardl. Marefoschi and four prelates to examine if the interests of the College were not sacrificed on this occasion: care has been taken to secure a proper determination by joining with the Cardl two Neapolitan Prelates, whose dependencies must necessarily influence their judgments against the novitiate. Perhaps likewise the other two are as sure tools, as any that have been employed for some time past in this kind of work. I know not whether I mentioned in my last that Marefoschi was likewise appointed Visitator (& Alfani his secretary) of a small college, called from ye prelate its Founder, Fucili College, which is destined for the education of a certain number of clergymen, & tho not immediately governed by the Society, yet entirely under its direction and superintendency. The deceased prefect founded a chaplainory disposeable by the Genl for a mass to be said every day at ye altar of S. Zavier of ye Gesu. The other day, the Cardl Visitor sent an order forbidding under pain of excommunication that mass to be continued. The order, & much more the strange sanction surprised every body, & appears very irregular for the very first notice sent to ye administrators. But I believe they are in the right, who imagine the Cardl by such proceeding has no other intention, than to impress the minds of the publick with an idea, that the most violent methods are necessary to inforce obedience from those refractory spirits. Another very serious affair here is, that the presses swarm with writings against the devotion to the sacred heart. What a revolution of ideas do all these proceedings produce in a mind accustomed to regard this city as the seat of Religion, and the bulwark against the incroachments of irreligion and impiety? Some of the most understanding as well as virtuous men here are persuaded entirely that the Jts will be expelled Rome, that they will lose the Roman College, Jesu, &c, but still that no essential alteration will be made in the Institute: but for the ground of their hopes, they can only alledge their trust in providence. My affte compliments as usual. I must sincerely congratulate you and your good fellow-professor for the ceremony

yesterday.   Drst Fr   Ever Yrs   J. C.   Remember me kindly to F. F.
Hodgson [&] Clifton

ALS   St

TO THOMAS ELLERKER   June 23. [1773]

My dear Fr   Mr. More[1] has probably left Liege by this time, and I shall
expect to hear from you the alterations his visit may have caused amongst
you, as well as your final determination concerning your visit to England. It is
a long time since I have heard any thing concerning my good Fr. Mercer, and
sincerely wish to be informed of his entire recovery. You will be pleased to
inform the Rector, that Mr. Stourton continues reacquiring his strength very
prosperously. In one of my late letters to Fr. Howard, I explained my
sentiments very freely on Neville's appointment to Philosophy, in the supposition of its not being a temporary measure, formed upon present necessity.
But if it should not be exclusive of Barrow, I dare say no one will have much
objection to it. I shall be glad to hear from you on this subject. Poor Austin's
misfortune excited, I doubt not, in you the same sentiments of grief &
compassion, which the reflection of so many hours spent amicably together
raised in my mind. He is indeed an example, which cannot but raise fears in
those, who lived with him in the course of his studies. Who can either depend
on himself or others, when a person of so religious behaviour, & so tender
conscience is come to so deplorable a condition?

Before this comes to your hands, Fr. Hothersall will have informed you
how far he has been affected by the late operations at Rome: however I will
venture to repeat, what we heard by yesterday's post. The Chancellor & Vicar
of Cardl. York Bishop of Frescati, by supreme order, as they signified, visited
a few days ago three houses of the Jesuits in order to search for printing
presses, which were suspected to be there. The houses were Monte Portio of
the Eng: College, Rufanella of the Roman, and ye residence of Frescati. In
the two last nothing was found, on which a suspicion could be hastend: but
in the Rector's room at Monte Portio was discovered a paper with some lamp
black in it, which is used to making blacking for shoes. I suppose this was
construed to be materials for making ink, & in consequence was carried off &
consigned to Cardl. York, who, I suppose is to present it to his holiness. Tho'
the visiters said their search was for printing presses, yet they extended it to
books &c, but with little success. They carried away from the R[ecto]rs.
room, besides the lamp-black, the offices of S. Pulcheria & Ven. Bede: &
hearing the Curate of the parish had a copy of the Bourg fontaine project,
they took that likewise away from him. The order for this visit was probably
occasioned by some late printed sheets scattered about Rome, some on the
Palafox cause, & others on the scandalous decision of Fr. Pisani's affair. In

particular, the Judge Alfani has been deeply wounded by a series of anecdotes, which have been published of him. The paper is badly written, but is wholly founded on truth, & exposes the Judge to the contempt, or rather the execration of the publick.

Another thing has happened at Rome, which gives much uneasiness & is probably the effect of some malicious enemy: for surely no friend could be so indiscreet, as to be the author of it. A letter was lately received by all, or at least by several Cardls, in which they are told, that the Spanish Ambassador is to come with peremptory demands for the abolition of the Society, & that his demands are to be accompanied with threats: that there is no vigor in the present government, or resolution to make a proper answer, as temporal considerations prevail so much over ye spiritual welfare of the church, which the writer endeavours to shew by many late facts: wherefore he advises the Cardls. to consult on the means for hindering the mischief, which may ensue.

The affair of the Roman seminary still remains in suspence. It is said that the Cardls. Vicar Colonna & Marefoschi are to hold a conference on the subject. The former is resolute in his opinion, that nothing be determined, without hearing the Seminary justify its conduct. Waterton is still at Rome. Has Fr. Stuart had another touch of the gout? Does he follow Dr. Cadogan's rules of drinking water, & eating only one thing? Could he abide by this regime during the Pentecost villa? Should one Fr. Pellegrini of this province pass by Liege, I hope the Rr. will shew him great civility. He is an eminent preacher & very fine writer. I know him only by reputation, & he is now travelling thro Germany & the low Countries, attended by his Br[other]. Count Pellegrini, a Gen[era]l. in ye Queen's service.   Complts.

ALS   St.   For date of this letter see to Eleanor Darnall Carroll, Sep. 11, 1773.
[1] Carroll's major superior, Thomas More (1722-95), Provincial of the English Mission of the Society of Jesus, with jurisdiction over the English colonies of North America, until the suppression of the Jesuits.

TO [ELEANOR DARNALL CARROLL[1]]   [Bruges, September 11, 1773]

I this day received a few lines from Daniel, of July 15, in which he complains with much reason of my long silence. My mind is at present too full of other things to make any apology. After spending part of the autumn of 1772 at Naples, and its environs, we returned to pass the winter at Rome, where I stayed till near the end of March, from thence came to Florence, Genoa, Tunis, Lyons, Paris, and so to Liege and Bruges. I was willing to accept of the vacant post of prefect of the sodality here, after consigning Mr. Stourton into his father's hands about two months ago, that I might enjoy some retirement, and consider well in the presence of God the disposition. I found myself in of going to join my relatives in Maryland, and in case that disposition continues, to get out next spring. But now all room for deliberation seems to be over. The enemies of the society, and above all the unrelenting perseverance of the Spanish and Portuguese Ministries, with the passiveness of the court of Vienna, has at length obtained their ends: and our so long persecuted, and I must add, holy society is no more. God's holy will be done, and may his name be blessed forever and ever! This fatal stroke was struck on the 21st of July, but was kept secret at Rome till the 16th of August, and was only made known to us on the 5th of September. I am not, and perhaps never shall be, recovered from the shock of this dreadful intelligence. The greatest blessing which in my estimation I could receive from God, would be immediate death: but if he deny me this, may his holy and adorable designs on me be wholly fulfilled. Is it possible that Divine Providence should permit to such an end, a body wholly devoted, and I will still aver, with the most disinterested charity, in procuring every comfort and advantage to their neighbors, whether by preaching, teaching, catechizing, missions, visiting hospitals, prisons, and every other function of spiritual and corporal mercy? Such I have beheld it, in every part of my travels, the first of all ecclesiastical bodies in the esteem and confidence of the faithful, and certainly the most laborious. What will become of our flourishing congregations with you, and those cultivated by the German fathers?[2] These reflections crowd so fast upon me that I almost lose my senses. But I will endeavor to suppress them for a few moments. You see that I am now my own master, and left to my own direction. In returning to Maryland I shall have the comfort of not only being with you, but of being farther out of the reach of scandal and defamation, and removed from the scenes of distress of many of my dearest friends, whom God knows, I shall not be able to relieve. I shall therefore most certainly sail for Maryland early next spring, if I possibly can.

L Brent, pp. 25-27.

[1] Brent indicates Daniel, Carroll's brother, as addressee, but the first sentence shows that it was some other member of Carroll's family, very likely his mother, for whom the letter was intended.

[2] Ferdinand Farmer and other immigrant German Jesuits stationed at Philadelphia, and Lancaster County, Pennsylvania.

A NARRATIVE OF THE PROCEEDINGS IN THE SUPPRESSION OF THE TWO ENGLISH COLLEGES AT BRUGES IN FLANDERS LATELY UNDER THE GOVERNMENT OF THE ENGLISH JESUITS　　　[1774]

When Queen Elizabeth had settled the Protestant Religio [n] in England, it is well known that several very severe laws were enacted against the Roman Catholicks, & the publick profession of their faith. Amongst other grievances to which they were subjected, was that of their children being deprived of the benefits of publick education, unless they conformed to the doctrines & worship of the established church, the government and direction of the universities and colleges being put entirely into the hands of Protestants; and all Papist[s] being forbidden under the severest penalties to erect or open schools within the realm. To supply the want of proper seminaries on this side of the sea, some zealous Catholicks found means to establish some on the other, destined to receive and educate the English youths, who should be sent thither. Among these Seminaries was that of S. Omer,[1] which was procured by the English Jesuits towards the latter end of ye reign of Elizabeth. It soon became very flourishing by the conflux of young English Gentlemen, & the [at] tention, which was constantly paid to ye securing of their morals from vice as well as ye improvement of their understanding in ye belles letters, & classical knowledge: insomuch that it was very well known at ye time that the honourable testimony given by Lord Chancellor Bacon to the method of education introduced [,or] rather revived by the Jesuits referred particularly to ye College of S. Omer. It continued with ye same reputation, till ye Expulsion of the Jesuits out of France in ye year 1762, when the English were likewise obliged to leave this their so long flourishing establishment. It is not in my subject to make at present any reflexions either upon the causes of ye general expulsion of ye Society out of France, or of the peculiar injustice done at that time to ye English Jesuits; tho' I am confident that a fair representation of their case might raise in ye reader still greater indignation for what has since happened.

When it became certain that the College of S. Omer would be taken out of the hands of the Jesuits, several towns of Austrian Flanders sensible of the advantage, they should derive from their forming a new establishment, made speedy application to draw them within their walls. As Bruges was foremost in making the invitation, & the situation of that town was very convenient for the purpose of an English College, they fixed upon that place, & contrived, to the great satisfaction of the respective parents, to remove with themselves the young students then in their College of S. Omer. After their arrival at Bruges, they were collected as soon as possible into ye same house, &, tho' subject to many inconveniences, schools were very soon opened, that too long interruption of studies added to the confusion of so extraordinary a transportation might not beget a habit of dissipation fatal to youth.

It is to be observed that about twenty years before the banishment of the Eng: Jesuits from St. Omer a new establishment had been formed by them for the still farther improvement of a virtuous education. For whereas the great College received only rich youths as were advanced sufficiently to enter upon their classical studies, a scheme was proposed and executed for forming another seminary into which children might to taken from the age of seven upwards to twelve, & taught reading, writing, arithmetick, book-keeping, with the first principles of Geography, and of their own as well as of the learned languages: in a word, this seminary was intended to fit and qualify them for entering into the greater college. This however was not the great object of the establishment: it is too well known to every one that the schools in England, even those where children of the tenderest years are taught their first elements, are in general extremely dangerous to morals, & that vice is often learned sooner there than the Alphabet. Fatal experience had shewn that boys entered from these schools into the college with tainted and corrupted morals, and there appeared no remedy so powerful to prevent the evil complained of as the forming of such an establishment, as the one I now mention, in which the children were treated indeed with all the kindness, which their tender years required, but at the same time kept from all occasions of learning vice by an unremitting watchfulness and attention. Malevolence and ignorance, and prejudice may continue to misrepresent the Jesuits principles and conduct, & persecute them even, when they are no more: but thinking men, who know them intimately and have followed them with very close attention, will allow that no motive, but a sincere and disinterested zeal for the virtuous education of youth, could induce persons of abilities, & learning & often of rank to pay so mortifying & constant an attendance on infants, especially when they had no expectations of the least advantage on profit to themselves. For the reader must remember, that these masters received not the smallest retribution; if the youth payed his boarding, nothing more was required: private perquisites were quite out of the case. This previous account of the two establishments lately destroyed at Bruges was necessary: it may serve in some degree to shew the reader how deserving they were of ye encouragement they found and to lament with members the greatness of their loss.

The students therefore of both these seminaries being brought to Bruges, and in some degree settled by consent and invitation of the magistracy, it still remained to obtain the sanction of government. Count Cobenze was at this time her Imperial Majesty's minister Plenipotentiary at Brussels for the low countries. An application being made to him, he easily saw that the erecting of two such colleges in his mistresses Dominions would be of considerable service as well to the country in general, as to the particular town, in which they should fix: he therefore interested himself warmly in their behalf; and obtained from his Sovereign letters patent, whereby the English Jesuits were admitted into the town of Bruges, and allowed there to buy ground, & erect the two colleges necessary to their plan of education. The Jesuits thus acquired a legal settlement and became entitled as well for themselves as their property to the protection of the laws of the country, into which they were admitted.

Their property indeed was the more entitled to this protection, and ought in right to be secured to them against any revolution, which might happen to their body, as they received nothing from the country, in which they acquired their new establishment. Great as their expences were on their sudden removal, they found not the least assistance either from the province of Flanders or town of Bruges, tho' the establishing of two such colleges was of such advantage to them. What the Jesuits could save out of the wreck of their fortunes at S. Omer, the benefactions of some generous friends, & above all the disinterested contributions of several individuals of their own Society enabled them by degrees to put matters again in some tolerable order. Improvements were every day made, and if the students were not lodged as conveniently as they had been at S. Omer, the same or greater attention was however paid to them in every other respect, & the plan of studies, far from suffering from the inconveniencies of situation, was greatly improved, and where all were zealous to arrive at perfection, and their views were directed by experience, every year opened some prospect of new advantage in the course of education.

The Jesuits therefore will be bold to aver, that they fully complied with the terms of their admission into ye Austrian States, & answered or surpassed the most sanguine expectations of the town of Bruges, with respect to ye temporal emoluments to be derived from the new settlements. The town has repeatedly given them this honourable testimony and latterly when alarmed by the bull of dissolution, the magistrate thought their duty to present a petition to ye Government at Brussells, praying that two Colleges so service-able in every respect to Religion and the country might still be allowed to subsist. This petition was not, as it often happens, the effect of private management: it was the voluntary expression of the sentiments not only of the body of magistrates, but of almost every individual in the whole town. It was founded not only upon the regularity, and discipline which they saw preserved amongst the students, but likewise on the constant and daily increase of their numbers, which was the effect of the constantly growing reputation of the Mrs. [members] & Superiors. The government itself became so sensible of the advantage to ye town and country, that it was sollicitous to secure to them the permanency of these establishments. They very well knew that when the Jesuits were expelled from France, they had left a very noble College ready built at S. Omer, and they feared that if by any new change in that kingdom the Jesuits should be recalled, it would be natural for them to return & take possession of their antient dwelling, rather than be at the expence of erecting a new College. These probably were the considerations, which induced the Government to send repeated orders to the new inhabitants of Bruges to begin the building for their new College; year after year were these injunctions given, and nothing could prevail upon the ministry to withdraw them, but the Jesuits giving demonstrative proofs of their total inability to set about such an undertaking.

This earnestness in the ministry to secure the settlements at Bruges is an irrefragable proof, that they were judged to be beneficial; that the Jesuits had given no cause of dissatisfaction or complaint; in a word that they had fully answered the ends of their admission into ye country. If they found themselves unable to undertake all, which the minister required, they at least did all they could, and full enough to give assurances of their intentions to remain in ye country, happen what would. They laid out £ St 4500 in ye purchase of a spot of ground in the town, whereon to erect the great college, whenever it should be in their power to build it. Near £ 3000 were likewise spent in buying the ground for the less College; and not content with this, being compelled by absolute necessity, they began & finished great part of the building for this latter establishment. I need say but little of the manner in which this was executed; let every one, Catholick or Protestant, who have seen this College (and many Englishmen of both Religions have seen it) speak from their own knowledge of the excellent accommodations for the tender Children, of the neatness, elegance, & order which was preserved amongst them. The tenderest Mother, on seeing this school, would not be afraid of trusting her darling child to it, & I shall only repeat, what has been said by thousands, that it had not its equal in Europe.

The pressing sollicitations and even the injunctions of the Court of Brussels to undertake the building of two new Colleges in the circumstances, in which the Jesuits then were, ought to be attended to. It was notorious at that time, that the princes of the Bourbon family had demanded of the court of Rome the utter extinction of the Society; and many events had evinced that the pope was not in the inclination to shew it the least favour, to use the most moderate expression. How far the Court of Vienna would allow the demand of the Bourbon family to operate with respect to ye Austrian States, was a secret to ye publick; but surely not to the Government of Brussels. And since the event has shewn, that the brief of extinction, when ever it should appear, was to be admitted in her Emm[inent]: Maj[esty's]: dominions in its full extent, it cannot but occur to every thinking man that the ministry of Brussels sought to engage the Jesuits in new expenses, in order to avail themselves of the plunder immediately after. This was indeed a poor return for the benefits, which had derived to ye Country from their establishment at Bruges, and an artifice to distress without resource the individuals of the Society, & injure their friends, without whose generous assistance such an undertaking could not be begun.

It however fortunately happened, that after the less College was built, & ground purchased for the site of the greater, so heavy a debt remained to be discharged, as utterly to disable the Jesuits from commencing any new building. They were obliged to continue in the house, they had hired from the beginning, & make amends for the inconveniency of their situation by redoubling their application to improve & perfect the education of ye young Gentlemen under their care. Both Colleges had the happiness to find that their endeavors to give satisfaction were approved: the conflux of students was constantly increased; and if ever the disadvantages arising from the general circumstances of ye. Society had been overcome, there is no doubt but the town and Country would have reaped a much larger profit from the Colleges, which already exceeded their most sanguine expectations.

It is therefore no wonder that the news of the dissolution of the order was received with ye greatest anxiety. The magistracy and citizens persuaded themselves, that the Government would not destroy two settlements so lately authorised by themselves, & that the bull would have no farther operation respecting the Eng: Jesuits, than to reduce them to ye condition of secular priests; but that they would be allowed, if they themselves were willing, to continue the same functions, they had hitherto discharged. Encouraged by these general expectations of the town, the Superiors of the two Colleges wrote a letter to Monssr. Neny, President of the privy Council at Brussels, who had often declared himself ye protector of the Colleges, & is thought to hold the first share in ye government. In ye. letter they expressed their alarms on account of ye situation of ye. Society; but withal desired to continue to render the same service to Religion and the instruction of youth, now they became secular Clergymen, as heretofore, whilst they were Jesuits: and if the government should not judge proper to allow any longer of the Colleges under their care, they prayed at least to have time to give warning to parents to remove their children; and especially reminded the minister of the necessity of such a delay arising from ye. situation of several American youths, who had no other friends in Europe besides the persons under whose care they actually were. To this letter Mr. Neny made a civil answer expressing his constant regard for the two Colleges, promising to do for them whatever should be in his power; & giving encouragement to the two Superiors to wait on him at Brussels. When they arrived thither, he immediately gave them an audience, in which he told them that he could say nothing positively to them because he knew nothing of the intentions of Vienna, that Court not having yet sent any orders relatively to ye Jesuits: that the whole of what was then written, was contained in a letter from the Empress Queen to his (Mr. Neny's) Brother, who chanced to be at that time at Brussels, in which her Majesty had these words: *Le 21 Juillet l'arret de mort a eté signé contre les Jesuites; je les ai toujours estimés.* "On the 21st of July (this is the date of their suppression at Rome) the death warrant of the Jesuits was signed; I always esteemed them." Several other publick persons, whom the Superiors saw at Brussels, gave them the strongest assurances of protection, and incessantly repeated to them that their establishments were of too great consequence to the Country not to be supported. And in all events, they said it was certain they would be treated with decency and regard; that their effects would be left them, or at least a provision made for their subsistance. Even Mr. Neny himself, when he heard from the Superiors that the English Jesuits on being expelled from France, were left without pensions, expressed his surprise & said it was a manifest injustice.

Some days after the return of the Superiors to Bruges, the Bishop received a commission from Court relative to ye execution of the bull. He immediately gave notice of his orders, & at ye same time said he was persuaded, that whatever change might happen in ye two Colleges, would only last for two or three days, after which everything would be allowed to go on as usual. Soon after this intimation from the Bishop, the lay Commissaries deputed by the ministry of Brussels likewise arrived, and on the morning of Sepr. 20th entering into the Colleges they ordered the doors to be shut, & placed guards over them; they assembled all the Jesuits, & having caused to be read the brief of their suppression and the Queens edict allowing it to be executed throughout Flanders, they then pursuant to private instructions forbad any Jesuit to go abroad, or have communication with persons abroad; to keep schools, or give any instruction to ye scholars either respecting learning or their duties of Religion; they declared them divested of all authority to administrate the temporalities of the Colleges, and assigned persons to do it in their stead &c. After which, a deputy from the Bishop revoked all the spiritual powers of adminis'[te]ring the sacraments, preaching or catechising, which had been ever granted, leaving them only faculty to say mass in their private chapel. The Bishop himself came shortly after, & having repeated his former assurances, he appointed two secular Priests at each College as President and Vice-President. Thus the scholars, without the least intimation being sent to their Parents, were taken out of the hands, which they had been intrusted by those alone, who had a right to dispose of them: and a farther injustice was, the suspension of their education, whilst parents were kept at the expence of paying for them, as if that had been duly attended to. The Jesuits were strictly inhibited from writing letters; and tho they represented the injury & hardship to absent Gentlemen not to be informed of the situation of their children, several of whom were almost infants, yet they could obtain nothing more from the Commissaries than a promise to write to Court to represent this grievance. When the answer came from Court, the leave it gave to write was so limited, that it could not be of any advantage. It restrained the Jesuits to write no more than this; that the students were in good health, & that the same care was taken of them, as had ever been. The letters were all to be delivered to, seald, and dispatched by the Commissaries. As such letters would have conveyed a manifest falsehood, whilst the education of the students was entirely neglected, none of the Jesuits would write at all to the Gentlemen of their acquaintance, at which the Bishop was not a little, tho' very undeservedly displeased. In the mean time, the Commissaries proceeded to make an inventory of all the effects in the Colleges, first obliging the two head Superiors of each house to make oath to discover them all fairly and entirely, and the inventory being finished, all the Jesuits were assembled to hear it read, and obliged likewise under oath to aver that it was a true Inventory, as far as they knew. They were admonished before hand, that if any fraud or concealment should afterwards be discovered, they would be treated with all the severity of the laws against wilful perjurers. It is to be observed that this oath was administer'd to ye rest after the Superiors had already attested the Inventory. Such treatment and such menaces were very strange with respect to persons, who were still complimented with flattering commendations of their care and application in instilling the principles of virtue in the minds of youth, and even with the promises of being still employed that way. The usage they now met with, besides being inconsistent with the Bps. assurances, had no other cause besides the wantonness of arbitrary power, and a disposition to add insult to the misfortune of men, amongst whom were several of a rank superior to that of their persecutors; for I think I may call them such; in particular one of the Superiors being Br. to a peer of G. Britain, & another nearly allied to several of the principal ones in this kingdom, to omit the connections & families of other private Jesuits, who were at Bruges exposed to these Insults.

The confinement of the Jesuits extended likewise, to the scholars. As it was an invariable rule for the latter never to go abroad without some Superior to attend them, the Commissaries allowed one to accompany them the very first day of the committment; but reflecting afterwards, that this indulgence might displease the government at Brussels, they would not grant it again for near a fortnight; and at the less College it was never permitted once during four weeks. The Jesuits were even so closely guarded, and all communication with persons abroad was so strictly inhibited, that Gentlemen and Ladies passing thro' Bruges, were often refused leave to speak with the Superiors of the Colleges concerning their relations, who were actually under their care: and if ever it was allowed to speak to them, it was to be in ye presence of the Commissaries or of their Substitutes, and in French, that they might understand what was said. A very respectable young Lady, just arrived from England, desiring to speak to ye Superior of the great College concerning her two Brs., who were students in it, was abruptly refused admission; and another Gentleman and Lady, who found means to enter into the less College, when they called for the Superior, were told they must depart: the Lady continuing resolutely to insist on seeing him, one of the Substitutes of the Commissary was so rude as to attempt violently to thrust her out of the room. Many adventures of this kind happened, which it is difficult to account for, as the sufferers were never charged with any crime, which could even furnish a pretext for such treatment. All this time, the letters directed to them were rigorously intercepted, tho' written by parents concerning their children; even those directed to the students were opened and examined; and there is great reason to believe that many of them were never delivered.

Had the Jesuits been charged in her Imp: Majesty's edict for ye execution of ye bull with any crimes, or if they had been accused of any felonious acts, the treatment they met with could not have been much more severe: it was equally felt by all; the old, and young, those concerned in the administration of the Colleges, and others who had no share in it, underwent the same hardships: With respect to them, one would think the laws had lost their whole force, and could no longer extend their protection to insure to them the rights common to the meanest individual. They were despoiled of them without trial or any reason assigned, and are yet at a loss to know, upon what foundation, besides the caprice and insolence of power, the privy Council of Brussels proceeded in giving orders so contrary to justice and the laws of Flanders.

In the midst of these hardships, the chief concern of the Jesuits was to see their scholars, thro want of employment, falling in[to] habits of indolence and dissipation. They incessantly represented to the Bishop and Commissaries the detriment, which must ensue to the young Gentlemen, from the suspension of their usual litterary exercises. The Bishop became persuaded of the bad consequences, & writ to Court to have something determined. In consequence of the answers he received, he proposed to the Jesuits (I continue to call by this name those, who were such before the pope's brief had secularised them) to continue their former employments, it being resolved that the two English Colleges should continue to subsist. The next day, most of the Jesuits, having answered that they were willing to remain in their several employments, as long as they could be of any service to Religion, and the education of Youth, the Bishop expressed great joy at their determination, said that every thing should be settled to their satisfaction in a few days, & even assured them that, as they now no longer formed a body, on which they might depend for a subsistance, in case of infirmity or age, they should be provided with competent salaries, as long as they were employed in the service of the Colleges; adding that he had received instructions to that effect. He & ye Commissaries even allowed them to open their schools anew, which were continued from this time, as long as the Jesuits remained, notwithstanding all the discouragements, which followed, as the reader shall soon be informed.

The Bishop not content with the assurances he had given to the Jesuits themselves, sent a circular printed letter to the parents of the Young gentlemen at the two Colleges, in wch. he informed them of the resolution of the Government to preserve those establishments; that he knew from good hands that the same masters would be preserved in them, and hoped the parents would continue to give the same countenance to the Colleges as heretofore. He moreover writ to ye Gentleman, who before the dissolution of their body, had been Provincial of the English Jesuits, in which he sent him a list of the persons he proposed to employ at Bruges, adding at the same time that he was exceedingly earnest to have the whole business settled to his satisfaction. These steps of the Bishop, which he said were warranted by the Government, quieted the fears of parents, who were alarmed and distressed for their children. Highly pleased with the idea of their continuing still under the direction of the same masters, they expressed in their answers the warmest acknowledgement to the Bishop for the pains he had been at. The Jesuits themselves after such authentick promises could hardly entertain a suspicion of the subsequent treatment they were to meet; tho during the interval of the Bishop's writing his letter, & the answers which were made to it, many things happened, which might naturally cause diffidence. All letters were still stopped; all communication from abroad severely prohibited; the Superiors were every day subjected to new interrogatories, that betrayed an earnest inclination in the Government to have some pretence to fall out with them [&] lay them under grievious imputations. When the inventory of effects belonging to the Colleges was first taken, each individual was advertised that what he claimed as his own, was not to form any part of it; that he might dispose of his own private effects how and in what manner he pleased. These effects were in general of so small value, that one would imagine they could never excite the attention of the ministry of Brussels. As the individuals of the Society were provided with all the necessaries of life, cloathing &c by the College, in which they dwelled, and as all luxury in furniture was excluded in private rooms, the chief riches of the Jesuits consisted in those books, which each one had purchased for his private use with the presents of money, he from time to time received from his parents or relations. However even these insignificant articles were to undergo a severe scrutiny. Tho every Jesuit had before sworn, that the inventory abovementioned comprehended all the effects belonging to the Colleges, yet each one was unexpectedly called upon by the Commissary to attend him to his room, and there to shew every article, & every penny he claimed as belonging to himself, & to swear again that he had concealed nothing, & that everything, he now averd to be his, was really so, & not procured either directly and indirectly with the money of the Society. After so many oaths, one would have expected no farther enquiries into this matter. But the spirit of rapine, which directed every step of the Council of Brussels, was not consistent with itself. Whilst they promised on one side to trust the Jesuits with the education of youth, & bestowed commendations on the care and assiduity, with which they formed their minds to virtue; they paid on the other no sort of regard to the oaths, which they still forced on the sufferers, and acted with them as with men not only unworthy of the great trust, which it was pretended was designed them; but likewise, wholly destitute of all principles of honour and conscience. For the very day after this last oath was administered the Jesuits were suddenly ordered to attend on one of the Commissaries in the same chambers, and as soon as they were assembled, they were required to deliver up all their keys, even of their most private papers. The Commissary then left them with guards to overlook & see that they did not depart from the place, where they had been assembled: He himself went to each particular's room, attended by a blacksmith, Masson and Carpenter, who were sworn to examine every part of the house, where they could suspect either money or other effects to be concealed. Every corner was thus diligently searched, every drawer was looked into, papers were turned over, & no precaution was omitted to discover the hidden treasures, which avarice had imagined to be concealed somewhere in the College. All this was conducted with so little ceremony, that the searchers did not allow themselves time to try the keys, but precipitately broke open several locks. They were however at length ashamed of their Commission, and some of them expressed a becoming warmth of indignation for being employed in such dirty work.

All these proceedings seemed calculated to vilify in the eyes of ye students, the masters in whom they had hitherto honoured & esteemed, & in whose tenderness they had placed all their confidence. But if such were the designs of the Court of Brussels, they entirely miscarried. Far from conceiving a worse opinion of their Masters by any thing which had happen'd, those generous young gentlemen were fired with indignation at seeing such contumelious usage, and it was no easy task for the Masters to restrain them from rash expression or other more significative proofs of their resentment. Perhaps it would have been impossible to keep them within bounds had they not still been deluded with hopes of remaining under the same teachers: for even whilst the Commissaries were executing these opprobrious orders, they said that they were still certain that the English Jesuits would be continued in their Colleges. They often expressed their surprise at the rigour (they were afraid to say, the malevolence) of their instructions, especially as they had repeatedly written that they were fully satisfied with the clearness, fullness and sincerity of the accounts laid before them.

For after the inventory was taken of all the effects actually in the Colleges, the Commissaries required an exact and specifick account of their incomes, interests, credits, & debts. This was clearly stated to them, first by laying all the books of [*illeg.*] before them, & latterly by making large extracts, which gave them a clear insight into the real circumstances of the Colleges. From the materials laid before them, the Commissaries stated an account of the income, & profits, and of the outgoings and debts, which they were to transmit to Court. But observing first that a considerable sum & large arrears were due for the boarding of several students, they required the names of those students, as well as of their parents, with the place of their residence. All this was sufficient to evince that some mischief was intended; but still, the continued assurances to the contrary, and above all the Bishop's circular letter, which he said was warranted by the ministry, diminished alarms, if they did not entirely quiet them. When the list of debts & names of creditors was collected, the managing Gentlemen thought they might safely carry their scheme into execution. It was calculated not only to injure and oppress, but likewise to surprise and deceive the sufferers: it was not adopted as a sudden measure, and speedily carried into execution; but previously & maliciously contrived, and at the same time artfully withheld from the knowledge of those, whom it was to affect, that the weight of their misfortune might not be alleviated by foreseeing the fate which was to befall them. The English Dominicans have a small settlement at Boerem, a village situated on the Scheld, a few miles from Antwerp. The ministry of Brussels made early application to these Religious to accept of the direction of the two Colleges at Bruges: they were ordered to be [in] readiness to set out for that place, but forbidden most severely to send any information to England, of what was intended, at least not so, that advice might be returned from thence by Octr. 14th. Every precaution was taken to prevent the Jesuits receiving the least notice of [what] was intended. On the very day of the 14th, the Commissary assembled them in the morning to hear the reading of the statement which had been formed of ye income, credits, & debts of the College: he went thro great part of it, and appointed an hour in the evening for finishing the whole; he added that he should be very glad when it was over; as the moment, that the reading of it would be finished, and affirmed under oath to be true, every individual would be at liberty, & their confinement at an end. He therefore requested, that all might be punctual to the time appointed, that when he returned in the evening, every thing should be in readiness to finish the business. It may easily be imagined that the prospect of recovering their liberty renderd every one punctual to the appointment. They were scarce met, when the Commissary enterd, attended by some of the magistrates of the town. Instead of restoring liberty, he came to announce more grievous oppression. He orderd all to leave the English Colleges, and attend him to that, which was still occupied by the Flemish Jesuits: the avenues leading to the doors were lin[e]d with guards, & coaches were ready to convey away the prisoners. No one was allowed upon any pretence to return to his own chamber, not so much as to take his hat. The coaches were escorted by files of soldiers with their fixed bayonets, which could not seriously have been intended by way of precaution, but only to add to misfortune the appearance of criminality. Other guards were in waiting to receive them at the Flemish Jesuits. Thus were they suddenly & violently separated from the young Gentlemen, who had been committed to their care, & who were now abandoned in a foreign country, without the comfort of one confidential friend to apply to, even in the greatest emergency. No doubt but ye Reader will recollect the petition, which was presented at Brussels, as soon as the suppression of the Society was known, in which it was desired, that time might be given to receive the Instructions of parents concerning their children, if it should be resolved not to continue the same masters. So equitable a request was not attended to, because the ministry of Brussels foolishly persuaded themselves that parents would implicitly submit to any insults and indignities they should put upon them.

The Jesuits were scarce removed, when the scholars, who were at that time collected together at their studies, began to [*illeg.*] the alarm: they soon discovered what had happened, and their resentment for the usage, they now received, broke out in the most violent manner. A regard, and constant attention to their welfare had endeard their Masters to them; and having no other friends in the country, their own feelings added weight to th[eir] sense of the cruelty exercised upon them. Their indignation was rou[sed] still higher, when they found how they themselves were to be treated. In every corner of the College, they met town serjeants, and soldiers with their screwed bayonets to awe them into order and silence all complaints. A committee of the magistrates was likewise charged to remain amongst them. The doors were shut, & none were allowed to go out, & remove from the scene of disorder, which was soon to ensue. Fired at this usage, it it [*sic*—is] not to be wondered at, if their indignation was no longer to be restrained. In the two Colleges there were near 220 students, and amongst them a great many youths of the noblest & most antient families of this kingdom. They refused to be awed by the soldiery or magistrates, & when the Commissary endeavourd to pacify them, told him, that no authority over them was given him by those to whom God and nature had placed the right of disposing of them. They had discoverd in the whole conduct of the Court of Brussels, from the first moment of the Jesuits confinement, such a spirit of minute enquity into the effects belonging to the College and to particulars, that they supposed this last proceeding to be the effect of rapine and avarice. They yet knew nothing of the intention to introduce other Masters: to prevent therefore those whom they esteemed plunderers, from reaping the whole fruit of their iniquity, they began to break and destroy whatever they could lay hands on. They saw themselves prisoners, yet still felt themselves Englishmen. In vain did the Commissary and magistrates require them to go to rest, when the night was advanced: many answerd only with their tears, others by giving loose to all the wildness of anarchy and despair. If the soldiers attempted to inforce the injunctions of their principals, they were soon compelled to desist by the united opposition of the students; and nothing was wanting to compleat the disasters of that night, but an order to the soldiers to fire amongst the young gentlemen.

What a scene would this have been to tender parents, had they beheld their children, now under no controul, and full of despair and indignation, engaged in a contest with soldiers, who kept their bayonets pointed against them. What an idea does such a proceeding convey of the government, which designedly brought matters to this issue! In the midst of this confusion, the Commissary finding every method of pacifying the students ineffectual, was forced to have recourse to those, who had been a little before conducted out of the College in so ignominios a manner. He desired two of them to accompany him back, & to persuade their former scholars to remain quiet. This gave occasion to a most affecting scene. No sooner was it known that two of the Jesuits were returned to the College, than they all ran precipitately to them; and bursting into a flood of tears, several earnestly besought the Fathers (for so they called them) to take pity of their situation, and to relieve them from the forlorn and friendless condition, to which they were now reduced. They threw themselves on their knees and clung to those of their former Masters. Such proofs of confidence and affection, joined to the reflection of their inability to render now any service to these helpless youths, quite overcame the resolution of those, who had hitherto been little moved by any hardships personal to themselves. They were only able to recommend to them to submit with patience to their present situation, till they could hear from their parents, who undoubtedly would hasten to their assistance: which being over, the Commissary reconducted them back to the Flemish College. They were no sooner departed than the sentiments of despair returned more violently upon the students, & the whole night was an uninterrupted scene of disorder and distraction. Some of the students found means to escape thro the College doors, forcing their way thro the guards; others jumped out of windows, others over walls, with imminent danger of their lives. It is even reported of one, that not finding any other means of escaping, he leaped over a part of the garden wall contiguous to a canal, & swam over it in the middle of the night. Books, beds and bedding, the house furniture, whatever in a word they could lay hold of, they threw out of the windows to the crowds of people, which this singular event had drawn together in the streets contiguous to the Colleges. The following days did not at all diminish the vivacity of their resentments. It was a lamentable and affecting sight to behold a great number of them, all the succeeding days, wandering thro' the streets, abandoned to themselves, and left exposed to the dangers arising from dissipation and independency. In vain did they sollicit leave to advise with, or speak to their antient Masters, even in presence of the Commissaries: many of the students, besides being placed by their parents under the Jesuits, as heads of the Colleges, were recommended to particular individuals of that order, owing to personal acquaintance of family connections. The necessity of such recommendations will appear to every one who considers the situation & helpless condition of the young Gentlemen in a foreign country. But no regard was now paid to these connections. A Brother, an uncle, a near relation was not allowed to see, or even give any direction concerning the students so closely allied to him.

It is true, that to replace the Jesuits, some Dominicans from the Convent of Borhem were put in possession of the two Eng: Colleges the morning after the removal of the first. . . .

AD   MPA   There are a considerable number of deletions, which reveal the attitudes of Carroll. Charles Plowden in 1807 wrote a similar narrative from notes taken at this time. See Hubert Chadwick, *St. Omers to Stonyhurst* (London, 1962), p. 326. As Secretary to Remonstrating Migrants, Carroll would logically compose the above narrative. See Melville, pp. 36-37. He was at Lord Arundell's Wardour Castle by early 1774, when the narrative was probably written.

[1] Carroll had his earliest education at St. Omers and in 1773 took up the office of Prefect of the Sodality at Bruges. (See to Eleanor Carroll, Sep. 11, 1773.) The Sodality was a religious confraternity, which also featured literary and other academic seminars.

TO [?]   [1776]

The Congress has done me the distinguished & unexpected honour of desiring me to accompany the Committee ordered to Canada, & of assisting them in such matters as they shall judge useful.

I should betray the confidence put in me by the honourable Congress, & perhaps disappoint their expectations, were I not to open my mind to them with the utmost sincerity, & plainly tell them how little service they can hope to derive from my assistance.

In the first place, the nature & functions of that profession, in which I have engaged from a very early period in life, render me, as I humbly conceive, a very unfit person to be employed in negotiations, of so new a kind to me, of which I have neither experience or systematical knowledge. I hope I may be allowed to add, that tho I have little regard to my personal safety amidst the present distress of my country, yet I cannot help feeling some for my character: and I have observed that when the ministers of Religion leave their duties of their profession to take a busy part in political matters, they generally fall into contempt; & sometimes even bring discredit to the cause, in whose service they are engaged.

Secondly—From all the information I have been able to collect concerning the State of Canada, it appears to me, that the inhabitants of that country are no wise disposed to molest the united colonies, or prevent their forces from taking & holding possession of the strong places in that province, or to assist in any manner the British arms. Now if it be proposed that the Canadians should concur with the other colonies any farther, than by such neutrality, I apprehend it will not be in my power to advise them to it. They have not the same motives for taking up arms against England, which render the resistance of the other colonies so justifiable. If an oppressive mode of government has been given them, it was what some of them chose, & the rest have acquiesced in. Or if they find themselves oppressed they have not tried the success of petitions & remonstrances, all of which ought, as I apprehend, to be ineffectual before it can be lawful to have recourse to arms & change of government.

Thirdly—Tho I were able to bring myself to think, (which, as objects now appear to me, I really cannot) that the Canadians might lawfully take up arms & concur with. . . .

ADf   AAB (Sp. C-F)   Charles Carroll of Carrollton was in Philadelphia in Dec., 1775, consulting about the commission to which he was ultimately appointed. It would not seem that John Carroll was informed of his role until at least a month later, and after possibly meeting with Charles and others about the difficulties mentioned, so that he ultimately joined the commissioners as an adviser.

TO ELEANOR DARNALL CARROLL [1776]

Not found. See May 1, 1776.

TO ELEANOR DARNALL CARROLL Montreal, May 1st, 1776

We have at length come to the end of our long and tedious journey, after meeting with several delays on account of the impassable condition of the lakes: and it is with a longing desire of measuring back the same ground, that I now take up my pen to inform you of my being in good health, thank God, and of wishing you a perfect enjoyment of yours.

We came hither the night before last and were received at the landing by General Arnold,[1] and a great body of officers, gentry, &c. and saluted by firing of cannon, and other military honors. Being conducted to the general's house, we were served with a glass of wine, while people were crowding in to pay their compliments, which ceremony being over, we were shown into another apartment, and unexpectedly met in it a large assemblage of ladies, most of them French. After drinking tea, and sitting some time, we went to an elegant supper, which was followed with the singing of the ladies, which proved very agreeable, and would have been more so, if we had not been so much fatigued with our journey. The next day was spent in receiving visits, and dining in a large company, with whom we were pressed to sup, but excused ourselves in order to write letters, of which this is one, and will be finished and dated to-morrow morning.

I owe you a journal of our adventures from Philadelphia to this place. When we came to Brunswick in the Jersey government, we overtook the Baron de W——, the Prussian general who had left Philadelphia the day before us. Though I had frequently seen him before, yet he was so disguised in furs, that I scarce knew him, and never beheld a more laughable object in my life. Like other Prussian officers, he appears to me as a man who knows little of polite life, and yet has picked up so much of it in his passage through France, as to make a most awkward appearance. When we came to New York, it was no more the gay, polite place it used to be esteemed: but was become almost a desert, unless for the troops. The people were expecting a bombardment, and had therefore removed themselves and their effects out of town: and the other side the troops were working at the fortifications with the utmost activity. After spending some disagreeable days at this place, we proceeded by water up to Albany, about 160 miles. At our arrival there, we were met by General Schuyler,[2] and entertained by him, during our stay, with great politeness and very genteely. I wrote to you before,[3] of our agreeable situation at Saratoga, and of our journey from thence over lake George to Ticonderoga: from this latter place we embarked on the great lake of Champlain, about 140 miles to St. John. We had a passage of three days and a half. We always came to in the night time. Passengers generally encamp in the woods, making a covering of the boughs of trees, and large fires at their feet. But as we had a good awning to our boat, and had brought with us good beds, and plenty of bed clothes, I chose to sleep on board.

L Brent, pp. 40-43.
  [1] Benedict Arnold (1741-1801) had retreated with his forces four months earlier in Quebec.
  [2] Philip John Schuyler (1733-1804), general in charge of the northern theatre.
  [3] Not found.

TO [BENJAMIN FRANKLIN]   Montreal May 11. 1776—

Among the inclosed papers is an open letter to Genl. Schuyler in recommendation of Mrs. Walker,[1] which yr. Br. Commissioners desire you would deliver to her.

If you can conveniently wait all tomorrow at St. Johns,[2] you will oblige me much, as I am uncertain whether I shall not join you.

Believe me, my Dr. Sr., that no one can wish your welfare more ardently, or bear a greater regard for you than, Dr. Sr.   Yr. affte & most obedt. servant   J Carroll

ALS   HL   Addressee is known from contents. Franklin was the Commissioner who departed in advance of the other two, Charles Carroll and Chase.
  [1] She and her husband provided a residence for Charles Carroll and possibly John during their stay. They both returned to Albany with John Carroll and Franklin.
  [2] One of the forts held by the Americans on the Sorel River and one of those supervised by the Commissioners to Canada at this time.

TO BENJAMIN FRANKLIN   May 11, 1776

[A brief note explaining that he is sending along letters from Franklin's fellow commissioners.]

AM   Huntington Library

TO CHARLES CARROLL AND SAMUEL CHASE[1] New York May 28th 1776

Dr. Gentlemen   I earnestly wish the dispatches mentioned in the Doctors[2] letter may find you in Canada, as I am persuaded they will give you pleasure, & enable you to do service. On our arrival here, we found Genl.

Washington gone for Philadelphia. Genl. Gates & Col. Mifflin are with him. The former of these two is made Major Genl. & Mifflin a Brigadier. As Genl. Ward at Boston has desired leave to resign, 'tis said Gates is to command there with Mifflin under him. I find that our officers will be much condemned, if they do not make a stand at Dechambeau. The Doctor & I are setting out this morning for Philadelphia. Tho I think you ought not to leave Canada without leave of Congress, yet as Governments are to be formed in the different Provinces, I wish you could both be spared in Maryland at this critical time. 'Tis said our province has offerd a reinforcement to Virginia or North Carolina, if wanted. If you should again see Genl. Arnold, assure him of our highest esteem, & present my complts. to all our friends, who crossed the S. Laurence with us. The Dr. has given you but a faint idea of the impertinence of our fellow travellers. The Lady had the assurance to tell us that the Commissioners had advised with & been governd by Tories. On enquiry who those tories were, she mentioned Mr. Frobisher. I suppose the woman had so dreamed; for I believe none of you remember having seen such a man, tho' I recollected his name in the list of Indian Traders. I am with earnest wishes for your happiness, Dr. Gentlemen   Yr. sincere friend & humble st.   J. Carroll

ALS   NYPL
    [1] Delegate from Maryland to the Continental Congress, had collaborated with John Adams and his scheme to win support of Canadians for the American colonies by approaching the Carrolls with commissions.
    [2] Benjamin Franklin.

TO CHARLES CARROLL OF ANNAPOLIS[1]   Philadelphia June 2d, 1776

Hond. Dr. Sr.   I arrived at this place the day before yesterday in company with Dr. Franklin. Cousin Charles & Mr. Chase left Montreal with me on the 12th of May, that they might not be in any danger from a frigate running up the River & getting between them, & the Eastern shore of S. Laurence. As Dr. Franklin determined to return to Philadelphia, on account of his health, I resolved to accompany him, seeing it was out of my power to be of any service, after the Commissioners had thought it advisable for them to leave Montreal.[2] Your son & Mr. Chase proposed staying at S. John's or in that neighbourhood, till they should know whether our army would keep post at De Chambeau: and the former desired me to give you notice of his being safe & well. Since I left him, it has not been in my power to do it before this day, as we unfortunately chanced to come to every post town on our road sometimes a day, sometimes a few hours too late for the mail. When I left him, he expected to follow us in a few days: but Mr. Hancock tells me that if an express, sent some days since from Congress, reaches them before they have left Canada, he is of opinion they will continue there for some time. I shall set out from hence next week, & propose doing myself the pleasure of calling at Elk-ridge. My affte. respectful complts. to Mrs. Darnall & Carroll with love to Polly.[3] Nothing new from Canada, nor indeed any advices at all since we left it. Great divisions here between the contending parties. I have presumed to trouble you to forward the inclosed, & remain, Hond. Dr. Sr.,   Yr. affte. Kinsman & hum. sevt.   J. Carroll

Ten tons of powder, 500 small arms came in yesterday. Cosn. Charles reced. large packets of letters from you a few days before we left Montreal.

ALS   MHS
[1] Father of Charles Carroll of Carrollton.
[2] The British advance toward Montreal prevented "any service" to French Catholics by his ministry.
[3] Rachel Brooke Darnall, her daughter (Mary or Molly, wife of Charles Carroll of Carrollton), and grandaughter (Mary). Rachel was John Carroll's aunt.

TO BENJAMIN FRANKLIN   Maryland, Rock Creek
                                                    near George Town Jan: 18 1778

My dear & venerable friend Will you allow your fellow traveller to and from Canada to take the opportunity of a vessel sailing from his neighborhood to renew his assurances of esteem & respect; and to congratulate you on the recovery of your health, which I have the pleasure to hear is now in a good state, after all your labours & fatigues? It is a great pleasure to me to reflect, that whilst you are employed by your country in so honourable and important a station, you are out of the way of suffering many inconveniences ill suited to your age; & now enjoy a pleasurable communication with men of the first character in every respect, & such as can both give you pleasure, & relish that, which you can return. I have seen in a Leyden Gazette some pretty French verses, *Le voila çe mortel* &c, written under your picture: I see by this, & many other things that you are much in mode at Paris; and as that is said to be every thing there, it is a good prognostick of your political success. To tell you the truth, we began to be a little out of humour at the delay of the Bourbon Princes in taking some decisive measures: and I am very well convinced that if they procrastinate much longer, every word of a letter in the supplement to the Leyden Gazette of June 14th., 1777, the author of which I could venture to swear to, will certainly come to pass.[1] If the vessel which carries this, goes safe to France, she will carry the melancholy news of poor Mr. Pliarnes death. He left his house, where I live with my Br[ethren]., the 6th. inst., & went over the next day to Alexandria[, Va.]. He was coming back across the Potomack the same evening, when he fell out of the boat, as he was sitting in an unguarded posture, & was most unfortunately drowned. Such is the account given by the Ferrymen: But it is now said that some circumstances raise suspicions to the prejudice of these men, & I hear just now, that they are taken up and put in irons. My Br. has been at Alexandria ever since to pursue this matter: notwithstanding all endeavours hitherto used, his body is not yet found. You cannot conceive the universal grief occasioned by this most unfortunate accident. He had endeared himself in a most extraordinary manner to all his acquaintances. Not only his friends, but I fear that the American states will feel his loss. I hear that his house have sent several valuable cargoes for the use of the army & publick.

Genl. Schuyler's oldest daughters have been married for some time; but I have not heard that the mild Miss Peggy has found a match to her liking yet. I mention this, because I am well convinced you can not but interest yourself in the concerns of that most amiable and hospitable family. We universally think here that the Genl. was cruelly used in being superseded in his command to the Northward. The assigned cause was no more than a pretext: the real one was that he was not the favourite of a great part of the forces, which were to compose that army. But I suppose you have better & more authentick accounts of all these matters. Our fellow traveller my Cousin is now at Congress. I have not seen Chase since we parted in Canada.

As I make no doubt but every man of letters in Paris is desirous of being introduced to you, perhaps you may have seen a very amiable & modest man L[or]d. abbé Brotierz an Ex-Jesuit, editor of a fine edition of Tacitus & author of some other performances, which recommend him much to the litterary world. When I was at Paris, he was proposing to publish from an original copy the correspondance of the Marquis of Torcy. If you either have, or should get acquainted with this valuable man, shall I beg of you the favour to assure him of my remembrance and affection? I have likewise to request of you to take care of & forward by the opportunities, which you know of, any letters, which may be recommended to you by some friends in Flanders, whom I have taken the liberty to direct to send them by that way.[2] You are undoubtedly happy in the Society of many agreeable persons & in the enjoyments furnished by a fine civilized country: but I still flatter myself that you will once again revisit this Western world. If you do, there will then be here a new order of things, a new combination of ideas & pursuits; indeed it will be truly *the new world;* you will be received with transport, & I hope I shall be one of the many to welcome your return.   In the meantime I remain, My Dr. Sr.   Yr. truly affte. & respectful friend   J.C.

ALS   American Philosophical Society Library
[1] On Mar. 20 Franklin and the other two American Commisioners met with Louis XVI and were informed of the conclusion of their treaty with France, the news of which reached America May 2.
[2] See Sep. 15, 1782.

TO CHARLES PLOWDEN   Maryland Feb: 28th–1779

My Dr Charles   I received about ten days ago your most agreeable favour from Paris of Novr 7th 1778. You will conceive how welcome it was to me, as coming from the person, I most wished to hear from, & being the first letter

received from Europe, either by myself or any of your acquaintance, since
the commencement of this war. I have wrote several times to England and to
Liege by many different ways, but cannot tell whether any of my letters
reached their destination. I cannot say that I wrote to you, being wholly at a
loss to know, where my letter would find you, as in the last letters I received
from you in the year 1775, you informed me of your & Mr. Aston's intention
of withdrawing yourselfs from the academy. Had it not been for this, believe
me, my Dr Charles, there is no person with whom I would chuse holding a
correspondence rather than with yourself, & thus renewing the memory of
those happy days, I spent with you at Bologna, & should have spent at Bruges
had not publick misfortunes damped all sense of private happiness. For the
future however, now that we have opened a channel of correspondence, I
hope we shall continue it uninterruptedly while we live: and indeed I
entertain some pleasing idea of making our correspondence personal, for a
few months at least, sometime or other of my life. I left so many dear friends
behind me in Europe, that I am at times determined to return thither for a
twelve month when peace is restored, & when I shall be enabled conveniently to bear the expense of a voyage thither & back again. I regret
exceedingly the loss of your letter of June last containing the full accounts
you mention of all my acquaintance & of their affairs. I have sent to Mr
Holker, who is well known to some of my friends, to enquire whether the
letter you refer to ever came to hand. I hope our letters will not long be so
liable to accidents, as I am informed that some accounts just received from
Europe give us a fair prospect of a speedy peace, which God of his infinite
goodness grant.

All our G'mn [Gentlemen] are, thank God, pretty well, except Mr.
Hunter,[1] who is often ailing. Messrs. Bolton & Roels are with him at P[or]t
To[bacco]. John is a good fellow, an active Miss[ione]r, & fully as much a
good fisherman & Hunter: as for Lewis Roels, if you can get his cup of Grog,
i.e., rum & water, he will never overturn states, or resettle our Independency.
Messrs Morris, Walton, Brent, Neal,[2] the two Boarmans[3] (John still as he was)
Jenkins are in the lower parts of the country, & I seldom see them: indeed I
have not seen the three former, since I came to Maryld. Messrs. Digges,
Aston,[4] & Diderick[5] are my nearest neighbours, & are well. The former
would be a favourite of yours, if you knew him. Messrs Matthews,[6] Lewis,[7]
Sewal & Mosely[8] live a great way from me; so do Messrs Frambach &
Pellentz. About three years ago, I saw Messrs Molyneux[10] & Farmor[9] at
Phila; the former the same good natured creature you ever knew him, as fat as
a porpoise, which occasions his neck to appear much shorter than it ever did,
& therefore fills him with dreadful apprehension of going off in an apoplexy.
I think I have now gone thro' the catalogue, as you requested to have them all
called over by name. I have only omitted two or three Germans in the back
settlements of Pennsylvania, whose names I do not recollect, & whose persons
I never saw: however they are well. No such division of property has yet

taken place here, as you mention in Engld: on the contrary, everything has hitherto been conducted as heretofore. I think the Engl: plan has too much of the *frigidum illud verbum.*[11] I think we unfortunate inhabitants of the foreign houses are doomed to be the outcasts of every society. Robbed & plundered at Bruges, dismissed without any consideration or reparation, excluded from a share in Engld, we must try if heaven will not make us amends hereafter for all our hopes here. As you are shut out from a share in Engld, so am I here. I have care of a very large congn; have often to ride 25 or 30 miles to the sick: besides which I go once a month between 50 & sixty miles to another congn in Virginia; yet because I live with my Mother, for whose sake alone I sacrificed the very best place in Engld, & told Mr. Lewis, that I did not chuse to be subject to be removed from place to place, now that we had no longer the vow of obed[ien]ce to entitle us to the merit of it, he does not chuse to bear any part of my expenses. One would think that some people are of opinion, that the change made in our circumstances by Ganganelli makes none in the authority, they ought to exercise over their former subjects. I do not mention this by way of complaint, as I am perfectly easy at present, & only mention it to you, as a friend to whom I would wish to communicate every thing without reserve. You enquire how Congress intend to treat the Cath: in this country. To this I must answer you that Congress have no authority or jurisdiction relative to the internal government or concerns of the particular states of the union: these are all settled by the Constitution & laws of the states themselves. I am glad however to inform you that the fullest & largest system of toleration is adopted in almost all the American states: publick protection & encouragement are extended alike to all denominations & R.C. are members of Congress, assemblies, & hold civil & military posts as well as others. For the sake of your & many other families I am heartily glad to see the same policy beginning to be adopted in Engld & Ireld: and I cannot help thinking that you are indebted to America for this piece of service. I hope it will soon be extended as far with you as with us.

I wish you had been so good as to have repeated in your last letter some things, which I suppose were in the preceding one, which miscarried; particularly I long to hear fully concerning Liege, Aston, Ellerker, Meynell &c: I have likewise a most sincere regard for your Br Frank: if the extension of toleration is obtained this session, as you expected it would, I shall expect to hear of Frank's making a conspicuous figure at the bar. Be sure when you write to him to remember me to him, & likewise to your sister Bern[?]ard; & Br Robert. I wish likewise that you had repeated what other deaths have happened besides those of Jos: Molyneux & Edm. Power, since July 1775 & yet I shall be afraid of reading the list, when it comes. Both those were men I had a very sincere regard for, & with whom I have spent many a social hour.

The last letter I had from Europe before yours informed me that Mr. Stourton was to be married in a short time to Miss Mary Langdale: did that marriage take place? I hope it did & that the Son proves a comfort to his aged

& venerable Fr. How does the good old Lord do? If you ever have an opportunity, let him & his Son be acquainted of my enquiries after them. Is Sr Wm Stanley well? I am sure he has turned out a Gentleman of real honour & sweet disposition. Was he not married before last March? I dare say he was; I often told him he would be in a great hurry, which he as positively denied: if he was, I have won of him a doz. of the Burgundy, which he must send me as soon as we have peace.

You are then going, my Dr C., to make another tour into Italy. The young Gentleman, that you call Maxwell Constable, is I reckon the one I knew by the name of Marmaduke. I dare say he has forgot me; but if he has not, present my complts to him. How many affecting sights will you have during your travels? I fear, more than Gothick waste and plunder: and what is still more distressing, many aged, venerable men worn out in the service of Religion doomed to drag out the remainder of their lives in want and poverty. No doubt, you will make it your business to find out all our agreeable companions at the Collo di Nobili; and you need not my directions to say every thing kind to them from me, Scotti, Bottaini, Muzzarelli, Bono, Rozalez, Signoretti, with his pupil Pisani. You will likewise surely see Giuliari, Cononici, Barotti, Zorzi, the younger Rozalez, & when you are at Venice enquire for Pasini, who was a Padrino at Sa Lucia, when the catastrophe happened. I should never end, if I made a list of all, whom I wish to be remembered to, & concerning whom I wish to be informed by you. When you are in that neighbourhood, there are several Gentlemen, who perhaps may remember me, & I must insist particularly that you pay a visit in my name to his Excellency Signor Francesco Rota, a Venetian Nobleman. When I knew him, he was Podestá of Padua; and a more kind & respectable couple than he & his incomparable Lady are hardly to be met with.

After your arrival at Rome, pray inform me whether Abbé Grant & Mr Honor are in being, & thank them in my name for the many civilities I received from them during my stay there. Tell Abbé Grant, that my young countryman of the name of Smith, whom I accidentally met with & introduced to him at Rome, is the same, who now a Lieutenant Col:. so bravely defended Mud Island fort in Delaware, the autumn before last. Meynell, I dare say, remembers him well. I am exceedingly anxious to hear what is become of Thorpe, Hothersall, Mattingly &c. If any of them should be at Rome, let me hear particularly concerning them. It was a great mortification to me that you did not give me an account of Lord Arundells having a son & heir: as soon as I can freely, I will not fail writing to that worthy & amiable Nobleman. You may depend on my letting no opportunity slip of writing to you. As I am well acquainted with Dr. Franklin, if you can get your letters put into his hand, he will forward them: or you may send them by the way of Phila to the care of Mr Molyneux; or if Mr. Garvy has any trade with America, letters sent to Baltimore will come safe to hand. at all events, write often & particularly to, Dr Ch., Yr most sincere friend & affte [humblest?] J. Carroll

ALS St

[1] George Hunter, S.J. (1713-79), superior in Maryland of the Jesuits, appointed 1759.
[2] Benedict Neale, S.J. (1709-87), not to be confused with Leonard Neale, S.J. (see May 18, 1783, n.1).
[3] Rev. John Boarmans, S.J. (1743-94?); and Rev. Sylvester Boarmans, S.J. (1745-1811), who attended General Chapter at Whitemarsh, 1783, and First Synod, 1791.
[4] John Ashton, S.J. (1742-1815), from 1769 served thirty-nine years at Whitemarsh, Md. Ms spelling omits "h".
[5] Bernard Diderick (sometimes referred to as John Baptist Diderick) (d. 1793) opposed founding of episcopate and Georgetown College. Was a native of Luxembourg.
[6] Ignatius Matthews, S.J., entered the order as a priest, was at General Chapters and opposed appointment of a bishop.
[7] John Lewis, S.J. (1721-88), superior of the Maryland mission at the time of the suppression of the Jesuits and continued under the Bishop of London as vicar general at this time.
[8] Joseph Mosley, S.J., missioner of Tuckahoe, Md., later opposed a bishopric.
[9] Robert Molyneux, S.J. (1731-1808) later became first superior of the American Jesuits when restored as an order.
[10] Ferdinand Farmer, S.J. (1744-86), native of Germany (Steinmyer was his original name), eminent clergyman and civic leader of Philadelphia, became a vicar general.
[11] Literally, "that cold word," i.e., lacking in liberality in what is legislated.

TO CHARLES PLOWDEN   Maryland Apr. 27–1780

My dear Sir   My last to you was in February 1779, which I flatter myself you received, as the vessel it went in, got safe to France, and it was inclosed, pursuant to your directions, to the care of Mr Garvey of Rouen. I have now an opportunity of forwarding this by a Brother of Notley Rozer, who is going to be settled in a commercial house there. I need not tell you how anxious I am to hear again & very frequently from you: and if you have no other more direct conveyance, Mr Holker, with whom it seems you are acquainted, will be a good channel for your letters to come through. I was exceedingly disappointed in not receiving the favour, you referred me to in yours of Novr 1778, especially as it contained so full an account of all our particular friends in Europe. Mr Holker informed a gentleman, whom I directed to enquire, that no letter for me had ever reached him, or he would have forwarded it immediately. Since my receiving that letter, we have never had any intelligence from our particular acquaintance in Europe, tho I have written to many of mine, and I cannot help thinking that opportunities are not wanting, as vessels are every day arriving from France, Holland, & indeed all other parts of Europe, except England.

I regret the loss of your letter the more, as besides the account of other friends, I doubt not it would have given me particular information respecting yourself, & the plan of life, you hereafter intend to pursue. I remember, that when I had the misfortune to be separated from you, a misfortune which I shall ever lament, you entertained thoughts of settling in France, & procuring letters of naturalization there. Are you yet in the same way of thinking? or will you not rather, after your second ramble into Italy, return to your own country, and enjoy that indulgence, & relaxation of penal laws, which the spirit of toleration has procured for you in England; and to which, as well as to the removal of the obstructions on the Irish trade, our American revolution has not a little contributed, by making it necessary for England to unite all parties at home, & stifle all opposition in Ireland. This is all I shall say upon politicks at present.

Since my last to you, died here universally regretted by his acquaintance Mr George Hunter. He was truly a holy man, full of the spirit of God, and the zeal of souls. His death happened during the hot months last summer, which always had a terrible effect upon his health. Your old friend Molyneux, with whom you have passed so many happy hours, is still at Phila; he is very anxious to be removed into this province, tho' he is now, as he writes me, in high credit, being teacher of the English Language to the Chevlr de la Luzerne the French Minister Plenipotentiary there.[1] Your schoolfellow Ashton lives about 25 miles from me, & is the most industrious man in Maryland: it is a pity he could not have the management of all the estates belonging to the clergy in this country: they would yield thrice as much as they now do. Mr Matthews, who succeeds Mr Hunter at Port Tobacco, promises, I am told, very well: but James Walton, who has as fine land as any in America, is said to make a bad hand at farming. This you, who know him, will not be surprised at. But if he does not succeed in temporals, he is indefatigable in his spiritual occupations. With him lives, among others, that man without guile, little Austin Jenkins. I am told he is almost adored by his acquaintances; and I dare say, very devotedly. Of the rest, I have only to say they continue as they were when I wrote last. The noted Lucas,[2] my unworthy scholar, I have never seen since I came to America. I hear that he has greatly involved himself, and leads a cat and dog life with the sweet partner of his bed. It is reported he is become very sottish tho' he lives at such a distance from me, that I can answer for nothing, excepting his having fallen into general contempt with all sorts of people. In the beginning of his apostacy, some share of vivacity, a good person, a joviality of temper over a bottle, & the novelty of a priest taking the steps he did, procured him some countenance even with leading people in this country. But a nearer acquaintance soon put an end to this, & he is now visited by none, nor well received, where he visits. Since my arrival into this country, I have heared such instances of his misbehaviour, long before he quite pulled off the mask, that it is astonishing, that he was not expelled [from] the Society much sooner. But the spirit of mildness, which was characteristick of our former happy government, often degenerated into a spirit of indolent forbearance; and irresolution was not only called, but by Superiors themselves thought longanimity. The original cause of this publick scandal was allowing him to leave the college, after what was known of his conduct at Spa[in] & in England; or rather, the ever allowing him to be promoted to orders. Alas!, my dear Charles, how many young men of much steadier virtue, than Lucas, have, by being turned adrift into the wide world, long before this fallen into all its prodigality and criminal excesses? What a number of these unfortunate young men will the unhappy Ganganelli have to answer for? God grant you may not now in Italy, in Flanders, & in England know or meet with many such instances amongst our common acquaintance.

In my last, I sent you a long list of names of friends in Italy, concerning whom you were to write me very particularly. As I am in no doubt of your having received that letter, I shall not repeat them all, but such only, as first occur, as Scotti, Canonici, & all our friends at San Saverio; Zorzi, Signoretti, Rozalez, Pasini, San Bontifacio, Muzzarelli, Bostaini & Boni: I find I cannot content myself with a general mention of my San Saverio acquaintance. If you have not passed over Lombardy & Stato Veneto, before you receive this, renew the remembrance of me with Counts Miniscelchi, Ferri at Padua, & Padre Giulian, & Nogarola & Ct Gazzola at Verona; Ct Stecchini at Vicenza; Ct Calini at Brescia &c: At Pisa forget not young Franchesci, & Signor Canonico Alleati. I am very anxious to hear what is become of Messrs Hothersall, Thorpe, Mattingly &c, whom I left in Rome. If they, or either of them are still there, you will not fail to assure them of my unalterable friendship & regard. I retain likewise a very singular affection for Messrs. Honor, & the Abbé Grant. Indeed, my dear Plowden, I every where received so many civilities, & such numerous instances of sincere goodwill, that I am sure of omitting, when I want to record my friends, the names of some of them: but you must supply dificiencies, & write to me as particularly about those I mention, as those I omit. If they are not now taken notice of by me, there are moments, when they are more strongly upon my mind, than some of those, whom I have mentioned.

If contrary to my expectation, this should find you returned from Italy, you will probably be in England or the neighbourhood of Liege. In either place, there are some who will be glad to hear of me, if I may judge from my own feelings: for I should be exceedingly happy to hear of them, particularly of your Brs, & Sister Bernard. What is become of Aston? Is he un gros chanoine? But I hope he will answer for himself as I intend writing to him by this opprty. Is the good Mr Ellerker, are Broning, Stuart, Mercer & Booth still at Liege? does that academy still subsist, & does Mr. Howard still preside there? is Mr. Scaristrick still alive, & does he still amuse his friends with his characteristical stories? I have written several times to Mr. T. T[albot?]. of Queen square, but can get no answer. Do he & Mr More still live together? are my excellent & noble friends, Ld & Lady Arundell yet happy in a son? Is good old Ld Stourton alive? & if not, does my pupil do honour to his station, & emulate his Frs virtues? I shall be very happy to hear of that excellent young gentleman, Sr Wm Hanley. As to myself, I continue as when I wrote last, living with my Mother in a retired part of the country, and enjoying great domestick felicity. My nephew Danl,[3] whom you may remember at the college, lives very near, being happily married, & by his conduct gives me great satisfaction. My Brother resides at Annapolis, our capital city, being in publick employ there.[4] I still retain the same inclination as when I wrote last to visit my European friends, but have little hopes of bringing it about. Amongst those, there is no one, whose company would give more pleasure than yours, as there is no one, whose sentiments and amusements would be better suited than yours to those of,   Dr Sr   Yr most affte friend & faithful Sert   J Carroll   Pray remember me kindly to Mr J Williams, & let me hear particularly about him—My M[othe]rs family & Mr Ign. Digges's,[5] especially Fr Thomas send their affte compliments—

ALS   St
   [1] Anne Caesar de la Luzerne, French minister to the U.S.
   [2] John Lucas, S.J., was later restored to the ministry.
   [3] Daniel Carroll, Jr., son of Carroll's brother Daniel.
   [4] Member of State Council, 1777-81.
   [5] Of Melwood, Md., who married Mary Carroll, Carroll's cousin and sister of Daniel Carroll's wife, (she being of the Carroll of Carrollton branch of the family).

TO THOMAS SIM LEE[1]   Rock Creek, March 13—1781

Dear Sir   I have been informed, that there was a foreign letter for me lying in the office at Annapolis; and I know that you will excuse me for taking the liberty of desiring you to direct some enquiry to be made; and if I have been rightly informed, to have it sent by some good opportunity to Mellwood, where my Sister Molly[2] will be in a few days, as she is to set out this morning for Mr Hill's[3]; or by the post to George-Town. Your weightier employments will not, I am well assured, diminish your readiness to perform the offices of friendship.

   You may be assured, that all this family sympathised sincerely with yourself & Mrs Lee, when we heared of her little Dolly's disorder, & of the rest of your family being in the same situation: and we were as much rejoiced to hear, they had got well of it. The same disorder has broke out very near us; & tho' most here have had it, yet enough are left to make us uneasy. My Mother, & Sisters present their love to Mrs Lee, & respectful complts to yourself, as I do to yr Lady, & love to the children, & remain with great esteem,   Dr Sir,   Yr most affte humble St   J Carroll

ALS   GU
   [1] Thomas Sim Lee, Governor of Maryland, 1779-83 and 1792-94.
   [2] Mary, who married Notley Young.
   [3] Probably Henry Hill. Daniel Carroll, John's brother, was related to this family through his wife, Eleanor Carroll, whose brother married Hill's daughter Mary.

TO THOMAS SIM LEE   Rock Creek, July 17, 1781

My dear Sir   The pleasure and happiness of being acquainted with you and of enjoying, as I flatter myself, some share of your esteem, has raised my credit greatly in the neighborhood. This you will understand from the earnest application made by the bearer of this for a letter in his favor. The young gentleman is son of the late Mr. Richard Beall, and grandson to Col. Sam'l Beall. I am not acquainted with him personally, but have heard his activity and diligence much commended. The good whiggism of his family is well known to you. He solicits a command in the militia to be raised immediately, and will conduct himself, I daresay from his character, with propriety and credit, if he should obtain it. I hope you will convince him that my interest with you is as great as it is supposed here. If you should not, I shall immediately experience a great diminution of the respect now shown me, for I look upon it to be more than a borrowed lustre darted upon me from some selfshining luminary. I find I have begun my letter on the wrongside of my paper. Your favorite Lord Chesterfield would write it over again, rather than send it in its present form: but you will excuse me for many reasons.

Your brother informed me that you had received some time since a letter from the Pres. of Congress, of which you would send me a copy when at liberty. I shall be very happy to understand from it, when I do see it, that there is any prospect of peace, an honorable one, I mean. We are very anxious here to know all the particulars of Genl. Wayne's action with Cornwallis. Three of my mother's grandsons are with the Marquis, and the uncertainty of their fate gives unceasing disquiet to this family.[1] My mother and sisters present their love to Mrs. Lee, and respectful compliments to yourself

T   GU   SC: Woodstock Letters, VII, 80-81.
    [1] Sons of Anne Carroll Brent, John Carroll's sister. June 10, Anthony Wayne reinforced Marquis de Lafayette in the Virginia campaign.

PLAN OF CLERGY ORGANIZATION   [1782]

The estates heretofore enjoyed by the Society in this and the neighboring province of Pennsylvania, still continue to be held by the former members of that body.[1] Thus they have it in their power to administer the same spiritual helps to the faithful, as heretofore, and have a fair prospect of perpetuating[2] the same services, which they now perform, to succeeding generations. It is certainly their duty to endeavour to do this good work. The obligations of justice to the benefactors, who took up or left these estates for pious uses; the sort of consecration which estates from such a destination acquire; the duty of charity to the present and future generations demand this service of them. To which may be added, that Almighty God seems in a particular manner to impose this duty upon them, by preserving in the same hands the property of the houses of the Society in these two provinces, while in almost every other country, its former members are not only deprived of any share in the administration of it, their antient possessions, but have scarce a miserable pittance allowed them to subsist upon.[3]

There can be no doubt but[4] that every one, who beares a love and veneration for his former profession, wishes to continue the same offices of charity to his neighbour, and to establish the same equal enjoyment of the common stock, and farther to make a proper provision for a due and equitable administration of it.

To effect these good purposes, nothing will so much contribute as the adoption of some system of administration, settled with the joint concurrence of all, and[5] founded on principles of justice and equality. It was the advantage of the government of the Society, that in the administration of its temporal effects, the managers of them were under the controul of checks, one rising above the other, and calculated to prevent alienations, or the abuses of waste, appropriation, and a partial [i.e., unfair] application of the yearly income. Thus the Procurators, besides being limited in their powers, were obliged to submit their books every month to the inspection of the Rectors; the Rectors were every year to lay the whole before the Provincial; the Provincial was to examine them with his Companion, and to put an immediate stop to maladministration, for which he was invested with an extraordinary power of deposing a Rector, when the necessity of the case was urgent, and admitted no delay.[6] The Provincial, besides being liable to be controulled by his Consultors and Admonitor, was to lay every third year the whole administration of the Colleges before the Provincial Congregations, who were to depute a Procurator with them to Rome; and was moreover to send to the General yearly accounts.[7] The General whom the Constitutions vest with a power energ[et]ically called superintendentia, could not alienate without manifest advantage, appropriate to himself, or make a partial application of any part of the estates possessed by Colleges: if he did, this was one of the cases deemed sufficient for his deposition. He was constantly liable to be checked by his admonitor and[8] advised by his assistants; who were authorised to depose him instantly, if his maladministration of the temporals rendered it necessary, and to call a general Congregation afterwards, to lay before them the necessity of the case; so that the last resort, on which rested the[9] final inspection into the temporal and all general interests of the Society, was the body of the Society prepresented by its Deputies.

These were undoubtedly wise provisions, and well calculated to prevent the effect of those passions, which are so apt to disturb the peace and happiness of all Societies and should be imitated as far as particular circumstances of the Country, and the necessary alteration arising from the dissolution of the Society will admit. At this time, is there any check on the administrators of the[10] priest's estates? If their conscience did not restrain them, might not they, who have the legal title to the lands, dispose of the yearly produce entirely to their own profit, without controul, or responsibility: and is not this an alarming consideration? It is happy for the priests, and indeed for the Roman Catholicks in general, that these estates are now vested in such persons, as having no interest in view but the general good, will be ready to concur in any measure to perpetuate the blessings of a Catholick ministry in this country. They, who succeed them in their trust[11] may not be equally disinterested and honest; and it would be unpardonable in the present trustees,[12] heretofore members of the Society, thro' indolence or inattention to let slip the opportunity of establishing a system of administration, which shall have for its object to provide an equitable support for all the present labourers in Christ's vineyard, and to transmit that same support to their successors in the ministry.

Whatever administration be adopted, it is of the utmost consequence that it should be settled by common consent. For, if it should be done by a junto or three or four, it will be sure, sooner or later, to breed disturbances and disgust; and the authority, by which the the administration is fixed; tho' this, if possible, would be very desirable; but that some might attend in behalf of all. Supposing, for instance, that the priests at St. Inigo and Newtown should depute one; those at Portobacco, one; those at the Marsh and its neighbourhood, one; those at Deer Creek, Bohemia, and Talbot County, one; those at Fredericktown, Conewago and Lancaster, one; and that (with the present Superior at their head), having met at a convenient place, and agreed upon such a plan as will appear best to them, and corresponding with the importance of the object, and the intentions of their constituents, they at their return lay it before them for their approbation. As the plan thus agreed upon would be intended for the future as well as the present time, there can be no doubt but all would divest themselves of partial considerations.

It has been observed already, that the preservation of the Catholick clergy's estates from alienation,[13] waste and misapplication, is to be the object and end of this meeting. But that they, who are deputed to it, may come better prepared for the consideration of these important matters, and that their views may all be drawn more to a center, it will not, 'tis hoped, be deemed impertinent to mark out with more precision the subjects of their deliberation. In the first place, by the present mode of conveying and holding the estates, is sufficient precaution taken to prevent their alienation, or their falling into other hands than those of the Clergy? 2ly. Is any or sufficient provision made to prevent the possibility (for not only what has, but what may happen, should be considered) of those persons, who enjoy the legal title to the lands, appropriating the whole income of them to themselves, their friends and relations, or dealing it out partially to their fellow labourers in the mission, more in some and less in others: 3ly. Will it not be proper to devise some sufficient securities, checks and controuls to prevent these mischiefs? 4thly. Should not a mode of application be determined in this meeting, or, as that will be difficult, ought not some general rules to be laid down, whereby they may be directed, who have in their hands the immediate management of the estates? 5ly. Would it be advisable to appoint by common consent some few persons, others than the managers[14] of the different estates, to revise the yearly accounts, and report on them, if they discover any waste or misapplication? Or would it be more expedient to have the different estates laid off in districts, and some in each district appointed as a check upon the managers? 6ly. If, after providing for the subsistance of the missioners (in which particular regard should be had for the old and infirm), there should remain a surplus in the hands of the managers, ought not the application to be for some purpose conducive to the good of Religion, as a fund for procuring more Priests, founding other places, etc. 7ly. If any clergyman is wanting to his duty by negligence or otherwise, ought he not to be deprived of all right to a subsistance, which was never intended to be the bread of idleness? and what authority is to determine, who is and who is not entitled to a provision?

If any objection is made to the establishing of some such securities and regulations, it is conceived that the objection will arise from the habits of thinking and living aquired in our former profession.[15] Accustomed to enjoy happiness and tranquility, and to see everything conducted smoothly under the government of our Superiors, we did not trouble ourselves with considering the many checks and restraints provided by the Constitutions against any abuse of power, to which we were indebted for that mild and equitable government. Considering the nature of mankind, when the present generation is past, and the spirit which animated the Society is no more, we must not hope that men, uncontrouled by any checks, will use power so moderately, or money so fairly and impartially, as we have seen it; and the sooner this is provided against, the better. Our Brethren in England have done so. They have rightly distinguished between the spiritual power derived from the Bishop, and which must be left in the hands to which he has intrusted it; and the common rights of the missioners to their temporal possessions, to which as the Bishop, or Pope himself have no just claim, so neither can they invest any persons with the administration of them.[16]

L Hughes, *Documents,* II, 611-14.

[1] I.e., legal title was in the name of specific individuals, only loyalty requiring them to share with all the others of their community the increment of estates. "Possessed by" is deleted in favor of "enjoyed."

[2] "Transmitting" is deleted.

[3] Carroll himself had sought to gain indemnities of English Jesuit colleges confiscated in France, two years prior to his return to America in 1774.

[4] Deleted: "a rightful."

[5] Deleted before "and": "the members of the former Society now in the country"; and after: "partaking, as much as circumstances will allow, of the former government."

[6] The Provincial could, however, act only through the General, who need not follow his recommendation.

[7] Actually these were triennial reports. There does not seem to be legal provision for the Provincial Congregation role indicated here.

[8] Deleted: "controuled."

[9] Deleted: "management." Carroll seems to ascribe too much power to the admonitor and assistants to the general, which was largely provisional in anticipation of a general congregation.

[10] Deleted: "lands and money of priests."

[11] Deleted: "the present holders of priests lands."

[12] A board of trustees did not yet exist, so that the reference here is to a few specific ex-Jesuits holding in their own names titles to the various estates that were handed down for common use of members of the order. Corporate ownership was unlawful prior to 1776.

[13] The term here is in reference to the use and application of the property, rather than the property itself. The estates as bequests were always designated for pious use or religious purpose, such as the support of the clergy or seminarians. The property could be alienated to gain an income that could be put to such uses. The reason for this is that these properties were not "ecclesiastical," being in the name of private individuals as far as civil records were concerned.

[14] It is not clear in this use of "managers" and in what follows, if Carroll understood some or all of these to be "those persons, who enjoy the legal title to the lands . . ." referred to in 2. above.

[15] No longer of one, legally existing religious order, the clergy now needs the systems of checks and balances always present, even if infrequently resorted to, in the old arrangement of the Jesuits and their constitution.

[16] The plan evidently does not require changing the old practice of specific individuals of the clergy retaining title as ex-Jesuits to the estates of the order in Maryland and Pennsylvania. The supervisory board appears to be a device which succeeds to the functions in the order which protected the use of property, as Carroll explained earlier in his plan. On developments from this plan, see below, June 27, 1783, Constitution of the Clergy.

TO CHARLES PLOWDEN   Maryland Feb: 20th 1782

My dear Sr   The last letter received from you was dated from Nancy June 1780. I cannot but persuade myself, that you have written several since that time; but I have not been so happy as to have them reach me. The pleasure I feel on receiving any is inexpressible: you know how many dear friends I left in Europe, and I can assure you that absence has not made me less sollicitous of their happiness, than I ever was. Now it is from you alone that I ever receive any information, tho I have wrote to Messrs Aston, Ellerker & Howard and Talbot. I regret exceedingly the loss of a former letter from Turin which you inform me you had sent with a full detail of every matter relating to our friends. By the time you receive this, I expect that you will be returned from Italy, and in all probability settled with your Sister Haggerston. At all events, I shall continue to direct to the care of Mr Garvy à Rouen. I have just heard that some of our Gentlemen here have advice from Liege, that the Epr. of Bavaria has renewed the foundn of his predecessor in favor of the academy. If so, that establishment may subsist, should it not fail for want of scholars: and I cannot help thinking that this latter may be the case, as R. C. are now allowed to open school in Engld. These same advices inform, as I hear, that Messrs Bruning & Mercer are deceased. R.I.P. Our Gentlemen here, thank God, continue, as when I wrote my last. None have died since Mr Hunter, of which you have been before advised.

I observe in your last letter, that some events had happened, and others were likely to follow, that afforded hope to the sanguine of a reestablishment of the Society. I rejoice indeed at these events, and particularly, that it has pleased God to vindicate & make known so publickly the innocence of the poor sufferers in Portugal. This was a great step towards a compleat justification, & with serious people might be a sufficient reason to call in question, & examine the other scandalous aspersions which were cast upon our dear Society. But I hope nothing beyond this: the spirit of irreligion, and, as I find from late proceedings in the Austrian government, of innovation is still prevailing. The reigning principle amongst the people is a spirit of independence not only of unlawful (which is commendable) but of all authority: and amongst rulers in Europe, it is a spirit of concentrating all jurisdiction within themselves, that they may be uncontroulable in the exercise of every act of despotism. Add to this, that the reestablishment, if otherwise probable, would be opposed by the united voice and efforts of all those plunderers, who have enriched themselves with the lands, the furniture of the colleges, the plate & treasure of the churches and sacristies. I can assure you, that one of my strongest inducements to leave Europe, was to be removed not only out of sight, but even out of the hearing of those scenes of iniquity, duplicity and depredation, of which I had seen and heard so much. This long war, which has raged between our Western continent, and your high-minded Island at the same time that it deprived me of the pleasure of hearing from my friends, has at least afforded me this consolation, that I have not been mortified with the recital of the rapines, with the defamation and insults, to which those, I love best, have been exposed. In my retirement here, I have scarce any other amusement than reading over and over the few books, I have and can borrow from my friends: and amongst others, I have been refreshing my memory by revising Muratori's account of the missions of Paraguay.[1] What a dreadful havock did irreligion make, when it tore up, root and branch, that noble establishment, the triumph of zeal, of humanity, and Christianity?

You will wonder, my Dr Charles, how I could fall into this long dissertation; but really when I write to you, or think on my friends in Europe, my grief, and, I fear, indignation, get the better of every other consideration. In your late travels thro' Italy, your pleasures were always blended with some such reflexions. I make no doubt, but you were exceedingly happy to meet with our numerous and kindest friends, the Scottis, Rozales's, Signorettis, Canonicis &c: but when you beheld those noble establishments, & seats of learning and virtue overturned, in the most melancholy sense of the word, & perhaps their former inhabitants labouring under indigence and distress, you could find little enjoyment in any thing else.

As I apprehend, that you are now at a great distance from Liege, I shall not expect a very minute account of my friends there from you, however agreeable it might be to me. But, at all events, write what you know of them, particularly of Aston, Ellerker, Ned Booth, Scarisbrick, Hodgson, Ned Wright &c. I should be likewise very glad to hear of poor Mr Wapelaer,[2] whose candour and artless disposition of heart always endeared him to me. What does he think of the great *overgetumbeling* of this American continent? I would dare aver that he is a strong advocate for your refractory colonies, to use the court stile of your country. A propos of politicks: I shall be much mistaken in mine, if in the course of the present year, we do not see some dispositions to peace. We wait with impatience to hear, how the news of Ld Cornwallis's surrender will operate in Europe, and what will be the first movements in your parliament. Should pacifick sentiments prevail, you may be assured, my Dr Charles, of my availing myself of them to cultivate a close & regular correspondence with so valuable and agreeable a friend, as you are. I should likewise have then an opportunity of renewing my sentiments of respect and veneration, or rather the declaration of them, to my most honourable and noble friend Ld Arundell & his incomparable Lady. I hope they will excuse me for not writing to them by so circuitous a conveyance as my letters must now be subject to; but I request of you to find some way of communicating to them my grateful and unfading remembrance of their gracious favours, and friendship. I was exceedingly happy to hear, that my goodnatured and honourable pupil is blessed with so fair a progeny. If his Fr good Ld Stourton be still living, assure them both of my best respects.

Whilst I am mentioning other friends, I must not forget your good Sister at Liege, to whose friendly offices I am so much indebted, nor your Brs, and particularly Frank, whom I heartily congratulate on his marriage; and proficiency, by this time I may say, his eminence in his profession.

Do you remember one Nichols at Bruges, a nephew of Mr. Church? He came into this country within a few months, after I did: I know not what scenes he had gone through; but his situation was not comfortable on his first arrival. He entered, as a private tutor, into a Gentleman's family; and having obtained much credit in that capacity, set up a Latin school, in which he meets with good encouragement; and if he supports it with diligence, and conducts himself with economy, he will earn a comfortable subsistance. While he behaves with propriety, I shall do every thing in my power to favour him, for the sake of his uncle, to whom you may give this information.

It is said, that the Emperor of Germany is a lover of justice, as well as of innovations; perhaps for this very reason, since it is so new a thing for crowned heads to be just or rather for them, who govern under them. You see, I have contracted the language of a Republican. If he really be just, ought not the E. Jess [English Jesuits] who were at Bruges, to present a state of their sufferings, representing that every thing belonging to them was seized (tho' none of it had been granted by the country), & they left without the smallest provision? To be sure, this has been thought of, and, if there can be a hope of redress, attempted. I heard from an Irish officer in the French service, that your Br in law Mr Gaaffe was promoted to the command of a Regiment: I am sincerely glad of it, as I have a very good opinion of his merit, and a very sincere affection for Mr Gaaffe. Can you tell me, whether old Col. Carroll, who lived at Cambray & was their intimate acquaintance, be yet living? I do not expect, that he is, but shall be glad to know certainly.

I find by late advices from Europe, that that madman Ld G. Gordon is beginning again to raise disturbances: this must keep many people in dread; for God forbid, that an ignorant multitude should be ever so deluded again. Pray was the Dr Brewer, whose house was demolished at Bath, my good friend John Brewer? I dare say, he will maintain, that he was as unmoved, as Horace's stedfast man, *si fractus illabatur orbis &c.* [if he is broken the whole world collapses, . . .] Hd [His Lordship] Mr Chaloner by this time is certainly no more. *Ejus memoria in benedictione erit.* [His memory will be held in veneration]. God has given a great blessing to his labours. Some of his writings, & particularly his Catholick Christian do infinite service here.[3]

The Clergymen here continue to live in the old form: it is the effect of habit, and if they could promise themselves immortality it would be well enough. But I regret, that indolence prevents any form of administration being adopted which might lend to secure to posterity a succession of Catholick Clergymen, and secure to these a comfortable subsistence. I said, that the former system of administration (that is, every thing being in the power of a superior) continued: but all those checks upon him, so wisely provided by our former constitutions, are at an end. It is happy that the present Superior is a person free from every selfish view, & ambition: but his successor may not; and, what is likewise to be feared, the succeeding generation wch will not be trained in the same discipline and habits as the present, will in all probability be infected much more strongly with interested and private views. The system therefore, which they will adopt, will be less calculated for the publick, or future benefit, than would be agreed to now, if they could be prevailed upon to enter at all upon the business. But ignorance, indolence, delusion (you remember certain prophecies of reestablishment) and above all the irresolution of Mr Lewis puts a stop to every proceeding in this matter.

I have not seen since my last, but often hear from our good friend Molyneux. When I have next the pleasure of meeting him I expect to find him perfectly metamorphosed. Phila is become a place of the greatest gaiety, the resort of all the rich people in America, and of the Fr[ench]. officers serving in this country. Molyneux has been Eng. master to the Chevr Luzerne, & undoubtedly often amongst the brilliant compny of his hotel. Now as you know his natural talents for elegant life and manners, you will judge of his proficiency.

What do you think of Abbé Raynal's work, lately imported into America, called the history of its revolution?[4] it is in every one's hands here. To me he appears the enthusiast, I had almost said, the Bedlamite of liberty. When a person, especially a Frenchman, born under an absolute Government had got his head full of the sentiments of an English Whig, he is sure to extend them, & push them to an excess. Like a sprig, which being bent too much one way, recoils to the other with too great violence. He is moreover very much mistaken as to facts, and even the geography of this country: and what I dislike most, is his fashionable jargon of substituting every where almost superstition for Religion. You inform me that poor Zorzi was once engaged in an Italian Cyclopoedia: Inform me farther, whether that work has made its appearance, and how it is relished. I fear the mischief of the first French Encyclopedie, and other works of the same stamp on Religious subjects, has operated too powerfully, & that the human passions are too much interested in countenancing them, to hope that any great revolution will happen in mens minds and hearts from the Italian publication. *They have Moses, and the Prophets; if they hear them not* &c. Let us, my Dr Charles, thank Alm: God for being brought up in a school, where we learnd the principles & saw the practice of those virtues, which will, I hope, ever make us despise & discover the shallow sophisms of irreligion, & pretences of immorality. May God ever bless you, my Dr friend; I am, Yrs most afftely   J. Carroll

ALS   St
[1] Luigi Antonio Muratori's "Account of the Missions of Paraguay" dealt with the famous Jesuit Indian Reductions, begun in 1609.
[2] William Wapalear [Wappeler], S.J., the Maryland missioner, once at St. Omers, probably while Carroll was there. See 1790, Establishment of Catholic Church . . .
[3] Richard Challoner, Vicar Apostolic of London, 1758 until his death in 1781. His jurisdiction extended to the original British colonies of North America; and he was the author of *The Catholic Christian Instructed* (1757).
[4] Abbé Guillaume Thomas Francis Raynal, educated by the Jesuits, ordained a priest, he left the ministry and wrote *Philosophical and Political History of the Indies.*

MEMORANDUM TO BENJAMIN FRANKLIN   Sep. 15. 1782

The Revd. Mr. John Carroll whom Docr. Franklin may remember by the Com[mi]ss[io]n. into Canada presents his comps. & requests the Docr. to do him the favor to forward the inclossd letter for Liege by post. His care is requested of the other [*ind.*] when a favourable opp[ortunit]y. offers.

MC American Philosophical Society Library.

TO POPE PIUS VI   1783

Most Holy Father   John Louis, Bernard Diderich, Ignatius Matthews, John Walton[1] and John Carroll, priests and missionaries in the thirteen united states of North America, assembled from the less remote stations, and with the consent of our fellow priests in distant places, as attested by letters, do in our name and in that of all of our brethren, and in the spirit of due submission, inform Your Holiness that because of the present arrangement in government in America, we are no longer able as formerly to have recourse for our spiritual jurisdiction to bishops or vicars apostolic who live under a different and foreign government. Again and again this fact has been urged on us in unmistakable terms by the officials of the Republic; neither could we acknowledge any such person as ecclesiastical superior without offense to the civil government. Wherefore, placed as we are in this difficult position, we have recourse to Your Paternity, and humbly beg that the ecclesiastical superior we now have, namely John Lewis, a priest fully approved by the Vicar Apostolic in London (to whom before the change in the political government this mission was subject) be again confirmed in that position, and that he be given the power to impart necessary faculties to priests who come to this mission; likewise that you graciously grant that the said superior be empowered to subdelegate the same power to one or another of the better qualified missionaries, as circumstances, and the remoteness and needs of places may demand.

Moreover, since there is no bishop in this country to bless the holy oils of which we have been deprived during the years of the war, no one to bless chalices and altar stones, and no one to administer Confirmation, we humbly pray Your Holiness that the aforesaid John Louis, priest and our superior, be authorized to do these things during our pressing needs and till Your Holiness has made other provision. We ask this lest the faithful who are exposed to many dangers be further deprived of the sacrament of Confirmation, and lest they die without the Extreme Unction according to the rites of the Church.

In like manner we pray Your Holiness to grant the Jubilee indulgences to this entire mission, as well as such extension of faculties, as may seem good, to the missionaries in this extensive and very remote region, plagued by a long and bitter war with concurrent and continuing disturbances. For the Jubilee to celebrate the elevation of Your Holiness to the see of Peter, and the Jubilee of 1775 could not be promulgated here, still less could they be celebrated or could we fully profit by them.

Holy Father, these are the favors which we, the aforesaid missionary priests in the United States of North America, humbly beg of the wisdom and providential care of Your Holiness for the good of the Catholic Religion.

D   PF   Probably a Roman copy. Italian notations in another hand and year 1784 inscribed at end of MS, indicating time of processing at Rome.

[1] James Walton, S.J., returned to Maryland in 1766, was legal owner of Jesuit property, and petitioned restoration of the order. He was a member of the first two General Chapters.

Bme Pater   Joannes Louis, Bernardus Diderich, Ignatius Matthews, Jacobus Walton et Joannes Carroll Presbyteri Missionarii in Tredecim confederatae Americae Septentrionalis Provinciis simul ex locis vicinioribus congregati et consentientibus in hoc, et per literas approbantibus fratribus nostris Presbyteris, qui in remotioribus hujusce Missionis partibus versantur, nostro et fratrum nostrorum communi nomine, cum omni obsequio exponimus Sanctitati Vestrae, nos sub moderno supremo dominio confederare, Americe constituto, non amplius posse recurrere ut olim, pro necessaria jurisdictione spirituali ad Episcopos et Vicarious Apostolicos in externo et alineo Dominio commorantes. Hoc enim saepenumero a Reipublicae hujus Magistratibus nobis significatum est gravibus verbis, nec quempiam illorum pro Superiore Ecclesiastico agnoscere absque aperta offensione hujusce Supremi Magistratus civilis, et Gubernii Politici. Quare in his angustiis positi recurrimus ad Paternitatem Vestram humiliter orantes ut quem modo Superiorem Ecclesiasticum habemus, nempe Joannem Louis presbyterum approbatum et confirmatum a Vicario Apotico Londiniensi (cui universa haec missio ante Gubernii Politici mutationem fuit subjecta) denuo confirmare dignetur, illumque delegare potestatem impertiendi Presbyteris in has Missiones venientibus facultates necessarias, prout expedire videbitur, itemque benigne concedere ut dictus Superior hanc potestatem uni saltem vel alteri Missionariis magis idoneis tamquam vicariis aut substitutis possit subdelegare, prout rerum et locorum necessitas et distantia postulaverit.

Deinde cum nullus sit in his regionibus Episcopus qui sacra olea conficiat quibus per plures annos inter belli tumultus caruimus, nullus qui calices et lapides ad usum Altaris necessaria benedicat, nullus qui sacramentum Confirmationis administret, suppliciter oramus Sanctitatem Vestram praefato Joanni Louis Presbytero Superiori committere ut in hac rerum necessitate et usque dum aliter a Sanctitate Vestra provisum fuerit huic Missioni, ista hic peragere valeat, ne nostri Fideles in multis periculis constituti diutius priventur Sacramento Confirmationis, neve moriantur absque extrema unctione juxta ritum Ecclesiae.

Denique oramus Sanctitatem Vestram, universae huic Missioni Jubilaum Indulgentiarum largiri, eamque facultatum amplitudinem Missionariis extendere quae opportunum videri potest in his vastis remotissimis regionibus acerbo diuturno bello exagitatis propter continuos annorum tumultus, neque Jubilaeum pro felici exaltatione Sanctitatis Vestrae in Cathedram Petri, neque Jubilaeum anni salutis 1775 promulgari potuit, multo minus celebrari et lucrefieri.

Haec sunt Beatissime Pater quae nos praefati Oratores Presbyteri Missionis in his Regionibus confederatae Americae Septentrionalis a Summa Sapientia et Providentia Sanctitatis Vestrae pro bono Catholicae Religionis humiliter supplicamus.

TO CHARLES PLOWDEN   Maryland May 18th 1783

Dear Sir   I have not had the pleasure of a line from you since the favour of your letter from Nanci, dated [*blank*] I answered that letter very soon afterwards, and directed it to the care of Mr Garvy at Rouen. The vessel, that carried my answer, got safely to France; and I was informed by Mr Johnson Mercht in Nantes, that the letter was forwarded agreeably to its directions, so that I hope it got into your hands. I have often wrote to you, that no letters I receive give me so much pleasure and information, as yours do: so that I flatter myself from your friendship, that you will often gratify me. I am at this time very anxious to know, whether you are yet quietly settled with your Sister at Ellingham after all your ramblings. If you are, I make no doubt of your enjoying much happiness, and that you have now and then the pleasure of the very important, tho' very good natured Mr Clinton's company, You know, my Dr Charles, how much I was inchanted with our common acquaintances at Bolonia. In your last journey to Italy, you saw, no doubt, many of them dispersed in the different towns of that fine country. Write me, whether their publick and private misfortunes had not cast a gloom around them, and extinguished the fire of their conversation. I mentioned in my last a long list of those, I wished you to enquire about: and if you ever received that letter, I shall expect from you to have them all particularly named. I am still living with my Mother, who, thanks to God, in her 78th year continues to enjoy as great a share of health, as can be expected, and as sound a mind, as can be wished. You may be assured that she retains a great affection for every thing, that was any way connected with your Mother, between whom and her there was an early and inseparable friendship.

I shall always to glad to hear of your Br Frank. Mr. Leonard Neale[1] lately arrived from Demarara into this country told me, that he was in high estimation in London; and I am entirely satisfied, that if he applies to business, he will both do himself credit, & raise a very comfortable fortune. I write by this opportunity to Liege, a young Gentleman going from hence to that academy; I do not fail to enquire of your good Sister there, whose goodness of heart will be always rememberd by me.

Since the death of Mr Hunter, we have lost none of our Gentlemen here. I find on the other hand, that mortality has swept away many in England. You, I hope, will live many years to be a comfort to your friends & to enjoy a comfortable repose after the storms and vicissitudes you have gone through. Do not fail to present my most affte compliments to all my acquaintance in your neighbourhood, & believe me with unalterable regard   Dr Charles,   Yr affte humble ser [*torn*]   friend   J Carroll

ALS   St
   [1] Marylander, Jesuit, President of Georgetown, 1798-1806, coadjutor to Carroll, 1800, and Archbishop of Baltimore, 1815-17.

CONSTITUTION OF THE CLERGY   White Marsh June 27. 1783
to October 11th. 1784

Proceedings at a Meeting of some of the Clergy in Maryland begun & held at the White Marsh June 27th. 1783.

There were present Messrs. Bernard Diderick, John Carroll, John Ashton, Leonard Neale, Sylvester Boarman and Leonard Neale.

It appeared to the meeting that a letter from several of the Clergy had been written to Mr Lewis the Bishop's Vicar for Maryland, Pensylvania &c &cc. and Superior at ye time of the dissolution of the Society, praying that he would attend at a Meeting, which they apprehended absolutely necessary for the preservation & well-government of all matters, & concerns of the Clergy & the service of Religion in these Countries; and that Mr Lewis in answer thereto, had expressed his entire approbation of the design of such a meeting without determining precisely whether he could personally attend.—It appeared further, that in consequence of Mr Lewis's answer, notice had been given generally to ye Clergymen in Maryland and Pensylvania of the time & place of this meeting & their attendance requested.

Messrs. Diderick, Carroll, Ashton, Sewall & Boarman attended in their own behalf as Clergymen in the service of this Country, and Mr Neale in his own & in behalf of Messrs. Ignatius Matthews, Lewis Roels, & John Bolton residing at Portobacco.

The object of this Meeting is agreed to be to establish a form of Government for the Clergy & to lay down rules for the administration & preservation of their property.[1]

Form of Government

1. There shall be one Genl. Procurator[2] and a Chapter or Representative Body of the Clergy with the Powers hereafter respectively annexed to each.

2. The Chapter shall be composed in the following manner: viz. The Clergymen residing in Pensylvania, and the Eastern Shore of Maryland shall choose two Deputies; Those on the Western Shore of Maryland as far as Charles County, exclusively likewise two, and those in Charles and St. Mary's County two.

3. If the members composing the District so laid off shd. increase or diminish considerably, the number of th[ei]r. Deputies to Chapter is to be increased or diminished proportionably, so that one Deputy be allowed for three members of a district.

4. The presence of at least two thirds of Chapter shall be necessary upon business.

5. The Procurator Genl. shall be chosen out of the Body of the Clergy by a Majority of Chapter.[3]

6. When the place of Procurator General becomes vacant by death or otherwise before the regular time of Election, the oldest member of Chapter shall act as Vice-Procurator Genl. during the Vacancy: And shall as soon as possible give notice to the different districts to collect the votes of the several members of Chapter for a new Procurator Genl., wch. votes shall be transmitted to the Vice-Procurator, and by him opened and in presence of one or two of his district, and he shall notify his Election to the Person having the greatest number of votes.

7. The Procurator Genl. must attend at Chapter, but unless a Member shall have no Vote in ths. deliberations.

8. At the expiration of his three years of Office, he shall be again eligible to the same Office and so on. He may likewise be deposed by Chapter before the expiration of three years; but at least two thirds of Chapter must concur in that measure.

9. The General Chapter shall be assembled at least every three years, and shall examin[e] the general state of the temporal affairs of the Clergy, the debts and credits, the improvements and losses on the different Estates: They shall direct on all needful occasions the observance of the general Rules of temporal Government: and when circumstances point out the propriety of establishing new Rules and altering those before established, such addition or alteration shall not take place, till it be confirmed by the subsequent Chapter, or in the mean time agreed to by a Majority in the different Districts. They shall hear and determine on complaints and appeals in temporal matters, and their determination shall be final.

10. The Chapter shall at all times have the power of judging of and finally determining the necessary measures for securing the publick Estates from all danger of alienation; whether by causing them to be vested in Trustees, and taking ample and indemnifying bonds, or by some other still more sufficient means, if any can be suggested: And the Chapter shall always have a right to call upon the Trustees to surrender their trust, or to make deeds of conveyance to such persons, as shall be named to them.

11. When the place of a member of Chapter becomes vacant, the Vacancy shall be instantly supplied by the District, to wch he belongs.

12. It shall be the business of the Procurator Genl., previous to the meeting, to get full information of, and report to the Chapter the particular condition of each Estate with the accomp[lishmen]ts thereof.

13. When any person not before incorporated into the body of the Clergy, desires to be admitted therein, the Superior *in Spiritualibus*,[4] on being well certified of his doctrine, morals and sufficient learning, shall propose him to the members of the Chapter of the District, where his services are wanted: and in case of his being accepted by them, some members of Chapter in that District shall lay before him the general Regulations of this Body of Clergy, and require him to sign his submission thereunto, and direct him to repair to the place allotted for his Residence. But if the Members of Chapter do not

agree to receive him in their District, then the said Superior is to propose him to any other, where there is need and proceed in the same manner as above. If no district will admit him, he is to be informed that he does not belong to this body of Clergy, that he owes no services and consequently is not entitled to any provision from them; and when any member of the body of the Clergy thro' discontent, leaves his former place of Residence without the approbation of lawful authority, and applies for another place, he is not to be imposed on any district without their consent, expressed by their members of Chapter.

14. With respect to Members actually forming part of the Body of the Clergy, there shall be no arbitrary power of removing them at will, or for greater convenience; but when a vacancy happens, which the good of Religion requires to be supplied, the members of Chapter of the District, in which the vacancy lies, shall endeavour to prevail upon the Person, they judge fittest to accept of the vacant charge, application having been first made to the Superior *in Spiritualibus.*

15. If complaints apparently reasonable should be made of the misconduct of any Manager in the administration of the Estate committed to his charge, the Procurator Genl. and members of the District Chapter are authorised to call upon him for his accounts, which he is to deliver into them; and if upon examination thereof, they find his administration injurious to the publick Good, they are to admonish him thereof: and no amendment ensuing, they are to refer to the General Chapter, if sitting; if not, to all the Members of his District to determine by a Majority of votes, whether he shall be continued in the management of the Estate.

16. When the Superior *in Spiritualibus* has withdrawn his Faculties from any Clergyman on account of his misconduct and irregularity of life, the Procurator Genl. and Chapter shall have power to deprive him of any maintenance from the Estates of the Clergy.

17. Neither Procurator Genl. nor any other Person shall have power to sell, dispose of, remove or anywise alienate the property of any plantation, without the consent of the General Chapter for real property, or of the District for personal Property.

18. In extraordinary emergencies the Procurator Genl. or a Majority of Members of Chapter in any two Districts, may convene the General Chapter.

19. The Person invested with Spiritual Jurisdiction in this Country, shall not in that quality have any power over or in the temporal property of the Clergy—.

Rules for the particular Government of
Members belonging to the Body of the Clergy—

1. Every Person to be admitted into the Body of the Clergy, shall first subscribe a form of promise, as appointed by the first General Chapter, to

submit to the common Rules and Regulations of Government, as long as he shall remain amongst them.

2. When two or more Clergymen live together in the same house; a system of equality must be observed, as far as possible, and every idea of dependance on, or subjection to the one to the other must be excluded. Good order and oeconomy require indeed, that one Person on each Estate have the management thereof, the disposal of the produce, the receiving of the profits, the ordering of the table &cc. But every person there living should have a reasonable sum to be determined by the Genl. Chapter, allowed him, to lay out in necessary and convenient uses.—And where any one's Mission is attended with an extraordinary expence, he shall be allowed for it accordingly—Every Manager of a plantation shall be on the same footing as his Collegues. The sums allowed is thirty pounds lawful Currency.

3. Any Person rendered by age or infirmity incapable of the common duties of a Clergyman, and so deemed by the General or District Chapter shall be entitled in all respects to the same maintenance as labouring Clergymen, as long as he remains in one of our houses. But if he chooses to retire in Europe, or live here with his Friends without giving disedification, he shall receive thirty pounds Currency annually out of the publick Fund, and no more shall be allowed him—Nor shall he be continued in or entrusted with the management of an Estate.—

4. No Clergyman living in a secular house shall be elected to the place of Procurator Genl., or be allowed a subsistence out of the effects of the Clergy, unless he be there placed with a consent of the Genl. Chapter.

5. To prevent scandals and publick disedification, all Persons admitted into this Body of Clergy, shall particularly promise to submit all difference between themselves and other individuals of the Clergy, to the determination of the Genl. Chapter, or to a standing commission of these to be appointed by the Chapter for that Genl. purpose. The Gentlemen chosen for this purpose are Mr. John Lewis, Mr. Thomas Digges and Mr. Ferdinand Farmer.

6. To preserve Charity amongst the Members of the Clergy in this mission, every one must frequently pray for each other, and say ten Masses for every Person dying in the service of this Mission: And the Members of the private Chapters may direct what masses or Prayers shall be said for other purposes in their respective Districts. Every Clergyman shall say one Mass every year for the Superior *in Spiritualibus* during his life time, and fifteen after his decease; and for the late Superior the Rd. Mr. John Lewis after his death also fifteen; And, particularly all shall be mindfull soon after the 2d. Novr. to say annually one Mass for deceased Benefactors.—

Regulations respecting the Management of Plantations—

1. Every Manager of an Estate shall have the sole ordering and direction for raising, disposing of and receiving the profits from the crops, rents, or emoluments thereof, the providing of necessaries for house-keeping & Servants: He shall pay the Person or Persons living with him the allowance determined, as is being directed. He is to be at all common charges for diet and lodging of himself and his Clergymen Companions. He is to find them with suitable and sufficient Horses, they providing themselves bridles and sadles. When Strangers come to his place of Residence, or are invited with moderation by himself or his Companion, he is to entertain them according to his or their rank with charity and hospitality, without rendering his house a place of great resort, or giving publick treats and costly Entertainments.

2. No Manager shall have power to dispose of real property, but under the same limitation as is mentioned above with respect to the Procurator Genl. nor of personal Property, so as considerably to diminish his original Stock: And he shall not contract debts beyond what he can speedily pay from the income of the Estate, nor commence Law Suits without being authorised by the Procurator Genl. and District Chapter.

3. On a Manager's entering upon the charge of a Plantation, an Inventory must be made and signed by himself & Predecessors, or some Person appointed by the District Chapters, and transmitted to the Procurator Genl. to be preserved with other papers of consequence. And the Manager must keep regular books of Debtor and Creditor, to be exhibited to the Genl. and District-Chapter, and Procurator Genl., when thereunto required.

4. The profits arising from the rented lands of St. Thomas's Manor in Charles County, and the rented land of St. Inigo's in St. Mary's County are hereby appropriated for uses at the disposal of the General Chapter, and to be lodged in the hands of the Procurator Genl.—The surplus money of the several Estates remaining in the hands of the respective Managers shall form a particular fund for supplying the deficiencies of their respective districts—and the persons appointed to receive these latter moneys are for the Northern District,—the Rd. Mr. John Lewis: for the middle the Rd. Mr. John Ashton and for the Southern the Rd. Mr. Ignatius Matthews.

5. When from the failure of Crops or other accidents the Manager of an Estate can not pay up the pensions he is charged with, he shall make known and justify his inability to the district-Chapter, & they shall make provision for the deficiency out of the District-Fund, as far as possible: And it is hoped that Individuals will sometimes rather submit to temporary inconveniences, than suffer the plantation to want necessary utensils.

6. The Estates under the different Managers are declared to be distinct from, and not liable for each others debts.

7. In extraordinary cases of great losses to any particular Estate the District Chapter shall relieve the distresses of the suffering Estate out of the surplus money lodged in the District-Fund.

8. If the Procurator Genl. should be Manager of an Estate, He is, like all other Managers, to be accountable for his administration, and shall exhibit his books to the oldest Member of Chapter in his District.

The Formula of promise to be subscribed by all Persons hereafter to be admitted into the Body of the American Clergy is as follows—

I promise to conform myself to the forms and regulations established for the Government of the Clergy residing in Maryland and Pensylvania, so long as I expect maintenance and support from them.

Be it remembered, that these regulations began to be formed by a meeting of some of the Clergy in Maryland held at the White Marsh June 27, 1783. Members those present [were] Messiers B. Diderick, J. Carroll, J. Ashton, Charles Lewis[,] Sylvester Boarman, Ld. Neale and were continued in another meeting held at the aforesaid White Marsh November 6th. 1783. Members present Messiers J. Lewis for the N. District Messiers B. Diderick and J. Carroll for the middle, and Messiers Ignatius Matthews and James Walton for the Southern; and finally concluded and determined at a 3d. meeting held at the id[em—same]. White-Marsh October 11th. 1784, and declared to be binding on all persons at present composing the body of Clergy in Maryland & Pensylvania[5] Members present, Messiers Joseph Mosley Deputy President-Vice [in the place of] Mr. John Lewis—N[orthern]. D[istrict]. Lucas Geissler Robt. Molyneux M[iddle]. D[istrict]. Bernard Diderick, John Carroll, Southern District. Ignatius Matthews, James Walton.

In witness thereof we here subscribe our Names—Joseph Mosley, Deputy of the Revd. Mr. John Lewis S[u]p[erio]r. Members of the Genl. Chapter[:] Lucas Geissler Robert Molyneux[;] of a N. District[:] Bernard Diderick of Middle District Igns. Matthews. James Walton of Southern District [all] Members of the Genl. Chapter[6]

Joseph Mosley. John Ashton Sylvr. Boarman Ferdinand Farmer J. B. Helbron [O.F.M.C.?] P: Helbron [O.F.M.C.?]

DS   AAB
[1] The foregoing is in a different hand from what follows.
[2] There is a second copy which goes to point 5 below and the term "Superior General" is employed with the first word deleted. It seems that the delegates from the Southern District favored this designation originally. Such a designation would have referred to John Lewis and then John Carroll as Vicar General and after 1790 as Bishop. The reasoning is defensive as implied in Carroll, *et al's* letter to the gentlemen of the Southern District (see below, 1787). In the event that Rome appointed a foreign jurisdiction in this office as Vicar General or Apostolic dependent upon a prelate of another country, he would not control property nor even appointments. The control of the Propaganda was also excluded in these matters.
[3] The preliminary draft referred to above deletes an explanation of the procedure at district chapters for selecting delegates to the General Chapter. (See unclassified folder

marked "WhiteMarsh Proceedings" in AAB.) Provision is not later made for this in the text that follows.

⁴ Carroll's MSS do not make it clear that he followed this procedure. The matter needs further study together with the role of trustees in pastoral appointments.

⁵ The remainder of this paragraph is found in the margin with two "X" symbols and "vide marginem" [see the margin] placed in the text at this point.

⁶ A series of brackets in three columns arrange the names in the first, the district in the second and "Members of the General Chapter" stated in the third column.

TO PASTOR OF MAINZ, GERMANY   July 17, 1783

Not found. See Lloyd P. McDonald, *Seminary Movement in the United States* (Washington, D.C., 1927), p. 7.

TO CHARLES PLOWDEN   Maryland Sepr. 26–1783

My dear Sir   Your favour, dated York Aug: 15–1782, after a circuitous and tedious journey, reached me only the first of this month. Ever since we received the happy tidings of peace, I had been in anxious expectation of hearing from you; and soon after it, wrote to you by some young Gentlemen going from hence to the academy at Liege: my letter was to the care of Mr. Talbot,¹ and I make ·no doubt of your having received it before this. I freely and joyfully accept your promise of a regular correspondance, and desire your letters to be directed to me at Rock Creek, near George town, Potomack River, Maryland: If you cannot depend upon Mr. Talbot's care of them at London (tho' I dare say you may) be pleased to get some friend to put them into the hands of Messrs. Wallace, Johnson & Muir, Merchts. in that city, and they will be safely sent.

Since my last to you, Messrs. Leonard Neale from Demara & Ch: Wharton have come into this country. I have seen the latter only once, but propose returning his visit in about a fortnight. I find him indeed possessed of considerable knowledge, and endowed with all those talents, which render Society agreeable: if upon a fuller acquaintance, I discover any of those blemishes, which some of his companions in Engld. though they did, it would give me great concern, and I should speak freely to him about them. But are there not, my dear Sir, some on your side of the water, as well as here, who brooding over undigested scraps of Theology, & never studying with any degree of liberality to enlarge their minds, throw indiscriminate censure on every person departing ever so little from the rules of thinking & acting they have laid down for themselves? I flatter myself, that Mr Wharton may have incurred blame only from such persons, or others prejudiced by their reports. He has surely too much knowledge, & is too well grounded in sound philosophy & sacred literature to adopt the incoherent & impious principles of modern infidelity. Our Gentlemen here continue, as when I last wrote. We are endeavouring to establish some regulations tending to perpetuate a succession of labourers in this vineyard, and to preserve their morals, to prevent idleness, & secure an equitable & frugal administration of our temporals. An immense field is opend to the zeal of apostolical men. Universal toleration throughout this immense country, and innumerable R. Cats going & ready to go into the new regions bordering on the Mississippi, perhaps the finest in the world, & impatiently clamorous for Clergymen to attend them. The object nearest my heart is to establish a college on this continent for the education of youth, which might at the same time be a Seminary for future Clergymen. But at present I see no prospect of success. Your information of the intention of the Propag[and]a [Fide, Congregatio de] gives me concern no farther, than to hear that men, whose institution was for the service of Religion, should bend their thoughts so much more to the grasping of power, & the commanding of wealth: For they may be assured, that they never will get possession of a sixpence of our property here, & if any of our friends could be weak enough to deliver any real estate into their hands, or attempt to subject it to their authority, our civil government would be called upon to wrest it again out of their dominion. A foreign temporal jurisdiction will never be tolerated here; & even the Spiritual supremacy of the Pope is the only reason why in some of the United States, the full participation of all civil rights is not granted to the R. C. They may therefore send their Agents, when they please; they will certainly return empty handed: my only dread, as I said before, would be the scandal that would result from the assertion of unjust pretensions on one hand, and of undoubted rights on the other: and these sentiments & communications you may make as publick as you shall think proper.

I have often thought, that an application to the Emperor, & true statement of our treatment at Bruges &c would procure an allowance, at least equal to the robbery committed on us: and I am glad that you had an audience and forwarded the memorial you mention. If the Emperor is desirous of establishing indeed the character of justice & impartial administration, which he so much affects, he cannot refuse demand so undeniably just. But perhaps his pretensions to the character of justice, affability, watchfulness over his ministers &c is only a cloak to cover his other designs against the rights of Episcopacy & Spl jurisdiction, and indeed of rivetting still faster & faster on his subjects the chains of despotism: for I cannot help thinking, that every prince, who strives so much to concenter all power in himself; to destroy every other exercise of authority, however respectable & antient; to render the condition of his subjects precarious by obliging many to relinquish the state, they were engaged in under the sanction of all the laws sacred & civil; I say, that I cannot help thinking that every such prince is in his disposition a despotical Tyrant. I cannot therefore, abstracting from religious considerations, come into the fashionable language of extolling the Emperor as a model of Princes. In my estimation, the late & present King of Sardinia, as far as I have heard of him, are much beyond the so much admired Joseph. But I live at so great a distance and hear these matters so imperfectly, that my opinion may be very erroneous.

You tell me, that you perceived, that in my last I was afraid of entering into Politicks; but that you will force me into the subject. Indeed, my Dr Charles, I had no such fears about me. I have the happiness to live under a government very different from that, I have been just talking of: & I have never had any cause to fear speaking my sentiments with the utmost freedom. But when I was writing to you I had so many other subjects nearer to my heart to talk of, that I suppose political matters did not occur to my mind, or I left them to the publick papers. You have adopted the language of some of the prints on your side the water by representing us as under imperious leaders, & the trammels of France: but alas! our Imperious leaders, by whom I suppose you mean the Congress, were at all times amenable to our particular assemblies, elected by them every year, often turnd out of their seats, & so little envied, that as their expences were often unavoidably greater than their profits, it has at all times been a difficult matter to get men disinterested and patriotick enough to accept the charge. And as to the trammels of France, we certainly have never wore her chains, but have treated with her as equals, have experienced from her the greatest magnanimity & moderation, & have re-payed it with an honourable fidelity to our engagements. By both of us proceeding on these principles, the war has been brought to an issue, with wch if you are pleased, all is well; for we are entirely satisfied. I am glad that you have not to fear a renewal of Ld G. Gordon's mobs: but cannot agree with you they were fomented or in any way encouraged by the leaders of the opposition of that time; or, as you call them foment[ers] of the *Rebellion* for I know that some of them were objects of the rabble's fury, such as Ld Sr George Saville,[2] Mr Burke &c; and principally on account of the very active part they took in procuring a relaxation of the penal laws.

I am not much surprised at your information of the prevalence of Sp: councils at Rome: the innumerable dependents on Naples, Parma, & Sp; itself must always give too much weight to the interposition of that obstinate & still more ignorant government. God grant, that the little beginning in White Russia may prove a foundation for erecting the Society upon once again; but I cannot help wishing that the proctectress of it were a more respectable character, than she has been often represented.[3] You gave me great satisfaction by your account of the academy: from your former letters, and especially your giving me the names of those, who were withdrawing themselves from it, & whom I knew to be its most capable professor &c, I concluded that it would decay fast.[4] But your manner of mentioning Aston[5] grieved me beyond measure: I cannot help hoping that you have adopted too slightly some disadvantagious reports of him. His unguarded expressions, his too great contempt of outward forms, the poignancy of his raillery, and the envy, which his superior abilities are apt to create, may have caused him to be much misrepresented. It is probable, that he may have committed faults; but I am greatly indeed mistaken in him, if he were ever guilty of such as you have heard, especially ingratitude. He perhaps may not be so lavish as others, of his expressions of acknowledgement; & probably will be so indolent, as to neglect even making those professional returns, which appear to be a duty: but if ever he misses an opportunity of doing a friend a substantial kindness; if he does not even sacrifice his own interest to serve them I am much mistaken in him.

May your Br Frank continue to deserve the character, you give him! I hope you will not omit any opportunity of expressing to him my sincere good wishes for him & my kindest remembrance, in which I beg you to include Messrs [torn] & Charles Sheldon, his law-brethren. I had many things to add; but hearing of a ship to sail immediately, I dispatch this, reserving myself to write farther in my next. I am with all sincerity,   Dr Sir   Yr most sincere frd &   humblest   J Carroll

ALS   St
¹ Thomas Talbot, S.J., procurator for the ex-Jesuits in England.
² Promoted the Roman Catholic Relief Act in 1775.
³ Catherine II refused to promulgate the act suppressing the Jesuits.
⁴ After explusion from colleges at Bruges, many English Jesuits went to the academy at Liege.
⁵ William Aston, S.J., was Rector of the academy of Liege.

CONSTITUTION OF THE CLERGY (CONTINUED)   Nov. 6, 1783

See June 27, 1783.

TO VITALIANO BORROMEO¹   Maryland 10th Novr. 1783

Dr. Sir   The missioners in Maryland and Pennsylvania having chosen some of their Brethren to convene & deliberate on matters of general concern, we, who have been thus delegated, have directed the Revd. Mr. John Lewis, one of our number, and Superior, to sign in our behalf this application to you: and we choose to address ourselves to you, well knowing your active zeal, and depending on the sincerity of your endeavours to promote an interest, which we have very much at heart.

You are not ignorant, that in these United States our Religious system has undergone a revolution, if possible, more extrordinary, than our political one. In all of them, free toleration is allowed to Christians of every denominations; and particularly in the States of Pennsylvania, Delaware, Maryland, and Virginia, a communication of all Civil rights, without distinction or diminution, is extended to those of our Religion. This is a blessing and advantage, which is our duty to preserve & improve with the utmost prudence, by demeaning ourselves on all occasions as subjects zealously attached to our government & avoiding to give any jealousies on account of any dependence on foreign jurisdictions, more than that, which is essential to our Religion an[d] acknowlegement of the Pope's spiritual Supremacy over the whole Christian world. You know that we of the Clergy have heretofore resorted to the Vicar Apostolick of the London district for the exercise of spiritual powers, but being well acquainted with the temper of Congress, of our assemblies and the people at large, we are firmly of opinion, that we shall not be suffered to continue under such a jurisdiction, whenever it becomes known to the publick. You may be assured of this from the following fact. The Clergy of the church of England were heretofore subject to the Bishop of London: but the umbrage taken at this dependance was so great, that notwithstanding the power & prevalence of that sect, they could find no other method to allay jealousies, than by withdrawing themselves, as they have lately done, from all obedience to him.

Being therefore thus circumstanced, we think it not only advisable in us, but, in a manner obligatory to solicit the Holy See to place the Episcopal powers at least such as recommended are most essential, in the hands of one amongst us, whose recognized virtue, knowledge, and integrity of faith, shall be certified by ourselves. We shall annex to this letter such powers, as we judge it absolutely necessary he should be invested with. We might add many very cogent reasons for having amongst us a person thus empowered, and for want of whom it is impossible to conceive the inconveniences happening every day. If it be possible to obtain a grant from Rome for vesting these powers in our Superior *pro tempore,* it would be most desirable. We shall endeavour to have you aided in this application by a recommendation if possible from our own country and the Minister of France. You will know how to avail yourself of the residence of so favourable a Russian minister at Rome; and if Mr. Thorpe will be pleased to undertake the management of the business there we will with cheerfulness and gratitude answer all expenses which he may incur in the prosecution of it. He will be the judge, how and whether the annexed petition[2] ought in prudence to be presented to His Holiness, but at all events the powers therein contained, are those which we wish our Superior to be invested with.

AL   AAB;   L Guilday, 172-73. MS is in decay and needs L to complete meaning. Guilday omits the first paragraph.

[1] A cardinal of influence with the Propaganda. Name not on letter.

[2] See to Pius VI, 1783. The reference here may possibly be to a second petition, which was not found.

TO CHARLES CARROLL OF CARROLLTON   White-marsh
Novr 11—1783—

Dear Sir   I have been informed, that some time after the establishment of our present Constitution, a law was continued relating to the administration of Orphans estates, in which amongst other provisions was a clause preventing Roman Catholicks from being guardians to Protestant children; & in consequence of this judgment a clause was obtained in the late Genl Court disabling one Philip Casey of Montgomery County from acting in that quality to his son in law. As this cause is inconsistent with that perfect equality of rights, which by our Constitution is secured to all Religions, I make no doubt but you will be able to obtain a general repeal of this and all other laws and clauses of laws enacting any partial regards to one denomination to the prejudice of others. Mr Judge Hanson will be able to point out to you the laws in question.

    I have been from home several days. You will be pleased to inform Miss [Mrs.] Darnall that her Sister was well, and her Fr as usual. I hope in a very short time to see you & make you a payment. My affectionate complts to Cousin Nancy, Miss Polly & your little ones. With sincere regard I am   Dr Sir   Yr affte Kinsman & hble Servt   J Carroll   P.S. I very much recommend to you and the other R.C. members of the assembly a business to be proposed to you by Messrs Lewis and Ashton.

ALS   MHS

ANSWER TO CHARLES WHARTON   Fall, 1784

[Charles Wharton, a Marylander and former Jesuit priest, left the ministry and the Church a few years before this time, while he was serving as a chaplain in Worcester, England. He returned to America and in May, 1784, delivered to a Philadelphia publisher an explanation of his defection by way of an attack on Catholicism, entitled *Letter to the Roman Catholics of Worcester.* He responded to Carroll's *Address* of 115 pages the following year with *A Reply to an Address to the Roman Catholics of the United States of America* (Philadelphia, 1785). Carroll made no rejoinder, fearing the bad effect upon inter-faith relations in America. See Carroll to C. Plowden, June 29, 1785, and other index references for his thoughts on the controversy.]

AN ADDRESS TO THE ROMAN CATHOLICS OF THE UNITED STATES OF AMERICA BY A CATHOLIC CLERGYMAN   [Fall,] M.DCC.LXXXIV.

SAINT Paul recommends to the antients of the church of Ephesus, in his last and earnest address to them, *to heed to themselves, and to the whole flock, over which the Holy Ghost has placed them overseers, to feed the church of God.*[1] This duty is at all times incumbent on those, who, by their station and profession, are called to the service of religion; and more especially at periods of unusual danger and temptation to the flocks committed to their charge: whether the temptation arise from outward violence, a growing curruption of manners, or *from men arising from your own selves, speaking perverse things to draw away disciples after them.*[2] For in the church of God, "the error of the teacher is a temptation to the people, and their danger is greater, where his knowledge is more extensive."[3] The antients and venerable author, who makes this observation, having instanced the truth of it in the departure from the catholic faith of several persons eminent for their knowledge and writings, concludes with an important instruction, and recommends it to be impressed upon the minds of catholics, *that they may know, that with the church, they receive their teachers, but must not with these abandon the faith of the church.*[4]

You will not now be at a loss to account for the occasion of the present address A letter to the Roman Catholics of the city of Worcester in England has been published here by one of their late chaplains; and had all the copies of it been transmitted to those, for whom *professedly* it is intended, I should not dedicate to animadversions on it the few moments of leisure left me from other employments incident to my charge and profession; especially with the scanty materials of which I am possessed; for I am destitute of many sources of information, and unable to refer to authorities, which I presume to have been collected on the other side with great industry. By the Chaplain's own account, he has long meditated a separation from us; and, during that time, he had opportunities of resorting to the repositories of science so common and convenient in Europe.

But the letter not only being printed here, but circulating widely through the country, a regard to your information, and the tranquillity of your consciences requires some notice to be taken of it. For the ministers of religion should always remember, that it is their duty as well to enlighten the understanding, as improve morals of mankind. *You are the salt of the earth,*[5] said Christ to his apostles, to his apostles, to preserve men from corruption of vice and immorality: and, *you are the light of the world,*[6] to instruct and inform it.

Our duty being so clearly delineated by the divine authors of our religion, if we have been deficient in the discharge of either part of it, if we have flattered your passions, or withheld knowledge from your minds, we have certainly deviated from the obligations of our state, and the positive injunctions of our church. For though you have often heard it reproachfully said, that it was both her maxim and practice to keep her votaries in ignorance, no imputation can be more groundless: and for a full confutation of it, we refer our candid adversaries to the ordinances of our councils, the directions of our

ecclesiastical superiors, and the whole discipline of our church, even in ages
the most inauspicious to the cultivation of letters. In those ages indeed, the
manners of the times had great influence, as they always will, on the manners
of the clergy: but every informed and ingenuous mind, instead of being
prejudiced by the vague imputations on monkish and clerical ignorance, will
remember with gratitude, that they owe to this body of men the preservation
of antient literature; that in times of general anarchy and violence, they alone
gave such cultivation to letters, as the inimproved state of science admitted;
and that in the cloisters of cathedral churches, and of monasteries, they
opened schools of public instruction, and, to men of studious minds, asylums
from the turbulence of war and rapine. The inference from these facts is
obvious: for if the ministers of religion, agreeably to the discipline of the
church, cultivated and taught letters at a time when they were generally
neglected; if the resurrection of sound literature was owing, as it certainly
was, to the most dignified of our clergy; who can impute ignorance to us, as
resulting from the genius of our religion?

I forbear to add other numerous proofs of the falsity of this charge: and I
can with confidence appeal to yourselves, whether your religious instructors
have not, to the extent of their abilities, and suitably to your respective
situations in life, endeavoured to suggest such grounds for your adhesion to
the doctrines of the church, as might make you ready always to *give an
answer to every man, that asketh you a reason of that hope that is in you.*[7]
We tell you indeed, that you must submit to the church; but we add with the
apostle, that *your obedience must be reasonable.* Now can obedience be
reasonable, "can any man give a reason for that hope that is in him, without a
due examination of the grounds or motives that induce him to it? No surely;
and therefore nothing ought to hinder you from examining thoroughly the
grounds of your religion. Nay, we exhort you to examine them over and over
again, till you have a full conviction of conscience, that it is not education,
but the prevailing force of truth, that determines you in the choice of it."[8]

But is not this recommendation a mere delusion? Can a consistent Roman
catholic be a candid inquirer in matters of religion? Why not? *Because,* says
the Chaplain (p.8.), *he cannot set out with that indifference to the truth or
falsity of a tenet, which forms the leading feature of rational investigation.*
Did the Chaplain weigh all the consequences of the doctrine here advanced?
Must we then suspend all the duties of natural religion and moral obligation?
Must a son divest himself of filial love and respect, that he may investigate
rationally, and judge impartially, of the obligations resulting from the tender
relations of parent and child? Must we neglect to train the tender minds of
youth in the habits of virtue, and to guard them from vice, by the prospect of
future rewards and punishments, lest they should be inclined to judge
hereafter too partially of those great sanctions of natural and revealed
religion? What an argument is here suggested to the impugners of all religion,

to the enemies of christianity? Suggested, did I say, or borrowed from them? For the learned Dr. Leland, to whose writings the cause of revelation is so much indebted, has informed us, that it has been long ago made use of by them; and his answer to it, more especially as he was a protestant, will save me the trouble of making any observations on this extraordinary assertion. "Another argument," says he, "with which he" (the author of *christianity not founded in argument*) "makes a mighty parade, is to this purpose, that no religion can be rational, that is not founded on a free and impartial examination: and such an examination supposes a perfect neutrality to the principles, which are examined, and even a temporal disbelief of them, which is what the Gospel condemns. But this proceeds upon a wrong account of the nature of free examination and inquiry. It is not necessary to a just inquiry into doctrines or facts, that a man should be absolutely indifferent to them, before he begins that inquiry; much less, that he should actually disbelieve them: as if he must necessarily commence atheist, before he can fairly examine into the proofs of the existence of God. It is sufficient to a candid examination, that a man apply himself to it with a mind open to conviction, and a disposition to embrace truth, on which side soever it shall appear, and to receive the evidence that shall arise in the course of the trial. And if the inquiry relateth to principles, in which we have been instructed; then supposing those principles to be in themselves rational and well founded, it may well happen, that in inquiring into the grounds of them, a fair examination may be carried on without seeing cause to disbelieve or doubt of them through the whole course of the inquiry; which in that case will end in a fuller conviction of them than before."[9]

But Roman catholics, it seems, are fettered with other obstacles to free inquiry. They cannot *seek religious information in the writings of* protestants, without incurring the *severest censures* of their church (Ch[aplain's]. Letter, p. 4): By the *Bulla Coenae* excommunication is denounced against all persons reading books written by heretics containing heresy, or treating religion. (Note ibid.)

It is indeed true, that the Bull referred to contains the prohibition, as mentioned by the Chaplain; and it is not less true, that in England, that protestant country of free inquiry, severe laws and heavy penalties were enacted, and, if I am well informed, still subsist, against the introduction, the printing and vending of books in favour of the catholic religion. I know, that within these last twenty years, these laws have been executed with severity. Such, on both sides, were the precautions suggested by a jealous zeal to preserve uninformed minds from the artificial colourings of real or supposed error. The heads of the respective churches considered it as their duty to guard their flocks from the poison of pernicious doctrines; and did not deem it essential to fair and full investigation, that their adversaries objections should be stated to the unlearned, to unexperienced youth, or to the softer

sex, with all the acrimony of invective, with the aggravations of misrepresentation, and powers of ridicule; weapons too common in controversies of every
kind. Without examining how far this zeal was prudent and justifieable in the
present instance, let me observe, that the proscription of books of evil
tendency is warranted by the example of St. Paul's disciples at Ephesus,
acting in the presense of, and probably by the instructions of their master.
Many of them, says holy writ, *that had followed curious arts, brought their
books together, and burnt them before all.*[10] And what inference follows? *So
mightily,* continues the inspired writer in the next verse, *grew the word of
God, and was strengthened.* What good parent, what conscientious instructor
feels not the anguish of religion, when they find, that promiscuous reading
has caused the rank weed of infidelity to grow in that soil, the tender minds
of their children and pupils, where they had sown and cultivated the seeds of
virtue?

But, be the prohibition of the Bull reasonable or not, I will be bold to say,
it was no prejudice to free inquiry. First, because the Bull not only was never
received into, but was expressly rejected from almost every catholic state. In
them it had no force; the very alleging of its authority was resented as an
encourachment on national independence; and in particular, the clause referred to by the Chaplain was generally disregarded. For this I will appeal to
his own candour. Throughout his extensive acquaintance with catholics, has
he not known them to read protestant authors without hesitation or repoof?
Did he not expect, that his letter would freely circulate amongst them? To
what purpose did he address it to the Roman catholics of the city of
Worcester, if he knew, that with the terrors of excommunication hanging over
them, they dare not read it? In the course of his theological studies, was he
himself ever denied access to the writings of our adversaries? Were not the
works of Luther, Calvin and Besa, of Hooker, Tillotson and Stillingfleet, and
all the other champions of the protestant cause, open to his inspection? In
public and private disputations, were not the best arguments from these
authors fairly and forcibly stated, in opposition to the most sacred tenets of
the catholic belief? Was not even literary vanity gratified, by placing objections in the strongest light, and wresting the palm of disputation out of the
hands of all concurrents? Knowing this, I must confess, that I cannot
reconcile with candour the following words; *I knew that to seek religious
information in the writings of protestants, was to incur the severest censures
of the church I belonged to.* (Letter, 1. 14.)

May I not then say with confidence, that rational investigation is as open
to catholics, as to any other set of men on the face of the earth? No; we are
told there still remains behind a powerful check to this investigation. This
article of our belief, that "the Roman church is the mother and mistress of all
churches, and that out of HER COMMUNION no salvation can be obtained,"
for which the Chaplain cites the famous creed of Pope Pius IV. (p.7), makes

too great an impression of terror on the mind, to suffer an unrestrained exertion of its faculties. Such is the imputation; and it being extremely odious and offensive, and tending to disturb the peace and harmony subsisting in these United States between religionists of all professions; you will allow me to enter fully into it, and rend, if I can, your vindication complete.

I begin with observing, that to be in the *communion of the catholic church,* and to be a *member of the catholic church,* are two very distinct things. They are in the *communion of the church,* who are united in the profession of her faith, and participation of her sacraments, through the ministry, and government of her lawful pastors.[11] But the *members of the catholic church* are all those, who with a sincere heart seek true religion, and are in an unfeigned disposition to embrace the truth, whenever they find it. Now it never was our doctrine, that salvation can be obtained only by the former; and this would have manifestly appeared, if the Chaplain, instead of citing pope Pius's creed from his memory, or some unfair copy, had taken the pains to examine a faithful transcript of it. These are the words of the obnoxious creed, and not those wrongfully quoted by him, which are not to be found in it. After enumerating the several articles of our belief, it goes on thus: *This true catholic faith, without which no one can be saved, I do at this present firmly profess and sincerely hold,* &c. Here is nothing of the *necessity of communion* with our church for salvation; nothing, that is not professed in the public liturgy of the protestant episcopal church; and nothing, I presume, but what is taught in very christian society on earth, viz that catholic faith is necessary to salvation. The distinction between being a member of *the catholic church,* and of *the communion of the church,* is no modern distinction, but a doctrine uniformly taught by antient as well as later divines. *What is said,* says Bellarmine, *of none being saved out of the church, must be understood of them, who belong not to it either in fact or desire.*[12] I shall soon have occasion to produce other authors establishing this same point: "We are accused of great uncharitableness in allowing salvation to none, but catholics. But this also is a mistaken notion. We say, I believe, no more, than do all other christian societies. Religion certainly is an affair of very serious consideration, When therefore a man either neglects to inform himself; or, when informed, neglects to follow the conviction of his mind; such a one, we say, is not in the way of salvation. After mature inquiries, if I am convinced, that the religion of England is the only true one, am I not obliged to become a protestant? In similar circumstances, must not you likewise declare yourself a catholic? Our meaning is, that no one can be saved out of the true church; and, as we consider the evidence of the truth of our religion to be great, that he, who will not embrace truth, when he sees it, deserves not to be happy. God however is the searcher of hearts. He only can read those internal dispositions, on which rectitude of conduct alone depends."[13] Let any one compare this explanation of our doctrine with the doctrine of protestant divines; and discover in the former, if he can, any plainer traces of the savage monster intolerance, than in the latter. Dr. Leland is now before me, and after transcribing from him, I shall spare myself the trouble of collecting the many other similar passages, which I remember to have read in protestant divines. "It seems to be obvious,["] says he, ["]to the common sense and reason of mankind, that if God hath given a revelation, or discovery of his will concerning doctrines or laws of importance to our duty and happiness, and hath caused them to be promulgated with such evidence, as he knoweth to be sufficient to convince reasonable and well disposed minds, that will carefully attend to it, he hath an undoubted right to require those, to whom this revelation is published, to receive and to obey it; and if through the influence of corrupt affections and lusts, those, to whom this revelation is made known, refuse to receive it, he can justly punish them for their culpable neglect, obstinacy and disobedience."[14]

Where then is the uncharitableness peculiar to catholics? Where is the odious tenet, that dries up the springs of philanthropy, and *chills by early infusions of bigotry and warm feeling of benevolence?* (Letter, p. 13) I am ready to do justice to the humanity of protestants; I acknowledge with pleasure and admiration their many charitable institutions, their acts of public and private beneficence. I likewise, as well as the Chaplain, *have the happiness to live in habits of intimacy and friendship with many valuable protestants* (Let. p. 9.); but with all my attachment to their persons, and respect for their virtues, I have never seen or heard of the works of christian mercy being exercised more extensively, more generally, or more uninterruptedly, than by many members of our own communion, though the Chaplain thinks our minds are *contracted by the narrowness of a system* (let. ibid.) Let him recall to his remembrance the many receptacles he has seen erected in catholic countries for indulgence and human distress in every shape; the tenderness and attention with which the unfortunate victims of penury and disease are there served, not by mercenary domestics, as elsewhere; but in many places, by religious men; and in others, by communities of women, often of the first nobility, dedicating their whole lives to this loathsome exercise of humanity without expectation of any reward on this side of the grave. Let him remember, how many men of genius he has known to devote themselves with a like disinterestedness to the irksome employment of training youth in the first rudiments of science; and others encountering incredible hardships, and, as it were, burying themselves alive, to bring savages to a social life, and afterwards to form them to christian virtue. To what society of christians does that body of men belong, who bind themselves by the sacred obligation of a vow, even to part with their own liberty, if necessary, by offering it up instead of, and for the redemption of their fellow-christians groaning under the slavery of the piratical states of Barbary? How often has the Chaplain seen the bread of consolation and the words of eternal life carried into the gloomy mansions of the imprisoned, before the humane Howard had awakened the sensibility of England to this important object? Need I mention the heroical charity of a Charles Borromeo, of a Thomas of Villanova, of Marseilles' good bishop, and so many others, who devoted themselves to the public relief, during dreadful visitations of the plague, *when nature sickened, and each gale was death?* The Chaplain's recollection will enable him to add greatly to those instances of *expanded benevolence;* and I would fain ask, if the virtues, from which they spring, are not formed in the bosom of the catholic church. Can a religion, which invariably and unceasingly gives them birth and cultivation, be unfriendly to humanity? Can so bad a tree bear such excellent fruit?

You may perhaps think, that enough has been said to free you from the imputation of uncharitableness in restraining salvation to those of your own communion. But you will excuse me for dwelling longer on it, conceiving it, as I do, of the utmost importance to charity and mutual fort earance, to render our doctrine on this head as persicuous, as I am able.

First then, it has been always and uniformly asserted by our divines, that baptism, actual baptism is essentially requisite to initiate us into the communion of the church; this notwithstanding, their doctrine is not less uniform and the council of Trent (sess[ion]. 6.ch. 4.) has expressly established it, that salvation may be obtained without actual baptism; thus then it appears, that we not only *may,* but *are obliged* to believe, that *out of our communion* salvation may be obtained.

Secondly, with the same unanimity our divines define heresy to be, not merely a mistaken opinion in a matter of faith; but an obstinate adherence to that opinion: not barely an error of judgment; but an error arising from a perverse affection of the will. Hence they infer, that he is no heretic, who, though he hold false opinions in matters of faith, yet remains in an habitual disposition to renounce these opinions, whenever he discovers them to be contrary to the doctrines of Jesus Christ.

These principles of our theology are so different from the common misrepresentations of them, and even from the statement of them by the late Chaplain of Worcester, that some, I doubt, will suspect them to be those palliatives, he mentions, to disguise the severity of an unpopular tenet, to which, he says, our *late* ingenious apologists *in England* have had recourse (p. 10.) But you shall see, that they were always our principles not only *in England,* but throughout the christian world; and I will be so bold to say, that so far from being contradicted *in every public catechism, and profession of faith,* as is suggested in the same page of the Chaplain's letter, they are not impeached in any one; so far from our teaching the impossibility of salvation out of the communion of our church, as much as we teach transubstantiation (Let. p. 10), no divine, worthy to be called such, teaches it at all.

I will set out with the French divines, and place him first, whose reputation, I presume, is highest. Thus then does the illustrious Bergier express himself, in his admirable work, entitled, *Deism refuted by itself.* "It is false, that we say to any one, that he will be damned; to do so, would be contrary to our general doctrine relating to the different sects out of the bosom of the church. First with respect to heretics" (the author here means those, who, though not heretics in the rigorous sense of the word, go under the general denomination), "who are baptised in Jesus Christ, we are persuaded, that all of them, who with sincerity remain in their error; who through inculpable ignorance believe themselves to be in the way of salvation; who would be ready to embrace the Roman catholic church, if God were pleased to make known to them, that she alone is the true church, we are persuaded, that these candid and upright persons, from the disposition of their hearts, are children of the catholic church. Such is the opinion of *all divines* since St. Augustin."[15]

The bishop of Puy, whose learning and merits are so much known and felt in the Gallican church, writes thus. "To define a heretic accurately, it is not enough to say, that he made choice of his doctrine, but it must be added that he is *obstinate* in his choice."[16]

The language of German divines is the same, or stronger, if possible. "Heresy,["] says Reuter, in a chrisitan, "or baptised person, is a *wilful* and *obstinate* error of the understanding opposite to some verity of faith.—So that three things are requisite to constitute heresy. 1st. In the understanding, an erroneous opinion against faith. 2ndly. in the will, liberty and obstinacy." The third condition is, that the erring person be a baptised christian; otherwise his sin against faith is called infidelity, not heresy. After which our author thus goes on. "The obstinacy requisite to heresy is a deliberate and determined resolution to dissent from a truth revealed, and sufficiently proposed by the church, or some other general rule of faith,[.]"[17] The same doctrine is delivered by all the other German divines, to whom I now can have recourse, and they cite to the same purpose Suarez, &c.

If the doctrine imputed to us could be found anywhere, it would probably be in Spain and Italy: But you have just heard Suarez, the first of Spanish theologians, quoted to disprove it; and with respect to Italy, Bellarmine's opinion has been stated; to which I shall add that of St. Thomas of Aquin, whose great authority and sanctity of life have procured him the title of the angel of the school. He teaches then, "that even they, to whom the gospel was never announced, will be excused from the sin of infidelity, though justly punishable for others, they may commit, or for that, in which they were born, But if any of them conduct themselves in the best manner they are able" (by conforming, I presume, to the laws of nature and direction of right reason) "God will provide for them in his mercy."[18]

You will observe, that in the passage quoted from Bergier, he says that the doctrine delivered by him *has been the opinion of all divines since St. Augustin.* This holy father, who usually expresses himself with great force and severity against real heretics, requires nevertheless the same conditions of obstinacy and perverseness, as the divines above mentioned. "I call him only a heretic,["] says he, ["]who, when the doctrine of catholic faith is manifested to him, prefers resistance."[19] Again: "They are not to be ranked with heretics, who without *pertinacious animosity* maintain their opinion, though false and mischievous, especially if they did not broach it themselves with forward presumption; but received it from their mistaken and seduced parents, and if they seek truth with earnest solicitude, and a readiness to retract, when they discover it."[20]

To these decisive authorities of St. Augustin might be added others, as well from him, as from Jerome, Tertulian, &c. but surely enough has been said to convince you, that we have no need to shelter our doctrines under the covering of modern glosses, and that the language of English and other divines of our church has in this respect been perfectly uniform.

Yet in spite of this uniformity, we must still have obtruded upon us the doctrine of confining salvation to those only of our own communion; for, without it, the *boasted infallibility of a living authority,* that *is no more.* (Let. p. 12.) Why so? Because "whoever admits this authority as an undoubted article of christian religion, must necessarily pronounce condemnation upon those, who *wilfully* reject it." (Let. ibid.) Therefore we must likewise pronounce condemnation upon those, who reject it through *ignorance and inculpable error.* Is this inference logical? And yet must it not follow from the premises to make any thing of the Chaplain's argument?

When I come to consider, how a man of genius and extensive knowledge, as he surely is, could bring himself to think, that we hold the doctrine imputed to us, I am at a loss to account for it. He received his education in a school, and from men, who have been charged, unjustly indeed, both by protestants and some catholics, with having too great latitude to the doctrine of invincible, or inculpable ignorance. He heard from them, that in certain cases, this ignorance extended even to, and excused from the guilt of violating the law of nature.[21] Can he then imagine, that we deem it insufficient to exempt from criminality the disbelief of positive facts, such as the divine revelation of certain articles of religion?

For all this, he still labours to fix on us this obnoxious tenet, with a perseverance, which carries with it an air of animosity. He says, that our controvertists make use of the argument cited in his 10th page; protestants allow salvation to catholics; catholics allow it not to protestants; therefore the religion of catholics is the safest. Hence he infers, that we deny salvation to all, but those of our own communion.

If his inference were conclusive, I should have cause to bring a similar charge of cruelty and uncharitableness against protestants. For their great champion, Chillingworth, answered the very objection stated by the Chaplain, expressly teaches, *that catholics allow, that ignorance and repentance may excuse a protestant from damnation, tho dying in his error;* "and this,["]

continues he, ["]is all the charity, which by our own (his opponents) confession also, the most favourable protestants allow to papists."[22] To this I shall add, that both Chillingworth and the Chaplain appear to misapprehend the argument of our controvertists; which is this. You protestants allow our church to be a true church; that it retains all the fundamental articles of religion, without teaching any damnable error; your universities have declared, on a solemn consultation, that a person, not pretending to the plea of invincible ignorance, may safely leave the protestant church, and become a member of ours, because it is a safe way to salvation. The Chaplain knows, that many of the most eminent protestant writers have asserted, that all the essentials of true religion are to be found in our communion; and surely the possibility of obtaining salvation is on of these essentials; he knows, that on a great occasion this was the determination of the protestant university of Helmstadt. But on the other hand, catholic divines always teach, that the true church of Christ being only one, inculpable error alone can justify a protestant for continuing out of her communion; and therefore that it is safest to become a catholic. Such is the argument employed by some of our controvertists. I do not undertake to make it good, but I mean only to prove, by stating it fairly, that the Chaplain is not warranted to draw from it that odious consequence, with which we are unjustly charged.

If then we do not hold the doctrine of exclusive salvation, can the horrible tenet of persecution, which, he says, is the consequence of it,[23] be imputed to us? I do not indeed see their necessary connexion; but I know, that protestants and catholics equally deviate from the spirit of their religion, when fanaticism and fiery zeal would usurp that controul over mens minds, to which conviction and fair argument have an exclusive right.

You now see, that neither the prohibition of reading heretical books, nor our doctrine concerning the possibility of salvation are any hindrances to free enquiry in matters of religion. If for so many years they with-held the Chaplain from making it, he was with held by unnecessary fears, and a phantom of his own imagination. Another cause too concurred, as he tells us, to hold him in ignorance. *I am not ashamed,* says he, to *confess, that it was the claim to infallibility, which prevented me so long from examining the tenets of the Roman church.* (Let. p. 22) Here indeed, if he means the claim of infallibility, as it rests upon proofs of every kind, I do not wonder at its preventing him from examining minutely all the difficulties to which some of our tenets singly may be liable. For if things beyond our comprehension are proposed to our belief, the immediate consideration should be; by whom are they proposed? When the authority, which proposes them, claims to be infallible, reason suggests this farther enquiry; on what grounds is this claim established? Is it found to be established on solid convincing proofs? Then certainly it becomes agreeable to the dictates of reason, and the soundest principles of morality, to assent to the doctrines so proposed, tho' we may not fully comprehend them, nor be able to give a satisfactory answer to every difficulty that human ingenuity may allege against them. This is the mode of reasoning used by all defenders of revealed religion; they first apply themselves to prove the divine revelation of scripture; having done this, they then infer, that its mysteries and unsearchable doctrines must be received, as coming from an unerring authority. And so far the Chaplain will surely agree with me.

I cannot therefore see, why he speaks so contemptuously of Bellarmine's creed, (p. 17) that *he believed, what the church believed; and that the church believed, what he believed.* For what do these words import more or less, than that he conformed his faith to that of the church; that to her decisions he submitted his judgment and belief so entirely, that the propositions recited from him were, in the language of logicians, convertible. And is not this the duty of every person, who believes the church to be infallible, as that great cardinal certainly did, after examining, if ever man did, all that was written against her infallibility. Where lies the difference between this *collier-like* (Let. ibid.) profession of faith, and that of St. Augustin conforming his religion to that of the fathers his precesessors, *I believe,* says he, *what they believe; I hold, what they believe; I hold, what they hold; I preach what they preach.*[24]

The Chaplain goes on to tell the catholics of the city of Worcester, that "if a man's belief be not rational, if he submit to *human authority* without weighing or understanding the doctrines, which it inculcates, this belief is not faith. It is credulity, it is weakness."[25] Who doubts it? But if he submit to *divine* authority, though he do not fully comprehend the doctrines delivered, is this weakness and credulity? or is it the rational obedience of faith? From his own account of the promises of Christ (p. 28), his church can never fail in teaching the *fundamental and necessary* articles of religion, and the *great and essential tenets?* For the Chaplain has told us, that they are proposed by an authority, which the promises of Christ, so far at least, guard from error and delusion. And yet amongst these tenets, there are some beyond the reach of human comprehension. The Trinity, the mystery of the incarnation of the Son of God, his being conceived of the Holy Ghost, his crucifixion and death, his descending into hell, are, I presume, those doctrines of christianity, which the Chaplain deems fundamental; for they are all contained in the apostles creed. He is certainly unable to *weigh* or *understand* them. Nevertheless he acts rationally in admitting and believing them, because he conceives them to be revealed by an infallible guide. Can it then be folly and credulity in you to believe for a similar reason these and all other articles of your religion?

The vainest therefore of all controversies, and the most ineffectual for the discovery of truth, is, to dispute on the metaphysical nature of the doctrines of christianity. For instance, to prove the Trinity, should we set about reading lectures on the divine persons and essence, on the eternal and necessary generation of the Word, &c.? This indeed would be folly, and we should speak a language unintelligible to our hearers and ourselves. In this and all similar cases, the only rational method is, to shew that the contested doctrine is proposed to our belief by an infallible authority. This undoubtedly would be the Chaplain's method in asserting against the Arians, Socinians, and modern sectaries, the Trinity, the Incarnation, and the eternity of future punishments; and such likewise is the method, by which we endeavour to establish the tenets, which he calls the *discriminating doctrines* of our church.

Apply these principles to all his reasonings in his 23rd, 24th, and 25th pages, and see what they will come to. Set him in competition with a Deist, an Arian, a Socinian; and how will he extricate himself from his own arguments, when urged to subvert the infallibility of scripture, or the christian doctrines of original sin, of the Trinity, the Incarnation and redemption of mankind? *Religion and reason can never be at variance,* will they say with the Chaplain, *because the most rational religion must always be the best.* (P. 25.) *The language of reason was never yet rejected with impunity—she will be heard—she must be respected,* &c. (ibid.) *Do then some controverted texts of scripture make* the Trinity and Incarnation of the Son of God *as evident to reason, as it is plain to the most ordinary capacity,* that three divine persons really distinct cannot be one and the same God? or that the eternal and immortal God cannot become a mortal and suffering man, which is a *stumbling-block to Jews; and to the Greeks, foolishness.* [26]

Will the Chaplain reply to the deist, and tell him, that the infallibility of scripture warrants his belief of these *seemingly* absurd tenets? He will be answered, that he begs the question; and in his own language, that *reason assures him* (the deist) *with greater evidence,* than the infallibility of scripture is proved, *that the Almighty requires not our belief of doctrines, which stand in direct contradiction to the only means, he has allowed us of arriving at truth,—our senses and understanding.*

Nor will the deist stop here; he will add, that the pretended *infallibility* of scripture *must prevent* the Chaplain *from examining the tenets of the* christian *church. Sheltered under the garb of so gorgeous a prerogative, impressed upon the yielding mind of youth by men of sense and virtue; backed moreover by the splendour of supposed miracles and the horrors of* damnation, *opinions the most absurd and contradictory must frequently dazzle and overawe the understanding. Amidst the fascinating glare of so might a privilege, the eye of reason becomes dim and inactive.* (P. 23.) Can the Chaplain or any other person tell us, why Bolingbroke, or a Hume had not as good a right to use this argument against the general doctrines of christianity, as the Chaplain had to urge it against the discriminating doctrines of the catholic church?

Such are the difficulties, in which men involve themselves by extending the exercise of reason to matters beyond its competency. Let this excellent gift of our provident and bountiful Creator be employed, as has been said before, in examining the grounds for believing the scriptures to be infallible; but let it go no farther, when that infallibility is fully evinced. In the same manner, let your reason investigate with the utmost attention, and sincere desire of discovering truth, the motives for and against the church's infallibility; but if your inquiries terminate in a full conviction, of her having received this great prerogative from Jesus Christ, *the author and finisher of our faith*, submit with respect and docility to her decisions. The Chaplain himself, when less rapt in extacy with the beauties of reason, can acknowledge this: *shew me*, says he, *the proofs of this infallibility*, and if I do not admit them with every faculty of my soul, you have my leave to brand me with the pride of Lucifer. (P. 23.)

You will not expect me to enter fully into this subject, and point out either to you or the Chaplain, the proofs which he requires. Neither my leisure, or inclination now allow me to undertake, what has been done by much abler hands. The Chaplain, and you too, I hope, know where to look for these proofs. Let him peruse the controversial works of Bellarmine, Bossuet, Nicole and Bergier, Mumford's Question of Questions, Manning's and Hawarden's writing on this subject; let him contrast them with Albertinus and Claude; with Chillingworth, Usher and Bishop Hurd. There is no answer for the impressions, which the minds of different men may receive from perusing the same authors. I can only say, for my own part, that as far as my reading on this subject has extended, I have generally found, on one side, candour in stating the opposite doctrine, fairness in quotations, clearness and fullness in the answers, and consistency of character in the controvertist; impugning and defending sometimes on the principles of a protestant, sometimes on those of a Socinian or deist, sometimes pretending to model his religion on the belief of the four first ages of christianity; and at other times finding corruptions immediately after, if not coeval with the apostolical times.

On this subject therefore, whatever disadvantage it may be to our cause, I shall confine myself solely to the defensive, and endeavour to satisfy you, that the Chaplain has given no sufficient reason to shake the stability of your faith with respect to the infallibility of the church.

He observes, that the *few scriptural texts*, "which seem to countenance infallibility, appeared no longer conclusive, *than he* refused to examine them." (P. 27.) Why he ever *refused* to examine them, he is yet to explain; especially as the duty of his profession, and the particular course of his studies called for a more attentive and fuller examination of them, than the generality of christians are obliged to. Surely he does not mean to insinuate, that he was ever discouraged from, or deprived of the means of making the

inquiry. Nor do I know why he mentions only a *few* texts, as countenancing
the doctrine of infallibility, since the writers above named allege so many
both of the Old and New Testament. The author of the *Catholic Scripturist,*
whom the Chaplain might have found an adversary worthy of his Chillingworth and Usher, enumerates thirty texts to prove this point, besides others,
to which he refers. Let us however hear the Chaplain's animadversions on the
few, he has though proper to consider.

Amongst other proofs of her infallibility, the catholic church alleges these
words of Christ to St. Peter, Mat. xvi. ver. 18 *Thou Art Peter, and upon this
rock I will build my church, and the gates of hell shall not prevail against it.*
The Chaplain observes (p. 28), that this text is wrongly translated, and that
the Greek words *hades* MANIFESTLY imports *death,* and *not hell.* The
alteration is not very material in itself, and might well pass unnoticed, were it
not for the sake of shewing, how unsafe it is to trust to private interpretation
of scripture, in opposition to the general sense and understanding of the
church in all its ages. The Chaplain has taken up this interpretation from
Besa, who, I believe, first suggested it. But I would fain ask these sagacious
Greek critics, whether *hell* is not meant by that place, out of which the rich
man (Luke xvi.) lifted up his eyes, and seeing Lazarus, wished he might be
allowed to cool with water his tongue; for *I am tormented,* said he, *in this
flame.* [27] Was not hell that *place of torments,* which he wished his brethren
might be warned to avoid, ver. 18? Now what says the Greek text in this
place? *And in hell,* en tô hadé, *lifting up his eyes, when he was in torments,
he saw Abraham afar off.* If I did not deem this scripture passage sufficient to
prove that the word *hades* does not *manifestly* import death, I could add
many others equally conclusive; and could support them with the authority
of some of the best Greek authors, as well as of Calvin, and even of Besa in
contradiction of himself. Among the moderns, the Chaplain will not dispute
the palm of Hebrew, and Greek literature, with Dr. Lowth, now bishop of
London, or with his learned commentator, professor Michaelis of Gottingen.
Let him read the bishop's elegant work, *de sacra Poesi Hebraeorum,* praelect.
7; and the professor in his annotations on that praelection, and he will find
them both decided in their opinion, that the Greek word *hades,* as well as its
correspondent Hebrew one, denotes not *death,* but the subterraneous recepta-
cle of departed souls, which is pointedly expressive of the popular idea of
hell.

But let us admit the Chaplain's interpretation; let Christ's words import in
their obvious sense, that the church shall never *fail,* not that she shall never
err. Does he not know, that the church fails principally by erring? How did
she fail in the countries over-run with Arianism? Was it not by error in faith?
and so in all countries corrupted by hersey. Thus likewise would the whole
visible church have failed, had she proposed any error to be believed, as an
article of faith. "For to do this, is to propose a lie, as upheld by divine

authority; which is to fall no less foully, than he should fall, who should teach God to be an affirmer and confirmer of lies. For whatsoever point any church held, as a point of their faith, they held it as a divine verity, affirmed and revealed by God. Therefore, if in any age, the visible church held any error for a point of faith, it did fail more miserably."[28]

The Chaplain's charge of unfaithful translation of scripture being thus removed, let us examine the meaning, he gives to the promises of Christ. The *obvious* one, he says is only this; "that neither the subtlety of infernal spirits, nor the passions of men, nor the violence of both shall ever succeed in overturning *his religion,* to which he has been pleased to annex perpetuity. *However feeble and disordered* his church may be at time, the powers of death shall never overcome her. She shall then only cease to exist, when time shall be no more." (P. 28.) If ever confident assertion stood in the place of solid argument, here surely is an instance of it. What? Does Christ's promise to his church *obviously* convey the meaning imported in the Chaplain's exposition, particularly in the first member of the second sentence of it, when there is not a single word to justify that meaning? The promise is unlimited and unconditional; what right therefore has he to limit it? or if he have, why has not any one of us an equal right to limit Christ's promises *to teach his disciples all truth,* which the Chaplain says (p. 27.) he undoubtedly did? Why may we not say, that he taught them truth so far, as to prevent their falling into any *fundamental* error, sufficient to overturn the great principles of religion? Why may we not say, that his spirit was so far with the evangelists, as to direct them in teaching the *essential* doctrines of christianity, but not in guarding them against errors of less consequence? And why may we not thus give a mortal stab to the authority of scripture itself, by limiting its infallibility to those things only, which it may please each man's private judgment to deem *fundamental?*

"The text,["] continues the Chaplain, ["]does not even *insinuate,* that the christian church should never teach any articles, besides such as are fundamental and necessary; or that some overbearing society of christians should not hold out many erroneous opinions as terms of communion to the rest of the faithful." If, by overbearing society of christians, the author mean not the church of Christ, he is certainly right; for to no such society was a divine promise ever made of its not falling into erroneous opinions; but if he mean, as he must to say any thing to the purpose, that it is not *even insinuated* in the promises of Christ, that his church shall never *hold out erroneous opinions, as terms of communion,* I am yet to learn the significa-tion of words. "For,["] says an excellent author, ["]if words retain their usual signification, we cannot charge the church of Christ with error, even against any one single article of faith, but we must draw this impious consequence from it, that he was either ignorant of the event of his promise, or unfaithful to it; and that after having in so solemn a manner engaged his sacred word to St. Peter, that the gates of hell shall not prevail against his church, he has nevertheless delivered her up to the power of Satan to be destroyed by him."

"This consequence will appear undeniable, if we consider the two following truths. 1st. *That faith is essential to the constitution of the church;* and 2dly, *that heresy destroys faith.* For it plainly follows hence, that if the whole church fall into heresy, she is without *faith;* and is no more the church, she was before, than a man can continue to be a man without a soul."[29] If the church of Christ hold out erroneous opinions as terms of communion, does she not, by public authority, establish falsehood instead of truth, and the lies of Satan for the genuine word of God? How shall we be assured, that these errors are not destructive of the *fundamental* articles of christianity? Suppose, for instance, she require an idolatrous worship, or teach those *mysteries of iniquity,* mentioned in the Chaplain's letter (p. 11.) *the denying of salvation to all out of her own communion,* and the horrible heresy will not *the gates of hell then prevail against her?* will not the promises of Christ be vain and deceitful?

But it seems, the promises were not made to the church; not against her, but "against the *great and essential tenets* expressed in the apostles creed, and adopted through every age by the most numerous body of christians, *the gates of death or of hell will never prevail—They* will ever retain sufficient light to conduct *each* upright and pious believer to *all* points of his duty, upon which his salvation depends." (Let. p. 28-29). So before, in giving us the *obvious* meaning of this difficult text, the Chaplain had found out, that the gates of hell were never to succeed in *overturning,* not the church, but the religion of Christ. (P. 28) Are then the *great and essential tenets of the apostles creed,* and the *church* one and the same thing? Is the *christian* religion, that is, the christian system of belief and practice, the same thing, as the *society of christians* professing that system? When we are directed, Mat.xviii. v. 16. *to tell the church* of our offending brethren, are we to go and tell their offences to *the great and essential tenets* of christianity, or to the *christian religion?* It is not difficult to discover the advantage, or rather the fatal consequences to christianity, which an able but irreligious controvertist might hope to derive from this alteration. He might lay down, as the only fundamental articles of christian belief, some few, which offer no violence to his understanding or passions; and such, as having for this very reason been little contested, were generally admitted by sectaries of all denominations. He might then contend, that the promises of Christ refer only to the upholding of these articles, and that *the gates of hell shall never prevail* to their extinction. The religious societies professing to believe them may all perish in their turns; but the promises of Christ will abide, if a new society arise adhering to the same supposed *fundamental* tenets; she may adopt many errors indeed, and superinduce them on the foundation of faith. But for all this, the promises of Christ would not be made void; these promises not being intended in favour of any religious society or church, however the letter of them may found, but only the fundamental articles of religion.

Will the Chaplain say, that he did not intend to put the charge upon his readers, and that the expressions, I have noticed, fell inadvertently from his pen? Will he acknowledge, that without prejudice to his cause, the word *church* may be substituted, agreeably to the scriptural text, where he has placed, *great and essential articles?* Be it so; and let not his candour be impeached. But let us now see, what will come of his exposition. *Against the* CHURCH *the gates of hell will never prevail–but* SHE *will ever retain sufficient light to conduct* EACH *upright and pious believer to* ALL *points of his duty, upon which his salvation depends.* (P. 29.) If this be true, and necessarily true in virtue of the promises of Christ, then even in the most *deplorable area of superstition and ignorance* (Let. p. 31), in every preceding and subsequent aera; even in that of the reformation, "the christian church retained sufficient light to conduct each upright and pious believer to *all points* of his duty, upon which his salvation depended." Need I point out the consequences ensuing to the first reformers from this doctrine; and consequently to those, who became their disciples? Need I tell you, that having separated themselves from the great body of christians throughout the world, they broke asunder the link of unity, and left society, in which *sufficient light remained to conduct* EACH *upright and pious believer to* ALL *points of his duty?* And since this society is the same now, it then was, or rather more pure, for, (the Chaplain says, *the Roman church is daily undergoing a silent reformation,* p. 12), it still retains that light, and consequently still has the promises of Christ pledged for its continuance. But what assurance has he, or any one, who leaves this society, of the promises of Christ extending to that, which he embraces in its stead?

Before I conclude upon this text, you will allow me to state the Chaplain's objection to the catholic explanation of it, and to give you the answer, as I find it ready made to my hands. The objection is, that the text might be as well alleged to prove, that sin and wickedness cannot prevail against the church, as it is brought to prove, that error and heresy cannot; for *vice is as formidable an enemy to religion,* as error; and *the christian system is as perfectly calculated to make us* good men, as orthodox believers. (P. 28.) "So far," the Chaplain "is in the right; that in virtue of this and many other promises of the word of God, sin and wickedness shall never so generally prevail, but that the church of Christ shall be always *holy* both in her doctrine, and in the lives of many both pastors and people living up to her doctrine. But then there is this difference between the case of damnable error in doctrine, and that of sin and wickedness in practice, that the former, if established by the whole body of church guides, would of course involve also the whole body of God's people, who are commanded to hear their church guides, and do what they teach them; whereas in the latter case, if pastors are guilty of any wicked practices contrary to their doctrine, the faithful are taught to do, what they say, and not what they do. Mat. XXIII. ver. 2, 3."[30]

To shew farther, that infallibility in faith is not necessarily attended with unfailing sanctity of manners, let it be observed, that tho' in time of the Old Testament, God was present with his infallible spirit to David and Solomon, when they wrote their books received into the canon of scripture; yet he did not prevent the first from committing adultery and murder, nor the second, from *going after Astaroth, the goddess of the Sidonians, and after Michom, the abomination of the Ammonites,* 1 Kings xi. ver. 15. Neither did Christ render his apostles and evangelists impeccable, though he conferred on them the privilege of infallibility. When the Chaplain has discovered in the decrees of the infinite wisdom the true reason of this conduct, he will at the same time be able to give a satisfactory answer to his own objection, and tell us, why it may not please Divine Providence to ordain the preservation of the church from error, and yet suffer the individual members of it to be liable to sin and immorality.

I now proceed to the promises of Christ made at his last supper, in that discourse, which "is, as it were, his last will and testament; every word whereof seems to be the overflowing of a heart filled with concern for his future church."[31] These promises the Chaplain has stated compendiously enough. "The divine author of the chrisitan religion promised,["] says he, ["]to teach his disciples all truth, John xiv. 15, 16. And he undoubtedly did so. But where did he so far insure the faith of their successors, as to secure them from building *wood, hay,* and *stubble* upon the foundation of the gospel?" (p. 17.) He promised to be *with his disciples to the end of the world,* Mat. xix. (should be xxvii.) ver. 20. And who denies it? He is with his church by his protection, by his grace, by the lights, he communicates to her, by the strength, which he exerts in supporting her against violence and temptation." (ibid.)

Such, according to the Chaplain, is the explanation of these passages from St. John. His reasons for so explaining them shall be presently examined. I will first set the texts down more fully, as they stand in the gospel. Our Saviour's words spoken to his apostles, and recorded by St. John in his 14th chapter, are these: *I will ask my Father, and he will send you another Comforter to abide with you* FOR EVER, John xiv. ver. 16. And soon after he informs them, who this Comforter is to be and to what end his Father will send him. *The Comforter,* says Christ, *whom the Father will send in my name, he shall teach you all things, and bring all things to your remembrance, whatsoever I have said unto you* (ibid ver. 16.) This promise is again repeated in the 16th chapter, which is a continuation of the same discourse. *I have yet many things to say unto you; but you cannot hear them now; however when the spirit of truth is come, he will lead you into all truth.*

In these texts, we see the means clearly and distinctly set down, by which the church is to be for ever protected, viz. the perpetual assistance of the divine Spirit teaching and leading the apostles and their successors, that is, the body of pastors, into *all truth* necessary and relating to the service of God, and salvation of man.

The Chaplain denies not the sufficiency of the means; he even acknowledges, that the Spirit of God *undoubtedly led the disciples into all truth;* but to them he limits the extent of the promises; the faith of their successors is left to be *tossed to and fro with every wind of doctrine;*[32] or at best, to be modeled upon their own fallible interpretation of scripture. For *where* says he, *did the divine author of our religion insure the faith of their successors?* (P. 27.) I answer, in the plain, unambiguous words, as I have cited them from John xiv. ver. 16; for they expressly say, that the Comforter, or Holy Ghost shall abide with the apostles *for ever;* which "though addressed to them, as the whole sermon at our Saviour's last supper was, yet like many other truths contained in it, could not regard their persons alone; for they were not to live for ever; but comprehended likewise all those, who were to succeed them in after ages. And that this was the intent of our Saviour's promise appears clearly from his last words before his ascension recorded by St. Matthew."[33]

These words of St. Matthew are in part cited by the Chaplain, as you have seen; but they deserve to be set down at large. All power is given unto me in heaven and earth. *Go ye therefore, and teach all nations, baptising them in the name of the Father, and of the Son, and of the Holy Ghost, teaching them to observe all things, whichsoever I have commanded you; and behold I am with you* ALWAYS (in the Greek, *all days*) *even unto* THE END OF THE WORLD.[34] Here surely Christ promises to be perpetually, even to the world's end, with them, who were to teach and baptise all nations. Were the apostles, to whom these words were immediately addressed, to perform that function for ever? He orders them, and consequently their successors in the ministry of the word, to teach *all things,* whichsoever he had commanded. Does not this evidently imply, that they were themselves to be assisted by the Spirit of God, to discover what those things are? Or did he impose upon them an obligation, without affording means of compliance? If they were to be assisted in discovering and teaching *all things* delivered by Christ; if they were ordered to *teach,* and he was to be present with them in the ministry of teaching, *even to the world's end;* does not this import a correspondent obligation in the hearers to receive and embrace the doctrines so delivered? Will any one say, that before he embraces them, he must be assured, that the doctrines, which he hears, are the things commanded by Jesus Christ? Will he say, that he must be satisfied, they are agreeable to the written word of God? I will answer him, that by this proceeding he would render the commission of teaching, entrusted by Jesus Christ to his apostles and their successors, vain and nugatory; he would transfer the ministry from them, and render it the duty of every person to be his own teacher; he would destroy the divine oeconomy of the church, in which Christ *gave some apostles, and some prophets, and other some evangelists, and other some pastors and doctors, for the perfecting of the saints, for the work of the ministry, for the edifying of the body of Christ*—Eph. iv. ver. 11, 12. The rational inquiry remaining, after a conviction of the divinity of the christian religion, is; are they, who deliver these doctrines, the lawful successors of the apostles? Can they trace to them their line of succession? If they can, we must *account of them as the ministers of Christ, and the dispensers of the mysteries of God,*[35] from whom we may learn certainly the truth of the gospel. For though each pastor be not so in his private capacity, yet as far as he teaches us in concert with the rest, I mean, in as much as he delivers the faith of the church, in that respect he is infallible.

The Chaplain in his comments upon the famous passage of Mat. xvi. 18. insinuated, that though the gates of hell should never prevail against the church to the suppression of the points of faith deemed by him fundamental, yet false opinions might be superinduced, and so far error might prevail. He here again would establish the same doctrine; and though compelled by the evident authority of scripture to confess, that Christ communicated infallibility to his disciples, he thinks this no security, that their successors will not build on the foundation of the gospel, *wood, hay and stubble.* If by these words, the Chaplain understand corrupt doctrines in faith and manners, it is plain from the very expressions of Christ that he is mistaken. For *all truth* in matters of faith and salvation, into which the spirit was to lead them, is exclusive of *all error* in the same line. In a word, either the promises of the assisting spirit of truth are confined in the immediate disciples of Christ, or not. If they are, then we have no assurance of the church's continuing even in the profession of fundamental points; if not, then upon what authority are the promises to be restrained to the church's being guided into *some* truth, when they expressly declare, that she shall be guided INTO ALL TRUTH?

But is not Christ *with his church by his protection, by his grace,* &c.? *Can he not be with her without rendering her infallible? Is he not with every just man,* &c.? (Let. p. 27.) Yes surely; he affords protection and grace; he might not have rendered her infallible; but when he informs us, that he will direct his church by the *spirit of truth,* consequently a spirit opposite to that of error; when in Mat. xxviii. he promises to the pastors of his church such a kind of presence, assistance, and guidance, as shall qualify them effectually to *teach all those things,* which he himself taught, and this for all times; shall we esteem him to be no otherwise with them, than with particular righteous men? Where has he ever promised these that singular and uninterrupted assistance of the spirit of *truth?* To private persons the Holy Ghost is given as the spirit of sanctification; but to the church as the spirit of truth, as well as sanctification, guiding her into all truth, and directly excluding all error from her.

I hope it will now appear to you, that the proofs of the church's infallibility from St. John, and Mat. xxviii. are not invalidated by the Chaplain's objections. I have adduced no arguments to confirm you in your belief of this capital doctrine; but meeting the Chaplain on his own ground have only endeavoured to defend it from his objections. whom we are grieved to have for an adversary. I forbear to allege other numerous testimonies of scripture, the concurrent authority of holy fathers, and the whole conduct of church government from the very days of the apostles, which necessarily supposes this, as an unquestionable article of christian faith. "I know very well, that no text of holy scripture is so clear, but persons of much wit may find interpretations to perplex it, or set it in a false light; but the question is not, whether the texts, I have produced, may with some pain and study be interpreted otherwise, than the Roman Catholic church has always understood them; but whether in their natural, obvious and literal sense, they do not lead an unbiased reader to the idea and belief of an infallible church. Now then let us suppose our Saviour had said to St. Peter, *I will not build my church upon a rock, and the gates of hell shall prevail against it.* Suppose he had said to his apostles, *I will not be with you to the end of the world. I will not send the Holy Ghost to abide with you for ever. He shall not teach you all things, nor lead you into all truth.* Would not all men of sound sense have concluded from such texts, that there is no such thing as an infallible church on earth? They certainly would, because the natural and obvious meaning of them is so plain, that it is impossible not to draw that consequence from them. Now if one part of two contradictories cannot but force a man of an unbiassed judgment to conclude against the doctrine of infallibility, the other part is surely of equal force to oblige him to conclude in favour of it. So that it is nothing to the purpose, whether protestants can, or cannot strain the texts, I have produced, from their natural and obvious meaning; but it is much to the purpose to consider, whether they can bring any evidence from scripture to disprove the infallibility of the church of equal strength and clearness to the texts, I have brought to prove it.["] [36]

The Chaplain's argument against infallibility next to be considered is that, which he truly calls a *hackneyed* one; After reading his answer, you may likewise judge, whether it be a *conclusive* one.

In the author of the Case stated between *the Church of Rome and the Church of England,* the argument is thus laid down. "You (Roman catholics) believe the scriptures, because the church bids you, and you believe the church, because the scriptures bid you." And he triumphantly adds, *that this is the circle, out of which we can never conjure ourselves.*

Let us now first examine the principles of logic, and find out, what is understood by a vicious circle. We shall find it to be that kind of argument by which two propositions reciprocally prove each other; and neither of them is proved by any other medium; as if a man were to attempt to prove that a stone fell, because it was heavy; and that it was heavy, because it fell, without being able to assign any other reason either of its falling, or its gravity. But if its gravity were demonstrable from other considerations, then from that property its falling might justly be inferred; and if its having fallen should, for instance, be attested by credible eye-witnesses, its gravity might be deduced from its falling; the cause in this instance inferring the effect; and the effect proving the existence of the cause.

Having premised so much, now let us analyse the catholic faith, and see if we reason as badly, as the Chaplain asserts.

The catholic reasoner has only to open his eyes, and he will discover, that his church is in the practice of determining controversies of faith by the concurrent authority of the episcopal body. But this view alone does not give him any undoubted assurance of the infallibility of her determinations. He is led therefore next to consider, when the church first exercised this authority. Did she assume it in ages of darkness and ignorance? Did she usurp it with a high hand, contrary to the usage of the first ages. What information will the christian collect in the course of this inquiry? He will find living monuments of this prerogative being always exercised, even from the days of the apostles and throughout every succeeding age. I say, *living* monuments; for they are now subsisting; and still afford as evident proof of the exercise of the authority, as if the facts had passed in our own time, and within our own memory; or as full proof, as we have of the courts of judicature of this state having heretofore decided the legal controversies of the citizens thereof. For instance, the abrogating of circumcision, and other observances of the Jewish law, is a still subsisting monument of the power of deciding being claimed and exercised by the church. Such likewise is the custom of not re-baptising persons baptised by heretics; such is the Nicene creed, and particularly the word, *consubstantial,* making part of it. These monuments, to omit innumerable others, owe their existence to the exercise of the definitive authority of the church in matters of faith. The inquiring christian will farther discover a most conspicuous monument of it in the canon of holy scripture. Many books therein received were some time doubted of; others were contended for; which are now rejected. The church interposed her authority, and the canon of scripture became established. On these facts, palpable, manifest, and of public notoriety, the christian will reason thus. The church, even from the apostles time, has always exercised the authority of deciding controverted points; her interposition would be of no avail, if her authority were not to be considered as definitive and infallible. The primitive christians so considered it. Whoever refused submission, was cast from the church, and reputed as a heathen and publican. On these grounds will the christian be induced to believe her infallibility; happy, that his belief arise not from a series of abstruse reasoning, but is built upon public, notorious facts, within the reach of the most common understanding. The church has always, from the first aera of christianity, exercised the right of judging in matters of faith, and requiring obedience to her decisions; the monuments attesting it are certain and visible. The exercise of such a right, without infallibility, would be vain and nugatory; therefore she is infallible. After thus discovering her infallibility upon the evidence of notorious facts, it is a subject of much comfort to the sincere christian, as well as a confirmation of his faith, to find the same truth attested by the words of scripture; and having before believed it for the evidence just mentioned, he now likewise believes it for the authority of scripture, at the same time, that he believes scripture for the authority of the church. Where now is the circle of false reasoning? Is not infallibility first demonstrated from other considerations, before it is demonstrated from scripture? And is not this alone, in the principles of sound logic, sufficient to destroy the magic of this famous circle, and the argument built upon it? But indeed this argument is many ways vulnerable, and you may find it otherwise destroyed in the authors referred to in the note.[37]

One word more concerning this hackneyed argument, and we will be done with it. Let it be taken for granted, that our process of reasoning runs round a circle; a deist, an infidel, a disbeliever of scripture might with propriety object to it. But how can the Chaplain do so, or any person professing his belief of scripture infallibility? For admitting this infallibility, he admits one of the propositions, which reciprocally prove each other; and therefore in arguing against him, we may logically infer the church's infallibility from texts of scripture; it being a common principle with us both, that scripture is divinely inspired; and no one is about to prove a principle admitted by his adversary.

The Chaplain produces against the Church's infallibility another argument, which he might likewise have called a hackneyed one; for it has been urged with great perseverance by our adversaries. He says, that *all Roman catholics are bound to admit an infallible authority; yet few of them agree, where or in whom it resides.* (P. 26. not[e].) When I have met with this argument in the writing of opponents little acquainted with our principles, of whom there are many, it has not surprised me. But that the Chaplain would likewise insist upon it, is really matter of astonishment. For he must know, that in the doctrine which we teach, as belonging to faith in this point, and as an article of communion, there is no variation; and with all his reading and recollection, I will venture to assert, that he cannot cite one catholic divine, who denies infallibility to reside in the body of bishops united and agreeing with their head, the bishop of Rome. So that, when the Chaplain, says, that *some schoolmen have taught the infallibility of the pope—some place it in a general council: others in the pope and council received by the whole church* (note ibid.), he is under a great mistake; for the last is not a mere opinion of schoolmen, but the constant belief of all catholics; a belief, in which there is no variation. Some divines indeed hold the pope, as Christ's vicar on earth, to be infallible, even without a council; but with this opinion faith has no concern, every one being at liberty to adopt or reject it, as the reasons for or against may affect him.

The Chaplain adds in the same place, that since the council of Trent, many things have been *unanimously taught* respecting the pope's authority, which are, I own, new to me, and which, I confidently aver, he cannot make good. Nay, so far are they from being taught unanimously since the council of Trent, that they are not taught at all, for instance, in France; and are expressly contradicted by the maxims and solemn determinations and theological schools there have constantly conformed.

Nor is it only in France, that many of the doctrines are rejected, which, he says, are taught *unanimously* amongst us; but they are exploded in every catholic country in the world. The body of bishops every where claim a divine right, in virtue of their ordination, to interpret the decrees of councils, and the ordinances of the popes. The Chaplain having discarded his former religion, appears likewise to have erased from his memory the theological principles of our schools.

He concludes his note with a curious piece of reasoning. *A christian,* he says, *may mistake the words of a pope* (the meaning of the words, I presume), *as easily as he can mistake the words of scripture.* So undoubtedly he may; and for this very reason a living authority is necessary to explain uncertainties, to remove ambiguities. But perhaps he means to carry his argument into the very heart of our principles, and deny, that even a living authority can speak a language clear enough to determine doubts and convict obstinacy. But few will be persuaded, that the powers of living language are so limited; as well might he attempt to persuade us, that when parties litigate on the interpretation of the law, the judges cannot deliver sentence in terms clear enough to determine the controversy.

You have hitherto seen the Chaplain endeavour to disprove the church's infallibility by his interpretation of certain passages of scripture, and by discovering fallacies and inconsistencies in our doctrines on this subject. Not content with thus attacking this capital tenet of our religion, he sets about to prove that the church may err, because in fact she has erred. To shew it, he aleges first, that she formerly taught doctrines as of faith, which she now rejects as contrary to faith. 2ndly, She suppressed for a time certain tenets, which ought to have been taught at all times, or not taught at all. 3rdly, She requires a belief of things, which are not contained in scripture, as is acknowledged even by some of our own divines.

How does he prove the first of these charges? By asserting (p. 29, 30.) that *the doctrine of the millennium,* now rejected by the church, *was maintained as an article of the catholic faith by almost every father, who lived immediately after the times of the apostles.* In opposition to this very positive assertion, I will take upon me to say, that not one of the primitive fathers held the opinion here mentioned as an article of catholic faith and communion. At the very time of its prevalence (for it was indeed adopted by Irenaeus, Justin the Martyr, &c.) it was combated by others not less zealously attached to the church's communion, as is acknowledged even by Justin himself, who speaking of the millennium says: "I have already confessed to you, o Trypho, that I and many others of the same mind with me, do think it will come to pass; but I have also signified that many, *who are of pure and pious christian sentiments,* do not think so."[38] Do these words indicate, that the millenarian doctrine *was maintained, as an article of the catholic faith by almost every* primitive *father,* as is asserted by the Chaplain? Do they not clearly prove, that even its ablest advocates, amongst whom Justin surely was, did not consider it as such, but as an opinion open to discussion and contradiction? And accordingly Eusebius in his Ecclesiastical History cites passages of a work written against this doctrine in the very beginning of the third century by Caius, a catholic priest,[39] the contemporary of Justin and Irenaeus.

I need take no notice of what the Chaplain adds,[40] that *it was the decided opinion of almost all the primitive fathers, that the souls of good men did not enjoy the beatific vision previous to the general* resurrection; for since he does not say, that this opinion ever became an article of catholic faith, as it certainly never did, I may be allowed to suspend any investigation of this subject, which has been ably and solidly discussed by Bellarmine long ago.[41]

The Chaplain argues secondly, that the church has erred, because *she regards some articles at present, as articles of faith, which for many ages were debated as matters of opinion.*[42] This we freely admit; and, I hope, without any prejudice to the claim of infallibility; though the Chaplain thinks, that a very forcible argument arises from this fact; for these doctrines having been delivered by Jesus Christ and his apostles, either as essential, or not; if the first, she forefeited her claim to infallibility by omitting to teach them for many ages; and if the second, she equally forfeits it by imposing as necessary to be believed, what neither Christ or his apostles did so teach.

Before I proceed to a direct answer, it may be proper to premise, that the distinction of *essentials,* and *not essentials; fundamentals* and *not fundamentals* in faith, to which the Chaplain so often recurs, is not admitted by us in his sense, and that of other protestant authors. We hold all revealed doctrines, when sufficiently proposed to our understanding, to be *essential* in this respect, that under pain of disobedience and heresy, we are bound to believe and submit our understanding to them; and the reason is, because we conceive of all doctrines so proposed, that they are revealed by God, who neither can err, or lead into error. Now whether the doctrine be in its own nature, or in our estimation of great importance, or not, it equally claims our assent, if divine authority is pledged for the truth of it. In another sense indeed, some points of faith are more essential and fundamental, than others;

for without our knowledge, or indeed without any revelation of some of them, christianity might subsist; whereas other points are so interwoven with the system and oeconomy of it, that the explicit profession and belief of them is implied in the very idea of a christian. But, as I before said, they both rest upon the same authority, that is, the word of God; and demand an equally firm assent, when sufficiently proposed to our understanding. Why are we obliged to believe every fact and circumstance contained in the Old and New Testament, as soon as we come to the knowledge of it? It is, because nothing therein is related, which does not affect the very vitals of christianity? or is it not rather, because divine authority is pledged for the entire truth of scripture?

This leads to a plain answer to the objection. All doctrines taught by Christ and his apostles were delivered as *necessary* to be believed, whenever the faithful should receive sufficient evidence of their divine revelation. But till they had that evidence, the belief was not obligatory; and christians were at liberty to discuss the doctrines with all freedom, provided they did so in an habitual disposition to submit to the authority established by Jesus Christ, whenever it should interfere in determining the uncertainty. So, before the holding of the first council at Jerusalem, some true christians maintained circumcision to be necessary.[43] And *when the apostles and antients came together to consider this matter, there was much disputing,* (v. 6, 7.) But after the decision of the council, *it pleased the apostles and the antients with the whole church* to issue their letter or decree against the necessity of circumcision, to which decree all were not obliged to submit under pain of heresy. Here I would fain ask, if there were no true catholicity of belief before this council; and whether this decision, all true christians *believed as an article of faith, what they before conceived to be matter of opinion.*[44]

The Chaplain's formidable dilemma (p. 33, 34.) turns out therefore a very harmless one; the doctrines, he refers to, were delivered as *essential,* that is, I suppose, essentially to be believed, whenever they came to be sufficiently proposed, as revealed by God, but they were not *essentially* to be believed, till they were so proposed. And the church, ever guided by the Spirit of God, sees when the dangers threatening her children from *false prophets arising and seducing many,* Mat. xxiv. v. 11. call upon her to examine the faith committed to her keeping and preserved in holy scripture and the chain of tradition. In these perilous moments she unfolds the doctrines, and presents them to christians as preservatives from the delusions of novelty, the refinements of false philosophy, and the misinterpretations of private and presumptuous judgment. Thus when Arius and his followers endeavoured to establish principles subversive of the divinity of the Son of God, to check the growth of this error, the church defined clearly and explicitly his consubstantiality with the Father. Previous to which decision, the fathers contented themselves with acknowledging his divine nature; but that the belief of it included consubstantiality, was not yet sufficiently proposed to them, and therefore could not be an object of their faith.

The principles indeed of the Chaplain would, if admitted, clearly prove, that neither his, nor the faith ony [*sic*—any] one, who admits all the books of scripture, is the same with that of the first christians; nay more, that the faith of these last was continually changing, as long as the apostles were alive. For he lays it down, that if any points are believed, as essential, today, which formerly were not so believed, there is no longer an unity of faith. (Let. p. 34.) Now the apostles at distant periods of their lives sent epistles and instructions to the different churches, which they then, and we now receive as of divine inspiration. But did they not from these writings collect information, which they had not before? and did they not believe the information given, as infallibly true? For instance, when St. paul wrote his second epistle to the Thessalonians, did they not understand from it, contrary to what they had before conceived, that the last general judgment was not immediately to happen? If so, then was their faith, according to the Chaplain, no longer the same it had been. Moreover, some of Christ's flock died before any, and many more before all the apostles; St. John, it is known, lived upwards of sixty years after his master's death, and wrote his revelation, and his gospel a very little while before his own. It follows then again, that the christians, who died without having either seen, or heard of his gospel, or revelation, had not the same faith with those, who afterwards saw and believed them. These consequences may be extended much farther; and, by adhering to the principles of the Chaplain, it may be shewn, that for many ages christians either did not believe *essential* doctrines; or that it is not *essential* now to admit many books of scripture, which nevertheless he who should reject, would not be deemed a christian. For it is notorious that long after the apostles time, several scriptural books were of uncertain authority, the authors of them not being ascertained; as for instance, the revelation, the epistle to the Hebrews, the second of St. Peter, the second and third of St. John, those of S. Jude and St. James. During all this time therefore, it was not *essential* to believe these writings to be divinely inspired; but will the Chaplain say, that it is not now essential to believe it? What would one of his controversial heroes, Dr. Hurd, say, if we were to deny the authority of St. John's revelation? For though I have not had an opportunity to see his *discourses on the prophecies,* yet I conclude from the occasion of his preaching them, that the revelation has furnished him his arguments, such as they are, to prove the *apostosy of papal Rome,* as it did his predecessor Jurieu, whose reveries the illustrious Bossuet exposed as completely as, I doubt not, all those of the lecturers of the Warburton foundation[45] will one day be.

To revert to our subject: Was all unity of faith destroyed in the church, when the above mentioned books of scripture were received into the canon? For it is certain that some things were then required to be believed, which before were not required. After St. John published his gospel, wherein are contained many things not related by the other evangelists, did not these things become objects of faith, which before had not been so? As long as the apostles lived, and preached, and wrote to the churches, *teaching them to observe all things, whichsoever their divine master had commanded them,* Mat. xxviii. v. 21. did not *new* matter continually arise to exercise the faith of their disciples? If then it be any objection to a *living authority, that the number of necessary tenets must increase, as decisions multiply* (Ch. Let. p. 34), the objection is as strong against the authority of the apostles, which the Chaplain admits (p. 27), as against that of a church equally endowed with infallibility in deciding on faith and morals.

The Chaplain's reasonings from page 30, to page 34, properly belong to the division, which we are now considering; but being desirous to place all his objections to particular tenets of our church in one point of view, I shall arrange them under the last division. On this I shall enter, after noticing that the Chaplain in the conclusion of his argument indulges himself in some declamation, which however carries no weight with it, as long as the church's claim to infallibility is not invalidated by other arguments, than those we have seen. For, supposing that claim well supported, his forebodings can never come to pass; and our faith has nothing to fear from the additions of any future pope Pius. And here, by the bye, it must be remarked, that though an intimation is thrown out (p. 34), that Pius the 4th, in his famous creed, imposed new doctrines; yet every article of that creed was long before him a point of our belief. This is known to every person conversant in the history of religion, and is candidly acknowledged by Dr. Bramhall, the protestant archbishop of Armagh, in his reply to the Bishop of Chalcedon: "For,["] says he, ["]those very points, which Pius the 4th comprehended in a new symbol or creed, were obtruded upon us before by his predecessors, as necessary articles of the Roman faith, and required as necessary articles of their communion."

To prove, that the church has fallen into error, it is urged in the third place, as was noticed above, that she requires a belief of tenets, which even some of our own celebrated divines acknowledge either not to be *found at all in the scriptures, or at least delivered in them with great obscurity* (p. 19.); and instances are given in the doctrines of *transubstantiation* and *purgatory, auricular confession,* and the *power of loosening and binding,* or *absolution.* These shall now be distinctly considered, as far as is necessary to vindicate them from the Chaplain's objections. For I propose proceeding here, as before, concerning infallibility; that is, I shall not pretend to allege other proofs of these contested doctrines, than such as may arise from the purely defensive system, I have adopted; and, God be praised, the grounds of our faith are so solid, that I trust the cause of truth and religion will not be injured, even in my hands, by this mode of repelling the attacks made against them.

But first, supposing it true, as the divines mentioned by the Chaplain are alleged to have said, that the tenets above cited are not to be found in scripture, does it follow, that they were not revealed by Jesus Christ? With what right does the Chaplain assume as a principle, that God communicated nothing more to his church, than is contained in his written word? He knows, that we have always asserted, that the *whole* word of God, unwritten, as well as written, is the christian's rule of faith. It was incumbent then on him, before he discarded this rule, to prove either, that no more was revealed, than is written; or that revealed doctrines derive their claim to our belief, not from God's infallible testimony, but from their being reduced to writing. He has not attempted this; and I will venture to say, he would have attempted it in vain, even with the assistance of his Chillingworth. Happy indeed it is for mankind, that no efforts to this purpose can succeed; for if the catholic rule of faith could be proved unsafe, what security have we for the authenticity, the genuineness, the incorruptibility of scripture itself: How do we know, but by the tradition that is, by the living doctrine of the catholic church, which are the true and genuine gospels? Can the Chaplain, with all his ingenuity, devise, for instance, any other solid motive, besides this already mentioned, for admitting the gospel of St. Matthew into the cononical writings? This gospel, according to the general opinion, was written in the vulgar Hebrew, or Syriack. The original text has been lost so long, that no traces of it remain; who translated it into Greek, is quite uncertain. Now, where is the *written* word of God assuring us of the correspondence of this translation with the original? Where shall we find, but in the tradition, that is, in the public invariable doctrine of the catholic church, any sufficient reason for admitting the faithfulness of the translator? Why shall we not reject it, as some early heretics did, the Manichaeans, Marcionists, Cerdonists, &c.? I mention St. Matthew's gospel, as coming first to my mind; but the argument is applicable to other parts of scripture, and to some with much greater force. The testimony therefore of the catholic church, certified in the tradition of all ages, is the ground, upon which we and others admit the divine authority of holy writ.[46] I do not suppose, that the Chaplain, after rejecting the church's infallibility, will place it, for the discrimination of true and false gospels, in an inward light administered to each sincere inquirer. I should be indeed greatly mistaken in him, if he entertain any such fanatical notions; his own Chillingworth would rise up against him. But if the testimony and tradition of the catholic church is to be necessarily admitted for receiving the scripture itself, which, according to him, is the *sole standard,* the *only rule* of protestant belief (p. 37), why is her testimony to be rejected, when offered in evidence of other points of faith? Why not as well admit it in favour of transubstantiation and purgatory, as of the lawfulness of infant baptism, of the validity of baptism administered by heretics, of the obligation of abstaining on Sundays from servile works, &c.? Scripture authority for these and other points admitted by protestants there is certainly none; and they, who have attempted to offer any, have only betrayed the weakness and nakedness of their cause. Wherefore St. Chrysostom, as I find him repeatedly quoted by authors, whose accuracy I cannot doubt, commenting on these words of St. Paul, *Stand and hold the traditions, you have been taught, whether by word, or by our epistle,* 2 Thess. ii. v. 17. alias 15. observes, that "it is plain, that the apostles did not deliver all things in writing, but many things without it; and these ought to be believed, as much as those; let us then give credit to the tradition of the church."[47] I have in preference cited this holy father in support of the catholic doctrine, not because numerous testimonies of others are wanting, both more antient, and, if possible, more full and express; but because the Chaplain in a note (p. 9.) insists much upon two remarkable passages, which, he says, are taken from the works of this eminent doctor.

I will not deny, that I was surprised when I read the first passage cited by the Chaplain; it appeared so opposite to the principles, which St. Chrysostom had laid down in several parts of his works. It was a mortifying circumstance, that I would not conveniently have recourse to that holy doctor's writings, nor minutely examine the passage objected, together with its context. I procured a friend to examine the edition of Chrysostom's works, belonging to the public library at Annapolis; he has carefully and repeatedly read the 49th homily on St. Matthew; and not one syllable of the Chaplain's citation is to be found in it. After receiving this notice, I was for some time doubtful, whether it might not be owing to a difference in the editions. I could not persuade myself, that he, who so solemnly calls heaven to witness for the impartiality and integrity of his inquiry, would publicly expose himself to a well-grounded imputation of unpardonable negligence, in a matter of such serious concern. But I have now the fullest evidence, that the passage, for which Chrysostom on Matthew, hom. 49. is quoted, is not taken from that father. It is extracted from a work of no credit, supposed to be written in the 6th century, entitled, *The unfinished work on Matthew.*[48] But had it even been fairly quoted from him, the Chaplain would not have had so much cause for triumph, as he imagines. For the passage, he adduces, carries with it equal condemnation of the protestant and catholic rule of faith. It asserts, that it is only then necessary to discover by *scripture alone,* which is the true church of Christ, when *heresy has all outward observances in common with her.* But if the outward observances are not the same, if the church and heresy do not agree in offering the same unbloody sacrifice; in administering the same sacraments; in the apostolical and uninterrupted succession of their clergy; in their liturgy, their hierarchy, the whole frame of their ecclesiastical government, &c. then *it may be evinced by various means,* other than scripture, *which is the true church of Christ.* But will this be admitted by the Chaplain, who *adopts the holy scripture for the sole standard of his belief?* Will it be admitted by the *protestant churches in general, which know no other rule?* See then how unsuccessfully this authority turns out for the Chaplain. In the first place, it lays him under the reproach of a want of impartial diligence; and 2ndly, if it militate against us, it is equally adverse to that religion, of which he now professes himself a member.

This disrepute of alleging the authority of Chrysostom so erroneously will not be compensated by the other passage, for which he likewise is cited; and which indeed I find to be noticed by Bellarmine, as genuine; but he observes that Chrysostom is not discoursing of doctrines obscurely delivered, or contested amongst different sects of christians; but of such, as being clearly and unambiguously taught in holy writ, are nevertheless disrelished or denied by worldly minded men; who contend, contrary to the evident declaration of scripture, that riches are more helpful, than hurtful to salvation; and of such Chrysostom says, that they ought to be disregarded, and all these things be estimated by the rule of scripture.

But if the Chaplain insist, that the direction here given is general to *all* men, who are advised to investigate all matters of faith in the scripture, without paying any regard to *what this or that man asserts for truth;* I answer first, that this direction is very different from that of Chrysostom above cited, in his commentary on the 2d to the Thessalonians; and of the learned Vincent of Lerins, whom the Chaplain quotes with singular complacency (p. 35.).[49] This venerable writer having observed, that all religious innovators accumulate texts upon texts to give credit to their different systems, enquires, *what catholics, what the children of the church must do?* How can they in scripture discern truth from falsehood? *They will take care,* he continues, *so to proceed—as to interpret holy writ agreeably to the traditions of the universal church, and the rules of catholic doctrine.*[50]

In the next place, I observe that the rule of investigation laid down as from St. Chrysostom is insufficient and inapplicable. Insufficient, because by scripture alone it is impossible to determine many points necessary to be believed and practised, and so received even by protestants themselves.[51]

The rule is moreover inapplicable to much the greatest part of mankind; and I am really ashamed to enter seriously on the proof of it, since it must be evident to every considerate man in the world. For if scripture, as interpreted *by private judgment,*[52] is the only rule, which *all* are to follow, *neglecting what this or that man asserts for truth;* if *all are to investigate all* disputed *things in the scriptures,* it plainly follows, that the laborious husbandman, the illiterate mechanic, the poor ignorant slave are to acquire the knowledge in languages, and the critical discernment necessary to compare translation with translation, text with text. For without this comparison and many other precautions, they never can form a reasonable judgment of the sense of scripture; nor can they be sure of that book being scripture, which is put into their hands, as such. If to relate this prodigious opinion be not enough to refute it, all argument, even demonstration itself will be of no avail.

The Chaplain seems to be aware of its glaring absurdity; and therefore in a note (p. 17, 18.) he says, that they, who are unqualified to enter upon such inquiries, as he made, *must rely principally upon the authority of their teachers;* and he quotes the bishop of Chester as recommending the same. Thus then after citing with so much complacency a pretended passage of St. Chrysostom; after bidding defiance to our divines to explain away the Saint's doctrine, requiring *all of us to neglect what this or that man,* even himself or the bishop of Chester asserts for truth, but *to investigate all things in the scriptures;* after this, I will not say, that he himself *unravels the difficulty with fine spun subtlety like a modern schoolman;*[53] but, like Alexander, he cuts the knot at once, and *refers us to the authority of our teachers.*

While the Chaplain's letter is before me, I feel other impressions too strongly upon my mind to indulge in the satisfaction, which it might otherwise suggest, to observe, that after decrying the *dead weight of authority* (p. 13), after exalting *private judgment,* as the sole interpreter of scripture (p. 9), he is obliged to confess, that the generality of mankind must be guided in religious matters *principally by the authority of their teachers;* for he will hardly deny, that the generality of mankind are neither *by education, or abilities, or leisure, qualified to enter upon the inquiries* necessary to judge for themselves. Did Jesus Christ then leave a *rule of faith* so adequate, as not to be capable of application to much the largest portion of mankind? Do the *protestant churches in general know* NO OTHER *rule* (letter p. 37), than one so miserably defective? and if defective, now, what must it have been, before the discovery of the art of printing, when the knowledge of letters was so rare, comparatively with the present times; and it was morally impossible to multiply manuscripts sufficient to supply every individual with the means, even if he had the ability to study scripture?

But who are the *teachers,* to whose *authority* the generality of mankind are referred? Are there any, however introduced to the exercise of that public function? This indeed may be a doctrine well enough suited to latitudinarians in religion, or the scoffers at all religion; but surely not very agreeable to the principles of a christian. Must the teachers then, whose authority is to be so respected, be the regular, and authorised ministry of the country? What if that country should be Turkey, and the ministers, the deluded disciples of Mahomet? What if it should be a country blessed like this with unlimited toleration, and giving equal countenance to the professors and teachers of every denomination of christians? In this case, the unlettered, that is, the far greater part of the community are directed indeed by the Chaplain and bishop of Chester to follow their teachers; but by what criterion they are to chuse their teachers, does not appear. If by their doctrine, if by scripture, all the labour recoils back again upon the uninformed multitude without *education, abilities,* or *leisure* to go through with it. On one hand, they are constrained to adopt Seneca's rule;[54] and on the other, they cannot possibly comply with it; they would fain follow the instructions of a faithful teacher; but now to distinguish him from a seduced or seducing one, they know not. I disdain taking notice of the insinuations so scandalously false, thown out by the bishop of Chester, as if we discountenanced free inquiry. From what was said in the beginning of this address, you may judge how undeserved they are. His lordship is pleased to add, that *whatever things are necessary to be believed, are easy to be understood.* (P. 18, note.) Are not all doctrines laid down in scripture, and particularly those contained in the apostles creed, *necessary to be believed?* So at least the Chaplain teaches. (P. 35.) In these is delivered the tenet of three divine persons, that of the Incarnation of the son of God, and of his descent into hell. Are these things easy to be understood? However they may appear to the bishop, they have been generally accounted mysteries incomprehensible to human understanding.

We likewise direct all to rely, in matters of faith, on their teachers, while they exercise their functions, uncontradicted and unreproved by the body of pastors, or their superiors in the hierarchy. But then their mission is established on a fact of public notoriety, the investigation of which requires no laborious discussion. They can trace an ininterrupted succession of their ministry to the apostles, and consequently to Christ himself. As Christ sent his apostles *to teach all nations, baptising and teaching them to observe all things, whichsoever he had commanded;* so did they send other pastors to discharge thes same functions, as themselves. They could not preach at all times; and in all places; they therefore appointed disciples to found other churches, as they themselves had founded, and to exercise therein the same ministry. The pastors, thus associated to the apostles, successively admitted others; and this apostolical body, that is, the body of the envoys of Jesus Christ has never ceased. When new members are incorporated into it, they receive from him the same commission of teaching, and administering the sacraments; the church of Christ cannot exist without the preaching of the gospel; and preaching, according to St. Paul, is not to be exercised without a mission; *how will they preach, if they be not sent?* Rom. x. v. 15. so that the church and this apostolical body must always subsist together, and can never be separated.

From these truths founded on a plain matter of fact, an argument is deduced equally clear and convincing. It is as certain, that the apostles appointed other pastors to succeed them, as it is, that they founded churches. The actual pastors then of these churches descending in a lawful and unbroken line of succession from them, are certainly sent by the apostles, and by Christ himself, since those churches have always subsisted, and still subsist. Thus our faith is as assured and well grounded, in believing the public doctrines delivered by these teachers, as it could have been in receiving the preaching of the apostles themselves.

No books, no erudition is here necessary. The illiterate, as well as learned christian can easily be certified of the fact, on which the reasoning is founded. The prerogative of tracing to the apostles an ordinary and regular succession of pastors is so peculiar a prerogative of the catholic church, that no other society can dispute it with her, or appropriate it to themselves.[55] To this succession the primitive fathers constantly appeal, as demonstrative evidence of the true church, and challenge sectaries to exhibit a like title to the divine commission of teaching and administering the sacraments.[56]

After having thus shewn both from the nature of the thing, and the Chaplain's own acknowledgment, that scripture alone is not a general and sufficient rule of faith, I might well contend, that *transubstantiation, purgatory, auricular confession,* and the *power of absolving,* are to be received as christian doctrines, on the authority of the church, though no mention were made of them in scripture. But for your entire satisfaction, I will now consider particularly all, that has been advanced on the other side respecting these articles of faith.

To begin with *transubstantiation,* the Chaplain asserts (p. 32), that *the doctrine conveyed by that word was not article of faith prior to the council of Lateran in 1215;* and for proof of it he refers to Scotus, as cited by Bellarmine, 1. 3. *de Euch.* c. 23. When I read this passage of the Chaplain's letter, I thought it remarkable in him to allege Scotus's testimony to prove a point of ecclesiastical history; the subtleties of the school were much better suited to that author's speculative genius, than a critical examination of historical facts. And it was becoming the Chaplain's candour to have acknowledged it, when he saw evident proofs of Scotus's inaccuracy in the place cited out of Bellarmine; who observes, that Scotus could never have seen the decrees of the councils held at Rome against Berengarius, the first of the year 1060, and the second 1079, in which the doctrine of transubstantiation was asserted; and Berengarius, who had impugned it, retracted his error.[57]

The Chaplain continues, that towards the beginning of the 9th century, *Paschasius Radbertus published his treatise upon the corporal presence of Christ in the Eucharist; and, as Bellarmine tells us, was the first, who wrote seriously and copiously concerning it.* (Ibid.) For this, he cites Bellarmine *de Scriptoribus Ecclesiasticis.* Does not every person, who reads this passage, understand it to import, that according to Bellarmine, Paschasius Radbertus was the first who *wrote seriously and copiously concerning* the corporeal presence of Christ in the eucharist? Now let us hear Bellarmine himself; and then let every one judge, whether the Chaplain has carried into his researches after truth all that impartiality and painful investigation mentioned in his seventh page. Thus then Bellarmine in the book cited by him.[:] "This author (Paschasius Radbertus) was the first, who wrote seriously and copiously of the reality of the body and blood of the Lord in the eucharist *against Bertram the priest, who was one of the first, that called it in question.* "[58] Is it the same thing to be the first to write fully on the real presence; and the first to write fully on that subject against Bertram, who impugned it? Does not the former sense suggested by the Chaplain imply, that Paschasius was the first to establish a *new* doctrine? and is not Bellarmine's real meaning, that

Paschasius was the first to defend an *established* doctrine against a recent *opposer* of it?

But let us proceed; and we shall find Paschasius himself clearly shewing, that his view and design was, not to set forth a new doctrine; but to expound that, which was common in the church; though the Chaplain says otherwise. *This monk*, says he, meaning Paschasius, *informs us himself, that his doctrine was by no means universal or settled.*[59] Let us now see, how he gives us this information; and let his letter to Frudegardus (for to that the Chaplain refers) determine the point. In this very letter then, he says, that "though some through ignorance err in this point, yet *not one* openly contradicts, what the *whole world* believes and professes."[60] Here you will observe, that Paschasius says, that *not one* was found openly to contradict his doctrine on the eucharist; and that it was believed and professed by the *whole world*. Is this to inform us, that his doctrine was by no means *universal or settled?* But let us hear him farther. "If any man," says he in the same place, "should oppose this truth, rather than believe it, let him take care what he is doing against the Lord himself, and the *whole church* of Christ. For it is a horrible crime to join in prayer with all, and not to believe, what truth itself attests, and what *every where, all universally* confess to be true."[61] From these passages it is evident, that the Chaplain could not make a more unfortunate reference to prove, what he intended, than to Paschasius's letter to Frudegard. But, continues he, Paschasius in this very letter, *speaking of the corporal presence, says, you question me upon a subject, about which many are doubtful.* (P. 34.) Does Paschasius indeed say so? It would strangely contradict, what he has already told us. Let us therefore return to the letter, and hear him himself. It appears from its contents, that Frudegard was a young monk, who had read in one of St. Augustin's works a passage, that perplexed him; and that he applied to Paschasius, as his master, to explain the difficulty.[62] I will venture to assert, that the passage in the note is all the Chaplain's foundation for saying, as if they were the words of Paschasius himself, that *many were doubtful* of the real presence in the eucharist. It is possible, that Paschasius should acknowledge this in the very letter, wherein he informs his scholar, that the *whole church* professes the doctrine, he delivers? That not even *one person* was found openly to contradict it? The young man himself acknowledges, that he had always believed the real presence, which shews, that it was at that time the common doctrine of the church, in which young persons were educated; he informs Paschasius, that a perplexity had arisen in his mind, not from hearing any public instruction of the pastors of the church contrary to the real presence; but from some expression of St. Augustin. He applies to Paschasius to explain the difficulty, relying on his knowledge and orthodoxy; he does not conclude from the passage of Augustin, that it inclined him to change his faith but expresses an uncertainity, as to its meaning. *I know not, how I am to understand it.* How then will the Chaplain make good his assertion, that Paschasius in his letter to Frudegard acknowledges, that *many doubted of the corporal presence of Christ in the eucharist?*

He next alleges Rabanus Maurus as one, who *about the year 847 wrote expressly against .the novelty of this doctrine in a letter to Heribaldus bishop of Auxerre.* [63] I apprehend, that here again the Chaplain has followed an unfaithful guide; whom I suspect to be the French huguenot Aurbertin, or Albertinus. For the Chaplain cites his work *on the eucharist,* as one of those, which operated in him a conviction of his former errors;[64] and I observe a great affinity between the mistakes already noticed in the Chaplain's citations, and those, which were detected in Aubertin by the author of *La pertpetuité de la foi.* Now, tho' I will not say positively, that Rabanus has no such words in his letter to Heribaldus, (for I really neither have, or can any where hear of its being to be found in America) yet it may, I think, be inferred from Fleury's Ecclesiastical History, that Rabanus did not write his letter to Heribaldus *expressly against the novelty of Paschasius's doctrine,* as the Chaplain says (p. 32); and I much question whether he so much as mentions it in that letter. For, according to Fleury, *Hist. Eccles. book* 49, an. 859, the express purpose of Rabanus's writing to Heribaldus was, to answer him on many penitential cases, concerning which the latter had consulted him, Rabanus being then archbishop of Mentz.

But as I wish to inform your faith, at the same time that I am endeavouring to confirm it, I will add from Fleury, that there is extant an anonymous writing against Paschasius, which is thought, with much probability, to be a letter from Rabanus to Egil, abbot Prum; and it is not unlikely, that the passage quoted by the Chaplain (p. 32), is taken from this writing.

But what is the purport of the letter? Is it to dispute the real presence, and transubstantiation? No certainly; for the author of it clearly professes these doctrines, and begins his letter with these words.[:] "All the faithful must believe and confess, that the body and blood of our Lord is true flesh and blood; whoever denies it, shews himself an infidel." And a little after; "I add, that as Jesus Christ is the true land of God, who is mystically offered every day for the life of the world; so by consecration and the power of the Holy Ghost, the bread becomes his true flesh, and the wine his true blood, which is so certain that no christian must doubt it."[65]

The purport of this writing against Paschasius, was, to censure some modes of speech used by him in explaining the eucharist. For he had said, that the body of our Lord, which the faithful receive in communion, is the same body, that was born of the Virgin Mary. This expression appeared to Rabanus particularly obnoxious, though it was undoubtedly authorised by former usage. It was therefore rejected by him and thought improper, as not conveying an idea of the different *manner,* in which Christ's body and blood exist in their natural state, and that, which they have in the sacrament. In the former, they are *palpable* and *sensible;* in the latter, they exist in a manner *supernatural* and *mysterious.*

Paschasius maintained the propriety of his language in treating on this subject, in which dispute many others took part. Ratramus, or Bertram wrote by order of Charles the Bald, a treatise *on the body and blood of our Lord,* but that *he was employed expressly by the prince to oppose* Paschasius, is a fact no where proved, though confidently asserted by the Chaplain. The French author of the *Perpetuity of the faith,* &c. says expressly, that Ratramus does not so much as mention Paschasius's name; he objects indeed to the expression used by him, but at the same time, he plainly asserts in many passages the catholic doctrine; and Boileau, the celebrated Sorbonist, has proved, that Bellarmine and others were mistaken in thinking, he was an adversary to it, as well as in saying that Paschasius wrote against him his treatise *of the reality of Christ's body and blood,* &c. For the occasion of Paschasius's writing was, to instruct the Saxons then lately converted to christianity.

I will not swell this address with copying from Ratramus many passages to prove his belief of the real presence and transubstantiation. Amongst others, this is one.[:] "The bread, which is offered, is, at consecration, changed into the body of Christ; as likewise the wine, expressed from the grape, is made blood by the significancy," or efficacy "of the sacred mystery; not indeed visibly, but by the invisible operation of the Holy Ghost. When they are called the body and blood of Christ, because they are received not for that, which they outwardly appear, but for that, which they are made by the intimate action of the divine spirit; and because they are quite another thing thro' invisible powers, than what they visibly appear."[66] This, I think, is abundantly sufficient to shew, that the disagreement between Paschasius and Ratramus consisted not in a difference of opinion respecting the real presence and transubstantiation.

We see, continues the Chaplain, *that the doctrine of the eternal presence was no sooner openly maintained, than some of the most celebrated doctors of the time arose to combat it without incurring any suspicion of heresy from their opponents.* (P. 33.) We have, I think, seen directly the contrary. We have heard Rabanus say, that *by consecration and the power of the Holy Ghost, the bread becomes the true flesh, and the wine the true blood of Christ, which is so CERTAIN, that no CHRISTIAN must doubt it.* And indeed it would be a most extraordinary thing, that Rabanus should *write expressly against the doctrine of the real presence;* and yet that Baronius, an historian so fervently attached to the doctrines of the catholic church, should style him the *brightest luminary of German.* (Ch. Let. p. 32.)

We have heard Ratramus, in the last paragraph but one, deliver no less clearly the doctrine of the real presence and transubstantiation; and if even *they* assert it so evidently, whom the Chaplain has selected out of all antiquity, as most favourable to his cause, I need not have recourse to other authors, their cotemporaries [*sic*], to prove, that a *suspicion of heresy* would have been incurred by those, who should have openly combated the above-said tenets.

Finally, we have heard Paschasius represent the doctrine of the real presence as that of the universal church, and publicly affirm, that it had not so much as *one* open adversary. Where then is the *convincing proof, that at the period* indicated by the Chaplain, *the doctrine of the carnal presence was regarded merely as matter of opinion, and so continued for 200 years.*[67]. I flatter myself on the contrary, that I have alleged from Paschasius and Rabanus *convincing proofs* of the doctrine of the carnal presence being at that time the established sense of the church; and other proofs more decisive will be added hereafter.

The Chaplain says, (p. 31), that the term *transubstantiation* was unknown, till an *obscure* bishop invented it eleven hundred years after the time of the apostles. The bishop here meant is Stephen of Autun, who lived about the year 950, that is 850, not 1100 years after the time of the apostles, St. John having lived to the year 101 of the christian aera, acccording to the common opinion. I mention this, not for the sake of any advantage I mean to make of the Chaplain's mistake, but merely to shew, that he did not bestow on his investigation all that scrupulous attention, with which he flatters himself. However Stephen was the first to make use of the term *transubstantiation;* I admit without hesitation, that it is not to be met with in any more antient author; but as our dispute is not about words, but things, the Chaplain can derive no more advantage from this fact, than an Arian, or Nestorian can from the terms *consubstantial* or *theotokos,* being never used before the first council of Nice, and that of Ephesus. The term transubstantiation was found to convey a precise idea of catholic doctrine, and so became adopted by the council of Lateran into ecclesiastical language; all which is perfectly agreeable to antient practice, as attested by Vincent of Lerins: "The catholic church,["] says he, ["]moved thereunto by the innovations of heretics, has always attended to this point in the decrees of her councils; that is, to transmit to posterity with the attestation of written authority, what she before received by tradition alone; comprehending much matter in few words; and for the better understanding, oftentimes expressing an *antient* doctrine by a *new* word of determinate signification."[68]

You have already seen, how much the Chaplain was mistaken in saying, that the doctrine conveyed by the word, *transubstantiation,* was no article of faith before the year 1215. But considering, that his assertions coincide with the prevailing prejudices in this country, I find myself obliged to sacrifice my desire of shortening this address to the necessity of fully manifesting an error adopted by Aubertin, or Dr. Cofin's *History of Transubstantiation;* for I cannot persuade myself, that he gave so much credit to Scotus, as to take it up on his authority.

In a council held at Rouen in Normandy, on occasion of Berengarius's heresy, an. 1063, the father of the council thus express their belief.[:] "With our hearts we believe, and with our tongues we confess, that the bread on the Lord's table is only bread before consecration; but that the nature and substance of bread is, at the very time of consecration, by the unspeakable power of God, *changed into the nature and substance of that flesh, which was born of the Virgin Mary*—and that the wine, which is mixed with water in the cup, *is truly and essentially changed into the blood,* which mercifully flowed for the world's redemption from the side of our blessed Saviour, when wounded by the soldiers lance."[69]

In the Roman Council, an. 1079, Berengarius retracted his error and professed the catholic faith in these words.[:] "I Berengarius with my heart believe, and with my tongue profess, that the bread and wine, which are placed on the altar, are, by the mystical prayer and words of our redeemer, *substantially changed into the true, proper, and life-giving flesh and blood of our Lord Jesus Christ.*"[70]

Six years after Berengarius's death, viz. 1094, a numerous council was held at Placentia of many bishops of Italy, France, Germany, &c. wherein it was again defined, "that bread and wine, when consecrated on the altar, are not only figuratively, but *truly and essentially changed into the body and blood of our Lord.*"[71] Eight or nine other councils were held during the same century, mostly in Italy and France, and all of them equally condemn Berengarius's opinion; so true it is, that the doctrine of transubstantiation was universally received as an article of faith, long before the year 1215.

When Berengarius first published his erroneous opinion of the real presence, and transubstantiation, between the year 1038, and 1050; it was instantly rejected universally, and concluded to be repugnant to faith. Adelmannus, who had been brought up with him under the discipline of Fulbert, bishop of Chartres, and became himself bishop of Brixen, wrote Berengarius a letter expressed with much tenderness and charity, wherein he tells his friend, that a "report was spread of his being "severed from the unity of the church by holding a doctrine contrary to the catholic faith, concerning the body and blood of the Lord, which is immolated every day on the altar." See the passage at length in the *Perpetuité de la foi,* 1st section. This letter was written, before any council had been held against Berengarius; and yet Adelmannus tells him, that his doctrine was deemed to be contrary to catholic faith and unity; a manifest proof of the real presence and transubstantiation being regarded as tenets of the church antecedently to Berengarius's error.

Lanfrank, who afterwards became archbishop of Canterbury, was present at the council held at Rome against Berengarius an. 1059, and wrote a treatise *on the reality of the body of Christ* in the eucharist. In the very beginning of it, he says that Berengarius first "began to entertain an opinion against the whole world;" and afterwards, that he "composed a writing against the catholic verity, and against the sentiment of *all* the churches."[72] And in his 18th chapter he thus states the catholic doctrine.[:] "We believe, that the earthly substances of bread and wine, being consecrated on the altar by divine institution, and the ministry of priests, are *changed by the unspeakable, incomprehensible, and miraculous operation of almighty power into the substance of our Lord's body.* —This is the faith, which the church, that being spread through the world, is called catholic, has held in all ages, and continues still to hold."[73] The same thing is repeated in many other places of his work; in his 22d chapter, he calls upon Berengarius to "question the Latins, to interrogate the Greeks, the Armenians, and generally all the christians of every country; and they will all with one voice profess this faith."[74]

Guitmundus, Archbishop of Aversa, another contemporary author, and who was probably present at the council of Rome an. 1059, reproaches the followers of Berengarius with holding a doctrine, "that was not received so much as in one borough, or even one village."[75]

In fine Berengarius himself was so much convinced of the universal belief being contrary to his new tenet, that he pretended, according to Lanfrank, "that the church had perished through the ignorance of those, who understood not her mysteries, and that she subsisted only in himself and his followers."[76]

With this, and much more similar evidence before me of the sense of the church concerning transubstantiation, at the rise of Berengarius's heresy about the year 1038, I may without rashness conclude, that the Chaplain was equally mistaken in saying that it only became an article of our faith in the year 1215; and in asserting, as we have before seen, that the doctrine of Christ's *carnal presence* in the eucharist was regarded merely as matter of opinion till the council of Rome under pope Nicholas in the year 1059, or 1060.

The testimonies, I have alleged, are so full and decisive, that the most learned protestant writers have admitted, reluctantly indeed, but still they have admitted, that the catholic doctrine had full possession of mens minds, when Berengarius first began to dogmatise. They assign its origin, increase and full establishment to the period between the publication of Paschasius's writings, and the aera of Berengarius above mentioned. This period they represent as the reign of darkness and absurdity; the Chaplain, without adopting their common opinion of the early prevalence of our tenets, has however caught the infection, and with wonderful sensibility laments the woeful degradation of reason, and the superstition and ignorance of the age. According to most of these authors, it was during this lamentable state of religion, virtue and learning, that our doctrine crept into mens minds; that it operated a total change in their faith; that parents, who had heard another lesson all their life-time, trained their offspring to the belief of the real presence, and transubstantiation; that the pastors of the churches did the same with their parishioners; that the faithful, instead of believing, as before, that they received Christ in the eucharist figuratively, or spiritually, now changed their creed, and admitted the tenet of the real presence so universally, that Berengarius could not in the whole world find so much as *one pitiful town, or a single village* to give countenance to his doctrine. What completes the wonder, is, that all this happened without any commotion or opposition. No council was called to withstand the growing evil; not one bishop throughout Christendom raised his voice against it. At all other times, the least innovation, the slightest departure from the received tenets occasioned disputes and contests; every heresy, however obscure, or speculative, was combated at its first appearance; but this doctrine of the real presence, which involved in its nature a point of daily practice, as well as of faith; which proposed to christians, as an object of inward and outward adoration, that, which in their former estimation it was idolatrous to adore; this doctrine gently insinuated itself without noise or disturbance into the minds of all christians during that long sleep, into which ignorance had lulled them; it operated this wonderful revolution so silently, that no historian either perceived it in himself or others, to transmit us an account of it. Can men, who will believe this, find any mystery in religion, even transubstantiation itself, too hard for their digestion?

But we are not yet come to all the wonders of this most extraordinary phaenomenon. The doctrine now held by the catholic church was, at the rise of Berengarius's error, and so continues to this day, the doctrine of all the eastern and southern christian churches, the Greek, the Armenian, the Cophtick, the Abyssinian; &c. so truly did Lanfrank, as above cited, refer to them as witnesses of the universal belief. Many of those christians, as the Nestorians, Eutychians, &c. were separated from the church of Rome, near four hundred years before Paschasius wrote on the eucharist. Within a few years after his writing his letter to Frudegardus, the Greek schism was in a great degree begun by Photius, and rent asunder the eastern and western churches, and bred between them especially in the former, an animosity, which they will with difficulty conceive, who are unacquainted with the ardent spirits of the Greeks. It is therefore incredible, I had almost said, impossible, considering the nature of the human mind, that in this state of resentment, the oriental churches should not only adopt the innovations of the Latins, but adopt them without reproach or opposition, of which not the slightest testimony is come down to us; and that these pretended innovations should be received and incorporated into their religion not only by the abettors of Photius's schism, but likewise by the Nestorians, Eutychians, &c. who had been so long separated from the communion both of the Roman pontiff, and the patriarch of Constantinople.

Obstinacy, or ignorance alone can deny, that our doctrine concerning the eucharist agrees with that of all the churches, I have mentioned. No point of history can be supported with fuller evidence, than this now is, that the real presence and transubstantiation are the invariable tenets of the eastern christians; and no other commencement of this general persuasion can be assigned with the smallest shew of probability, than the commencement of the christian religion itself.

From all that has been said, our inference is clear and conclusive. The doctrine of the real presence and transubstantiation were the established doctrines of the church, and not merely matters of opinion, long before the aeras assigned by the Chaplain, that it, before the years 1060, and 1215. They were universally taught previously to the Greek schism, which may be said to have begun an. 857, by Photius's intrusion into the see of Constantinople, and even before the Nestorian and Eutychian heresies, the latter of which was condemned in the council of Chalcedon, an. 454; and the former in that of Ephesus, an. 434. But if they were the general doctrines throughout the western and eastern churches at so early a period, what foundation can there be for assigning their commencement to any other aera, than that of christianity itself?

It imports then little to the present subject, whether in the interval between Paschasius and Berengarius, a gloom of dark and universal ignorance overspread the face of the christian world; and whether the bishops were unable to write their names;[77] for enough has been said, though much more remains unsaid, to prove to every dispassionate man, that the obnoxious tenets did not steal upon mens minds during this fatal interval. If it were at all material to refute the exaggerated imputations of supineness and ignorance, it would be no difficult matter; for the period so outrageously abused was not so fatal to the cultivation of letters, as is represented; and if through the tyranny of turbulent barons, and violence of contending factions, some few prelates, incapable of writing their names, perhaps not fit in all Christendom, were imposed upon different churches, there were many others, pious and well informed, who kept constant watch over the flocks committed to their charge. Whoever will read the acts of the council of Rheims, held within this period, viz. an. 992, will be satisified, that the bishops, who composed it, were perfectly acquainted with ecclesiastical discipline and sacred antiquity; and animated with a becoming zeal for the preservation of sound morals among the clergy. Baronius and Sigonius had their eyes principally turned on Italy, their own country, and especially on Rome, when they wrote so unfavourably of the age; and there indeed contending factions imposed some pontiffs on the chair of St. Peter, who disgraced their station by the corruption of their manners. But France, England and Germany, and even some parts of Italy were blessed with bishops of extraordinary virtue and knowledge, and with princes, who encouraged learning and endowed academies of science, in which if the true taste of literature did not yet flourish, at least the study of religion and zeal for improvement did, as is attested of the schools erected at Paris, Arras, Cambrai, Liege, &c.[78]

The Chaplain (p. 19, 20), cites some catholic divines, who acknowledge that the doctrine of transubstantiation is not to be found in scripture. It has been already observed, that nothing conclusive can be inferred from this, even supposing these divines in the right, and that they are fairly cited. But what if their meaning be only this, that in scripture there is no express declaration of the bread and wine being changed into the body and blood of Christ: Might they not say this, and still believe, that the doctrine of the real presence was so expressed in holy writ, as necessarily to infer the change, which we call *transubstantiation?* For I will venture to say, though I have never looked into some of these divines, that there is not one of them, who does not teach, that the words, *This is my body,* import Christ's real, corporeal, and substantial presence in the eucharist. Accordingly, Scotus says only, that there is no text of scripture so *explicit,* as *evidently to compel* our assent to transubstantiation?[79]

Melchior Cano's elegant work I have heretofore read with great pleasure; and I wish that the Chaplain had transcribed the whole passage referred to, that we might fairly judge of his meaning; for I own, that I grievously suspect Cano of saying, that transubstantiation is certainly implied as a necessary consequence of scripture doctrine, if not expressly delivered in it; and that the words of the institution of the sacrament of the *eucharist* would not be true, if they did not import a change of the bread and wine into the body and blood of Christ.

Alphonsus de Castro is very *orthodox,* and has the character of being a divine of some credit; but as to his being a *mighty name* in scholastic theology, I never before heard it; and I am sure, no divine can be entitled to that character, who gravely says, that in *old authors there is seldom any mention made of the transubstantiation of the bread into the body of Christ;* for so the Chaplain cites him. (P. 20) How little conversant with old authors he must be, who gravely advances such a proposition, will plainly appear from Bellarmine, Du Perron, Tournely, &c. I shall presently have occasion to recite some passages from old authors; but shall do it with a sparing hand, not forgetting that the purport of this address is not to establish, but to vindicate our doctrine from the attack made against it.

After exhausting his authorities against transubstantiation, the Chaplain begs leave to mention *two negative arguments, which seem to prove to a demonstration, that it was unknown to the antient church.*[80] How capable this is of demonstration, you may judge from what you have already heard. Was it unknown to the antient church, when Cyril bishop of Jerusalem wrote thus about the year 350? "Jesus Christ in Cana of Gailiee, by his will only, changed water into wine, which has some affinity with blood; and can we not believe, him, that *he changes the wine into his bood?* Let your soul rejoice at it, as a thing most certain, that the *bread, which appears to our eyes, is not bread, though our taste do judge it to be so,* but that it is the body of Christ; and that the wine, which appears to our eyes, is *not wine, though our sense of taste take it for wine,* but that it is the blood of Jesus Christ."[81]

Was transubstantiation unknown, when in the same century, Gaudentius bishop of Brescia thus expressed himself: "The Creator, and Lord of beings, who produces bread from the earth, *from bread makes his own body,* because he can do it, and has promised it; and he, that out of water made wine, *out of wine makes his own blood.*"[82] It is, I hope, needless to add to these, the testimonies of almost every christian father; and I think the Chaplain might contend with equal appearance of truth, that the doctrine of the necessity of baptism *was unknown* to the antient church, as that the catholic doctrine of the eucharist was.

We are now prepared to examine his *negative arguments.* The first is, that if the antient church formerly adored Christ in the eucharist, as we now do, catholics would, in arguing aginst Arians, have insisted on that adoration as a proof of Christ's divinity. (P. 24.) Such is his first demonstration; but does it not equally prove, that the antient church never adored Christ at all, in or out of the eucharist? For pray, would it not have been equally conclusive against Arians, and in favour of Christ's divinity, to have alleged the antient custom of adoring him out of the sacrament, for instance, as he is seated in Heaven on the right hand of his Father? Why therefore was this argument not insisted on by the antient fathers? for a very obvious reason; because the Arians, at the very time that they fell into heresy to avoid the pretended contradictions in the doctrine of the trinity, swallowed other real ones; and, as ecclesiastical historians observe, made no difficulty to acknowledge that Christ was a divine person, *true God of true God,*[83] *eternal, the same God with the Father, and possessing the same divine pre-eminence or dignity;*[84] and therefore an object of divine worship. In a word, they seemingly admitted every thing, but the term *consubstantial.* Adoration they did not refuse: and the catholics instead of having cause to reproach them with neglecting it, charged them on the contrary with introducing a plurality of Gods by paying divine honours to him, to whom, consistently with their principles, they could not be due.[85]

Before I proceed to the Chaplain's second argument, amounting likewise to *demonstration,* I must beg leave to detain your attention a little while longer on the first. This is his reasoning: The catholics, in their dispute with the Arians, did not object, against the latter, the supreme adoration paid to Christ in the blessed eucharist; therefore, since it was with-held, they did not believe in it. You have already heard a very satisfactory reason, why catholics did not object against the Arians, as the Chaplain thinks they would; to that then I shall say no more; but begging leave for once to quit my defensive plan, I shall build one argument in favour of our doctrine upon the foundation laid by the Chaplain. According to him, adoration of Christ in the eucharist imports a belief of his real presence; but primitive christians adored Christ in the eucharist; they therefore believed his real presence. The second, or *minor* position, which is the only disputable one, can be proved by the clearest evidence of primitive christians themselves. I shall omit relating passages to this point out of Ambrose, the holy bishop of Milan,[86] Chrysostom,[87] Gregory Nazianzen, &c. that I may come immediately to an authority still more authentic, the public liturgy of the church of Contantinople, which commonly goes under the name of Chrysostom, and was probably composed, and certainly used by him. In this liturgy, not only the external acts of adoration, expressed by incense, bending and prostrating the body, &c. are enjoined, but likewise internal adoration is clearly signified by the prayers addressed to Jesus Christ in the sacrament. "Lord Jesus,["] is the priest enjoined to say, ["] look down from thy holy habitation, and from the throne of thy glory, come to sanctify us, thou art seated in Heaven with thy Father, and who art here present with us in an invisible manner. Deign with thy powerful hand to grant us thy pure and unsullied body; and through us to all the people." Then adds the liturgy, "the priest and the deacon must make their adoration." And to shew, that this adoration refers to the body of Christ upon the altar, we need only note the farther directions of the liturgy. The priest taking up the consecrated bread, and bending his head before the altar, prays in this manner: "I confess, that thou art Christ, the son of the living God, who came into the world to save sinners, &c. Lord, I am not worth, that thou shouldst enter into my house defiled with sin; but as thou didst vouchsafe to enter the house of Simon the Leper; so likewise vouchsafe to enter my soul full of ungovernable passions, as a manger, or a house of filth and death, covered all over with the leprosy of sin." Thus is proved the adoration of Christ in the eucharist, not only by the testimony of the fathers, but by a law of ecclesiastical discipline, connected with daily and inviolable practice; and making part of the worship rendered to Jesus Christ agreeably to the public liturgy; and consequently, the primitive belief of the real presence is fully established.

The Chaplain's second negative argument, or demonstration against the catholic doctrine of the eucharist is, *that heathen writers would have retorted upon christians the accusation of idolatry in adoring a bit of bread, in reserving their God in gold and silver chalices*, &c. (P. 24, note.) Violent indeed must be his prejudices against the religion he has renounced, if such arguments appear demonstrations to him. For how little do we know of the disputations between christians and heathens? Some fragments of Celsus and Porphyry, and of the writings of Julian the apostate, together with the little, that can be collected from the early apologies for christianity, are almost all, that is come down to us on this subject. The heathens may have objected, as the Chaplain supposed they would; so may they have found, in the mystery of the Incarnation of the Son of God, in his nativity, in his crucifixion, an apparent apology for their fables concerning their own divinities. They may have grounded, on the christian doctrine of redemption, the same arguments, as the Socinians now do; and they may from the example it afforded them, have attempted to justify their own human sacrifices. Above all, they may have availed themselves of the tenet of the Trinity, to uphold, or, at least, explain away the absurdities of a plurality of gods. But, have we any authority for saying they did so? No; and except a single expression of the scoffer Lucian, which seems to glance at the Trinity; and a passage of Tertullian and Athanasius, implying, that some Jews and pagans reproached christians with admitting more gods than one; antiquity does not furnish us with any proof of these arguments being used by heathen writers. What wonder then, if they never made the objection proposed by the Chaplain, especially as of all the mysteries of our religion, the celebration of the eucharist was that, in which, during the reign of persecution and idolatry, the greatest privacy was observed.

The truth is, the heathens despised the christians too much to inform themselves minutely of their tenets. They knew little of them, but what appeared outwardly; their aversion of idolatry, and their profession of following the doctrine of Jesus Christ. Here their inquiries stopped; and Tertullian in his Apology, ch. I. upbraids them with neglecting in this point alone to seek information.

To these negative arguments, the Chaplain begs leave to add, "that the fathers of the 2d council of Nice expressly confirm the opinion that Christ's body in heaven is not flesh and blood; how therefore can bread and wine be changed into his body, if they become flesh and blood?" (P. 24, note.) For this most extraordinary passage, he quotes Labbe's collection of the councils, tom. 6. p. 541. This collection I know not where to find in America; but I aver, that no such doctrine was delivered or entertained by the fathers of that council; and will therefore, without fear of being convicted of rashness, undertake to say, that the Chaplain cannot support, what he has here advanced. Neither Cabasaffutius in his summary of the councils, nor Fleury, nor Natalis Alexander, who recite the decrees and canons of this council with much exactness, say one syllable of such a doctrine being taught in it. As in many other instances, so likewise in this, the Chaplain has suffered himself to be misled by authors, whom, I hope, he will deservedly mistrust for the time to come. Their unfaithfulness is eminently conspicuous in the present instance. In the fifth session of the council, some passages were read of a fabulous book, entitled, *The Travels of the Apostles*. Amongst other fables, it was there related, that John the evangelist had said, that Christ had no true body; that when the Jews thought they crucified him, he exhibited only the appearance of a body, but was in reality without any corporeal figure. But so far was the council from confirming this doctrine, that they rejected it with horror. This is the account given by *Fleury, Hist. Eccles.* Tom. 9. b. 44. an. 787. It would be curious indeed, if the authors, whom the Chaplain has followed, should have mistaken this fabulous writing for the acts of the council.[88]

Nothing, I think, now remains unnoticed of all, he has said against our doctrine of the eucharist, excepting the collection of supposed absurdities and contradictions, with which in the same page (24), he charges transubstantiation. In this, he uses a mode of reasoning not very liberal, and yet not unpracticed by many other writers against us. The objected absurdities and contradictions, whether real or imaginary, result more immediately from Christ's real presence in the eucharist, than from transubstantiation; but to impute them to that doctrine would not be quite so inoffensive. Some regards are due to protestant Lutheran brethren, and the doctrine of the protestant episcopal church, who admit the real presence, in their catechisms at least, and according to their earliest and most eminent writers. But as to the catholic tenets, too much cannot be said to render them an object of ridicule and detestation. *If* transubstantiation *be admitted,* says the Chaplain (p. 24), *the true God may be shut up in boxes, or devoured corporally by vermin.* Would to God, it were possible, in answering such objections (which indeed I never should have suspected the Chaplain capable of drawing from the foulest dregs of controversy) to keep up your respect for this great mystery of our religion, and adorable pledge of divine goodness towards mankind! *How can he give us his flesh to eat?* John vi. was the Jewish question; *and many hearing it, said, this saying is hard, and who can hear it?*

So likewise the Marcionites, and other enemies of the Incarnation, contended, that to be inclosed in a womb, and to be laid in a manger, was unworthy of the Divine Majesty. The Pagans and Jews ridiculed the credulity of christians in believing in a man crucified between two thieves; but the church despised their mockeries, being taught by the great apostle, that the mystery of the cross was indeed *a stumbling block to the Jews, and to the Greeks foolishness; but to those who are called—the power of God, and the wisdom of God.*[89] The divinity of Christ could not be inured by his mortal sufferings; and from them, great glory came to him, and utility to men. The same answer we may give to our opponents, when they compel us to take notice of objections so unworthy of the greatness and sanctity of the consideration. But if this will not satisfy them, I would beg leave to ask them, whether they do not believe, that the infant Jesus was confined in the womb of the Virgin Mary, and wrapped in swaddling clothes? Do they not believe, that he was, like other children, liable to be hurt, for instance, by the application of fire, or the stings of insects? If then he could suffer these things in his own natural body, and be liable to be hurt by them; why may he not render himself subject, in appearance, to the same accidents, when he is under the covering of bread and wine, and incapable of being hurt thereby?

I have already taken some notice of the objection, so often repeated,[90] and so often refuted, of transubstantiation contracting *our sense, and our understanding.* Ought we to trust our senses, more than God himself: When Joshua, who took the angel for a man, asked him, *art thou for us, or for our adversaries,* and was told, he was not a man, but *a captain of the heavenly host, he fell on his face, and worshipped, and said, what says my Lord unto his servant?* Joshua v. ver. 14; that is he believed him, rather than his *senses;* for to all his senses he appeared a man; but revelation informed him that what he saw, was an angel. In like manner, if God has revealed to us, that under the appearances of bread and wine is contained the body and blood of Christ; are we not to believe him, rather than those appearances? The evidence for the revelation may be tried by all the rules of criticism; but when the mind is once convinced of its existence, it must then submit, notwithstanding all seeming contradiction, or opposition of our senses. "Let us always believe God," says St. Chrysostom, speaking of the eucharist, "and not contradict him, *though that, which he says, seems to contradict our thoughts and our eyes. For his* words cannot deceive us; but our *sense* may be easily deceived. Since therefore he says, *this is my body,* let us be fully persuaded of it. How many say now, oh! that I could see him in his own shape! or his cloaths! or any thing about him! Believe me, you see him; you touch him; you eat him. You would be content to see his cloaths; and he lets you not only see him, but also touch him, and eat him, and receive him within you."[91]

As the Chaplain has added to his reasoning against our belief none of those *innumerable arguments,* which evince the meaning of Christ's words, *this is my body,* to be *figurative* (p. 25), I likewise shall gladly wave the controversy; only remarking, that he is neither terrified by the anathemas of Luther against the defenders of a figurative sense, whom he calls *blasphemers,* a *damned sect, liars, bread-eaters, wine-guzzlers,*[92] &c. nor by the severity of Dr. Cofin, bishop of Durham, in the beginning of his *History of Transubstantiation,* where speaking of the words of the institution of the sacrament, he says; *if any one make a bare figure of them we cannot and ought not either excuse or suffer him in our churches.*

Another of our tenets, which the Chaplain has selected as unsupported by scripture and antiquity, particularly in the Greek church, is, the belief of purgatory. But before he proceeded to impugn, he ought to have stated it; which not having done, the deficiency shall now be supplied. All therefore, which the church requires to be believed on this subject, is contained in the decree of the council of Trent, which defines, that there is *a purgatory,* or middle state, and *that the souls therein detained are relieved by the suffrages of the faithful, especially by the agreeable sacrifice of the altar.*[93] Concerning the nature, or extent of their sufferings, whether by fire or otherwise, the place of punishment, its duration, &c. we are not confined to any particular opinion. Now is it true, that this doctrine has no foundation in scripture and antiquity? The books of Macabees, which so decidedly establish it, must not be admitted of sufficient authority, because *they were not acknowledged for canonical scriptures* by *St. Hierom, Rufinus, Epiphanius, Athanasius. Gregory, and many other antient and eminent fathers.* (Ch. Let. 0. 21.) If it be a sufficient reason for rejecting the books of Machabees, that some early father doubted of their canonical authority, though afterwards, on a full investigation, they were received by the whole church, I wish to know, how protestants came generally to admit the authority of the epistle to the Hebrews, the 2d of Peter and of James, the revelation of John and others; for of all these, as well as of the books of Macabees, doubts were some time entertained, and the father held different opinions concerning them. But I expect no satisfactory account of this matter; and am well convinced, that the prevailing reason, which moved the compilers of the English Bible to reject the one, and receive the other, was, the support, which, they observed, the catholic doctrine of purgatory would derive from the book of Macabees.[94] But, though it were destitute of this, there are not wanting other passages of scripture to confirm the same, as the Chaplain may find in our divines, though he so positively says the contrary, and particularly in the *Catholic Scripturist,* with whom he ought not to be unacquainted.

As to the doctrine of antiquity concerning purgatory, and particularly of the Greek church, we shall meet with little difficulty. No article of the christian belief has stronger evidence from the testimony of the early fathers; they prove incontestably the practice of praying for the dead; they assert, that by the prayers of the faithful in this life, comfort and relief is obtained for those, who are departed out of it; which is estabishing as much of the doctrine of purgatory, as we are obliged to believe. St. Epiphanius, a bishop of the eastern church ranks Aerius amongst the founders of heretics, for teaching, that prayers and alms are unavailing to the dead;[95] and Augustin confirms the same, adding, that his heresy was condemned by the universal church,[96] Greeks therefore as well as others. Cyril, bishop of Jerusalem, another Greek father, expounding the liturgy in a catechistical discourse, says, "we remember those, who are deceased, first the patriarchs, apostles and martyrs, that God would receive our supplications through their prayers and intercession. Then we pray for our fathers and bishops, and in general all amongst us, who are departed out of this life, *believing, that this will be the greatest relief to their souls, for whom it is made,* whilst the holy and tremendous victim lies present."[97] If this address should chance to be seen by any one, who has access to the works of this holy father, I would entreat him to read the continuation of this passage, and see the perfect agreement of our doctrine with that of the Greek church in St. Cyril's time. The *enlightened* Greek doctor St. Chrysostom is equally decisive. "It is not in vain, says he, that in the divine mysteries we remember the dead, appearing in their behalf, praying the lamb, who takes away the sins of the world, that comfort may thence be derived to them—let us pray for them, who have slept in Christ; let us not fail to succour the departed; for the common expiation of the world is offered."[98] Here is surely evidence enough to prove the antiquity of our doctrine, and its entire conformity with that of the Greek church. I quote no Latin fathers, as the Chaplain appears to lay particular stress on the Greek; otherwise it were easy to produce the most unequivocal evidence of their perfect agreement with those just cited. The objection from the venerable bishop Fisher, that *to this very day purgatory is not believed by the Greeks*, &c. is either mistaken in him; or, what I am much more inclined to believe, he meant only to say, that the Greeks do not believe in a purgatory of fire, contrary to a common, though not a dogmatical opinion of the western church.

The Chaplain proceeds (p. 30), to tell us, that our present doctrine of the *divine* institution and necessity of confession was not always a settled point in our church. What if it were not? what harm would ensue? if for some ages this matter remained without minute investigation, and the faithful contented themselves with humble and penitential confession of their sins, not enquiring, whether the practice was derived from *divine* or *apostolical* institution? Must we, for this reason, refuse to believe the church, when upon full enquiry and examination of the tradition preserved in all the churches, she defines, that confession is an obligation imposed on us by *divine* authority? This would lead us back again into the question of infallibility. But let us hear the Chaplain's reasons. *The learned Alcuin,* says he, *during the ninth century tells us expressly, that some said it was sufficient to confess our sins to God alone.* Were the persons here mentioned catholics or not? Does it appear, that their opinion had any effect on the public practice, so that it might alarm the vigilance of the pastors of the church? Does he speak generally of all sins? Does he not refer to situations and cases of necessity, in which confession cannot be made but to God alone? Till these, and several other things relating to this passage are stated more fully, it is impossible to determine Alcuin's meaning. The same must be observed of the passage from the manuscript penitential of Theodore, the genuineness of which I much doubt; for I understand that Wilkins, the collector and editor of the British Councils, long since Usher's time, has not published it; and surely he would not have omitted so valuable a discovery; and morever [sic] because I find no mention of this passage in a comprehensive abridgement of Theodore's Penitential, which lies now before me. I do not hereby mean to impeach Usher's integrity, or, in general his judgment; but for the reasons just stated I conclude there were good grounds to question the authority of a manuscript, which does not appear to have had any of a similar tenor to support its credit. After all, to what do these authorities amount, supposing them both genuine and conveying the sense intended by the Chaplain? Only to this, that at the time, the church was not known to Theodore and Alcuin to have made any authentic declaration of the *divine* institution and necessity of confession. The practice of it we may fairly conclude to have been general from this circumstance, if all other proof were wanting, which certainly is not the case; that it was doubted, whether forgiveness could be obtained without it; and in such a situation, what prudent and virtuous christian, anxious to obtain reconciliation with his maker, would neglect the use of a mean, perhaps necessary to procure it?

These observations are equally applicable to the authority of Gratian, whether he was of the opinion attributed to him by the Chaplain and Maldonatus; or whether he only held, that the precept of confession was not obligatory immediately after the commission of sin, as I find his words understood by other divines. A general remark will not be improper in this place; that our faith is formed on the public doctrine of the church, and not on the opinions of private theologians. It is indeed requiring too much of us, to account for all the singularities, which any of them may have committed to writing. Does the Chaplain think, we cannot produce from protestant authors many concessions, many acknowledgments of the agreement of our tenets with the sense of antiquity, with the practice of the first ages, with the universal belief of early christians? Does not Dr. Cofin, in spite of all his animosity, acknowledge the possibility of transubstantiation? Does he not confess, that the water was changed into wine at the marriage feast of Cana in Galilee? Do not the translators of Dupin's history, and other protestant writers of eminence form the misrepresentation and objections of our opponents? Yet would the Chaplain think it worth his while to advert to these authorities, were they brought forth against him?

This however is his method against us. When he comes to object (p. 20), to the power of *loosening* and *binding* committed by Christ to his apostles and their successors in the ministry, he tells us, that the famous Lombard, The *Aristotle,* the *Newton* of scholastic divines, and some others, maintained that power to be only *declaratory* of forgiveness; Whereas *since the council of Trent, it is become an article of our faith,* that the priest has power to forgive sins. (P. 20.)

Peter Lombard, who lived in the 12th century, was indeed a man of acknowledged and methodical genius, and had the merit of reducing the scattered opinions of divines into a regular system or body, which has since been the groundwork of scholastic theology. But if the Chaplain, by calling him its *Newton* and *Aristotle,* mean to convey an idea, that all his opinions are held sacred, he is greatly mistaken; for many of them are controverted, many universally rejected. The opinion, for which he is here cited, is very different from that, which might be supposed by the Chaplain's imperfect representation of it. For the natural inference from his representation is, that the sacerdotal order not only do not exercise a ministerial and dependent jurisdiction over repentant sinners (which is what we teach) but likewise that they impart no absolution, that they have no power of loosening or binding; in a word, that no grace is administered through the instrumentality of their ministry, and consequently that there is no such thing as the sacrament of pennance. Now all this is expressly contrary to Lombard. He holds the divine institution of this sacrament; he teaches, that the ministry of absolution truly confers grace; that it has an inward effect on the soul; and though only declaratory with regard to the remission of the guilt of sin, is efficaciously and actively so with respect to the remission of the temporal punishment annexed to it. The council of Trent censured indeed the doctrine of the reformers in such terms, as appear to the generality of divines to import the falsehood of Lombard's opinion; but others do not think so; and the Chaplain might have remained in the bosom of our church, and still believed, that the power of absolution is only *declaratory,* in Lombard's sense, as Tournely[99] would have informed him.

I have now finished my observations on the argumentative part of the Chaplain's letter, with abilities far inferior indeed; but, I trust, with a superiority of cause, which has enabled me to leave nothing unanswered, that could carry trouble into your minds, or shake the firmness of your faith. Before he concludes his letter, he has thought proper to make a profession of his new belief, and shews a particular anxiety to vindicate to himself the appellation of a catholic. I am not surprised at his anxiety; it is an appellation characteristic of the true church. "My name is Christian," says Pacianus, "my surname is Catholic. That denominates me, this distinguishes me."[100] And St. Augustin; "we must hold the christian religion, and the communion of that church, which is *catholic;* and which is called *catholic,* not only by her own children, but by all her enemies."[101] But will the Chaplain now find this characteristic in his new religion, any more, than the sectaries of St. Augustin's times found it in theirs? This holy doctor having mentioned various reasons, which prevailed on him to remain in the communion of the church, proceeds thus. "I am held in this church by the succession of priests coming down even to the present episcopacy from St. Peter, to whom Christ after his resurrection committed the feeding of his flock. Finally, I am held to it by the very name of catholic, of which this church alone has, not without reason, so kept possession, that, though all heretics desire to be called catholics; yet if a stranger ask them, where catholics meet, none of them will presume to point out his own church, or his house."[102]

The Chaplain claims right to the title of catholic, because he "believes and professes every point of christian faith, which at *all times,* and in *all places* has constituted the creed of all orthodox believers." (P. 35.) For such, we are told, is Vincent of Lerins's description of a catholic. In the preceding, as well as subsequent part of his work, Vincent has explained the characteristics of catholicity so clearly, that it was impossible for the Chaplain to mistake them; and it was perhaps becoming his candour to have stated that author's

meaning, when he was alleging his authority to the Roman catholics of
Worcester. "It is necessary, says ye, to follow the universality, antiquity and
agreement of the catholic and apostolical church; and if a part revolt against
the whole; if innovation rise up against antiquity; if the dissent of one or a
few mistaken men disturb the agreement of all, or of a great majority of
catholics, let the integrity of the whole be preferred to the infection of a part.
In this same universality, let greater regard be had to venerable antiquity, than
profane novelty; in antiquity itself," (that is, with regard to doctrines, for
which antiquity is alleged) "let the *decrees of a general council,* if any exist,
in the first place be opposed to the rashness of a few; and if no such decrees
exist, let catholics follow, what is next in authority, *the agreeing opinions of
many and eminent fathers;* which thing being faithfully, soberly and anxious-
ly observed, we shall *easily* with God's help discover the pernicious errors of
rising heretics."[103] Will the Chaplain's catholicity stand the test of these
rules? Will the authority of the learned Vincent of Lerins justify the religion,
which he has adopted?

He next alleges, that the apostles creed is the standard of catholicity; but it
must be subscribed, he says, *in its full extent.* does he mean by these words,
that every article of the creed is to be received, without addition, in the terms
in which it is written? Or that it is to be received with such extension and
explanation, as may comprehend other points not clearly expressed, but only
implied therein? If this last be his meaning, who shall determine what is
implied? By what authority shall the Arian or Macedonian be bound to
acknowledge, that the divinity of Jesus Christ, and of the Holy Ghost is
taught in the creed? Will he, who receives the creed in the Arian or Macedonian sense, be a catholic? If it be the standard of catholicity, it surely
cannot be enough to admit its words; but the sense conveyed by those words
must be the object of catholic faith. I admit the creed, will each of these say,
which whoever admits *in its full extent,* according to you, *must be a* member
of the catholic church. (P. 35.) Shew me that I do not so admit it; shew me,
that by requiring my assent to your explanation and extension of it, you do
not require a submission to human authority, and thereby lay on us a yoke
heavier than that, with which you reproach the church of Rome; for when
she requires obedience, she does so in virtue of her claim to infallibility; but
you have no such pretention. Thus will the Arian, Macedonian, and other
sectaries argue; and I cannot see, how the Chaplain will get over their
objection consistently with the principles laid down in his letter; and therefore the creed, as subject to *extension* and *explanation,* cannot be with him
the standard of catholicity.

But if the Chaplain mean, that the creed contains the universal catholic
faith; that the profession of it alone, without understanding any thing more
to be implied, than is literally expressed, constitutes us members of the
catholic church; then are they not heretics, who condemn marriage, and

introduce a distinction of means; whom nevertheless the apostle describes as *giving heed to the doctrine of devils, speaking lies in hypocrisy, and having their conscience seared;*[104] nor they, who deny an eternity of punishment, or assert, that all the reprobated spirits in hell shall at length be saved; for none of these things are touched on in the creed. Where shall we find in it these necessary points, the profession of our obligation to love God, and to keep holy the Lord's day? For necessary those points certainly are, the omission or transgression of which is a damnable sin. Where does the creed speak of the necessity of baptism, or of the lawfulness of it, when administered by heretics? Did not the catholic church always assert the first, as an essential doctrine, and establish the other against the Donatists? Where finally, to omit many other articles, which not even the Chaplain would deny as belonging to catholic faith, does the creed propose to our belief, the receiving of the books of the old and new testament, as of divine revelation? It may therefore be concluded, and I think upon evident principles, and in direct opposition to the Chaplain, that a person may subscribe the apostles creed, even *in this full extent*, without being a member of the catholic church. I only make this exception, that by declaring his assent to these words, *I believe the holy catholic church*, he means not to acknowledge her unerring authority; for if he does, that acknowledgment imports the belief of every article, which she proposes as revealed by God.[105]

Another material objection to the Chaplain's doctrine is, that it admits into the communion of the church almost all those who in every age of christianity have been deemed heretics, and the corrupters of faith. The great council of Nice, which the first protestants pretended to respect as replenished with a truly catholic spirit, in their eight canon, speak of the Novatians as being out of the catholic church. Their errors consisted, 1st, in denying the power of the church to forgive sins, particularly that of apostasy from faith; 2ndly, in requiring the rebaptisation of those, who have been baptised by heretics; 3rdly in condemning second marriages. I doubt whether the Chaplain will find any of these errors reprobated in the apostles creed. St. Cyprian expressly teaches,[106] that the Novatians made use of no other creed, than that of the catholics; which undoubtedly was that of the apostles; and yet they were deemed heretics, and out of the communion of the church.

The Donatists in like manner, because they rejected baptism administered by heretics, were denied communion with the catholic church; but the creed they did not deny. "You are with us," says St. Augustine, "in baptism, *in the creed*, in the other sacraments of God; but in the spirit of unity, and in the bond of peace; finally, *in the catholic church* you are not with us."[107] I infer then again, that it was not the intention of the apostles to conclude in their creed the *universal christian catholic faith*.

You are now prepared to form a true estimate of the Chaplain's *universal belief*, as expressed in the place,[108] we have been considering. As I before said, almost every sect, that ever deformed the face of christianity, might be taken into it. Sabellians and Arians; Nestorians and Eutychians; Socinians and many Deists; and the disciples of that modern author (his name is celebrated in the literary world) who has lately discovered, that the doctrine of a pre-existent nature in Christ, that is, of his having existed before his Incarnation, is a corruption of christianity; all these however discordant in their principles would subscribe the apostles creed; and might say, that they *embraced no new religion, but only* discarded some doctrines, which had been engrafted upon the old one. Thus in a short time, under pretence of reducing our faith to the primitive simplicity of the creed, every tenet would be successively rejected, which curbs our passions, or subjects of our understanding. "If once this impious licentiousness be admitted," says the excellent Vincent of Lerins, "I dread to say, how great will be the danger of destroying and extirpating religion. For if any one part of the catholic doctrine be rejected, another and another will share the same fate; and at length it will become a practice, and deemed lawful to discard others; thus the tenets of religion being rejected one by one, what will finally ensue, but the rejection of the whole together."[109]

The Chaplain proceeds to tell the Roman catholics of Worcester, that his religion is that of the Bible; but that their religion is the doctrine of the council of Trent; insinuating thus an opposition between the two. But do not catholics, as well as he himself, recur to scripture, as the foundation of their religion? Does not the council of Trent profess the most profound veneration for, and implicit belief of every part of scripture? Does it not, in all its decrees and definitions of faith, assert the tenets of the church on the authority of scripture? If then both the council and Chaplain be solicitous to form their faith on scripture, which is most likely to discover the true meaning thereof? If the chaplain deem it his duty to rely most on his own private interpretation, the catholics of Worcester think it wiser, and more consistent with humility and obedience to follow that church, which Jesus Christ has promised to lead into all truth; and to hear those instructors, whim he has appointed *to teach all things, whichsoever he has commanded.*

I rely solely, says the Chaplain, *upon the authority of God's word* (p. 38); and do we not likewise rely *solely* upon the same authority? No, insinuates the Chaplain; *you* catholics *think it necessary to recur to unwritten tradition.* And, pray, what is the tradition, to which we recur, but *the word of God* delivered down to us by the testimony of the fathers, and in the public doctrine of the catholic church: Does not the Chaplain himself receive the *written* word of God from the same testimony and tradition? Why is it less to be depended on in witnessing the unwritten word of God, than in delivering down, and separating the true and genuine books of scripture from those, which are false or corrupted? He demands with St. Cyprian, *whence we have our tradition?* We answer, from the apostles, from their successors, from the attestation of christians spread throughout the world; and St. Augustin proves our right to assign this origin; because, says he, what the universal church holds and was not instituted in a council, but was always maintained, is most reasonably concluded to be derived from apostolical institution."[110] But St. Cyprian requires, *that it be commanded in the gospel, or contained in the epistles or acts of the apostles.* (P. 38.) What wonder, that St. Cyprian, while he was engaged, as he then was, in the error of the Donatists, should speak their language; and like all other opposers of the authority of the church, should call for scripture proofs, which can never be effectual, because they can always be explained away by human ingenuity? Therefore St. Augustin in his 5th book, 23rd ch. on baptism, against the Donatists, particularly refutes the writing now objected out of Cyprian; and it is wonderful indeed, if the Chaplain did not discover this in the very place, from which I presume he copied his objection. He sometimes cites Vincent of Lerins. Will he then allow one, who still retains the most sincere good will from him, to recommend to his reading the eleventh chapter of Vincent's excellent work: Will he notice, what Vincent there says of those, who endeavour to support their false opinions by quotations from Cyprian's works, written while he was engaged in the defence of error.

The Chaplain adds, that we deem the scriptures deficient and obscure; but he asks, *where is the deficiency? Where is the obscurity?* (Ibid.) Deficient they certainly are not, if it be meant, that they do not answer the views and designs of divine providence in causing them to be written; but in this sense they are deficient, that they do not contain all necessary points of belief and practice; which, I think has been sufficiently proved; and is declared by St. Paul in the words before cited; *brethren, stand and hold fast the traditions, you have been taught, whether by word or our epistle.*[111]

But where shall we find *the obscurity of the scripture?* We shall find it in almost every book of holy writ; we shall find it, where St. Peter tells us, it is to be found, in Paul's epistles, *in which are some things hard to be understood, and which, as well as all other scriptures, the unlearned and unstable wrest to their own destruction.*[112] But St. Chrysostom assures us, that *scripture expounds itself, and does not suffer the reader to err.* (P. 38.) The Chaplain is conversant in history; and undoubtedly a person of observation. Can he then seriously believe or imagine it to be Chrysostom's meaning, that the scriptures expounds itself in all points to every reader, so that he cannot err? Is every one able to make that conference and comparison of the different passages of scripture, which lead to its true interpretation? Can any thing more be intended by that great doctor, than that scripture directs every reader to such a rule of exposition, as secures him from error? But is his private interpretation this infallible rule? Or is it that of the church, manifested in her public doctrine by the ministers of her appointment? Hear St. Chrysostom himself; "Take the book in your hand; read a passage throughout; keep present to your mind, what you understand; but return frequently to the reading of those things, which are obscure and difficult; and if by repeated reading you cannot find out their meaning, go to a teacher, go to one wiser than yourself."[113] To the authority of Chrysostom might be added, I believe, that of every father of the church; and most of them have delivered their opinions of the insufficiency and obscurity of scripture, not in fragments of a sentence, but treating professedly and fully on this very subject. To these allow me to add an authority, which with many of our protestant brethren will weigh more, than that of all the fathers. Thus then Luther in his preface to the psalms; "It is a most audacious presumption in any one to say, that he understands every part even of one book of scripture."[114] Let the Chaplain recollect all the disputes and variations even amongst protestants themselves concerning the meaning of these words spoken by Christ at his last supper, this is my body. If innumerable arguments evince to him their meaning to be figurative, he cannot forget, that Luther and Dr. Cofin, a bishop of the church of England, pronounce anathemas against the maintainers of a figurative sense. After this, will he so confidently repeat his interrogation, *where is the deficiency, where is the obscurity of scripture?*

He is content, he says, to acquiesce in that authority, to which alone St. Austin, and St. Chrysostom refer us, (p. 38) insinuating hereby, that scripture is that sole authority. How he came to mention St. Augustin on this occasion, I am at a loss to conceive. This holy father has made a clear profession of receiving scripture itself, only because it came recommended to him by the church. "I would not,["] he says, ["]believe the gospel, if the authority of the catholic church did not move me thereunto."[115] In his controversies with the Manicheans and Donatists, he repeatedly appeals to the authority and practice of the catholic church; he tells the latter, that neither they, nor the catholics have any clear scripture for their different opinions concerning rebaptisation; but that the former, by refusing to submit to the church, resist not man, but our Saviour himself, who in the gospel bears testimony to the church.[116] The pretended authority from St. Chrysostom is no more his, than mine; it is a reference to the same exploded passage, as was cited in the Chaplain's note (p. 9), of which enough has been said.

I have now gone through a task, painful in every point of view, in which I could consider it. To write for the public eye, on any occasion whatever, is neither agreeable to my feelings, my leisure, or opportunities; that it is likewise disproportioned to my abilities, my readers, I doubt, will soon discover. But if reduced to the necessity of publishing, I would wish that my duty led me to any species of composition, rather than that of religious controversy. Mankind have conceived such a contempt for it, that an author cannot entertain a hope of enjoying those gratifications, which in treating other subjects may support his spirits and enliven his imagination. Much less could I have a prospect of these incitements in the prosecution of my present undertaking. I could not forget in the beginning, progress, and conclusion of it, that the habits of thinking, the prejudices, perhaps even the passions of many of my readers would be set against all the arguments, I could offer; and that the weaknesses, the errors, the absurdities of the writer would be imputed to the errors and absurdity of his religion. But of all considerations the most painful was, that I had to combat him, with whom I had been connected in an intercourse of friendship and mutual good offices; and in connection with whom I hoped to have consummated my course of our common ministry in the service of virtue and religion. But when I found these expectations disappointed; when I found that he not only had abandoned our faith and communion, but had imputed to us doctrines foreign to our belief, and having a natural tendency to embitter against us the minds of our fellow-citizens, I felt an anguish too keen for description; and perhaps the Chaplain will experience a similar sentiment, when he comes coolly to reflect on this instance of his conduct. It did not become the friend of toleration to misinform, and to sow in minds so misinformed the seeds of religious animosity.

Under all these distressful feelings, one consideration alone relieved me in writing; and that was, the hope of vindicating your religion to your ownselves at least, and preserving the steadfastness of your faith. But even this prospect should not have induced me to engage in the controversy, if I could fear that it would disturb the harmony now subsisting amongst all christians in this country, so blessed with civil and religious liberty; which if we have the wisdom and temper to preserve, America may come to exhibit a proof to the world, that general and equal toleration, by giving a free circulation to fair argument, is the most effectual method to bring all denominations of christians to an unity of faith.

The motives, which led the Chaplain to the step he has taken, are known best to God and himself. For the vindication of his conduct, he appeals to the dictates of conscience with a seriousness and solemnity, which must add greatly to his guilt, if he be not sincere. He is anxious to impress on his readers a firm conviction, that neither views of preferment or sensuality had any influence on his determination. He appears to be jealous, that suspicions will arise unfavourable to the purity of his intentions. He shall have no cause to impute to me the spreading of these suspicions. But I must entreat him with an earnestness suggested by the most perfect good will and zealous regard for his welfare, to consider the sanctity of the solemn and deliberate engagement, which at an age of perfect maturity he contracted with Almighty God. I pray him to read the two exhortations of that *enlightened doctor* St. Chrysostom to his friend Theodorus, who, like the Chaplain, had renounced his former state, in which by a vow of celibacy he had consecrated himself to God. "You allege," says the saint to his friend, "that marriage is lawful; this I

readily acknowledge; but it is not now in your power to embrace that state; for it is certain, that one, who by a solemn engagement has given himself to God, as his heavenly spouse, if he violate this contract, commits adultery, though he should a thousand times call it marriage. Nay he is guilty of a crime so much the more enormous, as the majesty of God surpasses man. Had you been free, no one could charge you with desertion; but since you are contracted to so great a king, you are not at your own disposal.[117] See here, how far St. Chrysostom was from considering the law of celibacy as *a cruel usurpation of the unalienable right of nature, as unwarrantable in its principle, inadequate in its object, and dreadful in its consequences.* He considered a vow of celibacy as an engagement, or contract entered into with Almighty God; independent therefore of the discipline of any society as to its binding power, and not to be leased but by God's relinquishing his right to exact a rigorous compliance with the sanctity of religion was interested in the performance of so sacred an engagement, according to Deuteron. xxiii. ver. 21.[:] *When thou has bowed to the Lord our God, thou shalt not slack to pay it, because our Lord thy God will require it.—That, which is once gone out of thy lips, thou shalt observe, and shalt do as thou hast promised to our Lord thy God, and has spoken with thy proper will and thy own mouth.*
THE END.

L Annapolis: Printed by Frederick Green. Numbers replace symbols for footnotes, all of which are Carroll's and were at the foot of their proper page reference. On date, see Sep. 18, 1784.

[1] Acts xx. ver. 28.

[2] Vinc[entius] Lir[ens]. comm[entaria]. cap[itulum]. 22.

[3] Ibid. ver. 30.

[4] Catholici noverint se cum ecclesia doctores recipere, non cum doctoribus ecclesiae fidem deferere debere. *Vinc. Lir.* comm. c. 23.

[5] Mat. v. ver. 13.

[6] Mat. v. ver. 14.

[7] 1 Pet. iii. ver. 15.

[8] England's conversion and reformation compared, Sect. 1.

[9] View of deistical writers, vol. I. Let. 10.

[10] Acts xix. ver. 19.

[11] Bellarm[ine]. de Eccl[esia]. milit[are]. 1. 3. c. 2.

[12] Bellarm. de Eccl. mil 1.3.c.3.

[13] The state and behaviour of English catholics.—London, 1780, (p. 155-6).

[14] View of deistical writers, vol. I. let. 10.

[15] Bergier, Deisme refuté par lui même—1. par[agrapha]. let. 4.

[16] Instruct[ion]. pastorale sur l'hersie—pag. 67. edit. in 4to.

[17] Reuter[,] theol[ogia]. moral[is]. p. 2. trac[tatus]. 1. quaes[tio]. 3.

[18] Si qui tamen eorum fecissent, quod in se est, Dominus eis secundum suam misericordiam providisset, mittendo eis praedicatorem fidei, sicut Petrum Cornelip. Comm. in cap[itulum]. 10. epis[ola]. ad Rom[anos]. lect[io]. 3.

[19] Nondum haereticum dico, nisi manifestata doctrina catholicae fidei, resistere maluerit. De bapt[ismo]. contr[a]. Donat. lib. 4. c. 16.

[20] Qui sententiam suam, quamvis falsam atque perversam, *nulla pertinaci animositate* defendunt, praesertim quam non audacia praesumptionis suae peperunt, sed a seductis atque in errorem lapsis parentibus acceperunt quaerunt autem causa sollicitudine veri-

tatem, corrigi parati cum invenerint, *nequaquam sunt inter haereticos deputandi.* Aug. epis. 43. ad Glorium & Eleusium.

²¹ I will set down two propositions, which the Chaplain will remember to have been generally taught in the schools of theology, which we both frequented. 1. *Possibilis est ignorantia invincibilis juris naturae, quoad conclusiones remotiores a primis principiis.* 2. *Ignorantia invincibilis juris naturae excusat a peccato.* I will take this occasion to thank my former friend for the justice he has done (p. 15. note) to the body of men, to which in our happier days we both belonged; and whom the world will regret, when the want of their services will recall the memory of them and the voice of envy, of obloquy, of misrepresentation will be heard no more. I am sorry, he mixed one word with their commendations, which cannot be admitted; and that he should ascribe ironically to the *tender mercy and justice of the church* those oppressions and acts of violence, in which she had no part, and which were only imputable to the unworthy condescension, and, I fear, sinister views of an artful and temporising pontiff.

²² Chilling. Religion of Protestants, &c. ch. 7. p. 306.
²³ Let. p. 11, 12.
²⁴ Aug. 1. 3. cont. Julian. c. 9.
²⁵ Let. p. 17.
²⁶ 1 Cor. i. ver. 23.
²⁷ Luke xvi. ver. 24.
²⁸ Mumford, Quest. of Quest. sect. 15.
²⁹ Manning, *Shortest Way to end disputes about religion,* chap. 1.
³⁰ Letter to a friend concerning infallibility. London, 1743.
³¹ Shortest way, &c.
³² Ephes. iv. ver. 14.
³³ Shortest way, &c. sect. 2.
³⁴ Mat. xxviii. ver. 20, 21.
³⁵ 2 Cor. 8v. ver. 1.
³⁶ Shortest way to end disputes, chap. 1. sect. 2.
³⁷ The true Church of Christ, p. 2. ch. 3. sect. 3. Shortest way, &c. part 2. sect. 2.
³⁸ Just. Mart. Dial. cum Tryph. p. 306. edit. Colon. ann. 1687.
³⁹ Euseb. Hist. Eccl. 1. 3. c. 28.
⁴⁰ Note, ibid.
⁴¹ Bell. de Sanct. Beatitud. 1. I.
⁴² P. 33.
⁴³ Acts xv. v. 1.
⁴⁴ See Chap. Lett. p. 34.

⁴⁵ Dr. Warburton, late bishop of Gloucester, founded an annual course of lectures to prove the apostasy of papal Rome. Dr. Hurd's discourses were the first on this occasion.

⁴⁶ See this acknowledged by Dr. Coffin, Bishop of Durham, in his Scholastic History of the Canon of Scripture, ch. 1 [*symbol*—section] 8. edit. London, 1672.

⁴⁷ Chrys. hom. 3. in 2 Thess. 2.

⁴⁸ *Opus imperfectum in Matthaeum.* The author adopts the Manichaean, the Montanist, and Arian heresies. In the first homily, he says, that *marriage is a sin.* In the 32d. that second marriage *is only an honourable fornication;* in the 49th, he calls the catholic doctrine of the divinity of Christ, the homousian, or consubstantiation heresy.

⁴⁹ In this author, the Chaplain may find the clearest condemnation of his new religious principles. I refer him to the 35, 36, 37, 39, and 39 chapters, which I wish I could translate without swelling this address to too great a bulk.

⁵⁰ Quid facient catholici homines, & matris ecclesiae filii? quonam modo in scripturis sanctis veritatem a falsitate discernment? Hoc scilicet facere curabunt, quod in principio commonitorii istius sanctos viros nobis tradidisse scripsimus; ut divinum canonem secundum universalis ecclesiae traditiones, & juxta catholici dogmatis regulas interpretenter. *Vince. Lir. Com.* c. 38.

⁵¹ See page 58, of this address, and Mumford's Question of Questions, point first and second.

⁵² Chaplain's note, p. 9.

[53] Note, p. 9.

[54] Omnia delibera cum amico; sed prius delibera de amico.

[55] See Bergier, *Deisme refute*, &c. let. 4.

[56] See *Irenaeus* contr. Haer. 1.3, c.3. *Tertul.* 1. de praeser, c. 32 *Opt. Milev.* 1.2 cont. Parm. *August.* in pl. contra par. Donati, & lib. contra ep. Fund. cap. 4.

[57] See Berengarius's retractations and his profession of faith in Bellarmine, 1. 3. de Euch. c. 21.

[58] Hic auctor primus fuit, who serio & copiose scripsit de veritate corporis & sanguinis Domini in eucharistia *contra Bertamum presbyterum, qui fuit ex primis, qui eam in dubium revocarunt.* Bell. de Scrip. Eccl. ad an. 810, de Paschasio Radberto.

[59] Letter, 0. 32.

[60] Quamvis ex hoc quidam de ignorantia errent, *nemo* tamen est adhuc in aperto, qui hoc ita esse contradicat, quod totus orbis credit & confitetur. *Pasch. Rabd.* epis. ad Frudeg. Bibl. P.P. tom. 9. par. 1. pag. 246.

[61] Videat, qui contra hoc venire voluerit, quid agat contra ipsum Dominum; & contra *omnem Christi ecclesiam.* Nefarium ergo scelus est orare cum omnibus, & non credere; quod veritas ipsa testatur, & *ubique omnes universaliter* verum esse fatentur. *Ibid.*

[62] Dicis te antea credidisse; sed profiteris, quod in libro *de doctrina christiana* Beati Augustini legisti, quod typica sit locutio: quo si figurata locutio est, est schema potius, quam veritas; nescio, inquis, qualiter illud sumere debeam. *Ep. ad Frude. ibid.*

[63] Let. p. 32.

[64] Note. p. 29.

[65] Fleury, ibid.

[66] Ratram. ap auct. *Perp. de la foi.*

[67] Let. p. 33.

[68] Vinc. Lir. Comm. ci. 32.

[69] See the decrees of this council published by the learned *Mabillon.*

[70] Ap. Bell. lib. 3. de Cuch. c. 21.

[71] Labbe, C.C. tom. 10. apud auct. *True Ch. of Christ.*

[72] Contra orbem sentire caeisti—contra catholicam veritatem; & contra *omnium* ecclesiarium opinionem scriptum postea condidisti. Lanfr. c. 1. apud auct. *Perp. de la foi.*

[73] Ibid.

[74] Ibid.

[75] Neque enim eis ulla civitatula, vel etiam una cillula concessit.

[76] Ibid.

[77] Chaplain's letter, p. 31.

[78] Histoire Litteraire de Fr. t. 6.

[79] Ut *evidenter cogat* transubstantiationem admittere. Scot. opua Bell. L. 3. de Euch. c. 23.

[80] P. 24, note.

[81] Cyril. Hier. Catech. Myst. 4.

[82] Gauden, Brix. Serm. 2.

[83] Socrates Hist. Eccl. 1. 2. c. 20.

[84] Ibid. c. 19. prope finem.

[85] Soc. Hist. Eccl. l. 1. c. 23. ed. Val.

[86] De Spir. fan. lib. 3. 12.

[87] Chrys. hom. 60. *ad Pop. Antioch.*—and, *de Sacerd.* lib. 6.

[88] Since writing the above, I have found, in the Annapolis library, Binius's Greek and Latin edition of the Acts of the 2d council of Nice; I have carefully examined these acts, but can meet with nothing similar to the opinion attributed to the council by the Chaplain, but the contrary doctrine repeatedly established, and the error rejected with horror, which ascribed to Christ only an apparent or phantastical body. See *Concil. Gener.* Vol. V. act. 5. p. 703, 4, 5, 6.

[89] 1 Cor. i.

[90] Ch. Let. p. 24.

[91] Chrys. hom. 82. (al. 83.) in Matt.

[92] Blasphemos in Deum, damnatam sectam, mendaces homines, panivoros, vini-bibones. *Luth. in parva Conf.*

[93] Conc. Trid. sess. 25.

[94] Neither Jerome or Gregory reject these books. The former says, they are not in the Hebrew canon (formed by Esdras, before they were written), nor universally received. But he himself held them to be of divine inspiration. *Comm.* in c. xxiii. Isaiae—in c. vii. & ix. Eccl—in c. viii. Daniel. And Gregory, who was posterior to the council of Carthage, which declared their canonical authority, can only mean, that they had not been so received by all the churches. As to Athanasius, if the Chaplain ground his assertion, as I suspect, on a writing entitled *Synopsis,* and bearing his name, that work is rejected by all the critics, as falsely imputed to him.

[95] Epiph. Haer. 75, alias 76.

[96] Aug. de Haeresibus—Haer. 53.

[97] Cyril. Hier. Catec. Myst. 1[?] 9. edit. Bened. *alias* cat. 60.

[98] Chrys. in i. ad. Cor. hom. 41—*alias* 51.

[99] De Poen. Qaes. 2. art.

[100] Ep. 1. ad Sympron. Nov.

[101] Aug. l. de Vera Rel. c. 7.

[102] Aug. cont. epis. Fundam. c. 4.

[103] Vinc. Lir. Com. c. 38.

[104] 1 Tim. c. 4.

[105] The Chaplain in a note (p. 35) obviates the meaning here insinuated, and attempts to shew an opposition between the exposition of this article of the creed in the catechism of the council of Trent, and that of many of our religious instructors. But they must be ignorant instructors indeed, who know not that by believing in God, we profess to believe both that he is, and that his word is infallible, as being founded in the divine perfections of infinite wisdom and truth; whereas by believing the catholic church, we make profession of acknowledging her existence; and that God communicates to us through her those truths, which we must receive, not as the words of man; but as they truly are, the words of God. Just so the Chaplain admits the scriptural doctrines delivered by the apostles and evangelists; nevertheless he does not fail *in making a sufficient difference between God and his creatures;* but he knows that divine omnipotence can render *mortal men* infallible in communicating revealed doctrines to others; and which must ultimately be believed for the authority of God alone.

[106] Cyp. ep. 76. ad Magnum.

[107] Aug. ep. 93 (olim 48) ad Vincentium.

[108] P. 36.

[109] Vinc. Lir. comm. c. 31.

[110] Aug. de Bapt. contra Donat. 1. 4. c. 6.

[111] 2 Thess. ii. ver. 15.

[112] 2 Pet. iii. ver. 16.

[113] Chrys. hom. 3. de Lazaro.

[114] Scio esse impudentissimae temeritatis eum, qui audeat profiteri unum scripturae librum a se in omnibus partibus intellectum. *Luth. praef. in Psal.* ap. bell. de R. P. 1. 3. c. 21.

[115] Ego vero evangelio non crederem, nisi me ecclesiae catholicae commoveret auctoritas. *Aug. cont. Epis.* Fundam. c. 5.

[116] Aug. lib. 1. cont. Cresc. c. 33.—& de Unit. Eccl. c. 22.

[117] Chrys. ad Theod. laps. Exh. 2.

TO MADAME GOUSÉS[1]   Feb. 12. 1784

Not found. See from same, Jan. 9. 1784 (8ARl).

[1] French emigrée nun, seeking refuge in Albany.

Eleanor Darnall Carroll (1703/4–1796)

Daniel Carroll of Upper Marlboro II and Rock Creek
(1730–1796)

Eleanor Carroll (Mrs. Wm. Brent) (1737- ?)

Charles Carroll of Carrollton (1737–1832)

Birthplace of John Carroll in Upper Marlboro, Maryland

A Replica of St. John's Chapel,
Rock Creek, Maryland

Old St. Peter's Church, Baltimore, Maryland

Chapel at Lulworth Castle

COMMENT ON THOMAS TALBOT LETTER Febry 28—1784

feasts & fasts—Advent wednesdays

AM   AAB (8Fl)

TO CHARLES PLOWDEN Maryland April 10th 1784

My Dr Sir   On the 4th I had the pleasure of receiving yours of the first of Novr 1783: By a letter of mine to you written some time last autumn, you will have before this received information of the happy, tho' late arrival of your favour of Aug: 1782: and if your other kind letters never came to hand, you have only to blame the unsleeping avidity of your own cruisers, whom I should call pirates, were I inclined to follow your example of abusing the political measures of our adversaries. For since the object of the war on your side, the right of parliamentary taxation is now confessedly & by every moderate man on both continents, acknowledged to have been unjust, surely every measure to attain that object must likewise have been unjust; and consequently your cruisers with all their commissions were nothing more than pirates. Thus much to retaliate for your stroke at our *faithless leaders* & *faithless allies;* after which we will be done with politicks. Your intelligence from Russia, tho' not quite new to me, is truly comfortable: what a wonderful display of the power of divine providence over the wily politicks of wicked and oppressive tyranny of powerful men would a general restoration of the Society exhibit? I say a restoration; for with all my penetration I cannot discover the arguments made use of to evince, that it was never totally destroyed: and I do not chuse to surrender the clearest principles of reasoning for the sake of supporting the credit of some pious prophecies & visions.

Poor Mr. Howard! what a dreadful loss to the Academy? & what an unexpected stroke to me? I had long considerd him not only as my friend, but as an active and zealous friend, on whom I knew I could depend, whenever I should have occasion to put his friendship to the test. I have already communicated the doleful intelligence to some of our Gentlemen; and I am sure that all, who knew him will feel his loss, as if it were peculiar to himself. I fear indeed, it will be fatal to the academy, when added to the stoppage of the Bavarian pension and its heavy debts. You treat poor Aston with great severity; indeed, my Dr Charles, I think with too much, after so close an intimacy, cemented by such severe common sufferings. You lived with him in the academy during the whole time, that he had any authority or administration in it. In your letter, which I still preserve, you bore the most ample testimony to his good conduct: were you not then more likely to discover his maladministration, than when you could have nothing to vouch for it, but the reports, perhaps the envious reports of others? If the revenues of the academy sufferd in his hands, I am satisfied it arose from indolence, and unbounded generosity, and perhaps from a fond persuasion that he should be able to replace the monies he made use of, not for his own emolument, but for his friends & to do honour to the academy. It is not uncommon for men of great & expanded hearts to let their generosity carry them too far. I do not mean to insinuate, that this is not blameable in an administrator; but surely it is an alleviation of their misconduct, that they did not apply the unaccounted sums to the improvement of their own fortune; which the state of his debts, and sequestration of his prebend, as mentioned by you, is a clear proof he did not. Poor fellow! I most sincerely pity him & heartily wish it were in my power to relieve one whom I shall ever remember with gratitude. And yet think not, that I was ever blind to his faults. No one, I believe, ever told him of them with more freedom, than myself; and he had some faults, which in a Religious man, or indeed in one professing a belief in the Xtian Religion, I greatly disapproved; such as holding some principles, which, if carried to their remotest consequences, appeared to me, tho' it was always denied by him to terminate in infidelity. I have wrote three or four times to him, & I know that he must have received some of my letters. But having had no answer, I shall trouble him no more; neither him indeed, nor my friend Ellerker. But my correspondence with you will, I hope, continue, as long as we both live.

I note what you write of the Propgda and Mr Jn Thyers.[1] Dr Franklin has sent in to Congress copy of a note deliverd him by the Nuncio at Paris, which I shall inclose in this. I did not see it before Congress had sent their instructions to their Minister in answer thereto; and the answer, I am well informd, is, that Congress have no answer to give, the matter proposed not being in their department, but resting with the different States. But this you may be assured of; that no authority derived from the Propagda will ever be admitted here; that the Catholick Clergy & Laity here know that the only connexion they ought to have with Rome is to acknowledge the pope as the Spirl head of the Church; that no Congregations existing in his states shall be allowed to exercise any share of his Spirl authority here; that no Bishop Vicar Apostolical shall be admitted; and if we are to have a Bishop, he shall not be *in partibus* but an ordinary national Bishop, in whose appointment Rome shall have no share.

Our Brethren have in a meeting held last Octr settled, or nearly settled a plan of internal government, which will meet with your approbation, being founded on Xtian and rational principles. You desire me to be particular about my friend and Relation Ch. Wharton for special reasons: I believe I know what those reasons are; for you mentioned them in a former letter; & Mr Thos Talbot has done the same. He lives upwards of sixty miles from me upon his own estate (with his Br) which is valuable, & will be renderd much more so by his activity & good sense. He has just had judgment, against the

Executors of his Frs will, for a large sum, near £St.1000: he brought in no faculties from the London district, to wch we were then subject, & therefore exercises none. He leads a life clear of all offence, & gives no handle to censure, tho' there are not wanting, who would be glad to find room for it. He is neither visionary or fanatick, *un peu philosophe,* but I hope not too much so. You may be assured he never made a friend of Hawkins;[2] tho' having received some civilities from him he returned them with politeness. His abilities I say nothing of; you know them well; and he left behind him few of our antient Brethren his equals, none, I believe, his Superiors. I am very happy to find, that you give so good an account to my pupil Ld Stourton. I infer from your letter, that Mr Strickland is your neighbour: I cannot think he will accept his appointment to the Presidency at Liege. Present my affte compliments to him & assurances of perfect esteem. Be sure to say something of both the Meynells in your next. Our Italian fellow traveller continues, I dare say, to laugh at all the world. Your Brother Frank's success gives me real pleasure. Whenever you write to him or good Bernard, be sure to remember me to them in the tenderest manner. Do you ever see Mrs Crathorne? for so she still continues, as Notley Roser, who arrived last Decr, informs me. If you do, present my most respectful compliments. My Mother is much obliged to you for the mention you make of her. Every thing is dear to her, that is any way connected with her dear friend Mrs Plowden. Poor Mr Peter Morris died suddenly the latter end of Novr 1783. Any letters directed to me near George-town, Potomack River, Maryland, & left at the house of Messrs Wallace, Johnson and Muir[,] Merchts in London, or at the house of Mr Uriah Forrest[,] Mercht[,] will be carefully forwarded.

Here is a copy of the paper delivered to Dr Franklin.[3]   Ever Yrs   J.C.

ALS   St

[1] John Thayer, former Congregational minister, was ordained a Catholic priest in 1783 and ministered in New England and Kentucky.

[2] John Hawkins, the ex-Benedictine, wrote in defense of Wharton against Carroll.

[3] Carroll enters here his own transcription of Giuseppe Doria-Pamphili's (Papal Nuncio in Paris) letter to Franklin, which was intended to dispose the Congress of the U.S. to accept a Catholic prefect apostolic from Europe as successor to the American vicar apostolic. Carroll had already acted to prevent this when the American clergy was organized at White Marsh and Franklin responded to the same effect, stating that the Congress was not empowered to deal with such spiritual matters.

TO JOSEPH BERINGTON[1]   Maryland, near George town
Potowmack River July 10–1784

Revd Sir   I very lately had the singular Pleasure of reading a Work published in the year 1780 on the *State and Behaviour of the English Catholics* &c, for wch I am told the Publick is indebted to you. The long

Interruption of all Correspondence between your Country and this prevented my having any Knowledge of it till towards the Close of last year; and I could not see if for some months after. If the small share, wch I formerly had in the Honour of your acquaintance, will not sufficiently account for the Interest I feel in the publick approbation your Work has met with, I hope you will allow a Brother Clergyman to rejoice in the eminent Service thereby done to the Cause of Truth and religion, and to give you his sincerest Thanks for employing your Abilities so effectually in their Behalf. The noble and generous Freedom, wth wch you disdain to deny, or palliate weaknesses, Errors or misdemeanors of Catholicks in different Periods of their History: the animated Picture, wch you draw of the Perfidy, the intolerant, & outrageous virulence of their Enemies; and your exact Delineation of the most Defective, and ill conducted foreign English Education, all claim an equal share of merit, by tending to correct & improve ourselves, &, if possible to wrest out of the Hand of Fanaticism the rod of Oppression. You have expressed on the Subject of Toleration those Sentiments, wch I have long wished to see come strongly recommended from eminent writers of our Religion; and which I am well persuaded, are the only sentiments, that can ever establish, by being generally adopted, a reasonable system of universal Forbearance, and Charity amongst Christians of every Denomination. Indeed their Operation may extend much farther; and as you have observed, such an unlimited Toleration giving an open Field to the Display of Truth and fair argument may greatly contribute to bring mankind to an unity of Opinion on matters of Religious Concern. That your writings have been censured by a few, even the Friends of Virtue and Religion, I have no Doubt; since you have dared to express yourself with Freedom on some Subjects, wch the timid wished never to be touched upon; and to declare openly your Opposition to many opinions, particularly on the Subject of Toleration, wch the authority of some of our great schoolmen had rendered too prevalent. But I am well persuaded from the Firmness of your mind visible in every Feature of your Compositions, that you will not suffer yourself to be discouraged from rendering to Religion the Services, you are capable of affording her. I shall hope that some Time or other, you will discuss two Subjects, which have long appeared to me to sollicit the pen of a Philosophical Divine. The first is, the ascertaining of the Extent and Boundaries of the Spiritual Juridiction of the Holy See. The other the use of the Latin Tongue in the publick Liturgy. I consider these two Points as the greatest Obstacles, with Christians of other Denominations, to a thorough union with us; or at least, to a much more general Diffusion of our Religion, particularly in N. America. With respect to the latter Point, I cannot help thinking that the Alteration of this Discipline ought not only to be sollicited, but *insisted on,* as essential to the Service of God & Benefit of Mankind—[2] In spight of all Evasions, the Latin is an unknown Tongue, and in this Country, still more than yours; either for want of Books, or disability to read, the greatest part of our Congregations must be utterly ignorant of the meaning and Sense of the publick Offices of the Church. It may have been prudent to refuse a Compliance in this Instance with the insulting and reproachful Demands of the first Reformers; but to continue the practice of the Latin Liturgy in the present State of Things, must be owing either to chimerical Fears of Inovation, or to Indolence & Inattention in the first Pastors of the national Churches, in not joining to sollicit, or indeed *ordain* this necessary alteration.[3] You are happily so situated, as to have it in your power to recur to monuments & books of every kind to aid you in these beneficial pursuits to the attainment of which, I would even dedicate my labours were it possible to execute the undertaking with any degree of credit or advantage, deprived as I now am of all sources of information and assistance. If your time is employed on other objects, I hope you will recommend these points to some of your learned & liberal friends, for the sake of the great concerns, which lie so near your heart, virtue, & Religion; and that you will impute to these the freedom of this address from, Revd. Sir   Your most obedt humble Servt   J Carroll   If you should please to favr. me with an answer, direct yr. letter to the care of Messr. Wallace, Johnson & Muir, Merchts. London. or to that of Mr. Thos. Talbot at Messr. Wright, Banker.

T   St; ADf   AAB.   ALS not found, but T is assumed to be of it. The ADf has deletions, one of some length (see below).
[1] Priest and author of the *State and Behaviour of the English Catholics from the Reformation to the Year 1780* (1780), from which Carroll quoted freely in his own *Address to the Roman Catholics of the United States of America* (1784). Berington was later to reply to John Hawkins, who supported Wharton against Carroll, with *Reflections Addressed to the Rev. John Hawkins* (1785).
[2] The following sentence was deleted in the ADf version.
[3] Deletion from this point: "Can there be any thing more preposterous, than for a small district containing in extent no more than mount Libarius & a trifling territory at the foot of it, to say nothing of the Greeks, Armenians, Coptits &c to have a liturgy in their proper idiom; & on the other hand for an immenser extent of countries, containing G. B., Ireland, all N. Am., the W. Indies &c, to be obliged to perform divine Service in an unknown tongue.

TO CHARLES PLOWDEN   Rock Creek Maryland Sepr. 18–1784

My Dear Sir   I received by Mr. Pile[1] your favours from London of Ap. 4–26; and have since had the pleasure of your additional favour from Ellingham of July 3d. You are indeed a most valuable correspondent, & will, I hope, never cease to communicate with me whilst we are both able to wield a pen. You need not be afraid, that political opinions will alter my sincere regard and friendship for you. I dare say, that I never again shall much interest myself in matters of that sort; and at no time would suffer my private connexions be hurt by a difference of sentiments on matters of a publick nature. You will hear before the receipt of this, that I was much deceived in my hopes of Wharton, and that your friends had too good grounds for their fears. He not only has renounced his Religion, but has published a pamphlet,[2] which, under the colour of apology, is a malignant invective & misrepresentation of our tenets. I never expected to class amongst the number of authors: but have been induced by the compulsion of all our Gentlemen to write an answer. I have just finished it, almost without books, or other necessary helps; & indeed without much leisure as is necessary to execute a work of this kind, with any tolerable success. As soon as it is printed, you & my other friends shall receive a copy both of Wharton's letter & my address.

Your kind & sensible directions, & informations concerning Rome are very useful; and the detail, into which you enter, concerning our affairs in Russia, is most pleasing to us all. Continue to write everything you can learn on this subject. You seem to signify in yours, that you had only received one letter from me since the peace which surprises me as I am certain that I have sent you three: and in particular, I remember to have answered in Decr. last your letter of Novr. 1st. Your information concerning poor Aston is really melancholy. Has he not only given up his reputation with the world, but likewise his duty to Alm: God? I can yet learn nothing more of Mr. Thyers, than what you inform me. My Br. enquired, at my request, of some of the Delegates to Congress from Massachusetts (the capital of which is Boston), but they knew him not. He perhaps did not come from Boston, but some of the other New England states, New Hampshire, Rhode-Island, or Connecticut: and as they all go under the general denomination of Bostonians in France, (Bostonois), this may have given occasion to the mistake. I most sincerely rejoice at your Br Frank's success, & hope you will so inform him. His writings in favr. of the Derwentwater family I will read, as soon as I have leisure: if his Ldsp succeeds, he ought to settle 1000 £ per an: on Frank, at least, for life: and therefore I most cordially wish him success: but I fear, your Parlt. has too many other things to settle, before they can attend to this business. You appear to me to be in the strangest situation, I ever knew a civilised government in my life. You blame Lords Stourton & Petre[3] for interfering in elections: if they have done so to the prejudice of their fortunes, they are censurable: but if they took part no otherwise, than as independent men, openly avowing their sentiments, I cannot see why they are to blame or why the King should be displeased with the R.C., because a few of that body opposed some of his minister's favourites. We certainly should not deserve the countenance of any government, if we were never to dare to act from the impulse of our reason, and as men having an interest in the common concerns of our Country. To be candid, I must think it betrays a littleness of mind in the king, to which a man, as knowing and well read as he is said to be, ought to be superior. Messrs Pile & Boone[4] I have not seen. As you could not prevent the latter from leaving you; so neither could we prevent his coming amongst us. If he will conduct himself well, we may perhaps find a station for him: if not he must provide a subsistance, where he can.

I now come to your favr. of July 3d, previous to which I had received similar intelligence from Talbut & Thorpe. I do assure you, Dr Chs, that nothing personal to myself, excepting the dissolution of the Society, ever gave me so much concern: and if a meeting of our Gentlemen to be held the 9th, of Octr, agree in thinking that I can decline the intended office without grievous inconvenience I shall certainly do so. I observe that your opinion coincides entirely with my own in believing that the propgda adopted the present measure merely thro' fear of our chusing a Bishop, & getting it recommended by the government here to have him made [*ind.*] To govern the spiritual concerns of this country, as a mission, is absurd, seeing there is a regular Clergy belonging to it; & with Gods assistance there will be in time, a succession of ministry to supply their places, as they drop off. The propgda hope, by appointing a Bp now, to establish the precedent of appointing one hereafter: but little do they know of the jealousy entertained here of foreign jurisdictions. In my last letter, I sent you copy of a note deliverd to Dr. Franklin by the Nunzio; & transmitted to Congress by the Dr.: I likewise told you the Congress's answer. Nothing can place in a stronger light, the propgda's aversion to the remains of the Socty, than the observation made by you of a negotiation being carried on, relative to the affairs of Religion, between the Ct. of Rome & Franklin, without the former ever deigning to apply for information to the Catholick Clergy in this Country. You have my sincere thanks for all the zeal you exert & express in our concerns. Continue to do so, & God will be your reward. I was sincerely glad to hear, that the Latin letter, sent off from hence last fall, was not presented in its rude form to his Holiness. Diderick, a good, but wrongheaded Walloon J[esui]t, among us, had prepared it before our meeting, and was so pleased with his perfor-manance that he had said, he would send it in his own name; if not adopted by the rest. We therefore agreed to send it, but left it discretional with Mr. Thorpe to present or not; which I was sure he would not do. However, I could see the other day, when I read your letter to some of our Gentlemen that he was not pleased.

This, I presume, will find you settled at Lullworth.[5] Be pleased to present my kind remembrance to your disinterested & generous Companion Mr. Clinton. How could he renounce London, & *la brillante direction* &c? I think, I have heared that Mr. Thos. Stanley[6] lives there likewise: if he does, I get you to assure him of my particular esteem & veneration.

When I first heared, that the Nunzio was treating with my old friend Dr. Franklin, I had thoughts of writing to him, & should certainly have done it, had I not been afraid of placing myself in a conspicuous point of view, & brought upon myself, what I now find is come to pass. I wished to give the old Gentleman a right understanding of the views of the propgda. Their paper delivered to him was insulting, and they deserved no management from us. Had I received timely information before Congress sent their answer, I flatter myself it would have been even more satisfactory to us, than the one which was sent, tho a good one. My Brs triennium in Congress has just expired; & Mr. Fitzsimmons,[7] the only Catholic member beside, had just resigned: these were unfortunate circumstances. You will perhaps sometimes see my good & old friend Mr. Jn Brewer. Pray remember me both to him & his Br. Tom very kindly, as likewise to all my old acquaintance: forget not John Edisford of Execter, if within your reach. My Mother presents her respects.   Dr Chs   Yrs &c   J Carroll

ALS   St
[1] Henry Pile, S.J., ministered in Yorkshire, England, returned to Maryland in 1784, and died at Newtown.
[2] *A Letter to the Roman Catholics of the City of Worcester* (Philadelphia, 1784).
[3] Robert Edward, 9th Baron Petre, played a leading part in the struggles for Catholic emancipation.
[4] John Boone, S.J., went to England in 1770, returned in 1784, and died at St. Ignatius Mission.
[5] Lulworth Castle in Dorset, residence of the Weld family, and place of Carroll's episcopal consecration.
[6] Rev. Thomas Stanley signed the official certificate of Carroll's consecration.
[7] Thomas Fitzsimons, a native of Ireland, signer of the Constitution.

CONSTITUTION OF THE CLERGY (CONTINUED)   Oct. 11, 1784

See June 27, 1783.

TO GIUSEPPE DORIA–PAMPHILI[1]   November 26 of the year 1784

I have had the honor, My Lord, of receiving the letter which your Excellency deigned to write me on July 5 of the same year. I have received it with the respect due to your illustrious birth; and with the veneration inspired by your Excellency's eminent qualities which I heard eulogized on every occasion during my stay in Rome in 1772. Mr. Marbois,[2] the Minister of His Most Christian Majesty to the United States of America, honored me by transmitting at the same time á packet from the Congr. of the Propaganda. It contained a mark of His Holiness' confidence, very flattering to me, but at the same time too far beyond my capacities to acquit myself in the manner demanded by the extremely delicate and laborious charge in this country. Your Excellency will understand easily this delicacy in reviewing in spirit the nature of our governments, and their jealousy of all foreign jurisdiction: a jealousy which has excluded Catholics from any part in the civil administration of several of our states. True, they are tolerated everywhere; but it is only in Pennsylvania, Delaware, Maryland, and Virginia that they enjoy advantages common to those of other citizens. The revolution from which we have just emerged has procured this advantage of toleration and of admission to civil functions.

We must use extreme circumspection in order not to give pretexts to the enemies of Religion to deprive us of our actual rights. It is very important that the prejudices entertained for so long against Catholics be eradicated. Above all, the opinion which several hold that our faith demands a subjection to His Holiness incompatible with the independence of a sovereign state, quite false as it is, cannot help giving us continual anxiety. To dissipate these prejudices it will take time, the protection of divine Providence, and the experience they will have of our devotion to the nation and to its sovereignty. The wisdom of the Holy See cannot fail to contribute to it. Your Excellency could, & I dare in the name of the Catholics to beg you to assure the Apostolic See that nowhere in the world has it children more attached to its doctrine or more filled with respect for all its decisions.

In finishing, My Lord, dare I request for myself the powerful protection of Your Excellency, and that you permit me, as long as I shall be in office, to address you in all the difficulties which will arise, and on all the occasions when I find myself having recourse to the Holy See. I can assure you that my intention is never to seek things of a personal nature, & to solicit your mediation only for the advantage and spread of Religion. I would do it with as great confidence as I am persuaded that Your Excellency never employs his influence with greater zeal than when favor of a weak portion of the church too far from the edifying examples which enliven the faith and piety in Catholic countries, and too exposed to the contagion of heresies not to need every support which it could derive from a spirit as enlightened and as devoted to the interests of Religion as is Your Excellency's.

In the letter for His Eminence, Cardinal Antonelli,[3] which I have the honor of transmitting to Your Excellency, I have informed him of the reasons which prevent me at present from sending the two young Americans to be trained in the Urban College. I will do everything to conform to Your Excellency's orders after having received the clarifications which I request His Eminence to communicate to me. The route from Marseilles would be less expensive, but I doubt that an opportunity will present itself from here for this voyage. The departure of vessels for Cadiz is rather frequent and in the event His Holiness maintains a consul there, I submit to Your Excellency whether it would not be preferable to send him the young men to be sent from there to Civita Vecchia or Leghorn rather than expose them to the expenses and discomforts of a journey on land from l'Orient or Nantes to Paris, and from Paris to Rome. I have deferred until now through necessity giving myself the honor of replying to Your Excellency. When I received your letter I was far from my regular dwelling, lacking moreover any favorable opportunity for sending the packets I intended to write. Since Christmas, when I have been able to be at home, our commerce has been interrupted by ice; it is only the last few days that it has opened for vessels destined for Europe. J.C.

ADf   AAB   The last two paragraphs seem to have been written on Feb. 27, 1785.
[1] Papal Nuncio at Paris.
[2] François, Marquis de Barbé-Barbois, successor of Luzerne as *chargé d'affaires* until 1785.
[3] Leonardo Cardinal Antonelli, Prefect of *Congregatio de Propaganda Fide.*

le 26 de Nov. de l'an 1784   J'ai eu l'honneur, Monseigneur, de reçevoir la lettre que Votre Exc. daigna m'écrire le 5 de juillet de la même année. Je l'ai reçu avec le respect du à votre illustre naissance; et avec la vénération, que, m'ont inspiré les qualités éminentes de V. Ex. dont j'entendis faire l'éloge dans toute occasion, pendant mon séjour à Rome en l'année 1772. Monsr. de Marbois, Ministre du roi très Chrétien auprès des Etats Unis de l'Amérique, me fit l'honneur de me transmettre en même temps, le paquet de la Congn. de la Propagande. Il contenoit une marque de la confiance de sa Sainteté, bien honorable pour moi, mais en même temps trop au dessus de mes forces pour pouvoir m'en acquitter de la manière qu'exige un emploi extrémement delicat en çe pais et très laborieux. V. Exc. en comprendra la délicatesse en repassant dans son esprit la nature de nos gouvernements, et leur jalousie de toute juridiction étrangère: jalousie qui a fait exclude les Catholiques de toute part à l'administration civile de plusieurs des Etats Unis. Ils sont en vérité tolérés partout; mais il n'y a qu'en Pennsulvanie, le Delaware, le Maryland, et la Virginie qu'ils jouissent en tout des avantages communs aux autres citoyens. La révolution dont nous venons de sortir, a procuré cet avantage de tolérance partout, et de l'admissibilité aux emplois civils en quelques états. La circonspection est extreme, dont nous devons user, pour ne pas donner des prétextes aux adversaires de la religion de nous chicaner nos droits actuels: Il s'en faut beaucoup que les préjugés entretenus depuis si longtems contre les Catholiques, soient déracinés. L'opinion surtout, que plusieurs se sont formés, que notre foi exige une sujetion à Sa Sainteté incompatible avec l'independance d'un état souverain, toute fausse qu'elle est, ne laisse pas de nous donner des inquiétudes continuelles. Ce sera au temps, à dissiper ces préjugés, à la protection de la divine Providence, à l'experience qu'on aura de notre dévouement à la patrie, et à sa souveraineté. La sagesse du Saint Siège ne manquera pas y contribuer; V. Exc. pourra & j'ose au nom des Catholiques la prier de l'assurer que la chaire apostolique n'a point au monde des enfans plus attachés à sa doctrine, ni plus pénétrés de respect pour toutes ses décisions.

Oserai-je, Monseigneur, en finissant, demander pour moi la puissante bienveillance de V. Ex., et qu'elle voudra bien permettre, tant que je serai dans mon emploi actuel, de m'addresser à elle, dans toute les difficultés, qui s'éléveront, et dans toute les occasions, où je me trouverai dans le cas de recourir au S. Siège. Je puis l'assurer, que mon intention est, de ne jamais importuner pour des choses qui me seront personnelles, et de ne solliciter sa médiation que pour l'avantage et l'accroissement de la religion. Je le ferai avec d'autant plus d'assurance, que je suis persuadé que votre Ex. n'emploie jamais son crédit avec plus de zéle, qu'en faveur d'une faible portion de l'église trop éloignée des examples édifians que animent la foi et la piété dans les pays Catholiques; et trop exposée à la contagion des heresies pour n'avoir pas besoin de tous les soutiens que peut lui fournir un esprit aussi éclairé et aussi dévoué aux intérets de la religion qu'est celui de votre Exc.

Dans la lettre pour son Em le Cardinal Antonelli, que j'ai l'honneur de transmettre a V. Exc., je l'ai informé des raisons qui m'empèchent pour le présent d'envoyer les deux jeunes Américains pour etre élevés au college Urbain. Je ne manquerai pas de me conformer aux ordres de votre Exc. après avoir reçu les eclaircissemens que je prie son Em. de me communiquer. Le chemin de Marseilles seroit moins dispendieux. Mais je doute que l'occasion se présente d'ici pour ce voyage. Le départ des vaisseaux pour Cadiz est assez fréquent; et au cas que sa Sainteté y entretienne un consul, je soumets à votre Exc. s'il ne seroit pas préférable de lui addresser les jeunes gens pour être delà envoyés à Cività Vecchia ou à Livourne, plutot que de les exposer aux frais et désagrémens d'un voyage par terre de l'orient ou de Nantes à Paris et de Paris à Rome.

J'ai différé a ce [moment?—*sic*] de me faire l'honneur de répondre a Votre Exc.: En reçevant sa lettre j'étois loin de ma demeure ordinaire: manquant d'ailleurs une occasion favorable d'envoyer les paquets que je me proposois d'écrire. Depuis le Noel que je me trouvois en état de retourner chez moi, notre navigation a été interrompue par les gelées. Ce n'est que depuis peu de jours qu'elle est ouverte pour les vaisseaux destinés en Europe.   J. C.

TO FERDINAND FARMER [Dec., 1784]

Revd. Dr. Sir   I have to inform you, & request you to transmit the same intelligence to the Gentlemen in your district, that I have received a decree of the Congregation of the Propaganda appointing me Superior of the *missions* in these thirteen states, *ad suum beneplacitum* . . . cum auctoritate ea exercendi, quo ad earundem missionum regimen pertinent, ad proscriptum decretorum Sacre Congnis, et facultatum eidem concessarum et non alias, *nec alio modo.*[1]

At the same time, I received an order of his Holiness empowering me to administer Confirmation in the said thirteen States.

And, finally, a letter from Cardinal Antonelli, Prefect of the Propaganda, advising me that his holiness has extended to these thirteen States the indult of the Jubilee, celebrated in Rome, an: 1775, & in the rest of the Christian world, an: 1776, & the time for gaining it to be, one year from the day of my receiving the decree, which was Novr. 26th. 1784.

The faculties, I have received, are much too confined for the exigencies of this Country; and there are moreover some circumstances in the granting of them which require the maturest consideration, They come, it seems, from the Congregation of the *Propaganda;* they are granted during their pleasure *only;* and they consider us as *missioners;* and our labours as employed in *mission,* I have likewise some other information, both publick and private, which inclines and indeed compels me to think, that the view of that Congregation is, to establish their authority here in such a manner, that no Clergymen be allowed, besides such, as are approved and sent into the Country by them.

I am moreover advised by Cardinal Antonelli, that his Holiness intends to appoint hereafter (but no term mentioned or even insinuated) a Vicar Apostolical with Episcopal character, and with such powers, as may exempt this country from every other Ecclesiastical dependence, besides that on the aforesaid Congregation. But not the slightest intimation is given of the person designed for that preferment.

Our real friends, both at Rome and in England, recommend the most perfect unanimity amongst ourselves: they advise that the slightest appearance of disagreement will be made a handle to push forward the schemes of those, who wish to leave no authority, whereever a member of our former Society must be employed in the exercise of it.

I will now take the liberty to communicate my observations on all this intelligence; and since unanimity is so much recommended, I shall be exceedingly happy to find that they harmonise with your own, since they will be the rule of my conduct.

1. I consider powers issued from the Propaganda not only as improper, but dangerous here. The jealousy in our Governments if the interference of any foreign jurisdiction is known to be such that we cannot expect, & in my opinion ought not to wish, that they would tolerate any other, than that which being purely spiritual, is essential to our Religion, to wit, an acknowledgement of the Pope's spiritual Supremacy, & of the see of S. Peter being the center of Ecclesiastical unity. The appointment therefore by the Propaganda of a Superior for this Country appears to be a dangerous step, &, by exciting the jealousy of the governments here may lend much to the prejudice of Religion, & perhaps expose it to the reproach of encouraging a dependance on a foreign power, & giving them an undue internal influence by leaving with them a prerogative to nominate to places of trust & real importance, & that *ad suum beneplacitum.*

2. The Congregation of the Propgda, if I understand its institution, was formed only for the government and superintendence of missions &c: and I observe, that they affect, in their Commission to me and other acts, to call our Ecclesiastical state here a *mission,* & the labourers therein, *missioners.* Perhaps this denomination was heretofore proper enough: but it cannot now be so deemed. By the Constitution, our Religion has acquired equal rights & privileges with that of other Christians: we form not a fluctuating body of

labourers in Christ's vineyard, sent hither, & removeable at the will of a Superior; but a permanent body of national Clergy, with sufficient powers to form our own system of internal government, &, I think, to chuse our own Superior, & a very just claim to have all necessary Spiritual authority communicated to him, on his being presented as regularly and canonically chosen by us. We have, farther reasonable prospect, which I soon hope to see realised, of forming an establishment for educating & perpetuating a succession of Clergy amongst ourselves: and as soon as that measure is in a promising forwardness, we shall have a right to a diocesan Bishop of our own choice. "Ought not the immense territory possessed by the thirteen United States to have an Ecclesiastical Superior as independent as the Bishop of Quebeck," says one of our zealous friends in England.

For these reasons therefore, I intend to represent strongly to Rome, 1st, that nothing but the present extreme necessity of some spiritual powers here could induce me to act under a commission, which *may* produce, if long continued, & it should become public, the most dangerous jealousy. 2ly, that the Clergy here consider themselves as a national Clergy, & not as missioners; competent to the choice of their Ecclesiastical Superior, and only wanting that spiritual connexion with the holy See, which shall be an evidence of our sincere attachment to & union with it. 3ly. that from our present prospect of instituting a seminary for the education of young Clergymen, we shall in a few years stand in absolute need of a Bishop; but that a Bishop Vicar Apostolic, would give great umbrage here, on acct of his entire dependance, both for his station and conduct, on a foreign jurisdiction, he must be a Diocesan Bishop; & his appointment must come, neither from his holiness, (for that would create more jealousy in our government, than even in France, Germany, or Spain) nor from the assemblies, or different executives which being composed of discordant Religionists, would be very improper for the business; but he should be chosen by the Catholic Clergy themselves; this having been the mode in which the Episcopal Protestant Clergy has been suffered to proceed.

With respect to the power of Confirmation, nothing can be done till I receive Blessed oil for that purpose.[2]

A general letter to the same purport, signed by each of us now in Maryld. and Pennsylvania, could not fail of commanding respect, and would evidence our perfect agreement and unanimity: as soon as it is known that a willingness prevails to join in such a measure a letter may be draughted transmitted for approbation, & then signed.

I propose shortly transmitting directions for publishing the Jubilee.

The same faculties, in the administration of the Sacrament of pennance, and with regard to dispensations, as have been heretofore granted by the Vicars Apostolical, are for the present, renewed to all the Gentlemen of yr. district.

Having said thus much concerning & in consequence of the advice from Rome I shall now communicate the observations of our most intelligent friends concerning the proposal at present on foot for erecting a College on the W. shore of this state. I make no doubt, you have seen these proposals, as they have been circulated thro' the Counties, and some of our Gentlemen appointed to solicit subscriptions.

The R. Catholics are too inconsiderable in point of wealth to erect & support a college; & we Clergymen are too few to supply a sufficient number of masters for the entire education of youth, if even such a College existed. In this situation the only reasonable prospect of raising a succession of ministers for the service of Religion here is, that in the number of Catholic Youth who receive their Grammar education in the College of Philada, & in those of Maryland,[3] there may be perhaps one or two every year, desirous of engaging themselves in the service of the Church to which will much contribute a good deal of attention on the part of the priest destined to attend these youths either in the Colleges, or in the towns, where they are or may be: it being an intended stipulation that provision be made, from the College funds, if necessary, to procure all of them opportunities to frequent their particular forms of worship. This joind to the suggestions of their parents, and other inducements will, with the blessing of providence, prepare some of the Cat. youth for a Religious vocation. After which, the business will be to form them to the virtues necessary for their state, and give them a Theological institution: and here will appear the necessity of a Seminary for yng Clergymen to the raising of which all our savings, all the contributions of our friends must be directed. In such a seminary, which may be contiguous to one of our own houses, we need have only one elderly Gentleman unfit for hard labour, but of approved virtue, & conduct to train the young men to the duties of their State, and one other, a man of learning & abilities to teach them Divinity. I know that we shall all discover inconveniencies & danger of immorality in these mixed Colleges but are we able to do any thing better. Is it not a good rule, to consider the advantages to be made of new institutions, rather than study to find out the objections which beset them. Being admitted to equal toleration, must we not concur in public measures, & avoid separating ourselves from the Community? Shall we not otherwise be marked, as forming distinct views, & raise a dislike which may terminate in consequences very disagreeable to us?

ADf   AAB

[1] "*according to its will* . . . with the authority of exercising it, insofar as what pertains to the governing of the same missions, according to the written direction of the decrees of the Sacred Congregation, and the faculties conceded to the same and no others, *nor in any other way.*"

[2] Two sentences, the last incomplete, are crossed out at this point. They inquire about an appropriate time for the Jubilee Year.

[3] St. John's and Washington Colleges.

SERMON ON GRATITUDE [1785]

God has visited you in particular by a signal instance of his mercy in removing obstacles which heretofore cramped the free exercise of our Religious functions. Our meeting together in this place to perform our public worship; that cross, the signal: of our faith & monument of its triumphs over the powers of idolatry & infidelity that altar erected to perpetuate the great sacrifice of the law of grace, & continued oblation of Christ's body & blood, as a propitiation for sin; these dear Brethren, are objects calculated to renew the memory of events, in which is displayed the eternal wisdom, reaching from end to end, embracing all space & ages, under its comprehensive arrangements & harmoniously disposing all things. In the events, to which I allude, they who attribute nothing in the affairs of Mankind to the government of providence; will only discover the result of human councel & passions, but they whose enlightened faith beholds in the history of Mankind the traces of a divine & overruling wisdom, will acknowledge the power of God continually exerted for the preservation of Religion. We particularly, dear Brethren, must feel a tender sentiment of gratitude towards the bestower of every good gift for the favours we now enjoy, whenever we recall to our remembrance the vicissitudes which have filled up the destinies of our church, since her first establishment by her head and founder Christ Jesus, down to this present day. Divine providence has so directed the course of human affairs; The Holy Ghost has so worked upon & tutored the minds of men, that now, agreeably to the dictates of our own consciences, we may sing canticles of praise to the Lord in a Country no longer foreign or unfriendly to us, but in a Country now become our own & taking us into her protection. In return for so great a blessing, your first duty was & I trust you forget it not, to render to Alm God the tribute of thankfulness due above all to him, & next to hear in your hearts, gratitude, respect & veneration for them, whose benevolence was the instrument of God's favour & mercy towards us. Let your earnest supplications be addressed to the throne of grace, that every blessing, temporal & eternal may descend on your fellow Citizens, your brethren in Jesus Christ. Be solicitous to extend, by your example & encouragement, the prevalence of Christian virtue to recommend your religion by the innocence of your manners & the sanctity of your lives; & especially by cultivating the first of Christian duties, that which is dearest to our Bd. & charitable Redeemer, a Spirit of peacefulness, & Mutual love, one for the other. Your particular circumstances call upon you for uncommon watchfulness over yourselves, & unusual exertions in all the exercises of a christian life. The impressions made by your conduct will be lasting impressions; & the opinion favourable or unfavourable to our holy religion, which shall result from observing your Manners, will have consequences extending down to the remotest times. I cannot therefore but comment some ontoward circumstances have disturbed that tranquility & harmony the preservance of which would have increased your happiness, & been singularly advantageous to the promotion of piety & truth. Of the cause of and circumstances of past misunderstanding, I wish to be entirely silent, & may the memory of them never be revived! May the blessed spirit be shed into your hearts, that divine Spirit, which drew & held the first Christians together in the bonds of perfect unity.

They buried all distinctions of birth & country in the happy & comfortable character of disciples of Jesus. Of Medes, of Parthians, of Jews of Proselytes of Elamites & the nations of Mesopotamia it was said, that their *heart was one & their soul was one.* To this heavenly disposition of mind & affection God now calls you. Jesus Christ the Prince of peace, solicits you by his grace, to forego all jealousies & contentions; & each one to have no other view in the service of God, but the advancement of his glory, & the salvation of his own & every one of his neighbors' souls. Thus will you each correspond with the visitation of Mercy, of which I have spoken. Again God has visited us by afflictions, by poverty, by Infirmity. In times of prosperity we turned our backs to him forgetting our continual dependance &c

T   GU   SC   Date was estimated by transcriber.

NOTATION ON MISSIONARIES   [1785]

Missioners to visit occasionally H. Lee to grant Indulgences—To remain a week together in a Congn. To instruct after the manner of the Jes[uit] Miss[ioners] from Europe—

AM   AAB (6J8)   On letter from Charles Plowden, Aug. 26, 1785.

TO BENJAMIN FRANKLIN   1785

Not found. See Feb. 27, 1785.

TO JOSEPH EDENSHINK   1785

Not found. See Apr.-June, 1786.

TO LEONARD NEALE   [1785]

Not found. See June 17, 1785.

TO THE CLERGY

Jan. 12—1785

Revd. Sirs   I have before informed you that his Holiness has extended the benefit of the Jubilee celebrated at Rom[e] an. 1775; and in other parts of Christendom ann. 1776, to all the Faithful subject to the thirteen United States. The commencement of this grant is to date from Novr. 26 1784, & it is to be in force till Nov 26 1785. A commission was sent me at the same time to publish it in all the countries subject to the States. Agreeably therefore to this commission, I now inform you, that as soon as you can conveniently, after receiving this notification you make known to the Congregations and faithful under your care, the publication of the Jubilee; and I make no doubt, but you will at the same time, and at all convenient opportunities afterwards, give such instructions, as may render them well acquainted with the nature, & advantage of a Jubilee, and of the necessary conditions for obtaining the benefit of it. I send you such extracts of the general grant, as may serve your direction. Dei ointntis Dei misericordia &c (p. 5) usque ad persistere decernimus ac declaramus—(p. 8).[1] To the general indult of the Jubilee is annexed the following declaration. *S. S. mus D. noster Pius* &c. [Our Most Holy Lord Pius, etc.]

To this His Holiness has [*fold*–sent a] commission empowering me to exchange the enjoined exercises of piety into other good works. Therefore, as the circumstances of the country do not admit of the faithful visiting four different churches in lieu thereof be pleased to direct,

1. That the inhabitants of towns, where there is a chapel convenient for the purpose, with the Bd. Sacrament kept in it, must visit the said chapel fifteen sucessive or interrupted days, & there devoutly recite either the litany of the Saints, or seven *Our Fathers,* & seven *Hail Marys* &c, for the intention expressed in his Holiness [*fold*] Constitution.

2. That they, who live in the country or other places not having the convenience of a chapel with the Bd. Sacrament kept in it; or who living in towns having such a chapel, are deprived of all opportunity of visiting it, being servants or slaves; shall likewise recite the Litany aforesaid, or seven times the Lds prayer & Ang. sal. [Angelic Salutation or Hail Mary] for the space of fifteen days, either continued or interrupted.

3. That on two fridays happening within the term of performing the devotions aforesaid all persons, obliged to keep the usual fasts of the Church and who are desirous of gaining the benefit of the Jubilee shall likewise keep fast: and they whose health, age, or other lawful cause exempt them from fasting at other times, on the fridays aforesaid shall recite either the seven penitential psalms or twice seven *our Frs* & Hail Marys.

You will observe in the extracts, which I send, that every Confessarius is authorised to give such directions to infirm persons, prisoners &c for the gaining of the Jubilee, as they can comply with; and to dispense with the obligation of communion where children have never before been admitted to it; but with all others this is a necessary condition. And I hope that you will appoint to your respective Congregations a time for the commencement of their devotions for gaining the Jubilee, which you may be & remain several days amongst them & that they begin their spiritual exercises by seeking in the Sacrament of pennance their reconciliation with Alm. God, & recovery of the state of grace, if needful; & likewise that they may have an opportunity to conclude all their other penitential works with receiving the Bd. Sacrament.

The faculties granted, you, for the Jubilee you will see in the extracts, transcribed above. But as they are not in some instances so extensive, as the general faculties, which I am empowered to grant, I now communicate to you till revoked by lawful authority, those, which you will find in the annexed sheet, a copy of which I request every Gentleman in your district to transcribe & keep by him. Concerning . . .

With very great regard and earnest recommendation of myself to your good answers I am Rd [*illeg.*] Finding it impossible, till I have better copy; of conversing with the several Gen[tlem]en, to fix a genl. & equitable rule of keeping lent for all the difrt. Congns, I request each of you to make such regula[ti]ons (for this year) for those under yr. charge as you shall in prudence think proper. Messrs Farmer, & Neale[2] —(Circular)—

ADf   AAB
[1] Indicates portions of extract from the Latin decree.
[2] Leonard Neale.

TO JOHN THORPE   Maryland, near George-town
                                                                                        Feb. 17—1785

Dear Sir   The official information of the advices sent by you June 9th 1784, was only received Novr.26th I did myself the honour of writing to you on the subject, immediately after receiving your letter, which was about the 20th of August, and of thanking you most cordially for your active & successful endeavours to render service to this country. I say successful, not because your partiality, as I presume, joined to that of my old cheerful friend Dr. Franklin suggested me to the consideration of his holiness; but because you have obtained some form of spiritual government to be adopted for us. It is not indeed quite such, as we wish; and it cannot continue long in its present form. You well know, that in our free and jealous government, where Catholics are admitted into all public councils equally with the professors of any other Religion, it never will be suffered, that their Ecclesiastical Superior (be he a Bishop, or Prefect Apostolic) receive his appointment from a foreign state, and only hold it at the discretion of a foreign tribunal or congregation.

If even the present temper, or inattention of our Executive, and legislative bodies were to overlook it for this & perhaps a few more instances, still ought we not to acquiesce & rest quiet in actual enjoyment: for the consequence, sooner or later, would certainly be, that some malicious or jealous-minded person would raise a spirit against us, & under pretence of rescuing the state from foreign influence, & dependance, strip us perhaps of our common civil rights. For these reasons, every thinking man amongst us is convinced, that we neither must request or admit any other foreign interference than such, as being essential to our religion, is implied in the acknowledgement of the Bishop of Rome being, by divine appointment, head of the universal Church; and the See of S. Peter being the center of ecclesiastical unity.

I am well aware, that these suggestions will sound ungrateful at Rome; and that the mention of them from us will be perhaps imputed by some of the officers of the propaganda to a remaining spirit of Jesuitism: but I own to you, that tho' I wish to treat them upon terms of sincere unanimity & cordial concurrence in all matters tending to the service of God; yet I do not feel myself disposed to sacrifice, to the fear of giving offence, the permanent interests of Religion. I mean candidly and respectfully to state our present situation; the spirit of our people; & the sentiments of the R. Catholics, the principal of whom are ready & desirous to transmit to Rome their opinion under their own signature, I am yet uncertain; I would wish to avoid giving the Congregation, or any other person the smallest reason to suspect a cabal to defeat their measures; and if plain and honest representation will not succeed with them, I shall fear the effects of intemperate obstinacy.

That you may judge of these matters yourself, I must inform you that my dispatches contained, 1st, a decree of the Congn. of the Propgda, appointing me Superior of the *missions* in the Thirteen U. States, *ad suum beneplacitum . . .* cum auctorae ea exercendi, quo ad earundem missionum regimen pertinent, ad proscriptum decretorum sacrae Congnis et facultatum eidem . . . concessarum, et non alias nec alio modo.[1] 2ly, an order from his holiness, empowering me to administer Confirmation. 3ly a letter from Cardl. Antonelli, advising that his holiness has extended to these States the Jubilee of 1776. 4ly. another letter from him, & one likewise from the Nuncio at Paris, desiring me to send two youths to be educated in the college of the Propgda. 5ly In the same letter Cardl. Antonelli wishes to know the number of our Clergy, & the *amount of our incomes:* for tho' the congregation means not to meddle in temporalities, yet conceiving & believing there are Church possessions here it is proper for them to know how many Clergymen can be maintained from them. 6ly He farther informs, that his holiness means hereafter to appoint a Bishop, Vicar apostolic; but neither insinuates when, or whom. 7ly In the faculties sent me which with respect to matrimonial dispensations are too much restricted for our exigencies, I am particularly charged to grant no powers or faculties to any who may come into the country, but those, *quos sacra Congregaeo destinaverit et approbaverit.*[2] Thus you see the outlines of our future Ecclesiastical government, as it is planned at Rome.

Our objections to it are—1st We conceive our situation no longer as that of missioners; and the Ecclesiastical constitution here no longer a mission. By acquiring civil and religious rights in common with other Christians, we are become a national catholic clergy; Colleges are now erecting for giving general & liberal education; these colleges are open, both to Masters and Scholars, of every religious denomination and as we have every reason to believe, that amongst the youth trained in these different Colleges, there will be frequently some inclined to the Ecclesiastical state, we Catholics propose instituting a seminary to form them to the virtues of their future state, & to instruct them in Divinity. Thus we shall, in a few years, with the blessing of providence be able to supply this country with labourers in the Lord's vineyard, & keep up a succession if we are indulged in a Bishop. We are not in immediate want of one, and it will be more agreeable to many of my Brethren not to have any yet appointed; but whenever the time for it comes, we conceive that it will be more advantageous to Religion, & less [*torn and fold*] that he be an ordinary Bishop; and not a Vicar-Apostolic & be chosen and presented to his holiness by the American Cat. Clergy. 2ly For two reasons we think it improper to be subject in our Ecclesiastical government to the Propaganda: the first is, that not being missioners, we conceive ourselves not a proper object of their institution: and the second is, that tho' our free and tolerant forms of Government (in Virga Maryld & Pennsylva.) admit us to equal civil rights with other Christians, yet the leading men in our respective states often express a jealousy of any foreign jurisdiction; and surely will be more offended with our submitting to it in matters not essential to our faith. I hope they will never object to our depending on the pope in things purely spiritual; but I am sure there are men, at least in this state, who would blow up a flame of animosity against us, if they suspected, that we were to be so much under the government of any Congn. at Rome, as to receive our Superior from it, commissioned only during their good will; and that this Superior was restricted from employing any Clergyman here, but such as that Congregation should direct. I dread so much the consequences of it being known; that this last direction was even given that I have not thought proper to mention it to several of my Brethren.

With respect to sending two youths, I shall inform Propgda that it would surely be very acceptable to us to have children educated gratis in so religious a seminary; and very acceptable to us all to have a succession of ministers of the altar thus provided for: but, as I suppose they will not receive any into their College, but such as shall afterwards be subject to their government; and it being yet uncertain what effect my representations may produce I shall delay that measure till farther information.

I shall in the mean time request permission to give faculties to other Clergymen, than those sent by the Propgda, of whose virtue & talents I shall have sufficient documents. For want of this power, the Catholics in the Jersies, N. Y., the great Western Country bordering on the lakes, & the Ohio, Wabash, & Mississippi (to say nothing of many in the N. England States & Carolinas) are entirely destitute of spiritual succours. The Catholics, in some of these settlements, have been at the expense of paying the passage in of some Irish Franciscans, & providing for their subsistance. These men have brought good testimonials; but I am precluded from giving them any Sprl powers.

I should deem it a singular happiness to have an opportunity of conferring with a person of your experience of the air of Rome before these representations are given in. But our distance is so great, that I must act according to the best of my own & Brethren's judgment, & commit all I can to your prudent management. At a meeting of some of us last autumn, it was ordered that £ St.20..0..0 should be remitted to you as a feeble acknowledgement of our sense of your services & to defray your expence of attendance &c. Mr. Jn Ashton who is chosen to be our manager general, either has or soon will transmit the necessary orders for it. Tho', since my late appointment, I do not intermeddle in our temporal concerns, yet I shall not fail to suggest the propriety of fixing on you, as our agent, a permanent salary: it will be proportioned, not to your zeal & services, but to our poor ability. At the same meeting, but after I had left it thro' indisposition, a direction was given to Messrs Diderick, Mosely & Matthews to write you a letter (I believe likewise a memorial to the Pope) against the appointment of a Bishop. I hear that this has displeased many of those absent from the meeting, & that it is not certain, whether the measure is to be carried into execution. Mr. Diderick has shewn me a copy of his intended letter to you of his memorial, & of a letter to Cardl. Borromeo. He had no other introduction to write to this worthy Cardl., than the information communicated to me by our common friend Plowden, of his great worth and friendly disposition to you. I made objections to some parts of his letters; & I cannot tell, as I mentioned before whether they will be sent. It is a matter of surprise to me that he was nominated to the commission of Three: he is truly a zealous, pains-taking Clergyman; but not sufficiently prudent, and conversant in the world, or capable of conducting such a business with the circumspection necessary to be used by us towards our own government, & the Congn. of the Propaganda.

My long letter must have tired you. But it has been so earnestly recommended to me to give you very minute intelligence, that I have ventured to trespass on your patience. I have two things more to request; 1st that you would please to present us all, & myself in particular, to Cardl. Borromeo, as penetrated with a lively sense of his virtue, & earnestly suing for his good offices to the service of Religion in this Country, wherever they can be usefully employed. 2ly that you would let Mr Thyers know (for I hear from Plowden that he is at Paris, & corresponds with you) that I shall be happy in being favoured with an epistolary intercourse with him: and in confidence of your introduction I shall probably write to him before I have your answer.

The little leisure, I have lately had, has been taken up in writing and publishing an answer to Wharton's pamphlet, which was held up as unanswerable by our adversaries, whom the elegance of his language, & their own ignorance in Religious controversy equally contributed to deceive. I have desired Mr. Talbot to transmit you a copy by the first opportunity. I doubt, I have not made my court to a certain party at Rome by my note on the destruction of the Society. Be pleased to charge us with all postage & other expences on our acct. A credit shall be placed in Engd. for discharging them. With perfect esteem I have the honour to be: Dr. Sir &c

ADf   AAB

[1] "At his good pleasure . . . with the power of exercising them where they apply to the rule of those missions, to the provisions of the decrees of the Sacred Congregation and of the facultities . . . granted and not for other purposes or in any other way."

[2] "Which the Sacred Congregation shall appoint and approve."

TO CHARLES PLOWDEN   Rock Creek Feb: 27—1785

My dear Sir   I have been favoured with your most acceptable letters of April 4—, July 3d—Sep. 2—& Octr. 2, 1784. The last was directed to me at London in consequence of some erroneous information given you of my being arrived at that place. Had it been so, how happy should I have been to have met so dear a friend, as yourself, & to listen to the many amusing relations and useful information with which you would entertain me? I have answered, at least, I think so, the two former letters: but lest I should be mistaken I will here again briefly repeat the substance of what I then wrote, or intended for you.

Your sentiments concerning the propaganda, and our rights, as a national Clergy, coincide entirely with my own: and as I am so happy as to find these sentiments adopted by our Gentlemen here I have written to Cardl. Antonelli, that the dependance of the R. Cath. of this country on any foreign tribunal or office, as to the appointment of their Ecclesiastical Superior, will not be tolerated by our jealous governments; that if the Clergy here are not allowed to chuse & present for approbation the person whom in their judgment they approve as best qualified, the consequences to Religion may be fatal. I have written very fully to our common friend Mr. Thorpe on all these matters,[1] & agreeably to your recommendation, have sent him every needful information. To you, my dear Sir, I am infinitely obliged for your excellent advices, and I can truly say that, I have that value for your correspondance, which it deserves: and this is saying very much. Mr. Tho. Digges, a most excellent,

holy, & sensible man whose judgment must be highly valued by all his
acquaintance charges me to present his most respectful compliments to you:
he claims an hereditary right to your friendship, having been intimate with so
many of your uncles. They were those, I suppose, of whom our good friend
Mr. Scarisbrick used to tell so many merry tales. He, I hear, is as young a man
as he was twenty years ago. The official communication from Rome of my
new powers came to hand only on the 26th of last Novr. I have before told
you that nothing since the dissolution of our poor Society ever gave me so
much uneasiness, as the first account of my being to be appointed a Bishop.
Luckily, the dispatches from Rome only mention that the Pope's intention is,
hereafter to appoint a Vicar Apostolic; but no intimation is given of time or
person. A Vicar Apostolic is quite unsuitable to our situation, geographical
and political, & so I write to Rome. Our gentlemen will, I hope, be unanimous in pursuing every firm and temperate measure to guard us against the
evils of a foreign dependance. The want of a Bishop will not be felt amongst
us, for some few years. Two Colleges are now erecting in this State, by private
contribution and public endowment. They are established on a liberal plan
open to Masters and Scholars of every denomination. Similar foundations
exist in other states. Notwithstanding the danger for morals in these mixed
Colleges, I still think that much advantage will be derived from them: & I
hope that as we R.C. are unable to raise or support one ourselves, providence
has ordained these as a resource for the exigencies of Religion. For in these
Colleges, I trust there will amongst the Catholic youth trained in them be
some from time to time inclined to an Ecclesiastical state. For these we
propose, what I hope our abilities will enable us to execute, a small seminary,
where they may be formed to the virtues of that state, and receive a
Theological education. Such is the plan now in my mind, and on which I
beseech Alm: God to grant his assistance, to which your prayers will greatly
contribute. How much I wish, that some young men of talents were now here
from Liege to offer themselves to fill the places of Professors &c in these
rising Colleges? The salaries will be liberal, and if I knew any of my
Countrymen in England & Liege likely to discharge these offices with reputation, I would earnestly sollicit their return. Messrs Semmes[2] & Mattingly[3] are
I doubt, engaged in employments, which forbid their revisiting this country:
You have heared of Wharton's proceeding and probably seen his pamphlet.
Notwithstanding all advices from you and others, I still hoped, that his
conduct in England was owing to great vivacity, and a more liberal view of
many things, than some of us educated in Colleges ever dare take. I was loth
to attribute it to the motives, which he has since avowed in his publication. I
dare say, that you will, on perusing it, find it carries marks of being written
long before it was published. The exultation of Protestants, and discouragement of R.C. compelled me to enter the lists with him. I wrote a hasty
answer, amidst continual avocations, & almost without any materials but

those, which my memory suggested. I have directed Mr. Talbot to send you a copy of it, which I hope you will read with the indulgence, to which the circumstances of writing it intitle me. Poor Aston! your account of him greatly distresses me. I am much obliged to you for sending your Brs writings on the great Derwentwater cause. I sincerely wish him success, and such increase of reputation as may be highly profitable and ornamental to him; & beg you to signify so much to him. We of this state are now engaged in a warm controversy, and I wish it may not tend to revive some animosities, which I hoped, were buried forever. In our new Constitution, it is fixed as a matter of natural justice, that every person has a right to worship Alm: God in that religious mode or from which his conscience dictates, as most agreeable to the divine will: that no person shall be compelled to support any minister, or any form of worship, which he does not approve; but that there shall rest with the legislature a power to be exercised at their discretion, to oblige all persons to contribute to the support of that particular Religion, and minister, which each one prefers. Our legislature or one branch of it has just proposed to the consideration of the people a law for this purpose, & require instructions against the next session. Where the law truly formed upon the principle of the Constitution, we R.C. should have no very great objection to it: but from certain clauses in it, and other circumstances, we, as well as the Presbyterians, Methodists, Quakers and Anabaptists are induced to believe, that it is calculated to create a predominant and irresistible influence in favour of the Protestant Episcopal Church,[4] as the Church of Engld. is now called; and therefore we shall all oppose it with might and main. We have all smarted heretofore under the lash of an established church and shall therefore to on our guard against every approach towards it. All other denominations were formerly subject to pay a heavy tax to the Clergy of the Ch. of England. As it is not unlikely, that your papers may take notice of the present ferment here I have thought proper to give you this state of the dispute, to regulate your judgment on what you may read.

I forgot to mention to you that my letters from Rome contained, first, a commission from the propada to be Superior in the thirteen United States, durante beneplacito [during its good pleasure] —2ly a grant from the Pope to confer confirmation—3ly faculties communicable to my Brethren, & some few peculiar to myself. But I am restricted fron granting faculties to any, but those, quos Sacra Congregao destinaverit; et approbaverit. This artful restriction renders a Superior of very little use; and if upon my remonstrance the restriction is not removed, & there should not be some appearance of an inclination to leave us that Ecclesiastical liberty, which the temper of the age and of our people requires, as well as the lasting benefit of Religion, I certainly will not hold my appointment very long.

In your letter of Octr. 2nd. sent to London, you mention some advices from our friend Mr. Thorpe containing his opinion of my present situation, &

which you wished to communicate to me. As you must have been informed of your mistake long ago, these advices are, I hope, now on their way to me.

The letter, which Mr. Thorpe wrote to me thro' the channel of Dr. Franklin, I have not yet received. In a few days, I shall write to that venerable old man[5] who will, I am sure give good information to the Nuncio at Paris concerning the impropriety of the Propgda intermeddling here. The Doctor wishes his country to be unconnected with Europe in every other way, than that of a communication of all useful knowledge, and upon that principle will be very far from giving Mgr Doria (from whom by the bye I have had a very polite letter) any flattering expectation of the power of the Propaganda being established here. I have some thoughts of commencing a correspondence with Mr. Thyers, as from your account of him I think he might be useful at [torn]. . . .

I was much pleased with your account of Lord Stourtons remembrance. If you shall again see him be pleased to assure him of my best wishes for his happiness here and hereafter.

Present me in the kindest manner to my respectable friends Messrs Stanley & Clinton and assure yourself of the constant regard and affection of Dr. Sir   Yr. most obedt & sincere friend   J Carroll   My good Mother begs to be remembered to the son of her dear friend Mrs Plowden. I fear my new appointment will oblige me to leave her, this residence not being convenient to my business.

ALS   St
[1] See Feb. 17, 1785.
[2] Joseph Semmes, S.J., a Marylander, at Stonyhurst.
[3] John Mattingly, S.J., a tutor.
[4] On Nov. 19, 1785, the House of Delegates of Maryland defeated the clergy salary bill. The 1776 constitution's allowance of this conflicted in practice, according to Carroll, with the broader provision of equality before the law. See Hanley, *American Revolution,* pp. 66-67.
[5] Not found.

TO CARDINAL ANTONELLI

From Maryland
27th of February, 1785

Most Eminent Lord   The letters for the 9th and 16th of last year, which your Eminence deigned to send me, did not arrive until the 26th of November. However, various documents did accompany the letters. 1o A decree of the Sacred Congregation for the Propagation of the Faith, by which it declares me, *ad suum beneplacitum,* the Superior of the missions in the thirteen United States of America. 2o The gracious concession of His Holiness in extending the universal Jubilee to all the Faithful in the thirteen United States of America. 3o Another concession of His Holiness by which I am granted the faculty of administering the Sacrament of Confirmation according to the norm of the Instruction accompanying it. 4o Finally, faculties granted me by our Holy Father and communicable to my Companions laboring in this vineyard of the Lord.

Because you manifested such benevolence toward me, Most Eminent Cardinal, and such an interest in the cause of Catholicism in this remote part of the world, in the letters by which you sent these documents to me, I want to express my sincerest gratitude. I would have expressed these sentiments earlier had not, first of all, a long absence from home, and later an unseasonable storm prevented my writing. I ask you then and humbly beg you to recommend me to the prayers of His Holiness, to attest my most devoted submission to the Holy See, and to offer thanks that the Holy Father did not think me unworthy of such a burdensome office.

These were my sentiments toward the Holy Father and you, Most Eminent Cardinal, when I realized your great benevolence toward me, and your sollicitous care for our holy Religion in this territory. There were some things, both in the beginning and later on, to my way of thinking, which were a source of fear and grave sorrow. At first I saw that office entrusted to me, the undertaking of which, I confess with sincere and deep feeling, I find myself altogether unequal to, and not at all endowed with the qualities of mind and body with which anyone must be equipped who girds himself for the faithful undertaking of that office. Secondly, that I may carry out the wishes of Your Eminence in wishing an accurate report on our affairs, I was not unaware that I must recount some things which would perhaps be less appreciated in the future, which, indeed, could foster suspicion of an obedience somewhat less than is due to the Apostolic See. However, I shall esteem these things less than the truth and a sincere exposition of our affairs. For I know, most Eminent Cardinal, nothing can be done safely or efficiently concerning us, unless our state of affairs is clearly understood.

First of all, then, of the thirteen states which were at one time subject to the King of England, there were only two, Pennsylvania and Maryland, in which Catholics could dwell in complete safety. Even in these states legal precaution was taken that Catholics could take no part in civil, military, or any other public office. Now that the English yoke has been thrown off, and new laws have been passed in all the States, Catholics are able to live in complete safety and can practice their religion. In many places, however, they are not allowed to undertake public offices unless they renounce all foreign jurisdiction, be it civil or ecclesiastical. Thus it happens that in many of these colonies, or States as they are now called, Catholics are excluded from government. In four states at least, namely in Pennsylvania, Delaware, Maryland, and Virginia, they enjoy the same rights as other citizens. How long we shall continue to have these benefits, however, whether of tolerance or of common right, I hesitate to say. Many of our people, especially in Maryland, fear that there is a desire among non-Catholics to exclude us altogether from holding office. I, however, who have always managed not to anticipate troubles, but, when they did arise, to tolerate them in any manner possible, nourish the hope that such a great harm will not come to us. Indeed, I truly believe that such solid foundations of Religion can be laid in these American States, that the most flourishing portion of the Church, with great comfort to the Holy See, may one day be found here. At this point I should recall those things of which I spoke earlier which should be known so that our ecclesiastical affairs may be correctly administered.

There flourished at one time, especially in this area, the Sect of the Anglicans whose ministers were dependent in religious matters on the Pseudo-Bishop of London. They referred to him for whatever Ordinaries they needed. After the war they could not depend on an English Bishop, or on any other foreign person for that matter, for ministers of that sect, although the Anglicans were the most numerous of all. They were, on the contrary, allowed to choose and select bishops for themselves, something they were already doing, although they did not yet have a bishop consecrated in their own rite. They prescribed for themselves the form of administering their religion. They want their religion to be called and treated as national, to the point where they now admit no Superior from another place. Finally, they are now so contriving, that some of ours fear them greatly.[1]

May the most Eminent Cardinal be persuaded that we will tolerate these grave burdens rather than renounce that divine authority of the Apostolic See. And not only we priests who are here, but also the Catholic Laity, seem to be so grounded in the faith, that they could never be swayed from the obedience due the Supreme Pontiff. Those same people, nevertheless, think the Holy Father ought to grant them some freedom which is clearly necessary for the preserving of the common law which they now enjoy, or for the repelling of the dangers which they fear. From what I have mentioned, and from the constitution of the government which exists here, your Eminence cannot fail to see how hateful all foreign jurisdiction is to these people. The Catholics, therefore, desire that the adversaries of our religion be given no handle for incriminating us on the grounds that we depend more than is proper on a foreign power. Let some reason be found, by which, later on, some ecclesiastical superior could be appointed to this area so that the spiritual jurisdiction of the Holy See may be altogether maintained. At the same time all occasion would be removed for objecting that we were admitting something harmful to the Independence of our country. Many outstanding Catholics were of a mind to point this out to His Holiness in a common letter, especially those men who either have a place in the American general council (which they call a Congress), or who are influential in the legislative councils in Pennsylvania and Maryland. However, I persuaded them to commit this message to the present letter. Perhaps the Holy Father will understand more clearly which is to be done in the matter, when he takes notice of the sixth article of the perpetual union among the United States of America. There it is laid down that no one who holds any office whatsoever in the United States shall be allowed to accept any gift, office, or title of any kind from any king, prince, or foreign ruler. Although this prohibition may seem to pertain only to those who are destined for civil offices, it will perhaps also be turned against ecclesiastical offices by our enemies. We desire, therefore, most Eminent Cardinal, to insure that in every way the integrity of the faith, and union with and proper obedience toward the Apostolic See may always flourish. However, at the same time we desire that whatever can be granted— with due respect to religion—to American Catholics on behalf of ecclesiastical government, should be granted. We are confident that the deep hatred and suspicion of the sects are lessening and thus our affairs can be made secure.

You pointed out, most Eminent Cardinal, that the mind and plan of His Holiness was that an Apostolic Vicar with the title and character of a Bishop should be chosen for these States. While this paternal sollicitude gives us great joy, nevertheless, it also gives rise to some fear. For we knew that on one occasion the non-Catholic Americans could not be persuaded to admit a Bishop to their sect while these States were still under the English King, although such an attempt was made. As a result, then, the fear has arisen that this permission will certainly not be granted to us. Some months ago during the convention of the Protestant ministers of the Anglican, or Episcopal Church, as they now call it, they decided that, by the very fact that they enjoyed the exercise of their religion by full authority of law, they therefore had the legal right to elect for themselves such ministers of religion as the need and discipline of their sect demanded: that is, bishops, priests, and deacons. Our legislators did not find anything wrong with this decree of the ministers.[2] Therefore, since the same free exercise of religion is granted us, and also the same legal right, we must comply as regards the scope of our State laws.

The situation being what it is, the most Holy Father will judge, and thus you, most Eminent Cardinal, will weigh carefully in your mind, whether the time is now ripe for appointing a bishop, what sort of a man he should be, and how he should be appointed. I shall recall a few points about these matters, not in order to impose my judgment, but to give a more complete account of the situation.

First of all, concerning the opportuneness, I would observe that there would not now be any disturbance if a bishop should be appointed, because the non-Catholic Protestants are thinking about appointing one themselves. Secondly, just as they hope to derive some esteem among the people of their sect from this Episcopal dignity, we also are confident that not only the same will hold true for us, but other great benefits will follow when the Church is administered the way Christ our Lord established it. On the other hand, it occurs to me that since the most Holy Father has already deigned to provide otherwise for the conferring of the Sacrament of Confirmation, necessity will not demand that a bishop be appointed for us before men are found suitable for the reception of Holy Orders, which we hope will be in a few years. The most Eminent Cardinal will understand this matter from information which I am planning to convey in a separate letter. However, when that time comes, perhaps we will be able to provide more suitably for the proper maintainance of a bishop than our limited sources now permit.

If, then, it shall seem good to His Holiness to assign us a Bishop, will he designate a Vicar Apostolic or will he establish an Ordinary with his own See, What person will serve more for the betterment of the Catholic position, for the removal of hatred toward Catholics, for removing the alarm over foreign jurisdiction? And I know that alarm will certainly be increased if the people know that an ecclesiastical superior has been appointed in such wise that he may be removed from office at the will of the Sacred Congregation for the Propagation of the Faith or of any other foreign tribunal. Or that he would not be allowed to admit any priest to perform the sacred functions whom that Congregation had not approved and appointed for us.

At present I shall say nothing more about the manner of appointing a Bishop than that we implore the divine wisdom and mercy to direct the judgment of the Apostolic See. If, then, it does not seem good to permit priests who have been laboring for so many years in this vineyard of the Lord to propose a man to His Holiness, whom they shall have thought more suitable, let them at least decide upon some way of nominating a bishop by which offense to our people both Catholic as well as sectarian may be averted.

Concerning the sending of the two young men to the Urban College,[3] there was nothing I could do, until I had understood your Eminence's mind more fully. If they had been unable to bear the expenses of the journey, I know that the Sacred Congregation would certainly have provided traveling expenses. I have, nevertheless, not sufficiently determined who should take care of those expenses. For ships' masters are not accustomed to receive passengers on board, unless the fare is duly taken care of before sailing, or unless they are certain from whom the money may be obtained. Therefore, what I mentioned concerning the appointment of a Bishop or Superior will perhaps suggest some change in the manner of handling our ecclesiastical affairs; and, perhaps the plan for training the young men in that college could be changed, which is something we scarcely hope for in the near future. Finally, it is agreed that the boys' parents be informed whether some promise, and of what nature, would be demanded of their sons before they return to their country. All possible care must be taken lest the Catholics, both laity and clergy, should seem to depend on some foreign power in matters of such great moment.

Meanwhile, while waiting for an answer, I shall take great care that two young men are chosen with special care, such as your letters, Eminent Cardinal, ask for. Moreover, I hope I can arrange that the expenses of the trip, at least from here to France, can be taken care of by the parents. If I do not meet with success in this matter, I shall urge them to be very saving. I understand, however, that for each boy making the trip and for the other expenses until port is reached it will cost 70 or 80 goldpieces.

The other matters about which you wanted to be informed, Eminent Cardinal, prompted by your religious sollicitude toward us, I thought could be more opportunely explained in a separate informal letter. Nevertheless, here I earnestly beseech again and again, that you take care to have removed from the faculties granted me that restriction by which I am prohibited from employing the labor of priests other than those whom the Sacred Congregation destined and approved. Unless this be granted, in a short time a great part of the Catholics will be altogether deprived of the sacraments and without priests. For our only remaining hope of quickly receiving replacements for our deceased associates, or those already on the verge of extreme old age, is to be found in those native priests who were sent to Europe before the war for their education and received Holy Orders there. I hear that some of them are thinking about returning to this country. Even if they do return they will be unemployed, however well prepared they are by character and learning to work in this vineyard. Therefore, with all reverence, but at the same time with complete trust, and from the full persuasion that it will concern the matter of religion, I ask, most Eminent Cardinal, that you exert your influence with His Holiness, and point out to him, that it is altogether necessary for the Superior in these United States of America that whatever priests His Holiness shall judge fit, may be added to the group of workers.

These are the matters, Most Eminent Cardinal, which I wanted to write to you freely and faithfully concerning religion. Perhaps by way of a supplement they will approximate a response to the three things you asked about, and which you will find mentioned in another letter. May I be allowed to commend to your singular piety and paternal benevolence myself and this portion of the Lord's flock and the pastors in it. I pray that you turn your eyes on those immense regions bounded by the limits of the United States. Day by day with every increasing number of immigrants, and from its own natural fecundity, the number of inhabitants is growing. Everywhere the true faith can be freely preached. There does not seem to be anything to prevent great fruits being reaped from this liberty except lack of laborers and the means of providing for them. We have recourse, then, to you with singular care, devotion, and authority to watch over the propagation of our religion, that in your wisdom you may wish to help us further our plans to this end, and that you may regard this region as entrusted to your supervision. As for myself, with greatest trust, Most Eminent Cardinal, I implore your piety, advice, and authority in the negotiations of this Church, and I pray almighty God that he vouchsafe to guard and preserve you for a long time for the salvation of souls and the spreading of the divine Faith. Thus wishes, Most Eminent Cardinal, Your Eminence's Most Obedient Servant   John Carroll

ADf   AAB
[1] On the Protestant Episcopal Church's autonomy, see Hanley, *American Revolution*, ch. 4. and Feb. 27, 1785, n. 4 above.
[2] Carroll spoke in favor of the Episcopal Vestry Act, when it came before the Maryland Assembly.
[3] Urban College of the Congregation for the Propagation of the Faith was founded by Pope Urban VI, 1727. See Feb. 17, 1785, for education plans.

Eminentissime Domine   Litterae, quas ad me destinare dignata est Ema Vestra, diebus 9a et 16a anni praeteriti, in manus meas non pervenerunt ante diem 26am Novembris. Varia autem documenta litteras comitabantur. 1o Decretum Sacrae Congregationis de Propaganda Fide, qua me Superiorem missionum in tredecim confederatae Americae provinciis ad suum beneplacitum declaravit. 2o Benignissima Suae Sanctitatis concessio et extensio universalis Jubilaei ad omnes Fideles in tredecim Confederatae Americae provinciis. 3o Altera ejusdem concessio qua mihi facultas tribuitur administrandi Sacramentum Confirmationis ad normam Instructionis, quam una recepi. 4o demum facultates a Ssmo D.N. mihi concessae et Sociis in hac Domini vinea laborantibus communicabiles.

Quod litteris, quibus haec ad me transmisisti documenta, Eminentissime Cardinalis, tantam erga me benevolentiam, tantum rei Catholicae in remotis hisce orbis partibus adjuvandae studium significaveris, gratias habeo et ago maximas, cujus quidem grati animi sensu certiorem te prius fecissem, nisi longa imprimis a domo absentia, postea autem intempestiva navigantibus glacies scribendi occasionem denegasset. Deinde rogo te ac humillime precor, ut Sanctitatis suae precibus me sistere, ac devotissimum erga Sedem Apostolicam obsequium testificari velis; gratiasque referre, quod tam gravi munere me indignum non existimaverit.

Hi sunt animi sensus quibus erga Bssmum Patrem, teque adeo, Cardinalis Eminentissime, affectus fui, ubi propensam utriusque in me benevolentiam, et sollicitam pro Sancta nostra Religione in his regionibus providentiam intelligerem. Fuere tamen aliquae, tum initio tum deinceps cogitanti mihi, magnum timorem, magnam etiam maestitiam incutiebant. Videbam imprimis illus mihi munus committi, cui subeundo, ut sincere et ex intimo sensu profiteor, imparem me omnino esse sentio, nec illis animi et corporis viribus praeditum, quibus instructum esse oportet, quiscumque se ad illud fideliter administrandum accinxerit. Deinde ut Eminae Tuae votis obsequerer accuratam de rebus nostris relationem desiderantis, aliqua mihi commemoranda esse non ignorabam, quae minus grata fortasse essent futura, imo quae suspicionem commovere possent minus prope suae in Sedem Apostolicam observantiae. Haec tamen omnia veritati postponam, et sincerae rerum nostrarum expositioni. Scio enim, Em. Cardlis, nihil tuto aut efficaciter circa nos agi posse, nisi quae sit nostra conditio plane intelligatur.

Imprimis igitur, ex tredecim provinciis, quae olim Regi Magnae Brittaniae parebant, duae tantum fuere, Pennsylvania et Marilandia, in quibus permissum erat Catholicis tuto degere. In his etiam lege cautum erat, ne officio civili, militari aut alio quovis frui possent. Excusso jam jugo Brittanico, novisque conditis legibus, in omnibus provinciis, Catholici sine molestia vivere et sacra peragere possunt. In plerisque tamen locis ad Reipublicae munera capessenda non admittuntur, nisi qui omnem jurisdictionem exteram, sive civilem, sive Ecclesiasticam, abrenuntiaverint. Ita fit, ut in plerisque his provinciis, seu Statibus, ut nunc vocant, nostri homines maneant a Republica exclusi: in quttuor tantum, nempe in Pensilvania, Delawaria, Marilandia et Virginia, eodem ac caeteri cives jure utuntur. Haec autem beneficia, sive tolerantiae sive juris communis, quamdiu simus habituri, non ausim pronunciare. Timent e nostris multi, in Marilandia praecipue, Acatholicis in animo esse, ut omnino a gerendis muneribus excludamur; ego autem, cui satis semper fuit mala non animo praevenire, sed, ubi advenerint, utcumque tolerare, spe foveor tantam nobis injuriam haud esse inferendam; imo vero confido tam firma Religionis fundamenta in his Americanis Statibus jaci posse, ut florentissima Ecclesiae portio, cum magna Sedis Apostolicae solatio, his aliquando sit futura. Hoc autem loco illa mihi commemoranda sunt, de quibus dixi superius, scitu necessaria, ut recte res nostrae Ecclesiasticae possint administrari.

Viguit olim in his regionibus praecipue secta Anglicana, rerum sacrarum apud illos ministri pendebant omnes a Pseudo-Episcopo Londiniensi; ad illum transfretabant, quotquot ordinari secundum sectae suae rationem cupiebant. Peracto autem bello, obtineri non potuit a sectae illius ministris, quamvis essent omnium frequentissimi ut ab Episcopo Anglo, imo ab extero quovis penderent. Concessum est illis potius, ut Episcopos sibi constituerent et eligerent, quod jam ab ipsis factum est, quamvis nullum adhuc suo ritu consecratum habeant. Religionis suae administrandae sibi formam praescripserunt; religionem suam dici et heberi nationalem cupiunt, eo quod jam nullum alibi Superiorem admittant; denique ita machinantur, ut ab illis timor ille incutiatur, quo nostrorum nonnullos percuti dicebam.

Eminentissimus Cardinalis persuasum sibi habeat, nobis gravissima omnia tolerabiliora fore, quam divinam illam Sedis Apostolicae auctoritatem abrenunciare; nec tantum Sacerdotes, qui his sumus, sed etiam populum Catholicum in fide ita videri stabilem, ut nunquam a debita Summo Pontifici obedientia sit dimovendus. Idem tamen ille populus aliquam a Bmo Patre gratiam sibi concedi, imo deberi existimat, necessariam sane sive ad juris communis, quo nunc utitur, conservationem, sive ad propulsandum periculum, quod timetur. Ex iis quae dixi, et ex rerum publicarum, quae hic sunt, constitutione, Emae Tuae ignotum esse non potest, quam invidiosa illis sit omnis extera juridictio. Hoc igitur a Catholicis desideratur, ut nulla detur ansa Religionis nostrae adversariis nos criminandi, quasi plus aequo a regimine externo pendeamus, et ut aliqua ratio ineatur, qua in posterum Superior Ecclesiasticus huic regioni destinari possit, ita ut spiritualis Sac. Sedis jurisdictio omnino servetur, et simul tollatur omnis occasio nobis objiciendi, quasi aliquid admittamus patriae Independentiae inimicum. Hoc ex praecipuis Catholicis multi, communi scripto, Sanctitati suae significare cogitabant, ac ii maxime, qui vel in generali Americae Concilio (Congressum vocant) sedem obtinuere, vel in Pensylvania ac Marilandia conciliis legislativis cum autoritate intersunt; a quibus tamen obtinui, ut in praesens ejusmodi scriptum differatur. Quid hac in re statui possit, Beatissimus Pater plenius forsan intelliget, ubi animam advertet ad sextum articulum *unionis perpetuae* inter Status foederatae Americae, quo Sancitur *nemini licitum fore, qui munere quovis fungatur sub Unitis Statibus, donum aliquod, officum aut titulum cujusvis generis accipere a Rege aliquo, Principe aut dominio extero.* Quae prohibitio etsi ad illos tantum pertinere videatur, qui ad munera Reipublicae destinantur, ab adversariis tamen nostris etiam ad officia Ecclesiastica fortasse detorquebitur. Cupimus igitur, Eme Cardinalis, omni modo providere, ut fidei integritas, et debita erga Sedem Apostolicam observantia et unio semper vigeat; at simul ut Catholicis Americanis pro Ecclesiastico regimine concedatur, quidquid salva Religione concedi potest. Ita minui sectariorum invidiam plenam suspicionis, ita res nostras stabiliri posse confidimus.

Significasti, Eme Cardlis, Sanctitatis suae mentem esse et consilium, ut Vicarium Apostolicum Episcopali charactere et titulo insignitum pro his provinciis decernat. Ut paterna haec pro nobis sollicitudo magna nos laetitia affecit, ita etiam aliquem initio incussit timorem. Sciebamus enim Acatholicis Americanis olim persuaderi nunquam potuisse, ut vel suae sectae Episcopum admitterent, cum id tentaretur, dum Angliae Regi hae provinciae subessent; unde etiam timor nascebatur, ne nobis quidem id permissum iri. At jam, ab aliquot mensibus, conventione facta Ministrorum Protestantium Ecclesiae Anglicane, seu Episcopalis, ut nunc vocant, decreverunt se, quod ex legum auctoritate plena suae Religionis exercitio gaudeant, eo ipso jus habere ad tales rerum Sacrarum Ministros sibi constituendos quales sectae suae ratio et disciplina exigit, Episcopos scilicet, Presbyteros, et Diaconos; cui illorum decreto non repugnaverunt, qui condendis legibus apud nos sunt designati. Cum igitur nobis eadem pro Religionis exercitio libertas concedatur, jus quoque idem, quantum ad leges nostras municipales spectat, competere necesse est.

Re autem ita se habente, judicabit Beatissimus Pater, tuque adeo, Eme Cardlis, animo perpendes, an tempus constituendo Episcopo opportunum nunc sit, qualis is esse debeat, et quomodo designatus; de quibus omnibus, non tanquam judicium meum impositurus, sed pleniorem relationem facturus, aliqua commemorabo.

Imprimis, de opportunitate temporis observari potest, nullam jam animorum fore commotionem, si Episcopus designetur, quod Acatholici Protestantes sibi aliquem constituere cogitent; deinde, ut aliquam suae sectae apud vulgus existimationem ex Episcopali dignitate conciliare sperant, ita etiam non solum similem nobis, sed etiam ingentia commoda obventura confidimus, cum hanc Ecclesiam eo modo administrari contigerit, quo Christus Dominus instituit. Ex altera tamen parte occurrit, quod cum jam Ssmus Pater aliter Sacramento Confirmationis conferendo providere dignatus sit, non prius Episcopum nobis constituere necessitas postulet, quam idonei aliqui reperiantur ad sacros Ordines suscipiendos, quod paucis annis futurum speramus, ut intilliget Eminentmus Cardinalis ex iis, quae separatim relatione distincta scribere cogito. Quod tempus ubi advenerit, commodius fortasse, pro decenti Episcopi sustentatione providere, quam nunc pro rerum nostrarum tenuitate poterimus.

Deinde, si Episcopum nobis assignare Sanctitati suae visum fuerit, praestabitne Vicarium Apostolicum, an Ordinarium cum propria Sede constituere? Quis rei Catholicae incremento, quis amovendae Catholicorum invidiae, terrorique illi de extera jurisdictione magis inserviet? quem terrorem auctum iri certissime scio, si Superiorem Ecclesiasticum ita designari noverint, ut ad arbitrium Sacrae Congregationis de propaganda fide, aut cujusvis alterius tribunalis externi ab officio possit dimoveri; nec fas illi sit Sacerdotem quemvis ad sacras functiones admittere, quem illa Congregatio non approbaverit, et ad nos destinaverit.

De modo autem Episcoporum designandi nihil aliud nunc dicam, quam implorare nos, pro Sedis Apostolicae judicio dirigendo, divinam sapientiam et misericoridiam; ut, si minime concedendum videatur Sacerdotibus in hac Domini vinea tot annos laborantibus iillum suae Sanctitati proponere, quem ipsi magis idoneum existimaverint, conveniatur tamen de aliqua Episcopum nominandi via, qua Nostratium, tam Catholicorum, quam Sectariorum offensio possit averti.

De duobus Juvenibus ad Urbanum Collegium mittendis nihil agere licuit, donec plenius de Emae tuae mente intellexero. Si itineris impensis impares fuerint, video quidem a Sacra Congregatione de viatico provisum iri; non tamen habeo compertum, cui demandatum sit illas impensas subministrare. Navium enim magistri in navem vectores recipere non solent, nisi naulum ante navigationem solvatur, aut certo sciant a quo repetendum sit. Deinde, ut quae dixi de Episcopo vel Superiore designando, aliquam forte mutationem suggerent circa modum res nostras Ecclesiasticas administrandi, ita quoque consilium de educandis in isto Collegio Juvenibus poterit mutari, quod tamen minime futurum confidimus. Postremo, convenit, ut juvenum parentes doceantur an juramentum aliquod et cujusmodi ab eorum filiis exigendum sit, antequam in patriam remittantur; omnis enim cautela abhibenda est, ut, quantum fieri potest, videantur Catholici, tam populus quam ministri, in rebus tantum omnino necessariis, ab extera potestate pendere.

Interim, dum responsum expecto, dabo operam ut juvenes duo summa cura seligantur, quales tuae litterae, Emin Cardlis exigunt; spero insuper me effecturum, ut itineris impensae, saltem hinc usque in Galliam a parentibus solvantur; si minus id obtinuero, omnem in illis moderationem adhiberi curabo. Intelligo autem pro unoquoque juvene navigationis et alios necessarios sumptus, donec portum attigerit, summam septuaginta vel octoginta aureorum circiter confecturos.

Reliqua de quibus instrui voluisti, Eme Cardlis, pro religiosa tua erga nos sollicitudine, opportunius separato scripto extra formam litterarum exhiberi posse existimavi; illud tamen hic iterum atque iterum obsecro, ut eam in facultatibus mihi concessis restrictionem tolli omni modo cures, qua aliorum Sacredotum opera uti prohibeor praeter illos quos sacra Congregatio destinaverit et approbaverit. Id enim nisi concedatur, brevi spatio magna Catholicorum pars omnino Sacramentorum expers erit, et Religionis ministeriis destituta. Unica enim quae nobis superest spes supplementi cujusdam cito recipiendi pro Sociis extinctis, aut jam ad extremum senium vergentibus, posita est in illis Sacerdotibus qui hic nati, ante bellum exortum in Europam educationis causa profecti sunt, ibique sacros Ordines susceperunt. Audio horum aliquos in patriam reditum cogitare, quibus tamen si advenerint, in otio erit manendum, utcumque moribus et doctrina comparatis ad hanc Domini vineam excolendam. Itaque, omni quidem reverentia, sed simul summa fiducia, et ex plena persuasione id e re Religionis fore, rogo, Emin Cardinalis, ut tuum apud Sanctitatem Suam studium interponas, illique significes, Superiori in his Foederatae Americae Statibus omnino necesse esse, ut quos Sacerdotes dignos judicaverit, hos in laborum Societatem possit scire.

Haec habui, Eme Cardinalis, quae libere fideliterque scriberem de rebus ad Religionem spectantibus, quibus veluti supplementum ad tria quaesita responsum accedent, quae altero scripto commemorata reperies. Mihi jam sit permissum hanc gregis Dominici portionem, pastoresq qui in illo sunt, meq ipsum singulari tuae pietati, paternaeq[ue] benevolentiae commendare; precariq, ut oculos conjicias in immensas illas regiones, quae foederatae Americae finibus continentur; indiesq magis ac magis immigrantium accessionibus, et ex naturali faecunditate, incolentium numero augentur. Ubique libere praedicari poterit vera fides, nec quidquam obstare videtur, quo minus magni ex hac libertate fructus decerpantur, praeter operariorum defectum, mediaque illis providendi. Ad te igitur, qui singulari cura, studio et auctoritate Religionis propagationi invigilas, re currimus, ut quae ad hunc finem meditamur, pro tua sapientia adjuvare velis, hancque regionem veluti tuae providentiae et fidei commissam intueri. Quod ad me spectat, ego summa fiducia, Eminentissime Cardinalis, in hujus Ecclesiae negotiis tua consilia, tuam auctoritatem, pietatem tuam implorabo, precaborque Deum omnipotentem, ut pro animarum salute, divinaeque fidei extensione te salvum et incolumem diu esse velit. Ita vovet   Eminentissime   Cardinalis   Eminae   Tuae   Servus Obsequentissimus   Joannes Carroll   Ex Marilandia, die 27ª Februarii, 1785

TO LEONARDO ANTONELLI   March 1, 1785

Report for His Eminence Cardinal Antonelli on the condition of religion in the sections of the United States of America.

1. Concerning the number of Catholics in the United States of America.

The Catholic population in Maryland is about 15,800. Of this number nine thousand are adult freemen, that is above twelve years of age; about three thousand are children, and the same number are slaves of all ages, come from Africa, who are called "Negroes" because of their color.[1] In Pennsylvania there are at least seven thousand but very few Africans. There the Catholics live more grouped together and near one another. In Virginia there are not more than two hundred, ministered to by a priest four or five times a year. Many others are said to live scattered here and there in that state and in the others, destitute of all religious services. In the state called New York I hear there are at least fifteen hundred, who recently, at common expense, brought from Ireland a religious of the order of Saint Francis;[2] and he is said to have credentials vouching for his excellent conduct and sound doctrine.

He had arrived shortly before I received the letter in which faculties were given to me which I could communicate to my assistants. I doubted for a while whether I could lawfully approve this priest for the administration of the sacraments. Then I decided as the feast of Easter was at hand, to use him as an assistant and the necessary faculties were granted. I trust my decision will be approved. Nothing certain can be said about the number of Catholics who live in the territory near the so-called Mississippi River, and in all that region which stretches from that river to the Atlantic Ocean, and from there to the boundaries of Carolina, Virginia and Pennsylvania. I hear that there are many Catholics in this territory once Canadians, who speak French. I greatly fear that they are left without ministers of the sacraments. Not long ago a certain German priest, who had come directly from France, went to them. He claims to be a member of the Carmelite order, but he had no adequate credentials that he had been sent by a legitimate superior.[3] I expect him any day to let me know what he is doing and in what condition Catholic affairs are there. The bishop of Quebec once had jurisdiction over part of that territory, but now, since the whole territory has come under the control of the United States, I have no idea whether he wants to exercise his jurisdiction.

2. Concerning the condition, observance and abuses of the Catholic population.

In Maryland a few of the outstanding and wealthy families dating back to the first founding of the colony still profess the Catholic religion brought here by their ancestors. The majority are farmers, and in Pennsylvania, apart from the merchants and workmen who live in Philadelphia, almost all are farmers. As for their observance, in general they are rather faithful to the practices of their religion, and in frequenting the sacraments. All fervor, however, is lacking, which usually is developed by constant exhortation to piety, since many congregations attend Mass and hear a sermon once a month or every two months. To this extent are we overwhelmed by the scarcity of priests, and even more so by the distances between missions and by the difficulties of travel. This refers to those born here; very different is the condition of the Catholics who pour in upon us in large numbers from various European countries. Since there are some of our own who do not approach the sacraments of Penance and the Eucharist more than once a year, usually at Eastertime, hardly anyone is found among the immigrants who observes this duty of religion. It is feared that their example will be especially harmful in the trading centers.

The abuses among the Catholic popuation are those above all which spring from the necessity of familiar relations with the non-Catholics and from the ideals derived from them. For example, the rather free conduct of the young people of both sexes, which endangers integrity of soul, and perhaps even of body; an undue propensity to dancing and other such things; and an unbelievable eagerness, especially among girls, to read novels which are brought here in large numbers. In general, then there is a lack of care in educating the children in religion, especially the African slaves. The whole care of education is handed over to the priests, and the result is that, since the children are busy with constant chores and can be with the priest only rarely and for a short time, most of them usually are uninstructed in the faith and very lax in morals. It is hard to believe how greatly cares and worries exhaust the pastors of souls.

3. Concerning the number of priests, their education and means of support.

In Maryland there are nineteen priests; in Pennsylvania five. Of these however, two are beyond, and three others are approaching seventy years, and thus they are totally incapable of sustaining the labor necessary for cultivating this vineyard of the Lord. Among the other priests some are already in poor health, and one has recently been approved by me for only a few months that I might test him. Such is the extreme need of laborers. I heard some reports about him which made me very reluctant to use his services. I will keep him under observation as much as I can, and if he does anything unworthy of priestly dignity, I will revoke the faculties I have given, however great the harm to many Catholics which would result. For I am convinced that the Catholic faith will suffer less if there are no priests for a short while than if, I do not say bad priests but those who are deficient in prudence and caution are admitted to the ministry. And this for the reason that we live among people of other religious beliefs. The other priests live lives in which labor abounds because they serve congregations far removed from one another, and they are constantly worn out by long and difficult journeys to the sick. For the most part the priests are supported by proceeds from their farms or by the liberality of the Catholics. Strictly speaking there are no ecclesiastical foundations here. The possessions by which priests are supported are held in the name of private individuals, and by will they are transferred to their heirs. This procedure was dictated by dire necessity while the Catholic religion is restricted by laws; nor have we thus far found a remedy for this inconvenience although during the past year we have tried hard to do so. It is not clear to us what we should do to insure successors in the ministry. In Philadelphia there is now a college, and there are plans for two in Maryland. Admission to them is open to Catholics equally with others as officials, professors or students. As we hope that some of them may wish to embrace the clerical life we are giving thought to building a seminary in which they could be formed in conduct and learning compatible with that state.

After this account may I be permitted to add what I judge absolutely necessary for the spiritual governance of Catholics. First of all the daily contacts with non-Catholics gives rise to constant danger of entering marriages with them. To avert this danger there grew up among us the practice of dispensing among Catholic blood relations as far as we were allowed. Experience has taught us that in this wise religion was not only safeguarded but also increased. The Holy Father has graciously granted me faculties communicable to my fellow workers of dispensing when the third degree touches the second, and for the lower degrees of consanguinity and affinity. In my name and theirs in all humility I ask that He may wish to extend, at least to the Superior of the mission, faculties for dispensing in the simple second degree, both of consanguinity and affinity. However, if he cannot grant this in general, although the distances between missions makes it most desirable, I pray that He grant me the faculty of dispensing in thirty cases at least. My colaborers most earnestly wish that dispensation could be granted here for the first degree of affinity resulting from illicit sexual intercourse. This impediment often obtains among the Africans, especially before marriage is entered into; and it is discovered by the priest accidentally only after the lapse of an extended period of time and many years of co-habitation.

I see also that it is desirable to extend the permission to celebrate Mass after noon to one oclock, because at times confessions cannot be heard in less than three hours. This has happened to me often when I heard confessions from early morning; and I believed that in such circumstances it was preferable rather than send home without Communion people who with great difficulty and inconvenience had come twenty or thirty miles or even further. And among them were pregnant women, some of them close to delivery. We wish His Holiness to express his mind on this subject.

If I should think of anything else that you would care to know so that the very eminent Cardinal may be informed I shall write about it fully.   John Carroll

ALS   PF

[1] The Catholic population of Maryland about this time was 12 percent, according to recent studies. (Total population of the state, according to the 1790 census was 319,728. See David C. Skaggs, "Maryland's Impulse Toward Social Revolution: 1750-1776," *Journal of American History* LIV [Mar., 1968], 771.)

[2] Charles Maurice Whelan, an Irish Capuchin, who reached New York in October, 1784. He later had a conflict with Carroll. See Apr. 16, 1785.

[3] Paul de St. Pierre, the Carmelite Missionary in the Illinois country. He came to Virginia about this time and soon returned again to Illinois. See Mar. 31 and Apr. 7, 1796.

Relatio pro Eme Cardinali Antonelli de Statu Religionis in Unitis Foederatae Americae Provinciis

1. De numero Catholicorum in Foederatae Americae Provinciis

Sunt in *Marilandia circiter 15,800.* Ex his sunt novem milla homines liberi aetatis adultae, aut supra annum duodecimum; pueri minoris aetatis fere ter mille, totidemque omnis aetatis servi (Nigros vocant a colore) ex Africa oriundi. In *Pensilvania* sunt ad minimum *septem mille,* inter quos paucissimi Africani, vivuntq Catholici collecti magis ac sibi invicem contigui. In *Virginia sunt non amplius ducenti,* quibus quater aut quinquies per annum adest Sacerdos. Dicuntur plurimi alii, tam in illa, quam in coeteris provinciis sparsim vivere, omni Religionis ministerio destituti. In provincia *Novum Eboracum* dicta, audio esse *mille quingentos ad minimum,* qui nuper communibus sumptibus ex Hibernia accersiverunt virum Religiosum Ordinis Sti. Francisci; diciturq optimis de moribus et doctrina documentis instructus esse; advenerat paulo prius quam litteras accepissem, quibus facultates Sociis communicabiles ad me sunt delatae. Dubitavi aliquando an jure possem hunc pro Sacramentorum administratione approbare. At jam statui, appropinquante maxime festo Paschali, ipsum pro Socio habere, facultatesq necessarias impertiri, quod meum consilium approbatum iri confido. Nihil certi dicere licet de numero Catholicorum, qui sunt in locis conterminis fluvio dicto Mississippi, omnique illi regioni, quae secundum illus flumium ad Oceanum Atlanticum pertingit, et ab eodem usque ad limites Carolinae, Virginiae, et Pensilvaniae extenditur. Hic tractus continet, ut audio, multos Catholicos, olim Canadenses, qui lingua Gallica utuntur, quos rerum sacrarum Ministris destitutos esse valde metuo. Transivit ad illos nuper Sacerdos quidam Germanus, sed ex Gallia ultimo profectus, qui ex ordine Carmelitorum se esse profitetur; nullo tamen sufficiente testimonio muniebatur, missum se esse a legitimo superiore. Quid agat, et quo statu ibi sint res Catholicae, edoctum me iri propediem expecto. Episcopi Quebecensis jurisdictio in aliquam regionis illius partem olim pertinuit; an nunc autem, cum omnes in foederatae Americae ditionem ceperint, potestatem illam exercere velit, haud equidem scio.

2. De Catholicorum conditione, pietate, abusibus, etc.

In Marilandia paucae ex praecipuis et ditioribus familiis, a primis provinciae fundamentis, fidem Catholicam a progenitoribus huc invectam adhuc profitentur; major autem pars sunt agricolae; et in Pensilvania fere omnes, exceptis mercatoribus et opificibus qui Philadelphiae degunt. Quod ad pietatem spectat, sunt, ut plurimum, in Religionis exercitiis et Sacramentorum frequentatione, satis assidui, sed sine ullo fervore, quem solet excitare continua ad sensa pietatis exhortatio; vix enim singulis mensibus, aut etiam bimestri spatio plurimae Congregationes rem divinam, et concionem sibi fieri audiunt; ita Sacerdotum inopia, multoq magis locorum intervallo, itinerisq incommodis opprimimur. Haec de indigenis dicta sint; alia enim longa est ratio Catholicorum, qui magno numero ex variis Europae nationibus ad nos confluunt. Cum enim ex nostratibus pauci sint qui non saepius per annum praecipue autem tempore paschali [ad] sacramenta Poenitentiae et Eucharistiae accedant, vix reperitur inter priores illos, qui officium hoc Religionis exerceat, quorum exemplum in urbibus mercatoriis maxime perniciosum fore timetur.

Abusus inter Catholicos sunt illi maxime, qui ex necessaria cum Acatholicis familiaritate et exemplis inde collectis oriuntur, liberior nempe se trac-

tandi ratio inter juniores personas diversi sexus, quam animi, aut forte etiam
corporis integritas patiatur; nimis propensum studium ad saltationes, et id
genus alia; et incredibilis aviditas (in puellis praecipue) legendi fabulas ama-
torias, quae magno numero ad nos advehuntur. Deinde, in coeteris universim,
defectus diligentiae in educandis in religione liberis, sed praecipue servis
Africanis, totius illius curae ad Sacerdotes transmissio; ex quo fit ut cum sint
continuio laboribus exerciti, raroq et non nisi ad breve tempus cum Sacerdote
esse possint, in fide rudes et in moribus turpissimi plerique esse soleant.
Incredibile est, quantum animarum pastoribus molestiae et sollicitudinis
facessant.

De numero Presbyterorum, studiis, et modo se sustendandi.

Sunt in *Marilandia Presbyteri novemdecim; in Pennsilvania quinque.* Ex his
autem duo sunt supra, tres alii proxime ad septuagesimum annum accedant,
adeoq omnino impares subeundis laboribus, sine quibus haec Domini vinea
coli non potest. Inter reliquos Presbyteros aliqui admodum infirma valetudine
utuntur et unus est nuper a me approbatus ad paucos menses tantum ut
experimentum illius faciam in extrema presbyterorum necessitate. Aliqua
enim de ipso narrabuntur quae vehementer me deterrebat ab illius opera
adhibenda. Ego quidem illi, quantum possum invigilabo; et si quid acciderit
gravitate sacerdotali minus dignum facultates concessas revocabo, quantum-
cunque incommodum multis Catholicis inde eventurum sit. Mihi enim persuasum est Catholicam fidem minus detrimenti passuram si nulli Sacerdotes per
breve tempus fuerint, quam si, ubi ita vivimus inter alterius Religionis homines, ad sacra ministeria assumuntur, non dicam mali Sacerdotes sed etiam
imprudentes et incauti. Reliqui omnes Sacerdotes plenam laboris vitam agunt,
quod unusquisque congregationibus longe dissitis obsequium praestet, adeoq
continuis, gravissimisque equitationibus ad aegrotos praecipue continuo fati-
getur.

Presbyteri sustentantur, ut plurimum, ex fundorum proventibus; alibi vero
liberalitate Catholicorum. Nulla hic proprie sunt bona Ecclesiastica. Privatorum enim nomine possidentur ea bona, ex quibus aluntur Presbyteri; et
testimentis transferuntur ad haeredes. Ita faciendum suggesit dira necessitas,
dum legibus Catholica Religio hic arctaretur; neque adhuc inventum est huic
incommodo remedium, quamvis multum a nobis anno elapso id tentaretur.
Ad procurandos in Religionis ministerio Successores, quid faciendum sit, non
satis intelligimus. Est jam Philadelphiae collegium, agiturque de duobus in
Marilandia extruendis, ad quae admitti poterunt Catholici aeque ac alii, tam
Praesides, quam Professores et alumni. Fore speramus, ut hos inter aliqui
vitam Ecclesiaticam velint amplecti. Cogitamus igitur de seminario institu-
endo in quo valeant deinceps ad mores et doctrinam statui illi convenientes
efformari.

Hac facta relatione, liceat nunc aliqua adjungo, quae omnino necessaria
judico ad spiritualem Catholicorum administrationem. Imprimis ex quotidi-
ano commercio cum Acatholicis oritur perpetuum discrimen ineundi cum
[eis] contractus *[illeg.]* quod periculum advertendum usus apud nos invalu-

erat dispensandi quantum nobis permittebatur, inter consanguineos Catholicos. Ita non solum conservari Religionem, sed augeri ab experientia didicimus. Ut igitur Ssmus Pater facultates mihi benigne concessit, Sociis etiam communicabiles dispensandi in 3o mixto cum 2o, et inferioribus consanguinitatis et affinitatis gradibus; ita humillime tam meo quam Sociorum nomine precor, ut saltem ad Superiorem extendere velit facultates dispensandi in 2o simplici, tam consanguinitatis quam affinitatis. Si autem illud generaliter concedi nequit, quod propter locorum distantiam maxime optandum esset, *pro triginta ad minimum vicibus* precor, ut ita dispensandi mihi detur facultas. Vehementer etiam a Sociis meis desideratur, ut possit his *dispensari in primo gradu affinitatis* ortae ex copula illicita. hoc enim impedimentum saepe subsistit inter Africanos praecipue ante matrimonium attentatum; nec tamen nisi longum post tempus. multorumq annorum cohabitationem Sacerdos impedimentum fortuito plerumq deprehendit.

Video praeterea dispensationem celebrandi missam post meridiem *ad unam tantum horam* extendi; cum tamen aliquando confessiones expediri non possint *ante tres horas,* quod mihi certe saepe contigit a prima aurora, illud ministerium auspicanti, credebamq in ejusmodi casibus legem charitatis validiorem esse, quam ut Sacramentorum expertes domum remitterentur, qui magno labore et incommodo viginti, triginta aut amplius mille passus venerant, et saepe in his mulieres gravidae et partui proximae. Hac item in re Sanctitatis suae mentem ulterius declarari cupimus.

Si quae alia occurant de quibus intellexero gratum fore, ut ad Emum Cardinalem relatio fiat, plene conscribam. Joannes Carroll Die 1a Martii 1785

TO JOSEPH EDENSHINK[1] [Apr.-June, 1785]

Dear Sir I have received your favour of Octr 4-1784 & was very glad to find that my former letter to you[2] had got to your hands. Your disposition to come to the assistance of your country, if sent or requested by the Presidt. of the Academy, is truly edifying, & convince me that if you have never had the happiness of being a member of our ever dear Society, you have at least imbibed her Spirit. I suppose from this, that you have entered into some engagement of a spiritual dependance on him; but for the sake of this country, I hope that it is not a perpetual engagement; or that Mr. Strickland will release you from it. We really labour under the most grievous necessity of supplies; and never, in my opinion, was a fairer field opened for the exertion of zeal, & the spreading of the truths of our divine Religion, than now offers here. Consider that in all the immense territory of the U.S. in general toleration prevails; that the part of it, which lies between the Mississippi & the frontiers of the old Colonies, is one of the finest climates & one richest soils in the known world; & for this reason is now filling very fast with

Inhabitants. Thousands of R.C. are wishing to remove thither, & nothing witholds them but the dread of wanting the ministrations of Religion. I have had repeated offers of liberal grants of land for the support of Clergymen there, if any could be prevailed on to go: and indeed some protestants, with a hope of having their lands speedily settled, have been induced to give their bonds for the conveyance to a Cath priest of very ample property. Add to this, that our prospects of spreading Religion are continually encreasing in the old States; that many of our Gentlemen are worn down with years and fatigue, & you will have some comprehension of our great distress for want of a reinforcement. It is generally conceived to be the duty of good citizens to assist their country sinking under the load of temporal distress: how much more therefore must all our able & healthy Countrymen be called upon to aid her in her present spiritual necessities, I beseech you therefore, my Dr. Sir; your Br. Charles, if his health permit it; Mr. Leonard Brooke, & all our other healthful Countrymen, to take our situation into their consideration, & resolve, as the interests of Religion and the glory of Alm. God shall direct. What an acquisition would not Messrs Mattingly & Semmes be to this country. But I fear, that they will be considered too precious in Europe. Do you know any young men of improved abilities, & good conduct, capable of teaching the different branches of science with credit & reputation? It is now in contemplation to establish two Colleges in this state,³ open to Professors & Scholars of all denominations, & handsome appointments are to be annexed to the professorships. To me it appears, that it may be of much service not only to learning, but to true Religion, to have some of these professorships filled by R.C. men of letters & virtue: and if one or two of them were in orders, it would be so much the better. I have reason to expect, that I may possibly have some interest with the Governors of these Colleges, & that my recommendation would have some weight. If therefore you know any such persons wanting employment & a comfortable subsistance, it may be in my power, on receiving your answer, to inform them of their prospects from these establishments. His Brs health Messrs Pile and Boone Mr Ellerker—Hothersal, Scar. Ash Ny Y. C. C., & Mr. Strickland

ADf   AAB   Dated by reference to previous and following letters in Carroll Letterbook.
¹Teacher at the Academy of Liege, soon to be ordained. Called *Eden* in America, he would participate in the First National Synod.
²Not found.
³Washington and St. John's Colleges.

TO ANTOINE DUGNANI¹   [Apr., 1785]

I had the honor of notifying your Excellency in the letter; which I believe I wrote in the month of February,² since I was far from my residence and cannot certify that I have the precise date, for lack of having at my side any copies from which to obtain the precise date; that I would send off to Rome in a short time two young Americans, to be raised at Urban College. I received instructions to this effect from his Em. Cardinal Antonelli. Your Excellency's predecessor at the nunciature of France, His Eminence the Cardinal and Prince Doria Pamphili, ordered me to address him an open letter, to be seen by the bishop, or Superior Eccles.: of the place of disembarkment, so that these young men can rely upon him in case of need: I will have them leave on a ship bound for Bordeaux: I know that there are other ports in France which might be prefered, or rather there are ports located so as to go more conveniently to Rome; but I thought that it would be better to entrust the travellers to a ship's Captain, a Catholic, a trustworthy man, rather than putting them into the hands of a stranger and of a sectarian, who would perhaps treat them harshly, or corrupt their morals.

The Congregation of the Propaganda had charitably offered to furnish the travelling expenses from America to France. But I advised the parents of these children to pay for that part of the cost. Your Exc. will be advised of their arrival at Bordeaux by the Archbishop or other ecclesiastical Superior: From that moment, they will be subject to your orders, for all the necessary arrangements in order to have them reach their destination. I take the liberty of recommending them to your kindness. Their parents are zealous Catholics. The one from Maryland is called Ralph Smith, who is . . . years old—the other from Pennsylvania is called . . . Dogherty, who is . . . years old.[3] I have the assurance that both are talented, and especially the latter. With the most profound respect I have the honor of being the very obedient servant of Mgr. your Exc.

ADf   AAB   Date estimated from Feb. 27, 1785. There is a second version (*ibid.*).
[1] Papal nuncio in Paris, succeeding Doria-Pamphili this year.
[2] See the 27th.
[3] Smith was twelve and Felix Dougherty nine. See to Antonelli, July 27, 1787, and to Dugnani, May, 1787.

J'ai eu l'honneur de prevenir votre Exc. par la lettre; que je crois avoir ecrite au mois de Fevrier (car etant loin du lieu de ma residence, je ne puis certifier la datte precise) faute d'en avoir aupres de moi, de copies pour en assurer la datte precise que je ferois partir pour Rome en peu de tems deux J[e]unes Americains, pour y être eleves au College Urbain. J'ai recu des Instructions à cet effet de son Em. le Cardl. Antonelli. Le predecesseur de V. Exc: dans la Nonciature de Fr. son Eminence, le Cardl. & Prince Doria Pamphili, m'a ordonné de lui addresser une lettre ouverte, pour être vue par l'eveque, ou Superieur Eccles: du lieu, du debarquement, afin que ces jeunes hommes puissent avoir recours à lui au cas de besoin: Je les fais partir sur un vaisseau destiné à Bordeaux: Je scais qu'il y a d'autres ports de France, qu'on peut preferer plutot qu'ils se trouvent de port [pour aller] le plus convenablement à Rome; mais j'ai cru qu'il valoit mieux confier les voyageurs [à] un Capitaine de vaisseau, Catholique, & homme de bien, que de les livrer entre les mains d'un etranger, & d'un sectaire, qui peutêtre ou les auroit traité avec dureté, ou auroit gaté leurs moeurs.

La Congregation de la Propagande s'etoit charitablement offerte à fournir aux frais du voyage de l'Amer. en France. Mais j'ai engage les parens de ces enfans à faire cette partie de la depense. V. Exc. sera avertie de leur arrivée a Bordeaux par l'Archeveque, ou autre Superieur Ecclesiastique: Des çe moment, ils seront soumis à ses ordres, pour tous les arrangements necessaires à les faire arriver au lieu de leur destination. Je prends la liberté de les recommander à ses bontés. Leurs parens sont Catholique zelés. Celui de Mariland s'appelle Rodolphe Smith, agé de [*blank*] ans—L'autre de Pensilvanie, est nommé [*blank*] Dogherty, agé de [*blank*] ans. On m'assure, que tous les deux ont de talent, & surtout le dernier. Avec le respect le plus profound J'ai l'honneur d'etre, Mgr de Votre Exc. Le tres humble & tres obeissant Serviteur . . .

TO CHARLES M. WHELAN   Rock Creek near F.T.[Frederick Town]
                                         Maryland April 16—1785

Revd. Sir   I heard at the beginning of the winter of your arrival at N.Y., which gave me great pleasure, it having been long my desire to have a clergyman settled there. I was very confident that a discreet and virtuous priest might there lay the foundation, on which a flourishing Congn. would rise. Soon after the news of your arrival, I received an appointment from his Holiness constituting me Superior General in the thirteen U.S. I was much mortified in perusing the powers sent me to find some doubtful expressions in my Commission, which appeared to restrain me from employing any Clergymen coming into the Country not immediately sent by the Congregation de propaganda. As you did not receive your approbation of mission from them I conceived my hands to be tied up in such a manner, that I could not give you faculties, & directed the Revd. Mr. Farmer so to inform you.

Since that time, I have been induced to consider more attentively the wants and necessity of the Catholics at New York,[1] and the terms of my appointment; & now conceive that you do not come under the aforesaid restriction: to think, you were arrived before I had my appointment. I sent therefore about a month ago, directions to transmit your faculties; I have been informed that you did not want to receive proper powers from me; and that you have assumed authority as well to administer the Sacraments, as to celebrate twice on sundays. you cannot be ignorant, that both the proceedings are irregular and very rigorously forbidden, by the Church. You will therefore oblige me much by informing Mr. Farmer, on what principles you proceeded, when you acted in this manner; and as I have the utmost confidence in that Gentleman's prudence and charity, the granting of faculties, or the continuation of them, if already transmitted to you, will depend on the reasons, which you are able to furnish for your past conduct. I sincerely hope, and flatter myself, that they will be such, as may not diminish the regard, with which I would always wish to continue, Rd. Sir,   Yr. most obedt humble Sert   J.C.

ADf   AAB
    [1] See Mar. 1, 1785, n. 1.

TO LEONARD NEALE   June 17, 1785

Dear Sir: I have received your favour of *Oct. 4. 1785* and was very glad to find that my former letter[1] to you had got to your hands. Your disposition to come to the assistance of your country, if sent or requested by the President of the Academy is truly edifying and convinces me, that if you have never had the happiness of being a member of our ever dear Society, you have at least imbibed her Spirit. I suppose from this that you have entered into engagement of a spiritual dependance on him; but for the sake of this country, I hope, that it is not a perpetual engagement or that Mr. Strickland will release you from it. We really labour under the most grievous necessity of supplies, and never in my opinion, was a fairer field opened for the exertion of zeal and the spreading of the truth of our divine Religion, than now offers here. Consider that in all the immense territory of the United States a general toleration prevails, that the part of it, which lies between the Mississippi and the frontiers of the old colonies is in one of the finest climates and richest soils in the known world; and for this reason is now filling very fast with inhabitants. Thousands of Roman Catholics are rushing to remove thither, and nothing withholds them but the dread of wanting the ministrations of religion. I have had repeated offers of liberal grants of land for the support of clergymen there, if any could be prevailed on to go: and indeed some Protestants, with a hope of having their lands speedily settled, have been induced to give their bonds for the conveyance to a Catholic priest of every ample property. Add to this that our prospects of spreading religion are continually increasing in the old states: that many of our gentlemen are worn down with years and fatigue, and you will have some comprehension of our great distress for want of a reinforcement. It is generally conceived to be the duty of good citizens to assist their country sinking under the load of temporal distress: how much more therefore, must all our able and healthy countrymen be called upon to aid her in her present spiritual necessities. I beseech you therefore, my dear Sir; your Brother Charles, if his health permit it, Mr. Leonard Brooke,[2] and all our other healthful countrymen, to take our situation into their consideration, and resolve, as the interests of Religion and the glory of Almighty God shall direct. What an acquisition would not Messrs. Mattingly and Semmes be to this country? But I fear that they will be considered too precious in Europe. Mr. Ashton to remit to England.

Do you know of any young men of improved ability and good conduct, capable of teaching the different branches of science with credit and reputation? It is now in contemplation to establish two colleges in this state, open to professors and scholars of all denominations, and handsome appointments are to be annexed to the professorships. To me it appears that it may be of much services not only to learning but to true religion to have some of these professorships filled by Roman Catholic men of letters and virtue: and if one or two of them were in orders, it would be so much the better. I have reason to expect that I may possibly have some interest with the governors of these colleges,[3] and that my recommendation would have some weight. If therefore, you know any such persons wanting employment in a comfortable sustenance, it may be in my power in receiving your answer, to inform them of their prospect from these establishments.

T   GU   SC
[1] Not found.
[2] Did not come until 1790, when he accompanied the Carmelite nuns from Holland as their spiritual director. He was a superior of the restored Jesuits.
[3] He held an honorary degree from Washington College and served on its board of visitors.

TO WILLIAM STRICKLAND[1]   June 17, 1785

I the undersigned by apostolic authority superior of the missions in the thirteen United States of North America affirm that Joseph Edenshink, a student of sacred theology in the English school at Liege, has made known to me his desire to take orders and serve God in these missions. Wherefore in my eagerness to get workers, of whom there is a great scarcity here, and in the full assurance of the said Joseph's virtue and learning, I most humbly ask the most excellent bishop and spiritual head of Lyons to confer orders on the said Joseph, by the title of activity on the missions, and I oblige myself and my successors to provide his due sustenance so long as he shall be active in this vineyard of the Lord.   J. C.

ADfS   AAB
[1] Rector and President of Liege Academy and Bruges College simultaneously in 1784.

Ego infra scriptus Apostolica auctoritate constitutus Superior missionum in Tredecim unitis provinciis Americae Septentrionalis fidem facio Josephum Edenshink, sacrae theologiae auditorem in academia Anglica Leodii, mihi significasse suum desiderium sacros ordines suscipiendi, Deoque in hisce missionibus inserviendi; quare permotus studio comparandi operarios quorum magna hic inopia, confidensque dictum Josephum virtutibus et doctrina idoneis, instructum, humillime precor Celsissimum Episcopum et Principem Leodiensem, ut dictum Josephum ad sacros ordines, titulo missionis, promovere dignetur; cui deinceps ut commoda fiat sustentatio, in me, meosque successores suscipio, quamdiu operam in hac Domini vinea debite exercuerit.   J.D. die 17 Junii, 1785

TO CHARLES PLOWDEN   Rock-Creek, June 29—1785—

My dear Sir   I begin with informing you, that I have had the pleasure of receiving your welcome favour of Feb. 28th; by which you will observe, that the post is a safe conveyance. I wrote to you in March last, and wish, that business may have called you to London about the time of that letter getting there; for it went under cover to Talbot, together with a letter for Thorpe, which I wished you to see; but which was too long to be copied for your perusal. With mine to you I sent a copy of my answer to Wharton and at the same time my own real opinion of it. That Gentleman has again just published a reply;[1] which like his letter, is written with spirit and elegance, and interspersed with many sentimental passages. He has boldly denied facts, which I did not expect, that any one now a days would have the effrontery to dispute: he has explained away his misquotations: he has vindicated particular passages in his letter by keeping his own words out of sight, of which you will see curious instances in his dissertation on the word *hades,* & in many places of his reply to my observations on Infallibility. I have no inclination to enter the lists again. The Catholics, I hear from all sides, are confirmed in their faith; and as that was my principal, and indeed, my only inducement to write at all, I shall forbear reviving a spirit of controversy, least it should add fuel to some sparks of religious animosity, which are visible at present amongst us. Mr. Wharton, soon after his departure from us, obtained a living in the Delawar State, consisting of a small glebe-land, & a subscription of the neighbouring members of the Protestant Episcopal Church, to the real annual amount of perhaps £ St. 100. I hear that he has now quitted this living, and is invited to another in this state. But it being in a very unhealthy part of the Country, & depending on precarious, and generally illpaid subscriptions, I presume he will not accept it. But there is no doubt of his writings and abilities recommending him to his new Brethren, so that he will have good offers enough from them to put it in his power to chuse that, which will please him best. A gentleman from London has lately presented me with Mr. Pillings *Caveat.*[2] With his opportunities of referring to any authors, he might want, he could have made his answer more compleat, especially had he been master of a more methodical genius, & graceful stile. However, there are excellent observations, & solid, as well as acute reasonings in it. You will see, that we do not agree in our character of Ganganelli; and I sincerely hope, that you will disabuse the world of the prejudices in his favour, which were first inculcated by the indefatigable industry of an inveterate faction. This puts me in mind of asking you to send me the history of the letters published in his name and translated into English. I am very sure, they are not his: but till I can give good proofs of it, I am not believed, when I say so. Let me recommend to you when you treat off that Pope's character, to give no way to your imagination; but support all your assertions with such authority, as shall convict the most hardened prejudices; and forget not to send me immediately, whatever you write on the subject. Your advice, and observations on our Religious situation here are always received with pleasure and gratitude. The prospect before us is immense; but the want of cultivators to enter into the field & improve it is a dreadful and discouraging circumstance. I receive applications from every part of the U. States, North, South & West, for Clergymen: and considerable property is offered for their maintenance: but it is impossible & cruel to abandon the Congregations already formed to go in quest of people who wish to be established into new ones. I have written in a pressing manner to all, whom I conceive likely to come to our assistance: and I hope you will urge the return hither of Charles & Francis Neale,[3] Leonard Brooke, & Thomson, if his health will allow it. Messrs Mattingly & Semmes would be sterling acquisitions; but, I fear, you will retain them in Europe. Encourage all you can meet with, Europeans or Americans, to come amongst us: we hope soon to have a sum of money lodged in London to pay the passages of six at least. And your charitable Gentlemen & Ladies will not fail in aiding so good a work. I was never more surprised, than at what you mention of Mr. Jas. Nelson. I am yet convinced, that tho' he may have been imprudent, perhaps even frail in a particular instance; he certainly is not vicious habitually and [*torn*] please God, find it so. Poor Aston! or rather, poor human nature! if your information concerning him is right, it must suggest the reflexions of Pope on the great Bacon—*Do parts allure Thee &c?*[4] I have written to him, & am sure he must have received my letters: but he never answered; & therefore I shall write no more. I was so pleased with Berington's pamphlet, *on the behaviour* &c *of the R.C.,*[5] that immediately after reading it, I wrote him a complimentary letter, which he has not been polite enough to answer. I know there are some reprehensible passages in it; but on the whole, I viewed it as a spirited & useful work: useful, as a vindication against our opponents; and as a corrective for ourselves. I find it very difficult where I now live, to attend the duties of my present station. It is inconvenient to some to apply to me here; and however painful it will be to my dear Mother, & myself, I apprehend that it will be necessary for me to remove to Baltimore as a more centrical situation. You shall know more particularly in my next. Be pleased to present my respectful compliments to

Messrs. Stanley and Clinton, and all the other Gentlemen within your reach. Mr. Reeves[6] translation of the history of the Bible has been lately reprinted at Phila. A most excellent work! which I recommend to every Cath. family in the country. My Mother, Mr. Thos. Digges, a great admirer of yours, & all your acquaintance desire their respects & Complts. &c Dr. Sir.   Yr. sincere affte friend & servt   J. Carroll

ALS   St
[1] *A Short and Candid Inquiry* (Phila., 1785).
[2] William Pilling, an English Franciscan Friar, author of *Caveat to the Catholics of Worcester against the Insinuating Letter of Dr. Wharton* (London, 1785).
[3] President of Georgetown College, 1804-12.
[4] Line 281 of "Essay on Man."
[5] See July 10, 1784.
[6] Thomas Reeves, S.J., church historian and biblical scholar, was once at Watten novitiate with Carroll.

TO THE VISITORS AND GOVERNORS OF WASHINGTON COLLEGE[1]

Rock Creek, July 1st 1785

Gentlemen—   I have been just informed of the very unexpected honour[2] done me at your late commencement. On this occasion, I feel a very lively impression of gratitude for the favourable and indeed too advantageous opinion, you are pleased to entertain of me: and at the same time, I receive additional pleasure from the diffusion of liberal and tolerating principles, which overlooking diversity of Religious sentiment, consider litterary merit alone in the collation of academical honours, flattering myself that your example and influence will perpetuate this spirit in Washington College, for the advancement of science and the happiness of our State. With sentiments of perfect respect, I have the honour to be, Gentlemen,   Yr. obliged and most humble Sert   J. Carroll

ALS   ACHSP
[1] Founded in 1782 at Chestertown, Md. under the leadership of William Smith, Carroll served on the board of visitors.
[2] Doctor of Divinity degree.

TO JOHN CAUSSE[1]

Aug: 16–1785

Reverend Sir   From your letter and that of Rev. Mr. Farmer I learned that you have already been in America a number of years, and that, with proper authorization of your superiors, you came to labor in this vineyard of the Lord. Indeed I rejoice and I thank the great and good God whenever He chooses to direct ministers of holy things to help us; and I should wish, now that the care of the Church in America is entrusted to me, to interpose no obstacle to any pious, learned and prudent priests whose services I could use.

Your reverence will learn from Mr. Farmer what are the limits of my authority. In view of the extreme needs of Catholics, the small number of priests and your long time in coming to America, I have decided to place you in Lancaster [Pa.]. From Mr. Farmer you will learn, if it can be done without inconvenience, that whatever faculties he gives to you are to be regarded as awarded by me, and I want you to know that they are to obtain until I decide otherwise, or till letters from Rome inform me how and on what conditions priests who come to America are approved. If, all things considered, Mr. Farmer should assign you to Lancaster you will get from Mr. Geissler[2] such directions as will in all respects be useful to you and to the congregations entrusted to you. You could not do better than follow in his footsteps and imitate his prudence and zeal for the glory of God. What pertains to the providing of temporalities lies beyond my jurisdiction; I shall, however, endeavor to bring it about that while you are at Lancaster proper sustenance is forthcoming. That this method of providing for you prove agreeable and satisfactory is my earnest wish till I shall have matured other plans which are turning over in my mind about you and your future ministry in this Church.   Reverend Sir, your very humble servant in Christ   J.C.

ADfS   AAB
[1] A German Recollect (Father Fidentius), he left his monastery without permission and came to Philadelphia. Farmer obtained pardon for him from his superiors.
[2] Luke Geissler, S.J., a German, came to Maryland in 1769, and died in Conewago, Pa.

August 15, 1785   Rde. Domine—   Ex tuis simul et Reverendi D. Farmer litteris primum intellexi te in America jam plures per annos versatum esse; et in illiam, ex tuorum Superiorum legitima auctoritate, advenisse, ut operam poneres in hac Domini vinea excolenda. Gaudeo quidem, et Deo optimo Maximo gratias ago, quandoncunque rerum sacrarum Ministros ad Religionis subsidium huc destinare visum ipsi fuerit, cuperemque, siquidem hujus ecclesiae Americanae cura mihi indignissimo committitur, nullum impedimentum intervenire quo minus cujusvis Sacerdotis pii, docti et prudentis ministerio uti possim. Intelliget autem Rev, Va. ex Domino Farmer quibus terminis mea concludatur auctoritas. Porro, perpensa Catholicorum extrema necessitate, paucitate sacerdotum, et diturno tuo in Americam adventu, statui tuam operam Lancastriae adhibere, ut ex eodem intelliges, si tamen viderit id absque incommodo fieri posse; quasque facultates ille tibi exhibebit, tamquam mea authoritate concessas, velim existimes, et tamdiu duraturas, donec aliud statuero aut Roma litterae adferantur, quibus de modo et ratione approbandi Sacerdotes huc migrantes certior fiam. Si, perpensis omnibus, Dom. Farmer te judicaverit ad Lancastriam esse destinandum, ex Dom. Geissler, praedecessore tuo, talem de omnibus instructionem colli quae maxime tibi et congregationibus tibi commissis, utilis esse possit: nec operam tuam melius impendes, quam illius inhaerendo vestigiis, prudentiamque et divinae gloriae studium imitando. Quod ad rerum temporalium subministrationem spectat, mei juris non est; conari tamen efficiam, ut suppeditetur, quod honestae sustentationi sufficiat, dum Lancastriae fueris. Haec de te providentia ut tibi grata sit, et commoda, sincere opto; donec alia, quae mihi in animo observantur, consilia maturavero de te, futuroque tuo in hac Ecclesia ministerio. Interim aestimari velim. Revde Domine, Servus in Christo humillimus   J.C.   Joannes Cause

TO[?]   Rock-Creek near George-town August 18th, 1785

Revd. Sir.   I had the pleasure of receiving last winter two of your letters from Baltimore, which I answerd, but you had left that town, before my answer reached it. Some time after, I was favoured with another from you, dated Pittsburgh; and finally, on the 9th. of this month, I had the additional pleasure of receiving your letter from Louisville, dated February the 18th. Nothing has prevented your hearing from me but the want of an opportunity. If I had known, that you would live so near Mr. Lancaster's family, I could have written, by an excellent opportunity, about three months ago. I am very much pleased to observe, that you propose extending your zeal to them, several times during the year: for tho' it is not yet in my power to give you *regular* jurisdiction, and spiritual powers, yet the necessities of Catholics in that country will justify a deviation from settled rules. The reason, why I cannot give you regular jurisdiction is, that when my appointment to be Ecclesiastical Superior arrived, I was directed & commanded *concedere facultates* &c illis Sacerdotibus, quos sacra Congregatio de Propaganda fide approbaverit et destinaverit, et *non aliis.*[1] If this restriction is not removed, there must soon be an end of the American Church, and so I have represented: but in the mean time we suffer great inconvenience. In this circumstance, it rests with you to consider, whether the situation of the Catholics with you does not realize that case, *in quo* praesumpta intentio et voluntas Ecclesiae supplet *defectum jurisdictionis.*[2] For my own part, I think, there can be little doubt of it, where the Clergyman is conscious to himself, that he lies under no Ecclesiastical censure, and has been regularly approved by the Ordinary under whom he last lived. I will be so candid with you, as to confess, that I heared with concern, that you did not bring with you any proper testimonial of your having come into America, this 2d. time, by authority and direction of your Religious Superiors. & that when 1st at Balt, you endeavoured to make the Congn. believe, that Mr. Ashton being an ex-jt [Jesuit], had no powers to administer the Sacraments. If my information in this respect should be wrong, as I hope it is, you will be kind enough to set me right. I shall annex to this letter a copy *Facultatum,* quae Sociis Sacerdotibus hic communicantur.[3] I cannot say, for reasons above mentioned, that I communicate them likewise to you, but leave it to your own prudence and charity to use them, as you in conscience *et coram Deo* think, you may. With regard to matrimonial dispensations, there is less difficulty: for wherever you think they ought to be granted, within the degrees contained in the annexed paper, so far I grant them, & you may inform the marrying persons, that they have them from the Ecclesiastical Superior in these States. But in no case whatever must you presume to marry, those, who are more nearly related, as the marriage would be null, & the parties would be obliged afterwards to separate.

It is not unlikely, that I may visit you in the course of next year; & hope to find abundant effects of your zeal, in the number, & still more in the piety of your Congregations: concerning the number of which, their distances from each other &c, I shall esteem it a great favour if you would inform me, agreeably to your promise. Wishing you every happiness, here & hereafter, & desiring to partake in your good prayers, I am with regard, Revd. Sir,   Yr. h. s.   J.C.

When you see Mrs. Lancaster, be pleased to inform her, that my Mother & the rest of her family continue well & present their tender love to her.   J. [*fold*] expect soon to live at Baltimore, & write in English, as I suppose you are now well able to understand it.

ADfS   AAB
 [1] "To grant faculties to those priests whom the Sacred Congregation of the Propagation of the Faith shall approve and appoint, and no others."
 [2] "In which the presumed intention and will of the Church supplies the lack of jurisdiction."
 [3] "Of the faculties which are here communicated to the priest members [of the Society of Jesus]."

TO CHARLES PLOWDEN   Rock Creek Decr. 15—1785

Dear Sir   I had the pleasure of receiving your favour of June 6th, on the 23d. of Septr. I had left home the day before on a progress to administer confirmation at Phila., N. York, and in the upper country of the Jersies & Pennsylvania where our worthy German Brethren[1] have formed Congregns. That at N. York, begun by the Ven: Mr. Farmer of Phila., he has now ceded to an Irish Capuchin resident there.[2] He arrived a few months before my appointment to my present station; and the great necessity of the Catholics there induced me to give a liberal construction to the terms of my authority, & approve him, upon the principle of his being in the Country, before I was restrained from employing any, for the time to come, not sent and approved by the propgda. The prospect at that place is pleasing on the whole: the Capuchin is a zealous, pious, &, I think, humble man: he is not indeed so learned or good a preacher, as I could wish, which mortifies his congregation as at N. York, & most other places of America, the different sectaries have scarce any other test to judge of a Clergyman than his talents for preaching:

and our Irish Congns, such as N. York, follow the same rule. Just before I got to that place, another of his Brethren arrived from Cork,[3] a man of good education, as he appeared to me; but he must remain in inaction till it shall please your favourite Congn. at Rome to enlarge my powers. I notice your advice, inforced by Mr. Thorpe's opinion, that I should not admit the appointment of a Vicar Apostolic; which I certainly will not, unless I see the matter hereafter in a very different light. I have just heared, that dispatches are come for me in the last French packet; I expect them every day, and hope they will prove such as the exigences of Religion here require. I see you have some suspicions of Thyers,[4] and of a French influence, in our Ecclesiastical concerns. On the latter subject, your apprehensions are unnecessary and totally groundless; & were you intimately acquainted with the nature of our governments, and the disposition of our people, you would not entertain them for a moment. If you adopt any of yr. ideas of America upon the credit of your News-papers, you recur to very bad sources. I often see those papers, & other publications from England; & more misrepresentation & idle nonsense I never remember to have read. Concerning Mr. Thyers, I can only tell you that I have had much conversation with Dr. Franklin about him; & that I find the Dr. does not greatly esteem him. He believes him sincere but does not think him wise. I rememberd what you wrote me, of Thyers having informed Mr. Thorpe, that a secret, respecting the future designs of the propada upon this country, had been communicated to him by the Nuncio Doria: I pumped the Dr. on this subject & he informed me that he was sure, Doria had communicated no secret to him as the Dr. knew, that Doria had no confidence in, not much regard for Thyers. I hope you will not neglect sending me the account of our Polish, or Russian Brethren[5] according to promise. Mr. Talbot, in his letters, is very urging for our reunion with them: but, I must own, that my ideas, nor those of the most intelligent amongst us, do not coincide with his, till we see more stability, an easier communication, and some alterations from our former system which may suit it better to the great revolution in political establishments & principles since P: Ignatius's time.[6] For instance do you think that our Governments here or almost any one in Europe would allow of the dependence such as formerly existed, on a general residing at Rome? Even before the suppression of the Society, this dependance began to be so much an object of dread & opposition that the curia of the professed house agreed to vest almost the whole powers of the General in some subject of the Venetian state for the territory of the Republick. You probably may have seen as well as myself, Fr. Ricci's[7] letter to Fr. Sagredo, Propositus of the professed house at Venice. Mr. Talbot has transmitted to me the 1st. vol: (a very short one for 2s6) of a sketch of Ganganelli's life & character, by an anonymous author. I find that the materials are chiefly drawn from 4 vol. of French letters; which Leonard Neale brought in with him. The materials however are much better digested &

arranged in the English, than French; but I wish that if Ganganelli's character was to be impeached by exposing the details of his private life, they had been accompanied with such proofs, as might silence opposition. For neither the [facts?] enumerated in the undigested French nor those in the [*torn*] English ones are attested sufficiently, to compel belief; and unless the authors English & French are possessed of authentic vouchers, I do not see, what reply they could make [*torn*] intrepid Franciscan who should boldly deny the principal & most disgraceful facts, & call the authors, Libellers. For which reason I have always thought, that a candid & well attested enumeration of the injustices done the Society, during that popes Government, & to many of its members both before & after the dissolution, would prove better; than any scandalous anecdotes, the innocence of the Society, and the infamy of its oppressor. I am sorry you did not compleat your plan; I dare say you would have exposed to public indignation the men & measures, which were employed in that iniquitous transaction. I am much indebted to the English author for his too favourable opinion of my *Address* &c.[8] Talbot sent me Hawkin's annotations upon it; a pitiful performance indeed! Wharton's reply infinitely surpasses it, in every thing but candor. There indeed they are on a level: but I have done with the controversy, which is now forgotten here. I long to hear, whether Mr. Strickland found any sincerity in the ministry at Brussels, and means to transfer the academy from Liege. Our papers have published some accounts from Spa[in] which lead to think that the Prince of Liege has assumed the unepiscopal office of protector of those public nuisances, gaming tables. No wonder then he gives little encouragement to learning and the improvement of taste amongst his subjects. The object nearest my heart now, & the only one, that can give consistency to our religious views in this country, is the establishment of a school, & afterwards of a Seminary for young Clergymen. I was surprised you had not received my *Address* &c when you wrote. I sent one to Mr. Talbot for you. The mutilated republication of it was an impudent liberty taken with another's performance. My respects to yr. excellent companions at Lullworth you must be happy together.   Dr. Charles   Yr.

AL St
  [1] Ferdinand Farmer, James Frambach, Luke Geissler, James Pellentz, and John Ritter.
  [2] Charles Whelan.
  [3] Andrew Nugent, Irish Capuchin, arrived in New York and at this time caused the first schism, when he displaced with the help of lay trustees the incumbent pastor Whelan at St. Peter's Church.
  [4] John Thayer, not Thyer.
  [5] The papal bull suppressing the Society of Jesus was not implemented in the dominions of Catherine II.
  [6] St. Ignatius Loyola (1491-1556), founder and first general of the Society of Jesus.
  [7] Lorenzo Ricci, general at the time of the order's suppression in 1773.
  [8] Carroll's reply to Wharton.

TO [JOHN HOCK] [1786]

[. . . .] From the foregoing your Excellency will know that I and my fellow priests think that it would contribute greatly to the welfare of religion if a seminary were established here. As for consultation with Congress on this subject it is neither necessary nor expedient. For the American Congress does not wish to treat of matters which concern one or another group of Christians, but to those who profess a certain creed it allows full liberty, without governmental interference, with respect to whatever pertains to its cult, discipline and internal organization, provided however that no harm ensues to the Republic.

Mr. Simon Creutzbourg will give this letter to your Excellency. He resided for some years in America; and I have been informed that he laudably maintained integrity of faith and morals. He says that he is very closely related to the distinguished Joseph Hertling the director of government in Mainz.

ADf AAB See Sep. 15, 1788, for the estimate of addressee.

exempla. Verum intelliget Do. Va. ex antedictis, ita me et confratres meos existimare, longe magis ad Religionis utilitatem collaturum, si apud nos Seminarium constituatur. Quod vero attenet ad deliberationem cum nostro Congressu hac super re ineundam, illud nullatenus esse necessarium, vel etiam expedire; quod Senatus ille Americanus nihil tractare velit de rebus hunc vel illum Christianorum coetum spectantibus, sed omnium Religionum professoribus permittat illa libere agere et ordinare sine politici regiminis interventione quae suum cultum, disciplinam, et regimen internum spectant, dummodo nihil in Reipublicae detrimentum statuatur.

Has litteras Eximiae Dom. Vae. exhibebit Dom. Simon Creutzbourg, qui aliquot annis in America versatus, et fidei et morum integritatem, uti mihi semper relatum est, laudabiliter conservavit, germanumque se esse affirmat amplissimi viri Josephi Hertling, Directoris Magistratus Moguntini.

TO LEONARDO ANTONELLI [1786]

My Ld. Cardl. Religion: learning have an hereditary claim on the Princes of yr. ancient family. It is therefore with great, but most respectful confidence, that an unknown Individual does himself the honour to present to the patronage of yr. Eminence, a proposed establishment[1] which being designed for promoting the best of causes, may greatly contribute to spread the empire of true Religion, and a respectful attachment[2] to the holy See.[3] Thus may [*illeg.*—Amer]ica console the friends of the Church, for the losses, she suffers in other Countries: and your Eminence, endeavours to obtain success for the present undertaking, will receive the grateful benedictions of the new world, as well as you attract the admiration of Europe. With the most profound respect & veneration I have the honour to be my Ld. Cardl.   Yr. Eminences most humble [. . .]'

ADf   AAB(8H6)   Written on letter from Thorpe, Dec. 2, 1786.
    ¹ Georgetown College
    ² The clause, "providence destines this country to . . . ," is not deleted and appears between the lines at this point.
    ³ Deleted: "in a country, which has hitherto been unfavourable to the progress . . ."

TO JOHN THORPE [1786]

Not found. Possibly several letters about this time. See May 26, 1788.

TO ANDREW NUGENT R. C. [Rock Creek] Jan: 17–1786

Revd Sir   I was called to Virginia immediately after Christmas, and at my return, some few days ago, I was honoured with your letter of Decr 19th. I am sorry, it is no more in my power now, than when I had the pleasure of seeing you to give you particular informations respecting Charleston. Tho I wrote to the Gentlemen of that place in June last, I have had no answer from them; & therefore shall again write to them, as soon as I am settled at Baltimore which will now be in a short time. Whenever it is in my power to give you the desired information, I shall at the same time insist on the utmost caution being used in the choice of ye Clergymen intended for that place; it being one of the most polished & improved in the U. States. I was lately favoured with an excellent letter from your good Br Mr Jones of Hallifax in which he paints so strongly the danger of receiving volunteer supplies, either of the secular or regular Clergy from Europe that I am determined to use all the precautions, which he most judiciously points out, especially for such a situation as Charleston. Besides, I will not venture to give encouragement to any to come in till I receive the enlargement of my powers, which, from late advices, I have every reason speedily to expect.

I now proceed to a more disagreeable subject. With your letter, I received others from N.Y. giving some account of unhappy disturbances in that Congregation: You will easily conceive my grief & distress at those advices. It cannot escape a person of your observation how fatal these dissensions may prove to that infant Congregation: and indeed now generally disadvantagious the impression of them may be thro the United States, of which N.Y., by the residence of Congress, may be deemed the capital. However, I am happy in one respect; which is, to find that you have justified my very favourable opinion of your discretion, zeal, & disinterestedness, by neither beginning or abetting the ill-advised measures of a part of the Congregation. But I must take the liberty of telling you, that I expect more from you; & that you not only do not approve, but openly discountenance, & oppose them with all the authority derived from your virtues, your Religion & your talents. I understand, that amongst other pretensions, the authors of the present disturbance have alledged, that they have a right to appoint & discharge their chaplain at their pleasure: which if true, render him liable to become the victim of the most capricious despotism. It is certain that the Congn of N. Y. received Mr W.[helan] as their Chaplain; that they agreed to support him; that even the few, who complain of him have no reproach to make against him, or immorality, or inattention to his ministerial functions, but only that his manners are some how unpleasing to them. At least, when repeatedly called upon by me they ownd that this & his not preaching to their satisfaction, were their only grounds of exception to him which if they be reasons sufficient for his discharge, I am afraid most of us must be involved in his sentence. I flatter myself, my Dr Sir, that you will enforce these sentiments with all yr authority & ability & that publickly & privately you will exert yourself to preserve unanimity & charity in the Congregn amonst themselves, & with the residing Clergymen: to which nothing will so much contribute as your joint example. I beseech you to forget every cause of complaint, if any exist against your Br, & give the Congregn the edifying spectacle of a zealous cooperation in promoting the glory of God, without any partial considerations. I must do him the justice to say, that he has never represented you, as author or fomenter of these unhappy dissensions, tho' I own he had conceived some distrust, which you have charity enough to excuse & remove. I am glad indeed not to be informed of the name of any one person, who either began or supported the late proceedings: it leaves me more at liberty to speak my mind without giving offence to any, which I most sincerely wish to avoid: and I reply on your friendship as well as zeal for the interests of Religion, to make my sentiments every where known. With great esteem I have the honour, to be &c   J. C.

ADfS   AAB

TO CHARLES WHELAN   Jan: 18–1786

Rd Dr Sir   At my return from Virg[ini]a the 11th inst, I received yours of the 19th ulto[last] & Mr Farmer transmitted yr former favr of ye 10th. You need not be told how disagreeable the contents proved. So scandalous a dissension in that new congregn, & in the eyes of all America, it is, yr city, being the residence of Congress, cannot fail having distressful consequences in N. Y., & perhaps in many other places by the impressions, which will be received in consequence of it. You may remember, that my uniform language to Mr. Nugent and others, was, that to you only I could give full powers for the admn of the Scmts [Sacraments] consistently with the rules prescribed to me. (have reason to believe, from his professions at N. Y. by word of mouth, & since by letter, that he will not attempt an unlawful exercise of Spiritual powers, and therefore trust, that the wild project of nominating him to the parish will die away, for surely he will be steady in refusing an offer, so repulsive to his understanding & sense of duty: and the persons, who devised or abetted so inconsistent a measure will soon discover its fatal consequence not only on the credit, but the very essence & vital spirit of our holy Religion. I shall always respect every decent & free representation or complaint of a congregation or a considerable part of it; but at the same time I hope God in his goodness will endow me with sufficient fortitude to resist every disorderly & tumultuary attempt to discharge or silence those Clergymen who have a lawful mission. In my letter to Mr Nugent I expressed these sentiments, & have taken with him a liberty, which, I know, you likewise will allow me. I have earnestly sollicited him to employ his best talents & industry in promoting a perfect and cordial unanimity in the Congregation, as well amongst one another as with the residing Clergymen & have intreated him as I now intreat you to be the first in giving so edifying an example; to forget all causes of complaint, you may have against each other, and to not only *be united* in heart, without jealousy, or partial views; but to let your union be conspicuous in the eyes of the public. Communicate freely with each other in all concerns of the Congn; and whenever your opinions differ, by mutual condescensions bring them to agree, or, without carrying them before the public, refer them for decision either to the Revd Mr Farmer, or myself.

I notice your complaints concerning Mr La Valiniere.[1] He applied to me lately for faculties to hear the French and Canadians. His credentials, strengthened by private and confidential accounts of his zeal & virtue & learning would have induced me to grant them for the satisfaction of those poor people; but I answered him, that restricted as I was, it was entirely out of my power; and that as you were at New York, & had full approbation & faculties, a necessity could not be supposed to exist sufici[en]t to justify me in a deviation from the orders of the propgda. Still however I am not unwilling that he should, by preaching & instruction, rouse his countrymen to a sense of their duty; and as Mr Farmer has granted him liberty so to do, I do not chuse to recall that permission. The letter you forwarded from ye *Propaganda* came safe; its contents I signified to you some time last month. Mr Silva &c . . .

I hope and indeed must require of you to make it an invariable rule never to exact any fee or reward for the admn of the Scmts: it having never been practiced in America I should be sorry to see it introduced. This does not restrain you from receiving any gratuity, that may be offered, excepting in the tribunal of pennance: where, as far as I have authority, I must expressly forbid any, not only being required, but even accepted on any pretence. Of this letter you may make any use that may be conducive to union & reconciliation. If I hear from you, that any thing farther is ncsry I shall address the Congn or Trustees, particularly if the latter continue to bring [*illeg.*] agreed in the precepts left in writing with you.

ADf   AAB

[1] Pierre Huet de la Valinière, a French priest, was deported from Canada because of his anti-British sentiments at the time of the American Revolution. He then served French Catholics in New York until his appointment in 1788 as Carroll's vicar general in the Illinois country.

TO DOMINICK LYNCH AND THOMAS STOUGHTON[1]

R.C. [Rock Creek] near George-town Jan: 24–1786

Gentlemen   I was honoured yesterday at the same time with your letters of Decr 22d 1785. & of Jan: 11–1786. You did me justice in supposing that the former was delayed in its way, or had miscarried: for I certainly should not have failed in my duty of immediately answering so respectable a part of the Congregation. You will however readily conceive, that this is not an easy nor, allow me to say, a very agreeable office in the present instance. One circumstance indeed gives me comfort; you profess to have no other views than for the service & credit of Religion: and as I make it my endeavour to be influenced solely by the same motive, I trust that proposing to ourselves the same end, we shall likewise agree in the means of obtaining it.

The first advices of any disturbances amongst you were transmitted to me in letters from Messrs Whelan & Nugent, which I answered on the 17th & 18th inst. Both these gentlemen represent the steps taken as extreme and improper; I spoke of them therefore in the same manner in my answers; and the more freely, as neither of them mentioned the name of one single person concerned. Having now received a communication of yr sentiments I shall likewise deliver mine with the respect due to your representations; & with the freedom and plainness becoming the responsible & burthensome office, of which I every day feel myself more unworthy in proportion as the duties & weights of it grow upon me. But I must first state to you the previous information, I had received; 1st that the Trustees denied having agreed to the articles, of which I left a copy with Mr. Whelan; & which, to my best apprehension, had been adopted at the meeting, I had the honour of having with those Gentlemen. 2ly That an opinion was made & propagated, of the Congregation having a right not only to chuse such parish priest, as is agreeable to them; but of discharging him at pleasure; & that after such election, the Bishop, or other Ecclesiastical Superior cannot hinder him from exercising the usual functions. 3ly that two of the Congregation, (by whose orders (I am not informed) on Sunday Decr 18th, after divine service, & in the face of all present in the Chappel, seized in a tumultuary manner & kept possession of the collection then made. The first part of this intelligence shocked me much both because it reflected on veracity, which in this instance, I will steadily assert; & because I considered the matters then agreed on, as right in p[oin]t of justice as the renewal of confidence & foundation of future union. The next point of intelligence was still more important. If ever the principles there laid down should become predominant, the unity and Catholicity of our Church would be at an end; & it would be formed into distinct & independent Societies, nearly in the same manner, as the Congregational Presbyterians of your neighbouring New England States. A zealous Clergyman performing his duty couragiously & without respect of persons, would be always liable to be the victim of his earnest endeavours to stop the progress of vice and evil example; and others more complying with the passions of some principal persons of the Congregation would be substituted in his room: and if the Ecclesiastical Superior has no controul in these instances, I will refer it to your own judgment, what the consequences may be. The great source of misconception in this matter is, that an idea appears to be taken up both by you & Mr Whelan that the officiating Clergyman of New York is a parish priest, whereas there is yet no such office in the U. S. The hierarchy of our American Church not being yet constituted, no parishes are formed; and the Clergy coming to the assistance of the faithful are only voluntary labourers in ye vineyd. of Christ, not vested with ordinary jurisdiction annexed to ye said office, but receiving it as delegated and extra-hierarchical commission. Whenever parishes are established no doubt, a proper regard, and such as is suitable to our Governments, will be had to the rights of the Congregation in the mode of election & presentation: and even now I shall ever pay to their wishes every deference consistent with the general welfare of Religion: of which I hope to give you proof in the sequel of this letter. The third article of my information was peculiarly mortifying; for I could not but fear, that a step so violent, at such a time & place, and probably in the presence of other Religionists, would breed disunion amongst yourselves, and make a very disadvantagious impression to the prejudice of the Catholic cause, so soon after the first introduction of public worship into your city.

I now return to the contents of your letters; and observe that after stating some very censurable instances of Mr Whelans conduct, you desire me to remove him; & imply, a desire that Mr Nugent, as being very acceptable, may succeed his office.

I can assure you Gentlemen that I have a very advantagious opinion of Mr Nugents abilities; & he shewed me very good testimonials of his zeal and virtue. I repeatedly told him as I did to many of yourselves; that nothing but my own want of suffct authority prevented me from giving him every power requisite for the exercise of his ministry; I hoped by this, to have that restriction of my authority removed; but as it is not, it remains still out of my power to employ him agreeably to your & my desires. If I am ever enabled to do it, I will certainly remember my assurances to him. But in the mean time, what can I do? can I revoke Mr Whelan's faculties, and leave so great a congregation without assistance? can I deprive him when neither his morals, his orthodoxy, or his assiduity have been impeached? especially while I am uncertain, whether his removal be desired by a majority of the Congregation: for I have received assurances, very much to the contrary. But even if a considerable part are still attached to him would the great object of unanimity, so be obtained by his removal? would not his adherents consider Mr Nugent, as coming in upon the ruins of his predecessor;? and consequently, would they not keep alive the spirit of discord? Upon these considerations, I have a resolution, which will, I hope meet your wishes, as well as of every part of the Congregation. As soon, as I am at liberty to grant them, Mr Nugent shall have powers from me to act as your joint-Chaplain: for the idea of parish priest is not admissible: he has repeatedly assured me that he never will accept of an appointment to the exclusion of his Br, in his letter, he says, a sufficient maintenance of both may be obtained. In the mean time, he has full authority to announce the word of God, & I promise myself he will do it with effect, especially by inculcating the great duty of charity & unanimity; He and Mr Whelan will concur in recommending this characteristic virtue of Christianity, by their example, as well as advice. Educated in the same school of Religion & connected by special ties to the same order, they will assist each other in the work of the ministry; & every part of the Congregation will have it in their power to apply to him of the two in whom they have the greatest confidence. I must not omit taking notice of Mr Whelan's address to the Congn, inclosed in yr last. I greatly disapprove it and shall so inform him. When I wrote the letter, to which he refers, I had heard nothing from N. Y. concerning your uneasinesses; I lamented, that my hands being still tied, I was prevented from giving full employment to Mr Nugents zeal: and I must add, for Mr La Valiniere's credit, that when I declined granting him leave to administer the Sacraments to the Canadian refugees, it was for the same reason, because I had no power to do it. Otherwise, I have such a conviction of his many good qualities, that I should gladly have indulged the wishes of these good people who sollicited [*torn*] and of this I beg you to inform him.

... [*torn*] of your last letter, you make some mention of eventually having recourse to legal means to rid yourselves of Mr Whelan. This insinuation makes me very unhappy. I cannot tell, what assistance the laws might give you; but allow me to say, that you can take no step more fatal to that respectability, in which, as a Religious Society, you wish to stand, or more prejudicial to the Catholic cause. I must therefore intreat you to decline a design so pernicious to all your prospects: and, protesting against measures so extreme, I explicitly declare, that no Clergyman be he who he may, shall receive any spiritual powers from me who shall advise or countenance so unnecessary & prejudicial a proceedure. I notice your observation, of the Church having received many wounds from the delays of men in power in preventing disorders of his [this kind?] : I am very sensible and if it be meant as a caution to me, I am sincerely thankful for your intimation and will endeavour to profit by it; without however forgetting, that precipitation & violence have perhaps done greater harm, than diffidence & procrastination. I hope you will implore the Fr of lights, that I may not be wanting in either respect, or of diligence in applying timely remedies to growing evils, of caution, or in applying proper ones. To this favr I reply you will likewise add that of lightening the burthen of my charge by cherishing a spirit of conciliation & [*illeg.*] condescension. Be pleased to communicate this answer to Messrs N. & Whe. if you have no objn I have the honr to be   Gentlemen &c   Messrs Lynch & Stoughton

ADf   AAB
  [1] Spokesmen for the Nugent faction at St. Peter's Church, New York.

TO PIERRE HUET DE LA VALINIÈRE   Jan. 27—1786—Extract—

I do not remember to have directed Mr Wh[elan]. to [*blank*] yr faculties. To the best of my remembrance my intention was, that you should enjoy them to the extent of the expressions & in the manner mentioned in my letter. I have been informed, that this good Gentleman announced to his Congregation on Sunday Jany 8—, that I had refused the sollicitations of the *French* for yr approbation. I am exceedingly morified at his using an expression, wch to some may appear particularly pointed; and indeed am greatly displeased that he mentioned my refusal at all, without adding, that I only refused it, because I had no power to grant it; which was really the case. But I will now add, that as I have very great deference for your judgment, so I will leave to your own discretion to assist the Canadians French, and others, so far as you think that I can empower you to do it, not only *in statu [torn]* (which is not my expression) but wherever I have any authority [*torn*] take notice, that as you know my confined and limited powers [*torn*] with your conscience, to what extent you may exercise any [*torn*] this permission, particularly in the tribunal of pennance. Mr. Farmer of Phila having authorised you to preach and instruct those good people I willingly confirm his act and likewise empower you to baptise and perform other pastoral duties, limiting however the powers for Confession to the dictates of yr own judgment & conscience.

Thanks for information concerning Gibau[1] & offers of sending for two priest—accept those offers for one, if a person to be fully relied on &c. I have given very plain directions to Mr Whelan not to exact any fees for the administration of the Sacraments, & never to receive even a present in the

Tribunal of pennance, as, I have heard, is the custom at Easter in Ireland. Mr Nugent had no other powers granted him than such as you have—and they were granted, when I expected Mr Whelan was leaving N. Y. & I supposed, necessity would justify my conduct. You will oblige me by collecting the best infn & sending me yr opn of the authors & causes in the dissensions in the Congn I shall rely on your advices preferably to any other. I mention this to you in confidence. J.C.

ADfS AAB
¹ Pierre Gibault was sent by Bishop Jean Briand of Quebec as vicar general in Illinois. When George Rogers Clark captured Kaskaskia, Gibault persuaded the inhabitants to submit.

TO CHARLES WHELAN   Jan. 28 [1786]

I wrote to you fully on the 18— Since which, have recd two long letters or rather remonstrances, the last of which is signed by more than 70 of the Congn You may be assured, I was sorry to find the number of malcontents so great, after hearing from you, they were not above five or six agst 500. I have so answerd those letters, as to shew, that I am determined not to use my authority for yr dismission, but to support you in the exercise of the ministry, while you continue to do it with zeal and the approbn of even a considerable part of the Congn I was sorry to receive with the aforesd letters, an address in yr own handwriting, to yr Congn, giving them notice of my continuing to refuse faculties to Messrs N[ugent] & La Val[inière], without adding, that this was done not on account of any exception to the conduct of those Gentn, but for my own want of power. Indeed, I wish you had never introduced the mention of it at all before the Congn. It must certainly lead them & Protest. of whom many, I hear were present, to believe that the Cath. Clergn are at variance amongst and jealous of one another. If those Gentn acted improperly, notice should have been given me, before an insinuation so public and offensive was made agst [torn] I know you did it with a good motive; and therefore still hope you will [torn] the line of conduct with Mr Nugt recommended in my last letter. As [torn] intimated a desire that he should not be associated with you & [torn] indeed intimated a wish to have him settled at N. Y., I have proposed the [torn] reestablish peace mentioned in my letter to Messrs Lynch &c, which I have [torn] shewn you. Pray, cultivate a good correspondence with Mr La Valinière

ADf AAB

TO LEONARDO ANTONELLI   From Maryland, 13 March, 1786

Most Eminent Cardinal   At the beginning of last December I received a letter in which Your Eminence wrote that the Congregation left it to my judgment, or rather recommended that the usual faculties be granted to Father Maurice Whelan,[1] a Capuchin. I had already done so, and my reasons were given in my letter of February 27, 1785. Upon the invitation of the Catholics of New York he had taken up residence there, and in the belief that his zeal would reap abundant fruit he spared no pains to bring this about. But at the end of autumn when Father Andrew Nugent, another priest of the same order and nationality arrived from Ireland, Father Whelan so completely lost favor with the people that he decided to leave. I intend to use him elsewhere where his talents can be put to better use than in a large city, and, if I may use the expression, in a metropolis of the United States. Meanwhile I am confronted with great difficulty in providing a priest for the Catholics of New York, for, while Father Andrew seems better qualified for that place he was not approved nor was he assigned by the Congregation. Thus I was faced with the alternative of leaving the faithful destitute of spiritual help or of being forced to risk going beyond the limits of my authority. Placed as I was in this predicament, and weighing the mind of the Fathers, I decided that it was certainly the mind of our Holy Mother the Church that provision be made for the welfare of souls through every appropriate means. Likewise I thought that my authority was utterly futile, or rather non-existent, if I could not come to the aid of people in such great danger. For this reason I gave the aforesaid Father Andrew faculties for preaching the word of God and for administering the sacraments of baptism and matrimony, and others also in case of necessity. In a word I said to myself that this was a case where necessity applied, not merely that extreme necessity which exposes souls to the great moral danger of falling into sin unless confession and communion are possible. In my judgment I had to do this until replies were had on this head, and in deep sollicitude I asked Your Eminence to intervene that the authority of the ecclesiastical superior be extended to the granting of faculties.[2]

In the same letter I made it known that in Maryland some disquietude of soul was aroused by the suspicion that some people were planning restrictions on religious liberty and practice. Already this fear appears exaggerated. But others have a plan which may be injurious to religion, namely the taxing of the properties which support Catholic priests. Their pretext is that since the ministers of the sects called as they are do not have such property but are supported by the contributions of the parishioners we should do likewise. As soon as the laws of England were abrogated freedom of religion was established, and we sought in every way to obtain a law permitting Catholic priests to form a corporate body and to hold property in common. In this wise we hoped to bring it about that property acquired from individuals would pass into the perpetual legal right and use of those who labor in the vineyard of the Lord, and thus be assured to religious use. We wished also to meet an ever present danger when an individual could transfer these properties to relatives or anyone else by legal instrument or will. So far we have made no progress because of the prejudice against the acquisition of property by ecclesiastics, or as they say, by mortmain.[3] If through divine favor our efforts should be more successful the Congregation will be informed.

I had written the above before March 27th on which date I received your letter of June 23rd of last year. At the same time I received various documents mentioned in the letter, especially a new listing of faculties, granting me the power to choose laborers whom I shall judge fully qualified. This letter evinced such benevolence that, in my name and that of my co-laborers, I offer most sincere thanks to Our Holy Father, to yourself and to the Congregation. And I trust that with God's help I shall so make use of this generous concession of His Holiness and the Congregation that the Catholic religion will be strengthened and spread in these united states. At present the greatest obstacles to this wished-for objective are the need of priests and the means of supporting them. To relieve this shortage we plan to build a school where boys will be trained in piety and in the discipline of the *litterae humaniores,* and at the same time a seminary for the education of priests, so that those who finish at the school and wish to give themselves to the sacred ministry can acquire the virtues and learning proper to that state of life. This cannot be accomplished by the charity of the Catholics and the extreme frugality of the priests, which . . . but we will try. . . . that these undertakings meet with success. I greatly desire the curriculum and disciplinary regulations for junior clerics in force in the most approved seminaries in Rome, and therefore, Most Eminent Cardinal, I beg you, if possible, to send me several such schedules. In this way I hope to provide qualified ministers of the sanctuary. In the meantime we suffer from a great shortage of them. Since my last letter two men of oustanding virtue have died; three others, broken by age and labor, cannot preach, attend the scattered congregations, or visit the sick. The first of those who died, himself a German, took care of three or four congregations of Germans. . .

ADf   AAB
[1] Charles Maurice Whelan.
[2] The fact that Whelan and Nugent were of the Capuchin Order further complicated acquiring faculties of the ministry under Carroll, who with most of his other priests was more directly under the congregation of the Propagation of the Faith.
[3] A legal incorporation of all American Church property under a native body would soon prevent any passage of property to a foreign jurisdiction.

Ex Marylandia die 13 Martii 1786   Eme Cardinalis   Sub initium Decembris anni proxime elapsi litteras accepi quibus Emus. Card. mihi jam fecit Sacram Congregationem de propaganda fide meo arbitrio remittere, imo commendare, ut Patri Mauritio Whelan, ordinis Capuccinorum, solitae facultates concedantur. Illud jam antea a me erat praestitum; quibusq rationibus adductus fecerim, scripsi litteris die 27 Feb. 1785 datis. Invitatus ille a Catholicis, Novi Eboraci incolis sedem apud illos fixit, magnosque ex ejus zelo fructus speravit et quidem nulli industriae pepercit, ut hos fructus colligeret. Cum autem a sub finem Autumni, alter ejusdem ordinis et nationis sacerdos, Pater Andreas Nugent ex Hibernia advenisset, post breve tempus animi Catholicorum a Patre Mauritio ita alienati sunt, ut inde discedendum judicaverit; cujus operam tamen alibi adhibere cogito, ubi illam collacare possit utilius quam in urbe incolis frequenti, et ut ita dicam, foederatae Americae metropoli. Interim, magna mihi suboritur difficultas de providendo Sacerdote pro Catholicis Novi Eboracensibus. Nam Patre Andreas, quamvis videatur illi stationi opportunior, tamen nec approbatus est, nec illuc destinatus a Sacra Congregatione de propaganda fide; under aut fideles omni spirituali adjutorio destitutos relinquere, aut inire periculum cogor auctoritatis meae limites excedendi. In his angustiis constitutus, ponderatis PP. sententiis, statui tandem Sanctae Matris nostrae Ecclesiae mentem omnino esse, ut omni opportuno remedio animarum saluti provideatur; et auctoritatem meam inanem, aut potius nullam esse, si in tanto periculo constitutis nullo modo possim succurrere. Unde praedicto P. Andreae facultatem concessi praedicandi Verbum Dei, et administrandi sacramenta baptismi et matrimonii; et reliqua etiam, ubi necessitas exegerit; verbo autem necessitatis dixi, me intelligere non solum *extramam* sed illam etiam, qua quis exponitur morali periculo graviter peccandi, nisi ad Poeni[tenti]ae et Eucharistiae sacramenta pateat recursus. Ita faciendum judicavi, donec ad ea responsum fuerit, in quibus omni sollicitudini Emae. Tuae studium interponi rogavi, et Superioris Ecclesiastici auctoritas pro facultatibus concedenis amplificetur.

Iisdem litteris significavi commotionem aliquam animorum extisse in Marilandia, ex qua suspicabantur aliqui periculum libertatis restringendae in negotio Religionis. Sed jam minus videtur timendum. Aliud autem quidam moliuntur, fortasse Religioni perniciosum, scilicet fisco addicere bona quibus sacerdotes Catholici sustentantur. Hoc eo praetextu, praecipue se velle aiunt quod Sectariorum ministri, ut vocant, bona nulla stabilia possideant, sed ex gregalium suorum collationibus victum repetant; unde et nos in eandem formam redigere cupiunt. Ubi primum abrogatis Angliae legibus, Religionis nostrae libertas plane constituta est, omni conatu legem obtinere studuimus qua sacerdotibus Catholicis in unum corpus coalescere liceat, ac communi nomine bona possidere. Hac ratione sperabamus fore ut bona ex privatorum manibus transirent in perpetuum jus et usum operariorum in hac Domini vinea; adeoque sacris usibus stabilitate manciparentur. Cupiebamus quoque periculo obviare quod semper adest dum in privati hominis potestate est, illa bona ad propinquos, aut alterius quemvis instrumento legali vel testamento transmittere. Huc usque vero nihil profecimus quod magna hic vigeant praejudicia de adeptione bonorum ab omnibus Ecclesiasticis, seu ut vocant, *manus mortuae.* Si posthaec divino beneficio conatus nostros melior successus commodaverit certior fiat Sacra Congregation.

Superiora scripserum ante diem 27 Martii cum tuae literae Eme. Card. mihi redditae sunt datae 23 Julii anni praelapsi. Accepi simul varia documenta, quae in illis memorantur, et maxime novum facultatum examplar, quibus mihi fit potestas eligendi operarios, quos dignos judicavero. Has literas tanta benevolentiae significatio comitabatur ut et Beatissimo Patri Nostro, et tibi,

Card. Eme. omnique adeo Sacrae Congregationi gratias et meo, et Sociorum nomine, maximas referam. Confido insuper ita me, divina ope, Sanctitatis Suae et Sacrae Congregationis, liberali concessione usurum, ut Religio Catholica non solum confirmationem sed et incrementum in his foederatis provinciis acceptura. Maxima nunc huic saluberrimo fini obstacula sunt, inopia Sacerdotum et media illos sustentandi. Ad sacerdotum sublevandam inopiam, cogitamus de schola erigenda in qua pueri ad omnem pietatis et humaniorum litterarum disciplinam informarentur; et simul de seminario stabiliendo pro clericorum institutione, ut qui schola egrediuntur Sanctuarii ministerio se devovere cupiunt virtute et doctrina imbuantur quae illi statui conveniunt. Haec et Catholicorum caritate, et omni Sociorum frugalitate non perficere, quod pro rerum nostrarum securitas [...] possumus sed id [...] conabimur; [...] omni successu quae molimina ut felicem successum sertiantur; rationem studiorum et domesticae pro junioribus clericis disciplinae ex probatissimis in Urbe seminariis multum desidero; audeoque, Eme Card, tuam autoritaem implorare, ut si fieri possit, aliquae ejusmodi rationes ad me transmittantur. Sic tamen idoneos Sanctuarii ministros providendos esse confido. Interim magna eorum penuria laboramus. Post ultimas meas litteras, duo eximiae virtutis Sacerdotes vita functi sunt; tres alii laboribus et annis fracti nec praedicare, nec dissitas congregationes obire, nec aegros possunt invisere. Qui primus vita cessit tres quattuorve congregationes Germanorum, et ipse Germanus, omni adhuc spirituali [....]

TO JOSEPH DE TRESPALACIOS[1]   Baltimore in Maryland 21 April, 1786

Most Reverend and Illustrious Lord—   Mr. Poey in the entourage of His Excellency Mr. Gardoqui[2] has greeted your illustrious and most reverend Lordship of Havanna. Since he is about to return to that place he graciously assented to the request of his petitioners that he appeal to the charity of the faithful for the funds to build a Catholic Church in this city. For this reason he has asked me for credentials to your Excellency and that I ask your permission for him to engage in this task. While I fear that I am perhaps too bold in doing so I could not refuse because I foresee that the building of a church here could contribute greatly to the preservation and propagation of the true faith. Moreover the zeal of the Spanish people for whatever pertains to the glory of God is so very well known. The most obedient servant of Your most reverend and illustrious Lordship John Carroll, Ecclesiastical Superior in the Thirteen provinces of America.

ADf   AAB
[1] Bishop of Havana. Louisiana and Florida as now under Spanish dominion were within his jurisdiction.
[2] Don Diego de Gardoqui was the Spanish minister to the United States at New York.

Illustrissimi et Reverendissime Domine—   Dominus Poey, qui in comitatu Excellentissime Domini Gardoqui Illustrissimam et Reverendissimam Domina-

tionem Tuam Havannae salutavit, nunc eodem rediturus, benigne annuit votis
rogantium, ut charitatem Fidelium sollicitaret pro construenda Ecclesia Catholica in hac civitate. Quare a me litteras petiit quibus id Tibi, Praesul
Illustrissime, significarem tuamque in has re auctoritatem implorarem. Quod
quidem, etsi nimis audacter a me fieri timeam, tamen recusare non potui,
quod videam Ecclesiae constructionem magno usui pro verae Religionis conservatione et propagatione hic esse posse; et Hispaniae nationis liberalitate
studium in iis quae ad divinam gloriam spectant, abunde compertum sit.

Interim omnia Reverendissimae at Illustrissimae Dominationi Tuae fausta
apprecabitur.   Reverendissime et Illustrissime Domine,   Servus obsequentissimus   Joannes Carroll   Superior Ecclasiasticus in Foederatis   Americae provinciis.   Baltimorae in Marylandia   die 21 Aprilis, 1786

TO CHARLES PLOWDEN   Rock Creek July 11th 1786

My Dr Sir   At my return to this place the 8th inst, after a long absence, I
found your two most acceptable favours of Aug:26th 1785, and March 19th
1786: and at the same time your invaluable ms: account of the remnant of
the Society,[1] miraculously preserved, as it seems, to be the seed of a future
generation. I have read it with great eagerness and infinite pleasure; but had
not time to make myself master of the history, before the impatient demands
of our worthy Mr Digges drew it out of my hands. To him I have now sent it;
and presume that it will go through the inspection, & contribute to the
edification of the curious amongst our Brethren, before I shall be able to
recover it. On this occasion, I cannot help congratulating myself, and even
returning thanks to heaven for the opportunities afforded me in Italy and at
Bruges to perfect my acquaintance & intimacy with you; as I owe to that, not
only the pleasure of your most valuable correspondence, but many advantages, public & private, which I have derived from it.

As you have so generously expressed a warm & zealous regard for the
interests of Religion in this country, my first information to you shall be on
that subject. About the end of March, I received dispatches from Cardl
Antonelli & Mgr Borgia[2] in answer to my representation of the insufficiency
of their first powers, sent in to me: and I was glad to see, that they have
granted them as ample as for the present, I could wish. I am authorised to
employ any Clergyman I may judge proper, & without having recourse to the
Propgda: as much latitude is allowed, with respect to dispensations, as ought
to be asked; the nomination of a Bishop is suspended, till I shall please to say
he may be serviceable: his appointment by a foreign tribunal is given up; and
wherever one is to be nominated, the Clergy here may chuse two of their own
number, one of whom shall be the Bishop. As our schools will not be able for
some time to bring foward young men sufficiently for ordination, that time
must be employed in endeavouring to remove the difficulty of its being left
to any foreign jurisdiction, to appoint even one, of two, to the Bishopric: for

this would be granting them a power & influence, inconsistent, I apprehend, with our laws. The only point of my letter, which the Cardl Prefect & Secretary have neglected answering, concerns the nomination of an Ordinary Bishop, instead of a Vicar Apostolic. Having obtained these essential points, you will perhaps think with me, that there is no present necessity of making a voyage to Rome. I conceive my presence of much greater consequence here; tho', were it otherwise, I would readily undergo the fatigue of it for the sake of establishing the American church on a proper footing. I cannot tell you, how much I am grieved, whenever I consider its present state. Many of the established Congregations are either without help, or receive it, only two or three times a year. The demands upon us for supplying those, who thro' all the other United States call for asistance are increasing every day; and yet I am quite unable to supply them. As I find so little inclination amongst many even of my Countrymen to return & enter upon the labours of this vineyard, I shall be under the necessity of calling in other assistants, besides those who were raised in the Society or under its former members. To preserve peace, & uniformity, I wish'd to avoid this in Maryland and Pennsylvania, and perhaps Virginia. A wider field I knew we could not embrace: but if larger supplies do not arrive soon, the great and prevailing consideration of charity will oblige me to admit labourers, wherever they come from, if their faith and morals are sound. I am well aware of the inconveniencies and mortification, which must result from this measure: but I cannot make myself responsible for the loss of many souls, which may be the consequence of a different conduct. It is probable, that you have an influence over Mr Leonard Brooke.[3] I am well informed, that he is not very necessary in his present station; indeed it has been suggested to me, that the Ladies of Ipres consider him rather as an incumbrance. Can you not prevail on him to join us? and if you think it will have weight, you may add, that I earnestly sollicit his assistance. His Br has informed me, that money has been transmitted to him for the purpose of his passage in &c; and if that resource has failed, Mr Ashton, our money agent, has established a credit in London, of which either Mr Strickland or Mr Talbot will give him notice, & direct the application. I hope Mr Beeston[4] will prove a valuable acquisition. I have directed him to Phila to live with poor Molyneux, who is continually solliciting to return to Maryland; but I cannot yet gratify his strange desire: for surely to a man fond of Society, Philada affords more opportunities, than any we have besides, at the same time, that it gives abundant employment to zeal. This year proves fatal to our most excellent & incomparable German Brethren. Fr. Jn Baptist de Ritter died towards the end of February.[5] Mr. Geissler,[6] a man of great merit, has followed him, I fear, by this time, he being in the last stage of a consumption when I heared of him: & that great Saint, Mr Farmer of Philada, is already unable to say mass; & worn down as he is, cannot survive the approaching autumn. Messrs Digges, & Neale hors de combat; & the same may al . . .

AL　St

[1] "Account of the Preservation and Actual State of the Society of Jesus in the Russian Dominions."

[2] Archbishop Stefano Borgia, Secretary of the Congregation of the Propagation of the Faith.

[3] Leonard Brooke, S.J., a Marylander.

[4] Francis Beeston, S.J., an Englishman, who came to Maryland in 1786.

[5] John Baptist de Ritter, S.J., a German who came to Maryland in 1765.

[6] Luke Geissler, S.J., died at Conewago, Pa., in August.

TO ANDREW NUGENT　　　　　　　　　　Rock Creek July 18–1786

Revd. Dr Sir　　　Excessive heats & our good people being in harvest having obliged me to interrupt my progress, I returned hither about ten days ago, & met your favr. of May 12th. It has not been in my power to answer it sooner: my hands have been full, in getting letters ready for Europe, which I had an immediate opportunity of sending away. I cannot conceive the grounds of your objection against applying to the Gentleman who acts as my Deputy, when convenient recourse cannot be had to me: I mean, in matters relating to the ordinary functions of our ministry: Every Ecclesiastical Superior has his Vicars &c: but this does not preclude any Clergyman from applying directly to the principal, in cases, which require secrecy. When I advised you to refer to Mr. Farmer, it was for the sake of convenience: I assure you I am happy in having a direct intercourse with you, whenever it can be carried on expeditiously. That good gentleman is entering, or perhaps has entered into eternity. God knows, When Philada. will get his equal, in virtue & zeal. I have just sent a Gentleman thither, who will in some degree, repair this heavy loss.

　　I am sorry you should consider my questions as serious charges. I am sure They were proposed merely for information. No transaction between you & me can justify your giving them such a construction: if I were capable of grounding charges on *ex parte* informations, I should be still more unworthy, than I am, of the place I hold. I cannot agree with you or rather with the Congn of N. Y., that Mr. Whelan was not admitted for their pastor, as much as a pastor can be in our unorganised Ecclesiastical state but I rejoice that he has withdrawn himself:[1] it has relieved me from a load of anxiety: I trust that your prudence and zeal will reconcile all people; preserve unanimity & promote the interests of virtue and Religion. I know and respect the legal rights of the Congn. It is as repugnant to my duty and wish, as it exceeds my power to compel them to accept & support a Clergyman, who is disagreeable to them, but I see no cause to depart from the principles laid down in my answer to the letter signed by Landry. I think Mr. Wh[alen]. was legally admitted: but having abdicated his charge, he has left me at liberty to recognise & empower you to act, as his successor: Which I do with pleasure upon this condition, that you hold your faculties, as every other clergyman in

America holds them, that is, *till they are revoked,* which is the most liberal manner of granting faculties, that I ever knew to be used; as it carries no limitation to any stated time. Your demand of having them, *quam diu tu bene gesseris,*[2] I never will yield to: and if you will accept them no otherwise, I must plainly tell you that you can have none. To grant them in that form is, I believe, unprecedented; & might be fatal in this country, where the words [of] that formula import that a person cannot be deprived of what he holds, without a formal trial: so that let a Clergyman give what scandal, or betray what ignorance he pleases, he must be first convicted in a court of law consisting altogether of lay members, & those not of our communion, before he can be deprived of his commission to administer the Sacraments & rights of exercising the most sacred functions of Religion. Apply these considerations to the state of things, & government in the U. S., & I am sure you will see the manifest impropriety of your demand.

With you, I am of opinion, that the oath of office required in your state[3] is inconsistent with our Religious tenets. Willing to suppose liberality in the framers of your Constitution, I endeavoured to reconcile it with Catholicity; but the more I consider'd it, the less able I was to do so. It is certainly of faith, that the successor of S. Peter is the visible head of the church, that is, in other words, *Ecclesiastical* Superior. If a legal and solemn decision could be obtained, that the words of the Constitution mean only to exclude all foreign temporal jurisdiction, right, or preeminence, on any plea *temporal* or *spiritual,* then I should see no difficulty: but the obvious, & I from private information, fear the intended meaning of the words is incompatible with our profession.

The declaration required of you in my last letter & which gave you so much pain, was not because I distrusted yr. tenets, but that your authority might stand against claims said to have been made by a great part of the Congn. To shew you, that I am not distrustful or difficult, I accept the principles contained in your letter as a sufficient disavowal of those claims. I have read over a copy of writing left with you. I do not conceive, you can consider the powers it gave as adequate to yr. present situation. It only contains faculties for cases of necessity in M. W. [Maurice Whelan's] absence. I shall wait yr. answer to send them in better and more ample form.

I am pleased and edified with the stedfast faith of the R.C. of N. Y.: You will not fail to use Your unwearied endeavours to encourage amongst them the union of works with faith, & particularly the frequentation of the Scmts. I am afraid, you will have much difficulty in prevailing over the contrary habits of grown people: but the rising generation may be formed to the practices best calculated to nourish and at least once a month, of a spirit of prayer & the fear of God.

My best wishes attend them all; and my particular respects wait on the families of Messr. Lynch McCready, and on your amiable friend Mr. Fitzgerald. Can you tell me what is become of Mr. Whelan? I wish to hear from him on a subject concerning which I wrote to him in the winter. As I can get no answer from Charleston I am inclined to think that if the Prov[incia]l of the Yr Dominicans wishes to employ his Brethren there, he would do well to select a discreet & learned man & to send them thither to make a beginning, a gentleman answering that description should have every encouragement in my power.

ADf   AAB

¹ In February, 1786, he went to his brother's home near Albany, N.Y.

² "As long as you act properly."

³ In the N. Y. State oath of allegiance for naturalized citizens, one must "abjure and renounce all allegiance and subjection to all and every foreign king, prince, potentate, and State in all matters, ecclesiastical as well as civil."

TO LEONARDO ANTONELLI   August 18, 1786

[. . . .] left without help. To the other place likewise inhabited by Germans there came from Germany a religious of the so-called Recollects, a son of Saint Francis, with testimonials from his religious superior who remained in Philadelphia for some years and won the approval of my vicar in that city. In this place other priests, one an Englishman, the other from lower Germany, recently lent us assistance. It is nevertheless very regrettable that such is the scarcity of workers here that I am obliged to use any whom I can get in any way rather than such as I should wish for. At the first opportunity two youths will leave for the Urban college and I shall do everything that they become such as your Eminence describes. To the present their departure has been delayed because their parents either failed to provide the cost of the voyage or were unable to do so. As to the Catholics who live on the extreme western frontier of the United States I write but little because the great distance and the difficulties of travel result in little intercourse between us. For the most part they are French; in their faith and their conduct they are said to be steadfast and innocent. A French priest whom the Bishop of Quebec highly recommended to my vicar general has gone there recently. I have directed him to write me faithfully about everything that touches on religion.

My delay in replying to Your Eminence's letter is due to the burden of four months of unbroken journeyings and labor. On the first opportunity I shall visit the various congregations. Since I began to administer Confirmation very large crowds have sought to obtain the benefit of this grace; not a day free from work. This must be resumed when the intense heat moderates. I see now that Catholics are much more numerous than I reported in previous correspondence.

ADf   AAB   Contents indicate Antonelli as addressee.

[....] adjutorio destitutas reliquit. In alterius pariter Germani locum successit vir Religionis ex ordine Recollectorum, ut vocant, Divi Francisci, qui ex Germania oriundus aliquot annis Philadelphiae commoratus est et Superiorum Ordinis litteris communitus, se meo in illa Urbe Vicario satis approbavit. Quo alii Sacerdotes, alter Anglus, alter ex inferiori Germania nuper nobis suppetias tulere. Dolendum tamen maxime est, ita nos operariorum inopia constringi, ut non quales cuperem, sed quales utcunque obtinere possim, cogar adhibere. Prima opportuna occasione, duo Juvenes ad Urbanum Collegium profiscentur et curam omnem adhibeo, tales ut sint quales Eminentiae tuae litteris describuntur. Obstitit hactenus eorum discessui, quod parentes navigationis sumptibus providere aut neglexerint aut non potuerint. De Catholicis qui in extremis Foederatae Americae finibus, Occidentalem versus, habitant, pauca scribo, quod nullum fere cum illis commercium propter ingentem distantiam et itinerum difficultatem et infrequentiam interveniat. Oriundi sunt ex Gallia, ut plurimum; dicunturque fide stabiles et moribus innocentes. Presbyter Gallus, quem Episcopus Quebecensis Vicario Generali multum commendat nuper illuc est profectus; quare huic commisi ut de omni Religionis negotio scribat ad me diligenter.

Quod Eminentiae Tuae litteris tam tarde rescripserim in causa fuit continua per quattuor menses itinerum et occupationum molestia. Primo vere, Congregationes diversas obire, et Confirmationis Sanctum coepi administrare ingens conventus ad hoc divinae gratiae beneficium obtinendum, neque ulla dies expers laboris; resumendus erit, ubi intensissimi aestus remiserint. Hac occasione video multo majorem esse Catholicorum numerum quam prioribus litteris memoraveram.

TO JOSEPH BERINGTON   Rock Creek, Maryland. Sepr 29th 1786

Dear Sir,   About a fortnight ago, I received your kind Letter of March 27th together wth your late excellent work addressed to Mr Hawkins.[1] Two Copies of the latter had reached America, before I was favoured with it; and it has been read with uncommon Approbation by every one, who had an Opportunity of seeing it. Some of my Friends are very earnest to have it reprinted here; and I am much disposed to concur in the Business, but for one Reason: This is that Religious Controversy being now at an End here, I am desirous it may never be revived. Wharton made a Reply to me, of which I never took Notice for this Reason, as well as because it really did not deserve any. I thought, for a Time there began to be a Sourness in the minds of our protestant Brethren, which might, if irritated, break out into Violence, and perhaps a renewal of those shameful and barbarous Laws, under which, we groaned so long, and you still groan. Thank God! the remembrance of the Controversy has now died away, and I see no Symtoms remaining of an intolerant Spirit. I hope we are approaching to that happy Term, when in the appointment of men to Offices of public Trust, it will never be considered what Religion does he profess; but only whether he be honest, and able to fulfill it. I have likewise the Consolation to find, that our own People are confirmed in their religious principles.

I have seen some Letters from England, by which I learn, that censure has not spared your late work any more, than it did your former on the *State and Behaviour of Catholics* &c. I have on this account redoubled my attention, and cannot discover any Thing to displease the most Scrupulous observer; unless perhaps a passage in p: 69. You there say, that the Pope *has indeed his Prerogative, but we have our Privileges* &c. The following words seem to import that he has no prerogative, which has not been surrendered to him by the Community: Is this quite accurate? is he not jure divino Head of the Church? and is not this a Prerogative independent of the Community? Pardon this Liberty: I have not a Doubt of the Orthodoxy of your Meaning; and am not sure that the words, taking in the Context, may not bear a sound sense. Every thing else to me appears unexceptionable and on the whole most excellent. I would only except the too flattering Expressions bestowed by your Partiality on me.

You wish to know the Situation of our Church, and its prospects. The Interest you take in its Welfare deserves full Information. Very unexpectedly I received from Rome, Novr 1784, an appointment to be Ecclesiastical Superior in the United States, and Information that I was to be created a Bishop, vicar Apostolic. In answer, I wrote that till our Seminary was completed for the Education of Young Clergymen, a Bishop was not necessary, as it might create an Expence prejudicial to our other Plans; that in two or three years, it would suit better, when we had a prospect of young men fit for Orders: that a Bishop appointed by a foreign Jurisdiction would give umbrage in this Country, and create unfavourable Prejudices against Religion; and particularly, if the Bishop were only a Vicar of a foreign Congregation, dependent on, and removable by them at pleasure; that if a Bishop was to be created, he should be chosen by the Catholic Clergy, and that an Ordinary Bishop would contribute much more to remove the Dread of foreign Interference, so reprobated in the Constitutions of the particular States, and general Confederation. To this I have received an answer, so far favourable, as to allow our Clergy here to chuse two, one of whom the Congregation is to nominate Bishop Vicar apostolic. But this will not suit our Jealous Governments, nor I fear be so advantageous to Religion, as a Diocesan or ordinary Bishop: I am unwilling to employ the Interference of our Rulers as they are men of so heterogenious Principles; but I am sure it will be better to do it, than suffer the Plan proposed by Rome to be carried into Execution. How greatly might your Friends in England assist us in this Negotiation, by demanding that Liberty for themselves, wch we must have here? Long before I left Europe, I used to be astonished, that the English Bishops did not exert themselves to obtain a more independent Appointment and Jurisdiction. And

I am more surprised now, since the rigor of the penal Laws is somewhat abated. I remain equally persuaded of the Expediency of using the vulgar Tongue in the public Offices of Religion. But hitherto I am able to do no more than express my Wishes, and inforce on my Brethren my own Sentiments. Most of them feel the Necessity of such a Change in this Country equally with myself. With best Thanks for your Offer of Service & sincere return of the Offer on my part and very great regard I am   Dr Sir,   Your most obedt affte Servant   J. Carroll   Present my respects to my earlier pupil your good Brother.

MSC St
[1] *Reflections addressed to Rev. John Hawkins* (London, 1785).

TO CHARLES PLOWDEN   Rock Creek Novr 13–1786–

My dear Sir   Three days ago I had the pleasure of receiving yours of June 28th It was a most agreeable relief to me on coming from a most fatiguing service which lasted from Easter till All Saints, during which time I have been employed, with the interruption of only a day now and then either in travelling from one Congregation to another, or at the confessional and giving Confirmation: If the service has been hard, the consolation has likewise been great. The grace of God has visibly shewn itself, not indeed as in the Apostolic ages by the speaking of strange tongues, and prophesying; but by returns of the heart to Almighty God: may he, who has poured down such a blessing, perpetuate the effects of his own mercy! my work is scarce more than half done; & must be resumed next spring, if I am well & alive. You expected that Mr Brooke[1] would deliver your letter; but with yours, I received one from him informing me of his disappointment in not finding cash ready at London as he had reason to expect it would be, from my letters. How this has happened, I cannot tell, but shall know in a day or two. Your schoolfellow Mr Ashton our very industrious and active money agent, is not often behind hand in the discharge of his business: and I relied on him so much as to suppose he would not be deficient. But as I know, that he made farther remittances about three months ago, I trust that Mr Brooke is now on his way to a country, in which he will be most welcome.

The Irish Capucin at New York, Mr Nugent, is likely to establish a flourishing Congregation: a very handsome church is built, and was to be opened the 4th inst, in honour of the King of Spain, who has been a considerable Benefactor, & whose minister to Congress laid the first stone.[2] I received a most pressing invitation from the Trustees to attend and perform the ceremony of the day; but I was then in our frontier counties, & received their letter too late. As I know, that even in this country, there may be malevolent people, eager to misrepresent every action of an Exjesuit, I should not be surprised to hear that my non-attendance was the effect of disrespect to his Catholic Majesty. To obviate such a misrepresentation I shall write a state of the matter to Don Gardoqui, the Spanish envoy, a man of sense with whom I have the honour to be acquainted. I am now just about sending another Irish Capucin[3] to the new settlement of Kentucky, down the Ohio River, towards Mississippi. Many poor Catholics, who hope to get land cheaper there than in this or the neighbouring states, are anxious to remove thither. I propose requesting the Capucins to take the entire charge of supplying that country with labourers, as for many years it will be out of our power. I am likewise extending my views to the southern parts of Virginia, and the Carolinas; but am every moment stopped by the obstacles of a want of fit and able hands. The money for their support would be found, as I am told, by the Congregations, that would be soon collected. I am greatly pleased with your account of Liege academy: it will not however prevent me from pursuing the great object of a school and seminary here. Deputies from our three districts meet this day, & one great point of their deliberations is to be this matter.[4] I shall proceed to join them tomorrow, or next day. You will not forget to urge my petition to Mr Weld,[5] and your other friends in behalf of Baltimore Church. I depended much on yr Relations, Messr Wright,[6] and was greatly affected at hearing the fatality, wch has befallen that worthy family. I hope the Survivor will do for the sake of the deceased & for himself, as much as if all were still living. If Mr Thorpe can remain at Rome with satisfaction to himself, I should be sorry to hear, he had left it. I informed you in my last of the receipt of your most valuable ms, which may be called, the history of a providential deliverance of the Society from utter destruction. If wickedness and an infidel spirit were not so prevalent, as to make us fear the effects of Gods justice, rather than his mercy, I should have most sanguine hopes for an union of the Greek and Latin Churches, and a consequent reestablishment of the Society. Indeed, as matters stand, I greatly hope it.

People here read Berington's last publication with other sentiments, than it excited in you. It is admired by all, who have seen it; and yesterday I heared, that a Lady of rank for this country & of the best connexions in it either has come, or is coming into the bosom of the Church, finally convinced by Mr Berington's work. Since my last to you I have repeatedly read it, always with pleasure excepting a great inaccuracy in page 69, respecting the Pope's prerogative, which he speaks of as derived solely from the faithful; and two or three other bold or unguarded expressions. In my last, I sent you the only foundation, he had for mentioning me in the manner he did.

I thought I had mentioned to you the proceeding of our Soidisans Episcopal clergy. They have torn up the Church of Englands thirty nine articles; they have abolished from their offices the Nicene and Athanasian

Creeds, & the Doxology, Glory be to the Father &c. Even the words, *he descended into* Hell, are left out of the Apostles creed. In all this, my unfortunate friend,[7] (for so I must call him tho' he is lately married) had a principal part. Had he not taken this last step of marrying, I should have entertained hopes of him, but now I fear, he has placed an insuperable bar to this return. Of late I have heared nothing more of him, than what I have just mentioned. He lives in the small state of Delaware, bordering on this and Pennsylvania. He there serves a Congregn upon a small subscription. I think, I have heard, that he likewise has some post in a College or school at Wilmington, near his residence. Pray, who is the Servile writer of a letter to the Author of Ganganelli's life,[8] which I accidentally found in a parcel of books brought in hither for sale? I find, he has been pleased to subject me to terrible consequences, in a conscientious way, for my note on the amiable and benevolent Pontiff. If the writer be an English Clergyman as some passages lead me to believe I would refer him to his Br Mr Honor at Rome; who, if he will speak as plainly to the letter writer, as he did to me, will tell him, that his hero had neither honor or integrity, or indeed an attachment to his Countrymen, if they chanced to be Catholics, tho' he shewed so much partiality to the Englishmen who were not. I think, I never read a writer, who ever avowed more servile opinions; or who endeavoured to cloak his secret approbation of our destruction under so flimsy a veil of submission & blind obedience. Be pleased to present my humble & sincere respects to the heads of Lullworth family, to Messrs Stanley & Clinton & all other friends. I remember having had the honour to see Miss Darell at Cambray. I presume she is the Mrs Jones, you mention, & to whom I desire a return of my respects. My Mother joins me in every good wish to you & all yr connexions. Mr D. was well & much attached to you in Sept From yr character of Mr Archer,[9] I shall be happy to see his sermons.   I am Dr Sr Yrs   J. C.

I shall be glad to see even your mutilated copy of the *Tartuffe Epistolaire*, if I cannot have the whole. The four volumes, with different titles, of *lettres à Mr Carroccioli* &c I have seen; They were imported by Leonard Neale, & have furnished, as I perceive, the materials to the *sketch of the life of Clem. 14th*.[10] To the author of the latter, I am obliged for his handsome expressions concerning me, & give him the merit of digesting his materials into better order, & method, than his original. But is there not sometimes a prolixity, which leaves what he writes, *sine nervis* [without vigor] &c?

I have lately written to Mr Thorpe; and therefore shall request you for the present to inform him, that the interval between this, & the appointment of a Bishop, shall be employed in bringing matters to such a state that we may have an Ordinary, instead of a Vicar Apostolic; that I can certainly have this point recommended by some branches of the civil power; that I am ready to enter into a correspondence on this subject with the Cardl Secretary, if he

thinks it would not give offence to those who at present shew a fair face &
are perhaps disposed to go unusual lengths of kindness, as they see, that
otherwise they cannot obtain any good purpose in this country.

ALS   St
    [1] Ignatius Baker Brooke, S.J., returned to America shortly after this, ministering and
tutoring near Port Tobacco in 1793.
    [2] St. Peter's Church on Barclay St., to which King Charles II of Spain had liberally
contributed.
    [3] Charles M. Whelan.
    [4] General Chapter of the Clergy: Robert Molyneaux, Northern District; John Ashton
and Bernard Diderick, Middle District; Ignatius Matthews and James Walton, Southern
District.
    [5] Thomas Weld of Lullworth Castle, Dorset, England, noted for his extensive chari-
ties, father of Thomas Cardinal Weld and host of Plowden.
    [6] Mr. Thomas Wright & Co., London bankers.
    [7] Charles Wharton.
    [8] Arthur O'Leary, *Defense of the Conduct of Pope Clement XIV* (1786).
    [9] James Archer, Vicar General of the London, England District, author of several
volumes of sermons, including *Sermons on Various Moral and Religious Subjects* (London, 1787).
    [10] Charles Plowden, *A Candid and Impartial Sketch of the Life and Government of
Pope Clement XIV* (London, 1785).

TO DIEGO DE GARDOQUI   November 14, 1786

Sir   The munificence of His Catholic Majesty and the noble favours
which he has seen fit to grant to the church of New York, united with my
gratitude and natural attachment, cause me to take the honor of offering to
Your Excellency (as representative of the great Prince) the due tribute of my
gratefulness; and if it is not too daring a presumption I would go so far as to
beg Your Excellency to convey the sincerest expression of gratitude and
respectful veneration which dominates them; and to tell the truth, the gift of
his Catholic Majesty not only will live in posterity by the exercise of our
religion, but will be the foundation for other establishments of the same
nature.

I hope from the constant prayers of those who enjoy the benefit of the
bounty of his Majesty that this great act will merit that Heaven pour down its
benedictions on His Catholic Majesty, his posterity and his kingdom; and if to
these sentiments of most profound gratitude towards the generous kindness
of His Majesty be united the vivid remembrance of the person through whom
the effect of the same has been received, then I humbly beg Your Excellency
to be sure that I shall never forget how much our faith owes to Your
Excellency's active and potent recommendation.

The untoward event which has prevented me from receiving in time the
invitation with which I was honoured by the Congregation for St. Charles'
Day was deeply regretted by me because it deprived me of the opportunity of

expressing to Your Excellency the great respect and esteem with which I have the honor of being the most obedient and humble servant of Your Excellency, J. Carroll

L Guilday, pp. 276-77.

TO JAMES FRAMBACH[1] [Dec., 1786]

R. Sir   I laid your letter from Conewago[2] of Novr 7–1786– before Chapter, which consisted of the following members, Messrs Matthews & Walton for the southern district; Messrs Diderick & Ashton for the middle, & Mr Mol[lyneux]. for the Northern. They have desired me to communicate their unanimous opinion & resolves thereupon. They have examined your charges; and on the other hand the payments made you, as entered in upon the books of Messrs Hunter, Matthews, Walton & Ashton. They made no charge against you for what you received from Pipe Creek,[3] or for monies & other values, which you had from the Conewago estate. They gave you credit for £800, continental. It is my earnest hope, that you are disposed to settle all disputes amicably. They are willing to give up all these claims, tho they might be justly brought to acct agst you.

After these deductions in your favour, and every allowance for depretiation, they offer to pay you £114.6.9, on your giving a receipt in full & disclaiming all farther demands. You may perhaps be surprised to find the offer so much below your expectations; but you will allow me to say that you have kept yr acct too irregularly, to be depended on. I will mention one or two instances. You say–*Anno 1778–solutum nihil* [nothing paid]. Now in Mr Hunters books, the payment made you by him Octr 25–1777, is thus enterd–pd to Mr Frambach for salary of *the ensuing year,* £50–Again; tho you say, 1778, *soluntum nihil,* yet Mr. Hunter's books shew that March 5–1778, you had sent to you by him thro' the hands of Mr Sewall[4] £100, continental equal to £20.0.0.

I had the pleasure to see the Gentlemen enter on this business not only with a desire of doing justice, & preserving charity; but likewise of using every indulgence consistent with the public interest.

I have hitherto been acting under the direction of Chapter. I will now add, that my sincere wish is to see you come into their proposal, that uneasinesses may be removed on every side.

ADf   AAB
    [1] Jesuit from Germany, arrived 1758, served at Hagerstown and Frederick in the later 1780's, and a vicar general for Carroll after 1790.
    [2] Lancaster County, Pa.
    [3] Frederick County, Md.
    [4] Charles Sewall, S.J., a Marylander, returned from Europe in 1758, and later became Rector of St. Peter's Pro-Cathedral at Baltimore.

TO ARTHUR O'LEARY   Baltimore [1787]

Revd. Sir   It is not quite a month, since I was honoured with your favour
of Aug: 23d. by Fitzgibbon. He arrived at this port during my absence, &
would not, at first, deliver your letter to my Companion, at this place: as I
did not return, till lately, he at length left it for me; so that I have not yet
seen him, but expect him in a few days. You may be assured, that I will do
every thing in my power for his welfare, both spiritual and temporal; not only
on his own account, from a general principle of charity and pastoral duty; but
as recommended by a gentleman, to whom I wish to give proof of my most
respectful esteem. It is somewhat unfortunate, that Fitzgibbon lives at some
distance from town, & in a Protestant family; tho' they do not debar him
from exercise of the Religion, which his conscience approves.

You will allow me to take this opportunity of returning my thanks for yr.
handsome; & indeed too favourable manner of mentioning the *address* &c in
reply to my unfortunate friend and Kinsman, Mr. Wharton, who has lately
concluded his defection in the usual manner, by associating himself to one, he
calls his wife. The defects of the address are many; & I will not be so modest
as to impute them all[1] to inability; some are chargeable on my continued
avocations; and others on the want of books to consult: But it was absolutely
necessary to publish something to check the triumph of our Protestant
Brethren, & to raise the spirits of our own people, who were depressed &
insulted. I have the comfort to find these purposes answered, notwithstanding
the elegant pen of our antagonist. To God may the praise be given. Your
writings, Revd. Sir, have in some degree contributed to this happy effect; I
mean not your review of the controversy begun here, (which review few have
seen), but your other publications: and I sincerely rejoice, that a person of
your forcible & distinguished talents had dedicated them to the service of
Religion; and particularly to the detection of those cruel misrepresentations,
which by calumniating us as bad citizens, endeavoured to render us[2] obnoxious to every free government. I find, that you are not pleased with my
note on the late Pope;[3] & that you think, I was mistaken in attributing to
him a time-serving policy. Peace be to his spirit! & may God have mercy on
his soul! but whatever allowance, charity may make for him, the pen of
impartial history will not join you & Mr. Pilling in attributing to his public
conduct (and to that the destruction of the Jesuits belongs) the virtue of
benevolence. You think, that your intimacy with the good Cardl. de Luines[4]
gave you opportunities of information, which I had not: on the contrary, I
think, that having spent in Italy the two years immediately preceding our
dissolution, and the last of them at Rome; & mixing in all companies, & not
being much with my own Brethren, I had means of collecting knowledge,
which were perhaps wanting to Cardl. de Luines himself: and certainly I saw
repeated instances of conduct, which upon the coolest & most unprejudiced

consideration appear irreconcileable not only with benevolence, but even with common humanity, & the plainest principles of justice.[5] At the same time, I do not take upon me to say, that the whole weight of this misconduct fell upon the Pope, unless it be, for withdrawing himself totally from business & trusting his authority to men, who so shamefully abused it.[6] for it was notorious to every one, who had access to the palace, that the Pope did no business himself, but spent the whole day in giving audience, playing at billiards, & the conversation of five or six persons of indifferent, if not to say, mean talents. I hope you will excuse this liberty: your writings express a free soul; and I cannot think you would wish me to dissemble the feelings of mine. But tho I communicate them to Mr. O'Leary, I have neither the ambition to make them public; nor, fear to do so if occasion requires. A few copies of Mr. Berington's late work had reached America before your letter; but I am not the less obliged to you for your kind intention of sending it. With that Gentleman, I had a slight acquaintance in Europe; and some correspondance has subsisted between us, occasioned by his former publication, *on the behaviour of the Eng: Catholics*. In a letter to him, and before I had a thought of ever being in my present station, I expressed a wish, that the Pastors of the church would see cause to grant to this extensive continent, jointly with England, Ireland &c, the same privilege, as is enjoyed by many churches of infinitely less extent, that of having the liturgy in their own language; for I do indeed conceive that one of the most popular prejudices agst. us is, that our public prayers are unintelligible to our hearers. Many of the poor people, & the Negroes generally, not being able to read, have no technical help to confine their attention. On this foundation, Mr. Berington's brilliant imagination attributes to me projects, which far exceed my powers, and in which I should find no cooperation from my Clerical Brethren in America, were I rash enough to attempt their introduction, upon my own authority. This & a few more passages, & that in which, by a slip of his pen (for I cannot think it any thing else) he ascribes to the Successor of St. Peter no (supremacy *jure divino*,) render his work exceptionable: but in many other respects, I view it as most excellently calculated to shew the weak sides of[7] the strong. . . .[8]

ADf   AAB   Date estimated by reference to Carroll's *Address* on Wharton and O'Leary's published work of 1786, which reviewed the controversy.

[1] An original seven lines are crossed-out at this point which reads with slight difference from the second version given here.

[2] Deleted: "object of public hatred . . ."

[3] Clement XIV.

[4] Paul d'Albert de Luynes, Archbishop of Senonen (Sienna), died in 1788 in Paris.

[5] Deleted: "I had almost said, with the clearest dictates of Religion."

[6] Deleted: "for it was notorious to every one, who had access to the palace, that the Pope did no business himself, but spent the whole day in giving audiences, playing at billiards, & the conversation of five or six persons of indifferent, if not to say, mean talents."

[7]"Protestantism" was crossed-out at this point, followed by "the strong" which is not.

[8] Between the last lines of this letter rendered here is another passage which reads: "In many other respects, I am far from viewing Mr. Berington's performance in so favourable a light, as it appears to you. He has indeed made a slip of his pen (for I hope it is no more) in attibuting to the Bishop of Rome no prerogative, jure divino, but only derivative from the faithful at large! or their representative body, the Bishops."

## TO THE GENTLEMEN OF THE SOUTHERN DISTRICT[1]					[1787]

Reverend Gentlemen & Brethren.			Pax Christi.		We have attentively & respectfully considered the contents of a letter sent by you to us, on the subject of some resolves passed in the last Chapter,[2] & have entered very fully into the weight & merits of every argument alleged by you in opposition to the plan of spiritual government adopted by Chapter, & of a school intended to be erected by subscription for the education of youth & perpetuity of the body of Clergy in this country. As to the mode of securing our estates to our Successors, it being referred to a Committee, the members thereof will be the fittest judges to determine thereon, after every argument pro & con is canvassed by cool reason. Our answer therefore now shall be confined to the two first points.

Before we answer either of these points in particular, we observe, that you lay down two principles as incontestable: viz. the injustice done to the Society, & the infringement of the Constitution, we have already adopted.[3]

We answer, that the existence of the Society & the existence of the Constitution are two things incompatible: for the injustice, you complain of, implying the existence of the Society, totally destroys the existence of the Constitution. The Preamble to the form of Government expressly says, that "the object of the meeting is agreed to be, to establish a form of Government for the Clergy, & to lay down rules for the administration & preservation of *their* Property." No mention is made of it's being the property of the Society; and a new form of Government to be established, presupposing the government of the Society extinct.

The 17th. article of the Form of Government reserves to the general Chapter a power to sell & dispose of real property; & to the District Chapter a power over personal property.

The same power is reserved to the Genl Chapter in the 2d. article of regulations respecting the management of plantations.

These articles of the Constitution would be nugatory, if the Chapter can not dispose of their property without an injustice.

A declaration made, after the form of Government was agreed to, says, "that the members thereof will in behalf of themselves, & as far as they are competent, in behalf of their Constituents, to the best of their power, promote & effect an absolute & entire restoration to the Society of Jesus, if it should please Alm. God to reestablish it in this Country, of all the property *formerly* belonging to it." This resolve is entirely consistent with the above mentioned; and being conditional has no object nor tie before the reexistence of the Society; and we are fully persuaded, that it is the sincere desire of every one to have it carried into execution at that happy period. But in the mean time the property is absolutely our own, agreeably to the first declaration & subsequent articles: which it would not be, if we could not dispose of it for pious uses, without an injustice to the not yet existing Society.

We observe moreover, that the property held in this Country did not belong at any period of time to the Society at large; but only to that portion of it residing here, or at most to the English province. The property of one College, & one mission was totally distinct from that of another. This principle was essential to good government & general security; and it was asserted & maintained by the General & all Superiors of the Society in opposition to the claims set up in France to make the whole Society liable for the debts of the Missions of Martinico.[4]

The reestablishment therefore of the Society in this Country, is a necessary preliminary for the reacquiring of its former property here: & if any more effectual means of compassing that reestablishment can be devised, than those adopted by Chapter, & which you do except against, we shall be very ready to join you in preferring them. A school will certainly be a nursery, from whence postulants can alone be expected; & an independent Ecclesiastical Superior is principally if not essentially necessary to render the school competent to all the purposes of its establishment. The application of some part of our estate, which may be spared to this purpose, & the honour of God & good of souls, being the end of this Society, & hereby intended, we hope will give it that blessing from heaven, which we all most earnestly pray for.

We are most firmly persuaded, that a Diocesan Bishop is preferable, to an Apost[olic]. Vicar, or Apost. Perfect, as at present, who must necessarily be under the control of a Congregation at Rome, that has always been unfavourable to the Society. and we know from the history of the late Society, that the Diocesan Bishops throughout Europe were the means of its getting footing & flourishing in all Catholic Countries, and were the most strenuous in the support of its existence in its last period. This Bishop will be of our own choosing, and undoubtedly one, who has been of the Society, & is yet known to be well affected towards it. His revenues will hardly exceed what is allowed to the present Superior; and can there be a shadow of injustice to ourselves to allow a decent maintenance to a Successor of the Apostles; a Pastor of Christ's Sheep, & a guardian of the depositum of faith? If this seasonable opportunity of petitioning such a one is passed over, when we have friends at Rome to promote our Interest, may we not expect, when one is asked for through the Propaganda, by the Clergy, who are now coming into this Country & who probably will soon exceed us in numbers that their petition will be most readily granted, though he should be supported at the expence of that Congregation (as it is in China & elsewhere) who will be such a thorn in our sides, as will frustrate our most zealous labours & render the vineyard of our Lord desolate.

We know the jealousy, that our exemption from Episcopal jurisdiction gave in Europe; and notwithstanding the grants of the Holy See, that few Prelates would indulge the Society in that point. It is true without faculties we could live; but would not the cause of God suffer, & our Estates in time from the refusal of ordination or non admittance of postulants from abroad, in whom we would confide, fall into profane & scandalous hands?

Such an extensive Continent as this can never be left long without a Bishop of some sort to superintend the Clergy, & it is to be feard, that many will soon want such an Ecclesiastical superior to watch over their conduct. We can not rationally carry our views so far as to form to ourselves the idea of a Society to be established in this Country sufficiently adequate to its extent; nor can we put such a clog on people's dispositions, as to leave no door for admittance to H. Orders, but thro' that of the Noviciate. Religious orders in the Church are only auxiliaries to the Ecclesiastical Hierarchy established by Christ, and we may hope that as Providence has provided for us, so it will provide for those, whom it calls in another way.[5]

To depend on strangers longer than it would be absolutely necessary, would be highly imprudent; for we know, that few such can be got to come in, who would not be a burden & scandal to us. We remember how we were served even by our own former Provincials; a very discouraging circumstance from having any dependence on a foreign subjection of any nature whatever, but what is essential. Ordination & blessing of oils are annexed to Episcopacy, & no foreign Bishop will ordain without dimissorials[,] a clear patrimony and acquiring the usual interstices, which would put us, or the candidate for orders to the trouble & expence of repeated & dangerous voyages, A Bishop on the Spot will see where operarii [missionaries] are wanting & be able to judge of the means of subsistance sufficient to induce him to give ordination. Schools & seminaries have generally been encouraged & protected by the Bishops, whether immediately under their own direction or the direction of the Society; and if she should be reestablished in this Country in our life time, there is no doubt but with the other property, the government of the school will likewise be surrendered into her hands.

The schools of the Society in Europe were not calculated merely to supply its order with members, or the Church with ministers, but to diffuse knowledge, promote virtue & serve Religion. This is just the end we propose by our school, & tho' no members should take to the Church, we conceive this end alone well worth our most earnest concurrence, since it is the object of our dayly labours & the establishment of this Mission. Seminaries may afterwards be erected & novitiates opened; the one under the care of the Bishop, the other under the care of the Society; and by the concurrence of both to the same end, we pray that God may be glorified & his H. Church edified. "Sum omni modo sive per occasionem sive per veritatem Christus annunciatur, & in hoc gaudeo, sed & gaudebo."[6]

The plan of education we conceive can not be less extensive, than the one proposed to answer the end of the academy: the sooner youths are put under virtuous & careful hands, the less danger there will be of corruption in their morals and principles. In Europe there was no occasion of the Jesuits teaching them the first elements: for they were taught every thing to prepare them for the learned languages even their Catechism in the Parish schools subject to the curates with great care & edification. As to the number of the scholars, to be sure it will not exceed the proportion of masters & school-room; & the Directors, we presume, will be attentive with the Clergyman, who will be Rector of the school, to see order, virtue & discipline kept up both by the masters & scholars.

The property allotted by Chapter for this end, never belonged to the Society, which has not been in existence here since it was acquired; hence alone every objection arising from the idea of justice is cut off on this head: tho' we are far from admitting, that the Clergy here can not contribute to a pious work in the use of their other property without injuring their successors. For this principle once admitted would perhaps operate too strongly against ourselves, & suggest uneasy thoughts of restitution to those, who may think themselves injured by donations made to our Predecessors & which we now enjoy, to the exclusion of the natural heirs to some of our best livings.

We now come to answer the particular reasons you have alleged for protesting against the three resolves of Chapter mentioned in your letter to us. The first. "That the form of Government, to which alone we do submit, shall be properly Episcopal."

1°. "You protest against this resolve & declare yourself no ways bound by the same."

Ans. We do not dispute the right you have of protesting; but if you will attend to the 9th. article of the form of Government, you will find, that if a majority in the different districts agree to establish new rules, or alter those before established, such alteration or establishment is binding on you, notwithstanding your protest. Whether this be the case or not, it remains only to be determined after all the voices are taken. Hence you will discover, that there was no occasion of taking the opinion of each individual before the passing of such a resolve in Chapter.

2°. "You protest against it as unjust, because the Society might hereafter be excluded from entering into the possession of her undoubted rights; or at least be clogged with the unjust burden of maintaining a Bishop for ever."

Ans. We deny that any right can be claimed by a non entity. A promise is made by Chapter as far as they are competent to reinstate the Society in her former rights, if she should ever revive in this Country; & it will never be in the power of a Bishop without the consent of Chapter to frustrate this resolve; particularly as he is secluded from all share of Government in our temporal affairs. The burden of maintaining a Bishop, if it can be so called, will be no clog to the Society, if it be now granted by the absolute proprietors before any claim can arise from a body not yet existing; which will on its revival have a right, under our promise, to claim the property we shall then be possessed of; it will also have a very ample support for its members. We do not see how "we should deprive ourselves of the power of reentering the Society, without forfeiting our rights to a maintenance from our present estates", when the members, who, it may be presumed, would reenter, are in possession & would keep possession of them till that period.

3°. "Because no material advantage is derived to compensate us for the maintenance of a Bishop."

Ans. We have in the first part of our letter, we think, sufficiently answered this objection; and we now add, that the expence of sending abroad for such necessaries as will be wanting, without a Bishop, joined to the expence of a Superior, who must naturally be a creature of the Propaganda in the present system of Government, will be more than sufficient to maintain a Bishop of our own choosing, & who must on that account alone be friendly disposed to us. We add that such a one tho' more expensive, would still be preferable to the former.

4°. "Because the maintaining a Bishop would disable us from providing for operarii, where the glory of God & good of souls might require."

Ans. We have been long in want of operarii without being able to procure a sufficient number, & the difficulty is likely to increase daily; shall we therefore by saving the expense of a Bishop deprive souls of every spiritual assistance, whilst we flatter ourselves with the hopes of seeing a Society, whose future establishment is a secret of Divine Providence. Was the Society instituted for the good of souls, or must souls be sacrificed for the sake of the Society?

Your second Protest is against a memorial being drawn up & sent to his Holiness to represent the present state of the R. Catholic Church in N. America & the determination of the Clergy thereon.

"You protest against this resolve being carried into immediate execution."

1°. "For the reasons above alleged."

Answered as above.

2°. "Because our form of Government directs," *that where circumstances point out* &c ord. 9. art.

This article of our form of Government, we conceive, militates against you so far as you declare yourselves not bound by the subsequent protested resolves. But where you only object to its being carried into immediate execution, we most readily join with you, till the sense of the different

Districts shall be taken on the same & notified to us; agreeably to which we mean to conduct ourselves in this affair.

3°. You declare against the mode or plan of erecting a College as proposed & resolved by the late Chapter.

1°. "Because the plan proposed is of so extensive a nature &c, & fear that the burden must fall on our Estates."

Ans. We are glad to find that you only object against the mode or plan. We do not see how it can be executed to answer the designed purpose on a less scale for the reasons given in the foregoing part of our letter. It will undoubtedly be the indispensible duty of the directors of the said College to see that nothing is undertaken or carried into execution but on the safest security of payment, without any danger of burdening or ruining ourselves by such an undertaking. Till the experiment is made, it is difficult to tell what the contributions of seculars will amount to; but most certain it is, that the plan ought to be proportioned to the said amount.

2°. "Because as we hold our Estates from the Society &c we conceive, that we have no right to alienate her property &c."

Ans. We will not take upon us to say, that we hold our estates from the Society; but we agree, that we are possessed of Estates formerly belonging to a part of the Society; and in case of her restoration here, have promised to each other to reinstate the Society in her former possessions; this, we conceive, does not deprive us in the mean time of the just right of applying part of them to some pious use, which the Society might formerly have done, & did do without any violation of justice to its successors.

3°. "Because the chief end proposed by erecting a College being to procure a continued supply of operarii &c."

Ans. We have above communicated to you our thoughts on this subject; & have now only to add, that the plan proposed is for the glory of God & edification of our neighbour, & such as St. Ignatius would glory in as coming from his most zealous children, whose spirit we wish may subsist amongst our Successors to the end of time, in spite of every opposition, which may be made to so laudable an undertaking.

To the question you ask; "Will it or can it be a benefit to the Society to be stripped of a considerable part of her property"? we answer: We deny the supposition of its being the property of the Society, or even of the English Province, which formerly held it; and we maintain it to be the sole property of the associated body of Clergy in this Country, as we have before observed.

We have but one observation now to make on the last paragraph of your letter to us: that as Chapter has ordered the subject of the Incorporation act to be discussed & determined on by a Committee at Port Tobacco, we do not conceive how you can with any propriety prejudge the point in suspense, before you have heard the reasons alleged on both sides. For we should deem it a great presumption in ourselves to declare that no reason shall move us to depart from the opinion, we may have already formed on this or any other subject submitted to our consideration. And therefore it is our opinion, that the resolve of Chapter with respect to a Committee on this point, ought to be complied with.

Wishing therefore that you would reconsider the subject of your letter to us after hearing our reasons, & knowing that we all mean one & the same thing, viz. the Greater Glory of God, we pray that his Divine grace may dispell every cloud, that is passing between us, & enlighten us to discover the truth wherever it lies.

Having animadverted on the general principles of your letter to us & answered your objections stated against the resolves of Chapter therein, we take this occasion to communicate to you our sentiments on the nature of our spiritual Government, which seems to us not rightly to be comprehended by you.

When the Clergy of these States first met together on the 27th day of June 1783 to take into their consideration the state of their temporal affairs, & the means that would be most conducive to the preservation of their property & the application thereof to the maintenance of those Clergymen, who should continue to do service to the faithful agreeably to the original design, for which it was intended; and to bind themselves by certain rules & regulations necessary to keep up order amongst the members thereof; it was never their intention to interfere with spiritual Government.

The subsequent Chapter, which met Novbr. 11. 1784, and by which the form of Government was drawn up & agreed to unanimously, declares that the object of the meeting is agreed to be to establish a form of Government for the Clergy & to lay down rules for the administration & preservation of their property.

Throughout the whole form of Government we do not find any regulation of a purely spiritual nature; but wherever it is necessary to make mention of the Superior in spirituals, it is always done in the abstract, as a matter not belonging to Chapter to decide upon.

The Chapter, which met Novbr. 13–1786 persuing the same plan & in conformity to the form of Government established by the foregoing Chapter, thought it not their province to establish a form of Spiritual Government, to which they were not competent; but finding a spiritual & temporal government already established, only explained & decided on points, that were not before settled & determined on.

We must here bring to your minds that doleful era of the dissolution of the Society of Jesus, when we were torn from our dear Mother, whom we saw sacrificed before our eyes to the designs permitted by Divine Providence. In consequence of this we were left without father, without mother, oppressed with grief, uncertain of our future destiny. In these melancholy circumstances a formula of Subscription to Episcopal Government was presented to us from our ordinary the Bishop of London, who was directed by the H. See to do the same. To this we all subscribed, & thereby bound ourselves to a new form of Ecclesiastical Government, to which we have been hitherto subject. For your information & satisfaction we do here subjoin the formula above mentioned.[7]

Since this period, we conceive that it is not in our power to alter the System of Ecclesiastical Government, to which we have submitted, without the consent of the H. See, which accepted of this our submission. As to those members of this body of Clergy, who have been admitted amongst us since the above period, we presume, that they by entering submitted to the form of spiritual Government, which they then found established amongst us, & have no more title to think themselves exempt from such a jurisdiction, than their fellow labourers in the Lord's vineyard.

But it not being determined by the above submission whether Episcopal jurisdiction should be *ordinary* & proper, or *extraordinary* under a Vicar Apostolic, the late Chapter after mature deliberation determined, as an assembly of the Clergy, that *ordinary* Episcopacy was better adapted to the exegenc[i]es of this Country, than such as would render us subject to a foreign jurisdiction known to be ill-affected to the members of the late unfortunate Society.

The only question therefore between us is this. Are you for a Bishop of your own choosing, & who in the nature of things will be well affected to us & the reestablishment of the Society? Or are you for leaving it to the Propaganda to appoint one over you, who in the ordinary course of things will be inimical to both? It is but natural, that one of our own choosing must be maintained by us; & we can not conceive how the present Superior can be maintained without an injustice done to the Society, if it would be an injustice to maintain a Bishop; unless you will admit, that an injustice can only be applicable to the *quantum* & not *ad rem.* —The Propgda. are absolutely bent on having a Vic. Apost: & it is only the remonstrance of the present Superior, that has suspended the appointment of one to a further time. They have even mentioned the appointment of a foreigner; but for the reasons alleged have suspended such design, & consented to leave to the Clergy of this Country, the choosing of him out of their own body. We therefore think, that this is the favourable time to have the business settled for ourselves & our successors, & earnestly sollicit your concurrence.

The school being essentially connected with the above system of Government submitted to, & the only resource for new members in case of a reestablishment, we most ardently entreat you not to impede so salutary & pious an institution, but to promote it with all your endeavours.[8]

That the spirit of God may open our eyes on this important occasion is the earnest prayer of J. Digges   J. Ashton   Cs. Sewall   Sylv. Boarman   J. Carroll

DfS   MPA   From Charles Sewall's hand, this MS evidently served as a faithful copy and is signed by Carroll. The other names affixed are not signatures but apparently from Carroll's hand. In view of previous and subsequent writings of Carroll on these matters, it is clear that the thoughts of this letter were very much his own. The letter Feb. 7, 1787 as well as Carroll's above references to the sequence of Chapters indicate that this letter was distributed in January.

[1] Leonard Neale seems to have been foremost in the opposition from the region of southern Maryland. Among other possible adherents were: Bennett Neale, Ignatius Matthews, James Walton, John Bolton, John Boarman, Augustin Jenkins, and Benjamin Roels. Neale gave way in the face of this explanation, and undoubtedly most of the others as well.

[2] Nov. 1786, which concluded the official Constitution of the Clergy.

[3] The correspondents mistakenly assumed that the property of the Jesuits during the interim between suppression and restoration in 1814 was not to be used by other clergy at all. Carroll makes the point that a promise of return alone was agreed to.

[4] The Caribbean Island of Martinique had a mission that incurred extensive debt to the French government. A deleted version of this paragraph grants the assumption of the English Province's jurisdiction, saying, however, that there was never any attempt at control of property in America.

[5] Carroll accepted the idea of exempt orders, such as the Jesuits, who were directly under the Bishop of Rome; but since that status no longer prevailed the only status remaining to ordained priests of the suppressed order was that of other priests under existing bishops.

[6] "I am in every way [desirous], whether through opportunity or through truth, that Christ be proclaimed, and in this I rejoice and will [ever] rejoice."

[7] The first letter of the Bishop of London, Richard Challoner, follows. Written in Latin, it calls for submission of all ex-Jesuits to the vicars apostolic of the bishop and to all the provisions of the decree of Clement XIV. A letter of Oct. 6, 1773 from Richard Debown [?], Vicar Apostolic to the missionaries in Maryland and Pennsylvania is quoted. He encloses a formula of submission which was to be signed by all.

[8] Deleted: "& to consider seriously in the sight of allm God, whither the opposition made, comes from power of Divine spirit, or whether the spirit of Darkness has not transformed himself into an Angel of light to oppose so holy, so beneficial & so essential a means to support the cause of God against Heresy, impiety & irreligion. We know that all pious institutions have met with great oppositions, & even from the most pious, till it pleased allm God to enlighten them with his Divine grace to see from whence the opposition came."

TO TRUSTEE OF GERMAN CONGREGATION IN PHILADELPHIA [1787]

Sir   I received a petition or remonstrance last night, signed by yourself, Messrs. Oellers and Premir, and was requested to direct my answer to you.

As the Congregations of this place[1] never before had the nomination of the Clergymen appointed to serve it, I now see no reason why I should depart from a right, which has been always exercised by my predecessors. In the present exercise of this right, I am governed by a nature, that acting in opposition contrary to them, I should esteem myself wanting to important & weighty considerations of justice, prudence & gratitude: so that I cannot make my determination agreeable to the wishes of the petitioners, & of the Gentlemen who wrote the remonstrance of last night.

This Congregation has ever flourished, & drawn on itself the admiration of all, who have visited Philada.: and I trust in God it ever will, unless it be disturbed by another interference, that has never been exercised before. In my way to New York,[2] I was requested to procure a German Clergyman:

This I promised to do as soon as in my power, & informed the Gentlemen, who did me the honour of calling on me, that I expected Mr. Cressler[3] to come expressly for Philada., with which they were much satisfied. I now see no sufficient reason for changing his destination. With great respect I have the honour to be, Sir   Yr. most obedt. Serv.   J. Carroll
Be pleased to communicate this to Messrs. Premir & Oeller.

ADfS   AAB   Reference to Graessl (Cressler) indicates date.
[1] St. Mary's Church, Philadelphia.
[2] 1785.
[3] Laurence Graessl, S.J., succeeded Farmer, who died at this time. Carroll misspells his name here and elsewhere. See to Antonelli, Mar. 18, 1788.

TO [LEONARDO ANTONELLI]   [1787]

My Ld. Cardl.   Religion & learning have an hereditary claim on the Princes of yr. august family. It is therefore with great, but most respectful confidence, that an unknown Individual does himself the honour to present to the patronage of yr. Eminence, a proposed establishment,[1] which being designed for promoting the best causes,[2] may greatly contribute to spread the empire of true Religion, and a respectful attachment to the Holy See. Thus may [*blank*–Amer]ica console the friends of the Church, for the losses she suffers in other countries: and your Eminence, endeavours to obtain success for the present undertaking, will receive the grateful benedictions of the new world, as much as you attract the admiration of Europe. With the most profound respect & veneration I have the honour to be, Most Rd. Cardl., Yr. Eminences most humble . . .

ADf   AAB   (8H6)   On letter from Thorpe, Dec. 2, 1786. Addressee and date established by reference to Jan. 12, 1787.
[1] Georgetown College, as seen from Jan. 21, 1787 letter.
[2] The following phrases have been deleted in passage to "This may . . .": "may greatly benefit . . . Religion, & letters . . . may hereafter become efficacious . . . Perhaps divine providence destines this country to . . . in a country, which has heretofore been unfavourable to the progress . . . "

NOTATION ON SEMMES FAMILY   [1787]

Petition from Mrs. Semmes children–A[nswer] To write to Dick Brent to draw up a proper power of attorney for Aggy Walsh [?] to execute & send it to Mr. Neale of P[or]t. Tob[acc]o.–

AM   AAB (6K2)   On letter from Charles Plowden, June 4, 1787 [or June 3?].

TO WILLIAM O'BRIEN   1787
Not found. See Dec. 9, 1787.

TO JOHN THAYER   1787

Not found.

TO LEONARDO ANTONELLI   12 Jan. 1787—

Most Eminent Cardinal   I enclose letters which I had composed from
time to time to be sent from which the Congregation will learn the status of
religion in these United States. Shortly after they were written we suffered a
great loss in the death of Rev. Mr. Farmer, who for many years in Philadelphia, gave evidence of every virtue and was untiring in laboring for the
welfare of souls. His life, full of merit, as we may believe, was closed with a
most happy death.

From a French priest, about whom I write elsewhere, I have discovered
that the Catholics who once lived near the Mississippi River for the most part
moved from there during the war; and that the same region is already taken
over by non-Catholics, among whom there is good hope of spreading the
faith. While I was thinking of extending my care to this territory word came to
me from Canada that the illustrious bishop of Quebec, to whose diocese the
territory belonged during the British regime, still claims it. To me this
arrangement would be acceptable, but I fear that those in authority here
would not tolerate under any condition the exercise of jurisdiction by a
prelate who is a British subject.

With this letter I had hoped to send the two young men to the Urban
College. When I thought that everything was arranged the parents of the one
from Pennsylvania suddenly changed their minds, so that another had to be
chosen and their departure deferred for about two months. The expenses of
both as far as Europe are taken care of, and thus the Congregation is relieved
of a burden.

Previously I spoke of a plan for establishing a school for Catholics. My
plans have partly taken shape after consultation with my associates. God
willing, next summer I shall push them to execution if the charity and
religious zeal of our people can be aroused so that some of the expense is
met. To expect them to bring the school to completion is out of the question.
Appeal will be made to the liberality of the faithful in Europe in the belief
that they certainly will contribute whatever they can to the preservation and
extension of the faith.

In New York I hope that the faith has taken root. Through the generosity
of the Most Catholic King they are building a very nice church. If it seems
good to the Holy Father I should wish for the faculty of blessing churches if
this faculty is ever given to a simple priest.

I enclose other sealed letters. When you have read them you will see to
whom they should be given. It is not clear to me in the case in point, and

when such remote territories are involved, whether recourse should be to the Sacred Penitentiary or to the Propaganda. I most earnestly ask that a reply be speedily given because the one concerned is greatly troubled in spirit and conscience.

To you, most eminent cardinal, and the entire Sacred Congregation, I and my associate priests and the laity entrusted to us, in all humility and respect commend ourselves.   Your most devoted and respectful   J. C.

ADf   AAB

12 Januarii 1787   Eme. Card.   Includo literas quas subinde mittendas conscripseram in quibus colliget Sacra Congregatio quo statu sint res religionis in his Foederatae Americae Provinciis. Paulo post quam scriptae sunt, gravissimam jacturam fecimus ex morte qua die Reverendus Dom. Ferdinandus Farmer, qui per multos annos Philadelphiae versatus omni virtutum generique laboris pro animarum salute se exercuit et vitam plenam meritis, sanctissima, ut credere par est, morte conclusit.

Non ita pridem intellexi ex presbytero Gallo, de quo in alteris litteris, Catholicos, qui olim ad oras fluvii Mississippi habitavere, ut plurimum fervente bello, inde transmigrasse; et eandem Regionem jam ab Acotholicis esse occupatam; magnam tamen spem affulgere veram fidem apud ipsos disseminandi. Dum ulteriores curas illis partibus impendere cogitarem; relatum mihi est ex Canada Illustrissimum Episcopum Quebecensem, ad cujus dioecesim regio illa, regnante Anglo: spectabat, etiamnum illam sibi vindicare. Quod certe mihi est ac prorsus erit gratissimum; id unum timeo ut qui rerum apud nos potiuntur, permittant quocumque omnino jurisdictionis exercitium Praelato sub Angliae regimine degenti.

Eadem occasione, qua hasce litteras, sperabam mittendos juvenes ad Collegium Urbanum; cumque omnia in promptu esse credebam, illius, qui ex Pennsylvania erat abiturus, parentes subito consilium mutavere, ita ut alter seligendus sit, ac utriusque profectio duobus circiter mensibus differenda. Amborum expensae usque ad Europam persolventur, atque illo onere levabitur Sacra Congregatio.

Superius dixi consilia scholam erigendi pro Catholicorum institutione. Illius operis formam aliquam jam apud me, et cum sociis constitui; ejusque executioni manum admovere, proxima aestate, Deo favente, cogito; si nostrorum charitas et Religionis studium ita poterit accendi, ut aliqua ex parte sumptui succurrant; nam ut plene proficiant, expectandum non est; sed Fidelium liberalitas in Europa sollicitanda est qui certe pro verae fidei conservatione et extensione utiliter conferent, quidquid ad scholae destinatae usum conferent.

Novi Eboracii vera fides, ut spero, firmas aget radices. Insignem ecclesiam ibi construunt Regis Catholici liberalitate multum adjuti. Vellem, siquidem Beatissimo Patri Nostro ita videretur, facultatem habere consecrandi ecclesias ritu solemni; si tamen ejusmodi facultas simplici Sacerdoti unquam conceditur.

Includo alias literas obsignatas, quas cum legeris, Cardlis Em. videbis ad quos sint referendae. Non enim compertum habeo utrum in causa degu agitur, ubi in his remotis regionibus intervenit ad Eme. Card. Penetentiarium recursus haberi debeat, an vero ad Sacram Congregationem de Propaganda fide. Plurimum ac instanter rogo, ut omni diligentia expediatur responsum, quod is, ad quem res spectat magno animi et consciae angore crucietur.

Tibi, Eme. Card. omnique Sacrae Congregationi, se, socios presbyteros, et fideles nostrae curae commissos omni humilitate et observantia commendat. Card. Eme. Devotissimus et observantissimus   J.C.

TO LEONARDO ANTONELLI   13 Jan. 1787

Most Eminent Cardinal   A Capuchin, whose name and fatherland I give elsewhere, has recourse to the Holy Father and presents his case so that, if need be, it may be examined by those to whom the Holy Father assigns it. He lived for some years as a lay brother under solemn vows. Without his superior's knowledge in April 1782 he changed his religious garb for secular dress, and as a layman he fled to America. Here, beyond the reach of religious obedience, he engaged in various businesses and employments, honorable in themselves but forbidden to a religious. He did not waver in his faith; he did not attempt marriage; his conduct never gave scandal. A few days ago he made a clean breast of all to me. He says that he is so conscience stricken that he is ready to do anything the Holy Father may enjoin on him, but that he lacks trust in himself and dreads the very prospect of returning to the severe rule of his order. Therefore, prostrating before the Holy Father, he pleads for release from his religious vows, and that he be allowed to devote himself to the service of some church or to a person in orders, and also that he be permitted to contribute the money made in business to some pious use. He does not ask to be dispensed from his vow of chastity while he lives secularized. While he awaits a reply he promises to observe the rules of his order so far as possible. At his request I have explained the situation, and now I leave the whole matter, as I should, to those to whom it rightfully belongs. Just one thing I add—he seems to be well disposed but so upset by mention of return to his order that I scarcely think he will have the courage to undertake it, should it be ordered. And this all the more because he is so situated that, should he resist, no assistance can be had from the external forum. Then too the urging of his friends will weaken and destroy his resolve because they will do everything to extinguish his pious sentiments.   Your Eminence's most respectful servant   J. C.

ADf   AAB

Die 13 Jan. 1787   Eme. Card.   Ad Bm. Patrem Nostrum humiliter pro sequenti casu recurrit vir religiosus ex ordine Capuccinorum, cujus nomen et patriam separatim obsigno, ut si opus fuerit, inspiciatur ab iis, quibus Sua Sanctitas rem commiserit. Cum esstet solemnibus votis obstrictus, et in Religione tanquam frater *conversus,* ut vocant, aliquos annos vixisset, nullo Sacro Ordine suscepto mense Aprilis an[ni] 1782 inscio superiore, dimisit habitum Religionis secularem induit, aufugit ita in Americam, ibique extra Superiorum obedientiam variis muneribus, et negotione se exercuit, per se quidem honesta, sed viro Religioso interdicta. Fidem constanter retinuit; matrimonium nunquam attentavit, moribus, publico scandalo non fuit. Paucis adhinc diebus rem mihi totam aperuit; se conscientia incredibiliter angi profitetur; ad omnia paratum esse, quae Beatissimus Pater injunxerit; sibi tamen diffidere, ac severissimam sui Ordinis disciplinam pertimescere. Hinc ad Sanctitatis Suae pedes provolutus, enixis ac ferventissimis precibus illius misericordiam ac auctoritatem implorat ut sibi a votis Religiosis dispensatio concedatur, et addicere se licaet ministerio alicujus Ecclesiae aut personae in sacris constitutae, ac ut bona ex negotione quaesita piis usibus valeat applicare. A voto castitatis, extra Religionem [illeg.] liberari non postulat. Interim, dum responsum expectatur, Ordinis sui regulas, quantum fieri potest, observaturum se promittit.

Haec secundum vota postulantis exposui, et rem totam, ut debeo, illis committo, ad quos de jure pertinet. Hoc unum adjicio, supplicantem videri quidem optime dispositum; ita tamen trepidare ad omnem mentionem reditus in Ordinem, ut vix sperem satis in eo futurum constantiae ad hoc suscipiendum, si juberetur; praesertim cum eo loco sit, ubi, si repugnaverit, nihil auctoritatis ad compellendum a foro externo derivari potest; et amicorum consilia ad constantiam labefactandam, et extinguendos pietatis sensus omnia dirigentur. Emae Tuae servus obsequentissimus   J.C.

TO ANTOINE DUGNANI   Baltimore Maryland 13 January 1787

My Lord   I have the honor of addressing to your Excellency the enclosed packet for his Eminence Cardinal Antonelli. My instructions prompt me to forward by your hands letters for the Congregation of the Propaganda: and I take this opportunity, with the greatest devotion, to express to Your Excellency the deep respect with which I am inspired not only by your rank and distinguished service, & the choice of His Holiness, but even more by your eminent personal qualities, which my European correspondents never stop praising to me.

Conforming to the request and to the charitable offer of the Congregation of the Propaganda, I intend to send in one or two months two young men from here to go to the Urban College in Rome. They will be sent directly to a port in France, which will probably be Bordeaux, L'Orient, or Havre de Grace. On their departure they will be accompanied by a letter for the bishop or Ecclesiastical Superior of the place where the vessel lands, in order that he may report their arrival to your Excellency, to receive your orders. I have received instructions to act thus.   With deepest respect, I have the honor to be   My Lord   Your most humble & obedient servant   J. C.

ADf   AAB

De Mariland, ce 13 Janvier 1787   Monseigneur   J'ai l'honneur d'adresser à votre Exc. le paquet çi-joint pour son Em. le Cardinal Antonelli. Mes instructions portent de faire passer par vos mains les lettres pour la Congregation de la propagande: et je profite, avec le plus grand devouement, de cette occasion à temoigner à Votre Exc. le profond respect que m'inspirent non seulement son rang et emploi distingué, & le choix de Sa Sainteté, mais encore plus ses eminentes qualités personnelles, dont mes correspondans en Europe ne cessent de me faire l'eloge.

Conformément à la demande et à l'offre charitable de la Congregation de la propagande, je me propose de faire embarquer dans un ou deux mois d'içi deux jeunes gens pour passer à Rome au College Urbain. Ils seront envoyés directement à un port de France, qui sera probablement ou Bordeaux, L'Orient, ou Havre de Grace. A leur depart ils seront accompagnés d'une lettre pour l'eveque ou Superieur Ecclesiastique du lieu, auquel le vaisseau abordera, à fin qu'il fasse rapport à votre Excellence de leur arrivée, pour en reçevoir ses ordres. J'ai reçu des Instructions pour ainsi agir.   Avec le plus profond respect, j'ai l'honneur d'être,   Monseigneur   De V. Ex.   Le très humble & très obeissant ser.   J. C.

TO CHARLES PLOWDEN   Rock Creek, January 22d 1787
                                         —Baltimore Feb. 28—1787

Dear Sir   About ten days ago, I received your welcome favour (for all from you are such) of Sepr 29th It appears from the contents, that you had not then got my letter of July, or the beginning of August; I do not remember which; since that, I wrote to you in November. In those letters you will find an account of several matters relating to our situation, & an acknowledgement of the receipt of your invaluable ms. concerning the Russian Jesuits. It continues to be read by all our Gentlemen with admiration and gratitude to the Giver of every good gift for the wonderful & evident tokens of his providential protection over that remnant of our ever regretted Society. Experience has indeed taught me to distrust my own hopes and expectations, however well founded I may esteem them, & however much they may appear to me purified from all selfishness, & vanity: but I must own, that at present it would seem too great diffidence, & even injurious to the goodness of God, not to believe that he has some extraordinary and salutary purpose to accomplish, by the singular preservation of our Russian Brethren: In what manner, & form and at what time it will please him fully to manifest his gracious purpose, must be left to his infinite wisdom. Your continued attention & earnestness for the prosperity of the American Church entitles you to every information concerning it. We have now two great undertakings on hand, for the success of which we stand in need of every support and best advice of the friends of Religion. We have resolved to establish an academy for the education of youth; and to sollicit the appointment of a diocesan Bishop: the latter is a necessary consequence of the former: for our great view, in the establishment of an academy, is to form subjects capable of becoming useful members of the ministry; and to these a Bishop, for Ordination, will be indispensably necessary: In the present temper of our Rulers, a Vicar Apostolical is the least calculated for this country of any, where a hierarchy is not already established: so that between no Bishop, & a Diocesan Bishop, there is no medium.

I shall send to London, either to Strickland or Talbot, a printed paper containing the general outlines of the plan for an academy.[1] It will be afterwards put into Mr Nihell's hands to be forwarded to you. But as it only contains as much as it was necessary the public should know; with you I will be more particular. In the beginning, the academy will not receive boarders, but they must provide lodgings in town: but all notorious deviations from the rules of morality, out, as well as in school, must be subjected to exemplary correction: every care & precaution that can be devised, will be employed to preserve attention to the duties of Religion & good manners, in which other American schools are most notoriously deficient. One of our own Gentlemen, & the best qualified we can get, will live at the academy to have the general direction of studies; & superintendence over Scholars and masters. Four other of our Gentlemen will be nominated to visit the academy at stated times, & whenever they can make it convenient, to see that the business is properly conducted. In the beginning, we shall be obliged to employ secular Masters, under the Superintendant, of which many, & tolerable good ones, have already sollicited appointments. The great influx from Europe of men of all professions & talents, has procured this opportunity of providing Teachers. But this is not intended to be the permanent system. We trust in God, that many youths will be called to the service of the Church. After finishing their academical studies, these will be sent to a seminary, which will be established in one of our own houses; & we have, thro' Gods mercy, a place & situation admirably calculated for the purpose of retirement; where these youths may be perfected in their first, & initiated into the higher studies; and at the same time formed to the virtues becoming their station. Before these young Seminarists are admitted to Orders, they will be sent to teach some years at the academy, which will improve their knowledge, & ripen their minds still more before they irrevocably engage themselves to the Church. You will observe, that the perfecting of this plan requires great exertions; and in particular, demands persons of considerable ability for the conduct of the academy; & will hereafter stand in farther need of able & interior men to take charge of the Seminary. The difficulties indeed perplex, but do not dishearten me. But I stand greatly in need of your powerful assistance to procure as soon as possible, a fit Gentleman to open, as Superintendant, the new establishment, which we hope may be next autumn, or at farthest, the Spring twelve-month. How often have I said to myself; what a blessing to this country would my friend Plowden be! what reputation and solid advantage would accrue to the academy from such a Director! and what a lasting blessing would he procure to America by forming the whole plan of studies and system of discipline for that institution, where the minds of Catholic youth are to be formed, & the first foundations laid of raising a Catholic ministry equal to the exigencies of the Country! Could the zeal of a Xaverious[2] wish a more promising field to exert his talents?

But, my dear Sir, I am sensible, that I can indulge this happiness only in idea: Europe will hold you too fast to spare you to America. But, if you cannot come yourself, is there no one on whom you can direct your views, capable of filling this place with credit and advantage? I trust this important concern almost entirely, to your management. You see, he must be a person old enough to carry a considerable weight of authority & respect; experienced in the detail of government for such a place of education; & capable of embracing in his mind a general & indeed universal plan of studies, of which the academical institution is only a part. He should have considerable knowledge of the world, as he will be obliged to converse with many different persons: and he should be capable of abstracting his mind from the methods used in the colleges, where he has lived, so as to adopt only as much of them as is suited to the circumstances of this country; and of substituting such others, as are better adapted to the vies and inclinations of those with whom he has to deal. You see I require a good deal; but all I mention, is necessary to give reputation & permanency to the plan; for you may be assured, that in the Institutions of other professions, they have procured from Europe some litterary characters of the first class: and this likewise makes me desirous of not falling behind hand with them. I have heard Mr. Kemper,[3] and Mr. Barrow[4] spoken of with great commendation. Can Liege spare them or either of them? and would either of them be willing to come to our assistance? You perhaps can point out some other able and proper person. I shall mention this matter to Messrs Mattingley & Semmes; and if you correspond with Liege, you will, I hope act in concert with them. We cannot afford, in the beginning, to offer very great encouragement: if the academy should prosper, we probably should have it in our power to make the Superintendants situation exceedingly comfortable indeed: but in the beginning, we dare not exceed an offer of £60. p.ann.

I again entreat you My Dr Sir, to exert your utmost industry in this business, & to give me immediate information of your success. You see the importance of the commission; and your exertions will, I hope, be adequate to the great concern at stake. Mr Kemper's uncle, the worthy Mr Wapelaer, having devoted so much of his labours to this country, may be a motive with the Nephew to sacrifice his own labours likewise to the perfecting the work begun by the former.

Next to the choice of a proper Superintendant, or Principal, your assistance will be requisite, principally, in the designation of proper elementary books for our establishment. You will therefore be so kind, as to write me immediately, which are the best of every kind, for teaching English, Latin, Greek, Geometry, & the first principles of mathematics. I remember, that the catastrophe of the Society came upon you, when you were engaged in simplifying the Latin Grammar & making it more easy to be understood. Did you, afterwards at Liege, finish your plan? or was any other grammar adopted there & with what success? what syntax, what prosody, what Greek grammar, and other elementary books of that language do you recommend? In the schools, established thro this country, I find they have adopted grammars, & syntaxes, both for Greek and Latin, much more concise, than our old ones of Alvarez & Gretzer:[5] whether they are equal in other respects I cannot tell excepting that they are preferable for containing the rules in English which the students understand; instead of being in Latin, which they do not.

Besides these elementary books, I wish you to recommend the best works, you know, for forming and improving the taste of students, & enlarging their minds without endangering their moral principles. I remember to have heard great commendations of the *cours de belles lettres*, by l'Abbé Batteux.[6] I never read it, as it did not lay in my line of studies at that time. You probably have, and, I hear it is translated into English. In a word, set your mind at work; & you will, I doubt not, send us a very good system. Above all, be not afraid of tiring me by descending into too great a detail: you may see by my enquiries, how much information I want, and particularly with respect to the minutiae of the business. At the same time, inform me, where the elementary books, the classics, maps, globes &c may be had on the most reasonable terms.

As to the other business of a Bishop, the negociation must be carried on in another place and our friend Mr Thorpe will, I hope, be eminently useful.

Amongst other difficulties, which we shall have to overcome in the undertaking of the academy, pecuniary resources will be a great one. I expect indeed, that considerable subscriptions, considering the abilities of our people, will be obtained amongst them; but the first expence of erecting proper buildings and securing the salaries for the Masters will be very great. Notwithstanding our debilitated circumstances, by the continuance of an expensive war, yet it so happens, that all services are paid higher here than perhaps in any country. The common Grammar masters in the colleges and academies amongst us have the enormous salaries of £150 to 180, & 200. I hope indeed to get ours at an underrate; but hardly for less than from £60 to £80 p ann:. On this occasion, may I not hope, that the opulent Catholics of Great Britain will contribute to a work so eminently useful, as the proposed one is; and that they will remember, that by giving it their assistance they probably render as essential and permanent service to Religion as ever will be in their power; and entitle themselves to the gratitude of millions yet unborn; besides the superior prospect of a transcendant reward in heaven. These motives and encouragements you, my Dr Sir, will know, how to place in a proper light; and in this, as well as in the matters recommended above I place great dependance on your zeal.

I am much obliged to you for your extract from the Italian criticism on the *Address to the R. C. &c.*[7] I thought, that the authorities quoted in that address were sufficient to vindicate it from so grievous an imputation as that, of having departed from the *fundamental principles* of Theology concerning the necessity of being in the external communion of the Church: and I am well convinced that nothing but my having been Jesuit could have drawn such a remark from one who sets himself up for a Divine: but if more authority be necessary in that point, I would recommend the critick to Fr Knotts famous work, *Charity maintained*[8] (if I remember right, such is the title of his book) or Dr Hawarden's treatise of *Catholics not uncharitable &c,*[9] where he will find the doctrine of the address much more fully stated. On this occasion I cannot help remarking that I have lately seen a catechistical & polemic work of Bp Hayes of Edinburgh, in two vol:, entitled the *faithful Xtian &c;*[10] where he carries to a more alarming &, in my estimation, unjustifiable length, the doctrine of no salvation out of the visible communion of the Church. The Bishop is certainly a good, zealous, & learned prelate; but not always accurate in his principles. You will find proof of this in a work of his, which I lately saw by accident, & wch is entitled, *Roman Catholic fidelity* &c. Look into pages. 56, and 57—of the second edition, printed by Coghlan 1779. I am astonished, how the author could publish, more especially in England, such an opinion as, that *persons excommunicated, while in that state* incur a suspension of *their right & title to the service of others under their authority* &c. Such doctrine coming from a Bishop was enough, had it been adverted to, to renew all the calumnies & misrepresentations, with which we used to be charged: and I am well convinced, the Bishop himself will disavow it, if he attends to & particularly examines it: as it is directly contrary to the doctrine of every Catholic school, in which the subject is ever now treated; tho' heretofore too prevalent in some. You well know, that it is universally agreed, that excommunication does not oblige us to shun that communication with persons excommunicated, which is necessary to fill the duties, we owe them. The wife of an excommunicated husband, the child of an excommunicated parent, must still perform the duties of their respective stations: and the subjects of an excommunicated prince remain bound to their allegiance. The Bp has, I think, some other very exceptionable passages, p. 40—41. Mr Nichs Sewall[11] has sent to his Brother a third volume of Ganganellis life; one of the letters of this volume takes notice of the publication adverted to in my last to you; and indeed treats the servile author with wellmerited severity & con-

tempt. The historian surpasses himself, where he treats of the fatal consequences, which would result from the Popes yielding only to the danger of a
schism. I find, that this is likewise the vindication offerd in behalf of
Ganganelli by the popular Fr O Leary, who pretends to great information on
the subject; but to us, who know much more of the secret history of the
court of Rome at the period alluded to he appears under a very glaring
mistake. I am likewise surprised to find that such a man as he, who really
possesses great strength & liberality of mind, should be an advocate for the
ungenerous measure of printing, in my name, a mutilated, and, in some
respects, a worsted edition of the *address.* It is curious to observe one of his
arguments to prove that the London editor has improved the language by cor-
recting an absurdity in the original, of the *church calling upon herself* &c. See a
note in O Leary; & then look at the Annapolis & London editions. The other
alteration of *may* into *might,* likewise approved by him, weakens the sense, I
intended to convey, by making me say, that Anti Christians had the *power* of
doing, what I allowed, they perhaps *actually* did. It gave me great pleasure to
hear that Miss Arundell, of whose great accomplishments much has reached
even this country, is to be disposed of to so amiable & worthy a Gentleman,
as must be Mr Clifford, if a judgment can be formed on his present conduct &
temper, from what they were thirteen years ago. To be sure our friend
Meynell must be surfeited of a wandering life: Again on the continent with a
boy at his heels; tell him to remember, *qui multum peregrinantur* &c. [those
who are given to much travel . . .] .

Remember me kindly to yr Brs Robert & Frank, & to your good Sister at
Liege, if you ever write to her. I most sincerely regret the deaths of the two
worthy Messrs Wrights.

I am afraid the postage of this long letter will come high; but the
importance of some parts of it required a full detail; & I had not leisure to
condense my matter into a smaller compass. My good Mother, in her 82d year
retains the perfect use of her understanding, her chearfulness, a slow, but
sufficient use of her limbs, & is always pleased to hear of you or of any of her
dear friend, Mrs Plowden's family. She has only to regret a great dimness of
sight: she is constantly disposing herself for that happy country, where, I
doubt not, she will be enlightened by the Sun of justice himself. She returns
her thankful respects. You will be pleased to present mine to Mr Weld &
Lady, & to Messrs Stanley and Clinton, & to all our other Gentlemen within
your reach.

We have had reprinted here Mr Reeves history of the Bible. It is greatly
admired, & by no one more than myself.

It has just occurred to me, that it may not be prudent to make too public
our intention of suing for a Diocesan Bishop.

Mr Ashton is now with me; a most valuable man to our affairs. He is the
general administrator of our temporalities, which improve under his method
and economy. He desires most earnestly to be kindly rememberd to you. Mr

Molyneux was down amongst us last autumn; & is as fat *comme un cochon.*
He laughs as much, as ever, and when he does so, he opens his mouth so wide
as to put me in mind of Gresset's description of one of his Jesuit Superiors, [12]
rit à la toise. He is wonderfully proud, as he desired me to inform you of his
funeral sermon on the venerable Mr Farmer being printed in all the News-
papers of Pennsylvania, and translated *even* into German. He defies you to
write any thing, that shall have so great an honour.

I am sorry to inform you, that since writing the above, an opposition has
broken out of some our good Gentlemen against the establishment of a
school, and an application for a Bishop. They act from this laudable motive:
that both these matters will occasion some alienation of property formerly
possessed by the Society, which they wish to restore undiminished to her, at
her reestablishment; and of this they appear to have no doubt, since they read
your Russian history. They positively assert, that any appropriation to the
school (tho' made by the representative body of the Clergy, as has been the
case) of estates now possessed by us, is a violation of the rights of the
Society; thus supposing, that a right of property can exist in a nonexisting
body: for certainly the Society has no existence here. As this objection has
arisen with a few, I hope they will soon change their mind, and remember,
that a very uncertain prospect of the revival of the Society ought not to
hinder so essential a service to Religion: that the Society was instituted to
save souls: & that souls were not made subservient to the temporal benefits of
the Society. You must know, that when we establish a form of government
for our temporal concerns, we severally promised to each other, that if it
pleased God to restore that Society in this country, we would surrender back
into her hands her former property; but at the same time a power was
expressly reserved, and indeed it is essential, for the chapter or representative
body of the clergy, to alienate for the common good, or for pious uses, any
part of the *real* property. Personal property may be disposed of with greater
ease. The few Gentlemen, who have objected, have considered the promise of
redelivery to the Society: but have not attended to the power expressly
granted to Chapter. I make no doubt but as soon as the matter is properly
explained, we shall all agree again, excepting perhaps a Mr Diderick, one of
those, whom as you once wrote, Mr Howards undistinguishing charity admitted into our province and sent hither. He has set all this in motion; and
the secret cause, tho perhaps unknown to himself, is, that your schoolfellow
Ashton is very strenuous for the measures adopted, as indeed are Molyneux,
Matthews, Pellentz,[13] Digges, Mosely, Sewall, Boarman, Lewis, & your humble
servt. Now Mr. Diderick makes it a point to oppose Mr Ashton; & I do not
believe, that I come in for a great share of his good will. I know not, whether
you are acquainted with this Man's history. I am told he was noted, & even
confined in the Walloon province for his turbulence. As much as we want
recruits, I should not be sorry, he would return to Europe: for I really fear,

he will do mischief sooner or later. This last part of my letter will be, I hope, to yourself. As no vessel is sailing from this to London, I write by a Liverpool ship, which will increase postage: but you must excuse it. You need not slacken in the measures recommended to you in the former part of this letter: for you may be assured, the Gentlemen will soon withdraw their objections. Mr. Strickland will deliver for you to Mr Nihell a copy of our printed proposals for the academy. Be pleased to present my very respectful compliments to Mr & Mrs Weld (excuse my repetition, for this latter part I write one month after the rest of my letter.) Has Mr Clinton no access to that eminently great Lady, Mrs Fitzherbert?[14] I think he was formerly a favourite & had general access into her Mother's family. With Mrs Fitzherbert I had myself the honour of some acquaintance. Is it impossible to obtain from her a donation towards our academy? Mr Chs Sewall now here, presents his compliments. I am, My Dr Sir   Yr most obedt humble st   J. Carroll

ALS   St   The first date appears at the beginning of the letter and the other at the end.

[1] See "General Outlines of a Plan for an Academy," 1787.

[2] St. Francis Xavier, sixteenth century Jesuit missionary to the Orient.

[3] Herman Kemper, S.J., a Westphalian, became Prefect of Studies at Liege Academy in 1794.

[4] Thomas Barrow, S.J. wrote a drama centering on the suppression of the Academy of Bruges and the story of Liege Academy.

[5] Manoel Alvarez, S.J. (d. 1582) wrote a Latin grammar that went through 400 editions; and Jacob Gretzer, S.J. (d. 1625) authored 229 books and 39 manuscripts.

[6] L'Abbe Charles Batteux (d. 1780) was a philosopher of aesthetics.

[7] Abbate Luigi Caccagui, Italian Rector of the Irish College in Rome, who saw only a mutilated British edition of Carroll's *Address* (1784).

[8] Edward Knott, S.J., *Mercy and Truth or Charity Maintained* (1634).

[9] Edward Hawarden, English theologian and professor of philosophy at Douai, author of *Charity and Truth* (Brussels, 1728), *etc.*

[10] George Hay, *The Sincere, Devout and Pious Christian* (1781-86).

[11] Nicholas Sewall, S.J., brother of Charles of Maryland, in 1821 became provincial of the restored Society of Jesus in England.

[12] Jean Baptiste Gresset (d. 1777), once an un-ordained member of the Jesuits, author of *Les Aides aux Jesuites.*

[13] James Pellentz, S.J., a German, came to Maryland in 1758 and died at Conewago in 1800.

[14] Plowden's brother Robert was chaplain to this family.

TO THOMAS SIM LEE   George-town Jan 25–1787–

Dr Sir   I have come to town this moment from Mr Youngs,[1] where Molly received a letter from Mrs Lee a few minutes before I came away. I regret that she did not know of Mr Magruders[2] being in town, that she might answer it. I have the pleasure to inform you that all your acquaintance are well, and exceedingly glad to hear of your family being so. I sent to Mr Frambach the proposals for our future academy to be communicated to you. I have the pleasure to inform you that we have flattering prospects for its encouragement: Col. Deakins³ & Mr Threlkeld⁴ have joind in granting a fine piece of ground for the purpose of building. I propose returning to Baltimore the beginning of next week; & with respectful compliments to Mrs Lee, & love to yr little family, I am   Dr Sir   Yr affte humble st   J Carroll

ALS   GU
¹ Notley Young, husband of Carroll's sister Mary (Molly).
² Alexander H. Magruder, captain of the 3rd Maryland Battalion of the Flying Camp in the Revolutionary War.
³ Col. Leonard M. Deakins, a Revolutionary soldier, who died in 1824.
⁴ John Threlkeld, Alderman of Georgetown (1789), and Mayor (1793).

TO [IGNATIUS MATTHEWS OR JAMES WALTON] Baltimore Feb. 7—1787—

Revd Dr Sir   The printed proposals,¹ accompanying this letter, were to have been sent long ago; but Mr Sewall could not meet with an opportunity. Be pleased to deliver one to each of our Gentlemen, & to those laymen who are appointed to sollicit subscriptions: to whom may be added any others, you judge proper.

From the generous subscriptions already received, I had conceived the most flattering hopes; & persuaded myself of the active cooperation of all our Brethren in a measure which has been long talked of amongst ourselves & strongly recommended from Europe. But Mr Sewall received a letter a few days ago from the G[entlemen]. of yr District reprobating the resolve of Chapter for a school; & another yesterday from Mr. Diderick, expressed in terms and containing insinuations and asser[tions] very injurious to the character of his Brethren in Chapter. The gentlemen thus censured will perhaps think proper to wipe off these aspersions agt their characters, if it be possible that any prejudice can arise against them from such unthinkable and groundless charges. As soon as Mr Sewall shewed me yr district's circular letter, I wrote to Mr. Leonard Neale concerning the unexpected opposition to a school, & shall hope to transcribe those first effusions of my heart, which were drawn from me by the earnest desire of seeing a prosperous issue of an undertaking, pregnant, in my estimation, with the greatest blessings. Thus I write to Mr Neale—"When amongst you I conversed on the subject of a school with every one of you excepting perhaps Mr Roels:² and it appeared to be the general and unanimous opinion that it was an advantageous and necessary measure. Indeed your letter excepts only to the extensiveness of the plan: not how the plan can be more contracted, yet still answer any of the intended purposes, and carry with it the reputation necessary for its success, I am at a loss to comprehend. With respect to Instruction, it is confined to the teaching of English, the learned languages, and the elements of mathematics: and with respect to discipline and morals, can less be proposed, than that a Gentleman of approved virtue & weight of character should reside as Superintendant over the conduct of Masters and Scholars, and to be always attentive to inspire virtue, & lead the youths to the practice of it? What added to my surprise at your opposition was, that it should come from those, who in a manner so exemplary, and with an affection so constant, have devoted themselves to the exercises of and preserved such an attachment to the Institute of S. Ignatius: for amongst all the means prescribed by him for the salvation of souls, every one, who considers the past services of the Jesuits, or the present decay of Religion in Europe, so generally complained of young people; the great scarcity of pastors & priest (as related to Chapter by Mr Pellentz); whoever considers these things must acknowledge, that the Society rendered no service more extensibely useful, than that of the education of youth.

When I first saw your letter, I own that I felt myself greatly disheartened: but consideration has in some measure revived my hopes. Alm: God suffers almost every design to be thwarted, and often times by the best men, from which eminent advantage is afterwards to be derived to his glory; that we may be made more sensible of his divine interposition in its final success. My hopes are perhaps too sanguine: but God is my witness, that in recommending a school at first, and in still persisting in that recommendation, I think I am rendering to Religion the greatest service, that will ever be in my power." So far to Mr Neale.[3]

The great objection to the school is, the appropriation of property, which is considered as an alienation injurious to the Society & a violation of justice. But in my humble opinion, whatever other objections may be against the appropriation complained of, that of violating justice is not well founded. In the first place, can individuals, can bodies of men retain rights of property, after they cease to exist? Do not Divines teach unanimously, that death extinguishes those rights in such manner, that they do not revive, even if the former possessor should be brought to life; 2ly, however, this may be, the property applied, either absolutely or conditionally, to the school, never was the property of the Society; the event, by which it lapsed into the present possessor, happening many years after the Society ceased to exist. Here therefore was no breach of *justice*. 3ly Were the Society existing at this moment, & in possession of the property alluded to; and if it had been granted to her without any particular destination from the Benefactor; my opinion would be, that it could not be applied to a purpose more conducive to the end of the Society.

I do not expect, that these considerations will entirely remove the objections of our good Gentlemen of yr district: but I hope, their private opinions will not hinder them from exerting their endeavours for & recommendations of the School: for surely the resolutions of chapter are binding in matters of this nature. As to other points objected to, I am glad the Gentlemen communicated their difficulties, before any steps were taken, in compliance with your resolves—and if my advice be followed by my colleagues of the committee, I will certainly suspend all proceedings, excepting in the school business, till a general, or nearly general harmony prevails amongst us. For charity is better than all our schemes, however well contrived they may seem to their authors. But I cannot conclude this without observing, that if Mr Diderick sent any letter to St Mary's[4] in the same stile & with the same imputations, as in that to Mr Sewal & Boarman he has not only conceived unfounded prejudices of, but has greatly misrepresented the proceedings in chapter. He says, the majority of chapter had contrived the business before-hand, kept matters secret from the rest, & with cunning & worldly policy carried their measures. You know, how contrary to fact these allegations are; that it was universally known, that the consideration of a school, of Incorpo-ration & I believe Ecclesiastical government was to come before chapter. I wish you would refer to Mr. Ashton's letter of convocation: and I beg you to recollect that the [*illeg.*] to settle a school were so much known, that Mr. Pellentz, not being able to attend personally, wrote his opinion on all those facts.

I am satisfied that we all aim at the same good end; that the perpetuity, the security, the extension of true Religion and piety are the objects of all in your, in this, and the northern district. When a diversity of opinion arises in the prosecution of these essential purposes, I know of no other method of proceeding, than by adhering to the government, we have adopted, & leaving contested matters to the determination of chapter, wherever chapter is competent, as certainly it is in the Institution of a school. And I rely so much on the charity, zeal, & good sense of our Brethren in St Mary's, as to promise myself, that, however they may agree in opinion with, they will at least discountenance the uncharitable suggestions of those, who impute sinister and unjustifiable motives to their fellow-labourer in the same common cause of virtue and Religion.

Be pleased to present my respects to our Brethren. With great affection and regard   I am Revd Dr Sir   Y^r obedt affte st   J Carroll   Fr John Butler dead in England fiant solita suffragia.[5] Be pleased to preserve this letter as I have no time to make a copy.

ALS   AAB   Addressee is given only as member of the Southern District. It is assumed that one of the two representatives given here was the recipient.

  [1] See Jan. 22–Feb. 28, 1787, and Feb., 1787, above.
  [2] Louis Rousse, S.J. (*alias* Roels), arrived in Maryland in 1761 and died in 1794 at St. Thomas Manor, Md.
  [3] Letter not found.
  [4] St Mary's was the second church built in Philadelphia after St. Joseph's.
  [5] "Let the customary offerings be made," i.e., masses, etc.

TO JOHN LUCAS   Baltimore March 9th–1787–

Dr Sir   Yesterday I had the pleasure of receiving yr letter inclosed in one from Mr Matthews. I do most sincerely rejoice, that it has pleased God to move you to a desire of reconciling yourself with him & making reparation for the evils, that probably have arisen from your former conduct.[1] In the process of this business, you shall always find me disposed to do every thing in my power, conducive to yr happiness & real welfare, and at the same time insist on no other conditions, than such as are essentially necessary to evidence the sincerity, & publicity of your repentance. You say, that I can; & therefore request that I would order your admission to the Sacraments. I have power indeed, my Dr Sir, to dispense with great part of the rigor of Ecclesiastical discipline, established in such cases, as yours, and I have already told you that I am inclined to use every indulgence consistent with the essential duties of Xtian pennance, & example due to the public. But, your admission to the Sacraments must rest with him whom you may make the depositary of your conscience. He alone can form a competent judgment of your dispositions, and the necessary removal from the occasions of sin. Your own reflections will remind you of what must be required and what you must do. Nothing is wanting but to rouse up yr own principles by earnest & penitential meditation. For which purpose, it is advisable & most necessary to withdraw yourself for some time from your present connexions & acquaintance, that you may devote your thoughts to the concerns of eternity more uninterruptedly: and if you will accept the proposal, I am going to make I will immediately give directions for its execution. Messrs Lewis, Pellentz, and Mosley are Gentlemen of the most approved virtue, & fatherly tenderness for all who place confidence in them—they live in retired situations, & can make a convenience for receiving you for a month, or six-weeks residence: with one of them whomsoever you may chuse, I propose you should make an eight or ten-days retreat, at least, & remain the time above: mentioned to renew more powerfully yr former practices of prayer & Religion: after which I am willing to abide by their determination concerning the propriety of your continuing in St Mary's County, which if public edification demands, that you do not frequent the house of Mrs Lucas's future residence.

In a matter of such weighty concern in which I assure you that I feel myself much interested, you will excuse me for being plain and explicit; and if any farther explanation be necessary, I will most readily grant it. With sincere and affte regard, I am &c—Respects &c—

ADf   AAB
[1] See Apr. 27, 1780.

TO CHARLES PLOWDEN Rock Creek March 29—1787—

My dear Sir   I wrote you very fully a few weeks ago. I have now only to add, that since the sending of that letter, the Gentlemen, who had shewn some opposition to the business mentioned in it, have seen the reasonableness of the intended establishment; of the application to Rome for a Diocesan; & are as urgent as any to have them carried into execution.

Out of this number I except the Gentlemen particularly mentioned in my last.[1] I have my doubts, whether any thing would remove his opposition, but an assurance, that the whole government of the Academy should reside in him; & that he should be the first Bishop of the American Church.

Therefore, as perfect unanimity now prevails amongst us, I recommend again & again to your consideration the points of my former letter: and I shall immediately write to Mr Thorpe[2] on the subject of both resolves, particularly concerning a Bishop. If possible, I will interest our government in the success of the application; but not till I find it necessary.

Repeating my most respectful compliments to the family of Lullworth, & to our good Brethren, Messrs Stanley and Clinton & others within your reach, I am   Dr Sir,   Yr obedt & affectionate Servt   J Carroll
I request you to apologise for me, if any apology be necessary, for directing to Mr & Mrs Weld a copy of our printed proposals, and an humble request to them to sollicit and receive donations for our intended school. I have taken the same liberty with other distinguished characters in England; and I promise myself good success from their exertions, especially those of the Ladies.

ALS   St
[1] Bernard Diderick, S.J.
[2] See Nov. 7, 1787.

TO BENJAMIN FRANKLIN   George-town April 2. 1787

Hond. & much respected Sir   Mr. Digges[1] will have the honour of presenting you these few lines. His business calls him to Philada. & he is desirous of paying his respects, where they are so justly due from every friend of his country, and indeed to human kind. He is my relation, & has often heared me speak of you in such terms, as have added to his veneration for your character. For I do with truth assure you, that I esteem it as one of the most fortunate and honourable events of my life, that I had an opportunity of forming an acquaintance with you &, I flatter myself with having inspired you with some sentiments of regard, & more than general benevolence towards me.

That you may long continue to be the blessing of your country, is the wish of all its friends: and that you may not only live to enlighten & better mankind, but continue to do so, with freedom from sickness & pain, is the earnest prayer of, Hond. & Dear Sir   Yr. most devoted & obliged [?]   J. Carroll

ALS   American Philosophical Society Library.
[1] Probably Thomas Digges, S.J.

TO CHARLES PLOWDEN   Rock Creek June 4–1787–

My Dear Sir   I returned to this place the last of May, having been absent about two months, travelling thro different Congregations in Maryland & Pennsylvania, & on both sides of the Chesapeak, administering Confirmation. This has been, and will be a very fatiquing service to me, as it regards not only young persons, as elsewhere, but all ages. My successors will not feel this burthen equally with myself: and the ministry of Confirmation would not be much of itself, if, for want of sufficient coadjutors, I were not obliged to bear a great share of the Confessionals wherever I go. At my return hither, I expected the consolation of a letter from you many ships having lately arrived from Europe: but in this, I am disappointed. Since my last to you none of yours have reached me; but I received a packet containing four volumes of Mr Archer's sermons, sent in your name. They found me at Baltimore where I reside great part of my time: but being then on the point of setting out & having left them there, I had only time to read one, & that I read with great pleasure indeed. In my next, I will say more concerning them; and do not doubt, but they will justify your character of your friend, the Author, whom I should be happy to call likewise mine. In my last, I took the liberty of requesting the exertion of your zeal, toward enabling us to begin the establishment of a litterary academy. I hope, that you & my good friends Messrs Stanley & Clinton will not let that object be forgotten.

A disagreeable affair has arisen between Mr Strickland & Jn Ashton, your schoolfellow, our agent general *pro temporalibus*. It regards a contract between Messrs Corbie[1] & Hunter; a debt from Maryland to the former Province; and a claim for a fair proportion of our share in the Province, or as you call it, the office stock. I wish the matter were amicably settled: and Mr Ashton has just informed me, that he has now offerred to Mr. Strickland to leave it to Referees, giving bonds mutually to abide by their determination: the referees to be chosen out of the former body. I long to hear more concerning Russia. I fear that the Empresses mind has been so taken up with her journey to Cherson, that she has attended to nothing else.

A few days ago, I received a very inquisitive letter from my old acquaintance Coghlan the Bookseller.[2] Amongst other enquiries, he asks, if the sentiments attributed to me in *Berington versus Hawkins,* as to the introduction of the vulgar tongue are really mine: then he goes on telling me, that the opinion, for which I am cited, is now openly espoused by many priests in London, as well as the expediency of abolishing the celibacy of the Clergy &c. Is it really true, that any are so bold, as to avow this latter sentiment; or even assert, that any single Bishop may alter the language of the liturgy, without the approbation of the Holy See, & a general concurrence of at least other national Bishops? I should be indeed sorry, if the few words of my letter to Berington should be tortured to such a meaning. Coghlan likewise informs me, that this Gentleman (Berington) had just published the history of Abelard and Eloisa: with what view or to whose edification I cannot conceive. From the specimens of his writings, which I have seen, I doubt not, he has treated with delicacy, a very indelicate subject. If you have a mind to know how indelicate, look into Natalis Alexander's Ecclesiastical history,[3] where are I remember, extracts from her original letters; & from wch I infer that she was not only an unfortunate, but most impudent woman in the former part of her life. In her latter years, I hope she made reparation. Assure of my humble respects Mr Weld & Lady, Messrs Stanley, Clinton & our other Gentlemen. My good Mother presents hers to yourself. Good Mr Bennet Neale finished a life of innocence with a holy death March 27th aged abt 78. With great sincerity I am, Dr Sir   Yrs afftely   J.C.

ALS   St
    [1] Henry Corbie, S.J., was Provincial of the English Jesuits, 1756-62.
    [2] P. J. Coghlan later published *An Address of Roman Catholic Gentlemen to George Washington* (1790) in England with a Preface by Carroll.
    [3] Natalis Alexander (d. 1724), French historian, Theologian and controversialist.

TO [P. J. COGHLAN]   Maryland June 13–1787–

Sir   I have received your favr of Feb. 15, inclosing two catalogues of books, to the amount of £43.6.7½, the other of £3.14.6– The latter I shall be glad to receive; tho I have no account of its being arrived. The former is too considerable for the present state of my finances: and if you have sent it, you misunderstood my former letter, which was only to know yr lowest price for the books therein mentioned, to direct my judgment in sending for such as I could pay for. I expect to see Capn James Fenwick in a few days, & deliver him your letter. He now commands a ship wch is to sail in a few weeks for Bordeaux. The letter to Mr Lloyd shall be carefully sent to Philada[;] you are misinformed with respect to his being Secretary to Congress: I doubt even, whether he is one of the Clerks in the Secretary's office: my Br, who was several years member of Congress, knows him not.

    Be pleased to return my respectful compliments to his Lordship, Bp Talbot, & to Mr Short: to Mr Pilling[1] likewise. I am sorry, Mr Berington's work in reply to Hawkins did not please. The few copies sent hither have met with a very different reception. If there be in it, as there are, some few exceptionable passages, yet it appeared to us to have great general merit, & to be excellently calculated &c. to humble & confound the licentious declaimers against the doctrine of the Church. If Mr Ber. should publish a 2d edition I doubt not, but he will rectify the inaccuracies of the 1st You inform that a passage in his work relating to me has raised of curiosity respecting my sentiments on the subject mentioned by him. My friends are well acquainted with them. If the Holy See & first Pastors of the Church should find cause to allow either generally, or in such a country as this, where so many poor people & Negroes cannot assist their attention by reading, liberty to have the divine office in a language generally understood, I should feel a satisfaction in it: but till they alter that point of discipline, I should think any single Bishop or Ecclesiastical Superior to blame for making such an innovation.

I am sorry to hear from you that an alteration is sought for by some English Clergymen in other points of discipline, which have been so long deemed of the most consequence to honr, piety & disinterested zeal of the priesthood. Their number, I trust, is inconsiderable, & their personal weight still more so. I will procure and send you by this occasion Mr Wharton's reply, which has been & will remain unnoticed by me; and indeed I may add, by the public; few have read it: not on account of their deeming it unworthy of notice; for there is in it much art & some merit & ingenuity, or rather too much art; but the spirit of learning & curiosity excited by the controversy was nearly over, when his answer came forth. I do not hear, that he intends to animadvert on Mr Pilling: some of his friends give out that he is much exasperated at Fr o Leary's[2] treatment of him & means to answer, but the latter part I do not believe it. I am Sir   Yr obedt Servt   J. Carroll

ADfS   AAB   The contents of the letter suggests the addressee assigned, since he was the London book publisher and dealer best known to Carroll.
[1] William Pilling, O.S.F., author of a *Caveat to the Catholics of Worcester against the insinuting Letter of Dr. Wharton* (London, 1785).
[2] Arthur O'Leary in 1786 published a review of the Carroll-Wharton controversy, in which he was critical of both men.

TO LEONARDO ANTONELLI   From Maryland, 2 July 1787

A few months ago, most eminent Cardinal, I wrote to you that at an early date two young men were to be sent to Rome, to be taught and trained in the Urban College, and then return to offer spiritual assistance here. They have already set sail for Bordeaux; they carry the letter of recommendation I was asked to write to His Excellency, the Papal Nuncio to the Most Christian King. You indicated that the Congregation would underwrite the expense of their passage, but I saw to it that the Congregation be spared all expense till the youths reached Bordeaux. The parents of both are excellent Catholics. The one, Rudolph [Ralph] Smith, fourteen years of age, comes from Maryland; the other Felix Dougherty from Pennsylvania is thirteen years old. Each of them, but especially the latter, is said to be talented and docile in temperament. May I suggest that while they are trained in all the forms of learning under college discipline they also be thoroughly schooled in their vernacular and cultivate acquaintance with the approved authors. In this way they will be much better prepared for work in the land of their birth. For, as the heretics cultivate elegant diction and delivery, the pastors of souls must make an effort that men be drawn to truth and piety through the pleasure of hearing them.

Words scarcely reveal the extent of our lack of laborers. Since my last letter death has claimed two,[1] one of them afflicted with the ills of age and almost unable to work, the other a man outstanding and, in the judgment alike of heretics and the orthodox, distinguished for virtue. Thus some congregations have no priest at all or are only occasionally visited by a priest, with consequent danger of the people gradually slipping into vicious habits or into the errors of the sectaries. In so far as possible I strive to combat this bad situation through a means that is effective and enduring, namely, by beginning a school, as you have already learned from me. Our resources are so limited that of themselves they are inadequate for such an undertaking. Everywhere we appeal to the charity of the faithful, and also to your benevolence and that of the Congregation; and I should be so bold as to ask the Holy Father to contribute if something should remain from other pious works.

From Germany I learned from some theology students that they wish to devote themselves to the saving of souls in these United States where there are many Germans. Working among these people are priests, both advanced in years, and one broken in health and strength.

Such is their desire to join the clergy in America and to secure dimissorial letters[1] so that without observing the intervals between orders they may be ordained as soon as possible and go to the assistance of souls. In view of the pressing need I should do this if it were clear that my authority applied. Because of the extreme need of the faithful, in a doubtful case I should not hesitate to give dimissorial letters for ordination and dispensation from observing the ordinary intervals between orders if my jurisdiction were beyond doubt. As a matter of fact I can only offer the assurance of a decent living to the young men who aspire to the priesthood, and urge that the Bishop in whose diocese they come, after consideration of the circumstances, advance them without delay to holy orders when he is fully assured of their learning and morals.[2] If in this [I] am at fault the Congregation will please ascribe it to my sollicitude for providing good pastors and not to presumption or arrogance.

Meanwhile we have suffered great loss, for although an abundant harvest of souls is at hand, nothing seems to prevent a great increase in our number except the dearth of priests of good life and sound doctrine. In New York all goes well. A religion of the Capuchin order is about to leave for the extreme western part of Virginia,[3] a region known as Kentucky, to which many Catholic familes have migrated. A certain priest has just come to Charleston in South Carolina,[4] but since he has no credentials from the archbishop of Dublin, His Ordinary, and I know nothing whatever about his life and conduct, till now I have put off the granting of faculties, even though the many Catholics there are destitute of spiritual help. It does not seem advisable ever to depart from the rule in this matter, mainly because so many are drawn here solely by a desire of a more abundant living. . . .

ADf   AAB

[1] John Ritter and Luke Geissler.

[2] An intervening sentence occurs that is obscure and might read: "After getting the necessary permissions, they shall place themselves under my jurisdiction."

[3] Charles M. Whelan.

[4] Probably John Ryan, O.P. See Dec. 16, 1797. There would be subsequent problems with Bishop Troy of Dublin, from whose jurisdiction Ryan and others came to America.

to Card Antonelli   Ex Marilandia die 2ª Julii 1787   Ante paucos menses, Eme Card., literas ad te direxi; ex quibus intellexisti duos Juvenes propediem Romam expediendos ut in Urbano Collegio optima doctrina moribusq exculti aliquando in patriam suppetias spirituales allaturi poterint reverti Navigationem jam ingrediuntur Burdigalam versus, litteris meis muniti, quibus illos curae committo Excellentissimi Nuncii Apostolici apud Regem Xtianissimum, prout in mandatis accepi. Significasti, Eme Card., provisum iri a Sacra Congne de navigaois sumptibus. Curavi, tamen ut omni Congnis sumptui pareatur donec Juvenes Burdigalam pervenerint. Ambo ex parentibus nati sunt apprime Catholicis. Alter Rodulphus Smith ex Marilandia, 14 anno habet, alter Felix Dogherty ex Pennsylvania habet annos tredecim. Uterque sed maxime posterior dicitur praeclarae indolis & ingenio docili. Liceat mihi suggere, Eme Card., ut dum ad omnem aliam doctrinam pro optima Collegii disciplina informantur in lingua etiam vernacula sedulo exerceantur ac in probatis illius idiomatis Scriptoribus multum versentur. Ita multo melius comparati ad labores in patriam revertentur. Cum haeretici eleganter dicendi et pronunciandi gloriolam aucupentur, allaborandum est animarum pastoribus ut eurium etiam oblectamento hoc: ad veritatem et pietatis sensum alliciantur.

Dici vix potest, quanta operariorum inopia laboremus. Post ultimas litteras, duos nobis mors eripuit; unum quidem aetate ingravescente, paene laboribus imparem; alterum vero virum insignem ac haereticis prope aequaliter ac Orthodoxis, pro virtute spectabilem. Hinc fit, ut aliquae Congregationes Pastoribus vel omnino careant vel saltem rarissime ab iis visitentur, non sine ingenti periculo in vitia et Sectariorum errores sensim delabendi.

Huic malo, quantum fieri potest, remedio aliquo stabili et efficaci occurrere studeo, scholae nempe institutione pro Catholica juventute educanda uti jam ex me didicisti, Eme Cardlis. Caeterum res nostra adeo sunt tenues ut cum per se tanti operis institutioni non sufficiant Fidelium charaem undique sollicitemus; tuamq adeo totiusque Sacrae Congnis benevolentiam et apud B.P.N. instantiam implorare ausim, ut aliquid suppeditare dignetur si de caeteris pietatis operibus quidquam reliquum fuerit.

Ex Germania relatum ad me est de quibusdam Theologiae Auditoribus qui cupiunt se devovere animarum saluti in his foederatae Americae provinciis quas quidem multi incolunt Germani. Inter quos tamen supersunt, sacerdotes et uterque provectae aetatis, et alter viribus & valetudine confectus.

Ita ascribi desiderant clero Americano et litteris dimissoriis communiri ut non servat interstitionum more quam primum ordines sacros suscipere et ad subsidium animarum profisci queant. Ego quidem lubens id facerem, attenta necessitate, si de mea ad hoc auctoritate constaret. In re dubia nec dubitarem spectata fidelium summa necessitate, et literas dimissorias pro ordinatione, et ab interstitiis servandis dispensatione concedere si de mea ad hoc jurisdictione constaret. In re dubia id tantum praestare potero de congrua sustentatione certos reddere juvenes qui ad presbyteratum aspirant, et ipsum regare in cujus veniunt diocesis, ut ipse, attentis rerum circumstantiis, eos sine mora ad sacros ordines promovere ubi de doctrina et moribus abunde constiterit. [ordiariorum obtenta licentia, meae jurisdictioni ses subjecerunt?] Si quid in hac re peccatum [mihi?] fuerit, illud Sacra Congregatio non vanae praesumptioni aut arrongantiae sed sollicitudini pro providendis pastoribus ascribi dignabitur.

Interim dum tanta nobis ex pastorum defectu ingruit calamitas, magna scilicet messis offert, nec videtur aliquid deesse ad magnum religionis incrementum praeter sacerdotum probae vitae et doctrina inopiam, et media illis victum providendi. Novi Eboracensi res prospere procedunt. In procinctu est vir religiosus ex ordine Capuccinorum ad profectionem in extremam oram Virginiae, occientem versus, ad plagam quae dicitur Kentucky, qua jam multae familiae Catholicorum migraverunt. Sacerdos quidam ad Caropopolim, Carolinae meridionalis, modo prevenit sed cum nullas a proprio Archiepiscopo Dubliensi praebet litteras, nec mihi ullo modo de vita et moribus constet, facultatum concessionem hucusque distuli, nec unquam mihi videtur ab hac regula discedendum, praecipue cum tot eo usque avehuntur qui uberius vivendi [*illeg.*] unice quaerunt. . . .

TO JEROME CHAMION DE CIRCE[1]   Mariland the 19 of July, 1787

My Lord   The Congregation of the Propaganda at Rome wishing to obtain some priests of the sanctuary in the United States, has charged me with the care of sending two young Americans to be students at the Urban College in Rome. The Nuncio of His Holiness close to S.M.T.C., in writing me on the subject, speaks thus, "You will see to it—in case of necessity."

In conformity with these orders, I have the honor to write you, My Lord, and to send you unsealed my letter for Mgr. the Nuncio at Paris, who should give his orders, and furnish my young compatriots the means of going on to Rome. I confide in the charity of Your Grace for the prompt sending of my letter to Mgr the Nuncio, and for the assistance which will be necessary until Your Grace shall have received the answer of His Excellency, who should reimburse all expenses.

With the most respectful devotion, I have the honor to be   My Lord   Your Grace's   Most humble and very obedient serv.

ADf   AAB
[1] He was Archbishop of Bordeaux from 1781-1801, and then of Aix until his death in 1810.

Mariland ce 19 Juillet, 1787   Mgr   La Congregation de la Propagande à Rome desirant de procurer des ministres du Sanctuaire aux Etats Unis de l'Amerique, m'a chargée du soin d'envoyer deux jeunes Americains pour étre elevés au College Urbain à Rome. Le Nonce de SS. auprés de S.M.T.C., en m'ecrivant à çe sujet, J'enonce ainsi "Vous verrez de—au cas de besoin".

En consequence de ces ordres, j'ai l'honneur de vous ecrire, Monsgr, & de vous envoyer ouverte ma lettre pour Mgr le Nonce à Paris, qui doit donner ses ordres, & fournir aux moyens pour faire passer à Rome mes jeunes Compatriotes. Je me remets à la charité de V. G. pour le prompt envoi de ma lettre à Mgr le Nonce, & pour les secours qui seront necessaires jusq' à ce que V. G. aura reçu la reponse se Son Exc., qui doit rembourser tous les frais.

Avec le devouement le plus respectueux, j'ai l'honneur d'etre   Mgr   De V. G.   Le trés humble et tres obeissant serv.

TO THE EDITOR OF THE COLUMBIAN MAGAZINE   New Jersey,
Sept. 1, 1787

SIR,   One of your correspondents sends you a fabricated history of a Cardinal Turlone, who never existed, and which you inserted in a former Magazine: this history he enriched with inflammatory comments; but he had neither the justice nor candour enough to undeceive your readers by informing them that the whole was a malicious fable.

A very small part of your Monthly Miscellany is devoted to the article of *news,* for this you are commendable: we can readily refer to other collections for that commodity. But when you condescend to relate events of modern times, you might, once in a month, make selection of a few articles of undoubted credit and general importance, and not deal out the malicious and mischief-making forgeries of persecuting Europeans. Thanks to the genuine spirit of christianity! the United States have banished intolerance from their systems of government, and many of them have done the justice to every denomination of christians, which ought to be done to them in all, of placing them on the same footing of citizenship, and conferring an equal right of participation in national privileges. Freedom and indpendence, acquired by the united efforts, and cemented with the mingled blood of protestant and catholic fellow-citizens, should be equally enjoyed by all. The Jersey state was the first, which, in forming her new constitution, gave the unjust example of reserving to protestants alone the prerogatives of government and legislation.[1] At that very time the American army swarmed with Roman-catholic soldiers; and the world would have held them justified, had they withdrawn themselves from the defence of a state which treated them with so much cruelty and injustice, and which they then covered from the depredations of the British army. But their patriotism was too disinterested to hearken to the first impulse of even just resentment. They could not believe, that the state, which was foremost to injure them, would continue, or that any others would imitate, her partial and iniquitous policy. It seems they were not acquainted with the bitter spirit which dictated the unjustifiable exclusion: they trusted to the wise and generous sentiments which pervaded every corner of the American continent. For who, that remembers our cordial unanimity in rejecting the claims of foreign oppression, could imagine that any of us would impose on fellow-soldiers and citizens, the degrading mark of distrust, or the galling yoke of inferiority? Such, however, was the treatment they found, not because they were less warm or less profuse of their blood in the defence of our common rights, but because the authors of injustice, who could resent and oppose British counsels, levelled against their own rights of legislation, wanted the greater fortitude of emancipating their minds from a slavish subjection to the prejudices imbibed during a narrowed British education.

The malicious fable of Cardinal Turloni's assassination would not have extorted these reflections, had I not seen in your magazine for June or July, certain *Considerations on Religion,* by A.Z. So sacred a subject requires a heart more purified by charity and candour, and an understanding better versed in theology and history. It may help to feed the prejudices of ignorance, and it may confirm the tales of many a nursery and many a pulpit, to be told, that Roman Catholics *reverence as Deities, Mary, Peter, Paul, &c.;* that these are the substitutes of the Heathenish *Jupiter and Juno,* and are often times addressed in terms not expressive *of bare intercession,* but of an inward sense of their divinity. For *ora pro nobis* [pray for us], is frequently repeated: and this supplication, according to the considerer, can be offered only to God. So undoubtedly St. Paul used it, when he said to the Thessalonians 1c.5.–25. *Brethren pray for us;* and again to the Hebrews, c. 13–18. pray for us. What a multitude of Gods did this vessel of election worship.

Your correspondent knows our tenets better, than we ourselves. When we address the Virgin Mary and other holy powers, we hope to obtain more readily, through their greater interest and favour in Heaven, the graces needful to our salvation; but he discovers in our hearts all the turpitude of idolatry. He is shocked at the *absurdity of the interposition of a mortal between God and man.* It happens well for us that the interposition of departed saints, is exempt from this absurdity; for they are no longer mortal. St. Paul was not quite so happy, when he interposed the prayers of christians still liable to death, between the divinity and himself.

What could conduce this unprovoked aggressor of the Roman Catholics to say, after some inflammatory controvertist, that they request the Virgin Mary to command her son; *impera filio*²? Did he ever read such a prayer in any of their public authorised missals, breviaries or liturgical books; Did he ever hear it used in their churches? Do not all their publications at the throne of mercy through the intercession of the Virgin Mary, evidently denote her immense inferiority to, and entire dependance on the divinity? And was it not clear from all this that if any rapturous devotee in his private exercises of piety ever used those obnoxious words, he meant only that he, who deigned to be *Subject to his parents* at Nazareth (Luke 2.51) will in heaven grant his mother's requests with a promptitude that may almost seem the effect of obedience? Mistake me not: I intend not to justify such a prayer, which is indirect, and in a literal sense, even impious. But have no children of the reformation poured forth prayers, in the paroxysms of fanaticism, infinitely more shocking and blasphemous? Must we therefore say, that their extravagances are imputable to protestantism? *With what measure you mete, it shall be measured out to you again,* Matt. 7.

Excuse me, Sir, I find, that I am insensibly engaging in controversy, on a subject for which your Miscellany is not calculated; my design was only to recommend fairness, truth and equity. Correspondents uniting these qualities with real knowledge, will render your undertaking a benefit to the public and acceptable to your humble servant, A READER. New Jersey, Sept. 1, 1787.

L *The Columbia Magazine or Monthly Miscellany* ... Vol. 1. (Philadelphia: Printed for T. Seddon, W. Spotswood, C. Cist, & J. Trenchard), For December, 1787. Pp. 881-82. For authorship see to Carey, Jan. 30, 1789, and Guilday, pp. 112-14. Carroll's original MS was longer, as he told Carey. The given origin of the letter as New Jersey may have served assurance of anonymity; or Carroll may have departed for New York earlier than it first appears, passing through New Jersey at this time.

¹ New Hampshire, Connecticut, North and South Carolina, and Georgia also had established forms of Protestantism.

² Latin phrase for the previous three words.

TO JAMES FRAMBACH   —Balt[imore]. Sepr. 20—1787

Revd. Sir.   Having been informed, that your state of health continues such, as to disqualify you for the laborious services dependent on the station of Frederic-Town, I have appointed Mr. Cerfoumont to succeed you, *at least* till a recovery of your strength enables you to resume your former labours. In the mean time, an offer is made to you of retirement to any of our houses in Maryland which you shall chuse, and in which there is room for your comfortable accommodations. There you shall be treated with the attention and entitled to the provision established by our regulations. I expect that Mr. Cerfoumont¹ will soon return to Frederic, and take charge of every thing temporal and spiritual, at that place— Commendo me²— I am &c

ADf   AAB

¹ Stanislaus Cerfoumont sat at the Synod of 1791. He was not available for the above appointment, so that the letter may not have been sent.

² "I commend myself [to you in your Holy Sacrifices....]"

SERMON SUSPENDING ANDREW NUGENT   [Oct. 1787]

Dr. Christians, and most beloved Brethren in Jesus Christ; Before we proceed
any farther in the service of this day,[1] I esteem it necessary, for causes well
known to you all, to address you with all the fervor of charity, with all the
concern for your eternal happiness, & all the interest for the honour of our
holy Religion, which my duty and superintendence over the welfare of this
Congregaon require from me: If the ministers of Christ must always feel a
sollicitude for the interests of their heavenly Master, how greatly must this
sollicitude increase, when his holy Religion is in danger of being dishonoured
by dissensions, by indocility, or the mischievous operation of any other
passion; and especially if this should happen on its first introduction into a
country, where before it was only seen thro the false colouring of prejudice
and misrepresentation. It is then, Dr Xtian Brethren, under the impression,
which these considerations have made on me, that I appear before you this
day; & that I beseech you to recall to your remembrance the principles of
your holy faith, & the maxims of church government, by an adhesian to
which, nations have been brought out of the darkness of paganism into the
light of the Gospel; and your forefathers in particular preserved in their own
country & to the present day, the purity of the faith delivered down to them
from the first Apostles of Christianity; they preserved it under every temporal
discouragement, and against the influence of every worldly interest. And how
did they obtain this great effect? Was it by intruding themselves into the
sanctuary? Did they, did you before you crossed over into this country,
assume to yourselves the rights of your first Pastors? did you name those
Clergymen, who were charged with the immediate care of your souls? did you
invest them with their authority? did you confer on them those powers,
without which their ministry must be of no avail; No, Dr Xtians, neither you
Forefathers, nor you assumed to yourselves those prerogatives: you never
plunged that fatal dagger into the vitals of true Religion. Too dearly was it
impressed on your minds, that the ministry of the word & the administration
of the Sacraments cannot be given in charge, but by his divine authority,
whose doctrine is to be preached, & who has enriched his Sacraments with
the treasures of grace & salvation. You cannot but remember, that when Jesus
was on the point of ascending up into heaven, and to leave his church under
the visible government of his Apostles, and their Successors, he communicated to them that spiritual & sublime jurisdiction, which the world cannot
give, and which extends itself not over the bodies, but over the souls of men.
A jurisdiction [is this] which cannot be derived, but from God; which cannot
be acquired merely under the sanction or by the sole authority of any human
laws. To fill our minds with a due sense of the sublimity of this sacred
jurisdiction Christ, before he bequeathed it, as his last legacy to his Apostles,
addressed to them these awful and solemn words recorded by St Matthew

c.28, and *spoke to them saying all power is given to me in heaven and in Earth.* Having thus brought to their recollection the heavenly ministry, which he himself had dispensed on Earth; that he had received it not from Man but from his Fr, who is in heaven; and that power was given to him to transmit it to others for the salvation of the world; *as my Fr sent me, so do I send you;* John 22. he thus continued his discourse: *Go ye therefore and teach all nations, baptising them in the name of the Fr, and of the Son, and of the Holy Ghost, teaching them to observe all things, whatsoever I have commanded you; and behold I am with you all days, even to the consummation of the world.* The Apostles having received this commission from their heavenly Master, proceeded in the work of the ministry, they dispensed the Sacraments, they announced the good tidings of Salvation, they appointed Pastors to the Congregations, which were gathered together. To those pastors so appointed others succeeded, and so down to the present day, deriving their power of exercising the sacred functions of Religion not from men, but from the same sacred source as the Apostles themselves. That the Catholic church possesses a spiritual jurisdiction, so transmitted thro every age, is her distinguishing and glorious prerogative: and if it were possible for her to lose this prerogative, she would cease to hold any spiritual authority. Sometimes she has had cause to deplore the indocility of some of her Children who have attributed powers to themselves, which God alone could bestow: and whenever these undutiful children have obstinately resisted the charitable admonitions of their first pastors, & have not soon returned to an acknowledgment of spiritual subordination they rapidly advanced in the tract of disobedience & compleated the course of their iniquity by bidding defiance to the Church herself. I shall not here mention any examples to establish the truth of what I have said: they are known to you—and you had them undoubtedly in your mind, when on a very late occasion you publicly acknowledged the just right & power of him who now speaks to you, to constitue & appoint Clergymen to the care of souls, within the extent of his jurisdiction, & namely in this very Church. In making this acknowledgement, you did not consider my imperfections, or personal unworthiness; but you considered the source, from which my authority is derived; and you knew, that it could be traced up to Christ himself, the author and fountain head of all spiritual jurisdiction. With this firm persuasion on your minds, you admitted the lawfulness of my delegation, and my right to appoint the Clergyman to have charge of your souls. You admitted this in a manner the most explicit, & with a zeal, for which my thanks are not worthy of being offerred you, since you receive those of Religion herself.

In the exercise therefore of a power so well established, both by our present discipline, (which is protected by the laws of this state) and by your own admission and acknowledgement, I proceed to give you public notice, that having heretofore granted to the Revd Mr Andrew Nugent, during my pleasure powers for preaching, and administering the Sacraments of baptism, pennance, Eucharist to sick persons, extreme unction & matrimony, I hereby recall those powers: and my duty demanding of me at the same time to provide a pastor for the care of your souls, I have invested with all necessary & requisite powers for that purpose the Revd. Mr. William O Brien,[2] of whose zeal, virtue and talents for the work of the ministry I have received the most ample testimony and assurances & whom I recommend to your benevolence & regard.

This is not the time for enlarging on the motives, which brought me to my present determination: but I intreat you to believe, that it was formed without passion, or unfavourable prejudices: & that if I had not conceived it my duty to act in the manner, I have done, my authority should never have been exerted to the purposes, of which you were just now informed.

And now Dr Xtians, allow me to entreat you to join with united hearts in presenting at the throne of grace and sacred victim, who is going to be offerred on this altar; and earnestly to beseech Alm: God, the bestower of every good gift, to behold with complacency the living body and blood of his blessed Son, held up & presented by us all to him, as a propitiation for our crimes; and that it may draw down on this Congregation every heavenly blessing, & above all perfect charity, well grounded hope, & unshaken & active faith: may these virtues rest with you for ever & bring you to eternal life.   Mr Molyneux[3] &c.

ADf   MPA
    [1] At St. Peter's Church in New York city. See Jan. 17 and July 18, 1786.
    [2] After sixteen years of ministry in the Diocese of Dublin, he came to America, serving in Philadelphia and New Jersey. He and his brother were both Dominicans, Matthew acting as William's assistant in New York in 1801.
    [3] Possibly Carroll's vicar in the area, following the recent death of Farmer, with whom Molyneux ministered at St. Mary's Church, Philadelphia.

TO JAMES FRAMBACH   Baltimore Oct. 1,–1787

Revd Sir: Having been often informed, that your state of health contin- ues such as to disqualify you for the laborious services dependent on the station of Frederic-town I have appointed Mr Smyth,[1] a G. newly arrived, to succeed you *at least* till a recovery of your strength enables you to resume your former labours. In the mean time, an offer is made to you of a retirement to any of our houses in Maryland, which you shall chuse, & in which there is room for your comfortable accommodation.   Yr most obedt & humble st   J. Carroll
Mr Smyth will either be the bearer of this or soon follow it. I hope you will give him every information respecting the services, he must perform, & the Congns he must visit, as well as put him in possession of the temporalities

annexed to your station. I shall set out for N. Y. to morrow. you will probably have made your choice at my return. Should you chuse to continue at Frederic with Mr Sm, perhaps matters may be so settled, that you may please yourself, & take such share of labour, as may suit your health. I know that Mr Smyth wishes for a companion, and I think, that you will find him a sensible one.   J.C.

ADfS   AAB   "Sp. 20" is crossed out in the dating of the letter.
[1] Patrick Smith, Dunboyne, Ireland, author of the attack on Carroll, *The Present State of the Catholic Missions* (Dublin, 1788). See Smyth to Carroll, Apr. 8, 1788, which has intimations of his grievances as he prepares to leave for Ireland. The reference to him as "a G." is an abbreviation for "Gael."

TO CHARLES PLOWDEN   New York Novr 7–1787–

Dear Sir   The departure of the packet to morrow morning gives me the opportunity of acknowledging your favour of July brought by the two Germans.[1] Your letter was sent hither two days ago, where I have been for four weeks, to inquire into the foundation of complaints lodged against Mr Nugent, the Capucin, Incumbent of this place. Unfortunately I find myself obliged to remove him & have substituted in his place a Mr o Brien, Dominican well recommended by Archbishop Troy of Dublin,[2] But I still expect violent opposition. Soon do I begin to experience the sad effects of taking up with the volunteer clergymen Emigrants to America. We have at this time three of the same nation in the U. States, who injure the reputation of the priestly order by unhappy excesses. I send a short state of this matter to Mr Thorpe to be communicated, where need may be. I shall write to you very soon, & fully. I can add no more at present, than respects & Compliments. Two German Capucins are come to Philada.[3] With the assistance of Messrs Cresler[4] & Edenshink, we may do tolerably for numbers. Adieu. Yrs sincerely   J. Carroll

ALS   St
[1] Probably Capuchins mentioned in n. 3 below.
[2] Archbishop John T. Troy of Dublin, a Dominican, who became bishop in 1776.
[3] John and Peter Heilbron Dominicans came to Philadelphia from Ireland the previous month. John was elected Pastor of Holy Trinity in 1789, precipitating a ten year period of controversy and schism.
[4] Laurence Graessl.

TO JOHN THORPE   New York 7 Novbre., 1787

A certain Father Nugent, an Irish Capuchin, not an ignorant but rather a sufficiently talented man, arrived here from Cork two years ago, bringing along good recommendations from Father O'Leary (another Irish Capuchin) and producing for inspection faculties previously granted him in various dioceses of France and, I think, of Ireland. His predecessor, Whelan by name, a friar of the same order and the first to settle in New York, a respectable man but not a learned one, left his post in disgust a little after Nugent's arrival, and now I have learned that he was compelled to do so to a great extent by Nugent's schemings. As soon as the increase of my faculties made it possible for me, I granted Nugent approbation for this place at my good pleasure; having received information only from him, I deluded myself and wrote to the Sacred Congregation of the Propagation of the Faith that the affairs of this place were prospering. On the last day of August I received a dispatch from the overseers of Catholicism in this place with serious accusations of immorality against Nugent; since he protested against them, it was necessary, in order to discover the truth, to subject both sides to an examination. For this purpose I came here, and before starting the trial, both sides signed an agreement obliging themselves to accept and abide by my decision. I deemed that necessary in order to prevent any recourse that they might have to secular courts and to give force and strength to a decision that neither one could receive from the civil power. After a troublesome and long examination of countless witnesses, I withdrew the approbation and spiritual faculties granted to Nugent and invested with them a certain William O'Brien of the Order of St. Dominic, who arrived here from Dublin recently, a man gifted with learning and manners that indicate a good reasoning power, and well recommended. But here the disturbances began. In two or three letters Nugent let me know that as long as he lived, Mr. William O'Brien would never be able to officiate in St. Peter's Church (that is, in the church of New York) and that the Gazette of that day would carry the first of a series of letters that he intended to address to me in this way. I learned furthermore from him and his party (for he has on his side a large number of the basest persons) that a contrary declaration and protest would be made against my decision in favor of Mr. William O'Brien; and it was reported to me several times that we would not be spared open violence and bloodshed. I leave it to you to consider how harmful to the religion this regrettable affair must turn out, especially in a city in which [Catholicism] was established barely three years ago and in which Congress, and consequently many persons from each of the States, reside. In the course of the examination one testimony among others came to light which ought to have rendered more cautious those who recommended Nugent for the service of the mission in America, that is, that he had been suspended for incontinence and expelled from his diocese by the late Archbishop Carpenter of Dublin;[1] from there he betook himself to Cork and, taking advantage of the excessive credulity of the unfortunate apostate Lord Dunboyne, who was then bishop of that city, he obtained the faculties of the ministry. Observe that when I approved him, I did it by granting him faculties with the clause "donec revocentur [until they are recalled]," and now I have withdrawn them. And yet he is so much in the dark as to the nature of this approbation, or to be more exact, he so deceives himself and his friends in this respect, that they presented me with a sheet notifying me of their appeal to the Holy See.

I am troubling you with this long account (because it is not possible for me to write to the Sacred Congregation by the mail which is going by ship tomorrow morning) to ask you to communicate the first news of this business to the same Sacred Congregation.

C   PF   A heading designates this an extract. There would not seem to be much more than this in the original. See to Plowden. Nov. 7, 1787.
[1] John Carpenter was archbishop from 1770-1786.

Estratto di Lettera del Rev.do Sig.re Carroll Vico. Aposto negli Stati Uniti dell'America Settentrionale in data di Nuova York 7 Novbre, 1787 al Ab. Giovanni Thorpe dimorante in Roma.

Un certo P. Nugent Cappuccino Irlandese, non ignorante e di talento sufficiente, giunse qui da Cork, due anni sono, portando seco buone raccommandazioni da P. O'Leary (altro Cappuccino Irlandese) ed esibendo facoltà anteriomente concessegli in varie Diocesi di Francia, e mi par d'Irlanda. Il suo predecessore, per nome Whelan Fr. dello stesso Ordine, ed il primo che si stabilisce a New York, uomo dabbene, ma illetterato, poco dopo l'arrivo di Nugent lasciò disgustato il suo luogo, ed ho adesso rilevato, astrettovi in gran parte dalli costui raggiri. Subito che l'accrescimento delle mie facoltà me lo permise, concedetti a Nugent un'approvazione a mio piacimento per questo luogo; ne ricevendo informazione che da lui, mi lusingai, e scrissi alla Sagra Cong. de Prop. Fide, che gli affari di questo luogo andavano prosperamente. L'ultimo di Agosto ricevei un dispaccio da Soprain-tendenti del Catolicismo di questo luogo, con gravi accuse di immoralità contro il Nugent: contro le quali protestandosi egli, convenne per iscoprire la verità, sottoporre ambe le parti ad esame. Io per tal motivo me sono qui portato, e prima di porre mano al processo, ambe le parti sottoscrissero uno strumento obligandosi ad accettare e stare alla mia determinazione. Ciò stimavo necessario per impedire qualunque ricorso, che si potesse fare a Tribunali secolari, e per dar vigore e forza ad una decisione, che niuna potea derivare dal poter civile. Dopo un noioso e lungo esame di innumerabili testimoni, ritirai l'approvazione e spirituali facoltà concesse al Nugent, e ne ho delle medesime investo un certo Guglielmo O'Brien dell'Ordine di S. Domenico, qui giunto da Dublino ultimamente, uomo dotato di dottrina e maniere che indicano una buona razione, e ben raccomandato. Ma qui comminciano i disturbi. Nugent in due o tre lettere mi ha fatto sapere, che vivente lui, il Sig.re Guglielmo O'Brien giammai potrà uffiziare nella Chiesa di S. Pietro (cioè nella Chiesa di New York) e che la Gazzetta di questo giorno rapporterà la prima di una serie di lettere, che egli ha, per questo mezzo, intenzione di indirizzare a me. Io ho inoltre da lui e dal suo partito (perchè egli ha da sua parte un grande numero de' più infimi suoi personi) che alla mia determinazione in favore del Sig.re Guglo. O'Brien, si farà una contraria dichiarazione e protesta: e mi è stato più volte riferito, che aperta violenza e spargimento di sangue non si sarebbe risparmiato. Lascio a voi di considerare quanto pernizioso alla Religione debba riuscire questo malaugurato affare, specialmente in una Città, dove conta appena tre anni del suo stabilimento, e dove il Congresso, e per conseguenza molte persone da ciascheduno degli Stati risiedono. Nel progresso del sudetto esame tra le testimonianze, una venne a luce, la quale avrebbe dovuto aver resi più cauti quelli i quali raccommandarono il Nugent al servizio della Missione in America, cioè che per incontinenza egli era stato sospeso ed espulso dalla di dui Diocesi dal fu Monsigre. Carpenter Arcivescovo di Dublino, donde portatosi a Cork ed abbusandosi della soverchia credulità dell'infelice Apostata Lord Dunboyne allora Vescovo di cotesta città, ottenne le facoltà di operare. Osservate che quando lo approvai, ciò feci col concedergli facoltà colla clausola "donec revocentur" le quali ho al presente revocate. Eppure cotanto è egli al oscuro circa la natura di simile approvazione, o per dir meglio, tanto egli si prende giuoco, ed inganna i suoi amici circa tal materia, che mi presentarono un foglio intimandomi il loro appello alla Santa Sede.

Vi incommodo con questo lungo racconto (perchè non mi è possibile lo scrivere alla S. Congrege. per la posta, che si mette alla vela domattina) per pregarvi a communicare alla medesima S. Cong. la prima notizia di tale facenda.

TO WILLIAM O'BRIEN   Nov. 8—[1787] Washington—

—He (Goetz) must likewise know, that he owes, & it is my duty to insist on a reparation of the scandal given and mischief produced, as public as the offence—By his encouragement, assertions and sermons, as well the printed one,[1] as those he generally delivered, the unlearned were drawn into & the better informed[,] confirmed in their open resistance[,] to an outrageous contempt of ecclesiastical authority. It is requisite for him to make a public disavowal of the principles of independance contained in these acts; and disabuse, as far as he now can, those unfortunate persons, who were misled or obstinate as to receive absolution from his ministry, after notification of the withdrawing of his faculties, his syspension & excommn. If he consent to these terms, his censures will be removed, and after compleating the term of his pennance, he will be readmitted to the functions of the priesthood. Previous to absolution, explicit act of faith & declaration of his religious principles; because in one of his sermons, he spoke as a Deist., and Latitudinarian, advocated the conduct of Jos[ep]h. 2d & freemasonry—[2]

Conclude with mentioning the well grounded report of his attempt at Philada.; that if a satisfactory answer is received of his submission to the terms required, he need not come to Balte; that Mr. o Brien or some other, as the case may be, will be appointed to act in my name[3]

ADf   AAB   "Extract & heads of my answer to Mr. o Brien—" at head of MS. Year determined by O'Brien's letter of Aug. 15, 1796 (5U5).

[1] See Carroll's extracts and comment regarding the sermon, Feb., 1797.

[2] Holy Roman Emperor (1760-90). In his system of Josephinism the principle that the state should regulate ecclesiastical affairs is referred to here.

[3] Goetz was in New York at this time with the intention of getting O'Brien to intercede with Carroll, claiming that he was duped by the trustee Oellers.

TO JOHN EDISFORD[1]   Nber 9. 1787

A printed Letter, dated Aug. 6th 1787, concerning the nature of our temporalities, was not long since put into my hands. From a combination of various circumstances I cannot hesitate to suppose it was written by our worthy friend, Mr Joseph Reeve. If my conjecture be right, I request you would present my compliments to him, and acquaint him, that I be pleased to rectify two mistakes which he has undoubtedly fallen into. One is, that he supposes I maintained the propriety of consolidating the property of several Districts; a doctrine I always reprobated as much as he could possibly do. Some indeed ventured to say something about pensions, but it was with doubt and diffidence, and "with deference to better judgments." But it was always my opinion, that whatever was appropriated to a particular place, or a particular county, or the mission at large, must remain so appropriated to the end of the world.[2] The other is, that he makes me say what I never said, viz. That "many thousands of pounds have been justly seized upon, and withdrawn from the common stock." I never said that many thousands of pounds had been withdrawn, much less that they had been withdrawn from the common stock. My words are these: "Individuals associated, and took to themselves, in their own separate and exclusive property, several thousand pounds that belonged to the Community." For instance: The members of the London District associated, and took to themselves, as their own separate and exclusive property, the whole property of the London District, which consisted of several thousand pounds. This is an undeniable fact, not raised on the ground of impeachment, but fixed on the solid basis of truth. It remains to be known, whether the property of the London District does or does not belong to the Community. I say it does, because before the dissolution of the Society, every individual of the Community had a right to become a member, and eat the bread of the London District, when placed therein by legal authority, and because the Clementine Brief did not alter the destination of the funds, or alienate them from the use originally intended. The members, therefore, of the London District could not in justice take the property thereof to themselves, as their own for life, separate and exclusive. Nor is this kind of language to be deemed obloquy; for I throw no censure upon individuals; I have all along declared, "I had rather make any imposition, than harbour a thought for a single moment that those gentlemen would intentionally commit injustice." The censure falls upon the general plan of operation. Our gentlemen took for granted what ought to have been taken into consideration, and by that means suffered the members of Districts to take District property to themselves, as their own for life, separate and exclusive, which they had no more right to than you or I had.

It gives me great pleasure to find, that Mr Reeve not only maintains, but proves unanswerably, that before the suppression of the Society, the members of a District were not proprietors of the stock belonging to it. I have had agreements with Mr Ellerker and Mr Power[3] upon that subject, and I own I was astonished to find, that two first-rate men, such as they certainly are, should hold the Affirmative with great earnestness. They told me they could not comprehend my distinction between a College and the members of a College.

Mr Reeve says, that "in virtue of the separate and exclu[sive] appropriation of funds to certain Districts of the English Province, those Districts must consequently exist tho' the Society is no more." And he adds, that "the douay Clergy are possessed of separate funds of the like nature, appropriated to certain counties and Districts." If this be his idea of a District, I will allow him the existence of as many Districts as there are foundations in all England. But how will the existence of those secular-clergy Districts, now no longer of the Society of Jesus, apologize for those gentlemen who have taken District property to themselves, as their own for life, separate and exclusive?

Mr Reeve does not discuss the main question, which is, Whether, upon the dissolution of the Society, the members of a District had a right to take to themselves the revenues thereof, as their own for life, separate and exclusive; but from his words it may fairly be inferred that they had not.

Thus Mr Reeve admits the three principal points respecting the present subject, namely, that before the dissolution of the Society, the members of a District were not proprietors of the stock belonging to it; That the Colleges and Districts of the late English Province of the Society of Jesus do not actually exist; and that upon the dissolution of the Society, the members of Districts had no right to take District property to themselves, as their own for life, separate and exclusive. Other questions such as, Whether the foundations should or should not have gone to the Bishops; whether or not it required three years to settle our affairs, before a general Meeting could be held; and perhaps one or two more are so unimportant, that they may be granted or denied without any prejudice to the main argument. So that upon the whole matter, I am really of opinion that if we understood one another, Mr Reeve and I should find our principles to be much the same, except it be, that he is for palliating, and I am for exposing, the absurdity of the measures hitherto pursued.

ADf   AAB   "Carroll London" adjoins the date, which is written vertically on the right margin at the conclusion of the letter, possibly in another hand of the period.

[1] Evidently a resident of England and a clergyman, but not a Jesuit.

[2] See Feb. 7, 1787, for Carroll's principles as applied to his plan for a college.

[3] Probably James Power, S.J., once at Bourges as tutor to Charles Carroll.

TO [WILLIAM O'BRIEN] Baltimore, Dec. 8, 1787

Revd. Sir   I received two days ago your kind favour of Nov. 26th, and thank you much for the full communication of the events at New York, however shocking and scandalous they are. I cannot say, that they surprised me, as I have perhaps more reason, than any one to know, how totally abandoned Nugent is to the sway of his passions; how much he is now aching and against the conviction of his conscience; &, what is still worse, drawing others into the same fatal precipice, into which he has plunged himself. The rashness & falsehood of his late declaration, that every thing was settled on the sunday, afterwards was undone by my going to dine with his enemy Mr. Lynch, may perhaps provoke me to publish some matters concerning this unhappy man, which yet have never passed my lips, & which must hold him up to the execration of even his own party, if they have a spark left, I do not say of Religion, but even of common honesty and these matters rest on his own acknowledgment to myself, in, what he called, a confidential way; but his lies, his atrocious calumnies, his excesses in every kind of infamy may possibly lead me to believe, that no regard ought to be shown to the pretended confidential communications of a man who can so grossly abuse that silence which I have held hitherto, & from which both Religion & honour may now perhaps acquit me while these horrible scenes are exhibiting at New York,[.] I am greatly obliged to you for bestowing on me one sentiment of congratulation, for being removed at such a distance from them: but I do assure you, that they are almost as constantly on my mind, as if I still remained with you: and I will likewise tell you, that I have felt no small apprehension, that you might become disgusted at the prospect before you; or that the virulence of Nugent & his desperate part against you might be carried to the most outrageous excesses. In the first place therefore I have to recommend every prudent precaution against violence: and in the next place to beseech you not to lose courage: for if you should, I candidly own, that I do not know, where to find the Clergyman in the U. States, who could replace you. I really consider your arrival in America, at so critical a period, as a providential designation of you to repair so dreadful scandals, & heal such dangerous wounds given to Religion, at its first introduction into New York.

I wrote to you a letter from Philada.,[1] inclosing a very material letter of Nugent, which in my estimation must be fully sufficient evidence against him & his party with respect to my jurisdiction. You now write, that the minutes of the enquiry, and all other letters will be wanting. I own, that I cannot see the smallest necessity for any other part of the minutes, that the joint agreement of the Trustees & Nugent to abide by my determination: and to yourself only I will own, that if the minutes are called for, the whole must be produced. Now in them, there are facts so disgraceful to Mr. Connell,[2] & such expressions of his are sworn to, respecting his being threatened by the Secretary of the Sp[anish]. Legation, in case he did not retract his certificate in favour of Nugent, that I think Mr. Gardoqui would turn Connel head and shoulders out of his house, as a vagabond in the streets, if these matters should ever be brought into Court. Till I know from you for certain, whether these papers will be insisted on, I must suspend my application to Mr. Gardoqui in behalf of Mr. Connell: for I am sure, I should incur blame from him for interceding for one, against whom such matters were said, & who himself had spoken things so dishonourable to the conduct of one of the ministers of his household. All other papers in my possession, in relation to the business, shall be sent to Philada. by the first safe hand.

ADf   AAB
[1] Not found.
[2] It is not certain that this is James Connell, later Carroll's agent in Rome after 1790.

TO BERNARD DIDERICK   Dec. 10, 1787

Not found. See July 25, 1788.

TO FRANCIS BEESTON   [Jan. - Mar. 1788]

LS Not found. See Mar. 22, 1788.

TO PATRICK SMYTH   Feb. 20, 1788

Not found. See July 9, 1799.

TO CHARLES PLOWDEN   Maryland March 1–1788–

Dr Sir   In my letter of Novr. last from New York, I had just time to acknowledge the receipt of your favours of July 29th, I now likewise thank you for your additional one of Sept. 2d, both of 1787. I was sent for to New York by the principal Gentlemen of the Congn, to investigate the conduct of an Irish Capucin, Nugent, who had been the incumbent at that place for two years. I really had conceived a favourable opinion of him: he shewed me good credentials, when he first arrived, and amongst others, a strong recommendation from Fr o Leary. I have reason now to suspect, that it was forged; for Nugent has been detected to be a most infamous fellow; & there is no excess, of which he does not seem capable. I began with revoking his faculties: his audacious resistance soon compelled me to suspend him. He disregarded it, and proceeded to such outrages, that the civil power has laid hold of him &

the grand Jury have found a bill & presented him as a rioter: his trial is to come on in May. I have appointed an Irish Dominican[1] who appears a very decent man & is well recommended, to succeed him: he has just got possession of the Church, which Nugent forcibly held, till the presentment of the grand Jury. I cannot describe to you the horrible scandal, that has arisen from this affair. I am afraid, it will be often repeated, as long as I am obliged to employ such Irish priests, as come over unsollicited. When they bring good characters, and Congregations are destitute of other help, I cannot refuse availing myself of them: and yet I know, that characters are too easily obtained in Ireland, even from most respectable persons. There is now in Maryland, & in employment, an Irish priest of the name of Smyth[2] (author of a new translation of the Imitation of Christ) a man of some knowledge, and decent in his manners. His manner of coming, & even his discourse at times has something mysterious. He shewed me a letter from the priest, Hussey of London[3] (whom I have heard mentioned as a man of address and intrigue), in which Hussey writes to him as an Intimate, and wishes him *success* in the object of his voyage. These things create a suspicion of his being an emissary for particular purposes. But I am much at ease about any dark manouvres, that may be meditated. We stand on such a footing, by our laws, that we may bid defiance to any insidious attempts, which however, I hope are not thought of. If you can learn any thing of this Gentleman you will oblige me by informing me of it. He says he was Parish priest at Dunboyne, the seat of the unhappy Ld. Dunboyne late Bp of Cork,[4] and that he left Ireland, with the approbation of Dr. Plunket,[5] Bp of Meath in whose diocese Dunboyne stands. Perhaps Mr. Thorpe may be able, at Rome, to trace the intrigue, if any there is. Mention it to him. I am sending to him our memorial to the Pope for the erection of an Episcopal see in the U. States. We ask moreover, that the choice may be with the officiating Clergy here. I am promised, that the memorial shall be backed by the Court of Spain: it is to go thro the hands of Count Florida Bianca,[6] & Mr. Thorpe is furnished with an authentic copy only for fear of accidents. I hope to have it backed by other powerful supporters. You, I suppose, would only laugh at me for thinking of France in her present state of humiliation, and whilst you Britons are insulting her poverty and misgovernment. Indeed, she makes a despicable figure, since the death of that great and good man, Monsr. de Vergennes. I sincerely rejoice, that the Son of my favourite, the late Lord Chatham, conducts himself with such ability and integrity. You did not perhaps expect so much from an American: and indeed, we should be excusable, (if not as Xtians, at least politically) for not bearing you much good will, in return for all the lies and misrepresentations, which many of your soured & indignant Countrymen are every day coining about us. You have certainly cramped our trade by some regulations, not merely selfish, but revengeful. Your Merchants will find, that, without warfare we have immense resources, & the means of redress in our power; as soon as the establishment of our new federal government will allow those means to be called forth.

March 13th Last fall, two German Capucins (brothers) arrived at Philada,[7] very decent men to appearance. They came in consequence of letters sent by our German Brethren here, complaining to their European friends of the want of assistance. Their coming in a very expensive manner from Rotterdam put us to heavy charges for passage &c. I now wish they had remained in Germany, especially since I had your intelligence from Augsburgh: we are unable to pay the expences of any more Germans, or support them here; unless I should be obliged to come to extremities with the Capucins, who are accused, with too great appearance of truth, of fomenting some discontents & divisions, which have broken out amongst the German part of the Congn. in Philada. I appointed to that station Mr Grosl,[8] a most amiable, modest, & learned, as well as singularly virtuous Gentleman: but the Capucins, who, thro our friend Molyneux's supineness, remained six weeks in Philada. after their arrival, living in their free way with some of the poorer part of the Germans & other jealous of a pretended preference given to, what is called, the English part of the Congn, got a petition presented to me for one of the Capucins to remain there instead of Mr. Grosl, who arrived just after them. This I positively refused, & with other reasons of my refusal, gave without disguise the following: viz:, that as long as there was an Exjesuit alive, willing and capable of serving a Congregation, which had been raised by that body of men, he should have preference. The malecontents are trying to erect another Church for the Capucin, both of whom I have disposed of in exceedingly good places, with which they need be well content; and which may be called paradises in comparison of what poor Mr. Wapeler and his Companions found at & long after their settlement. I am determined, that if I get certain intelligence of these Friars fomenting discord, I will revoke their faculties, by which, according to our articles of Ecclesiastical government they will lose their maintenance. Your communications from Mr. Thorpe shall be attended to, particularly concerning my writing to Cardl. Borromeo. I regret most exceedingly the loss of a very large packet of letters, which I sent off in August 1786.[9] There was a very long one to you & some part of it interesting. In it, I gave you a full account of my opinion of Beringtons answer to Hawkins, and several other things, particularly of the grounds he had for mentioning me in the manner he does. His last work, the history of Abelard and Eloise, I have not seen: Mr Francis Neale of Liege writes me a bad account of it, that it is a disgrace to his profession &c. I feel great disquietude in the thought, that a man who manages his pen so well, & might do it with so much credit to Religion, should be snatched from her service by running after fleeting & dishonourable applause. I have received from him no answer to my letter, containing much commendation of & some strictures on his answer to Hawkins. How came you never to mention to me, that you were proposed for Coadjutor of the Bprick of London? This information I owe to Mr. Strickland. It is perhaps selfish in me to recommend to you an acquiescence in that, which I so much dread myself. But I cannot avoid saying to you that I most cordially wish you were raised to a station, for which you are so excellently qualified. It would moreover add to the relief of our minds, to see public honours conferred on the merit of those whom calumny & tyranny have oppressed so long. We shall begin the building of our Academy this summer. In the beginning, we shall confine our plan to a house of 63 to 64 feet by 50, on one of the most lovely situations, that imagination can frame. It will be three stories high exclusive of the offices under the whole. Do not forget to give & procure assistance. On this academy is built all my hope of permanency, & success to our H. Religion in the United States.

I know not, what is got into Mr. Ths. Talbot's head. I write to him constantly; and for 18 months cannot get from him one word of answer. I suspect, that he imputes partly to me some proceedings of yr. schoolfellow Ashton, who is our temporal Agent. I had no part in the business, except certifying, when called on by Ashton that he is the agent of the Clergy here for their temporalities: and an excellent agent he is for the substance, tho ungracious oftentimes in the manner. The *suaviter in modo* so much recommended by the courtly Chesterfield, is wanted to temper the vigor of his exertions, the *fortiter in re.*[10] I fear he has offended both Strickland & Talbot, & drawn even on me in the displeasure of the latter. Present my respectful compliments to Mr. Weld & his Lady, to Messrs Stanley & Clinton, and all our other Gentlemen within your reach. My Mother & Mr. Ths. Digges send theirs to you. The former I have not seen for two months being obliged to reside much at Baltimore as a place of more ready communication with many places, where my business lies. She was very well lately. Mr. Ashton likewise desires to be rememberd to you. I am with the greatest esteem & affection, Dr Sir,   Yr. sincere friend & humble st   J. Carroll

March 25—After writing, as above I received your favour per packet of Nov. 13. You load me with obligations, which I prize more than any money, or diamonds of Golconda: for really your correspondence is most valuable to me and, I hope, to the cause of Religion. You write that your good Sister Bernard had received the last Sacraments; and on the 19th inst. I had the misfortune to lose a dear Sister in Virga,[11] whom I earnestly recommend to your prayers & those of Messrs. St[anley]: & Clinton. Her loss will be severely felt, I fear by two daughters, young women just grown up; who being surrounded by none but Protestants, will be in great danger of placing their affections on some of them. Mr Thorpe has had reason to think, that I neglected him; but it was not the case. Agreeable to notice from him & you I declined sending the proposed memorial,[12] till I could get it supported by powerful interest. I write a very long letter to him by this occasion.[13]

ALS   St
¹ Matthew O'Brien.
² Patrick Smyth.
³ Thomas Hussey, after 1767 chaplain to the Spanish embassy in London and rector of the Spanish Church there, was made president of a new college at Marymonte, Ireland and shortly after this Bishop of Waterford and Lismore in the 1790's.
⁴ John Butter, 12th Baron of Dunboyne in County Meath, Bishop of Cork until 1786, when he left the Catholic Church, returning in 1800.
⁵ Patrick J. Plunket.
⁶ Josè Monino, Conde de Floridablanca, Spanish Ambassador to Rome at the time, collaborating in the suppression of the Jesuits, was Premier of Spain 1777-87.
⁷ Heilbrons.
⁸ Lawrence Graessl, S.J., was ordained as a secular priest, came to America in 1787 and to St. Mary's Church, Philadelphia, and became embroiled in the Heilbron controversy. Appointed a coadjutor to Carroll, he died before the papers arrived from Rome.
⁹ See Carroll to Plowden, Aug. 18, 1786 (AAB).
¹⁰ "Gentle in manner" and "Vigorous in action."
¹¹ Eleanor. wife of William Brent of the Richland Manor in Virginia.
¹² See Feb. 17, 1785.
¹³ Not found.

TO THE GERMAN CONGREGATION IN PHILADELPHIA¹

Baltimore March 3d—1788

Gentlemen: I was honoured last thursday, with your favour of Febr. 23d. requesting my approbation of your design to erect a new church in Philada. principally for the accomodation of the German congregation. After thanking you for your very obliging reference to me in this matter, you may be assured, that I can not but approve, and encourage every well digested plan for the accomodation of our congregation, and their better instruction in their religious duties. As far therefore, as your design is conducive to these purposes, it has my hearty approbation. Besides, I think that this farther benefit may result from your undertaking, to animate the pastors of each church, in all future times, by mutual example, to greater exertions of zeal, & labour in the service of God.

On the other hand, I am not enough acquainted with your ability to provide a house, and maintenance for your new pastor, to enable me to judge, how prudent your plans may be at this time. I hope, there is no danger, of causing such a separation amongst roman catholicks, as will prevent divine service from being performed with the same concourse, and general approbation, as at present. By embracing too many objects, we some times fail in all; and pull down old establishments, by endeavouring to raise new ones. I hope, that you have weighed these matters maturely, and dispassionately. Many of you are well acquainted with Mr Pellentz, and know his merit, virtue, and attachment to his countrymen. I could wish him to be consulted on this occasion.

If your letter had not given me assurances to the contrary, I should have felt a suspicion, that your design arose from some resentment, at my refusing to appoint Mr. Heilbron, agreably to your recommendation. As I then acted from the conviction of my mind, and in the exercise of my rightful authority; so now do I see no reason to repine at my determination. I shall even have an additional reason to be pleased at it, if it should become the occasion of so great a good, as the raising of a new church, provided with the means of its own support, without injuring that, in which most of you were born again to Christ, and were so often fed with the bread of angels, and the words of eternal life. Above all things, be mindful of charity, and brotherly love; avoid contentions, never assume the exercise of that spiritual power, which can only be communicated to the ministers of Christ; let the election of the pastors of your new church be so settled, that every danger of a tumultuous appointment be avoided, as much, as possible, In any country this would be hurtful to Religion: in this, it would totally destroy it. Do not think, that you are abridged of your rights, when you have not this appointment in your own hands: in the country of your forefathers, there are very few instances, if any, of its being in the hands of the people at large: and I hope, you will not attempt to fix it in that manner. As you undertake to raise your church at your own charge, and with yr. own industry, it is probable, you may have it in view, to reserve to yourselves the appointment of the clergyman, even without the concurrence of the ecclesiastical Superior. On this matter I request to hear again from you, as I conceive, it may involve consequences to Religion of the most serious nature.

I have now told you my mind fully, on the subject of yr. letter: your professions of zeal, and submission required a free communication from me. Wishing most sincerely an increase of the kingdom of Jesus Christ, that your present designs may contribute thereunto, and that you may be governed by his spirit in all your proceedings, I have the honour to be with great respect, and attachment,   Gentlemen,   Yr. most obedt. and   devoted Servt. in Christ

ADf   AAB

[1] Early in 1788 Adam Premir was elected chairman of a German Catholic committee, which acquired a lot at 6th and Spruce Sts., future site of Holy Trinity Church. Carroll respected the general feeling that the Germans would benefit from this, but with reservations about how it would be provided. He was uneasy at Premir's action.

TO ANTOINE DUGNANI   Maryland March 5, 1788

I profit, My Lord, from the departure from New York of the merchant ship of his Most Christian Majesty to acknowledge to Your Excellency the letters of July 2 and October 9, 1787, with which you honored me; and which filled me with gratitude by the kind expressions which they contained. I do not conceal, My Lord, that I was very flattered; and please God I may continue to enjoy the esteem of so worthy a prelate.

It was a very great pleasure for me & for the parents of our two young Americans[1] to learn of their arrival at Bordeaux. I do not doubt that they are now well established at the Urban College. Their friends unite with me in thanking your Excellency for the particular attentions owing to you after their arrival in France.

At present I am busy preparing dispatches for My Lord Cardinal Antonelli which I will have the honor of addressing to Your Excellency. They contain the detail of a frightful scandal given by an unworthy priest in New York,[2] who was in charge of the Catholics of that city. Your Excellency will be informed of it by the Reverend Bandol,[3] who will have the honor of giving you this letter. He has been in America for ten years. A chaplain of the French legation, and in a situation full of perils for a clergyman who does not have the fear of God constantly before his eyes; he has never given bad example nor betrayed his holiness, and if Your Excellency could be useful to him in his pursuits you would be rewarded by a gratitude which will never be denied.

I have the honor to be with the most profound respect, My Lord, Your Excellency's most humble, etc.

ADf   AAB   "(Le Nonce a Paris)" precedes the date at the head of the letter.
[1] Ralph Smith and Felix Dougherty.
[2] Patrick Smith.
[3] Seraphim Bandol was celebrated for his sermons honoring the Declaration of Independence at St. Mary's Church, Philadelphia in 1779 and 1781.

(Le Nonce a Paris)   de Mariland çe 5 Mars 1788   Je profite, Mgr, du depart de la Nouvelle York du paquebot de S. M. Très Chrétienne pour faire part à V. Exc. que les lettres du 2 de Juillet, & du 9 d'Octobre de 1787, dont elle daigna m'honorer; et qu'elles m'ont penetré de reconnoissance par les expressions obligeantes, qu'elles contenoient. Je ne cache pas, Mgr, que j'en ai eté très flatté; et plut à Dieu que je puisse continuer à jouir de l'estime d'un prelat aussi recommandable.

C'etoit pour les Parens de nos deux jeunes Americains, & pour moi un très grand plaisir que d'apprendre [leu]r arrivée à Bordeaux. Je ne doute point, qu'ils ne [soient ?] presentment bien etablis au College Urbain. Leurs amis s'unissent à [*illeg.*] pour remercier V. Ex. pour les attentions particulieres dont ils sont redevables apres leur arrivée en France.

Je suis occupé à present a preparer des depeches pour Mgr le Card. Antonelli, que j'aurai l'honneur d'envoyer à l'adresse de votre Exc. Elles contiendront le detail d'un scandale affreux, qu'a donné à la Nouvelle York un prétre indigne, qui etoit chargé de la conduite des Catholiques en cette ville. V. Exc. en pourra etre instruite par Monsr. l'abbé Bandol, qui aura l'honneur de lui remettre cette lettre. Pendant dix ans celuici a eté en Amerique. Aumonier de la legation de France; et dans une situation pleine d'ecueils pour un Ecclesiastique qui n'auroit pas la crainte de Dieu toujours devant les yeux; il n'a jamais donné mauvais example ni trahi la sainteté de son etat, et si V. Exc. peut lui être utile en ses poursuites, Elle sera payée [*illeg.*] par une reconnoissance, qui ne se dementira jamais.

TO PIUS VI   Baltimore in the State of Maryland
March 12, 1788

Holy Father—   We the undersigned petitioners of the Holy See in all due respect kneeling before you, humbly make known what follows: —we priests, especially deputed by our brother priests who exercize the ministry with us in the United States, in the first place offer Your Holiness our utmost thanks for the truly fatherly care which you have exhibited towards this very distant portion of the vineyard of the Lord. This very sollicitude has aroused all of us to continue and increase our labors for the upbuilding and extending of faith in Christ Our Lord in these areas where the errors of the sects abound. In so doing we are convinced that we evince a proper obedience to God, do what is gratifying to the common Father of the faithful, and fulfill the duties of our station. Moreover, in response to such care, we believe that we are under obligation to make known to Your Holiness all that in our long experience in these States we feel you should know, so that your pastoral care of us may be exercised as profitably as possible. His Eminence Cardinal Antonelli signified to one of the petitioners in a letter of July 23, 1785, that it was the intention of the Sacred Congregation of the Propagation of the Faith to establish an Episcopal Vicar Apostolic for these States as soon as the same Congregation thought it expedient; and he wished that, when the time seemed opportune, the one to whom the letter was addressed should give due notice. Not he alone but all of us, in the name of all our co-laborers, declare that in our opinion the time has come, and that episcopal dignity and authority are highly desirable. We pass over other weighty reasons; but we find more and more under the very liberal constitution of the Republic, that if among the clergy there are some men of intractible character, who are restive under ecclesiastical discipline, they offer as the reason for their unruliness and disobedience that they are bound to obey a bishop who wields personal authority, but not a simple priest who has only delegated authority, such as is forbidden by our laws. This was recently done in New York by those who wished to throw off the yoke of authority. In seeking an excuse for their obstinacy they stressed a reason most likely to win favor with the heterodox, namely, that the authority of the ecclesiastical superior put over us by the Sacred Congregation was illegal, because it was set up by a foreign tribunal and was dependent on this tribunal both as regards its exercise and its duration. We refrain from explaining at greater length because we know that certain original documents were sent to Rome. From them it will appear what degree of authority should belong to the office to which the ecclesiastical governance of these States is entrusted.

We explain all these things to the Pastor of the faithful on earth so as to ascertain how the authority of our Superior as now constituted, can be restored; and the same would hold for a bishop who enjoys vicarious and not ordinary powers. For this reason, Holy Father, expressing the desire and speaking in the name of all, it seems to us that the religious situation in the States demands such a form of ecclesiastical governance as would, first of all, provide effectively for the integrity of faith and morals, enduring union with the Apostolic See, and proper obedience and respect for it. And besides, that the choice and authority of the bishop, if we are to be granted one, should arouse the least suspicion and opposition among those with whom we live. To this end two things will contribute greatly—the first is that the Holy Father in the applying of his authority over the Church, establish an episcopal see in the United States of America, one immediately under the Holy See; and, secondly, that the choice of the bishop, at least in this first instance, be left to the priests here who have the care of souls. When a bishop is chosen and established in the first American see the Apostolic See in its foresight and care of us will see to it that a fixed procedure be agreed upon for the future selection of a bishop.

Holy Father, in fullest devotion to the Holy See, we have thought these matters should be brought to the attention of your priestly sollicitude; and, from our hearts, we protest that in offering this advice to Jesus Christ the divine bishop of souls, we have no purpose other than the increase of our holy faith, the growth of piety, the flourishing of ecclesiastical discipline, and that the false teachings disseminated by the heterodox about the true religion be entirely eradicated. May the Great and Omnipotent God preserve, you, Holy Father, unharmed for a long time, so that you may regard this church in America not only benignly as you have done, but may also safeguard it with every spiritual aid, and establish it firmly. May you wish to impart to us prostrate before you the Apostolic and paternal blessing.

Thus plead the most devoted and obedient sons of Your Holiness,   John Carroll   Robert Molyneaux   John Ashton[:] priests

C   PF

Bme Pater   Nos infra scripti oratores ad Sedem Apostolicam omni debita veneratione accedentes, et ad Sanctitatis tuae pedes provoluti, ea quae sequuntur humiliter exponimus; nos scilicet Sacerdotes specialiter deputatos fuisse a fratribus nostris sacerdotibus religionis ministeria nobiscum exercentibus in Foederatae Americae Provinciis, ut imprimis Sanctitati Sedi ingentes gratias referamus pro sollicitudine plane paterna quam in dissitam hanc Dominicae vineae portionem extendere dignatur; ac deinde significamus nos omnes hac tanta sollicitudine excitatos fuisse ad labores nostros continuandos, augendosque pro conservandi et ampliandi Xti Domini fide in his provinciis quae omnium sectarum erroribus replentur; ita nempe faciendo persuasum habemus nos non solum debitum Deo obsequium exhibere sed etiam communi Patri fidelium gratum, acceptumque reddere officium. Praeterea ut tantae sollicitudini respondeamus muneris nostri esse credimus illa omnia Sanctitati Tuae patefacere quae pro diuturnae nostrae in his provinciis experientia scitu necessaria videntur, ut Pastoralis Tuae in nos providentia, quam fieri potest, utilissime administretur. Itaque cum Em. Cardlis Antonelli uni oratorum significaverit litteris datis die 23 Julii, 1785, Sacrae Congregationis de Propda Fide mentem fuisse pro hisce Provinciis constituere Episcopum Vicarium Apostolicum quamprimum eadem Sac. Cong. illud opportunum fore intelligeret, cuperitque de congruo ad eam designationem tempore certior fieri ab eo, ad quem scripsit Em. Cardinalis; inde est, Bme Pastor, ut non ille tantum sed omnes communi omnium operariorum nomine profiteamur, nostra quidem opinione, tempus jam advenisse, quo dignitas et auctoritas Episcopalis maxime desideratur. Ut enim alias gravissimas rationes omittamus, magis ac magis experimur in hac liberrimae Reipublicae constitutione si qui sint vel inter ipsos Sanctuarii Ministros indocitis ingenii homines ac disciplinae Ecclesiasticae impatientes, eos suae licentiae et inobedientiae [uti] rationem praetendere quod Episcopis quadam propria auctoritate utentibus obedire teneantur; non autem simplici Sacerdoti vicariam quamdam ac legibus nostris interdictam jurisdictionem exercenti. Haec nuper Neo Eboraci jactitarunt qui auctoritatis jugum cupiunt excutere, et cum prae ceteris pervicaciae suae praetextum quaesiverunt, qui esset ad capessendum heretedoxorum favorem maxime idoneus, contendere siquidem auctoritatem Superioris Ecclesiastici, quem nobis Sae. Cong. constituit, esse illicitam, utpote a Tribunali externo praefectam, ab eodemque dependentem quoad durationem et exercitium. Haec Sanctitati Tuae fusius exponere supersedemus quod documenta quaedam originaria Romam Transmissa ipsi cognovimus ex quibus intelligetur qua auctoritate ipsi muniri conveniat, cui Ecclesiasticum harum Provinciarum regimen committi [illeg.].

Ad haec supremo in terra Fidelium Pastori exponimus illa omnia ex quibus manibus reddi potest auctoritas Superioris prout nunc constituitur; militaturae etiam contra Episcopum cui vicaria volum modo et non ordinaria potestas concederetur. Igitur Bme Pater, communi voto ac nomine, significamus nobis videre Statum politicum religiosum harum Provinciarum exigere ejusmodi formam regiminis Ecclesiastici per quam imprimis efficaciter pro videatur Fidei, morumque integritati, adeoque unioni perpetuae cum Sede Apostolica, debitisque erga illam observantiae et obsequio; deinde ut Episcopi, si quis nobis concedendus est, designatio et auctoritas redditur quam minime suspecta aut odiosa illos quos inter vivimus. Ad quem finem duo videntur nobis multum collatura; primum ut Beatissimus Pater, pro sua in Xti Ecclesia Auctoritate, novam sedem Episcopalem erigat in his Foederatae Americae provinciis, Sedi Apostolicae immediate Suffraganeam; deinde ut Episcopi electio, saltem prima vice, permittatur Presbyteris qui nunc religionis ministeria hic [debite] exercent, curamque agant animarum. Illo autem constituto et redacto, in primam Americana Ecclesia curabit provide Sedis Apostolicae sollicitudo ut ratio aliqua stabilis concludatur secundum quam in posterum Episcopi deligantur.

Haec sunt, Bme Pater, quae maxima animi devotione Sanctitati Tuae pastorali sollicitudini submittenda esse existimavimus, ex animo profitentes et tamquam [rectam] rationem nostri consilii divino animarum Episcopo Jesu Xto, nihil nos prae oculis habere quam ut sancta nostra fides augeatur, crescat pietas, vigeat disciplina Ecclesiastica, atque falsae opiniones quae heterexodorum animi de vera religione insederunt, omnino evellantur. Deus Opt. Max. Xtiano populo Te, Beatissime Pater, diu servet incolumem ut hanc Ecclesiam Americanam non solum benigne [foveas] ut fecisti, sed etiam omni spirituali subsidio custodias, penitusque constituas, utque nobis ad pedes tuos procumbentibus Apostolicam ac paternam benedictionem velis largiri.

Ita precantur   Sanctitatis Tuae   Devotissimi et obedientissimi servi et filii   Joannes Carroll   Robertus Molyneaux   Joannes Ashton[:]   Presbyteri

Baltimore in provincia Marylandiae, Martii die 12, 1788

COMMENT ON PATRICK SMYTH LETTER   Mar. 15, 1788

[In his letter to Carroll, Smyth expresses his gratitude and reasons for leaving for Ireland. One Burrowe gave him financial assistance before his departure, Carroll later reimbursing him.] Note—Burrowe is a young man at New York, who paid some expences of Mr. Smith at that place, which were repaid him by mr. J. Carroll. True copy—Testd. J. Carroll.

AM   AAB (8B G6)

TO LEONARDO ANTONELLI   From Maryland, 18 March, 1788

I hope, Most Eminent Cardinal, that you have already received the letter which I entrusted to the two American students who left Maryland in July, for Rome and the Urban College. Since I wrote at due length about all religious matters I can add very little about affairs in general. Recently very great and much wanted assistance came to us from Germany with the arrival of two secular priests and two Capuchins so that all German congregations can be supplied.[1] For good reasons I have a change in New York in October, and towards the end of November I informed you,[2] Most Eminent Cardinal, that a Capuchin priest, Andrew Nugent by name, was located there. Relying on his credentials I thought that religion was well provided for, but in August some very serious accusations were made against him. When he denied them both he and his accusers committed the case to my judgment. After a careful inquiry I decided to withdraw my previous approval and grant of faculties to this Capuchin, and to this decision I was moved by his conduct so improper in a religious and a priest. Further investigation revealed that some years ago he was suspended by the Archbishop of Dublin for incontinence. This made me wonder that when he set out for America he was given favorable credentials by his superior of his order. When I notified him that I would recall his faculties some of his friends presented a document, an appeal to the judgment of the Holy See, implying that even contrary to my wish the Holy Father could restore faculties to those who were under suspension, but meanwhile, since he was deprived of all spiritual jurisdiction, Nugent would not exercise any ministry. It seems to me that it was the good Providence of God that at this juncture brought to America a priest of the order of Saint Dominic, who, as is attested by a letter of the Archbishop of Dublin, spent sixteen years in that diocese in commendable activity. As soon as the Capuchin discovered that I intended to replace him with this Dominican he wrote a letter threatening that this appointment would not take effect, and that he would not permit the Dominican to enter his sanctuary or celebrate Mass at his altar. A second and a third letter renewed these threats. On my part I pleaded that he should not increase the scandal or force me to sterner measures. But all in vain. On the following Sunday as I prepared to offer Mass before a large congregation, including as usual many heterodox, previously informed as he was of my intention, he intervened, maintaining that he had the right to say the so-called parochial Mass, and that he would not yield his right unless I promised that I should not mention him in my sermon. I replied that I could scarcely make such a promise for it was my duty to warn the faithful whom they should beware of, and to whom they should have recourse in their spiritual needs. And when I attempted to do this he shouted in a still louder voice. When he charged his accusers with perjury some of the parishioners accused him of the gravest misconduct. A tumult ensued, abusive language, most unbecoming the sacredness of the place, was exchanged between him and others.

Eventually it came to this that he denied that I had any authority to recall his faculties. Some of his adherents who are with one or another exception people of little importance and Irish did not hesitate to assert that since my jurisdiction comes from the Holy See it was foreign, and for this reason in conflict with the law. The unlettered people did not get this idea from any source but from himself. Therefore when I saw that such was the situation that it was critical I decided in so far as possible to put an end to this scandal, and, collecting my thoughts and omitting the previous denunciations which otherwise were in place, I stated in public that I suspended him from divine services because of his contumacy, and I admonished those present not to assist at the Mass he celebrated. Without delay I withdrew with the majority of the faithful who were of sounder mind to celebrate [the Mass] in the domestic chapel of the Legate of the Most Christian King. It is not without great sorrow that I add that nevertheless the suspended priest celebrated Mass on this day in the presence of a few people, some of whom were contumacious and others simply ignorant. Later rumors were circulated in the city by his followers that I had no more authority than a simple priest, except that I could administer confirmation. They added that the laws of New York forbade all foreign jurisdiction whether civil or ecclesiastical; and they cited with approval some unhappy decrees of certain European princes against the authority of the Holy See. When I was made aware of this I thought that I should at once combat such destructive rumors. I drew up a notice, a copy of which in English I include.[3] I add merely that by their signatures all sincere Catholics eagerly supported my stand. Meanwhile those in charge of the church took new measures to exclude this contumacious man. On the next Sunday I planned to instruct the people on the nature and source of jurisdiction, and what an offense it is to receive the sacraments from one to whom their administration is forbidden. But before I reached the church he and some of his group, by night as we suppose, broke down the door and took possession of the church. When I arrived I saw that a tumult was taking place so that neither a sermon nor the Holy Sacrifice was possible. I opposed those who would resort to violence; and after I had said a few words about those who openly and in ignorance shouted that the authority of the Church was nullified by the civil law, he who was the cause of this uproar returned to his residence and I repaired to the Spanish chapel.

When the situation had become such that nothing could be effected merely by ecclesiastical authority I left New York, and the custodians of the church decided to appeal to the civil law. Fortunately, it happens that the very New York law which regulates the administration of the temporalities of our church and other churches ends with the very wholesome provision— nothing in this law shall be construed or understood as in any way affecting the right of freedom of conscience or judgment, or as making any change in the religious constitution or government of any church, or society, as regards their belief, discipline or origin. Thus there is good ground for hoping that this unruly and defiant man will shortly be reduced to order, because he not only strives to overthrow our discipline but he likewise opposes Catholic doctrine. For, as I learned from a letter of the Franciscan[4] mentioned above, Nugent celebrates Mass on Sundays and preaches, and he deplores his stupidity in every acknowledging me, a priest of no account, as his superior; and, finally, it is an abjuration of the faith for him to assert in a sermon that he will not recognize the pope or anyone except Christ and the civil authorities of New York.

It is greatly to be regretted that such a scandal should have occured within three years of the introduction of our religion in that city. He surely gave occasion for this scandal who sent to America with his recommendation a priest already notorious for misconduct. I have been rather detailed in this account because I want the Sacred Congregation to understand very fully what I have done, and I want to be instructed if I have failed in implementing the power which the Holy Father has given me, however unworthy I may be. I almost forgot to mention what this unhappy man stated in a public sermon before I took up his case, a sermon which I wanted him to submit to me. When discoursing on the virtue of charity he began to rave against those who impose restraints on others in the matter of religion, and he gave utterance to many sentiments more appropriate to the pulpits of the heterodox than those of Catholics. "The detestable slaughter of St. Bartholomew! The field of Jarnac[5] stained with the noblest blood of France! Is this the gospel of the meek Jesus? German heretics! The Spanish Inquisitors! Portuguese hypocrites! Do you believe that the religion of Christ is established by persecution? Etc." Then he digressed into extended denunciation of those who opposed him, even mentioning them by name.

I admit that I am very eager that this first attempt at resistance to ecclesiastical jurisdiction be repressed, even by recourse to civil authority. Here Catholics live among every variety of the heterodox, so that I greatly fear that unless this be done priests of unruly character, guided by this example, will throw off the yoke of obedience, and the laity will be flattered into believing that they too should claim the power of determining their pastor just as they see the sectarians do.

While we ponder these and other things, my priestly brothers, whose labors and experience in America are of long duration, believe that the time has come, provided it seems so to the Holy See and the Sacred Congregation, for the appointing of a bishop over the Church of America, because his very title and dignity may be effective in coercing those of intractible disposition. I am not unaware, Most Eminent Cardinal, that there may be some who will suspect me of sinful ambition, but I would rather risk this and even greater suspicion than by silence pretend that religion is not menaced. In addition to the fact that the authority of a bishop will be more weighty in church government, the sect which professes the Anglican religion gained no little glory and esteem with the public by introducing bishops, whereas formerly the very name was abhorred in the states of America.[6] Another result was greater observance and attention to morals on the part of their so-called ministers. For these and other reasons we thought it well to offer a petition to His Holiness which he undoubtedly will send to the Sacred Congregation. In it our reasons for the suggestion are explained more fully. In this connection my only comment is that you, Most Eminent Cardinal, and the other fathers who watch over the propagation of the faith so carefully and with such success, seriously weigh the spirit and the prejudices which prevail in these States, and that you so arrange the naming of a bishop, and give him such authority that, while union and due obedience to the Apostolic See is maintained, in so far as is possible, he be freed from the suspicion of any kind of subjection which is not absolutely necessary.

April 19, 1788   While I was waiting for an opportunity to send the above letter I received that of Your Eminence, dated Rome, 8th of August 1787, with the reprints of the Mass for the Propagation of the Faith, and the dispensation for the apostate Capuchin. I am unable to say whether it was more with pleasure or with confusion that I heard of the opinion entertained of me by the eminent fathers, expressed in a general meeting on June 18. On the one hand when I call to mind what I believe could be done for increasing the glory of God, or on the other when I realize how little I have accomplished of what I planned to do, I am almost driven to resign and give back my office to the Sacred Congregation so as to be relieved of the burden of such responsibility. But I admit that I am greatly consoled by the approbation of the Sacred Congregation, and in all reverence and gratitude I heartily thank you, the most eminent Prefect of the Congregation and the other fathers, that, prescinding from my merits, you were moved by such singular regard. Your commendation will not move me to any vain ostentation but it will prove a stimulus to arouse me from torpor and to greater diligence in promoting divine interests.

I hope shortly to have a law by which the Catholic priests will be permitted to unite into one body and to hold their possessions in common; and, with some limitations, to acquire other possessions when, as we hope, the ministers of the sanctuary will be more numerous.

The building of the school began a few days ago. That it be brought to successful completion we must trust to divine providence most of all, perhaps altogether. I think that the preservation of religion in these States depends entirely on this beginning. In no other way will the organizing of an ecclesiastical seminary be made possible, or a sufficient numbers of pastors be obtained to care for the faithful and work for the extension of religion.

As respects affairs in New York—That unhappy priest and author of schism a few days after my departure, goaded on by men of unbridled disposition, retained possession of the church and continued to celebrate Mass. In a short while he was driven out both by the application of force and the authority of the law. Before the judge he was charged by twelve men with arousing sedition and disturbing the peace. In May a verdict will be given. Meanwhile, he and his supporters bought a private home where he continues to preach and celebrate Mass sacrilegiously. Although such an instance of the very worst example seems to demand the application of extreme ecclesiastical penalties, for the present I have thought it best to abstain from further censure of him and those of his faction. Next autumn I shall make a change in New York. I have repeatedly consulted the very excellent Spanish Representative[7] about the state of religion and its spread throughout the States. In his wisdom *he too is of the opinion that the title and authority of a bishop is necessary,* and of his own accord he volunteered to send our request to the Holy See. I entrusted it to his care, and I enclose an authentic copy of this letter. In all possible respect and devotion there commends himself to you, Most Eminent Cardinal and the other eminent fathers   Your Eminence's   Most humble and obedient   John Carroll

C   PF   ADf   AAB

[1] Laurence Graessl, Joseph Edenshink (Eden), and the Heilbrons are referred to here. Graessl was from Munich and arrived in Phiadelphia in Oct., 1787; was later named coadjutor to Carroll but died before receiving the papers from Rome. The name *Cresler* seems to be a mispelling by Carroll in some places at this early stage of Graessl's residence in America.

[2] See Oct., 1787. This document in copy seems to have been presented to Antonelli by Thorpe, who received it from Plowden as Carroll's intermediary. See Nov. 7, 1787.

[3] Apparently this was the same "Suspension . . ." with signatures later affixed to the document in a second copy sent to Antonelli.

[4] O'Brien was a Dominican, not a Franciscan, as Carroll shows he understands in other references.

[5] In southwest France; it was here that the Catholic partisans defeated the Huguenots in 1569 as a phase of the Wars of Religion, the St. Bartholomew's Day Massacre being a more infamous episode.

[6] William White was consecrated in England in 1787 and led the formation of the Protestant Episcopal Church.

[7] Don Diego de Gardoqui.

Ex Marilandia die 18 Martii, 1788   Literas jam accepisti Eminentissime Cardinalis, uti sperare fas est, quas commisi duobus alumnis Americanis qui ex Marilandia solverunt, mense Julio, Romam ad Collegium Urbanum profecturi. De rebus ad Religionem spectantibus tunc scripsi satis copiose, neque multa de generali earum statu adjicienda supersunt. Magnae nuper, multumq desideratae suppetiae ex Germania nobis advenere Sacerdotes, duo saeculares, duoq ex ordine Capuccinorum, quo fit ut omnibus Germanorum Congregationibus succuri jam queat. Gravibus de causis *Neo Eboraci* substiti mense octobris, et fere ad finem Novembris Tibi Eminentissime Cardinalis, olim significavi in ea urbe versari Sacerdotem ex ordine Capuccinorum *Andream Nugent.* Ejus literis fretus, credidi omnia recte procedere in negotio Religionis cum delatae ad me sunt, mense Augusto, atrociores aliquae adversus eum criminationes; quas cum veras esse negaret, tam ipse, quam delatores rem meo judicio definiendam commissere. Post diligentem inquisitionem, statui approbationem et facultates Capucino antea concessas omnino subtrahendas; ad quod me movebant illa praecipue, quae hic ab illo acta sunt viro Religioso et Sacerdote prorsus indigna. Accessit deinde quod dum cetera investigarem, compertum fuerit ipsum ante aliquot annos ob incontinentiae crimen a Dubliniensi Archiepiscopo defuncto suspensum fuisse; quo mihi magis mirari contingat, litteras honorificas illi in Americam proficiscenti datas fuisse a sui ordinis Superiore. Postquam ipsi significavi reventurum me ad facultatum revocationem, quidam illius amici chartam porrexere, Sanctae Sedis judicium interpellantes. Quibus respondi facultates a Beatissimo Patre restitui posse, vel me invito; interim tamen praedictum Sacerdotem, dum omni spirituali jurisdictione spoliatus, nullam debere exercere. Magna, uti confido, Dei providentia his temporibus in Americam navigavit *Sacerdos ex Ordine D. Dominici,* qui, uti ferunt, literae Archiepiscopi Dubliensis hodierni, sedecim annos in illa Diocesi cum laude transegit. Quamprimum revenit Capucinus hunc suo loco a me designari, minacibus literis mihi significavit designationem meam locum non habituram, neq permissurum se, ut nuper adductus Dominicanus *suum* Sanctuarium unquam ingrediatur, vel celebret in *suo* altari. Quod altera ac tertia vice repetivit. Interim ego ipsum precari, scandalum ne augeat, neve me adigat ad aliquid gravius de se statuendum. Omnia tamen frustra fuere. Sequenti Dominica, dum me comparo ad celebrandam Missam coram frequenti populo, et multis etiam, ut fit, Heteredoxis, ille quamvis antea monitus esset de meo consilio, se interposuit, jus se habere dictitans recitandi Missam, ut vocat, parochialem neq se jure cessurum, nisi ipsi promittam me nullam sui in dicendo mentionem facturum. Respondi id a me promittendum haud esse; fidelibus significari debere, et a quo cavere, et ad quem in spiritualibus necessitatibus recurrere debeant; cumq, hoc adstantibus dicere conarer, ille validiori voce pleraq suppressit. Inter haec ipse suis accusatoribus perjurium improperare, et vicissim ex adstantibus quidam gravissima illi crimina objicere; ita ut omnia foedo tumultu complerentur, et verba plurimum injuriosa, lociq sanctitate omnino indigna ab ipso et paucis aliis ultro citroq jactarentur. Eo tandem devenit, ut ullum mihi esse jus negaverit facultates suas substrahendi; et aliqui ejus asseclae qui omnes uno alterove excepto sunt inferioris notae homines, et fere Hiberni, asserere non dubitabant jurisdictionem meam, tanquam a sede apostolica profectam, extraneam esse, adeoque legibus contrariam. Hoc ignari homines non aliunde, quam ab ipso didicere. Igitur ubi res conspexi ita turbari, statui, quantum potui, scandalo finem facere, meque paulatim colligens, publice significavi, omissis praeviis denuntiationibus, quae aliter necessariae forent, me propter notoriam ejus contumaciam ipsum a divinis suspendere, monuique adstantes, ne interessent Sacrificio, ipso celebrante: statimque cum majori et saniori fidelium parte discessi, celebraturus in domestico sacello Excellentissimi Legati Regis Catholici. Non sine magno dolore adjicio suspensum sacerdotem missam nihilominus eadem die celebrasse, paucis vel contumacibus, vel propter ignorantiem assistentibus. Rumores subinde spargi per urbem ab ejus asseclis, me nihil habere auctoritatis, quam quae simplici sacerdoti competit, praeter facultatem administrandi confirmationem; leges Neo-Eboracenses prohibere omnem jurisdictionem extraneam, sive civilem, sive Ecclesiasticam: citari et commendari infausta edicta quorundam in Europa Principum adversus Sanctae Sedis auctoritatem. Haec ubi rescivi, statim tam perniciosis rumoribus obviam eundum esse credidi, et scriptum condidi, cujus exemplar Anglica linqua, ut i rat conceptum una adjicio, quodq avide omnes sinceri Catholici suis subscriptionibus firmaverunt. Inter haec, Ecclesiae Curatores legum muniti auctoritate novam seram templo imponunt, ut contumacem excludant; et ego sequenti Dominica populum instruere cogito de natura et fonte spiritualis jurisdictionis, quantumq crimen sit Sacramenta ab eo suscipere, cui illorum administratio interdicitur. Ante tamen quam templum adiissem ipse cum quibusdam suae factionis hominibus, de nocte ut creditur, portam effregit, templumq occupavit. Cum advenissem, omnia iterum tumultu turbari animadverti, ut neq concioni aut sanctissimo sacrificio celebrando locus esset. Vim adhibere cupientes repulsi; cumq contra eos pauca dixissem, qui palam et ignoranter clamitabant Sanctae Sedis auctoritatem legibus explosam esse, ipse auctor harum turbarum domum rediit, ego ad Sacellum Hispaniae.

Cum res hoc statu essent, ut nihil sola auctoritate Ecclesiastica perfici posset Eboraco discessi et templi curatores ad leges civiles recurrere statuerunt. Etenim opportune accidit ut eadem lege, qua Novi Eboraci statuitur de administratione bonorum ad Ecclesias sive nostras sive alienas spectantium, haec etiam saluberrima provisio concludatur; nihil ea lege contentum ita intelligi aut sumi debere ut minuat, ullove modo afficiat jura *conscientiae fruendiq judicii, aut quamvis omnio mutationem faciat in* Religiosa constitutione aut *regimine cujuscumq Ecclesiae, congregationis* vel Societatis *quantum spectat ad earundum doctrinam, disciplinam et initium.* Unde merito sperare licet contumacem Sacerdotem brevi in ordinem reductum iri; cum non solum *disciplinam* nostram prorsus evertere conetur, sed etiam Catholicae doctrinae se nunc aperte opponat. Audio enim ex litteris Patris Dominicani, de quo supra, ipsum jam aperte celebrare missam diebus Dominicis et concionari, et suam stoliditatem deplorare quod me Sacerdotem nullius momenti tanquam Superiorem unquam agnovisset; ac deniq quod plane erit fidem abjurare inter concionandum asserere, se neque Papam, nec alium omnino supra se agnoscere praeter Christum et magistratus Neo Eboracenses.

Dolendum maxime est tam grave scandalum in ea urbe ortum esse intra triennium ex quo in eam Religionis nostrae cultus primo est introductus; cujus scandali occasionem ille certe praebuit qui Sacerdotem tanta infamia quidem notatum tanta tamen commendatione in Americam oblegavit. Prolixior fui in hac narratione facienda quod cupiam a sacra Congregatione plene intelligi imprimis quae a me facta sunt, et ab ea edoceri si quid peccaverim in exercenda jurisdictione, quam mihi immerito Sanctissimus Pater communicavit. Paene oblitus eram commemorare quae homo infelix in publica concione dixerat antequam illius causam coepi tractare; quam concinionem mihi exhiberi ab ipso volui. Cum de charitatis virtute tractaret vehementer *in illos coepit debacchari qui alios Religionis ergo, fraenis plectunt,* ac plura dixit quae Heterdoxorum pulpitis magis quam Catholicorum consonant. "Caedes execrabilis Sancti Bartholomei! Campi de Jarnac foedati nobilissimo Galliae sanguine! Hoccine est mitis Jesu Evangelium? Haertici Germani! Inquisitores Hispaniae! Hypocritae Lusitani! Creditisne prosequendo Christi Religionem stabilire, etc?" Hinc digressus est ad injuriosa multa in illos dicendo singulatim qui ipsi adversabantur.

Fateor quidem valde mihi cordi esse ut primus hic conatus adversus jurisdictionem Ecclesiasticam reprimatur, legum etiam civilium auctoritate. Ita enim omnis generis professionis Heterodoxis permixti vivunt Catholici, ut valde timeam id nisi fiat, indocibilis ingenii Sacerdotes aliquando hinc exemplum sumpturos ad excutiendum oboedientiae jugum, et Laici ablandiendo persuasuros, ut ipsi eandem sibi auctoritatem assumant parochos suos constituendi, qua vicinos Sectarios vident possidere.

Cum haec aliaq multa perpenderemus et ipsi fratres mei Sacerdotes, quorum diuturnior est in America usus et experientia, credidimus tempus jam esse, si etiam ita Sanctae Sedi et Congregationi videretur, *Episcopum Americanae Ecclesiae designandi,* cujus auctoritas et nomen petulantia ingenia fortius possit cohibere. Non me latet, Eminentissime Cardinalis, futuros fortasse qui haec a me pravae ambitionis intuitu dicta suspicabuntur. At vel huic suspicioni vel gravioribus etiam malam subjacere, quam tacendo periculum dissimulare quod Religioni imminere videtur. Nam praeterquam quod Episcopi auctoritas majoris momenti futura sit in regimine Ecclesiastico non parum sibi splendorem et existimationem apud vulgus comparavit Secta quae Religionem Anglicanam profitetur, Episcopos nuper introducendo quorum nomen erat antae Americanis provinciis invidiosum. Hincq etiam major errata est in illorum Ministris, uti vocant, observantia et morum custodia. His aliisq causis libellum supplicem ad Suae Sanctitatis pedes deponere visum est nobis quem ipse Beatissimus Pater Sae Congregationi procul dubio communicabit, in quo [scilicet] nostri Consilii rationes fusius exponentur. Nihil aliud ea de re commemoro nisi ut te, Cardinalis Emenintissime, obtestor ceterosq Eminintissimos Patres qui tecum fidei propagationi ita sedulo et enixe invigilant, multum diligenterq perpendatis genium et praejudicia his Provinciis vigentia, velitisq ita fieri Episcopi denotionem, *taliq ipsum instrui auctoritate ut unio cum Sede Apostolica* debitaq obedientia sarta tecta conservetur, ac simul quantum his salvis fieri potest, ut eximatur Episcopus a *suspicione cujusvis subjectionis externae* quae non sit plane necessaria.

Aprilis die 19, 1788   Dum superiora mittendi occasionem expecto, allatae ad me sunt litterae Emae Dominationis Tuae, datae Romae die 8 Aug anni 1787 cum inclusis exemplaribus impressis Missae pro fidei propagatione, et dispensatione pro Capucino Apostata. Nequeo decere, utrum majore animi voluptate, an vero confusione audiverim, quae Emi Patres de me censuerint in Congregatione generali habita die 18 Junii. Quippe, ubi ex una parte mente recogito, quae in hisce provinciis pro divina gloria augenda fieri posse credo; ex altera autem, aestimo, quam parum effecerim, vel ipsarum rerum quas exsequi statueram, eo fere redigor, ut munus mihi commissum deponam in manus Sae Congregationis, et tantae sollicitudnis mole me penitus eximam. Fateor tamen multum me recreari approbatione Sae Congregationis, atq omni reverentia et grati animi sensu, et Tibi Eme. Congregationis Praefecte, caeterisq Emis Patribus summas refero gratias, quod me non pro meis meritis, sed pro singulari vestra humanitate tam honorifice commemoraveritis; qua ergo commemoratione non ad vanam aliquam ostentationem utar, sed tamquam stimulo ad excitandum torporem meum, et augendam in rebus divinis diligentiam.

Maxime jam confido legem brevi obtinendam qua Sacerdotibus Catholicis *in unum corpus coalescere* permittetur, ac communi nomine bona possidere; et cum quadam restrictione, alia acquirere, si quando, ut speramus frequentiores fuerint Sanctuarii Ministri.

Scholae aedificatio ante paucos dies incepta est; ut autem ad felicem exitum perducatur Divinae providentiae subsidia praecipue aut unice fidendum. Ab hoc incepto Religionis conservatio in his provinciis omnino pendere existimo; non enim aliter aut Seminario Ecclesiastico constitutendo locus erit, aut Pastores sufficienti numero provideri poterunt qui curam agant Fidelium et pro religionis extensione laborent.

Ab excellentissimo Sedis apostolicae in Gallia Nuncio, atq ex litteris ipsorum adolescentium, qui ad Urbanum Collegium designabantur, intellexi de felici illorum adventu in Galliam, eosq jam Romae feliciter degere confido.

De rebus Neo-Eboracensibus haec scribenda supersunt. Infaustus ille Sacerdos, et Schismatis auctor, aliquamdiu post meum discessum, paucis effrenatae conditionis hominibus stipatus, Ecclesiam retinuit, neque a Sacris celebrandis destitit. Brevi tamen et vi et legum auctoritate exturbatus est, et coram judice de seditione excitanda accusatus a duodecim hominibus qui adversus pacis perturbatores questionem instituunt. Mense Maio causam dicturus est. Interim cum suis asseclis domum quamdam privatam conduxit ubi diebus Dominicis concionari pergit, et Missam sacrilege celebrare. Haec sunt quidem perniciosissimi exempli, et severissimam Ecclesiasticae disciplinae animadversionem exigere videntur. Ab ulteriori tamen censura adversus ipsum et illius factionis homines hucusq abstinendum duxi, cujus consilii rationes intelliges, Cardinalis Eminentissime, ex iis quae superius conscripsi. Dum proximo autumno Novi Eboraci substiti, multa cum Excellentissimo Hispaniarum Legato de statu Religionis, illiusq per has provincias amplificatione tractavi; atq ille pro singulari sua sagacitate *Episcopi nomen et auctoritatem plurimum necessarium esse commemoravit* atq ultro in se suscepit transmissionem libelli supplices ad Sanctitatis suae pedes; quem his diebus illius carae committo, cujusq exemplar authenticum hisce literis includo.

Omni qua possum reverentia et devotione Tibi, Eme Cardinalis, et ceteris Congnis Emis Patribus se commendat   Emae Tuae   Humillimus et obsequentissimus   Joannes Carroll

TO FRANCIS BEESTON   Baltimore March 22d—1788—

Revd. Dr. Sir   Since Mr. Bussy's[1] departure, I have reconsidered with all the attention, which I could command, the subject of your letter, and all the events, which have passed, relatively to the German Seceders (if they may be called such) as far as I have been concerned in these transactions—; and I must still think, notwithstanding your complaint against me, that when a number of people, disclaiming all pretence to independance of spiritual jurisdiction, request my approbation to build a church, I cannot refuse a qualified approbation of a work which may terminate in the honour of God. That this idea arose from their disappointment in not gaining Mr. Heilbron, I believe; and that this motive may be uppermost in the minds of some of the most active persons, I likewise believe: but I cannot help entertaining a hope, that some of the party have better principles of conduct; and, whether in this I am deceived or not, I can console myself, & I know, that you will, with St. Paul–Phil. 1. 17–*"Some out of contention preach Christ, not sincerely; supposing that they raise affliction to us: but what then? so that every way, whether by occasion, or by truth, Christ be preached; in this also we rejoice, yea & will rejoice.* ["] Read the following verses, in which you will find encouragement, & the true principles, by which the Society always governed herself, & finally merited superior esteem, has followed her in her dissolution and even encreased, if possible. I considered farther, that it is very uncertain, how long the spirit of the Society will be kept alive, at least in this country. I am afraid, not much longer, than they live, who have been trained under its discipline: and into what hands will our religious establishments and possessions fall hereafter, if our proposed school & seminary should fail of success, which certainly is not beyond the bounds of probability? The expence of a Liège education, at the advanced price of £ 40 per ann: for young Ecclesiastics, renders it impracticable for many Americans to profit by that excellent institution; and even that (without a restoration of the Society) is liable to degeneracy. In case therefore of our own school failing, our houses & foundations will probably fall into the hands of such missionary adventurers, as we have lately seen. Supposing this the case of yr. house & church at Philada, will it not be a comfort to good Xitans to have another Church there; in one of which at least there may be some zeal, some regard for public edification: and this I meant to insinuate in my letter to the German petitioners, when I mentioned, that exertions might be the greater, where there was mutual example &c. Read all Ecclesiastical history; and you will find the best Bishops, a St. Ch. Borromeo, a St. Francis of Sales &c, sollicitous to multiply Religious establishments. I know very well, that the circumstances were somewhat different, and that, generally speaking, those undertakings were conducted with harmony; but even the history of the Society, & the passage of St. Paul above recited, furnish contrary examples. In opposition to these consideration, you will observe–1o–that I encourage a spirit of revolt & defiance of pastoral authority–2: that I foster a schism, or at least, an uncharitable division amongst the Congregn. of Philada.

To the first, I answer, that I have letters from Mr. Molyneux, which I supposed, he had communicated to you, wherein he describes the German petitioners as avowing deference to spiritual jurisdiction, and as having taken occasion indeed from my rejecting their application for Heilborn, not to originate, but to renew an idea, some of them formerly entertained of building themselves a Church. He requested me to answer their petition, if any should be sent, agreeably to his own communication with them, that their plan appeard to be founded on resentment; that they would do well to consult Mr Pellentz; that the attempt would probably end in ruining themselves & their children. He added, that Mr Farmer used sometimes to wish they had a Church on the North of the town. In their petition to me, they say, the ground alone in that part of Phila would have made a difference to them of £ 2000. With all this information I never conceived, that you could be hurt at my giving so guarded an approbation, as is contained in my letter. You should have been more explicit & expressly marked your entire disapprobation, not only of the motives of the attempt, but of the thing itself. When their petition came to hand, I consulted my good Companion, & Mr Ashton, who happened to be here; they both said, they did not see, how I could refuse people leave to build a church provided they did not arrogate the right of making the Pastor. If hereby I gave them a pretence for triumph over you, it was certainly from not being informed, that you had ever manifested any public opposition. Consider my situation: I knew indeed that some of the most respected Germans disliked the attempt; but that a majority of that body opposed it, was unknown to me till I heard it from you. Could I avoid supposing, that advantage would be taken of my refusal (if I had seen cause to give a refusal) to spread the flames of discontent; & to raise a clamour; that the Jesuits were determined, no churches should be created, but by their agency & direction. So far I have spoken in opposition to your charges. I now add—1o, that if you will communicate any particular; well ascertained, & notorious facts of Oillers,[2] or others, of a *schismatical* nature (i.d, tending to a rapture of communion with the Cath Church), or of evidently pernicious example, I will reconsider the sentiments of my short letter by Mr. Bussy, written in great hurry & confusion, as he can inform you of circumstances.[3] If it should be necessary to proceed to the censures of the Church, every matter must be conducted with regularity, and the previous monitions must be given. 2o that I shall write to the Germans, as p. copy; that their conduct in the affair of Incorporation betrays a spirit very dissonant from the expressions of their petition &c; and that if I can make any certain discovery of their being abetted by Messr Heilbron, I shall immediately take some vigorous steps with them. 3o that if you are quite assured, that so considerable a majority, as you represent of the Germans, are opposed to them, you ought to lose no time in getting their names to some instrument of writing (memorial or petition) expressive of their sentiments.

ADf   AAB

[1] Ministered in N.Y., Va., and N.J., but little else is known of James Bussy. Guilday misspells his name as Bushe.

[2] James Oellers, lay advocate of a German parish under Heilbron, and later head trustee of Holy Trinity, who defied Carroll.

[3] Letter not found. See 1788, "To Beeston."

TO ROBERT MOLYNEUX   Mar. 26, 1788

Not found.

TO GERMAN CONGREGATION OF PHILADELPHIA   White Marsh,
[March 31, 1788]

Gentlemen.   I should have written to you sooner, had I not been obliged
to leave Baltimore very suddenly on Easter Sunday. The Sentiments contained in your last Letters so expressive of regard for your pastors, & of a
desire to live in great Harmony with your Brethren did not prepare me for the
information, I have since received; & from which I learn, that some of you,
upon the ground of a most causeless apprehension, put in their council against
the passing of an act of Incorporation; & after that cause of uneasiness was
readily removed, the same persons continued, on frivolous pretenses, to
oppose a measure, which had been argued, & sollicited these several years.
Thus were divisions stirred up, at the very time, that assurances were sent to
me of the most perfect dispositions to cultivate peace, & that in consequence
of these assurances, I had given my conditional assent to your proposal of
building; more indeed for the preservation of charity, & in the hope of its
being hereafter conducive to the interests of Religion that for any conviction
of its being necessary at this time. I am sorry to add, that some of the
persons, most active in opposing the petition for incorporation, endeavour to
raise up a spirit of Discontent against their present pastors, for no other
reason, than that they received their education from those men, to whose zeal
this country in General, & your congregations in particular are solely &
intirely indebted for the examples & monuments of Religion which subsist
among them.[1] When I hear of such proceedings, my fears return upon me,
that motives suggested by disappointment, rather than piety & charity, lie at
the Bottom of some late proceedings. I am far from imputing these motives
to all. I doubt not, but many virtuous & wellmeaning Christians have been
misled by specious pretexts. The Authors of dissensions & sowers of discontent between Pastors, & their flock have been always punished by the church
with exemplary Severity; And I should be wanting in my duty, If I did not let
her censures fall on them, who should contumaciously persevere, after charitable admonitions, in such sinful practices, & so destructive of our Religion.
       I should never forgive myself; could I conceive that my conditional
approbation of your Building would be construed into an argument of my
approving likewise the measures, which some have lately pursued. God will
not bless undertakings begun with such a Spirit of Bitterness. Little will it
avail to raise temples to him, if through want of Charity & docility to your
Pastors, you destroy the Temple of the holy Ghost in your hearts.
       Mr. Beeston will have a copy of this,[2] that I may be informed by him,
whether I have overcharged any beyond their desserts.
       With the most Sollicitous regard for the preservation of christian charity,
Subordination, & your eternal Welfare, I have the honor to be Gentlemen,   Yr. most devoted Servant in Christ   J. Carroll.

LS   AAB   No addressee given on this MS, but there is one on a copy by Beeston that is wrongly dated Mar. 3; also ADf   AAB (9K1) with deletions.
   [1] Reference to Jesuit clergy, which carried on the ministry in Maryland and Pennsylvania. The present pastors were Molyneux and Graessl.
   [2] In AAB. This copy does not have this paragraph and has a few minor variations.

TO DON DIEGO DE GARDOQUI   [April 1788]

   The inclosed memorial—what it contains—Request his excy to represent the expedcy of the grant—Prospect of success in the new fed. Govt—

H[onored]. S[ir].   The Trustees of St Peter's Church[1] have lately represented to me the very wretched state of its temporalities, & that, after having made so great exertions to vindicate the honour of Religion, they find themselves unable to make any farther advances at present, for its support & relief. Experience has taught them, to regard your Excys destination to America by yr. most gracious sovgn—not only as an event calculated greatly to promote for the interests of his kingdoms; but likewise to preserve & favour the extension of divine worship. They are too sensible of the generosity and success of your former interposition in their favour to request it in the same manner as heretofore, by importuning your Excy with any supplications to be carried to the foot of the throne: but they earnestly pray you (& yr. goodness will allow me to unite my earnest prayer with theirs) to allow the Revd. Mr. O'Brien to proceed to Sp America & sollicit in behalf of St. Peter's Church charitable contributions from private persons. From the accounts sent me I have reason to think, that the preservation of the Church & divine service must depend on the success of this their applicaon to yr. Excy—

ADf   AAB
   [1] In New York.

TO PATRICK SMYTH   Rock Creek April 8—1788

Revd. Sir   I was favoured on the 5th inst. with yours of the 3d. America I find, has no charms to detain you from your friends. When I requested you to settle in Frederick, I flattered myself with having compleatly provided for that place & the congregations depending on it. Your departure makes a chasm which God alone knows how to fill. I am sorry that you had any cause of dissatisfaction with Mr. Framback. You know, that I apprehended it, & prepared you for such an event. His unhappy temper, &, I fear, an attachment to money, without one reasonable view of enjoying or employing it, always have, & always will make him an impracticable man. Indulgence & forbearance have had no effect upon him: and I am afraid of using with him violent measures tho I begin, more than ever, to perceive the necessity of removing him from Frederic. What I am afraid of is, that strong and authoritative proceedings may work on his passionate disposition, & precipitate him to farther irregularities, than he has hitherto committed. The manner, in which you condemn, the harshness of your expressions, in yr note to him, leaves me no room for censure, if even I had the inclination. I expect to be at Baltimore about the middle of next week. But as some unforeseen event may take place I inclose an attestation of the favourable reports, made to me of your zealous exertions, which will be sufficient evidence to your Bishop in Ireland, that your conduct in America has been the same as I doubt not, he always knew it in your own Country. I have letters from Mr. o Brien of March 24th & 30th, by which I find, that your Br. is in New York, & that Mr. o Brien had, thro' regard for you agreed for his boarding and lodging, till he hears from you. He says he has written to you on this subject. I was surprised to hear, that your reception at Messrs Darnalls[1] gave you so little encouragement to return thither. Mr. o Neill, your Countryman, a respectable Mercht at George-town; and their intimate friend informed me some months ago, that he met you there, & that all the family, as well as himself, were exceedingly pleased with you. This makes me suspect, that you mistook their, & particularly the elder Mr. Darnall's natural reserve & seeming coldness of behaviour for a mark of disgust, & contempt. On fuller acquaintance with them you would have been convinced, that you were mistaken. If by any accident it should be my fate not to have the pleasure of seeing you before your departure, I request you to accept of my sincere thanks for the services, you have rendered to Religion in our Country; and to be assured of my wishes for yr prosperous voyage, & happy return to yr friends. I am with great respect,   Revd. Sir   In D[omino]   J C

ADfS   AAB
[1] John Darnall of Frederick County.

TO THE TRUSTEES OF ST. PETER'S CHURCH, NEW YORK
R[ock] Creek, April 13–1788–

Gentlemen: This answer to your most obliging favr of March 26th, will reach you much later, than you might reasonably expect. I have told the Rev. M. o'brien the melancholy occasion of my absence from Baltimore, & of my coming for these three weeks to a country place remote from the post road. I owe you every acknowledgement for your generous & perservering exertions in a cause, in which the honour & welfare of Religion were so deeply concerned: your vexations were great; but the blessing, which God gave to your zeal by rescuing your Church out of the sacriligious hands, which kept possession of it,[1] cannot now fail of giving you comfort; it must be considered, as a token of his farther designs of mercy towards the Congregation of N. Y. I should not cooperate with your services to Religion, if I hesitated to employ all my interest with Mr. Gardoqui (tho' you estimate it much too highly) in the manner you wish. I shall write to him therefore with great earnestness solliciting his consent for Mr. o'Briens departure to the Havannas &c,[2] by all the most powerful inducements for it, which I can suggest to myself. The property and time, which you have devoted to the establishment and increase of our Religion in the place of your residence, require every return from me not only of commendation, but likewise of exertion to assist & relieve you: and Mr. Gardoqui's consent & recommendation if obtained will open the most ready & indeed the only source of relief, that I can think of.

I feel myself much honoured with your request to me of residing some months at N.Y.; tho it is not in my power to gratify you in it.

Were I to reside there during the whole of Mr. o'Brien's absence; the whole weight of detail of service and attendance on every call of that one Congn would absorb the time, which must be devoted to the general super-intendance over every part of our American Church. Last fall thro' my long detention at N.Y. I was under the necessity of leaving some Congregations unvisited and unsettled, who are now loudly calling upon me. The utmost, that I can promise (and that even will depend on certain contingencies) is, to pay you a short visit; & concert with you some arrangements for averting the evils, which your zeal so much dreads & wch must be averted in so con-spicuous important a Congregation. If I do not consent to your proposal, you may be assured, that I am withheld only by necessity & a sense of other duties.

ADf   AAB
[1] See "To Gardoqui," Apr. 1788.
[2] Reference to Nugent's schism.

TO DON DIEGO DE GARDOQUI   Apr. 19, 1788

Your Excellency will be pleased to recollect a conversation with which I was honoured during my residence in New York. It related to the expediency, and indeed the necessity of introducing Episcopal Government into the U. S., as no other would carry sufficient weight to restrain the turbulent Clergymen, whom views of independence would probably conduct into this Country. This opinion appeared to be strongly impressed on your Excellency, and is the natural result of your thorough penetration into the nature & necessary effects of our Republican governments. You noticed at the same time their great opposition to foreign jurisdiction, and the prejudices, which would certainly arise against our Religion, if the appointment of the Bishop were to rest in a distant Congregation of Cardinals; and if he were to act only as their Vicar, removeable at their pleasure: for which reasons, you thought, that the Bishop should be chosen by the American Clergy, approved by the Holy See for the preservation of unity in faith, & ordained to some title or see to be erected within these states with the ordinary powers annexed to the Episcopal character. You even were so obliging as to offer to support with yr. recommendation a petition addressed to his Holiness, for this purpose; & to transmit it to the Count of Florida Blanca, with a request to his Excellency to have it presented with the great additional interest of his recommendation.

In consequence of this generous offer, your Excellency will receive from one of my Brethren at Philada, the R. Mr. Beeston, the original petition to be sent to his Holiness,[1] & which, I doubt not you will be so kind as to forward in the manner, you were pleased to mention. I am so much concerned to preserve the favourable regards, with which you have hitherto honoured me that I must request you not to impute the petition to views of ambition. Such a passion will be poorly gratified by such a Bishoprick, as ours will be: Labour & sollicitude it will yield in plenty, & I trust those heavy burdens will never fall on my shoulders.

I received great satisfaction from yr. condescension to my request in favr. of the R. Mr. Connell, & I hope he has not since rendered himself unworthy of your kindness.

Our Convention for the ratification of the new Govt meets on the 21st inst. We have every reason to expect a happy issue, & that there will be, in favr of federalism, a majority of 64, against only 12 antifederalists—: but I cannot help regretting, that the exertions of the latter prevailed in one of the Counties, where some of my Relations expected to be chosen. Son & secretaries,[2]

ADf   AAB
[1] See Mar. 12, 1788.
[2] This is evidently a notation intended to remind Carroll that he should send good wishes to Gardoqui's son and members of the Spanish ministry staff.

TO VITALIANO BORROMEO[1]   April 19, 1788

For a long time, Very Eminent Cardinal, I have been hearing of your activity and ardent desire to spread the faith in these parts of America; of the singular benevolence with which you encompass those who labor in this vineyard of the Lord; how through your advice you assist in guiding an administration abounding in difficulty; and how you arouse the workers to strive for better things as becomes one who professes Christ. As to matters of religion—I cannot express in words my joy at learning that a prince of the name and house of Borromeo was not only advanced to the College of

Cardinals but made a member of the very Congregation whose wonderful solicitude for the Church in America is manifested in action. From the letter which I wrote to the eminent Prefect of the Congregation the state of things here will be made manifest, and what is still needed to bring about a school for the instruction of Catholic youth. And it will also reveal that my efforts and those of the other priests for the spread of religion have effected very little of a durable or substantial character.

Continuation to Cardinal Borromeo, April 29th 1788.

I have seized upon this occasion for writing, Most Eminent Cardinal, because Reverend Mr. Thorpe, who I understand is known to you, in his letters to me always lauds your character, your zeal and your kind regard for us who are fighting in this very distant region, and, if I may so speak, in this sink of all errors.

Most Eminent Cardinal I have presumed to include in this letter another for the father mentioned above which I greatly desire should reach him safely; and I did not think it could be done readily save by entrusting it to your benevolence.[2]

All the ministers of the sanctuary who are here look to you and we feel that you are bound to us through your zeal for spreading divine worship. In turn we are bound to you by ties of a deep sense of gratitude, of respect for your outstanding virtue, of regard for your noble family, and respect for the memory of Cardinal Borromeo. And I above all profess my devotion of mind and heart.   Most Eminent Cardinal   The most obedient servant of your Eminence and Lordship   J.C.

ADf   AAB

[1] Cardinal Borromeo was now a member of the Congregation of the Propagation of the Faith.

[2] An obscure paragraph of a few sentences is deleted from this point.

De Vestra Excellentia Cardli Borromeo   Die 19 Aprilis   Jam dudum Eminentissime Cardinali ad me relatum est de tua opera et ardenti studio fidem in his Americanis provinciis amplificandi simul de singulari charactere et humanitate qua ope in hac Domini vinea laborantes adeo complecteris, et omni esse ope in hac difficili administratione consilliis tuis dirigere, cura et commemoratione ad meliora incitare tamquam Christi professorem invocat. Religio: nec dicere possum, qua laetitia receperim Principem nominis et gentis Borromeae non solum in Cardinalium Collegio, sed in illa Congregatione sedem tenere, cujus pro Americana Ecclesia mira sollicitudo exercetur. Ex litteris, quas Eminentissimo sacrae illius Congregationis Praefecto conscripsi, intelligi poterit, quo statu res nostrae sint, quidquid adhuc desiderari videatur ad perfectionem regiminis Ecclesiastici formam, scholaeque constructionem pro Christiana juventutis instructione; quae nostri reliqui mei conatus pro Religionis incremento nihil stabile ac duraturum efficient.

(Continuation to Cardinal Borromeo, April 19, 1788.)

Hac scribendi, Eminentissime Cardinali, inde animum sumpsi quod Reverendus Dominus Thorpe, quem tibi notum esse intelligo, suis ad me literis nunquam non praedicat characterem tuam, tuum zelum atque animi affectum ergo nos in his dissitis provinciis, atque in hac, ut ita dicam, omnium errorum sentina pro fide dimicantes.

Ausus sum, Eminentissime Cardinale, hisce literis alias includere pro dicto Reverendo Domino quas multum cupio ad ipsum salvas pervenire, nec alia ratione id ita commode fieri posse existimavi, quam tuae benevolentiae illas commundando.

Quotquot hic sumus Sanctuarii ministri ad te respicimus, Eminentissime Cardinale, teque nobis devinctum aestimamus, studio tuo divini cultus ampliandi; nosque tibi vicissim intimo grati animi sensu, ac summa virtutum tuarum, tuae nobilissimae familiae et pro Domini Cardinalis memoria, veneratione. Atque ego prae caeteris omni mentis et cordis devotione ita de me profiteor.   Princeps Eminintissime,   Eminentiae Dominationis Tuae servus obsequentissimus   J.C.

TO LEONARDO ANTONELLI   April 19, 1788

While I look forward to an occasion of sending more distinguished things, letters of Your Eminent Lordship have been sent to me, given at Rome on the 8th day of August, in the year 1787, with the enclosed embossed copies of a Mass for the Propagation of the Faith, and the dispensation for the apostate Capuchin.[1] I am unable to say whether with greater pleasure of mind, or indeed confusion, I have heard what the Eminent Father decided about me in the General Congregation convened on June 18. As a matter of fact, when, on the one hand, I deliberate on that understanding about what I believe can happen in these provinces for the increase of divine glory; however, on the other hand, [when] I judge how little I have accomplished, even of those things which I have resolved to accomplish; I am practically brought to such a point, that I will set aside the office entrusted to me into the hands of the Sacred Congregation, and I will free myself of so great a care, poorly acquired by me through experience. I confess nonetheless that I am greatly refreshed by the approval of the Sacred Congregation, and by every reverence and feeling of a satisfied spirit, and to you of the Eminent Congregation. Certainly, I express to the other Eminent Fathers all thanks, because you have mentioned me in such an honorable way, not for my merits, but because of your singular humanity: therefore, I employ this mention, not for some vain display, but as a stimulus to arousing my torpor [*sic*], and for increasing in diligence for divine things.

Above all, I now trust that a law will shortly be obtained by which it will be permitted to Catholic priests *to gather together in one body,* and to possess their goods in a common name; and, with some restriction, to acquire other goods, if at any time we hope that the Ministers of the Sanctuary will be more numerous.

The *construction of a school* was begun a few days ago; however, that it may reach a happy conclusion is to be trusted principally or rather entirely, to the help of Divine providence. From this beginning, I think the preservation of Religion in these states depends entirely: for otherwise there will neither be a place for establishing an ecclesiastical seminary nor can pastors be provided in [*illeg.*] numbers to take care of the Faithful and to labor for the extension of Religion.

From the most excellent Nuncio of the Apostolic See[3] in France and from the letters of the young men themselves, who were marked out for the Urban College, I learned of their safe arrival in France, and I trust that even now they are living contentedly at Rome.

About affairs in New York, these things remain to be put in writing. Unfortunately, that Priest[4] and author of schism, for a short time after my withdrawal, was surrounded by a few men of malevolent condition, held the Church, and did not desist from celebrating the sacred rites. Nevertheless, in a short time, he was called to account both by force and by the authority of the laws, and in the presence of a judge he was accused of having stirred up a sedition by twelve men, who initiated a proceeding against disturbers of the peace. In the month of May, the case will be decided. In the meantime, with his adherents, he serves at a certain private home, where he undertakes to preach on Sundays, and to celebrate Mass sacrilegiously. These are indeed the most pernicious examples and demand the most serious attention of ecclesiastical discipline. You will understand, however, Eminent Cardinal, from those things which I have written above, the reasons taken for this counsel, of abstaining from further censure against him and that faction of men up to this time. When I came in the Autumn, I tarried in New York, I treated many things in detail with respect to Religion throughout the Provinces with the most excellent Secretary of the Spaniards,[5] and he, in his singular wisdom, mentioned that the name of a Bishop and his authority was most necessary. Spontaneously, he undertook by himself a transmission of a petition to the feet of His Holiness; which in these days, I commit to his care, and an authentic copy of which I include with these letters.

May it be permitted with all grace, and reverence and devotion to You, Eminent Cardinal and the other most Eminent Fathers he commends himself to your Eminence the humble and dutiful servant John Carroll

Adf. AAB   Addressee's name not given on MS, but clear from contents and conclusion.
[1] The Heilbrons were the only Capuchins arriving in the country this year. By "apostate" Carroll probably meant a case of unauthorized departure from the jurisdiction of a local superior in Europe.
[2] Georgetown College.

³ Antoine Dugnani.
⁴ In Oct. of 1787 Carroll went to New York and suspended Andrew Nugent, who is referred to here.

Dum superiora mittendi occasionem expecto, allatae ad me sunt litterae Emae Dominationis Tuae, datae Romae die 8 Aug. anni 1787 cum inclusis exemplaribus impressis Missae pro fidei propagatione, & dispensatione pro Capucino apostata. Nequeo dicere, utrum majore animi voluptate, an vero confusione audiverim, quae Emi Patres de me censuerint in Congregatione generali habita die 18 Junii. Quippe ubi ex una parte, illa mente recogito, quae in hisce provinciis pro Divina gloria augenda fieri posse credo; ex altera autem, aestimo, quam parum effecerim, vel ipsarum rerum quas exequi statueram; eo fere redigor, ut munus mihi commissum deponam in manus Sae Congregationis, & tantae sollicitudinis male me penittu eximam. Fateor tamen multum me recreari approbatione Sae Congregationis atq omni reverentia & grati animi sensu, & Tibi Eme Congregationis. Praefecte, caeterisq Emis Patribus summas refero gratias, quod me non pro meis meritis, sed pro singulari vestra humanitate tam honorifice commemoraveritis: qua ergo commemoratione non ad vanam aliquam ostentationem utar, sed tanquam stimulo ad excitandum torporem meum, & augendam in rebus Divinis diligentiam.

Maxime jam confido legem brevi obtinendam esse qua Sacerdotibus Catholicis *in unum corpus coalescere* permittetur, ac communi nomine bona possidere; & cum quadam restrictione, alia acquirere, si quando speramus frequentiores fuerint Sanctuarii Ministri.

Scholae aedificatio ante paucas dies incepta est; ut autem ad felicem exitum perducatur, Divinae providentiae subsidio praecipue aut unice fidendum est. Ab hoc incepto Religionis conservationem in his provinciis omnino pendere existimo; neque enim aliter aut Seminario Ecclesiastico constituendo locus erit, aut Pastores sufficienti numero provideri poterunt qui curam agant Fidelium, & pro Religionis extensione laborant.

Ab excellentissimo Sedis Apostolicae in Gallia Nuncio atq ex litteris ipsorum adolescentium ad Urbanum Collegium designabantur, intellexi de felici illorum adventu in Galliam, eosq jam Romae feliciter gere confido.

De rebus Neo-Eboracensibus haec scribenda supersunt. Infaustus ille Sacerdos & Schismatis auctor, aliquamdiu post meum discessum paucis desperatae conditionis hominibus stipatus, Ecclesiae tenuit, neq, a sacris celebrandis destitit. Brevi tamen & vi & legum auctoritate exturbatus est, & coram judi[cem?] de seditione excitanda accusatus a duodecim hominibus, qui adversus pacis pertubatores quaestionem instituunt. Mense Maio causam dicturum est. Interim cum suis asseclis, domum quamdam privatam conduxit, ubi diebus Dominicis concionari pergit, & Missam sacrilege celebrare. Haec sunt quidem perniciossimi exempli & severissimam Ecclesiasticae disciplinae animadversionem exigere aidentur. Ab ulteriori tamen censura adversus ipsum & illius factionis homines hucusq abstinendum duceri cujus consilii rationes intelliges, Cardinalis Eminentissime, ex iis quae superius conscripsi. Dum proximo Autumno Novi Eboraci substiti, multa cum Excellentissimo Hispaniarum Legato de Statu Religionis, illiusq per has provincias amplificatione tractavi; atq. ille pro singulari sua sagacitate *Episcopi nomen & auctoritatem plurimum necessariam esse commemoravit* atq. ultro in se suscepit transmissionem libelli supplicis ad Sanctitatis suae pedes; quem his diebus illius curae committo, cujusq. exemplar authenicum hisce litteris includo.

Omnia qua passum, reverentia et devotione Tibi, Eme Cardinalis & caeteris Emis Patribus se commendat Emae Tuae Humillimus & obseq suus Servus   Joannes Carroll

TO ANTOINE DUGNANI
Baltimore, Maryland
April 20, 1788

My Lord   I had the honor of notifying Your Excellency by my letter of March 5th of this year that I would take the liberty of addressing to you my dispatches for Rome. They are destined for their Eminences, the Cardinal Prefect of the Congregation of Propaganda,[1] and Cardinal Borromeo. The scandal which has broken out in New York, of which I notified Your Excellency in my last letter, still exists because it is impossible to use the means made to uphold spiritual censures. However there is reason to hope that next month will put an end to the sacrilegious entreprises of the unhappy apostate, who has done so much harm to Catholicism in New York, that we will not know how to undo it for many years.

I have the honor to be with devotion and most profound respect, My Lord

ADf   AAB
[1] Cardinal Antonelli.

De Baltimore en Mariland le 20 d'Avril, 1788   Mgr le Nonce—   J'ai eu l'honneur de prevenir V. Exc. par ma lettre du 5 de Mars de cette année, que je prendrois la liberté d'addresser à elle mes depeches pour Rome. Elles sont destinées pour leurs Eminences, le Cardinal Prefet de la Congn. de la Propagande, & le Cardl. Borromeo. Le scandale, qui a eclaté à la Nouvelle York, dont j'ai prevenu V. Ex. dans ma derniere lettre, subsiste toujours parce qui'içi il est impossible d'employer les voyes de fait pour soutenir les censures spirituelles. Cependant il y a lieu d'esperer, que le mois prochain mettra fin aux entreprises sacrileges du malheureux apostat, qui a fait un tort au Catholiçisme à la N.Y., qu'on ne saura reparer pendant plusieurs années. — J'ai l'honneur d'etre avec le devouement et le respect le plus profond, Mgr

TO ADAM PREMIR AND HY. HORN[1]
Baltimore, Ap. 23d. 1788

Gentlemen.   On returning to Baltimore, a few days ago, I was hond. with your letter of the 12th inst. From its contents, I find that tho' you consulted Mr. Pellentz, yet you paid no deference to his opinion, and are determined to proceed in your undertaking. Perhaps it would have been more respectful to his age & merits, to have expressed your absolute determination, before you referred yourselves to him, & induced him to take such a journey. Excuse me for saying that I should think better of your proceedings, if your conduct in the business of Incorporation did not suggest a doubt to my mind. I know nothing of the naming of the Trustees mentioned in the bill, than what you have been pleased to tell me. But I clearly see in the bill itself a provision for a free annual election. Is there any likelihood of the Trustees having any management for these twelve months whc. can endanger yr. . . . Does not this sufficiently secure rights and privileges? admitting even that there had been some irregularity in the first appointment, as it stands in the bill; was it worth your while, or could it be attended with one good effect, for you to put in a counter petition, & thus inform the public that you are a dissatisfied & divided people? Can it tend in the smallest degree to the benefit of Religion, or the glory of God, to exasperate each other more & more & widen that breach already made? Supposing that to humour you, a new election should be agreed to: & some of the Trustees changed; is the obtaining of this pitiful point a compensation, or will it atone for the evils, springing from your opposition? Bring then the matter home to your consciences, & see if yr. late conduct, does not savour more of sourness and animosity, than of the meekness & charity of Christ. Will not this induce you to withdraw your opposition, & use your influence to reconcile your less informed Brethren. You used some expressions in your letter, which surprised & alarmed me. You say that Church censures are *odious* & *obsolete:* This is most irreverent language, & even worse, for it is inconsistent with Catholic doctrine; the power of censuring being transmitted from Xt to his apostles & th[ei]r. suc[cessors]. can never be obsolete, & never odious; it is a power ordained for the salvation of souls, it was so used by St. Paul, & all good pastors; such it has been always esteemed by the Church; & is expressly declared by the Council of Trent to be the sinew of Ecclesiastical discipline. Your language has been unadvisably taken from the enemies of our faith & is just the same as is used every day by them: I expect a retraction of it, as a necessary evidence of your Catholic sentiments, & veneration for authority derived from Xt, & essential to the govt. of his Church. My earnest prayers and hope is, that your intended Church (if built), may be productive of great service to Religion: but I have many reasons to decline going to Philada at present, if I can avoid it; & therefore you will excuse my not accepting your invitation; especially while you refuse to withdraw your opposition to the bill of Incor[por]a[ti]on?

ADf   AAB

[1] Evidently a member of the committee led by Premir in March, which now had a board of trustees for the future Holy Trinity Church.

TO FILIPPO OR ANTONIO FILLICHI [May 1-9, 1788]

Not found. See May, 10, 1788.

TO JEAN FRANÇOIS HUBERT[1] Baltimore May 5, 1788

My Lord   I find myself compelled to ask your Lordship for some light upon a rather delicate matter, and this necessity at the same time gives me an opportunity to assure you of the esteem I entertain for your character and episcopal virtues.

Encouraged by the favorable recommendations with which Mr. Huet de la Valinière was supplied by his ecclesiastical superiors in Canada, I gladly accepted his offer to go to the Illinois, and appointed him my vicar general there. Since he left, I have received letters written by another priest, Mr. Gibeau of Post Vincennes, in which he complains bitterly of the tyrannical conduct of the new vicar general, and informs me that he himself had formerly been vicar general for the Bishop of Quebec. It is about this matter, my Lord, that I wish to be informed; and about reports which have been made previously relative to the conduct of Mr. Gibeau, whom they have painted to me as very unsavory in his conduct. I venture to beg you, my Lord, to tell me what you know of the aforementioned, since it concerns the interests of Religion, and perhaps the rendering of justice to a priest whom I have wronged on the basis of false reports.

I learned, some months ago, that your Lordship disapproved of me for interfering in the ecclesiastical government of the country of the Illinois, the Wabashes, &c. I did so because I believed it was included within my jurisdiction, and I had not the slightest idea that your Lordship was concerned with these countries since they were ceded to the United States. No motive of ambition was involved; and if you are willing to provide for the spiritual needs of these poor Christians, you will relieve me of a great encumbrance, & rid my conscience of a burden which weighs heavily upon it. In such an event, my only remaining anxiety would be that the United States might not perhaps wish to allow for long the exercise of power even of a spiritual nature by a British subject.[2]

I have the honor of being with most respectful devotion to your Lordship, Monsignor,   The very humble & obedient servant   J. Carroll, Ecclesiastical Superior in the United States Letters sent by way of New York reach me safely.

ADf   AAB;   ALS   AAQ   The ALS lacks last portion of second paragraph.

[1] A missionary to the Huron, he became a coadjutor in 1786, and then succeeded Briand as Bishop of Quebec.

[2] The following conclusion is taken from the ALS, there being none in the ADf.

Mgr   La necessité, dans laquelle je me trouve, de demander à V. Grandeur
des eclaircissemens sur une matiere assez delicate me procure en même tems
l'honneur de temoigner à Elle la véneration, dont je suis pénetré pour son
caractere et ses vertus Episcopales.

Encouragé par les attestations favorables, dont Monsr. Huet de la Valinière
etoit muni de la part de ses superieurs eccles. de Canada, j'ai reçu de bon gré
ses offres pour aller chez les Illinois, et l'y ai nommé mon Vicaire General.

Dupuis son depart j'ai reçu des lettres écrites par un autre prêtre, Monsr.
Gibeau du Poste St. Vincent dans lesquelles il se plaint amèrement de la
conduite tyrannique du nouveau Vicaire Genl., & m'annonce que lui même a
eté çi-devant le Grand Vicaire de Monsgr de Quebec. Voila, Monsgr, sur quoi
je voudrois être instruit; et sur des rapports qui ont eté faits çi-devant
relativement à la conduite de Mr. Gibeau, qu'on m'a depeint comme très
déréglé dans sa conduite. J'ose vous prier, Monsr., de me communiquer çe que
vous pourrez savoir la dessus, puisqu'il s'agit des interets de la Religion, et
peutêtre de rendre justice à un prêtre à qui j'aurois fait tort sur un faux
exposé.

J'ai appris, depuis quelques mois, que V. Gran. trouvoit mal à moi de
m'ingerer dans le gouvernement ecclesiastique du pays des Illinois, Ouabaches,
&c. J'ai le fait, parce que je les croyois compris dans ma jurisdiction, et que je
n'avois pas la moindre idée, que V. G. s'en melât depuis que ces contrées
étoient cedés aux Et. Unis. Aucun motif d'ambition n'y a çoncouru; et si elle
veut bien pourvoir aux besoins spirituels de ces pauvre Xtiens, elle me tirera
d'un grand embarras, & dechargera ma conscience d'un fardeau qui lui pese
extremement. En çe cas, la seule inquietude qui me resteroit, seroit que les
Etats Unis ne voudroient pas peutêtre souffrir longtems l'exercice du pouvoir
meme spirituel d'un sujet Britannique.

TO PETER GIBAULT   Baltimore, May 5, 1788

I received three months ago the letter with which you favored me from
Post St. Vincent, without date other than the year 1788. It was accompanied,
however, by a certificate of last September 29. I knew only a short time
before the departure of Mr. Huet de la Valiniere for the Illinois, that there
was any other ecclesiastic in all your districts, except Mr. de St. Pierre: and
still less did I have information that he had been there exercising the powers
of Grand Vicar, named for that purpose by the Bishop of Quebec.[1] I take
advantage of this first occasion to write you by General Varnum,[2] who has
the kindness of burdening himself with this reply.

I very much fear I have done you harm, although without design, in
depriving you of your authority; and [hope] you can be convinced, sir, that I
am quite disposed to render justice to your Apostolic work during the twenty
years of your work among the savages and the scattered Christians. I wait for
this purpose some explanations from Canada; and I write on this occasion to

Mr. Huet to suspend all power of authority in your regard until I order otherwise.[3] His conduct, which gives you pain, surprises me so much the more, after the particular letters from Canada and the certificate from the Vicar General at Montreal, speaking a great deal in his favor.

I wait for the adoption of the new system of government formed at Philadelphia last summer, in order to direct the prayer to substitute for the *God Save the King* etc., and the exact wording for the United States.

The feasts and fast days presently observed here, and which should be observed in your districts, are as below. The unworthy Ecclesiastical Superior who commends himself to your prayers, calls himself John, I have the honor to be, etc.—

Feasts[4] January—Day[:] 1. The Circumcision 6. The Epiphany March 25 The annunciation of the Holy Virgin August 15 The assumption of the Virgin November 1 All Saints December 25 Christmas

Movable feasts Easter Monday The ascension of Our Savior The Monday of Pentecost Corpus Christi The Wednesdays & Saturdays of the year (expect the Saturdays between Christmas and the Purification of the Holy Virgin) & the rogation days For Lent: you will regulate it as you have done before for the Bishop of Quebec.

The fast days besides Lent and the four seasons—are,[:] The eve of Pentecost[;] of Sts. Peter & Paul[;] of the Assumption[;] of All Saints[;] the Wednesdays & Fridays of Advent[;] Christmas Eve

ADfS   AAB

[1] Carroll seems to have understood that Gibault had vicar powers from Quebec prior to this time. See to Hubert, May 5, 1788.

[2] James Varnum, from Rhode Island, member of the Congress under the Confederation, and active in western land development.

[3] Not found.

[4] The French version of the remainder of the letter will not be given. The following covered much more space in the original, which arranged the topics schematically.

Monsr. Gibeau, Prêtre, au poste St. Vincent   Baltimore ce 5 Mai 1788—

j'ai reçu il y a trois mois, la lettre dont vous m'avez honnoré du poste St. Vincent, sans autre date que de l'an 1788. Elle etoit cependant accompagnée d'un certificat du 29 de Septembre passé. Je n'ai sçu que peu de tems avant le depart de Monsr. Huet de le Valinière pour les Illinois, qu'il y eut d'autre Ecclesiastique dans tous vos cantons, excepté Monsr. de St. Pierre: et encore moins avoir je connaissance, qu'il y en eut un, en exercise des pouvoirs de Grand Vicaire, nommé à cet effet pas l'Eveque de Quebec. Je profite de cette premiere occasion de vous ecrire par Monsr. le General Varnum, qui a la bonté de se charger de cette reponse. Je crains beaucoup vous avoir fait tout en vous destituant, quoique sans dessein, de votre autorité; et vous pouvez être persuadé, Monsieur, que je suis très disposé à rendre justice à vos travaux Apostoliques pendant les vingt années de votre residence parmi les Sauvages, & les Chrétiens dispersés.

J'attends à cet effet quelques eclaircissements de Canada; et j'ecris à cette occasion à Monsr. Huet de suspendre tout acte d'autorité à votre egard, j'usqu' a çe que j'ordonne autrement. Sa conduite, telle que vous la peignez, me surprend d'autant plus, que des lettres particulieres du Canada, et le certificat de Monsr. le Vicaire general à Montreal, en disoient beaucoup de bien.

J'attends l'adoption du nouveau système de Gouvernement formé à Philadelphia l'eté passé, pour regler l'oraison à substituer au Domine salvum &c, & la formule pour les Etats Unis.

Les fêtes et jeunents s'observent presentement içi, & qui doivent être observées dans vos cantons, sont comme çidessous. L'indigne Superieur Ecclesiastique, qui se recommande à vos prieres, s'appele Jean. J'ai l'honneur d'être &c—

TO JAMES WHITE[1]   Balt. May 5—1788

Sr   Yr. letter to Mr. Molyneux of March 26—was sent to me abt. a week ago, and I was requested to give you an answer. After returning you my very sincere thanks for your attention, in the present instance to the interests of Religion, and to that body of wch. most of our American Brethren of the Clergy belonged, I take the liberty to inform you that the parochial Clergy appear to have a natural right of succession to & are the natural representation of the holders of property, which was formerly granted to the Society for parochial purposes; and which was in fact the means of supporting those who in the western Country exercised the functions of religion. I depend therefore greatly on the continuance of your attention to this object. As long as the lands in question can be appropriated to their original destination (the maintenance of the ministers of Religion) so long does it appear reasonable, they should be reserved for that purpose. There is now living at Post S. Vincent[2] a Clergyman of our Church;[3] and if God pleases to bless our designs, it shall be regularly & more fully supplied. There are likewise lands and Clergymen at the Kaskaskias and Kaokias,[4] 20 ligues distant. Your watchfulness will, I hope, be likewise extended to those places. If you think it necessary for me to take any farther steps, as Superior of the Roman Cath. Clergy, by petition or informaon to Congress, I shall be govd. by your advice. I have the honr &c—

P.S. Maryland & Pennsylvania afford a precedent in this case. The dissolution of the Society no wise affected the rights of the R. Cath. Clergy to the lands or estates formerly possessed by them for their maintenance. Their successors to the same Religious functions enjoy them now in the same manner. The late changes introduced into the forms and creeds of the Ch. of England leave the Episcopalians in America still in possession of the same property.

ADf   AAB

[1] A North Carolinian, at this time at the site of Knoxville, Tenn. He was a North Carolina assemblyman when the Constitution was ratified in 1789 and later served in the Tennessee Assembly.
[2] Vincennes, Ind.
[3] Pierre Huet de la Valiniere.
[4] Kaskaskia and Cahokia, Ill.

TO WILLIAM O'BRIEN

Baltimore May 10–1788–

Revd Dear Sir   Immediately after receiving your favour of the 30th April, I wrote to Mr Felicchi,[1] & hope my letter will reach him before his departure. The loss of so amiable an acquaintance must be very painful to you. I mentioned to him something concerning our views for an Episcopal government: tho' I own, that I never enter on this subject without reluctance; & for two reasons. One is, that if that government is introduced into our Ecclesiastical police [policy] in America, I have some reason to apprehend, that I may be thought of for it, and it is without affectation, or pretended shew of humility that I declare of you, and every where else, a dread of being ever invested with such an employment. Another reason is, that they, who know not my sincere sentiments, may attribute any activity, they discover in me for the establishment of Episcopacy, to an ambition of having a mitre placed on my head. This is the reason why I have taken so little notice of your many generous & too partial recommendations both of me & to me on that subject. However, I shall now open myself more fully to you. About a year & half ago, a meeting was held of the Clergy of Maryland & Pennsylva. on their temporal concerns; and conversation devolving on the most effectual means of promoting the welfare of Religion it was agreed on to attempt the establishment of a School & seminary for the general education of Catholic youths, & the forming of Ecclesiastics to the ministry of Religion: and since the Ecclesiastics would want ordination, the subject of Episcopacy was brought forward, & it was determined to sollicit it. Two other Gentlemen were appointed besides myself to transact this business, & they, as it happens to easy people like myself, devolved the whole trouble of framing memorials, petitions &c on me. Being very unwilling to engage in this last affair, I delayed it, till Nugents misconduct convinced me, it was no longer safe to do so: and a prospect having opened itself of procuring a Bishop, eligible by the officiating Clergymen in America, instead of being appointed; by a foreign tribunal (which would shock the political prejudices of this Country) the memorial for that purpose is now gone to his Holiness. This is the business, which, you may remember, I said to you, I should have to communicate; but which was afterwards put out of my mind by the unhappy events, which followed.

I have had no answer from Mr Gardoqui; but presume he has made his intentions known to you or to the Trustees. If his answer be favourable, I shall feel myself happy in your having behind you a character so willing and so capable of rendering service, as you describe the French Chaplain;[2] to whom you will be so obliging as to present my compliments & thanks for his services amongst his Countrymen. There are now some affairs to be transacted here, which will not admit of my presence on any account; so that it will be impossible to visit N. Y. so soon, as you wish and expect. And indeed I cannot do it immediately, for another reason without putting myself under obligation to other persons, which I wish to avoid. Your embarassements distress me & the more so, as it is entirely out of my power to relieve them. Mr Smith, who left us about eight days ago, left ten dollars with Mr Sewall for his Brs expences, of which he informed you. That Gentleman's insincere & dark manouvres have come to light since his departure. I gave you notice before that some circumstances made me fear he was a prey to suspicion. He wrote me letters late in March & frequently before, acknowledging in the most forcible expressions his grateful sense of the utmost generosity and tender regard, with wch. he had been treated every since coming into America: he was with Mr Sewall & self near four weeks waiting for a passage to Dublin, & no attention I am sure was wanting to him. On hearing accidentally some conversation in town (wch; I am now convinced, was occasioned by him) I brought the Gentleman, who retailed the conversation, to my house, & to Mr Smyth: told Mr Smyth, what that Gentleman & another had said of Smyth's being compelled, by bad usage, to quit America; & desired him as an honest man to speak the sentiments of his heart before them. Upon wch. Smyth repeated, what he had often said to me before that he was shocked, that such reports should be spread; that it was impossible he could have been treated with more openness or generosity, & enumerated many instances to prove it. Such was his language whenever I called on him. Will you believe after this, that this dark man, whose character shall follow him to Ireland, left a letter behind him full of the most groundless insinuations, & betraying a heart so treacherous, that I should be afraid of ever placing myself in his power; and that after saying to every person, with whom he conversed, that he came not to America to stay in it, but only to reclaim his Br[other]; he has now the effrontery to say, that he leaves it, because he finds, that every priest, who has not been a *Regular*[3] is considered as an Intruder. I have done and shall do what I can to promote subscriptions. & am R. D. Sir   Yrs. most sincerely   J. C.

Capn. White carries Valrechhi, 3 vol. If you go to New Spain, be pleased to send them back. My respects to Yr Sister &c. Forward by a conveyance the letter to the Bp of Quebec.

ALS   AAB
[1] Either Filippo, American Consul, or Antonio Fillichi, merchant in Leghorn, Italy. One of the brothers offered his good offices for Carroll and the American Church upon his return. Letter not found.

[2] Seraphim Bandol has been ten years in America.

[3] Jesuits were considered "Clerks Regular," or men in religious orders with members exercising the priesthood.

TO CHARLES PLOWDEN   Rock Creek May 26–1788

Dear Sir   I have duly received your favour of March 2d, but not the preceding letter, which you mention as having written in answer to the few lines from N. York.[1] I have since informed you of the issue of that unhappy affair. Your account of the innovating spirit of many English, both Clergy and Laity, is an alarming symptom of the propagation of indocility, and independance on all authority, however well established. God grant, we may not experience it here! not indeed amongst our own Brethren, nor, I believe, amongst our native R. Catholics: but some specimens of it have appeared amongst the Irish & Germans. Some of the latter, at Philada., have asserted a claim similar to that, which, you say, is countenanced by Mr Berington at Bristol, of nominating their own Pastors. I cannot express, how fatal such a right, if made good, would prove to Religion in this Country. You and our friends are alarmed at the introduction, or rather, at the arrival of Irish priests & Fryars into our Country; but, my Dr. Sir, can I reject them if well recommended, and exclude numberless Xtians from every opportunity of frequenting the Sacraments? I know from my own little experience that they are a poor resource, not for want of knowledge (for they have proved, in general, men of much information), but for want of virtue, temper, & disinterestedness. As to their being sent with ambitious views, it may be so: but their prospects, when once arrived, will quickly deaden their ambition.

I have written very fully to Mr Thorpe, & very frequently, so that I hope, he will have no reason to regret the want of information from America.[2] He has now a negociation on hand, which will call forth all his talents. It concerns, what I have mentioned to you already, the introduction of Episcopal government. I have the happiness to inform you, that our Academy is begun, and we have some hopes of seeing it covered in this year. Do not forget your promise of some assistance. Mr Francis Neale will be a favourable opportunity. But when the academy is compleated, that is, the house, what shall we do for a general Director or President of it? Liege absorbs all those, who would be willing to lend their assistance; & others have probably settled themselves for life. Do look out for some Gentleman of abilities & judgment, & inspire into him a desire of rendering this eminent service. As to Masters, we can do for a little time, with some to be collected in the Country: and our own Institution will, in time, supply them.

I was very sorry to hear of the death of our very worthy Mr Wheble, and of the bad health of Messrs Angier & Thomson, our worthy fellow prisoners:

and I perfectly agree with you that there are not in England two more respectable priests. Since my last to you we have had the misfortune of losing, March 24th, our worthy Mr. Jn. Lewis. Yr. friend Molyneux who was quite tired of Philada.; replaces him at Bohemia (residentia St. Xaverii) where he may indulge his love of ease: he is the same man, you knew him, with this different that time & experience have made him a valuable Counsellor. I wish I could always have him with me. He has left at Philada, Messrs Beeston and Graesl,[3] both rather too young, without an older head to superintend at that place; but necessity has no law. I am sorry to see no more done yet in Russia. The Empress is growing in years, &, we are told, is intemperate in drink: if the great business is delayed too long by the war, she may lose that warm eagerness, with which she seemed inspired some time ago. I wish to hear more of the wonderful woman Donna Maria Antonia,[4] whom you slightly mention. Female missioners are not much to my taste! but I hope, I shall not be blind to the wonderful works of God, if he chuses to make use of such instruments for the salvation of the world. When you write to yr. Br. Robt., remember me to him most affectionately as well as to Frank tho I was not pleased with yr last [torn] of him. My good Mother presents her respects. You will not fail in mine to Mr Weld & his Lady, nor to Messrs Stanley & Clinton. How came the latter to renounce London so entirely and confine himself to a country retreat? I thought the devout Ladies would never suffer it. I am with great affection   Dr. Sir,   Yr. ever devoted servt.   J. Carroll

I expect Mr Thayer very soon. As to his nuns, I hope he will let that alone till he has made some progress in Boston. Mr Chs. Neale of Antwerp is eager to introduce Teresians. I wish rather for Ursulines. When you write by the packet, direct to me at Baltimore where I reside much of my time.

ALS   St
  [1] See Nov. 2, 1787.
  [2] Few of these letters have been located.
  [3] Francis Beeston, S.J., age 37 and Lawrence Graessl, S.J., age 35.
  [4] After the suppression of the Jesuits, Donna Maria Antonia de San Jose de la Paz had remarkable success in promoting the Spiritual Exercises of St. Ignatius, or retreats.

TO ADAM PREMIR   Baltimore June 15–1788

Sir   Yesterday, at my return to this place, I received your favour of the 20th, containing a retractation of the unguarded expressions, contained in a former letter, & promising likewise to decline any opposition to a bill of incorporation, provided the little property belonging to the German Congregation be excepted out of the act. I hear, that is already done; tho' it appears to me, that as a very considerable and respectable part of the German Congregation does not unite with you in the new building, & separation from the old congregation consisting of all nations, you are not warranted to make such a demand. However, if they are willing to give you this satisfaction, I have no objection. Perfect, and general charity must be obtained, where ever it can be obtained without a sacrifice of the essential interests of religion: for if these give way, charity so purchased will neither be sincere, or lasting.

As I have just heard, that the corner stone of the new building has been blessed, it is now unnecessary to send any farther directions concerning that matter.

Cultivate peace, and unity with all; forsake all wrangling; renounce all anger; and bitterness. Thus will you render to the cause of God more essential services, than any others, you can perform. I have the honour to be Sir Yr most obedt. servt. in Christ John Carroll

ADfS AAB

TO THE GERMAN CONGREGATION[1]   Baltimore June 15–1788.

Gentlemen   When I first answered your most obliging letter brought by Mr. Bussy, as I had not that letter with me, I conceived, it would be necessary to write you more fully afterwards. But when I returned hither, and examined again, your favour to me, I did not find in it any matter requiring particular dissension and have therefore contented myself, till this time, with the acknowledgement, I have made already not only of my own obligations to you, but of those of religion itself. I cannot however delay any longer informing you, that I received the greatest satisfaction from your steady adherance to the principles of Xtian piety, your docility, & your good understanding, & harmony with your pastors. The example, you have ever given, will perpetuate virtues, & blessings in the congregation, long after you are gone, as I doubt not, you will go sooner, or later, to receive the reward in heaven of the good works, and particularly of the regularity, charity, and obedience, of which you were patterns here. I earnestly beg you to recommend in your devotions to God, the restoration of peace, and concord; to encourage by word and example frequent recourse to the sacraments; & to promote a spirit of sobriety, and moderation in worldly amusements; & to employ for these good purposes all the authority, which you derive from your experience, from the esteem, in which you are universally held, and the confidence, which is placed in you. With great respect I have the honour to be Gentlemen Yr. most obedt. & humble St. J. Carroll

ADfS AAB

[1] "Messrs Joseph Erk & others of the German congregation" is the given addressee at the end of this letter. Adam Premir was "President of the Society of Germans" which bought the land referred to in the previous letter. Carroll puts the Erk group apart from Premir and his committee and society formed earlier in the year.

TO[THOMAS BETAGH[1]]   Baltimore July 9th 1788—

Revd. Sir   I claim the liberty, as having been a fellow member of the
same body, of writing to you on a subject, disagreeable indeed in itself but
which may be of some consequence to Religion in these states. With this
liberty, I am sure you will not be offended, when you know the occasion &
the motive of my address.

The Revd. Mr. Patrick Smyth, a Clergyman of the Diocese of Meath,
presented himself to me in Baltimore some time in Sepr. 1787—, desiring to
be employed in the ministry of Religion & exhibiting testimonials of his good
conduct & ability &c from his Diocesan, Dr. Plunkett. He remained with me
some days to my great satisfaction and I found myself happy in receiving a
Clergyman so capable & well recommended, being much in want of men of
that character. I immediately appointed him to a place; to which is annexed a
salary of £ St.53.6.8 pr. ann., with exceeding good dwelling house, an
inclosed garden, & grass lot. Twenty guineas were immediately paid him in
advance, and a horse was provided for him. He went to take possession of his
place, to which indeed, as to all our other settlements much labour is
annexed. In the course of his labours, an intercourse of letters subsisted
between us, in which he always expressed a warm sense of, & perhaps over
rated the little civilities, it was in our power to shew him. On the 17th of last
March he wrote me a letter, expressing in stronger terms, than ever, his
acknowledgment of the kindness he had met with, and at the same time
intimating his resolution to return to Ireland, which resolution he imputed
solely to the urgent sollicitations of his friends & Relations there, the
dissatisfaction his absence gave them & his own too great weakness for the
ties of flesh & Blood. This intimation of his intended return to Ireland gave
me much concern both because he had discharged the duties of his station
very much to the satisfaction of his different Congregations, & because it
then was, & still is out of my power to find him a Successor. He came to this
place I being then absent, immediately after Easter, & engaged his passage for
Ireland; before I returned to Balt., he informed me by letter of some
pecuniary dispute between himself, and the Clergyman, who had been his
predecessor in the station of Frederic town,[2] & remained there in a disabled
condition. Their dispute was concerning a difference of, I believe, about four
pounds Stl. He applied for payment of his claim to the Clergyman who is
appointed our Agent Genl. for all temporalities.[3] This gentleman thought it a
private matter between them in the settlement of which he had no concern;
neither did I interfere in it, both because it was not in my department; nor
was I applied to for the purpose, but barely was told the matter agreeably to
Mr Smyths statement. On coming to Baltimore I found him at the house of
my residence, & there he continued till his departure, entertained all the
while about four weeks, as well as my companion the Revd Mr Sewall &

myself, knew how; or could afford to do—& communicating in the greatest familiarity with each other. About a week, before his departure, I fell in company with a gentleman who intimated that Mr Smyth was leaving the Country, because he found, that not having been a Jesuit he was not well used. I immediately conducted to my house a friend of that gentleman, who was present at the Conversation & finding Mr Smyth within, I told him in presence of the Gentleman's friend, the conversation, I had just heard, & called on him (Smyth) as a man of candor, to declare whether he had ever found bad usage from any of us, or any treatment that indicated the least disinclination for his services. Mr Smyth immediately replied, that if any person had thrown out such an insinuation, it was a very unjust one; that tho' he arrived an entire stranger, yet as soon as he came he presented his papers, he was appointed to a comfortable situation; that he was treated with as much generosity & attention, as if he had been an old & intimate acquaintance & friend &c; that if any person had any right to complain of his usage, it would surely be himself, whereas he could confidently say no cause of complaint had ever been given him. This, I can safely attest, was the substance of his reply. Some day soon after this was appointed for his sailing: & to my great surprise, he left the house without seeing or leaving a civil word to either of us—, which immediately filled me with a suspicion that some thing unknown to me, and certainly undesigned had given him offence: for I had heard some matters, which convinced me, he was unhappily susceptible of most groundless jealousies. However, it turned out that the vessel did not sail that day, & just before dinner time I accidentally met him in the town, & immediately, in presence of two Gentlemen expostulated with him on his manner of going off in the morning, & told him, I was afraid he had taken some thing amiss. He declared he had not, made a frivolous excuse, & promised he would come to dinner with me, as he did, & where I again requested him to tell me candidly, if he had taken any thing amiss, & what it was. He again denied the least offence, tho I observed a blush & a downcast countenance which confirmed my suspicion. He sailed a day or two after, & when it was supposed he was out of reach, a letter was brought to me of which I inclose you a faithful copy. You will observe, that in this letter he assigns, as the proof of my want of confidence in him my letter of Feb: 20th,[4] which he acknowledges to have received the 25th of the same month; and that his letter to me, in which he gives intimation of his designed return to Ireland; & expresses so much gratitude for the usage he received here is dated on the 15th of March following. An attention to these dates suggests a full confutation of his most groundless charge.

The letter left behind him was under cover to an acquaintance, he made in this town; & in the few lines to his friend, he insinuates, that his services were discouraged, because he was not a *regular;*[5] than which nothing is falser; for my fixed resolution is, as I informed Mr. Smyth in an early stage of our acquaintance to embrace alike the services of the secular & regular Clergy, and make no difference but in proportion to their respective merits. I even wrote to him, that I would prefer the secular clergy to Regulars, unless the latter, when here, remained still under subjection & obedience to their own Religious Superiors & kept their particular rules, as far as it was possible, out of their convents. I wish indeed to see prevailing amongst them that discipline of our ever dear Society, which, if two went together on a mission, constituted one Superior of the other, & if only one went, made him subject to the nearest Superior of the order, Had this practice prevailed amongst the Capucins, now in N. America, great part, if not the whole of the scandal might have been prevented, which has subsisted for some time past at N. York.

My reason for troubling you with this tedious detail is, that you may have it in your power to prevent the impressions of Smyth's misrepresentations. Otherwise, some good & virtuous Priests, well inclined to devote their services to the cause of Religion here, may be deterred from embarking in so good a cause. In particular, I wish that the Right Revd. Dr. Plunket could be informed of this transaction, not to prejudice Mr. Smyth (who is an able &, tho uncandid in this matter, to the best of my knowledge, a virtuous priest) but to vindicate my Brethren & myself from the narrow, ungenerous sentiments now imputed to us.

If any of our former Society reside in D[ublin]., be pleased to present my respects to them & request a communicaon of their prayers—.

ADf   AAB
¹ A former Jesuit in Dublin, source of possible influence with the bishop there. At the head of the letter is the following: "Mr. Mulhall, or Betagh (olim Soc. Jesu) Dublin." The first name is an *alias.* Carroll hears that the right name is neither of these, but Mulcaile. See to Troy, July 2, 1789. Later correspondence, however, shows that this is Thomas Betagh.
² James Frambach.
³ John Ashton.
⁴ Not found.
⁵ "Clerks Regular," or members of religious orders and here specifically the Jesuits.

TO REPRESENTATIVES OF THE SOUTHERN DISTRICT July 15—1788—

Revd. Gentlemen   I wrote to Mr. Leond. Neale some time ago, requesting him to propose to you an adjournment of yr. intended meeting at P. Tobo., till we had cooler weather. The gentlemen at a distance who might be inclined to meet you must be deterred by the season of the year. At least, I find this reason operating on myself. A matter of immediate and urgent necessity would overcome this objection; but the present case is not such. Having received no answer from Mr. Neale, I presume, that you have not agreed to postpone, and tho I did not sign yr. circular letter,¹ for reasons not necessary to be mentioned now, yet I have no doubt of your readiness to hear my opinion, and give it as much weight, as you may find it to deserve. In forming this opinion, I have endeavoured to make the general interest of Religion my first concern; and the restoration of the Society, my next. The last, if really effected, would be of great advantage to the first: but if it be attempted unsuccessfully, especially by any application at Rome I fear the attempt would be hurtful not only to the cause of the Society, but even of Religion.

To revive the Society here, the express consent of the Holy See is necessary. The Clementin Brief[2] has had its full operation here. We stand in the same situation in that respect as our Brethren at Liege, in Poland, & everywhere else but in Russia. You have amongst you a copy of the late Vicar General's letter to Mr. Howard, in which he mentions the difference in this respect, between the Society in White Russia, and the former members of it at Liege. And the M. S. history of the preserved Society in Russia[3] thus speaks of the Polish Jesuits, p. 107. "The Jesuits having undergone in Poland the whole effect of the Clementin Brief, cannot reassume the practice of their Institute and all its functions without being duly authorised to do so." That Brief contains the following words—*"per praesentes prohibemus, ne ullus amplius in dictam Societatem excipiatur, et ad habitum ac novitatum admittatur."* [For the present, we forbid that anyone be received into the above-named Society, and clothed in a habit and admitted to a novitiate.] This Ecclesiastical law having been published & submitted to by all of us, has had on us its full effect, and we cannot, here resume our habit and former institute, till we are empowered by the same authority, which destroyed the Society here, & forbad its renewal & our resumption of the habit & government. For these reasons, it appears evident, that the concurrence of the Holy See is necessary for the revival of the Society here—; not only in consequence of the general law of the Church, as made in the last Council of Lateran[4] concerning Religious orders, but likewise from the tenor of the destructive brief, and the general sense entertained by our Brethren of other Countries. Indeed the Jesuits of Russia, tho' the brief was never published to them appear nevertheless to have thought themselves incompetent to admit Postulants to their probation, or Novices to their vows without being authorised by the Holy See; as is evidently seen in the above mentioned history. Whether in this they judged right, I cannot pretend to say. But certain it is, that they were not satisfied of their power to open a novitiate & receive simple vows, till the Archbp of Mohilow[5] authorised them to do it, using to that purpose the power, which was delegated to him from Rome, with the hope as was believed, that he would employ it in the annihilation of the remnant of the Society.

If the approbation & authority of the Vicar Genl. in Russia were sufficient to reunite us to the Society, without any farther countenance or consent from Rome, that difficulty would be removed, and it would only remain to consider the expedience of a reunion formed under his authority. But this is not the case. The Vicar Genl. in his letter to Mr. Howard says, that white Russia bounds his jurisdiction: and it is evident, on very slight consideration, that it must be so: his authority can reach no farther, than that of the Archbishop of Mohilow. It was in consequence of the special Delegation from the Holy See to this prelate to visit, & reform *the Regulars, who exist in the parts of his diocese under his government* (ms. p. 48) *in pristinum redintegrare ac de novo condere,* [to restore it to its former vigor and rebuild it entirely] that he, instead of destroying the Jesuits, as was expected seconded the views of his sovereign, and empowered them to open a novitiate, to receive Novices to Religious vows, to chuse a Vicar Genl. &c. "The Delegation, says the M. S. history p. 56—most evidently empowered him to make new establishments or revive old ones, not repugnant to the canons and decrees of the Council of Trent, *for any Regular Religious existing within his diocese,* and such establishments are declared to be the work of the Holy Apostolical See . . . Now the Jesuits had never forfeited their canonical existence in the Countries subject to the jurisdiction of the Bishop; nor did the Canons or the Council of Trent[6] oppose the opening of a new Noviciate of this order. The Bishop then had the power to establish a new noviciate, and the establishment itself became the work of the Holy See." p. 56-57.

But it may still seem, that the Vicar Genl. being now constituted, he succeeds to the authority of the Genl., who had authority, wherever the laws of the State did not prohibit it, to open Novitiates, Colleges &c, and extend the Society into all Countries. But it happens unfortunately, that the Vicar Genl. does not succeed to this extent of power. The power of the Genl. was communicated to him by the Holy See which alone is competent to grant spiritual jurisdiction all over the world: and this was expressly & authentically granted to him over the members of the Society everywhere, & for the purposes of extending & governing it. But did the Archbp of Mohilow's delegation empower him to grant such extensive jurisdiction? could he give more than he possessed himself? and is it not, by express words, limited to his diocese?

Moreover, the destructive brief of Clem. 14 *prohibits,* as we have seen *any one from being received into the Society, to the habit of it, or Novitiate;* this therefore revokes & annuls all power to the contrary, wherever the brief was published, till the Holy See restores the power so revoked. But no such restoration has been made. And even the supposed approbations of his Holiness & his *viva voce oracula* [verbal pronouncement] are all confined to the Russian Jesuits. The Vicar Genl. then of Russia has no power to establish Jesuits in foreign countries, or exercise jurisdiction over them; & vows made as under his authority & promissory of obedience to him as to the Superior of the Society, would be null out of Russia; at least they would not be vows of Religion, which must have the sanction of the Head of the Church.

Thus then it is certain, that the consent of the Holy See is necessary for the revival of the Society here. It remains therefore to consider, whether there is any probability of obtaining this consent: and whether an application to the Pope, if it should prove unsuccessful, would not be injurious to the great and general interests of Religion.

As to the first, you may judge of the probability of obtaining the pope's consent by the following extract from the Russian history (p. 85). "It is well known &c." Now, tho this promise to do nothing derogatory to the Clementine Brief left his Holiness at liberty to suffer & even privately favour the measures taken in Russia to which the brief was never extended: yet surely it will prevent his reestablishing the Society here, since the reestablishment would be derogatory to the Brief. In fine, if all the interests of Religion and policy, which combine to make the Pope gratify the Empress's desire by some public act, have not been able to induce him to do it, & disentangle him from the trammels of Spain, it must be obvious, how slender our foundations are to expect such an exertion for us. And yet without a public act nothing can be done. A *vivo vocis oraculum,* delivered to authorise our resumption of our habit, besides being a violation of the promise, & therefore not to be expected, could not operate here as in Russia. We have been secularised by a law actually promulgated; they not. The effect therefore of such a law cannot be destroyed but by a repealing law equally public, & vested with equal formality. A succeeding Pope might regard the *oraculum* as a fiction, & declare null all engagements made under it, as standing in opposition to a law published & received. I omit many other reasons, & articles of intelligence wch uniformly describe the Court of Rome as being fearful of taking one step, which may meet the disapprobation of the Bourbon princes.

An application then to his Holiness in all human probability, will have no success. And if unsuccessful, will it not be even hurtful? I do not mean hurtful to the persons applying, but to the general interests of Religion. Must we not then expect to be, more than ever, objects of distrust and jealousy to that Congregation, to whom the Pope has committed the spirtl government of this Country? Will not the priests amongst us who were never Jesuits, always be attended to, in preference to us? will not every proposal from us for the benefit and enlargement of Religion, be imputed to some particular view, & consequently discountenanced? will not the very measure, we are now pursuing for the establishment of ordinary jurisdiction, and obtaining a Diocesan Bishop, be deemed an artifice to promote the restoration of the Society, & not calculated for the general service of Religion? and above all, will it not raise great difficulties agst our strong demand to have the election of the Bp left to ourselves?

Must we then do nothing towards a revival of the Society? God forbid I should advise or harbour such a plan of conduct, but we ought not to go to work, like blindmen, without seeing a step before us; or say, that no objections however reasonable they may be shall withold us. My clear opinion is, that we ought not to risk the first of all concerns for a delusive & unfounded hope of obtaining one of likewise very great, the inferior moment. What then shall we do in this matter? In the 1st place, I would recommend a compliance with the advice, & pursue the means of restoration suggested by the Vicar Genl. to Mr. Howard; for which purpose I am willing to unite with our other Brethren in some stated prayers, & exercises of devotion & zeal to draw down that blessing from heaven. 2ly to consult Mr. Thorpe at Rome, and any other of our best informed Gentlemen who may be suggested, & after communicating to them the earnest desires of many of us, request their advice & assistance in so momentous a business. Such, R. Gen., are my sentiments on the present subject. I have revolved it often & with great attention in my mind. If my opinion be not so favourable to the object of yr wishes, as you perhaps expected, you must consider, that I could not controul the principles, on which my opinion is founded: I hope it is needless for me to say, how much I honour and cherish the memory of our dear Society, and how sincerely I wish for its reestablishment on such a footing, as may justify a prudent man for engaging himself to it. Be pleased to inform me of the result of your deliberations.   I am &c

ADf   AAB

[1] Among others, Beeston, Molyneux, Walton, Matthews and Graessl signed the document. See MS of Apr. 25, 1788, MPA and Hughes, *Documents,* II, 683-84.

[2] Suppressing the Jesuits.

[3] Carroll had the MS (MPA). The reference is probably to John Howard. S.J., or some member of his titled family.

[4] In 1512 under Julius II.

[5] Catholic ecclesiasical province in union with Rome when formally recognized by Pius VI in 1783.

[6] 1545-63.

TO BERNARD DIDERICK   Balt. July 17—1788—

Revd. Sir—   I received yesterday yours of the 10th inst. The restoration of your faculties will depend on yourself. I deprived you of them, because for the 2d time, you endeavoured, by misrepresentation, to cause dissensions amongst our Brethren. I did not then know the contents of what is called, your apology.[1] I have since seen it, & shall retain it by me, at least for the present. I am sorry to tell you that I scarce, if ever, read any thing more reprehensible, & in which there were greater deviations from truth. It would justify me, for inflicting heavier penalties on you, than you have yet experienced. But this I shall forbear for the present. When I receive sufficient assurances, that you will not again endeavour to sow divisions, amongst us, and are willing to make a retractation of the most exceptionable parts of your apology, to be shewn only to those who have seen the latter, I will willingly restore yr. faculties; with this condition however, which will not be peculiar to you but common to all, that you do not *habitually* exercise your functions within the Congregations allotted to other Gentlemen.

Mr Molyneux informed me, that you were disposed to live at Conholloran's. I wish to hear as much from yourself, and then I will endeavour to procure an arrangement for your comfortable subsistance there. Wherever almost I have been I was shocked to hear, that you had reported yrself to have been denied a home or subsistance: and I see as much in some of your writings. I need only refer you to the conversations between us, and to the recollection of the different proposals I made you for a full confutation of these assertions even now, I have no doubt but this district will make you every reasonable allowance till the present time. As soon as I receive your answer, I shall determine what more is to be done in the subject of your letter. The gratification of individuals, however respectable is too feeble a motive either to move me to take, or relent in the resolution, which has been notified to you. I wish to oblige them in every thing consistent with duties of a superior order.   I am Revd Sr. &c

ADf   AAB
[1] See July 25, 1788.

TO PETITIONERS FOR FRANCIS FLEMING[1] Balt. July 21, 1788

Gentlemen.   I was honoured the 17th inst. with your favour of the 11th. Mr. Fleming being an utter stranger to me, & the Revd Mr o Brien not pretending to any personal acquaintance with him, I cannot take upon me to write to Lisbon for him, and especially with a promise of placing him at Philada. If he be really desirous of coming to America, and will bring with him sufficient vouchers for his good conduct & ability, I will be exceedingly glad of his service, receive him with cordiality, & give him employment suitable to his profession. But I have many reasons not to make a previous agreement of fixing him in your town: and the one, I am going to mention, will, I am confident, appear very sufficient to you. I have great cause to expect, that a Bishop will be appointed over us, in a few months: and it is more than probable that Philadelphia will be the Episcopal See. The Bishop will undoubtedly chuse to have near him Clergymen of his own appointment and if Mr. Fleming should not be his choice he might think himself ill used not to be retained at & employed [in] Philada, after being sent for at your desire, with the expectation of remaining there.

I am now treating with a Clergyman to live in Newcastle County, Deleware; in which case he will attend the Country Congregations, that so often call Mr. Beeston out of town: Both yr Pastors will then be generally with you; & will, I hope, be adequate to the labours required of them till the future Bp make the arrangements, wch I wish to leave to his determination.

ADf   AAB
[1] A native of Ireland, in time he became Carroll's vicar general for the northeastern part of his diocese.

TO BERNARD DIDERICK   Balt. July 25–1788–

Revd. Sir   I was much pleased to find in your letter of the 19th inst. a disposition to retract the exceptionable passages of your apology. I do not mean that you should make yr. retractation public, but only communicate it to me for those who have seen or heard your apology, & have imbibed from it false or disadvantageous opinions of the persons therein mentioned. The reprehensible passages, and erroneous statements are I fear too many for a letter. However I shall now refer to some of them; & recommend a particular & general disavowal of all assertions or insinuations, tending to impute crimes or injustices to those against whom none have been found. I am very anxious for your speedy resolution concerning yr. residence in the Delaware state. Fresh complaint, being made from Philada. within these three weeks of the frequent absence of their Pastors, a new arrangement is become necessary and another person must be procured to serve the Congregations now depending on that place. As the labour will not be great, I shall be happy to accommodate you at Conhollarn, if agreeable to you & if we can adjust happily all other matters.

You say that you never wilfully endeavoured by misrepresentations to cause dissensions amongst our Brethren. I hope you did not: but you must be sensible, that external actions must be my rule of judgment. Recollect then, Revd. Sir, your proceedings after the last genl. chapter, & consider whether they did not tend to irritate the minds of our Bn. & induce them to overset by an irregular combination the resolves of Chapter, which has the supreme legislative authority in matters of internal government. Remember the expressions of yr. circular letter to several of our Gentlemen in which you represented the advocates in chapter for the measures disapproved by you as having acted from most unworthy & the basest principles; cunning & interest I think, were yr. expres. Remember, the ferment caused by this misinformation.

Again, you stated to the Cn. convened at Newtown,[1] that in your old age and after all your services, you were deprived of a home, obliged to wander all the winter &c, & had no resource but in their protection. To them you never mentioned, that I offerred you a residence at Deer-Creek;[2] & even a temporary one with us at Baltimore till a final settlement was made to yr. satisfaction: and when you chose to reside with Mr. Bolton I immediately acquiesced: and I have now by me answers to the letters, I sent soon after to that District, intimating your desire. To this same meeting you had read yr. apology, with all its partial & erroneous statements. In consequence of wch, a paper was signed, wch could not fail of exasperating & provoking a dissension: With this paper, you travelled thro Maryld. & Pennsylva., sollicicting subscriptions, tho it was apparent, how fatal it might prove to Religious harmony: and you did not fail to shew yr. apology, not only those parts of it, which were intended for yr. own justfcn (& for this I should not have blamed you); but those likewise, which without exculpating you had a direct tendency to blacken the characters of others.

I subjoin some of the exceptionable passages which I have noted in your apology & am &c.

1° The insertion into yr. apology of all matters degrading of Mr A.[3] copied from the supplt. of the paper given in to Mr P.[4] & myself. The relating of some of these to us two may not have been blameable but yr. communicating of them to others could not tend to yr. justfcn [justification], but rather aggravated Mr A. charge agst you of defamaon. In particular, you yourself told me that the adventure of Phillis being seen &c, was at the very time that one of the parties was entirely deprived of his reason by the violence of a burning fever. Now, as you knew this, how can you justify yourself for concealing that circumstance when you related the tale told by Duval & the Negro-man? Did it contribute to yr. vindication to tell all our Brethren & some seculars the hearsay & unproved contents of No 6. of yr supplement . . ? to lay before them the most indecent oath of Kelly before Mullikin?

2° In page 20 of yr. apology, can you justify the generality of your application of the words of the psalm, *testes iniqui?* . . . you make a list of articles, which Tomalty should have added to his deposition; but as he never did add them, or give any hint of them, tho' interrogated by you, you surely should not publish them now, especially as they tend to disgrace another, without exculpating you: and therefore it is incumbent on you who alone have divulged them to our Gentlemen, to retract them; that is, to contradict your knowledge of the truth of his belief, reports, or suspicions; and your own assertion, that he ought to have added them to his deposition.[5]

3° pag. 21. You say that *B. allowed her &c* . . . . . . p. 22, that *she herself &c* . . . . Consider the imputations conveyed in these words, and the impressions, they must make. Was it necessary for you to say all these cruel things, in order to convince your Brethren and acquaintance, that you had done nothing to injure, even occasionally, your Companions character?

4° p. 27. you say, speaking of Kelly's affidavit, that *if it is so, you take it to be a forced oath* &c. Is this a vindication of your conduct, or a most cruel insinuation agst another?

5° p. 23. your reflexions on Mr. B. deposition are very reprehensible: and your assertion that Mr Graesl[6] could contradict him you now know to be a mistake. This is one erroneous statement. p. 25—You say of Mr E. *jurat in verba magistri.* What an imputation! p. 26. Of Mr Sewall you say p. 25. that he never told you, that Mr A. *forced* him to swear in prison &c: and yet I have a letter from you in your own hand-writing, where you say directly the contrary. This then is erroneous.

6⁰ p. 16. You say *K. oath was totally disregarded.* How do you know, that the credibility of it was not thoroughly weighed? and does this assertion tend to justify you or impeach Mr A. judges of shewing him undeserved favour? p. 27. you say, that *not dreaming of Mr A. having so heavy a charge &c, nor knowing the particulars* &c, it was *impossible for you to answer in an hours time* &c. By this you would lead your readers to believe, that you had no previous information given you of Mr A. charge. before you met Mr P. & self about Jan. 26.; that no particulars were communicated to you; that you had but one hours allowance to make yr. defence &c. On the contrary, you were informed by my letter of Decr. 10–1787,[7] as follows. *"Mr A. has presented a formal complaint of your having* &c. *I therefore give you this notice* &c. *I refer you* to the letter itself. 3ly from all which it results, that you had not only one hour, but six weeks notice of the charge against you. This then is a very erroneous statement.

7⁰ p. 28. you say, *you were informed* (it does not appear by whom) *that Mr P. was determined to give sentence against you, as he condemned K. unheard.* In my letter just referred to, you received a notice directly contrary to this, and a full communication of the evidence which affected you. Here again you gave erroneous information to your readers.

8⁰ p. 30. You say *that Mr C. knew of the discredit &c; that having heard of the first reported transgressions &c, admonished you not to mention &c.* This is altogether erroneous—for I solemnly declare, that I never heard the least insinuation of the last imputation against Mr A., till after my return from N. York: and as to the 1st, I never heard it but in a light manner from Wharton who picked it up somewhere in his travels: and if such imputation may be said to bring discredit on the ministry, its reputation must be destroyed long since, as I heard the very same person say, that similar reports were circulating agst as respectable a Clergyman as any in America; and I have reason to believe & know, that they are sometimes circulated agst everyone of us upon genl. Protestant prejudices. You cannot therefore ground any vindication of yr. conduct on a pretended similarity of obligation between us to prevent the growth of scandal.

p. 31. you say that you wrote to me *some years ago about Mr A. & that I shewed your* letter &c. & *that was the reason Mr A.* &c. This is totally void of truth. You never wrote to me about, & consequently, I never betrayed your letter to Mr A., & therefore no such thing happened to make Mr A. quit going to you. p. 33. you insinuate that Mr A. is commended by his judges *for knocking his servants down* &c. Where can you find this commendation? Is not this another erroneous statement? . . . ibid. You say, *all the evidences of the people of the White marsh* &c. This again is a most erroneous statement, totally void of truth. p. 34. you say, *you were forced to wander to & fro during the winter &c; &* p. 37., *that you were equally destitute of a home & maintenance &c.* Is not this, what in your last letter to me, you deny having said?

These, R. Sir, are some of the very obnoxious passages of yr. apology: and I must insist, that you make sufficient satisfaction for them: wch being done I will readily restore yr. faculties, with the condition expressed in my last letter. There are some other offensive passages, wch, I have omitted, and the reason is, that I really am tired, as well as sorry to have such to transcribe. I am &c—

ADf   AAB
    [1] A mission in St. Mary's County, Md.
    [2] St. Joseph's Mission, Harford County, Md.
    [3] John Ashton served as treasurer for the Catholic clergy under Carroll. It was with him that Diderick lodged his financial claims.
    [4] James Pellentz was designated by Carroll to serve as judge of the claims Diderick brought against Ashton.
    [5] Diderick disagreed with the principles by which Carroll and the conference of the clergy agreed to deal with property formerly held by the Jesuits. See Jan. 22-Feb. 28, 1787.
    [6] Lawrence Graessl.
    [7] Letter not found.

TO NORFOLK CONGREGATION   [Aug., 1788]

The Rev. Mr Roan[1] has exhibited to the underwritten Eclessiastical Superior of the Clergy in the United States of America letters testimonial from the Archbishop of Dublin, certifying that the said Mr. Roan was duly promoted & ordained to the priesthood: he likewise has informed the Superior, that the R. Catholics of Norfolk & Portsmouth in Virginia expressed their desire to him to have a clergyman resident amongst them, whom they promised decently to maintain: As this intelligence was peculiarly agreeable to the Superior; and he is most sincerely disposed to comply with this desire of the R.C., as far as in him lies; he has empowered Mr. Roan to proceed to Norfolk, and there to enquire particularly, what prospect there is of a sufficient maintenance for a Clergyman; and if Mr. Roan finds such a prospect, as may induce him to embrace any offer made him; the Superior will then give him powers to exercise the regular spiritual functions provided however, that such farther certificates of Mr. Roans good conduct be furnished as are required in such cases—J.C.

ADfS   AAB   Date estimated from reference in May 8, 1789.
    [1] Carroll distinguishes this man from Rohan, (See Aug. 1, 1794.) He had a zealous career in the ministry in Kentucky. Guilday (p. 688) attributes the full name of William de Rohan to him, not taking account of Carroll's remark on the name.

TO DON CASIMIR Baltimore, August 11, 1788

I wrote to your Reverence some months ago to inform you of the great zeal and services Father Charles Whelan of your order rendered to Religion in the United States. I have received some letters from him recently, dated at Kentucky at about 800 miles from this place, where he lives with a large number of Catholics who have emigrated from this state to assure their posterity of a piece of good land in a very delightful climate. The reports which he has sent me are very consoling. Not only does he uphold the spirit of Religion among the Catholics, but he also succeeds in making a great increase in the Church of Jesus Christ by converting the different sects. There is only one thing which gives me uneasiness in his regard, that is the fear that he has not obtained permission from his Superiors to stay there longer. Exclusive of his zeal, he is actually accustomed to the habits and harsh life of those people, he is veritably an apostle among them and changing him would deal a mortal blow to Religion and probably destroy the fruit of his labors. That is why I beg very earnestly that your Reverence allow him to stay there for the service and consolation of so many poor souls, as well as for the advantage of those who are yet to be born.

I do not doubt that with the help of Heaven he is establishing a flourishing church, and that he is forming a nursery to furnish good subjects for his Order, perhaps even to found a Convent, which is certainly much to be desired in view of the great decline in Religious orders in the other parts of the world.

Another subject of anxiety for me as well as for Father Whelan is that there is no other priest with him. He ardently desires, and with reason, a companion of his Order, a man of proven virtue who is not looking for the good things of the world but only the service of God in the salvation of souls. The object of his choice would be Father Danally, if you could spare him and he wished to undertake a task so holy and so meritorious. I would be very relieved and very happy to receive him and would contribute to procuring the means for him to make the voyage. I recommend the mission of Father Whelan to the prayers of your holy Community and have the honor to be etc. J. Carroll Superior of the Clergy United States

C PF The following is at the beginning of the letter: "A copy and translation in French of a letter from Father Carroll prefect of the missions of the united states of North America, to Don Casimir of Dublin, Provincial of the Irish Capuchins, given at Baltimore the 11th of August 1788."

J'ecrivis à votre Révérence il y a quelques mois, pour l'informer du grand zèle et services que le Pere Charles Whelan de votre Ordre rendoit à la Religion dans les États Unis. J'ai reçu des lettres de lui dernièrement, dattées à Kentucky à environ 800 miles de ce lieu, où il Demoure avec un grand nombre de Catholiques, qui ont émigré de cet état pour assurer à leur Posterité un espace de bonne terre dans un climat des plus Délicieux. Les relations qu'il m'en a envoyées sont très consolantes. Non seulement il entretient l'esprit de la Religion parmi les Catholiques, mais encore il reussit à faire une grande augmentation a l'Église de Jesus Christ par la conversion des Differentes Sectes. Il n'y a qu'une seule chose qui me donne de l'inquietude à son égard. C'est la crainte qu'il n'obtienne pas de ses Supérieurs la permission d'y rester plus long tems. Abstraction faite à son zèle, il est actuallement accoutumé aux moeurs et à la Vie Dure de ce peuple, il est veritablement un apôtre parmi eux et son changement porteroit un coup mortel à la Religion et detruiroit probablement tout le fruit de ses travaux. C'est pourquoi je supplie très instamment votre Révérence de le permettre d'y rester pour le service et la consolation de tant de pauvres ames, ainsi que pour l'avantage de ceux qui sont encore à naitre. Je ne doute pas qu'avec le secours du Ciel, il n'etablisse une Église fleurissante, et qu'il ne forme une Pépiniere pour fournir de bons sujet à son Ordre, peut être même pour en fonder un Couvent qui est certainement beaucoup à desirer, vu la grande decadence des ordres Religieux dans les autres parties du monde.

Un autre sujet d'inquietude pour moi aussi bien que pour le Père Whelan, c'est qu'il n'a point d'autre prêtre avec lui. Il desire ardemment et avec raison un compagnon de son Ordre homme d'une vertu a l'epreuve, qui ne cherche pas les bonnes choses de ce monde mais seulement le service de Dieu dans le salut des ames. L'objet de son choix seroit le Père Danally, si vous pourrez vous en passer et qu'il veuille entreprendre un état si saint et si meritant. Je serois très aise et très heureux de le recevoir et contribuerois lui procurer les moyens pour faire le voyage. Je recommande la mission du P. Whelan aux Prières de votre Ste. Communauté et a l'honneur d'être &c.   J. Carroll Superior of the clergy   United States

TO JOHN TROY   Baltimore, August 11, 1788

My Lord,   I was honoured with your Grace's letter of May 16th, by the Rev. Mr. Ryan,[1] who arrived at Philadelphia the first of this month, and is now with me. I am happy in taking this occasion to open a correspondence with a prelate of your distinguished character, and hope your Grace will allow me to apply to you with confidence and liberty in all matters which may intervene between this country and Ireland relative to the welfare of religion. Mr. Ryan I will endeavour to place, agreeably to himself and advantageously to some Catholics destitute of all spiritual assistance. He is not willing to accept an appointment in the country, in one of the western counties of Pennsylvania, where a large colony of Irish Catholics are soliciting a priest, and offer him a maintenance. He has turned his eyes on Charleston, South Carolina, where a clergyman is likewise wanted.

My very good friend, Mr. O'Brien of New York has informed your Grace of the reason I have to be dissatisfied with the unaccountable conduct of the Rev. Mr. S[myth], lately returned to Ireland. I should remain perfectly easy in the self-conviction of having afforded him no cause of dissatisfaction, but quite the contrary; were it not that misrepresentation may deprive this country of the services of some valuable assistance from Ireland. To prevent this, I have written fully to a gentleman of your city, Mr. Mulcaile,[2] whom Mr. O'Brien recommended to me, and with whose character he brought me acquainted. I shall desire him to communicate the contents to your Lordship, that you may be convinced, with how little candour Mr. S[myth] has conducted himself in this business, and that no impressions may be received as if I were not disposed to give employment to as many virtuous and well-informed clergymen as a maintenance can be procured for. But one thing must be fully impressed on their minds, that no pecuniary prospects or worldly comforts must enter into the motives for their cross the Atlantic to this country. They will find themselves much disappointed. Labour, hardships of every kind, coarse living, and particularly great scarcity of wine (especially out of the towns) must be borne with. Sobriety in drink is expected from clergymen to a great degree. That which in many parts of Europe would be esteemed no more than a cheerful and allowable enjoyment of a friendly company, would be regarded here in our clergy as an unbecoming excess. Your Lordship will excuse this detail, and know how to ascribe it to its proper motive, that gentlemen applying to come to this country may know what to expect.

I have the honour to be, with the greatest veneration and respect,   My Lord,   Your Grace's most obedient and humble servant,   J. Carroll

L   Moran, III, 504-05.
  [1] Denis Ryan ministered at Charleston, S. C., this year, dying two years later.
  [2] See July 9, 1788.

TO THOMAS BETAGH Sep.–Nov., 1788

Not found. See to Troy, Mar., 1789.

TO JOHN HOCK[1] Baltimore in Maryland, 15 September, 1788

At the beginning of August I received the very welcome letter of Your Lordship dated March 25 of this year; and at the same time a letter came for Father Farmer, born Steinmaier, who had died about two years ago, namely on August 17, 1786. He ended a life adorned by every virtue with a very happy death. The letter which your Lordship writes that you sent me last year never reached me. Great admiration and no less joy were mine, when in reading your letter I observed that such religious zeal for these states animated so generous a person, and that despite the distance separating us and the fact that no bond united us save the common bond of charity. Now in response to such good will I shall faithfully but briefly tell you how things are here.

There are thirteen United States some of which equal or even surpass Germany in extent. Before the break with the British government Catholic priests were in only two states, Maryland and Pennsylvania. In the other states there were few or none of the faithful, and from most of them priests were excluded by severe laws and the threat of capital punishment. With the overthrow of English rule freedom of religion was everywhere established, and in many states Catholics, no less than others, became qualified to participate in the governance of the Republic and to hold other office. Thus, immediately after the war ended priests from Europe tried to extend the ministry of our faith to other states, and they continue to do so. A great obstacle however is the poverty of the Catholics who are neither able to build churches nor provide for the upkeep of the clergy. For the possessions of the ex-Jesuits, about which you have been informed, scarcely suffice for the support of those who labor in Maryland and Pennsylvania. And if there be a surplus all of it is usefully applied to a school under construction for the education of Catholic youth and a seminary for young clerics.

In these states there was recently a great shortage of priests, above all for the German speaking people; but last year two Capuchins[2] from the diocese of Treves came, impelled, so I hear, by certain letters in the public press of Mainz. With their accession the Germans can be provided for till the arrival next year of two newly ordained secular priests of approved learning and conduct. As you remember they were supported by some persons in the English Seminary while they learned the English language without which they scarcely can be used here. Generally speaking it is necessary for anyone who gives himself to this vineyard of the Lord to learn this language. For the present our poverty will not permit us to avail ourselves of the good will of those priests of the diocese of Mainz under your supervision who are prepared to come to America. Nor can the church in America bear the expense of sending young men to Mainz or the archiepiscopal seminary. Indeed if Providence smiles on our efforts, as I and my confreres are attempting to do, we may be able to build a school for the education of young men under our direction, and later a seminary for clerics of limited means, in secular and sacred learning. This will be preferable to expending great sums on travel to and from Europe. This is what we are attempting with indifferent success at the beginning. With all due gratitude and respect we appeal to the very illustrious and most reverend suffragan, and with special trust to your Lordship that we may rejoice in the blessing of a seminary for American young men; we likewise entreat that priests of approved conduct and learning be allowed to come to us, or be exhorted to do so. Once again I urge that a school and seminary be built[,] for in them I place the sole safeguard of religion. For this reason I earnestly appeal to your well known charity and zeal for religion, and that you explain to the Archbishop and elector, to the other canons of the church in Mainz, and to other outstanding individuals how much it contributes to the preservation and spread of the true faith, and how much to the glory of God, that they contribute what they think proper to so salutary an undertaking. I enclose a printed form in English respecting the building of a school which you may wish to show to other very worthy persons.

With respect to your Lordship's proposal about travel to America let me say that I admire what is said about setting up a seminary in Mainz for educating clerics, as it truly reveals your concern for their welfare. I also hold it in deep respect as truly apostolic and quite unusual.

ADf   AAB
[1] Suffragan Bishop of Mainz, described as follows by Carroll: "Eccl. Counsellor at Mainz, Pastor of B.V.M. [Blessed Virgin Mary] Collegiate Church, canon and scholar at St. Maurice's."
[2] John and Peter Heilbron.

Admodum Revd. ac perillustris Domine—   Principio mensis Augusti accepi gratissimas Rev. Do,. litteras, quas dedit die 26 Martii anni currentis; simulque allatae sunt aliae ad Revd. Dom. Farmer, vere Steinmaier destinatae qui biennio fere antea e vivis exceperat, die namque 17 Aug. anni 1786; vitam omni virtutum genere excultam sanctissima morte conclusit. Quas anno superiore ad nos perillustris Dom. scribit se misisse litteras, nunquam mihi sunt redditae; ita ut magnam admirationem nec minorem laetitiam in me expertus sim, cum legendo Dom. litteras animadverterem tantae Religionis studio in has provincias flagrare virum amplissima tam longo intervallo sejunctum, nullaque cum illis rei necessitudine connexum, nisi communi genuinae charitatis vinculo. Ut igitur tam Religiosae in nos voluntati respondeam, fideliter sed breviter rerum nostrarum statum communicabo. Tredecim sunt foederatae   Americae   provinciae,   quarum   aliquae   Germaniam ipsam extensione aequant, vel etiam superant. Ante disruptam cum Anglis regiminis societatem, in duabus tantum provinciis Catholici sacerdotes sedem habuere, Marylandia nempe et Pennsylvania. In reliquis nulli, vel paucissimi Fideles; et in plerisque severissima lege, et capitis poena cautum fuit, ne Sacerdotes in illas ingrederentur. Excesso Angliae jugo, libertas cultus ubique stabilita, et in multis provinciis Catholici, non minus quam caeteri, ad Reipublicae Dominationem et caetera munia fiunt habiles. Unde statim post bellum finitum Religionis ministeria in alias provincias extendere conati sunt, acemnum conantur, advecti ex Europa Sanctuarii ministri. Magno tamen obstaculo est Catholicorum paupertas, nec Ecclesias construere valentium nec satis sustentationi Sacerdotum providere. Bona enim Exjesuitarum de quibus ad Dom. V. relatum fuit, vix eorum qui in Marylandia et Pennsylvania laborant, sumptibus sufficiunt; et si quid superest, id omne ad Academiam quae nunc pro Catholicae juventutis educatione construitur, et seminarium pro junioribus ecclesiasticis utiliter conferetur.

In his provinciis magna nuper extitit penuria Sacerdotum, pro Germanis praecipue; sed anno superiore advenere duo ex Diocesi Trevinensi Capuccini, excitati, ut audio, litteris quibusdam, quae in chartis publicis Moguntiae sunt impressae. Hoc subsidio Germanis succurri poterit, donec anno sequenti advenerint tres Neo Sacerdotes saeculares laudatae vitae et doctrinae, qui in Seminario quodam Anglicano ex bonis quorum meministi, sustentantur, donec linguam Anglicanam didicerint, sine qua vix usui hic esse poterunt; et generatim necesse est, ut quisquis se huic Domini vineae devoverit, illo subsidio instruatur. Quare nec in praesens, rerum nostrarum tenuitas patitur, ut optima voluntate eorum Sacerdotum utamur, bui ex Moguntiae Diocesi sub Dominationis tuae auspiciis parati sunt ad transmeandum in Americam; neque ut adolescentes sumptibus Ecclesiae Americanae Moguntiam ad Seminarium Archiepiscopale transmittantur. Et quidem si divina providentia conatibus nostris arriserit, ut quod jam moli cum meis confratribus, scholam pro juventutis educatione in bonis literis sub nostra disciplina hic erigere valeamus ac deinceps Seminarium Ecclesiasticum pro Clericorum instructione, minus dispendiosi, hic ad literas tum profanas, tum sacras efformabuntur, quam si magnis sumptibus iter in Europam reditusque in patriam essent instituenda. Tamen quod efficere conamur; minus prospere ceperit; cum omni gratissimi animi obsequio, ac summa veneratione, et ad Illm. et Revdmum. D. Suffraganeum; et speciali confidentia ad amplissimam Dominationem Vestram confugiam, non solum ut Seminarii beneficio pro quibusdam Americanis adolescentibus gaudeamus, sed etiam ut probae vitae et doctrinae Sacerdotes, quatenus fieri poterit, et ubi necessitas exegerit, ad nos venire permittant, aut, ut veniant, exhortentur. Interim tamen, omni studio in id incumbo, ut scholae institutio et Seminarii Ecclesiastici ad effectum perducatur, quod omne fere Religionis tutamen in illis constituo, atque pro eximia Dominationis Vae charitate ac Religionis zelo enixe precor, sollicitudinem interponere ut ostendere velit Em. Archiepiscope et Elect., allisque excellentissimis Ecclesiae Moguntinae Canonicis, et nobilissimis viris quantopere ad verae fidei conservationem et incrementum hoc consilium conferat, quam utiliter ad divinam gloriam conferetur, quidquid in tam salutare opus conferre ipsis visum fuerit. In hunc finem includo chartam impressam, lingua Anglica de scholae aedificatione quam istis praeclarissimis viris velim ostendere dignetur V. Do.

Quod attinet ad D. V. propositum de itinere in Americam, ut tractat de constituendo Moguntiae Seminario pro Clericorum educatione, id quidem testimonium eximiae tuae pro animarum salute ardore non tantum admiror; sed veneror tamquam plane Apostolicum, et longe supra hujusce aetatis.

TO CHARLES PLOWDEN Baltimore Nov. 12—1788—

My Dear Sir   Your most acceptable favours of June 30th & Sept 20 (by the packts) are now in my hands. Continue to favour me with your interesting letters, & let our correspondence be terminated only with our lives. Our academy is going on & I have not lost hopes of having it under cover this year. Your intentions are truly generous, & you will have your reward in heaven. I hope you will not be disappointed this fall, for your own sake as well as the academy's. If you have been able to obtain nothing from others as yet I trust you will not despair. A few more friends may perhaps be prevailed on to add a few more £50—to your own generous bequest, & they will help the work forward with great expedition. I sent two years ago many papers of the plan &c to Mr. Talbot,[1] to be offerred to several of my principal acquaintance amongst the Catholics. But I have had no answer from him since that time. Do you not think, that Sr. Wm. Meynell, Sr. Carnaby Haggerston[2] &c would do something? Mr. Francis Neale arrived at this port yesterday after a three months passage from Amsterdam. I am much pleased with & promise myself great assistance from him. By letters from Mr. Thorpe, I find that he was told that every thing had been done, as I wished. I suspect Monsignr. Borgia gave him premature, if not erroneous information. I have no accounts from Rome posterior to the receipt of my letters to the Propgda. But since finishing my letter of today to Mr. Thorpe I have one from the Sp Minister at Congress, informing me of his expecting to be *soon* acquainted with the news of the petition being granted. He adds indeed of my being nominated to the Bpk; but that would be a departure from the purport of our petition which was, that the Clergy might, in the first instance, chuse their Bp, & afterwards concert with his holiness a regular plan of electing in future; which I hope will never be vested in the whole body of officiating clergy; but only certain select persons &c—. The issue of the expectations of the poor Span: Exiles, who instead of being recalled into their country, are dispersed & separated from one another, is another proof of that credulity, with which we have been so constantly infatuated. God be praised, matters at New York are happily terminated. The wretched Nugent was found by the Jury guilty of a riot. His counsel pleaded, that being the lawful pastor, he could not be guilty of a riot in going to take possession of his Church; that the person, who deposed him received his jurisdiction from the Pope that is, a jurisdiction contrary to the laws of N. York. This plea was overruled; and verdict given against him. Was the Cardinal Branciforte, mentioned in your letter of June 30th, the hopeful Legate of Bolonia in our time?

You must excuse the shortness of this. I will make amends soon. My good Mother was well on Saturday last. I am sure, she would send her respects, if she knew of my writing; so would Mr. Digges, who is decaying fast, being troubled with a sore leg. I have lately sent an Irish priest,[3] recommended for his piety, but, I fear, not eminent for learning to Charleston, S. Carolina. Next year if possible, a priest must be established in the Jersey. I am surprised, Mr. Thayer is not yet arrived. I wrote to him above a year ago, but never got an answer, tho I know, he got my letter. My respectful compliments to the Lord & Lady of Lullworth; & every good wish to Messrs Stanley & Clinton. Mr Sewall my worthy Companion salutes you. I am   Dr. Sir   Yrs Affectionately   J.C.

ALS   St
    [1] Letter not found.
    [2] Sir Carnaby Haggerston of Northumberland, England, representative of the Northern District to the Catholic Committee in London, elected 1782.
    [3] Denis Ryan.

TO THOMAS TALBOT   Nov. 12, 1788

Not found. John Carroll Committee notes indicate the item.

TO CLAUDIUS DE LA POTERIE[1]   Baltimore Dec. 24–1788–

Since you have started to learn English, I shall take the liberty of writing to you partly in that language, since I do not doubt that you can readily understand it, and to give me more facility in communicating to you my sentiments.[2]

I am sorry that I had not the pleasure of receiving your letter of Novr. 19th before the 22d inst. I had left Baltimore for some weeks & the Chevalier d'Armour kept your letter till after my return, which was on the 20th. This delay will prevent your having the spiritual powers, which would be so beneficial to the Catholics of Boston during this holy time of Xtmas. The Chevalier communicated to me the letter of Mr. Baury de Bellerive; I pay it the respect, due to the merit of the Gentleman who wrote it: I request you likewise to present my respectful compliments to him, and sincere thanks for his assistance in promoting & encouraging the introduction of divine service into Boston.

You can be assured, Monsr., that I learned, with the greatest pleasure and with a feeling of most profound gratitude towards the Father of mercies, that he deigned to take you to Boston through a series of unexpected events in order to open the exercise, and to lay the foundations, maybe even to erect there the structure of our holy religion. I admit to you, that since the American revolution, I have always thought that Providence was reserving an even more extraordinary revolution in the order of grace: and who knows, would you not be destined to be the instrument in the hand of God to bring about this great work? Your disinterestedness, your avoidance of the vain praises of the world; your readiness to embrace sufferings are for me true signs of this. Allow me to beg you fervently to persevere in these sentiments so necessary in Apostolic life, through a continual watch over yourself, and an inviolable and constant application to meditation; which are all the more necessary for you as you are lacking one of the great preservatives against indifference, and slackening in the service of God, that is to say, that you lack opportunities to revive your fervor through the sacrament of penance. I do not know what prevents you from having this consolation by the arrival of Mr. Thayer, which has been announced for so long. I can only be alarmed by that which you tell me in reference to him. I had already seen something about it in the public newspapers, which I attributed to slander and to the rage of heterodoxy. Anyway, I know Mr. Thayer only through my correspondance to Europe; they informed me that he is well thought of in Rome, Paris and elsewhere by the most eminent figures in the Church, and the most respectable in their piety; that he won the friendship of the Superiors at the St. Sulpice Seminary; that he went to London during the summer of 1777, where he was appreciated by the Apostolic Vicar of this city, and by other most estimable Ecclesiastics; that he was given for use by Bostonians a very beautiful and large collection of books of piety and of Religion, and other necessary articles for the establishment of the divine service. I had with him no direct relationship, except for a letter, which I wrote him in 1777,[3] but to which I received no reply.

You will find enclosed the necessary powers for the administering of sacraments, and to give dispensation in matrimonial cases for certain degrees of parentage and affinity. It is not possible for lack of opportunity at this moment, of sending you the oil for the sick, and for baptisms. If you would address yourself to Mr. O'Brien, a priest in New York, where the opportunities arise much more often, I think he will be able to furnish you with them. We used to have the directories[4] sent from London; but they came so late, and so infrequently, that for the last few years, we have not been requesting any, and each year one is made in manuscript. I will not fail to send you some books of piety for your congregation for the education and edification of the faithful, and the newly Converted of your flock, books of piety; as soon as the winter is over, if Mr. Thayer does not arrive before that time abundantly furnished with all that is necessary in that respect. I do not know if I can let you count on more help from here, Catholics are generally poor and cannot manage to build churches for themselves, which are lacking, or to see to their up-keep. At any rate, you must count on my efforts, and communicate to me without reservation, anything I could help you with, you, Sir, or the faithful, to whose service you have just given yourself.

For the time being, since you have no private cemetery, and supposing that the Protestant ministers would not think kindly of your exercising any ministerial function in the cemeteries, where they have jurisdiction, I think that you could follow the usage observed in England. The service is performed at the chapel or at the deceased's home, and the requiem prayers are done over a pile of blessed earth, which is placed inside the coffin of the deceased, before he is carried over to the public cemetery to be interred. But,

in case it would not be frowned upon if you performed the function in the
cemetery, I think that it would be proper to accompany the body, and to
bless the grave, *toties quoties* [as often as needed], according to the formula
of the Roman ritual. If Catholic men are married to Protestant women, or
vice versa, by a Protestant minister, they must be subject to a public penance
before being absolved. At least, that is the ordinary procedure here. In case of
necessity, and upon the representations brought to me, I may give dispensation for marriages in 2o gradu consanguinitatis & affinitatis—; and even in 1o
gradu affinais ex copula illicita &c.[5] I inform you of all this, so that you
know whom to refer to, in case you ever find yourself in a situation which
requires such dispensations. Indulgence monthly. Lent.

ADf   AAB
[1] Arrived in Boston from Europe in 1788, he had been a chaplain under Rochambeau.
He made pretentions to ecclesiastical honors in Europe, as well as assuming himself to
have a vice-prefecture and apostolic missionary status in Boston. Later in debt, probably
from initiating a school (see to Poterie, Apr. 3, 1789), he fled to Quebec and then to the
West Indies.
[2] The following paragraph is in English.
[3] Not found.
[4] Probably the liturgical calendar.
[5] "Marriages in second degree of blood relationship and affinity and in the first degree
where unlawful relations were had . . . "

Puisque vous vous etes mis à l'etude de l'Anglois, je prendrai la liberté de
vous ecrire en partie en çette langue, ne doutant point que vous ne soiez en
etat de la comprendre, & pour me donner à moi même plus de facilité à vous
communiquer mes sentimens.
   [Paragraph in English follows.]
   Vous pouvez être assuré, Monsr., que j'ai appris, avec le plus grand plaisir
& avec des sentimens d'une profonde reconnoissance au Pere des miseri-
cordes, qu'il a daigné vous conduire à Boston par une suite d'evenemens
inattendus pour y ouvrir l'exerçise, & pour jeter les fondemens, peutêtre
même pour eriger l'edifice de notre Ste Religion. Je vous avoue, que depuis le
revolution Americaine, je me suis toujours mis dans l'esprit, que la providence
se menagoit une revolution plus extraordinaire encore dans l'ordre de la
grace: et que sai-je, si vous n'etes pas destiné pour en être l'instrument en la
main de Dieu pour operer çe grand ouvrage? Votre desinteressement, votre
degagement de vaines louanges de çe monde; votre promtitude à embrasser les
souffrances m'en sont des gages assurées. Permettez moi de vous prier instamment de vous entretenir en ces sentimens si necessaires dans la vie Apostolique, par une attention continuelle sur vous même, & une assiduité inviolable à faire usage de la meditation; qui vous sont d'autant plus necessaires,
qu'il vous manque un de grands preservatifs contre la tiedeur, et le rallentis-
sement dans le service de Dieu, c'est à dire, que les occasions vous manquent
de ranimer le ferveur dans le sacrement de la penitence. Je ne sais, çe qui
empêche, que vous n'aiez cette consolation par l'arrivée de Monsr. Thayer,

qui est annoncé depuis si long tems. Je ne puis qu'etre inquieté par çe que vous me mandez à son sujet. J'en avois deja vu quelque chose sur les papiers publics, que j'attribuois à la medisance et à la rage de l'heterodoxie. Du reste, je ne connois Monsr. Thayer, que par mes correspondances en Europe; m'ont appris qu'il est fort estimé à Rome, à Paris, & ailleurs des personnes les plus eminentes dans l'eglise, & respectables par leur pieté; qu'il s'est attiré la bienveillance de Superieurs du Seminaire de St. Sulpice; qu'il a eté à Londres pendant l'eté de 1777, ou il se fit estimer du Vicaire Apostolique de çette ville, & d'autres Ecclesiastiques de plus estimables; qu'on lui a donné pour l'usage de Bostoniens une tres belle et ample collection des livres de pieté et de Religion, & autres choses necessaires pour l'establissement du service divin. Je n'ai point eu avec lui aucune relation directe, si çe n'est une lettre, que je lui ecrivis en 1777, mais à laquelle je n'ai point eu de reponse.

Vous reçevrez çi joint les pouvoirs necessaires pour l'administration des Sacremens, & pour dispenser en cas matrimoniaux pour certains degrés de parenté et d'affinité. Il n'est pas possible faute d'occasion à çe moment, de vous envoyer de l'huile des Infirmes, & pour le baptême. Si vous voulez bien vous addresser à Monsr. O'Brien, prêtre à la Nouvelle York, d'ou les occasions sont bien plus frequentes, je crois qu'il sera en etat de vous en fournir. Nous etions dans l'usage de faire venir les directoires de Londres: mais ils venoient si tard, & avec si peu de certitude, que depuis peu d'années, on n'en demande plus, & chaque an s'en fait un en manuscrit. Je ne manquerai pas de vous envoyer de livres de pieté pour votre Congn l'instruction & l'edification des Fideles, & nouveaux Convertis de votre troupeau, des livres de pieté; aussitot que l'hyver sera passé, si Monsr. Thayer n'arrive point avant ce terme abondamment pourvu de tout çe qui est necessaire en çe genre. Je ne sais, si je dois vous faire esperer d'autres secours d'ici. Les Catholiques generalement sont pauvres & ne peuvent point reussir à se batir les eglises, qui leur manquent, ou fournir à leur entretien. Du reste, vous devez conter sur mes efforts, & me communiquer sans reserve, en quoi je pourrai vous etre utile, à vous, Monsr., ou aux fideles, au service desquels vous venez de vous consacrer.

En attendant que vous aiez de cimitiere particulier, & supposant, que les ministres Protestans ne vous verroient pas de bon oeil exercer aucune fonction ministerielle dans les cimitieres, ou ils ont jurisdiction, je crois, que vous pourriez suivre l'usage qui s'observe en Angleterre. L'office se fait à la chapelle ou à la maison du defunt, & les prieres de sepulture sont accompagnées d'un tas de terre benite, qui se met dans le coffre du defunt, avant qu'il ne soit transporté pour etre inhumé dans le cimitiere public. Mais dans le cas, qu'on ne trouveroit pas mal à vous de faire la fonction dans le cimitiere, je crois, qu'il seroit convenable d'y accompagner le corps, & de benir la fosse, *toties quoties,* suivant la formule du rituel Romain. Si les Catholiques se font marier avec des Protestantes, ou *vice versa,* par le ministre Protestant, ils doivent être assujettis à une penitence publique avant que d'etre absous. Au moins, c'est l'usage ordinaire içi. En cas de necessité, & sur les representations, qui me sont faites, je puis donner dispense pour les mariages in 2o. gradu consanguinitatis & affinitatis—; et même in 1o. gradu affinâis ex copulâ illicitâ &c. Je vous en instruis, afin que vous sachiez ou vous addresser, au cas que vous vous trouviez dans une situation à demander pareilles dispenses. Indulgence monthly. Lent.

RESPONSE TO PATRICK SMYTH[1] [1789]

The following pages will be written for the sake of those only who delight more in truth than slander; and who feeling themselves interested in the cause of Religion, think no information beneath their notice, which tends to ilustrate its history. When the ministers of the Church are publickly accused of pursuing a system of iniquitous policy, instead of promoting the interests of virtue, the imputation recoils generally on Religion itself. If the imputation be calumnious, the calumny reaised against them receives aggravation from the circumstances of its eventually bringing scandal on the cause, with which their reputations are so nearly connected, and the gradation of guilt will be carried much higher, if a Clergymen himself by traducing his Brethren, essentially injure the the credit of that sacred cause which he is bound to protect.

Nor is he less guilty who sacrifices to the preservation of some selfish and local interest the happiness of numerous Christians and the extension of the Kingdom of Jesus Christ, and for the sake of a particular body of men, to screen them from deserved infamy, and to secure to them an exclusive enjoyment of ease and plenty, refuses to receive fellow-labourers in the vineyard, while he himself with the companions of his indolence beholds it overrun with thorns and briars. Estimating his duty by these principles, the writer of these lines conceives it incumbent on him to assert the honour of Religion by repelling unmerited attacks on its ministers. He will be led unavoidably to give a real statement of some facts, which may prove a better direction to a future historian of the Church, than the pretenders to a —[*illeg.?*] of registering Ecclesiastical Memoirs. The attacks now to be repelled are grievous indeed, and it is uncertain, whether they would not have been borne in silence, had not a threat been denounced more injurious to the honour of the ministers of Religion, than even the attacks themselves. It is said that if an answer be made, authentic records are to be produced, capable of shaming the most impudent liar into silence (p. 46) and that it is owing to the *bounty* of this tender aggressor, that the extravagant Constitutions of Ecclesiastical government in the United States and certain *private documents* to be shown in an unguarded moment are not laid before the public.

Disgusting indeed is his prospect, who knowing Mr. Smyth's propensity to literary controversy, is called to a review of his late publication; and they who have experienced the effects of his proneness to suspicion (to say nothing of other more dangerous weapons to which he sometimes resorts) have reason to fear[,] that as soon as one monster is destroyed he will conjure up another to alarm the public concern. Hercules might subdue Hydra; but it is impossible to exhaust the fecundity of suspicion. What could induce him, a Clergyman, a man of education, who puts in a claim of truth and integrity, to publish to the world what every man in America knows to be void of foundation: that the *liberty of the press* is liable to be restrained in this country by a *violent and opulent party?* (p. 5, 6), that no one *dares mutter a complaint against a Jesuit;* that the Catholic religion was never extended to Pennsylvania before Mr. James[2] sent German missionaries; that poor Catholics instead of removing farther back in quest of plenty and independence are made to hover and starve round the superb seats of the Clergymen and rich squires, conspiring together in a system of oppression? Did he ever visit those superb seats, of which he speaks on the banks of the Potomack? or go to rouse the zeale of slumbering shepherds, whom he describes as basking in the luxuriant climes of the Eastern shore of Maryland? (p. 17.) No; he never saw them, but has trusted to an imagination, pregnant with suspicion, to give colouring to his picture. A word, a hint that he had improved on; and fancy, but not sportive good-natured fancy, has furnished the price.

I presume that considerate men would not deem it criminal in the former missionaries of Maryland, even tho' they were Jesuits, had they honestly built comfortable houses for their retreats, when returning home exhausted with labours, or when age or infirmities rendered labour no longer practicable to them. But either insensibility in their own sufferings or inability, or perhaps, the mismanagement so common to men not trained to the cultivation of landed estates, have in many instances deprived them of even this comfort;— and in contradiction to Mr. Smyth's unwarranted assertions, it is here declared in the case of thousands, who are eye-witnesses to the fact, that of three houses on Potomack ever inhabited by Catholic clergymen, only one enjoys the most ordinary conveniences of a comfortable habitation; that even this with an elegant external appearance, presents no more refined accommodations for the gratification of sensuality, than are found in the families of the middle ranks of Society in America; that the other two houses are so far from being superb are mean and despicable; and in other respects as little calculated as the former, for those enjoyments, which are suggested to the reader in the expressions chosen by Mr. Smyth. If curiosity should be excited by his misrepresentation,[3] should it go to the Eastern Shore of Maryland, it will find there but two clergymen. One of these lives on the confines of Maryland and State of Delaware, in a house not only inelegant, but ruinous and scarce affording shelter from the weather. The other occupies a cell such as the woman of Sumanite prepared for the prophet Eliseus (4th Book of Kings, c. 4), containing just space enough for a bed, a table and a stool. Such are the establishments formed on the Potomack and the Eastern Shore, and yet preserved for the benefit of Religion by that Society, which could not bury obloquy in the same grave with itself, and whose memory Mr. Smyth, in grateful remembrance *of his beloved departed friend* of the order (p. 30) is preparing to consign to perpetual infamy: this he proposes by a *new* translation (I can inform him, that he is not the first to perform this laudable exploit) of Pascal's letters; that is, of a work, branded as false and calumnious by the most respectable tribunals, civil and Ecclesiastical; and therefore not an improper appendix to *the present State of the Catholic Mission.*

In reading over this last performance, one is every moment surprised to find, how easily a pretended history may be compiled without any of the materials, which ought to enter into its composition. Does the Rev. Gentleman treat introduction into the first progress of the Catholic Religion in Maryland, Pennsylvania, New York, and Kentucky? Does he pretend to delineate its actual state, and the conduct of those who by profession are its guardians? Instead of aunthentic history, as might be expected from his self-praised talent of registering Ecclesiastical Memoirs, we meet with little, except mistakes generally springing from malignity, respecting past transactions, to say the least of them of late occurrences.

Where did he find that a few Jesuits attended by a Treasurer,[4] followed Lord Baltimore at his first settlement of Maryland? I have always understood (and my materials, I think, are to be depended on) that only one Jesuit of the name of White, came first into this country with no other treasure than his virtue and no other means than his zeal of preserving the infant colony in the Religion which he brought from Europe; that he returned to England after spending some years in America; and having collected a few fellow labourers, he revisited it again, and that the successors of these first missioners have continued to this day to labour in the vineyard which they planted, and to be the instruments of Divine Providence in enlarging it.

Mr. Smyth laments that they have been so indolent, or so unenterprising, as to confine their feeble services to Maryland alone; (p. 14) that not a single effort of *consequence was made by them,—to extend their missions to their neighbours, or even to assist with any degree of regularity the back countries of Maryland.*

How true this is will be seen hereafter. But were it even so, that they confined themselves to the limits assigned by Mr. Smyth, what cause of reproach can he find in this? Few in number as the English Jesuits always were, unable even to supply the demands of their parent country, and much less those of Maryland; bound by the ties of Gratitude and justice to devote their services to that province for the sake of which they obtained their livings in it; did it belong to them to leave the Catholics of Maryland without pastors, and go, in defiance of their sacred duties, into the neighbouring provinces where no Catholics dwelled, or, at least, none professed their religion? Was it in the opinion of this Rev. Gentleman, a crime in the Jesuits, to leave the harvest of their countries free to the workmen, who [were] never disposed to labour in it? Did they put obstacles in the way between England or Ireland, and New England, New York, Virginia, and the two Carolinas? Why did not this country which could not suffer by sparing a few super-numerary priests, send them forth to the assistance of those abandoned provinces? Why did not they, like the first Jesuits of Maryland encounter poverty and wretchedness to spread and preseve the true faith, and thus by patience and persevereance found useful establishments of Religion? Were the pains and deaths denounced against Catholic Clergymen presuming to enter these provinces, sufficient to damp their zeal? Would not the venerable Dr. Challoner[5] and his predecessors, Bishops of the London district, have joyfully concurred in seconding their Apostolick enterprises had any been formed?

Were those worthy prelates withheld by any imagination of the Jesuits from extending their solicitude to so great a portion of the countries under their charge?

But no such enterprises were formed. The Jesuits were not in sufficient number, and Mr. Smyth ought to say what kept dormant the zeal of others. Since the dissolution of the Society some have come forward across the Atlantic; and if suspicion were as congenial to others as to him, they might invent some plausible reasons for this new appearance of zeale. However, that may be, the public ought to be informed that the few surviving Ex-Jesuits owe to Religion one more service in addition to those which they have already rendered in Maryland, and that is to secure from waste and misappli-cation, and to transmit undiminished to the future ministers of the Church, the property, which was acquired for its advantage, and preserved by their predecessors.

Of this their sincere attachment to the cause, which they served so long, the journals of the Assembly of Maryland bear ample testimony; with whose concurrence they hope to see their view carried soon and finally into effect. Had these Ex-Jesuits been such as Mr. Smyth represents them, deaf to the voice of conscience and eager *to share the spoils,* (p. 33) what could have hindered them from converting their lands and Negroes into portable prop-erty, as soon as the Society was destroyed, and enjoying in indolence the fruit of their sacrilegious plunder? With the same laudable view of fixing a stigma on the ministers of Religion in Maryland, our church historian says that the Catholic Religion ceased from being an established Religion in Maryland. (I wonder from what register of Ecclesiastical Memoirs he learnt this curious fact, unknown before, that it ever was the established Religion.) [*sic*–; that] That the Marylanders *branched out into various forms of worship,* while the great *body of the Irish* had invariably adhered to the Religion of their Fathers. This the reader cannot but understand [as] a delicate stroke of the gentleman's pen at those pastors of whom he somewhere says, that they are *slumbering in the vineyard.*

But if indeed they have slumbered more than others, it is a consolation to know, that Providence has graciously interposed to prevent in great measure the bad effects which would naturally arise from their drowsiness. For it is notorious that few of [the] original Catholic Families in Maryland, which did not emigrate to the other parts of America, have abandoned their religion; and many others have embraced it. They are reduced much indeed in point of prosperity and [influence, both because like other men they have been][6] liable to carelessness and extravagance; and because during the prevalence of the British Empire, they were most iniquitously excluded from the favours of government and even from professing the most lucrative employments, [; yet] their numbers have daily increased and their congregations have multiplied.

But Mr. Smyth says there is no vestige of Catholic Religion in Annapolis, the capital of Maryland. In vain will the traveller (there) seek for such a monument of the zeal of its ministers and first planters. On this occasion he might at least have given them the credit of not being ambitious to establish themselves near the seats of grandeur such as our country affords, and which I suppose flatter the human mind, in proportion equally with the more splendid greatness of richer and higher polished cities. But the reader will not find Mr. Smyth once deviating from his line of composition into praise and commendation. If he cannot distort a fact into a subject of censure, he will be wholly silent on it. When he pretended to write a sketch of the history of Religion and its ministers, he ought to have known, that while Catholics bore any share or had any influence in the government of Maryland, the town of St. Mary and not Annapolis was the capital. A church was built very early near to that, and has been rebuilt again, and subsists to the present day; Under all the discouragement of subsequent times the great body of inhabitants in the neighbourhood (for the town subsists no more), are still of the Religion of their Forefathers, besides many who are gone to people Kentucky. When after the Revolution in England, the seat of government was removed to Annapolis, it was carried into the heart of the Protestant interest. Thither crowded all officers and placemen, among whom no Roman Catholic could be ranked; there sat the Assemblies, which kept always over them a jealous and watchful eye, and sometimes attempted their total suppression. In a small town where every inhabitant was exposed to notice and scarce any settled, but with a view to preferment, is it a matter of wonder that our Religion thus discouraged and persecuted, should make little progress? And yet in this very town, and not merely in the *neighbourhood* as is asserted by our *candid and well-informed historian,* there has always been and still is a decent chapel visited every month by a clergyman.

With respect to the past and present state of Religion in Baltimore, as well as the other historical scraps gleaned from his registry of *Ecclesiastical Memoirs,* he is misinformed in, or he misrepresents almost every circumstance. Baltimore began to grow into notice not more than 25 or 30 years ago. Before that it was an inconsiderable village, which afforded neither employment or sufficient living even for a minister of the established church, who derived his living [support] not from the few inhabitants of the town, but from a general tax on people of every denomination in the parish, which comprehended a large portion of Baltimore County. As the town increased, so did the number of Catholics; and through much opposition, and by great constancy both in the Congregation and the Clergyman who occassionally visited it, they were amongst the first to build a small church, which is now receiving considerable enlargement. A house for the residence of a Clergyman was added some years after [this] chiefly by the contributions of the congregation: the *better informed* Mr. Smyth says, it was done at the private expense *of a Jesuit in order to claim the property on a future occasion.*

He concludes his account on the State of Religion in Baltimore by some injurious reflections on the Rev. Gentleman, who officiates for the congregations of that place. This is his return [of] generosity for the continued civilities and hospitality, with which he has treated for a month by that very gentleman, who needs not my vindication from the groundless aspersions of his Guest.[7] The goodness of his heart; the [his] zeal for the welfare of his flock; his punctuality in his pastoral duties are conspicuous to all, and are not to be heightened by my descriptions of them. As a writer his compositions would have no cause to shrink from the eye of the critic, tho' placed in view of those of his Detractor; he is incapable of uttering a falsehood; and he has solemnly declared to me that he has never used the expressions ascribed to him because he never entertained the sentiments which they convey. But is Mr. Smyth equally entitled to credit; who had the confidence to commit to press, that the Catholic Religion in Baltimore *may be assimilated to an almost consumed taper glimmering in the socket?* The fact is, that as many witnesses may be produced as there are inhabitants in that town, that thro' the providence of God, our Religion has increased and does greatly increase in numbers. The person who with Mr. Smyth's means of information asserts the contrary, may discover the grounds of his assertions in those malignant passions, which too often agitate the human heart.

Perhaps he hoped to avail himself of the prejudices raised against a late Society; thinking, that if it could but bring Ex-Jesuits into view, thousands would be ready enough to believe them capable of every offence, which malignity should be pleased to assign to them. Their time (says this humane man) is employed not in the apostolic functions of instructing the ignorant, of visiting the sick, or catechising with patience and condescention poor unheeded slaves; but in goading these wretched being, *and whipping and almost flaying them alive* (p. 18).

Mr. Smyth knows and should not forget, that a calumniator cannot atone for his guilt, but by making his retraction as public as his offence, and that the weight of his obligation is, at least, commensurate to the heinousness of the slander. Beyond all question reparation is a debt, which he owes to many persons, whose reputation, from the nature of their functions, is of some importance to the community as well as to themselves. This obligation they

call on him to discharge; let him think of it, before he presumes again to
make his offering on the altar of the God of justice and peace. They deny in
the face of all Maryland (I would say of Heaven itself, if Mr. Smyth had not
made a most unrighteous appeal to the God of Heaven–p. 18–at the very
moment he was devoting his pen to the office of defamation),[;] they deny
his most atrocious charge, a charge equal at least, to that of cool and
deliberate murder. They deny that he ever saw one single instance, in any
clergyman of America, of the horrible crime which he imputes generally to
them all. On the contrary, they say that a few amongst them are concerned in
the management of estates of negroes that they . . . [sic] . . . [illeg.?][8] no
such avocation from their pastoral duties; that the few to whom this management is committed, treat their negroes with great mildness and are attentive
to guard them from the evils of hunger and nakedness; that they work less
and are much better fed, lodged and clothed, than labouring men in almost
any part of Europe; that the instances are rare indeed, and almost unknown,
of corporal punishment being inflicted on any of them who are come to the
age of manhood; and that a *priest's negro* is almost proverbial for one, who is
allowed to act without control.

Besides the advantage of this humane treatment, they are instructed
incessantly in their duties of Christianity and their morals watched, I may
say, with fatherly solicitude. By this treatment they are induced to conceive
an attachment for their masters and the habitations of which they have given
the strongest evidence. During the late war the British cruisers landed often at
and hovered almost continually around the plantations of the clergy; they
pillaged their houses; they drove and slaughtered their sheep and cattle. What
an opportunity for their slaves to desert from their cruel treatment described
by Mr. Smyth.

But how was the fact? While the negroes belonging to the neighbouring
plantations were crowding aboard the British ships, those of the Priests, tho'
whipped and scourged and almost flayed alive, refused every invitation to go,
and even force used to carry them on board. Of the whole number belonging
to Clergymen, two only were seduced away, one of them [whom][9] took the
first opportunity of returning. The rest either absolutely refused, or ran into
the woods to prevent being carried off. The fact alone furnishes the most
complete refutation of the charge made by Mr. Smyth. When he seemed to
boil with indignation against the crimes, conceived only in his suspcious
bosom, are we to consider his expressions as genuine effusions or as the
affectation of humanity? Can defamation coexist with humanity? Can we
expect the delicate feelings of sympathy, when even justice is violated? Can
we suppose that Mr. Smyth will not indulge himself in colouring certain
objects too highly?

With the same spirit of bitterness he proceeds to an erroneous history of
progress and present State of Religion in Pennsylvania. Like a good Irishman,
full of resentments for the evils his country has suffered from England, if he

cannot withhold commendation from some Jesuits, he will take care however
not bestow it on English Jesuits. The writer of these sheets owes as little
favour to Britain as to Mr. Smyth; but he owes great respect to truth. And
truth obliges him to contradict Mr. Smyth, and inform others, what everybody in Philadelphia knows, that the exercise of the Catholic Religion was
begun there long before the arrival of any German Jesuits: that the first
chapel was opened by the Rev. Greaton, and the new church, in which Mr.
Smyth saw divine service performed with so much decorum, was raised by the
exertions and under the auspices of the late Rev. Mr. Harding. The relation of
Mr. James' foundation is likewise discordant with the fact. From Mr. Smyth's
account one would imagine that Mr. James was a Protestant and lived in
America, when he solicited for German Jesuits; the fact was otherwise. He
then was a Catholic in England, and had become a Catholic by meeting
accidentally with the life of St. Francis Xavier, and afterwards by conversing
with the late excellent Dr. Challoner. It is unnecessary to follow thro' all the
mistakes in this subject. But he concluded his account of Pennsylvania with
an anecdote of which he observes that it [may help the main drift of his
paper (p. 12). I think so too For nothing] [10] is more apt to promote the
growth of calumny as an anecdote high[ly] seasoned with that commodity.
Here is the real fact: A year or two before the death of the late Rev. and
much revered Mr. Farmer he received information, by letters from Germany,
of the character and estimable qualities of Mr. Graessel who had been in the
novitiate of the Jesuits at the time of their dissolution. Mr. Farmer wrote to
him earnestly inviting him to give his services to that country which he
himself had burdened with his sweat and expressing the pleasure he should
feel in having a cooperator who had been trained in the same school and
discipline as himself. After receiving this letter Mr. Graessel resigned a
handsome employment and flattering prospects of preferment, in order to
join his venerable correspondent. But when he reached Philadelphia, Mr.
Farmer was no more. About the same time arrived likewise from Germany
two Capuchin Priests,[11] worthy and able labourers in the Lord's vineyard. The
ecclesiastical Superior appointed each of his respective station and nominated
Mr. Graessel to remain in Philadelphia. He was induced by several considerations: 1st. Mr. Graessel, in consequence of Mr. Farmer's invitation quitted his
employment and prospects in Bavaria bringing with him the original letter of
invitation, and in full expectation of remaining at Philadelphia; 2ndly. His
education having been the same as that of those who were to be his
companions in Philadelphia, and they having expressed their wish for his
appointment, the Superior thought so much was due to their services and
enjoyment, not to refuse their request. 3rd. He thought likewise it was a just
way of rewarding the members of the body, who, under God, had brought
Religion to its present state in Philad., provided their talents were equal to
their charge. Let the Catholics of Philadelphia say, whether Mr. Graessel has

not appeared as such. Mr. Smyth says that another Gentleman had recommended himself in Phila. by superior talents at least for preaching. He makes assertions without the least support of truth; neither of the candidates had been heard in Philadelphia, when the appointment was made; and I nearly believe, that oneone of them has never been heard there, even to this day; tho' I am sure he would be heard with pleasure. A part of the German Congregation but not the most numerous or little more than the most numerous part, some of whom had contracted a friendship for the worthy son of St. Francis, were dissatisfied with the appointment—they even took some measures, the impropriety of which they themselves afterward avowed; they applied to the Superior for his approbation to build a new church for their nation, and, as they said to preserve their native tongue. The Superior instantly granted their request. He (Mr. Smyth) adds that the new church [12] will continue a *monument of German resentment.* For my part I rather trust it will be a *monument of German piety.* He says that it is only separated by the street from the old one. The eyes of all Philadelphia behold it at least 400 yards distant.

[(Summation of remainder:)[13] In substance it states that Father Farmer was the first priest appointed by the Superior.

It praises the zeal of Fath. Farmer and tells how he visited N.Y. before the revolutionary war, when the legal punishment was death for priests or Jesuits presuming to set foot on that Province. He denies the *universal faculties* attributed to Fr. Whelan by the Rev. Mr. Smyth. He shows that Whelan's spiritual powers were granted to him by the Superior. He then refers to the arrival of Fr. Nugent.

Note 6. Lord Baltimore never came to Maryland. His brother Leonard brought over the settlers. Two Jesuits came, White and Altham, no treasurer.[14] Baltimore did not provide for them, they came as Gentlemen adventurers.

7. To call priests like Frs. Hunter, Molyneux, Copley, etc. the refused (or refuse?) of both countries is shameful.

James was not a convert and a Catholic; he lived in England not America, and put his fund in the V(icariate). A(polstolic). of London.

11. The Jesuits had no control of the fund and could not fling it into the common sewer.

13. The German Ex-Jesuit alluded here to was the holy Mr. Graessel.

16. Catholic never State Religion in Maryland. The Maryland Protestants are not the descendants of fallen Catholics but of Protestant Settlers.

16-7. Annapolis.]

L Guilday, pp. 313-21 and *Researches,* XXII (N.S. I[July, 1905]), 194-206. ADf   AAB not found. Guilday's appears to be the more accurate and was corrected here and supplemented by *Researches* where needed. The latter has page references to Smyth's work and underlines (italics) quoted passages from it. Other adjustments are noted

below. In cases of doubt on punctuation and spelling Carroll's prevailing practices are
followed. On date and context see Carroll to Troy, July 2, 1789 and to William O'Brien,
May 10, 1788. May 21, 1789 to Carey refers to the item.
   [1] Rev. Patrick Smyth, *The Present State of the Catholic Missions Conducted by the
Ex-Jesuits in North America* (Dublin, 1788).
   [2] Sir John James, biographically noted by Carroll later in his Response, died in 1741,
but his bequest was not applied to Bishop Challoner's care until ten years later.
Benefactions and supports for the clergy then came regularly to Pennsylvania thereafter.
   [3] The next four words are from *Researches* version.
   [4] John Lewger is evidently referred to here. He appears to be a priest while in
America, although it is not clearly established, and he later sought to become a Jesuit.
He served as Secretary of the Province and handled financial affairs.
   [5] Richard Challoner was Vicar Apostolic of London with jurisdiction over America
through much of the American Revolutionary War period.
   [6] *Researches* addition in brackets.
   [7] Reference to Charles Sewall, S.J.
   [8] The first brackets are Guilday's the second the Editor's.
   [9] *Researches* version.
   [10] *Ibid.* additions.
   [11] Probably the Heilbrons.
   [12] Holy Trinity Church.
   [13] The remainder is from *Researches,* which attempted an intepretation of the highly
illegible passage at the end of the Response.
   [14] Reference to Lewger, who is discussed in note 4 above.

TO THE CLERGY   1789

Not found. See Apr. 8, 1789 to Carey.

TO PETER GIBAULT   Jan., 1789

Not found. See Dec. 27, 1790, to Churchwardens of St. Vincennes.

TO [THOMAS LLOYD[1]]   Baltre. Jan. 12–1789–

Sir   With this you will receive the list of subscribers for the *unerring
authority* &c–, at least, such as I have been able to collect. For notwithstanding my request to have the names of subscribers returned by Christmass,
many have neglected it. My occupations here have prevented my seeing many
persons, who would, I know, have added their names to the list: but tho I
cannot no authorise you to put them down as subscribers, I expect to be able
to do so in a short time.

   I mentioned to you that Coghlan the London Bookseller had written to
me something concerning a gentleman of your name, which I could not then
recollect. He sent a letter at the same time, which I sent, not having the
pleasure of knowing you then, to Mr. Molyneux, requesting him to enquire for

the person, to whom it was directed. I think M. Molyneux never gave any answer on the subject. I have now referred to Coghlans letter, & find as follows.[2]

I am with great regard, Sir   Yr. obedt. & most hle st.   J Carroll

In Mr. Sewall's list of subscribers, two names are not filled up, they not being legible. They shall be obtained on another occasion. Mr. Robert Welsh has some names likewise on his paper; but I cannot see him, before Mr. Beeston's departure.

ALS   ACHS   See footnote 2 for addressee identification.
[1] Served as clerk of the Continental Congress.
[2] Coghlan sought to pass an inquiry from a friend for Lloyd through Carroll, regarding the fact of Lloyd's connection with the Congress. This identifies the addressee of the above.

TO ARTHUR ST. CLAIR[1]   Baltimore Jan. 29–1789–

Sir   I take the liberty of addressing you by Mr. Tardiveau, who will, I presume, have the honour of paying you his respects in his progress to Kaskasias. After offering to your Excellency my best wishes for your health and happiness in the fine climate, which you now inhabit, I presume to recommend to your protection those interests, to which I am bound by my station to pay an attention. I have heard, that complaints have been transmitted to you & Congress, against the Revd. Mr. La Valiniere of the Kaskasias. As I only know him from character, I cannot form a very competent judgment of his merit or demerit in the cases complained of. Your Excellency has it in your power to form much a more accurate estimate. He offered me his services for those of our Religion in the Illinois country, & produced the best certificates of his moral & Religious conduct from the Ecclesiastical Superiors, under whom he had lived. He was, to my knowledge, a great sufferer for his attachment to the cause of America. These reasons induced me to vest him with a superintendence over the other clergymen residing in the same country. I have since had reason to fear, that he has used his powers indiscreetly & vehemently, & even exceeded them. But perhaps your Excellency will find, on enquiry, that he had some persons to deal with, who having been a long time withdrawn from the inspection of any Superior, had lost the virtues of their state, &[2] required a tight government to bring them into a sense of their duty.

I am far from offering this as a full vindication of his conduct; but as some alleviation. When I heard from him last, he was in impatient expectation of your Excellency's arrival, from which he promised himself ample justice; but, at the same time, he expressed an intention of leaving his residence. If he has effected this, I have perhaps given you unnecessary trouble by laying these things under your consideration.

If Genl. Varnum be with you, I take the liberty of requesting that my humble respects be presented him—& of adding to you both, as I know the congeniality of your sentiments, that the cause of federalism is so fully triumphant in this state, that the whole federal ticket, for Representatives & electors of the President, has been carried without the mixture of any other character.

I have the honour to be with the greatest respect, Sir   Yr. Excellency's most obedt. st.   J. Carroll

ALS   LC (Peter Force Papers, 1789).
  [1] Governor of the Northwest Territory at this time.
  [2] The preceeding evidently refers to the conflict of jurisdiction which Valiniere had with Peter Gibault, who had earlier possessed powers from the Bishop of Quebec.

TO MATTHEW CAREY[1]   Baltimore Jan. 30—1789—

Sir   I have just now, been favoured with yours of Jan. 26—& the inclosed proposals for publishing the Doway Bible—, by which I presume you mean the Doway Bible, agreeably to the last corrections made in it by the late Bishop Challenor. I still retain the same desire of seeing it in the hands of our people, instead of those translations, which they purchase in stores & from Booksellers in the Country, & you may depend on my exertions for the encouragement of a liberal subcription.

But at the same time, I must communicate to you my fears, that you will not be sufficiently supported to carry through so expensive an undertaking. I know, it will be a difficult matter to obtain 1200 dollars paid in hand, before the work is begun. I cannot tell, how consistent, what I have now to propose, may be with any reasonable prospect of advantage to yourself; but if the present proposal should prove impracticable, I am well satisfied, that an edition of the New Testament, in a moderate 8vo., would meet with good encouragement. My good Br. & companion Mr. Sewall is indeed very desirous that the proposed edition of the old & New Testament should be in separate volumes, of an 8 vo. size, such as it was printed in England. This advantage will attend that form, that many, who would not be able to purchase the whole, might get only the New Testament, and for their accommodation you would probably take off more copies of that part of Scripture.

I must take this occasion to thank you sincerely for some very pertinent observations interspersed in your Museum, on the illiberal treatment of R. Catholics in some, indeed in most of the United States. After having contributed, in proportion to their numbers, equally at least with every other denomination, to the establishment of independence, & ran every risk in common with them, it is not only contradictory to the avowed principle of equality in Religious rights, but a flagrant act of injustice to deprive them of those advantages, to the acquirement of which they so much contributed. I wrote & sent a few reflexions on this subject for the Columbian magazine about 18 months ago:[2] but the Editor, after violating his engagements, made in the outset of his work, & delaying the publication for many months, printed it at length with unjustifiable retrenchments. I am with respect, Sir   Yr. mst. humble st.   J. Carroll

ALS   HSP

[1] A native of Ireland, from which he recently came, he was active in Irish emancipation and had a long career as a publisher and book dealer in Philadelphia.
[2] See Sep. 1, 1787.

TO GIUSEPPE DORIA-PAMPHILI   Feb. 23d. 1789.—

Not found. See AAB (8A-I4).

TO [JOHN TROY]   [Mar., 1789]

.... myself indebted for the honour of the candid communications, it contained. About ten days before, I had the pleasure of receiving your letter, Mr Smyth's extraordinary *account of the Catholic Mission in America*[1] was sent me by a friend from Philada. I do not know whether Mr. Mulcaile (thro' misinformation I wrote to him under the name of Mulhall) has communicated to your Grace the letter, I sent to him from New York during the last autumn.[2] That letter might serve to show that Mr. Smyth was of a most suspicious character (which is seldom the case of men of an open & honest disposition); but, I did not imagine that his mind was depraved to the degree of treachery & falsehood, of which I now find him guilty. Your Grace requests me not to answer him: and, on the other hand, I am urged by many of my brethren not to let so grievous imputations remain unrefuted; for silence, they say, will be construed into a consciousness of guilt, especially as Smyth threatens the publication of such *authentic records, as shall shame the most impudent liar into silence.* My time has been so incessantly taken up, since his publication was received, that I have not had a moment's leisure, even to determine myself, by a careful perusal of his work, what counsels to follow. That with which Your Grace honoured me, will have very great weight indeed, and if I shall finally conclude to animadvert on any passages of so injurious a libel (I call it so on your most respectable authority), my animadversions shall be transmitted to Your Grace in the first place, and merely be communicated, with a view whether they may serve to do justice to injured reputations, without meaning to gratify malevolence towards any person whatever.

May I presume to request your Grace to present my most cordial and respectful thanks to their Graces the other Archbishops, who with so much readiness & & [*sic*] so great a desire of preventing the propagation of calumny contained in the condemnation of a work, calculated to injure that very interest, which it pretends to promote. I lament with them that there are so few clergymen spread over these States: but it ever must be the case, unless it please God to inspire good Xtians to make provision for them, or the clergymen [to] have courage to suffer greater hardship [. . .]

The intelligence concerning an Agent to serve here with the powers of a Nuncio was without foundation. A Mr. Thayer, heretofore a Presbyterian minister, became a Catholic at Rome about seven years ago, studied Divinity in the Seminary of St. Sulpice at Paris, has received Orders, & is now expected in Boston. I have urged his coming with all expedition. But he is not to be invested with such powers, as you have heard. On the contrary, His Holiness has lately empowered all officiating Clergymen of the U. States to proceed to the election of an ordinary Bishop to derive his title from some town of the U.S. And I[. . . .]

ADf   AAB   On estimate of addressee and date, see July 2, 1789.
    [1] *The Present State of the Catholic Missions* (Dublin, 1788).
    [2] Letter not found. It may be that Carroll was thinking of a letter to the same of July 9, 1788, given above.

TO JOHN THORPE   Mar. 1789

Not found. See from same, Oct. 18, 1788 (816).

TO MATTHEW CAREY   Balt. March 19–1789

Sir   Since I received yours of the 10th inst., with the altered proposals, I have circulated these, as much as opportunity has allowed, and hope there will be a satisfactory subscription. I have little doubt indeed of it, if my Brethren will exert themselves generally. I desired Mr. Beeston to inform you, that I have not had any returns yet from them; and to add a few names to the Subscribers for your museum, the gleanings from the neighbourhood of George town, left by your Brother, as I was informed, in his passage thro' that place. An obstinate cold & sore throat has prevented my seeing as many in this town, as I expect will subscribe for the Bible. I am with esteem, Sir   Yr. most obedt. st.   J. Carroll

ALS   HSP

TO CHARLES PLOWDEN   Baltimore March 20–1789–

Dear Sir   Your favours of Sept. 15th & Novr. 1st (the last being crowded into Mr Thorpes of Octr. 8th) are received; and the edifying accounts of Donna Maria Antonia. The works of God are wonderful indeed: his graces are adapted not only to the various dispositions, & situations of the moral creation but likewise seem to be fitted to the nature of the country &c. How many provinces and kingdoms are there, which would feel all the severity of want and famine, if such a number of hands were taken for so long a time from the labours of agriculture as, it appears, have been in S. America without any such consequence ensuing? Do not the ways of providence appear to you more and more mysterious, when you consider the great good, which even yet results to Religion, from the past services, & practices introduced by the Society? How far does it surpass our estimate of things, that providence should ordain the destruction of the Society, at that time, when in our judgment its services would appear most necessary? Your favouring me with a continuation of the wonders performed by the agency of that extraordinary woman will be very agreeable.

I received only about the middle of last month Cardl Antonelli's letter, dated in July last; by which he informs me, that his Holiness had granted our request for an Ordinary Bishop the see to be fixed by ourselves, & the choice to be made by the officiating Clergymen. This matter will be gone on immediately, & God, I trust, will direct to a good choice. This confidence is my comfort; otherwise I should be full of apprehensions of the choice falling, where it would be fatal indeed.

I do not know, on what principles your respectable V.V.A.A.[2] govern themselves, by opposing the appointment of Ordinaries for England. I think, it would remove many plausible objections agst. the Catholic Religion, give a more decided authority to the Prelates, & introduce an Ecclesiastical government more consonant to other churches & the established discipline. You have frequently recommended to me to send the characters of Messrs Hunter, Farmer &c to be inserted in the work now preparing by Fr. Termanini. I have as often recommended it to our friend Molyneux, who enjoys the only sinecure, I know of in the U. States: and yet he is so lazy, as to alledge want of time & refer me to Mr Elliotts friend, Austin Jenkins,[3] who has labours enough to kill a less zealous man. However, I expect to see Molyneux in a few days, & if other means will not do, I will engage your schoolfellow Ashton, who will be with us, to discipline him into compliance. Your very gracious intentions with respect to our [*torn*–academy] claim all our gratitude; and tho you have been hitherto disappointed, I hope it will not be always the case. Be not disheartened by past denials from exerting your influence to procure some farther assistance to our undertaking.

To give you in return for your political sketches, something in the same way; we have been the longest while, I ever remember, without hearing from Europe: nothing since Decr. 11th, before to day; when I observe in the paper published this morning, that the Prince of Wales is become sole Regent, and a revolution is made in the ministry. I think, your country will lose a most valuable Minister in Mr Pitt; and if I have any political sagacity, he will be forced upon the Regent, before any very long period be elapsed. You may conclude, that when I discourse with you on politics, I am come nearly to the end of my letter.

My good Mother is always mindful of & respectfully thankful for your kind attention. Messrs Digges and Ashton present their compliments. Mine very respectfully to the honble family, in which you live, & to Messrs Stanley & Clinton. I am my Dr. Sir   Yr. most obedt. & affte friend & st   J. Carroll

Our Religion is introduced into Boston by a French Clergyman, of whom I conceived a very good opinion from the accounts sent me, his certificates, & the sentiments expressed [in] his letters. I now fear he is too assuming & [*torn*—not] very prudent. His name, La Poterie. An Irish priest[4] is settled [*torn*—in] Carolina.

ALS   St
  [1] See May 26, 1788, n. 4.
  [2] Vicars Apostolic.
  [3] Augustin Jenkins, S.J., a Marylander, stationed in 1781 at Newtown (d. 1800).
  [4] Matthew Ryan.

TO THE CLERGY OF THE NORTHERN DISTRICT   Baltimore
                                                    March 25th—1789

Rev. Gentln.   We the Subscribers having been appointed by the Genl. Chapr. began Novr. 13, 1786 to draw up and send to His Holiness a Memorial representing the State of the Rom. Cath. Church in the United States of North America, and petitioning that the Clergy thereof be empowered to choose a Diocesan Ordinary Bishop to govern the same—did in consequence thereof apply to His Holiness and stated the necessity of leaving the members of the Clergy at full liberty in their election of the same: We also petitioned that in the first instance the officiating Clergymen might have a Vote in the Election, leaving to future Regulation the permanent form of election to be adopted hereafter.

His Holiness has been pleased in consequence to grant the prayer of our petition, and to appoint us to see that the said Election be properly conducted and with as much dispatch as possible.

We do therefore hereby notify to all our Brethren, that in order to carry his Holiness' and your own intentions into immediate effect, we have adopted the following mode of election viz.

1⁰. that in each district two of its members be appointed in conjunction with one Agent to open & inspect the several votes taken in their respective districts, viz the Rev. Messrs. Beeston and Graessl with Rev. R. Molyneux as Agent to examine the votes of the Northern district at Philada. the Rev. Messrs. C. Sewall & Sylv. Boarman with the Rev. Mr. J. Carroll to examine the votes of the Middle district at Baltimore; and the Rev. Ig. Matthews & J Walton with the Rev. Mr. J. Ashton to examine the votes of the Southern district at Newtown.

2⁰. that on the votes being opened and examined, a fair list be made thereof, without inserting the names of the Voters, and signed and certified by the Agent and the two members of the district to be a true State of the Votes, and so transmitted for the information of all the Agents. But the original votes with the names of the Voters annexed must not be destroyed, but left in the possession of one of the members of the district deputed to examine them, till advice return of the Election being confirmed by His Holiness.

This mode is adopted for the greater freedom of election, as by that means the names of the Voters will be concealed from the person chosen.

3⁰. That the time limited for compleating the Elections in all the districts be from the date hereof till the last day of April ensuing. When the votes of all the districts are thus taken and laid before all the Agents, one list shall be made of the whole, and whoever has the majority of the Votes from the collective Body of the Clergy will be the person duly elected and whose election shall be notified to all the districts as soon as possible.

As it will be necessary for us to meet again to examine the Votes of the different districts, so it is necessary to have a fixed period stated for the elections; our orders being to have the business finished with all possible dispatch. Therefore the votes will be summed up at the expiration of the above period and the returns thereof made to Rome for the confirmation of His Holiness.

To the end that this business may be carried on and happily compleated to the greater honour of God and good of Religion, We invite All to join Us in saying a Votive Mass of the H. Ghost, before they give in their Votes, and to recommend it earnestly to Alm. God in their other prayers. We are with the greatest respect, Revd. Gentlemen   Yr. most obedt & humble Servants   J. Carroll   R. Molyneux   John Ashton

ALS   MPA

TO CLAUDIUS DE LA POTERIE   Baltimore, April 3d—1789.

R. Sir   I received on the 19th. of March a large packet without date, containing many sheets of paper, your pastoral instruction & other prints; a few days after your manuscript & written letter of March 3d; and finally another printed copy of your pastoral instruction. I was sorry to find in these papers many passages, highly improper for publication in this country, & of a tendency to alienate from our Religion, & disgust the minds of our Protestant Brethren. I am [*sic*] cannot help therefore censuring my own conduct very severely, in sending you the spiritual powers, which I did, till you had time to be better acquainted with the temper & habits of thinking in America; where more caution is required in the ministers of our Religion, than perhaps in any other Country. I have moreover heard complaints of your conduct from one of the principal persons of the State of Massachusetts; and I see in your publications the grounds of the complaints. Amongst other things, it is said, you have rendered our Religion most execrable to the people of Boston & have even exasperated the legislation agst. it. I therefore find it absolutely necessary for the preservation of Religion, to commission the Revd. Mr. o Brien, of New York, to inform himself of all matters concerning your conduct; & (if he finds it necessary) to revoke the faculties, which I sent you, till farther regulations can be made. I am particularly displeased to find, that [*illeg.*] of dissatisfaction with the French Consul at Boston, you would print any thing relative of your differences with him and thereby inform the publick of dissensions, breaking out amongst you, as soon as ever the exercise of our Religion was opened in Boston. I saw likewise with surprise in your pastoral Instruction, (which it was very unnecessary to print) that you give yourself the titles of Vice prefect, Curate of the Church of the Holy Cross and Prothonotary. I certainly did not constitute you Vice-prefect, which implies a jurisdiction over other Clergymen if any should come to Boston: nor Pastor of that Congregation, tho' you have faculties for the administration of the Sacraments;: and as your announcing yr. title of Prothonotary, &c you could hardly do any thing more offensive to the Govt. of America: for it will be supposed in consequence that you will undertake to legalise certain acts, in virtue of a foreign authority: whereas nothing of the sort ought to be done, but in virtue of the laws of the state in which you live. In the formulary of your Sunday's discourse you pray publicly for the King of France which it is not proper to do; because it will be concluded, that your Congregation considers him entitled to some sovereignty over them: and, without any authority you have excluded certain classes of people from the communion of the Church, contrary to the discipline existing in America, or in any other Country, that I know of, excepting France; for instance, Comedians &c. I do not pretend to excuse their profession; but only to blame the precipitation of your censure: And you have moreover furnished ample matter of ridicule, by copying from some ritual, not suited to this Country, your exclusion of those from our Communion, who *by witchcraft prevent the use of marriage.* The title, you give me of *Lord* Carroll, tho' a mark of your politeness, is very odious in America, & no wise due to me.

I write to you with great plainness, agreeably to your desire; & think it best for us both. I request you to print nothing more for the present. You will find in the 6th. paragraph of your faculties the case of *homicidium* [*sic*] *voluntarium* comprehended: if not, I grant it you now *pro casu de quo agitur,* & provided the person concerned has already had recourse to your ministry.[1]

ADf   AAB

[1] Probably "homocidium" is meant, or voluntary homicide. The second Latin phrase, "for a case in which action is being taken," has the force of concluding but not first taking up a problem of conscience of a parishioner.

TO MATTHEW CAREY   Balt. Ap. 8–1789–

I have just received your letter of the 6th. inst., but not the advertisements, which were to accompany it. I have dispersed many of those, received before. It is impossible for me to get returns this evening from the different persons employed to take subscriptions. On my own list, I have upward of twenty. I do not expect to get returns from my Brethren till the middle of May, when I shall probably meet several of them. I have written to them,[1] as you do to me, that it will be a disgrace to Catholics not to make up so small a number of subscriptions, as is required. In many parts of Maryland, they have been so long used to receive, as presents from their Clergy, the Religious books, they wanted, that they have no idea of purchasing any.

I have repeatedly & very urgently recommended subscriptions for your undertaking from the altar; & I hope, not unsuccessfully. Some active persons have undertaken to solicit.

I am obliged to you for your communications from Massachusett. The establishment of our Religion there has enkindled the fanaticism of the puritans. I am afraid, the French Clergyman's imprudence,[2] & imperfect knowledge of the habits of this Country will inflame it still more. I wish it were in my power to fix a sensible & discreet Gentleman in his place. There is a prospect of making it a very serviceable, as well as comfortable station.

To the list of Subscribers to your Museum, (I sent you some names before) be pleased to add Mr. Chs. Carroll of Carrollton, & send it to him at New York. He left this [city] yesterday to take his seat in the Senate there.[3] He will pay the advance on demand.

In my next to Mr. Beeston, I shall advise him of what has been done here for recommending your undertaking, & encourage him to do the same.

Of those, who have subscribed with me, I have not yet taken the advance; but they are such, as will pay at the moment; and as soon as I know, that a sufficient number is made up to determine you to proceed, I will instantly collect it. I am Sir   Yr. most humble st.   J. Carroll

ALS   HSP

[1] Not found.
[2] De la Poterie.
[3] Possibly with the letters of Jan. 30, Mar. 19, 1789, but were not found with these letters. The *American Museum* began publication by Carey in Jan., 1787 and its seventh volume of 1790 was dedicated to Carroll.

TO LEONARDO ANTONELLI   From Baltimore in Maryland,
                                                      14 April, 1789

Most Eminent and Reverend Lord:—   Last year on the 5th of August I received a letter from your Lordship dated January 19; and again on February 18 of this year another written on July 12, 1788.

That the two students[1] from the United States have found patrons in Rome they owe largely to the Sacred Congregation. That they continue to commend themselves by their good conduct and talent gives me great satisfaction. In their letters to their parents they speak favorably of the benevolence of all in their regard. God grant that they may always enjoy this good reputation, that it grow, and that they do not disappoint your Lordship's hope that in time they will become worthy ministers of the church.

Not in vain was my hope that through the civil law assistance would be given towards ending the spiritual jurisdiction and boldness of the man who has given so much scandal in New York.[2] For the civil judges to whom he appealed, on the principle of full religious liberty which I mentioned in my letter,[3] have judged that since he was condemned by his ecclesiastical superior according to the precepts of our faith, he should no longer be deemed fitted for the pastoral office. Thus peace was restored to that church.

At the beginning of last autumn I sent to Charleston, the largest city of the state of South Carolina, a priest from the diocese of Dublin.[4] His bishop, from whom I could wish greater promptness, testified to the man's probity. From the letters of this man I find out that there are not a few Catholics but some of them conceal their faith while others are wanting in all sense of piety.

For a long time I have eagerly looked for the arrival of Mr. Thayer, whose reputation I doubt not must be known to your Lordship. I had heard that with the approbation of the Sacred Congregation he was assigned to these States so that in his native city of Boston he could begin to preach and conduct Catholic services. Meanwhile at the end of last year a Frenchman, La Poterie, chanced to come here. I mention this because he writes that he lived a long while in Rome and was well known to many cardinals and other prelates. While he strove to attain some proficiency in the use of our language he insisted that I grant him faculties to administer the sacraments, and he had several people submit testimonials on his behalf. I agreed to this temporarily. At once he opened a school and began to exercise the sacred ministry.

Moreover, all that he did or planned to do he broadcast in the press perhaps somewhat indiscreetly. I began to suspect that he was unduly tenacious of his opinion and that zeal rather than prudence guided him. While both are desirable, prudence is most desirable, and particularly in Boston.

I continue to stress a school as patently necessary for the preservation of our faith. However we must proceed slowly because of the expense to which we are not equal. For this reason I derived the greatest satisfaction from the assurance that your Lordship would, if possible, bring it about that at some time financial help would be applied to this pious use.

Now I take up the letter of your Eminence, dated July 12, by which my two confreres and I were informed what our Holy Father, on the advice of the Congregation, had deigned to decide about the establishment of a bishop. As one man we reply briefly. With all due respect we express our common sense of gratitude. I must say that we heartily thank His Holiness, the Sacred Congregation, and its very eminent Prefect, that in so weighty a matter, they put their trust in us. In developing this matter there would have been no lack of diligence on our part, but the unusual delay in the passage of letters intervened, together with the remoteness of the priests from one another. Then Lent and Easter impeded communication. This April the suffrages of all can be collected. After that all the other points contained in your instruction will be taken up in due order, and the reasons for our decision will be forwarded to Rome.

ADf   AAB
[1] Ralph Smith and Felix Dougherty.
[2] Andrew Nugent.
[3] April 19, 1788, above.
[4] Matthew Ryan.

Ex Baltimorae in Marilandia die 14 Aprilis, 1789   Eme et Revdsme Domine   Die 5a Augusti anni elapsi literas accepi quas 19 Januarii Eme Dominatio ad me destinavit; atque iterum 18a Februarii anni currentis alias sub data 12 Julii, an. 1788.

Quod duo alumni ex his foederatis Americae provinciis et Roman hospites acceperint, et Sacrae Congregationi tantum debent, bonis moribus et ingenio sese commendare pergant, et quidem mihi maxime gratum accidit. Illi admodum satis suis ad parentes suos literis universam omnium erga se benevolentiam possunt commendare. Facit Deus, ut bonam hanc in se existimationem semper sustineant ac majorem in modum augeant, neque spem frustrentur, quam Ema. Dominatio Tua de ipsis concepit, fore scilicet, ut excellentes Ecclesiae ministri suo tempore evadant.

Non me fefellit spes, quam mente conceperam, fore ut ex legum etiam civilium auctoritate robur aliquod accederet et ad jurisdictionem spiritualem frangendam illius audaciam, qui Neo Eboraci tam gravis scandali auctor fuit. Judices enim, ad quos ille provocavit, inhaerentes illi principio, quod meis literis memoravi, de plena Religionum libertate, judicavere ipsum, utpote a Superiore suo Ecclesiastico juxta Religionis nostras regulas condemnatum, non amplius pastorali muneri aptum censeri debere, Ita pax illi Ecclesiae restituta.

Sub initium autumni anni elapsi, destinavi Caropolim, quae est urbs metropolis Provinciae Carolinae meridionalis, Sacerdotem ex diocese Dublinensi, probum quidem, ut ex Archiepiscopo cognovi, in quo tamen majorem expeditionem desiderarem. Ex ipsius literis comperio, plures admodum ibi esse Catholicos, sed partim occultos, partim omni pietatis sensu destitutos.

Diu atque avide expectavi adventum Domini Thayer, quem Eme. Dominationi Tuae fama esse cognitum non dubito. Audivi enim ipsum, cum Sacrae Congregationis commendatione, ad has provincias fuisse destinatum, ut in urbe sua nativa, quae dicitur Bostonia, Catholicam Religionem praedicare et exercere inciperet. Interim sub finem anni praeteriti illuc casu advenit Sacerdos Gallus, La Poterie, quod ideo adjicio, quia scribit se diu Romae vixisse ac multis Em Cardinalibus, aliisque praelatis probe notum esse. Cum aliquam nostrae linguae notitiam comparasset, magno studio facultates pro Sacramentorum administratione postulasset, atque quorundam in sui gratiam testimonia subministrasset, illius votis pro brevi spatio annui; unde statim Eccesiam aperire ac Religionis ministeria coepit exercere; atque omnia sibi facta, sive agenda, typis evulgare et fortasse non satis caute; incipit suboriri mihi aliqua suspicio, hominem esse sui judicii plus juste tenacem et zelo magis quam prudentia valere; cum tamen utrumque desideratur, sed praecipue prudentia, et maxime Bostoniae.

Pergo urgere scholae institutionem, utque plane, pro Religionis conservatione necessarium; lente tamen procedendum est propter expensas, quibus non sufficimus; unde gratissimo animi sensu accepit effecturam Em. Dom. tuam, siquidem fieri potest, ut aliquando pecuniae subsidium in tam pium opus decerneretur.

Venio nunc ad literas tuas, Eme, Cardinalis, diei 12 Julii quibus confratribus meis duobus, quid ex Sacrae Congregationis consilio Beatissimus Pater Noster statuere dignatus sit de Episcopo constituendo. Communi quidem nomine ad has literas breviter scriberemus; et gratos omnium sensus, ea quae decet, veneratione significabimus. Interim hoc mihi dicendum existimo ingentes suae Sanctitati et sacrae Congregationi, et Eminentissimo illius Praefecto gratias deberi, quo ita nobis in tanto negotio fidant; in quo maturando nulla deficisset diligentia nisi inusitata mora in literarum reditione intervenisset; ac deinde magna operariorum a se invicem distantia; Quadragesimae, festorumque Paschalium interventio conciliorum obstitisset.

Aprilis omnium vota colligi poterunt, deinde reliqua quae habemus in mandatis, recto ordine fiant, atque Romam ratio factorum.

TO ANTOINE DUGNANI   Baltimore, April 14–1789

My Lord   I had the honor of notifying Your Excellency in my letter of February,[1] by way of Bourdeaux that I had just learned from His Eminence

Cardinal Antonelli that His Holiness had decided to erect here an Episcopal See, & to impower the Priests, workers in this vineyard of the Lord, to proceed with the election of the first Bishop. The votes of the various members of the Clergy can not be gathered before the end of this month, given their great distance from one another. As soon as the election is made, those of my colleagues who are responsible with me for executing the designs of His Holiness, will hasten to inform Your Excellency of all that was done on this occasion.

I venture to beg Your Excellency to forward the enclosed letters to those for whom they are destined.

ADf   AAB
¹ Not found.

J'ai eu l'honneur de prevenir V. Exc, dans ma lettre du mois de Fevrier, par la voye de Bourdeaux, que je venois d'apprendre de Son Em. le Cardinal Antonelli que S. S. s'etoit decidée à eriger içi un Siege Episcopal, & à donner charge aux Pretres, ouvriers en cette vigne du Seigneur, de proceder à l'election du premier Evêque. Les voix de differens membres du Clergé ne peuvent etre recueillies avant la fin de ce mois, vu leur grand eloignement l'un de l'autre. Aussitotque l'election sera faite, ceux de mes confreres qui sont chargés avec moi pour faire executer les desseins de S.S., ne manqueront pas d'informer V. Exc. de tout ce qui sera fait à cette occasion.

J'ose prier V. Exc. de vouloir faire passer les lettres çi jointes aux P.P. pour lesquelles elles sont destinées.

TO VITALIANO BORROMEO   Apr. 14, 1789

I have learned by a letter from His Eminence Cardinal Antonelli that His Holiness has decided to erect in the United States of America an episcopal see & to leave the choice of the Bishop, this first time, to the Apostolic workers in this vineyard of the Lord. I know how much this church owes this privilege to Your Eminence, and how much you have done in all this to contribute to strengthening and expanding it. The great distance my colleagues are from each other, & the various arrangements necessary and preliminary to the election, will not permit gathering their votes before the end of this month. May Jesus Christ, the Shepherd of his Church, direct them toward that, which more than all else, will make zeal and piety reign in the Priests & the people. The great means will be the establishment of Catholic schools & a seminary. Cardinal Antonelli has had the kindness to write me that he will try to obtain help, to this effect, from the Sacred Congregation of the Propaganda. I am persuaded that Your Eminence will not fail to support his advice and his recommendation. I have learned that Your Eminence is an admirer of tobacco from Virginia. I take the liberty of sending you by the first vessel leaving here for the Mediterranean some different varieties.

ADf   AAB   The date is assumed from the fact that the draft appears immediately below a letter to Dugnani of the same date. The contents of both letters are similar.

J'ai appris par une lettre de S. Em. le Cardl. Antonelli que Sa Sainteté s'etoit decidée à eriger dans les Etats Unis de l'Amerique un siège Episcopal, & de laisser le choix de l'Evêque, cette premiere fois, aux ouvriers Evangeliques en cetter vigne du Seigneur. Je scais, combien cette Eglise est redevable de cette grace à V. Em:, et combien elle prend part à tout çe, qui poura contribuer à l'affermir et l'etendre. Le grand eloignement, ou sont mes confreres l'un de l'autre, & les divers arrangemens necessaires prealablement à l'election, ne permettront pas que les voix se rassemblent avant la fin de çe mois. Que J. C., Pasteur de son Eglise, les dirigent vers celui, qui, mieux que tout autre, fera regner le zele & la pietè dans les Pretres & le peuple. Le grand moyen sera l'etablissement des ecoles Catholiques & d'un Seminaire. Le Cardl. Antonelli a eu la bonté de m'ecrire qu'il tacheroit d'obtenir du secours, a cet effet, de la Sacrée Congn de la Propagde. Je suis persuadé, que V. Em. ne manquera point de soutenir son avis et sa recommendation.—J'ai scu que V. Em. etoit amateur du tabac de la Virginie. Je prendrai la liberté d'addresser à Elle par le premier vaisseau qui partira d'ici pour la Mediteranée des diverses qualités.

TO MATTHEW CAREY'S ASSOCIATE   [May, 1789]

Let Mr. Carey know that in my late excursion to George Town I sollicited subscriptions for his Museum; but his Br. had been just before me, &, I hear, obtained almost from everybody in town. However I got two more, viz.: Thos. Sim Lee, Esq., E Notley Young, Esqr. Their Museums must go to G. Town and Mr. Lee's be put into the hands of Messrs. Waring, Merchts G. Town. Mr. Lee has just paid me some money in advance which I will send by the 1st opportunity; & tho' Mr. Young forgot it, yet I will advance it, if necessary.

L *Records,* IX, 366 (HSP, Letter 292 of Carey Coll.) MS not found, but said to have "Extract from Mr. Carroll's Letter" marked on it, according to *Record* version. Date estimated by reference to May 3, 1789, to Carey. The addressee may have been Steuart, to whom reference is made in this period in letters to Carey on similar business. See July 12, 1791.

TO MATTHEW CAREY   Baltimore May 3rd. 1789—

Sir   Returning last night, after a short absence from Baltimore, I found here your very kind favour of April 27th. with Mr. Smyth's publication inclosed.¹ I have not yet had leisure to read it thro, but have read enough to convince me of something, I only suspected before, but now have full evidence o̲f, that truth is not a leading principle in his character. I am sincerely sorry, that he should employ good talents on a subject, which he has opened by betraying confidence, misrepresenting some matters, falsifying letters & inventing things, which never happen'd. I have not yet come to any resolution about answering it. I have materials in my possession, sufficient, I think, to invalidate every one of his charges, & on the clearest evidence. But contention, I know, is his element; & he has abilities to carry it on. To me it is odious, & I want both time & many other ingredients to engage in contest with such a man. I shall consult my friends: and if I finally conclude that the credit of Religion require it of me (for nothing personal to myself shall draw me into a controversy) you may be assured of having the offer of my manuscript, either to print it yourself, or to be advised by you conce[rning–*illeg.*] the sending it to some of your correspondents in Ireland, under the direction however, of some friend of mine there.

I beg you not to despair yet of publishing the Bible. It is true, I have not as yet very favourable returns, but quite the contrary. There is, however, to be a meeting of many of our Clergy about the middle of this month. I then will urge, with my most earnest endeavours, a renewal of exertions in favour of a work, which I conceive to be eminently necessary for the instruction of our flocks, & for the credit of Religion.

I hope you send your Museums to the Gentlemen, whom I mentioned to you. Their money will be paid, whenever called for by your agent at George-Town. I received myself the 1st. payment from Mr. Lee, & forgot to send it you by some opportunities, which offered. In the mean time, it cannot have been any detriment to you to have witheld it. I am, Sir   Yr. most obedt. st.   J. Carroll.

ALS   HSP
¹ Patrick Smyth, *The Present State of the Catholic Missions conducted by the Ex-Jesuits in North America* (Dublin, 1788). Smyth served briefly at Frederick, Md. and returned to Ireland, expressing gratitude to Carroll for his consideration of him. He soon attacked Carroll for alledgedly favoring the former Jesuits and generally criticized the condition of the American clergy as well as Carroll.

TO CHARLES PLOWDEN   Baltimore May 8–1789–

Dear Sir: Since my last in March, I have been favoured with yours of Feby 2d by the packet. & March 2d. Be pleased to inform Mr. Thorpe (I reserve myself to write to him fully in about a fortnight) that a pamphlet has just made its appearance here, sent from Ireland, with which you, I presume, are well acquainted. It is written most rancorously by the Mr Smyth, who returned to his own Country after a stay of six months here.¹ You know, that I had my suspicions of this mans views in coming, & he has justified my suspicions: notwithstanding the cause I had to question the disinterestedness & purity of his intentions in coming to America, yet I treated him with so much confidence & attention that I hoped his malevolence would be disarmed, if he brought any along with him. His invectives against the Jesuits, against our Brethren here & especially against me; his misrepresentation of facts; divulging & falsification of private letters, betray to those, who are acquainted with all circumstances, as malignant & dishonourable a character, as ever I was acquainted with. May 25—Since the above was written, I have recd your short favour of March 2d, & have written fully to Mr. Thorpe concerning Smyth.[2] I have within these few days had a letter from Dr. Troy, A Bishop of Dublin, informing me that Smyth's pamphlet has had no effect but to bring him into ridicule and to draw on it a condemnation by the four Archbps, notified personally to Smyth himself. The Archbp has requested me not to answer it, saying this will be the greatest mortification which Smyth can meet with. I have excellent materials to prove him a liar, & calumniator; and I have been told by my Brethren, that I owe it to their, if not to my own character, to answer it. But I can assure you I have had no time since I saw it to set about such a matter, or even to determine on answering or not.[3]

Communicating freely with you as I do, you would not forgive me were I to omit informing you that a grant has been made to all our officiating Clergy to chuse one of their body, as Bishop; & it is left to our determination whether he shall be an Ordinary, taking his title from some town of our appointment; or a *titular* Bishop, by which I understand A Bishop constituted over a country without the designation of any particular See. (V[*ide*]. Tomassin de la discipline de l'Eglise.[4]) Our Brethren chose to have an Ordinary Bishop, & named Baltimore to be the Bishops title, this being the principal town of Maryland, & that State being the oldest & still the most numerous residence of true Religion in America. So far all was right. We then proceeded to the Election; the event of which was such as deprives me of all expectation of rest or pleasure henceforward, and fills me with terror, with respect to eternity. I am so stunned with the issue of this business, that I truly hate the hearing or the mention of it; and therefore will say only, that since my Brethren, whom in this case I consider as the Interpreters of the divine will say I must obey, I will e'en do it; but by obeying, shall sacrifice henceforth every moment of peace & satisfaction. I most earnestly commend myself to your prayers & those of my other friends. In your Br. Robert's,[5] I always had great confidence, & hope he will bestow them on me now.

I hope the doctrine broached, as you informed me, by some Priests in England, does not gain ground—, that there is no need of Approbation for the exercise of spiritual functions. This country, as every other, would be shortly overrun with the most profligate Clergymen. I have been grossly deceived in one from whom I expected much & who opened his ministry in Boston. He is a Frenchman calling himself La Poterie, and procured [suitable—*torn*] recommendations, but has turned out a sad rasc[al—*torn*] The same thing has happened with a French Dominican,[6] whom I sent last winter to the Illinois Country on the Mississippi to assist the old French settlers there. He turns out an Apostate. You see, what fine encouragement I have with the Nugents, & Smiths & Roans from Ireland: and these latter French men—O poor Jesuits! when shall we have you again? You communicated in your last some dubious information concerning them. I have been so often the dupe of my hopes, that I am become very incredulous to reports of any favourable turn in their affairs.

My good Mother is always pleased at your mention of her, as well as our old & worthy Mr Digges. Molyneux has left me this afternoon after staying exactly one week longer, than he proposed: and if a Gentleman who was to travel the same road, had not dragged him away, he would still be here. He is the same man you know him; fond of beginning mischief, but sure of being worsted; never calculating to day for to morrow; more absent, if possible, than ever; but of sound judgement, in things, where he is not to be an actor: but of the greatest timidity & irresolution possible, where he is. In other respects a most valuable man. Be pleased to present my humble respects to Mr. & Mrs Weld: and to Messrs Stanley, Clinton &c—, as well as to all our other friends. Pray inform me, whether Messrs James Porter[7] & Jn Brewer be living near you. I once heard of the former being very ill—; but news of his recovery or death never reached me. I am, Dr. Sir   Yrs affely   J. Carroll   Do not forget our academy

ALS   St
    [1] *Present State of the Catholic Missions conducted by the ex-Jesuits in North America* (Dublin, 1788).
    [2] Not found.
    [3] See Reply to Smyth, 1789.
    [4] Louis Thomassin, French Oratorian and theologian, author of *Ancienne et nouvelle discipline de l'eglise touchant les benefices et les benefiiers* (3 vols.; Paris, 1678-79).
    [5] Robert Plowden S.J., was in Bristol, England for nearly thirty years. From 1815-20 he was chaplain to the Fitzherbert family.
    [6] Pierre de la Valiniere.
    [7] Possibly a brother of Rev. Thomas Porter, who would take part in Carroll's episcopal consecration and sign the official document.

TO CHARLES PLOWDEN   May 20, 28, 1789

Not found. See from same, Mar. 2, 1789 (6L1).

TO MATTHEW CAREY   Baltimore May 21—1789—

Sir   The day before yesterday, I returned from a conference with some of my Brethren on matters of general concernment: and sorry I was to find, that little progress had been made in subscriptions for the Doway Bible. But I cannot yet reconcile myself to the idea of your renouncing this undertaking. I have urged it more forcibly than ever, & prayed them to use every possible exertion: Besides requesting them to procure all subscriptions they can from Individuals, the Clergymen there present agreed to subscribe for one copy for each of the Congregations served by them, and to encourage the same to be done by all their Brethren of their respective districts. And they farther promised to collect & send the lists, immediately after allowing a reasonable time for these new endeavours. You may be assured that I will leave nothing untried for your success in this undertaking.

Yesterday, I received a letter from the M. Revd. Dr. Troy, Archbp. of Dublin, in which he writes as follows—[Troy explains that the bishops of Ireland have censured Smyth for his *Account of the Catholic Mission in America,* making it advisable for Carroll to remain silent as the matter had now quieted down.]

I am not sure, that I shall follow the Archbps advice altogether. I have been so much urged by others to take notice of Mr. Smyth's mischievous misrepresentations & false statements, & have been told with so much earnestness, that the reputation of my Brethren in this vineyard of Christ is concerned in the controversy begun by him, that it is possible I may draw up some remarks. But if Mr. Smyths pamphlet circulates no more here, I shall not wish to give publicity either to his accusations or the answer to them. I shall inclose the latter to some friend in Ireland to publish or not, as it may then be found expedient: and in that event, shall request him to prefer any person you, will be plea[sed—*torn*—r]ecommend for the publisher, if so trifling an object c[an—*torn*] be a consideration with him. Thus do I now view this subject. But I have had no time yet to write a single line, & fear it will be some weeks, before I shall.[1] Finding myself in arrears for your museum, I will pay in a day or two my deficiency to your Correspondents here as well as for Messrs. Lee & Young. The Revd. Mr. Henry Pile, at Newport, Charles County, & the Revd. Mr. James Walton, St. Inigo's in St. Marys County wish to be subscribers to it, & promised me to send the money, as early as opportunity offers. I believe they must be lodged with me to be spent, as I can meet with a conveyance, as I do not find, you have correspondents in their neighbourhood.

I am, Sir   Yr. obedt. & humble st.   J Carroll

ALS   HSP
[1] See Reply to Smyth, 1789 above.

TO WILLIAM STRICKLAND [May 25, 1789]

Not found. See comment on letter from same (7V8):
Mr. Strickland Jan. 21—1789—Rcvd. May 25. 1789—Communication to be made to Mr. Ashton of some matters herein inclosed—

TO JOHN THORPE   May 25, 1789

Not found. Two letters. See from same, Oct. 18, 1788 (8I6); Jan. 31, and Feb. 24, 1789 (8J3).

TO MATTHEW CAREY   George town June 6th. 1789—

Sir   Your favour of May 28th. has been forwarded to me at this place. I herewith a list of subscriptions received by myself, with a few from other Gentlemen. Others are not yet come to hand, since my pressing & earnest recommendation of renewed exertions. I beg you not yet to renounce the undertak[ing;—*torn*] the advance money for those, who subscribed with me shall be got for you, as soon as you you [*sic*] are determined to proceed. The Gentlemen of Baltimore, on whose exertions I depended, did nothing at all.

I think I shall be able to dispose of 100 copies of the *Vade mecum*,[1] and perhaps more. But my present engagements are so many, that I dare not take upon me, to be responsible for more, than I can part with.

My absence from Baltimore will make this come later to hand, than you might expect. I am writing a few observations on Mr. Smith, as I have leisure—so that I proceed [*torn*—slow]ly. I quite forgot to have the money for Museums r[eturned—*torn*] from Messrs. Young & Lee as well as my own. I hope no inconvenience will arise from it, tho if payable to G. Town to any correspondent there, I can call for it on monday. I am, Sir,   Yr. most obedt.   st.   J Carroll.[2]

ALS   HSP
    [1] Douai version of the Bible.
    [2] A list of 37 names follow, Charles Carroll of Carrollton among them.

TO JOHN FENNO[1] OF THE *GAZETTE OF THE UNITED STATES*
                                                          June 10, 1789

EVERY friend to the rights of conscience, equal liberty and diffusive happiness, must have felt pain on seeing the attempt made by one of your correspondents, in the Gazette of the United States No. 8, May the 9th, to revive an odious system of religious intolerance.— The author may not have been fully sensible of the tendency of his publication, because he speaks of preserving universal toleration.[2] Perhaps he is one of those who think it consistent with justice to exclude certain citizens from the honors and emoluments of society, merely on account of their religious opinions, provided they be not restrained by racks and forfeitures from the exercise of that worship which their consciences approve.—If such be his views, in vain then have Americans associated into one great national union, under the express condition of not being shackled by religious tests; and under a firm persuasion that they were to retain when associated, every natural right not expressly surrendered.[3]

It is pretended that they, who are the objects of an intended exclusion from certain offices of honor and advantage, have forfeited by an act, or treason against the United States, the common rights of nature, or the stipulated rights of the political society, of which they form a part? This the author has not presumed to assert. Their blood flowed as freely (in proportion to their numbers) to cement the fabric of independence as that of any of their fellow-citizens: They concurred with perhaps greater unanimity than any other body of men, in recommending and promoting that government, from whose influence America anticipates all the blessings of justice, peace, plenty, good order and civil and religious liberty. What character shall we then give to a system of policy, for the express purpose of divesting of rights legally acquired[,] those citizens, who are not only unoffending, but whose conduct has been highly meritorious?

These observations refer to the general tendency of the publication, which I now proceed to consider more particularly. Is it true as the author states, that our forefathers abandoned their native home; renounced its honors and comforts, and buried themselves in the immense forests of this new world, for the sake of that religion which he recommends preferable to any other? Was not the religion which the emigrants to the four Southern States brought with them to America, the pre-eminent and favored religion of the country which they left? Did the Roman Catholics who first came to Maryland, leave their native soil for the sake of preserving the Protestant church? Was this the motive of the peaceable Quakers in the settlement of Pennsylvania? Did the first inhabitants of the Jerseys and New York, quit Europe for fear of being compelled to renounce their Protestant tenets? Can it be even truly affirmed that this motive operated on all, or a majority of those who began to settle and improve the four eastern States?[4] Or even if they really where [*sic*— were] influenced by a desire of preserving their religion, what will ensue from the fact, but that one denomination of Protestants fought a retreat from the persecution of another? Will history justify the assertion that they left their native homes for the sake of the Protestant religion, understanding it in a comprehensive sense as distinguished from every other?

This leading fact being so much mistated, no wonder that the author should go on bewildering himself more and more. He asserts that the *religion* which he recommends, *laid the foundation of this new and great empire;* and therefore contends it is entitled to pre-eminence and distinguished favor. Might I not say with equal truth, that the religion which he recommends exerted her powers to crush this empire in its birth, and still is laboring to prevent its growth? For, can we so soon forget, or now help seeing, that the bitterest enemies of our national prosperity possess the same religion as prevails generally in the United States? What inference will a philosophic mind derive from this view, but that religion is out of the question? That it is ridiculous to say, THE PROTESTANT RELIGION IS THE IMPORTANT BULWARK OF OUR CONSTITUTION? That the establishment of the American empire was not the work of this or that religion, but arose from a generous exertion of all her citizens to redress their wrongs, to assert their rights, and lay its foundations on the soundest principles of justice and equal liberty?

When he ascribed so many valuable effects to his cherished religion, as that she was the nurse of *arts and sciences,* could he not reflect, that *Homer* and *Virgil, Demosthenes* and *Cicero, Thucydides* and *Livy, Phidias* and *Apelles* flourished long before this nurse *of arts and sciences* had an existence? Was he so inconsiderate as not to attend to the consequences, favorable to Polytheism, which flow from his reasoning? Or did he forget that the Emperor Julian, the subtle and inveterate enemy of christianity, applied this very same argument to the defence of Heathenish superstition? The recollection of that circumstance may induce him to suspect the weight of his observation, and perhaps to doubt of the fact, which he assumed for its basis.

But he tells us that Britain owes to *her religion her present distinguished greatness:* a gentle invitation to America to pursue the same political maxims, in heaping exclusive favors on one, and depressing all other religions!

But does Britain owe indeed the perfection and extent of her manufactures, and the enormous wealth of many individuals to the cause assigned by this author? Can he so soon put it out of his mind, that the patient industry so natural to English artificers, and the long monopoly of our trade, and that of their dependencies, by increasing the demand and a competition among her artizans, contributed principally to the perfection of the manufactures of Britain? And that the plunder of Indian provinces poured into her lap the immense fortunes which murder and rapacity accumulated in those fertile climes? God forbid that religion should be instrumental in raising such greatness!

When the author proceeds to say, that the clergy of that religion, which operated such wonders in Britain, *boldly and zealously stepped forth and bravely stood our distinguished sentinels to bring about the late glorious revolution,* I am almost determined to follow him no further: He is leading me on too tender ground, on which I chuse not to venture. The clergy of that religion behaved, I believe, as any other clergy would have done in similar circumstances: But the voice of America will not contradict me, when I assert that they discovered no greater zeal for the revolution, than the ministry of any other denomination whatever.

When men comprehend not, or refuse to admit the luminous principles on which the rights of conscience and liberty of religion depend, they are industrious to find out pretences for intolerance. If they cannot discover them in the actions, they strain to cull them out of the tenets of the religion which they wish to exclude from a free participation of equal rights. Thus this author attributes to his religion the merit of being *the most favorable to freedom,* and affirms that not only *morality* but *liberty* likewise must expire, if his clergy should ever be *contemned* or *neglected:* all which conveys a refined insinuation, that liberty cannot consist with, or be cherished by any other religious institution; and which therefore he would give us to understand, it is not safe to countenance in a free government.

I am anxious to guard against the impression intended by such insinuations; not merely for the sake of any one profession, but from an earnest regard to preserve inviolate for ever, in our new empire, the great principle of religious freedom. The constitutions of some of the States continue still to intrench on the sacred rights of conscience; and men who have bled, and opened their purses as freely in the cause of liberty and independence, as any other citizens, are most unjustly excluded from the advantages which they contributed to establish. But if bigotry and narrow prejudices have prevented hitherto the cure of these evils, be it the duty of every lover of peace and justice to extend them no further. Let the author who has opened this field for discussion, be aware of slyly imputing to any set of men, principles or consequences, which they disavow. He perhaps may meet with retaliation. He may be told and referred to Lord Lyttleton, as zealous a Protestant as any man of his days, for information, that the principles of non-reistence *seemed the principles* of that religion which we are not told is *most favorable to freedom;* and that its opponents *had gone too far in the other* extreme![5]

He may be told farther, that a Reverend Prelate of Ireland, the Bishop of Bloyne, has lately attempted to prove, that the Protestant Episcopal Church is best fitted to unite with the civil constitution of a mixed monarchy, while Presbyterianism is only congenial with republicanism. Must America then yielding to these fanciful systems, confine her *distinguishing* favors to the followers of Calvin, and keep a jealous eye on all others? Ought she not rather to treat with contempt these idle, and generally speaking interested speculations, refuted by reason, history, and daily experience, and rest the preservation of her liberalities and her government on the attachment of mankind to their political happiness, to the security of their persons and their property, which is independent of religious doctrines, and not restrained by any?
PACIFICUS.

L *Gazette of the United States* (New York, June 10, 1789) [No. XVII], p. 1. Authorship established by Brent's use (pp. 97-105). "Mr. Fenno" introduces the letter. Matthew Carey's *The American Museum* . . . Vol. VI (Philadelphia, July, 1789), 43-45, carries the entire letter with some modification in punctuation, as well as the letter that gave rise to Pacificus.

[1] (1751-98), a Federalist with Alexander Hamilton's favor, published the Gazette in New York from April, 1789 to Apr., 1790 and in Philadelphia thereafter until his death.

[2] Signed "E.C.," "The importance of the Protestant religion politically considered," by indirection calls for established Protestantism, when he portrays its service to the Republic and calls attention to the poverty of the clergy at the present time. Carroll does

not advert to this last feature of his adversary's letter. Massachusetts, Connecticut and a few other states provided clergy salaries for the state denomination. E. C.'s is a very early statement of the popular nineteenth century theme of Protestant Nationalism, which Martin Marty portrays in *Righteous Empire* (New York, 1970).

³ The letter is properly understood in the context of the ratification of the Federal Constitution and the First Amendment. Similar ideas are presented in Carroll's letter to the *Columbian Magazine,* Sep. 1, 1787 above.

⁴ Massachusetts, Connecticut, New Hampshire and Vermont.

⁵ An asterisk occurs here and refers to this note by Carroll at the end of the letter: "See dialogues of the dead, 1st dialogue." George, First Baron Lyttleton of Frankley, published this work in 1760. He opposed the Stamp Act.

TO JOHN TROY Dumfries, Virginia, July 2nd, 1789.

My Lord, A few days before I left Baltimore with a view of visiting some of our scattered congregations, I was honoured with your Grace's letter of February, in which you have, in a manner the most obliging, communicated to me the intelligence of Mr. S[myth]'s, pamphlet—shall I call it— or libel.[1] I had received, a week or two before, the pamphlet itself from a printer in Philadelphia. I reserved to myself to write to your Grace with the thankfulness which is due to you, and fully, as soon as I should return to Baltimore. But having this moment met, accidentally, a gentleman of character, who sails in two days for Cork, I would not omit the opportunity of informing your Grace, that I will draw up a few observations on the pamphlet as soon as I can get a little leisure, and send them for your reading and that of those other Rev. Prelates who have, in a manner so obliging, prevented the intended bad effects of the malicious publication.[2] You will add to other obligations that of presenting my respectful thanks to those Fathers of our Church, and will excuse this uncouth piece of paper, the best I could get in a little tavern where I found the bearer of this.

I have the honour to be, with the greatest respect, My Lord, Your Grace's most obliged and humble servant, J. Carroll.

L Moran, III, 506
  ¹ Patrick Smyth, *Present State of Catholic Missions . . .*
  ² See Reply to Smyth, 1789.

TO CHARLES PLOWDEN Baltimore July 12–1789–

My Dear Sir Your favours of Feb. 3d, April 1st. & May 3d. are before me. I gave you a short notice of the issue of our election: If I could persuade myself, Dr. Sir, to follow your example, in refusing peremptorily to submit to the choice of my Brethren I have much reason to think, it would be better for our H. Religion & certainly to my greater ease of mind: but having previously used all my sincere endeavours to divert them from such a choice, I cannot but acquiesce in it, as it was unanimous, excepting one vote.[1] At the same

time, my own knowledge of myself informs me better, than a thousand voices
to the contrary, that I am entirely unfit for a station in which I can have no
hopes of rendering service but thro his holy & continual direction, who has
called me to it, when I was doing all in my power to prevent it. God grant the
Catholics of England the exemptions, they sollicit, & to make a right use of
them. It is however humiliating to owe them to oaths and declarations, which
bear such marks of suspicion, or contempt. How far distant is the policy of
your country, in respect to Religious freedom from the benevolent principles
prevailing here?

I find, that you have not seen a most venomous & false libel, printed in
Ireland by the Mr. Smyth who left us last summer, & was mentioned formerly
to you. As he is a confident of Mr. Hussey,[2] I make no doubt, but this
Gentleman is well supplied with copies.

Archbp Troy of Dublin has sent me a most obliging letter, in which he
informs me, that he & his Brethren the 3 other archbps, who happened all to
be at Dublin, had censured the work severely, & notified the censure to
Smyth. The having been Jesuits is our original sin. Sometime ago, I was much
pleased with the letters (which were written in the language of an Apostle) of
a French priest, who had wandered to Boston. I received several letters of
strong recommendation, testimonials &c; all which, joined to his own sentiments of submission, induced me to grant him faculties for a short term. He
proceeded with great rapidity to open divine service, introduce music; celebrate all the ceremonies of a cathedral &c—and he proceeded to make some
publications, which soon convinced me of his imprudence. He soon after
discovered himself to be of an infamous character: his faculties are revoked,
& he now proceeds to every abuse agst me, as a Jesuit, aiming at nothing in all
my manouvres, but to reestablish the order here under the title of American
Clergy. It is singular enough, that some of our own friends are blaming me for
being too irresolute or indifferent, for not adopting their most intemperate
councils with respect to restoring the Society, whilst on the other hand,
Smyth the Abbé[3] & others are accusing me of sacrificing to this intention the
good of Religion. You will be kind enough to transcribe the heads of this
information to Mr. Thorpe.

The abbé has been at Rome & pretends an acquaintance with Cardl. York[4]
& other consequential characters there: he is exceedingly insinuating, & as
great a hypocrite in his letters, as I ever knew. If he be only slightly known he
may impose: but I am sure, he has resided no where long, without betraying
his infamy. I think he has lately discoverd such knavery, that I should not
wonder at his using the most iniquitous means of pursuing his resentment.
Before his faculties were recalled, I directed him not to use as he had done,
public prayers for the King of France, in the Sunday service as is done for our
own ruling power; because a government jealous of its independence might
construe it into an undue attachment of American Roman Catholics to a

foreign prince. He first acquiesced in the propriety of my direction [*torn—he*] now says; I forbad prayers for the K. of France because the French expelled the Jesuits: & I think him capable of writing, such falsehoods to Europe, & even to his ministry. His name is La Poterie. Luckily the french corps diplomatique here are well acquainted with his character. Mr. Thayer will have much to do to repair the scandals caused by this man.

Adieu, my Dr. Sir—I have been travelling thro' excessive heats for six weeks, arrived hither the day before yesterday; find numberless letters to answer; shall be too late for your packet, if I do not send them off to night—; & this is Sunday, a thronged & busy day. My respects to yr. excellent family, to W[a]rd[e]r. Castle of Messrs St[anley]. & Clinton. My good mother always salutes you. Dr. Sir. Yrs &c. J.C. I answer Fr. Humilis to day,[5] accepting his services.

ALS St
[1] In addition to his own against himself.
[2] Richard Hussey, attorney general to the queen mother of George III.
[3] Poterie.
[4] Henry Benedict Stuart.
[5] Not found.

TO [?] HUMILIS[1]   July 12, 1789

Not found. See July 12, 1789.

[1] No evidence found that he took up a ministry.

TO BENJAMIN RUSH[1]   Baltimore July 18—1879—

Sir   I have no better apology for my long delay in acknowledging your interesting favour of Feb. 9th, than that I have been almost always absent from home.

I see continuously, & have much cause to lament the fatal effects of spirituous liquors; and often times incline to wish, that those effects were the unavoidable & necessary consequences of their use: for then there would not remain a doubt with a reasona[b]l[e] moralist of their being absolutely and entirely forbidden. As a matter is, morality, and religion cannot, in my apprehension, proceed farther, than to condemn & reprobate the abuse; & repeatedly to caution against using them at all. The ministers of Religion must not presume, without the warrant of the highest authority, to inforce as a precept, the entire disuse of them. To draw the cords of duty, moral or religious, too tight, may restrain for a short time, but men will soon break loose from the restraint, & run perhaps the more easily into the opposite extreme, whenever reason will support them in rejecting the rigor, not only of their past forbearance, but likewise of the principles, on which it was enjoined, as a matter of obligation.

I do not therefore see, that any principle of Religion will support an ordinance for the total abolition of spirituous liquors, unless it come in aid of the civil law, first prohibiting the manufacturing or importation of them. The late proceedings of Congress afford little prospect of such an event. The utmost therefore, which we can do, is to inculcate the obligation of being moderate in the use of them, & the great expediency of totally abstaining from them; & in many cases, the indispensable necessity of doing so. In this I promise you my best assistance, & that of my Brethren, both in our public instructions, & in our personal conferences with our respective flocks. Habitual offenders are commanded by us never to taste them. This injunction is often ineffectual: but exclusion from the Sacraments of pennance & the Eucharist is the penalty of a relapse.

I applaud very sincerely your zeal for the reformation of morals: and wish it were in my power to go as far in the subject recommended by you, as you wish. I am with very great esteem   Sir   Yr. most obedt & humble St   J. Carroll—

ALS   LCP
[1] The noted scientist had opened a dispensary in Philadelphia in 1785, after publishing the previous year *An Inquiry into the Effects of Spirituous Liquors on the Human Mind and Body.*

TO MATTHEW CAREY   Baltimore July 23—1789—

Sir   Your request being so earnest to have the list of subscribers *by return of post,* I set down to transcribe them, tho very much hurried to answer other letters this evening. I have no other objection to your mention of my approbation of the intended publication of a Catholic prayer book, excepting that it seems to convey a consciousness of my own importance far above what I feel. I am in haste, Dr. Sir,   Yr. most obedt. servt.   J. Carroll[1]

ALS   HPS
[1] About seventy-six subscribers are listed, carrying over to a third MS page.

TO [JOHN HEILBRON]   July 24—1789

Reverend Father in Christ: Yesterday, letters of your Reverence were given to me, which you wrote on the 15th of this month, and in which he indicated his own intention of setting out for Philadelphia,[1] and of acting as Pastor and Rector of souls of those who invited him. Indeed, Your Reverence also added the reasons by which the right of patronage prevailed over those opposing his residence, and he pointed out to me my power and office for arranging that suitably enough, for whomsoever they themselves have presented.

He seeks reasons from the decree of Innocent 3rd *Concerning the Right of Patronage:*[2] indeed, he indicates the powers of my office from common practice and right according to which he has been presented for benefices; and [claims] the rights of patronage belong to those who possess it. There is no doubt but that he would be installed. He succeeded in being presented, [and] no incapacity impedes him.

But in fact, it has neither been conceded to Philadelphia by what means to construct a new Church as Parochial;[3] nor does any need of the Faithful lead in that direction. Then, where the power for constructing a new Church is given by me, I have added on my own that condition, [*i.e.*] lest a Church had been constructed by him,[;] and they used this as the pretext for assuming that it had been designed for them by him, and in that place he performed holy rites [*ind.*], with respect to whose status they attached a common name and witnesses of his consent [and] sent to me letters, testifying its authenticity. Wherefore, although the right of Patronage would truly be acquired through the construction of a Church, nevertheless, he who renounces this right on his own, and acknowledges that it will reside without interruption within the Superior of the Church, he is unable, without its violation, at last to arrogate that to himself. But, indeed, this decree of Innocent, by which it endeavors to strengthen your opinion of Your Reverence, does not have the force of law among us,[;] not at all, however, is it conceded to favor him. For the words cited treat of the individual person preparing a Church by his own undertakings,[;] he does not [*ind.*—regard] his own work enviously and use force with respect to those trampling upon it.[4]

For this reason, I have written that it is evident both from the words of the decree itself, and from the Council of Trent, session 14 "de Ref." chapter 12, cited according to this decree, which spoke thus. For no one, of whatever dignity, ecclesiastical or secular, unless he shall have newly founded and constructed a Church, benefice or chapel, or once erected [such], [or] shall have endowed it competently with his own patrimonial goods, is able to or ought to beseech or obtain the right of patronage. Moreover, let Your Reverence see chapter nine of the third letter of the decretal, concerning churches to be built, which [chapter] is customarily inscribed at the end of the Council of Trent, where he will find Ecclesiastical rules,[;] thus, if for parochial convenience, a new parish is to be established, the Rector of the major or mother Church, from whose domain new parishes to be brought forth[,] acquires the right of patronage, not indeed, he who constructs or founds a church.

Now these things have been said, that Your Reverence may understand that the right of patronage is not at all evident, that it has been acquired from the disposition of Canon Law, by them who undertook the work of constructing a new temple in Philadelphia. Therefore, neither I nor Your Reverence has been able to define what force there is in these regions in the matter of a benefice. Canonical right is absent. From such a definition, finally, if that right here turns out to be his full [*ind.*] it is thus to be understood, that he who has built it yields the Patrimony of the Church; that it cannot be argued in this case in which the builders of the temple have voluntarily foresworn the right of patronage, and [*ind.*] [. . . .]

[. . . .] it belongs to the common [authority?] to confer all benefices in behalf of the Diocese, as Thomassin has clearly showed in his *Treatise on the Ancient and Modern Discipline of the Church* and is held to be taken of all Basilicas; confer "nullus oĩo 1697 Cap. Conspurcute 16 de off. *Ordo* [*ind.*] *de Instit.*

ADf   AAB   Addressee learned from context.
[1] Peter Heilbron was at Lancaster, Pa.
[2] Innocent (d. 1216) had effectively reversed the feudal and secular decentralization of the the Church through his contests with the kings of England and Germany in particular.
[3] Nearby St. Mary's in Philadelphia.
[4] A deleted section of nine lines follows at this point, dealing with the case of Bristol, England.

Revde in Christo Pater: Heri redditae mihi sunt literae Rae Vae sub quas scripsit 15a hujus quibusque sententiam suam expresse significat Philadelphiam proficiscendi, seque ut coram pastorem et animarum rectorem gerendi, qui ipsum invitavere. Rationes etiam adjecit Ra Va, quibus et jus patronatus in invitantibus residere evincat, et meum mihi munus et officium ostendit illum instituendi, modo idoneum, quemcumque ipsi praesentaverint.

Rationes petit ex decreto Innocentii 3i *de jure Patronatus:* mei vero officii munera suggerit ex communi praxi & jure secundum quod praesentatus pro beneficia et aliunde capax jus patronatus legitime ad praesentantes spectaret, dubium non est quin is instituendus esset praesentationem obtinuit, nulla subest incapacitas.

At vero neque concessum est Philadelphi quibus novam Ecclesiam tanquam Parochialem, construere; neque ulla Fidelium necessitas ad hoc compellit. Deinde, ubi Ecclesiae construendae facta est a me potestas, illam conditionem expresse adjeci ne illi quorum opera construerenda erat Ecclesia, eo praetextu uterentur ad assumendam sibi designationem illius; que ibidem sacra ministeria ageret, cui conditioni illi communi nomine subscripserunt, suique consensus testes ad me literas, foa authentica miserunt. Quare, tametsi verum fore jus Patronatus acquiri per Ecclesiae constructionem, tamen qui huic juri expresse renunciat, profiteturque illus penes Superiorem Ecclscum continuo fore, sine hujus laesione nequit illud sibi denuo arrogare. At vero ipsum Innoc. decretum quo sententiam tuam Reva. Va.roborare nititur, illi minime favere quamvis concederetur, decretum illud vim legis apud nos habere. Etenim verba citata agunt de singulari persona Ecclesiam suis sumptibus construente, non [*ind.*] suam operam invide aque conterentibus viusus [*ind.*].

Idcirco scripsi quod constat et ex verbis ipsius decreti, et ex Conc. Trid. sess. 14 de Ref. c. 12 quod ad hoc decr. citatum ita loquitur. *Nemo etiam cujusvis dignais Ecclesiastiae vel saecularis, quacunq raoe nisi Eccliam, beneficium aut capellam, de novo fundaverit, & construxerit, seu jam erectam - de suis proprisi et patrimonialibus bonis competenter dotaverit, jus patronatus impetrare aut obtinere possit, aut debeat.* Videat praeterea Ra Va cap. 9 lit. 3 decretal. *de ecclesiis aedificandis* quae solet imprimi ad calcem Conc. Trid. ubi reperiet regulae Ecclesiasticae esse, ut, si propter Parochianorum commodum nova Parochia erigenda sit, Rector majoris seu matricae ecclesiae, ex cujus ambitu nova parochia desumenda est, jus patronatus acquirat, non vero ille, qui Ecclesiam construxit aut fundavit.

Atque haec dicta sunt, ut intelligat Ra Va non minime constare jus patronatus, acquisitum ex dispooe juris Canonici ab ipsius fuisse, qui ad novum templum Philadae construendum tuam operam contulerunt. Deinde, neque ego, neque forte Ra Va definire poterit, quam vim in his regionibus in materia beneficiali, abstineat jus canonicum. Denique si jus illud hic plenum suum effectum sortiretur, intelligendumq ita et, ut Patronatum Ecclesiae illic conferret qui ipsam ercuere; id [*ind.*] contendi in hoc casu non posset, in quo templi aedificatores jus oe patronatus ab se abdicaverunt, atque amovere illud [*ind.*] fore usi [. . . .]

[. . . .] communi competit conferre oia beneficia prae diocesis, ut fuse ostendit Thomassin. *Traité de la discipline de Ecles ancienne & moderne* et habetur capi [*torn*] *omnes basilica, c. nullus oio* 1697 [*torn*] *Cap. Conspurcute* 16 de off. Iud Ords *Bus* [*ind.*] *de Instit.*

TO MATTHEW CAREY [Aug., 1789]

Sr. Sir I will have ready for you all that can be collected, which will, I hope, be the whole. With my own, I have ready for you about six or seven pounds cash if you want it to carry to Frederick, it is at command. I did not mean to say, you would attend the Gentlemen thro town; but mentioned your being in town, as a reason for their having their subscription money ready. I have devoted tuesday to making a circuit thro town myself. I return you Mr. Goddard's paper, & with it send two, I have received from my Br. In the *Daily advertiser* you will find some farther information respecting the Rom. Cat. petition.[1] I am Sir yr. obedt. st. J. Carroll Sunday afternoon.

ALS HSP Date estimated from letter to Carey at this time. See Sep. 10, 1789.
[1] Evidently of Catholics in England for relief from civil disabilities

TO LEONARDO ANTONELLI Balt. Aug. 5—1789—

Most Reverend and Illustrious Lord Rev. Mr. Hock, and still more my own deep sense of gratitude impel me to tell your Lordship how I welcome your letters, and thank you for your interest and your fostering of religion in our America. I have already expressed to Canon Hock my sentiments on the benefits to be derived from a seminary. If, as we think, God will soon deign to place this least vineyard of the Lord under the authority of a bishop the first appointee to this see will gladly consult you. Meanwhile, because of your benign and very friendly attitude towards us, I recommend that you read the account of the state of religion which I subjoin, and, in particular, the building of a Catholic school which I regard as the bulwark of religion, and bear in mind that because Catholics are spread over a very vast region the support of priests is next to impossible. Perhaps you will then wish to seek help from the charity of the faithful to bring about the removal of so many obstacles to religion and its spread. Good health, the esteem of men, a happy temporal and eternal life is the prayer and wish to your very reverend and illustrious lordship from your most devoted and humble [. . .]

To all who may see this, eternal well-being in the Lord. Since we were informed that many persons distinguished for piety and zeal for the true religion, and, moreover, men who occupy places of dignity in the church and civil government wish to know the state of the Catholic religion in these states that make up the United States, we have been led to draw up a brief account. As long as these states were subject to the British king Catholics were excluded from most of them, and capital punishment was threatened lest a priest enter them. In Maryland and Pennsylvania there was greater liberty of conscience as it was called, but even in these colonies there were many restrictions. Thus it came about that there were only a few priests, Englishmen and Germans, active as ministers of religion. They led a simple and plain life, supported not by the contributions of Catholics (outside of Philadelphia such contributions were unheard of) but by the farms which the first missionaries acquired by purchase and transmitted to their successors, not as ecclesiatical but as private possessions. With the overthrow of British rule a great change came about. Everywhere freedom of religion was established, and in some states Catholics do not differ from others as regards legal rights and general conditions. From this situation came an excellent opportunity for introducing our religion into all of the states. Hitherto, however, great obstacles were the difficulty of supporting priests and churches, the building of chapels, the providing of such sacred furnishings as chalices and vestments. Greatest of all was the problem of building a college for the education of Catholic youth. To meet these problems and needs our efforts and desires are directed, and we earnestly appeal to the faithful, especially to those in places where spiritual assistance suffices, to give from their abundance what they judge will greatly contribute to the increase of faith, the reform of morals, and the dignified and proper carrying out of divine worship.

ADf   AAB

Balt. Aug. 5, 1789   Reverendissime et Illustrissime Domine   Excitatus sum tum ad Amd. Rev. D. Hock, tum maxime intimo grati animi sensu, ut

Ressm. et Illustrissimam D. tuam litteris salutarem, eique gratias, quam possum, maximas referrem, quo ita benigne hanc nostram Americam et religionem in illa statum complecteretur, foveretque. Ipsi D. Canonico Koch jam significavi, quae de proposito Seminarii beneficio dicenda nunc videbantur. Si Deus O. M. exiguam hanc Dominicae vineae portionem sub legitimi episcopi auctoritate, uti credimus, brevi constituere dignatus fuerit, cum Revma. D. tua consilia laetus inibit qui primus ad Novam in America Sedem promovebitur. Interim eidem benignissimae et propensae in nos voluntati commendo, ut perlecto rerum nostrarum statu, quem hic subjicio, ac praecipue scholae Catholicae molitione, quam magnum Religionis praesidium fore confido; ut attenta deinde Catholicorum per vastissimam regionem dispersione, atque exinde imparibus ad Sacerdotum sustentationem facultatibus; adjumenta quaedam ex Fidelium charitate sollicitare velit, quibus tanta obstacula, quae Religioni officiunt, dimoveantur.

Revdme. ac Illustrimae. D. vitam, famam, felicem temporalem ac aeternam ex animo precatur   Revmae. ac Illusmae. D. Devotissimus et humillimus.

Omnibus has visuris, salutem in D. sempiternam - Cum nobis significatum eit viros multos insignes pietate et zelo verae Religionis, et praeterea dignitate in Ecclesia Dei, et in regimine politico excellentes scire desiderare quo statu res Catholicorum sint in Foederatae Americae Provinciis, ideo brevem illius statum hic declarandum duximus - Quamdiu hae provinciae Angliae Regi suberant, Catholici a plerisque fuerunt exclusi; capitisque poena cautum fuit, ne in illas sacerdos Catholicus ingrederetur. In Marilandia et Pennsylvania major, sed in his quoque multum restricta fuit conscientiae, ut vocant, libertas. Unde in his pauci sacerdotes, Angli et Germani, Religionis ministeriis vacabant, tenuiter vitam sustentantes non ex collationibus Catholicorum (hoc enim extra Philadelphia erat inauditum) sed ex certis terrae fundis, quae primi missionarii pretio conquisitos in successores suos deinde non tamquam bona ecclesiastica [*illeg.*] sed tamquam privatorum possessiones, fuere transmissi ac si in alios. Excusso Angliae jugo, alia rerum facies. Ubique libertas religionis stabilita, et in quibusdam provinciis Catholici eodem jure ac eisdem conditionibus utuntur, ac caeteri. Hinc nata est optima Religionem in omnes provincias invehendi opportunitas-Sed ingenti obstaculo huiusque fuit difficultas subveniendi sacerdotum expensis et sustentationi, Ecclesias, aut saltem sacella construendi et sacrae suppellectili, puta calices, vestes sacerdotales, et comparandae; praecipue vero colegii erigendi pro Catholicae juventutis educatione. Ad haec consequenda, conatus nostros, ac studia dirigimus, ac enixe rogamus Fideles, in istis praecipue partibus, ubi spiritualia omnia adjumenta suppetunt, ut de sua abundantia benignissime conferre velint, quae ad fidei incrementum ad morum reformationem, ad divini cultus amplitudinem et decorem augendum maxime conducere judicaverint.

TO LEONARDO ANTONELLI   Baltimore 6 Aug. 1789

Very Reverend and Illustrious Lord   More than four weeks ago Rev. Mr. Fromm[1] arrived with proper credentials from your reverence. I was not at home at the time. Ten days later, upon my return to Baltimore, I found him in great distress because the captain of the ship impounded his baggage till he should pay his passage. Your letter reveals that he had received money for this purpose but he had spent it on clothes and books. It was imprudent of him to do this after my letter to you which he admits seeing. At some inconvenience assistance was given him, a sacrifice which I hope will help the Catholic cause, but I urge that no others undertake so great a journey unless they have the necessary funds. I have already given warning that the Catholics here cannot meet such expenses. Those things which John Schorb recalled, he gave the first consideration and indulged in gross exaggeration, if indeed he was the author of what was published in Mainz some years ago.[2] Right after the end of the war when more gold and silver was in circulation it was not too difficult to secure the sums required for the passage of one or two priests; and this money, as I hear, was consigned to John Schorb. Now, however, it is much more difficult to do this.

I assigned Rev. Mr. Fromm to Conewago where Mr. Pellentz and another priest of his own order and likewise from Mainz,[3] are stationed. Fromm must learn English to extend the field of his activity. I observe that of the priests who come to America the majority use every means to secure location in the principal centers of population, and are less willing to be in the country among the farmers where there is greater opportunity to promote the glory of God; and if they do not obtain these coveted places they complain that they are mistreated. For this reason I want as missionaries men who are learned and prudent but also humble, men not covetous of money but intent solely on the welfare of souls, men inspired to even greater regard for the uncultured and the people in the country than for the more refined city dwellers. In a word I want men who preach not themselves but Jesus Christ, men who seek not what is their own but what belongs to Jesus Christ.

All this I have made known unreservedly to your reverence so that you direct your attention to this end, and select as ministers of the sanctuary those who, placing fullest trust in divine providence, are not afraid to come here to work even though as yet no assured sustenance is provided. This is how our religion began in most places in the Christian world; this is how it found entrance into this part of America. As I said elsewhere we are hampered by a distinct shortage of laborers of this type. As for those for whom I must provide a living all these places are already filled.

On this occasion I write briefly to your reverend suffragan as you suggested, so that his benevolence and experience in religious matters may come to the relief of our poverty, especially with regard to the building of a Catholic school in which I place the highest hopes.

Rev. Mr. Fromm who recently left Conewago and is now here will assuredly give you full details concerning Mr. P. Miller his cousin.

I do not know how to return adequate thanks to your reverend suffragan and to the whole vicariate general for the signal favor of sending to the episcopal seminary students who, after due training, will come to these missions. There is very good reason for believing that within a few months an episcopal see will be established in one of the cities of the United States, and the first occupant of the see named. When this is done, what I have just mentioned, and the sending of American students to the seminary, will be arranged more easily and on a more solid basis. Meanwhile in fullest gratitude and esteem I wish to be regarded   Your reverence's   Most obedient and humble servant.

ADf   AAB

[1] Francis Fromm, a Franciscan from Germany, came in conflict with Carroll while ministering in Westmoreland County, Pa., shortly after this. From 1791-98 Carroll sent several letters to him.

[2] This incident suggests a defense by Schorb and Fromm against alleged preferment by Carroll as unfavorable to the Germans, who would be justified in the use Fromm made of the funds. Schorb as well as Carroll made reports to Antonelli.

[3] Theodore Brouwers, a Franciscan. Though stationed at Conewago, he soon undertook establishment of a congregation in Westmoreland County at Greensburg, acquiring an estate for support of the church. He died shortly after this. Fromm laid claim to succession and the property of this congregation. A schism ensued in the 1790's, ending in a civil suit.

Baltimore, die 6 August 1789   Admodum Rde ac perillustris Domine—
    Quattuor et amplius abhinc hebdomadis advenit Rdus. D. Fromm, munitus benevolentissimis litteris adm. Rvdae ac perillustris Vae Dom. Domo ipse abfui; post dies decem redux Baltimoram, hic ipsum deprehendi magna in molestia quod navis Gubernator sarcinas ejus retineret, donec ipse ad sumptus itineris solvendos pecuniam conferret; quam enim in hunc finem acceperat, ut D.V. literae ferunt, ad librorum et vestium usum applicuerat; quod parum prudenter ab ipso factum fuit post visas meas ad D. V. litteras; quas sibi exhibitas fuisse agnoscit. Subventum tamen ipsi fuit, cum incommodo quidem aliquo, sed, uti spero, cum rei Catholicae utilitate. Suadeo tamen, ne alii tantum iter ingrediantur, nisi rationem solvendi perspectam sibi habeant. Jam enim monui, Catholicos sumptibus non sufficere; quae Joannes Schorb memoravit illa dixit praeponere ac omnia in immensum exaggeravit, si ipse eorum auctor fuit quae aliquot abhinc annos Moguntiae edita. Statim ac bellum finitum fuit, cum major esset auri et argenti [*illeg.*] non difficulter conflatum fuit quantum transvehendo uni vel alteri Sacerdoti foret satis, idque in Joannis Schorb manus, ut audio, fuit consignatum, nunc tamen multo est difficilius.
    Revdo Domo Fromm stationem assignavi in Conewago apud Dominum Pellentz, ac alium sui Ordinis sacerdotem, tente Moguntinum. Quo latius labores suos impendat addiscenda est ipsi lingua Anglica. Animadverto ex Sacerdotibus, qui in Americam veniunt, plerosque omni ope niti, ut in praecipuis civitatibus sedem obtineant; minus autem libenter ruri inter agri-

colas degere, ubi tamen multo major augendae Dei gloriae opportunitas; et si minus has sedes obtineant, non recte secum agi queruntur. Missionarios ergo desidero, doctos quidem et prudentes, sed etiam pios et humiles, neque pecuniae in [*illeg.*] iantes, qui uni animarum saluti intenti, curas suas eadem, vel etiam majori animi affectione impendant rudibus, et rusticis hominibus, quam cultioribus urbium incolis. Uno verbo eos requiro qui non seipsos, sed Jesu Christi praedicent; non sua, sed quae Jesu Christi sunt, quaerant.

Haec omni animi libertate apud Rev. Dom. V. effundo, ut sua optima in nos studia eo dirigat, talesque ubi exegerit, Sanctuarii ministros seligat, qui divinae providentiae plurimum fidentes, non metuant illuc suos labores dirigere, ubi nulla adhuc certa media pro sustenatione provisa fuerint. Ita Religio primum in plerasque orbis Christiani partes invecta. Ita primo in has Americae regiones ingressum habuit. Magna quidem, ut prius erat significatum hujusmodi Operariorum inopia laboramus: sed, si de iis agitur, quibus ego victum parare debeam, comnes jam stationes plenae sunt.

Hac occasione pauca scribo ad Rev. D. Suffraganeum uti mihi a V. D. Significatum fuit, ut ex illius benevolentia et auctoritate in usus Religionis, et maxime ad scholae Catholicae confectionem, in qua summam spem colloco, nostrae paupertati subveniatur.

R. D. Fromm, qui nunc hic est, et nuper ex Conewago discessit, R.D.V. haud dubie certiorem faciet de omnibus, quae suum Patruelem, virum optimum D. P. Miller, respiciunt.

Nescio plane quas gratias digne referre possim pro singulari beneficio, quod nobis exhibere designatus est R. D. Suffraganeus cum toto generali Vicariatu, de mittendis in Seminarium Episcopale alumnis, qui omni necessaria disciplina instructi, in has missiones denuo destinentur. Verum omnino credendum est intra paucos menses sedem Episcopalem in una ex foederatae Americae urbibus esse Constituendum, designandumque primum illius Episcopum; quod ubi perficietur, tam id, quod modo humanissime propositum est, quem aliud de studiosis Americanis ad idem Seminarium transmittendis opportunius et solidiori modo concludetur.

Ego interim cum omni gratiarum et venerationis exhibitione aestimari opto   Adm. Revae. Dom. Suae   S. Obs. et hum.

TO MATTHEW CAREY   Balto. Sep. 10–1789–

Dear Sir   I am just returned to Baltimore, where I find your favr. & packages of Aug. 15. My health at present, or rather a most severe rhumatic complaint, which has seized me, put it out of my power to answer you so fully, as I would wish. I am sensible of the expence of your undertaking, & proposed, in my late absence from Balt., to have made great exertions; but was obliged to remain inactive, the first attack of my present indisposition having prevented me from seeing any one, or doing any thing, as proposed. I do not find in your list of subscribers five or six additional names, sent some time ago to you to M. Beeston; to which you may add the Revd. Mr. Thomas

Digges, 1. the Revd. Mr. James Walton, *twelve* instead of *four,* John Lee Gibson Esqr., Clerk of Harford County, one; & William Herbert, St. Mary's County, one. I sent you £9..0..0, tho Mr. Beeston, about a month ago; & have eleven or twelve more now ready for you.[1] But I do not chuse to subject myself to the acceptance of an order as I foresee, it will not suit my opporunity to make the whole collection myself, & must depend on the diligence of others.

I am very sorry indeed, that the delay in receiving your letter prevented me from forwarding letters for the Eastern Shore, agreeably to your request. The pain, I feel from writing, which increases every moment, would prevent me from doing it now, even if it were not too late.

I am unacquainted with Wetham's translation. I have occasionally, tho' several years ago, examined part of Nary's, which then appeared to me too paraphrastical; & would not, I think, be approved of equal authority with the Doway translation; to which I would have you adhere, tho you have pointed out some & I know, there are other imperfections. But as it is the only English translation, which has the long established credit of faithfulness &c.; and it is quite out of my power to [*torn*–compare?] the other translations with it. & would be deemed presumption to alter it, I cannot take upon me to do it. I heared some years ago, that Bishop Geddes (of our Church, Coadjutor, I presume to Dr. Hayes) was preparing a new English Bible: but whether a translation from the Vulgate, or from the Hebrew & Greek, I cannot tell; tho I think it was the latter, after the manner of Fr. Houbigants latin translation from the original languages.

Excuse the inaccuracy of this, & attribute it to my painful situation. I am with esteem & great regard, Dr. Sir   Yr. most obedt. st.   J. Carroll

ALS   HSP
[1] See Aug., 1789.

TO JOHN HEILBRON   Baltimore the 10th of Septr.–1789

Reverend Father: The letters written by Your Reverence at Lancaster, under date of August 18, were received at Baltimore two days prior to my return. First of all, I sincerely regret his grievous illness; no less does it pain me that he wrote that no assistance had been supplied to him for his support, for which reason he came to Lancaster. I certainly understood from the Reverend Mr. Pellentz that a sufficiently notable sum of money had been received in his name by Your Reverence from a certain inhabitant of C[G]oshenhopen,[1] and which he left to be applied to your use, until the Procurator General would be paid: then, I heard that other aid had been supplied, when the affairs of the residents of Lancaster were being discussed in Chapter. I have asked Your Reverence about all these things so that he might inform the Procurator as soon as possible, with whom I wish a monetary matter should be transacted directly, not however through me, whose care has been extended in so many other very grave matters. The things which I have written concerning the statutes of the Chapter[2] are certain; indeed, I have taken those things from the acts whence a sum recorded daily by me was paid out at the Lancaster station.

Now I return to the matter of Philadelphia; it is not my plan to examine those things which you have noted in my previous letters. I have, previously, written a few things, so that I might subjoin reasons for doubting about those things, which you have proposed as certain; for, in truth, they [my remarks] seem to me to be in accord by and large with Theological discipline; however, I have not written so that I might enter into an argument, because reasons neither of time nor of my office permit. And thus, other things having been laid aside, I devote my attention only to this, that in those things concerning the pact or declaration of Philadelphia with respect to the Right of Patronage,[3] whose cause you thus treat at this point, so that it certainly is evident to me, that not only have their subterfuges been related, but Your Reverence also supported their efforts, so that in some manner, you defended this violation of good faith. For, first of all, he says that the word *appointment* means consent to know approval—*agreement* or *approbation,* so that some person is established in a certain office: however, this is altogether beyond common use, since all our languages or men hardly skilled know that the word *appointment* is the same as a designation to a certain function. However, what else is a designation in the present matter; than an exercise in the Right of Patronage? And thus it is evident then that it has been understood by the residents of Philadelphia because Mr. Premir asked me in their name during the past autumn that I should designate some priest for them, which I took upon myself to do, when some of the congregation would inform me of reliable support for him: in this matter, since Your Reverence ought to know those things in my letters, I hesitate that my faith in you should even thus be called into doubt, so that he may deny that the Philadelphians have renounced in writing or [*ind.*] the Right of Patronage. And thus he was able to judge that his argument had been taken from the word *concurrence;* since they who demand that those things happen, are rightly involved in the designation of a pastor, and they undertake among themselves to provide entirely for his sustenance.

Then, Your Reverence adds that the Philadelphians, if in truth they have renounced their right, did that for the sake of *redeeming their anger* for those things which they had done invalidly. How unfitting it may be by and large for such actions with respect to their objects, and inconsonant with your accustomed humanity, and what happened even undeservedly beyond the truth of the matter,[–] all know by what means their letters were communicated to me, which I do not doubt was recounted for Your Reverence. For thus they write in their letters of him, by which they take away from themselves the Right of Patronage, and they give thanks to me, because I acquiesced immediately in their first demand for a Church to be built— "Monday last,["] thus, they write, etc.

I ask, Reverend Father, whether those who write thus, think that they are harassed, and are deprived violently of their right, or, on the contrary, that they have been treated benignly and very humanely. Then, I ask, whether even with respect to your Superiors in Religion, or their predecessors, under whose authority you have otherwise conducted the sacred ministries, have you so undeservedly and unfittingly dared to object that their "harassment" is unjust, or, if you had, whether they themselves had not been responsible for the penalty of of an unjust accusation, which, nonetheless, is far from my intentions: but, I further beseech that you considerably mistrust yourself, your teaching, however clear it is, and also your friendships, and then, that you will recall to mind [the things] which you yourself have written to me in your first coming to America, and have promised, since I store up jealously a monument of your piety, observance, and zeal.

Therefore, Your Reverence thus understands that I have clearly determined that I will render an account in everything considered before God, and my service to Him, however brief it may be; that I will not promise that the right will be usurped by others, which stems from the use of previous times, or, by another title, belongs to an Ecclesiastical Superior: Then, I do not see in what manner Your Reverence seeks to be immune from blame as being a defender of the Laity in his attempts against the Rights of the Clergy. For such principles add that there would follow from them in almost all Churches in America that the Right of Patronage resides in the Laity: though generally indeed they were constructed by their contributions.

Your Reverence adds that the question of Patronage, having been suspended, I may transfer you by my own authority to Philadelphia: as if indeed that translation might not be a matter of future discussion,[.] I do not acknowledge the right of those who, without having consulted me, have proceeded to an election, and by their own authority have established the *sole rights* as a parochial authority; and they have asked me to confirm the de facto election: and because for this reason, it strengthens more this interpretation of fact, [that] there will be a certain testimonial before many months, transcribed by Your Reverence, in which, as I hear, you have added the title of Pastor of the Church of the Holy Trinity to your name: For thus it was related to me by the Reverend Mr. Rousselot, a French priest, recently expelled from the coast of Hispanic America, who witnesses that he has seen that testimonial.

I add further, for fuller information, that there is not the same jurisdiction for the faculties of all priests in the Missions; but they are limited at the free will of the Superior: because the spiritual administration itself of the social fabric altogether demands that this be done; how utterly contrary in those rules of the Missions, which, without foundation, in so far as I know, Your Reverence seems to hold: which [rules] indeed, so far are they from being the rules of the Missions themselves, that Benedict 14[4] instituted altogether different rules for England, and this among others, lest any missionary, under most grave penalty and deprivation of faculties travel into another's district of his own accord, and exercise the ministries of Religion.

After this, I will set aside from myself every argument. I desire that a priest be established for the Church of the Most Holy Trinity; but according to ancient custom and agreement made with me. Beseech the omnipotent God that all things be done rightly and in order; so that He may even remove me from this administration to which I feel more unequal day by day; or that he shall make me worthy. Thus, I am in spirit, for Your Reverence,   Your Humble Servant in Christ,   John Carroll   P.S. I began the above letters on the 10th Day of September; but, afflicted with most severe pains of rheumatism, I was compelled to interupt them even to this 15th Day of the same month.

ADf and CS   AAB   The first paragraph is missing from the CS and is supplied by the ADf, which has the date and which begins at the bottom of the letter received from Heilbron. The ADf is not complete and has many deleted and indecipherable passages not noted specifically in the editing that follows here.
[1] In southeastern Pa.
[2] Second General Chapter of the Clergy in Nov., 1786.
[3] Heilbron's letter to Carroll, Aug. 18, 1789, gives a full presentation of this right, not merely as taken from Germany, but with adaptation to America as the discussion with Carroll developed. In essence: the parish might present a priest, but not appoint him; the ecclesiastical superior might appoint only after a parish presentation. It seems that Carroll led Heilbron to this more acceptable understanding by his restraint; but even this formulation did not prove satisfactory for practical reasons. See Fecher, pp. 17-19, 211-13.
[4] Author of *De Synodo Diocesana,* Rome, 1748.

Rde. Pater   Baltimoram ante duos dies redeunti oblatae sunt literae Rae. Vae.. Lancastria scriptae sub die 18 Aug. Doleo imprimis & sincere de tentata ipsius valetudine; neque minus fere me angit, quod nullum sibi ad victum subsidium subministratum fuisse scribat ex quo Lancastriam adiverit. Ego certe ex R. Dom. Pellentz intellexi summam pecuniae satis spectabilem suo nomine a Ra Va ex quodam Coshenhopensi incola acceptam fuisse, quamque vestris usibus applicandam reliquit, donec Procr. Genlis solvendo eet: alia deinde subsidia subministrata fuisse audiveram, ubi res Lancastrienses in Capitulo discutiebantur. De his omnibus Ram Vam rogi ut Procuratorem quamprimum certiorem faciat, quocum rem pecuniariam directe transigi cupio, o autem per me, cujus sollicitudo tot aliis negotiis gravissimis e distenta. Quae scripsi de Capituli statutis, certa sunt; quippe illa ex actis desumpsi unde Lancastrensi stationi summa a me memorata quotannis solvenda e.

Nunc ad Philadelphiense negotium revertor: non est mei consilii illa expendere, quae prioribus meis litteris reposuisti. Pauca prius scripsi, ut suggererem causas dubitandi de iis, quae tanquam certa proposuisti; mihi vero sunt Theologicae disciplinae passim consentanea; non scripsi autem ut disputationem ingrederer, quod nec temporis nec officii mei rationes permittunt. Itaq caeteris praetermissis, ad illud unice advertam, quod eis de pacto seu declaratione Philadelphiensium circa jus patronatus, quorum causam ita agis in hac parte, ut inde mihi certo constet, non tantum illorum subterfugia commemorari, sed etiam R.Va. studia sua interponere, ut hanc fidei datae violationem aliquo modo defendet. Dicit enim imprimis vocem *appointment* significare consensum sive approbationem—*agreement* or *approbation,* ut persona aliqua in certo munere constituatur: hoc autem est omnino praeter usum communem, cum omnes linguae nostrae vel parum periti sciant vocem *appointment* idem esse ac designationem ad certum munus aut officium. Quod autem aliud est designatio in re praesenti; quam juris patronatus exercitium? Remq ita a Philadelphiensibus intellectum fuisse inde constat, quod autumno praeterito ipsorum nomine Dominus Premir me rogaverit, ut pro ipsis Sacerdotem aliquem designarem, quod facturum in me suscepi, ubi de congrua ipsius sustentatione certiorem me facerent: quod cum Rae Vae notum esse debeat ex meis litteris, moror ipsi meam fidem usq adeo in dubium vocari, ut neget Philadelphienses scripto vel [*ind.*] juri Patronatus renunciasse. Atq hinc etiam argumentum suum ex *concurrentiae* verbo depromptum aestimare poterit; cum illi sane in pastoris designationem influant, qui postulant, ut illa fiat, & suscipiunt in se omno illius sustentationi praevidendi.

Deinde adjicit Ra Va Philadelphienses, si revera juri suo renunciavissent, id fecisse causa *redimendae vescae,* adeoq irrito fecisse. Quae objectis quam parum decens sit, atq absona a solita vestra humanitate, quamq etiam immerito & praeter rei veritatem fiat, omnes norunt quibuscum ipsorum ad me literae sunt communicatae, quos inter Rae Vae recensendam esse non dubito. Ita enim scribunt iis ipsis literis, quibus a se abdicant jus patronatus, mihiq gratias agunt, quod primo ipsorum postulato de aedificanda Ecclesia statim acquievissim—"Monday last," ita scribunt &c &

Rogo, Rde Pater, an qui ita scribunt, vexari se sentiant, & juro suo violenter privari? an non potius se cum benigne & humaniter agi? Rogo deinde, an vel tuis in Religione Superioribus, vel praelatis, sub quorum auctoritate sacra ministeria alias perfecisti, tam immerito ac indecore injustam suorum *vescam* objicere ausus fuisses? aut si fecisses, an non ipsi injustae criminationis poenam exegissent? quod tamen a meo consilio longe abest: sed precor potius, ut tibi, ut doctrinae tuae, quamquam praeclara est, ut etiam amicitiis tuis aliquantum diffidas; deniq ut in memoriam revoces, quae primo in Americam adventu ipse mihi scripseris, promiserisqe, quod ego tuae monumentum pietatis, observantiae, ac zeli petiose conservo.

Intelligat igir Rae Va ita me plane statuisse, se omni secundum Deum considerata & tamquam administrationis meae rationem ipsi, brevi fortasse, redditurus; non promissurum me, ut ab aliis jus usurpetur, quod ex praecedentum temporum usu, vel alio titulo spectat ad Superiorem Ecclesiasticum: deinde me non videre, quomodo Reva. Va immunis esse queat ab incusatione tanquam defensoris laicorum in suis adversus Cleri jura conatibus. Talia enim adstruit principia, ut ex iis sequeretur omnium ferme in America Ecclesiarum jus patronatus penes Laicos esse: pleraeqe enim ex illorum collationibus constructae fuerunt.

Suggerit Ra Va ut, suspensa quaestione de patronatu, te propria auctoritate Philadelphiam transferam: quasi vero illa translatio non argumento futura sit, jus ipsorum agnosci, qui, me inconsulto, ad electionem processerunt, & tanquam propria auctoritate *jura stolae,* hoc est, parochialia constituere; meq interpellaverunt, ut electionem factam confirmarem: quodq eo magis hanc facti interpretationem roboraret, foret charta quaedam ante paucos menses a Ra Va subscripta, in qua ut audio, Pastoris Ecclesiae Sa Trinitatis titulam tuo nomini adjecisti: Ita enim mihi relatum fuit a Rdo Do Rousselet, Presbytero Gallo, nuper ex Hispaniae Americanae oris appulso, qui chartam illam se vidisse testatur.

Adjicio demum ad pleniorem informationem, non omnium in Missionibus Sacerdotum eandem esse jurisdictionem ad facultates; sed ad arbitrium Superioris esse ita limitatas: quod ipsa regiminis spiritualis administratio omnino fieri exigit; contra prorsus quam in illis regulis Missionum, quas, sine auctore, quantum scio, Re Va visum est cohibere: quae quidem, tantum abest, ut reipsa regulae Missionum sint, ut Benedictus 14 pro Anglia regulas omnino contrarias instituerit, ac hanc inter caeteras, ne quis Missionarius sub gravissima poena ac facultatum privatione in alterius districtum suo nutu excurrat, & ministeria Religionis exerceat.

Post haec, omni argumentationi hac de re supersedebo. Sacerdotem pro Ecclesia Smae Trinitatis constitui cupio; sed juxta priuscum morem & conventionem mecum factam. Precare Deum O.M. ut omnia rite & ordine fiant; atqe ut me vel ab hac administratione submoveat, cui me in dies magis imparem sentio; vel ut dignum faciat. Ita ex animo,   Rae Vae Servus & Xo humillimus   Joannes Carroll   P.S. Has literas inceperam die 10 Sepris; sed cruciatus gravissimis rhumatismi doloribus interrumpere coactus sum usq ad hanc 15d ejusdem mensis.

TO AN EPISCOPALIAN   Sep. 11, 1789

Not found. Listed as in Ethan Allen Collection, Maryland Historical Society.

TO THE TRUSTEES OF HOLY TRINITY CHURCH, PHILADELPHIA
Balte. Oct. 11—1789—

Gentlemen—   Your letter of the 4th. instt was delivered to me too late to answer it by the return of post. The delay you complain of, is not imputable to me; I have been willing & ready for this long time to appoint, or procure you Clergymen for Trinity Church; but I have told you before the reasons of my refusing to approve of your appointment & proceedings in it. You cannot conceive that any person should be so uncharitable or unjust, as to question your right of patronage, it being so well established & grounded in Ecclesiastical & civil law. I must own, that I not only question but, after considering every thing alledged in behalf of yr claim, am convinced, you are not entitled to it, by either Ecclesiastical, or civil law; and especially by the former, in which I am more conversant.

You say, that the expressions in one of your former letters, which I placed in opposition to your proceedings, in chusing Mr. Heilbron slipped inadvertently from your pen & were not intended in the sense wch. the words convey. I refer to yourselves, whether such an allegation is even admitted in the transaction of business between two parties? Could any letter appear more to be the result of deliberate attention, than that which was sent to me signed by Mr. Premir, as president, countersigned by Mr. Horn[1] as secretary, & tested as being written by order of the German Society in Philada. and its vicinity? And if you will refer to the extracts heretofore sent you you will find it was written, not as a protestation against allegations to yr prejudice but expressly in answer to mine, in which I cautioned you against founding a claim to a right of patronage, on the ground of your having built a church.

In my last I referred to Mr Premir's conversation with me, as collateral evidence that you did not always claim this right of patronage. He now declares he conversed with me, without authority or commission; I cannot tell how that may have been, but I know that I thought, I was treating with him as the presidt. of the German Society, and with them as such (& I think Mr. Oellers was present) I discoursed on many other matters relative to your Incorporation act. This I know; I should conceive myself now bound by any convention, which I might have made with them, or any assurances given them. It was natural therefore to infer, that I ought to place the same dependance on them.

You say, you despise Former customs as despotic. I am sorry to hear such a sentiment come from you, because it prepares me for more innovations. But I endeavour to persuade myself, that you will soon discover the danger of departing from established rules in Ecclesiastical matters.

I can assure you, that I am impartial in this business, & have neither ambition or inclination to keep in my hands the apointment of a Clergyman for your new Church. So far from feeling any such desire I sincerely wish, I were divested of all power whatever, either to appoint or govern one person in the United States. If my deference for those, whom I ought to respect & trust more than myself, had not compelled me in a manner, to resist my inclination, I should have resigned all pretensions to superiority long ago. But, while providence is pleased to keep me in office, it is my duty to fulfill its

388 *Holy Trinity Church (Philadelphia) Controversy*

obligations as faithfully, as my judgment and abilities enable me. I act in conformity to this principle when I continue to disallow of your late election

ADf   AAB

[1] Henry Horne associated with the society at an earlier date.

TO JOHN HEILBRON   Balt Oct 13–1789

R. Sir   I have received yours of Sepr. 30th. The Rev. Mr. Rousselet[1] is a French secular priest, lately from Carthagena in New Spain, with an excellent character of zeal & virtue. Many poor Creatures brought back from Carthagena & saved by his fatherly kindness, will bear testimony of his merits. He is now gone to Boston. He described to me the instrument of paper so particularly, with the great seal of Trinity Church annexed to it, and to which your name is affixed, that I have no doubt of his having seen it, as he related. But, since you say (& I doubt not of your veracity) that you did not sign it yourself, I imagine some of your acquaintance presumed, they might make free with your name. This I well remember, that he told me of it, before I had ever mentioned to him your name, or any circumstance concerning Trinity Church.

If your very Revd. Fr. Genl.[2] has received the powers, which formerly belonged to the Genl. of the Jesuits, that does not give him authority to confer any spiritual jurisdiction here excepting to the Religious of his order over one another. The Jesuits, sent hither formerly by their Superiors, could exercise no jurisdiction over the laity, unless power was given to them by the Vicar Apostolic of the London district, to whom we continued subject till the year 1784–, to whom then I succeeded by appointment of his Holiness. I hope yr. Revce will be always so much govd. by the rules & universal discipline of the Cath. Church, as not to act in direct opposition to the authority established by the H. See. This I must prevent by all means in my power. I have told yr. Revce. before I will not dispute with you any more. But I cannot help informing you that you are entirely mistaken in your observations on the practice of England, & Benedict 14ths regulations.[3] There is not a vestige remaining there of former dioceses or parishes. The Bishops are all Vicars Apostolic & Bishops in partibus Infidelium.[4] The jurisdiction over all England is divided amongst four of these.

ADf   AAB

[1] Louis Rousselet, a French priest, granted powers of ministry by Carroll, departed in 1791 for Guadeloupe, where he became a victim of the French Revolution.

[2] Of the Capuchin Order.

[3] Pope Benedict XIV (d. 1759) in *De Synodo Diocesane* (Rome, 1748), which adapts general ecclesiastical law to diocesan administration.

[4] Titular bishops of sees, mostly in Asia and Africa, no longer occupied by bishops of the Roman jurisdiction.

TO CHARLES PLOWDEN Baltimore Oct. 23–1789–

My dear friend   Your favours by the August and Sept. mail are safely arrived, and claim, as all others from you, my warmest thanks. The interest you take, in a late event, proves the warmth of your friendship; but it proves likewise, how blind & partial friends are liable to be. Your condolance would have suited better the situation of my mind: every day furnishes me with new reflections, & almost every day promises new events, to alarm my conscience, and excite fresh sollicitude at the prospect before me. You cannot conceive the trouble, I suffer already, & still greater, which I foresee, from the medley of clerical characters coming from different quarters, & various educations, & seeking employment here. I cannot avoid employing some of them, & they begin soon to create disturbances. As soon as this happens, they proceed to bring in Jesuitism, & to suggest, that every thing is calculated by me for its restoration; & that I sacrifice the real interest of Religion to the chimerical project of reviving it. But of all classes of such persons, who have been yet amongst us, I have found the Capucins, both German & Irish, most intolerable. To a great deal of ignorance they join most consummate assurance. Add, that they seem to have no principles of Religious life. We have some German *Recollets,* & some Irish Dominicans, & some secular priests, who behave properly, & even commendably.

No news is yet received from Rome of advice being got to the Propaganda of our proceedings here: But I have a letter of July 20th. from Bourdeaux, acknowleding the receipt of the packet, wch. had reached them, & of its being forwarded to the Nuncio at Paris. I request you to make my most respectful compliments to Mr. Weld, and to return him the best thanks, you are able, for his most kind & honourable invitation. But as nothing is yet received from Rome, & I hate even to think of my promotion, and still hope that something may turn out to prevent it, I can give no positive answer on this occasion. Should I finally determine on going to England, I will not fail sending you previous notice. The only pleasing view, which this prospect of Episcopacy affords, is that of once again seeing some of my ever esteemed friends. I am solicitous and very uneasy at the critical situation of Eng: Rom: Catholics.[1] The advantage taken by their enemies, of the divisions caused by the famous oath of allegiance are fresh in our memory. It behoves all you, whom God has blessed with talents, & filled with an enlightened zeal, to consult with each other in great moderation, &, by giving up unessential points, to let every one of your resolutions be the result of common consent. Union being thus preserved amongst Catholics of character, & of the best regulation of their learning, you need not fear, but the whole body will act uniformly. I congratulate with Mr. Weld & his amiable family for the mark of favourable attention which they received from the Royal family.[2] In the midst of convulsions in France, I have been sollicitous to hear, how Religion would be treated there. Your last justifies my fears. I have long thought that almost every man in that kingdom above the rank of mediocrity, & many even of these, are lost to every feeling of Religion. We have many of them in this town, Traders & others. It is the case generally throughout the United States. They are every where a scandal to Religion, with very few exceptions; not only that, but they disseminate, as much as they can, all the principles of irreligion, of contempt for the church, & disregard for the duties, which both command. They have corrupted here almost entirely, the principles of a numerous body of Acadians, or French Neutrals, & their descendants, who being expelled by the English from Nova Scotia in the war of 1755, settled & increased here.[3]

I am greatly obliged to you for still remembering our Academy, which is indeed to be our main sheet anchor for Religion. We now hope to get it under way, to continue my sea language, early next summer. But what shall we do for a principal? Is it impossible to inspire so much zeal into any of the distinguished [torn—masters] at Liege? For God's sake try to provide us such a one.

Religion is making some progress with us, at least in some parts of America. The exercise of It was, you know, introduced into Boston by a French Abbé La Poterie, who proves to have been a most infamous character, as appears by a certificate sent unto me from the Vicar Genl. of the Diocese Blois. Luckily, La Poterie had been detected in some misconduct before, & was discharged from Boston, without having committed very flagrant scandals there. Another French priest,[4] who is well recommended, and speaks English succeeds him; & I suppose Mr. Thayer is arrived, as I heard from him, then at Paris July 1st, that he would leave France in a few days.

Charleston, in Sth. Carolina, affords a favourable prospect. I sent thither, Sepr. 1788, a very pious Irish Priest, named Ryan; but a man of very moderate abilities. God has blessed his labours. His edifying deportment has gatherd. together a congn., who now sollicit a second priest in which I hope soon to gratify them. Other places likewise are receiving priests.

Having now filled my paper almost in your manner, except as to the agreeableness & variety of narration, I must take leave of you for the present & prepare for a journey to morrow towards our back settlements, where I propose spending ten days in visiting some Congns, I have not yet seen. My best respects to Messrs. Stanley & Clinton. Yr. friends here salute you. My good M[othe]r. is always happy to hear of you & so is the respectable Mr. Digges—who approaches near being the Dean of the former Province.   Dr. Sr. Yrs. &c.   J.C.   I beg you not to forget or omit to convey to Wardour my most grateful & respectful remembrance of that every honb. and amiable family.

ALS   St

[1] Mitigated oaths were offered in the decades preceeding the Relief Act and the Catholic Committee sought to mediate with the government as well as factions among Catholics regarding acceptability of the oaths.

[2] The visit of George III, first by royalty to a Catholic family since the Reformation.

[3] Large numbers resided near Carroll's Church of St. Peter's in Baltimore.

[4] Louis Rousselet.

COMMENT ON CHARLES PLOWDEN LETTER   Oct. 25–1789

Rebecca Riley 6 weeks old, daughter of John (Acatholicus) & Elizabeth Riley—Sponsor John & Mary Logsdon

AM   AAB (6L6)   Date of letter is Aug. 30, 1789. May be an isolated memorandum.

TO JOHN HEILBRON   [Nov. 1789]

[. . . .] instead of about twenty Diocesan Bishops, as formerly—Not one parish remains, as in Catholic times; there has never been a succession in them, any more than in the Bishopricks. I inform you farther, that almost all the Churches and Chapels in America have been built, or are now building by contribution of the Catholics living in their neighbourhood, & not by donations collected far and near. But if it had happened really, as you state the matter, I ask if contributions for Trinity Church were not gathered from distant parts of Pennsylvania, from Protestants, Quakers &c. & I mean not this as a reproach, but to convince yr. Revce. the insufficiency of your distinction of presentation,[1] & to shew you to w[ha]t. a state of vassalage your doctrine would reduce the American Church. You use some expressions, which I must not pass unnoticed. *Non ex collationibus laicorum in unum corpus, seu paroeciam ex condicto coadunatorum, uti in casu Philadelphiensium.*[2] The supposition involved in these words contains principles subversive to all subordination, and of the very essence of any Ecclesiastical benefice, especially a parochial one. Divines give this definition of a benefice. You conclude—with lamenting & imputing to my fault, that many souls in Philada. are without a pastor, without spiritual food, without sacraments &c. What does all this mean, but that no one can be their pastor but your Revce.? That those, who are appointed, & who continually administer the scts, & the word of God by due authority, are not the pastors of the flock of Philada. &. but that he will be the pastor, who shall go thither without mission, & assume a jurisdiction, without authority or appointment? I wonder that your Rev. should call for my final resolution after receiving it so fully in my last.[3] I should be wanting to my most sacred duty, if I allowed the intended encroachments on my right of office, and still more, if I were to countenance your intended proceedings, after you had told me, as in yr. last that you were determined to proceed to Philada. to execute, what you have neither authority or commission to execute; and under pretence of serving those, who are amply provided already with the means of salvation, to quit those,[4] who without you must be destitute of all spiritual assistance. I give you notice therefore, that if you proceed, without my farther authority, to exercise any pastoral functions in Philada., you will do so *invalide* and *illicite;* as I thereby revoke the faculties granted you formerly, so far, as they may be deemed to extend to Philada., or within ten miles from it. I am exceedingly sorry to come to these extremities: but your violent declarations have compelled me. I am &c.

ADf   AAB   First portion not found.
   [1] The reasonableness of the *jus patronatus,* or right of patronage, in the laity of the congregation and of their "presentation" of a pastor for episcopal approbation derives from the fact that the whole formation and building of the local church was by these laymen. This was not verified in the case of Holy Trinity, Carroll says, as it may have been in parishes of Germany.
   [2] Heilbron's letter with this garbled Latin has not been found.
   [3] Of Oct. 13, 1789.
   [4] At Lancaster County, Pa.

MEMORANDUM FOR JOHN HEILBRON   [Nov. 1789]

1. To know by what authority Mr. H[eilbron]. proclaims certain feasts not appointed to be kept in the U.S. Says that he published them agreeably to a list of Mr. Fermon [Farmer].

2. To see the lists of his Easter Communicants. 400—

3. To know the reason of his not obeying my orders.

4. To inform him of the impropriety of admitting any foreign Priest to say mass without a written permission from the Bishop or his Vicar, who is Mr. Fleming for Philada.

5. To know by what rights he keeps the clock belonging to Lancaster.[1] He says that the clock was Mr. Cause' private property, and given by him to Mr. Helbron.

6. To make inquiry concerning his attention to catechism etc. They are educated in catechism at school, in the church and his own house.

7. To examine into the state of temporalities of Trinity Church.

ADf   AAB   The following was deleted at the top of the MS: "Rules to be observed at Philada. by H." On date estimate see Heilbron to Carroll, Oct. 8, 1789, and Guilday, p. 649.
   [1] Lancaster County, Pa., and its congregation.

TO JOHN TROY   Baltimore, Nov. 9th, 1789.

My Lord,   I did myself the honour of writing a few lines to your Lordship from Virginia, the last of June, or the beginning of July.[1] I then returned my sincere thanks for your great and generous endeavour to discountenance a pamphlet full of falsehood and malignity, and I requested your Grace to be the interpreter of my sentiments of gratitude to the other most Rev. Prelates who joined your Lordship so readily in condemning it.

I lament with your Lordship that there are not more clergymen in the United States. They are large enough, and offer a field wide enough for many more labourers. But unfortunately almost all who offer their services have great expectations of livings, high salaries, &c.; and these our country does not afford. Most of the stations to which salaries are annexed, are occupied; and I find few, or, to speak more properly, I find none willing to commit themselves entirely to the care of Providence, and seek to gather congregations, and livings, of consequence, by fixing themselves in places where no missioners preceded them. Your Grace knows, it was thus that religion was propagated in every age of the Church. If clergymen animated with this spirit will offer their services, I will receive them with the greatest cheerfulness, and direct their zeal where there is every prospect of success; and will make no manner of distinction between Seculars and Regulars. I am, with great veneration and respect, My Lord, Your Lordship's most obedient and humble servant, J. Carroll.

L   Moran, III, 506-07
¹ See July 2, 1789, above.

TO MATTHEW CAREY Baltimore Nov. 14—1789—

Dear Sir   I received to day your letter by Mr. McCoy, & as soon as the packet thro Mr. Rice come to hand, I will forward the sale of the books, as quickly as possible. I am glad you have at length got the bible under press; I shall now be able to satisfy the numerous interrogatories, that assail me. I send you some dollars, & must accuse my own inattention for not collecting more, which might have been done in this town. As to distant subscribers, I cannot take blame to myself. I have directed Mr. Beeston to add some names to your list of subscribers. But as he has been frequently out of Philada, he may have neglected it, & I repeat the names underneath. Mr. Sewall joins in compliments to you: I am, Dr. Sir   Yr. most obedt. servt.   J. Carroll   (turn over) [*eight subscribers named*] I shall have a better oppor[tunit]y. of sending the dollars in a few days.

ALS   HSP

TO JOHN HEILBRON [Dec. 2, 1789]

Since you have violated in various ways and seriously the rules of Ecclesiastical discipline, first of all, by deserting, on your own authority, the Congregations committed to your care; by accusing your Ecclesiastical Superior falsely of a most serious crime; and by denying utterly his whole authority over you; and especially by usurping spiritual jurisdiction against his express prohibition; thus, I warn you for this first time, that you bring an end to scandal; otherwise, you should know that you will be burdened with a grave censure. I earnestly beseech the all-high God, that He may deign to inspire upon you salutary counsels— John Carroll, Superior in the Provinces of the Church of the Federated States of America.

He has been notified in Philadelphia on the . . . Day . . . in the Year In the Presence of the Witnesses

ADS AAB There is also in AAB an ADf with a slightly different arrangement of the concluding section. (See below.) For the date see to Beeston, Dec. 2, 1789, who would determine the actual date on which this and subsequent notes were delivered to Heilbron.

TO JOHN HEILBRON [Dec. 2, 1789]

You have, on your own authority, deserted the Congregations committed to you by your Superior in these ecclesiastical matters, and you have dared to bear witness against the Superior himself, as being mistaken. Since you have shown contempt for his jurisdiction by words and deeds, and have fore-sworn beyond his precept and expressed will without any faculty, you have not feared to conduct spiritual duties; and you persist in hardening yourself obstinately in rebellion. Therefore, by this first warning to you, I give you notice that a grave censure is to be imposed upon you, unless you recover your senses as soon as possible. and for the grave scandal whose author you were, you offer fitting satisfaction. That you will act as from your heart, I earnestly beseech Almighty God— John Carroll

He has been notified by us (or, by me) by those set aside (or the one set aside) for this, on this day —in the year—in the presence of N.N. Witness (Witnesses).

ADf AAB from which the preceding item was made. Another ADf exists in AAB; and, though shorter and without the detailed conclusion, it is substantially the same as the above. Still another has the full conclusion found in the copy sent to Beeston, but the whole text was deleted, apparently by Carroll.

Rdo Patri, Joanni Carolo Helbron, Sacerdoti ex ordine Minoritarum Capuccinorum. Congregationes tibi a Superiore his Ecclesiasticis commissas ppria auctorae deseruistis ipsum Superiorem tanquam fallarium insimulare exausus: Illius jurisdictione verbis et factis contempta, et ejurata praeter illius praescriptum. et expressam voluntatem sine ulla facultate, munera spiritualia exercere non metuisti; atque emorum in rebellione pervicacit te obdurare pergis—Hac igr prima monitione tibi significo gravem in te ferendam ee censuram, nisi quam primum resipiscas, et pro gravi scandalo, cujus auctor fuisti, satisfactionem competentem praestes—Quod ut ex animo facias, Deum oiptentem enixe precor— Joannes Carroll

Significatum fuit a nobis (vel, a me) ad hoc deputatis (deputato), hac die —ann.—coram—N.N. teste (testibus).

MEMORANDUM FOR JOHN HEILBRON [Dec. 2, 1789]

1. Your Reverence will publicly declare that he acknowledges that no authority belongs to him or to other priests, for the administration of the Sacraments, or for preaching, or for other parochial functions, unless and in so far as they shall have been approved by an Ecclesiastical Superior, whom the Holy See has designated—and in order to remove all doubt, or controversy hereafter concerning the meaning of this declaration, he will prescribe some means to this end, and he will give [it] over into the hands of the forenamed Superior, in which the very words themselves are contained, since it has been rendered in the Latin language; by this means, the declaration will be understood to be public.[1]

2. In the case in which it shall have seemed good to the Superior to designate Your Reverence, so that he may exercise spiritual ministries in some manner in the Church of the Holy Trinity; it ought to be demanded from those, who strive only for the right of patronage, or, in their name, from the custodians of the Church, that they declare in writing that they do not understand and acknowledge, a declaration of this kind done by a Superior, not [*sic;* as?] from the force of some pretended presentation, but from the judgment of the Superior himself.

[Notations in English on the back of the MS for the above:] If the German Congregations consist of Roman Catholics, they must profess the doctrines of their Church; consequently, supremacy of the Bishop of Rome, which is a most material article of their creed—He has supreme visible past [or]

Right of presentation & approbation Contract with the Bp.

R C Roman Catholics, cannot exist without being subject to the pastoral authority of the Bp.

ADf and ACS AAB Except for English notations, a fair copy. Contents indicate addressee. Date and circumstances established by to Beeston and Heilbron, Dec. 2, 1789.

[1] Reference to English passage below.

1. Ra Va publice declarabit se agnoscere nullam sibi aut caeteris Sacerdotibus auctoritatem competere, pro Sacramentorum administratione, aut praedicatione, aut aliis functionibus parochialibus, nisi & quatenus approbati fuerint a Superiore Ecclesiastico, quem Sa Sedes designavit—et ad tollendum omne dubium, aut controversiam posthac de sensu hujus declarationis, instrumen-

tum aliquod subscribit, et tradet in manus praedicti Superiori, quo con-
tineantur ipsissima verba, latino sermone reddita; quibus declaratio publica
concipienda fit.

2. Casu, quo Superiori visum fuerit Ram Vam designare, ut ministeria
quaedam Spiritualia in Ecclesia Smae Trinitatis exerceat; exigi debet ab illis,
qui modo pro jus patronatus contendunt, vel, eorum nomine, ab Ecclesiae
curatoribus, ut scripto declarent se agnoscere & fateri, hujusmodi designationem fieri a Superiore non ex vi praetensae alicujus praesentationis, sed ex
ipsius Superioris arbitrio.

TO JOHN HEILBRON   Balt. Dec. 2, 1789

I have already [repressed?][1] the exercise of yr faculties, I now revoke
them entirely, & recall all spiritual powers & authority, which you ever
received from me.

ADf   AAB   Delivered Dec. 7, 1789. (See below, to Heilbron, Dec. 31, 1789.)
[1] Deleted passage starting at this point: "the faculties you had from me, for the
administration of pastoral functions & administration of sacraments in Philada., and ten
miles round it."

TO HOLY TRINITY CONGREGATION   Baltimore, Decr. 2, 1789

The undersigned Ecclesiastical Superior in the United States[1] of America is
called on by the Sacred respect, which, he owes to the lawful administration
of the Sacraments, to the preservation of discipline, & the tranquillity of the
consciences of the faithful under his charge, to make known to all, whom it
may concern, that in virtue of his authority derived from the Holy See, he has
restrained the Rev. Mr. J.C. Helbron from exercising any functions whatever;
& namely from preaching, or administering the Sacraments of baptism, the
Eucharist, as viaticum to the exped, pennance, extreme unction, or matrimony. All therefore, who shall knowingly have recourse to his ministry for
any of the abovesaid services, unless in cases of extreme necessity, will incur a
heavy guilt; & absolution given by him in the Sacrament of pennance, will be
null and void.   J. Carroll

ADf   AAB   Addressee not given on MS.
[1] At this point the following was deleted: "The Rev. Mr. John Charles Helbron having
openly, publicly, & contumaciously in disobedience contempt of the rightful authority
of his Ecclesiastical Superior."

TO JOHN HEILBRON   19 Dec. 1789.

Reverend Sir: Such a great delay is not necessary for Your Reverence to
reply to a simple proposal,[1] nor is it necessary for this Synod, as you call it,
or a gathering of the Curators of the Church. (With respect to those things)

which pertain to them, they perhaps will not have thus a difficult outcome, if only Your Reverence shows beforehand an example of necessary docility. At nine o'clock tomorrow: I will await him, since he does not write that he is able to assemble earlier. [To] I.H. [John Heilbron]   J.C.

ADf   AAB   Date is at the end of the letter.
[1] Possibly a reference to Carroll's Memorandum to John Heilbron [Dec. 2, 1789] above, calling for public acknowledgment of Carroll's authority.

TO JOHN HEILBRON   Dec. 20, 1789

Not found. See to Heilbron, Dec. 21, 1789.

TO JOHN HEILBRON   Monday morning Dec. 21, 1789

Rev. Sr.   The message, which I sent you yesterday[1] was very sufficient to satisfy you in my intentions in desiring a conference. After that, you might have forborne your indelicate interrogation in the beginning of your note of this morning. You can have no better opportunity at your house for a personal interview between us two alone, than we may enjoy here. After coming so far, I shall expect you to meet me here, & as soon as possible. I am Rev. Sir, &c.
    Be pleased to inform me of the hour, at which you can come.

ADf   AAB   At the head of MS appears: "(Answer)."
[1] Not found. Carroll may have been referring to his letter to Heilbron of Dec. 19, 1789.

TO JOHN HEILBRON   Philada. Dec. 24, 1789

Rev. Sir   Unless you will make an explicit acknowledgement publick & give it in writing signed by yourself, that you cannot exercise any parochial functions, till I restore your faculties, it is in vain to expect, that we can come to any agreement: and therefore, till this point is settled, we need not treat on any others. I am &c.   J.C.

ADf   AAB

TO CHARLES PLOWDEN   Philada. Dec. 28–1789

Dear Sir   I am indebted to you for some very affectionate letters, since I wrote last; and I have reason to expect I may find others in Baltimore, at my return, as the October & November packets are just arrived; the former having had a very long passage. I acknowledged in my last Mr. Weld's most generous and (to me) honourable invitation. But it is impossible to determine on accepting it, till I have the bulls, & see the tenor of them. These I have reason to expect every day, according to advices lately received from Mr. Thorpe. My business in this town is exceedingly disagreeable. A Capucin German friar,[1] who arrived here two years ago, & has since been employed in some country Congregations, felt an ambition to display his talents in this city; & having found a party of his countrymen willing to receive him here accepted their nomination of him to a new Church they have built, & pretended a right to exercise faculties & jurisdiction here, contrary to my express injunctions, & limitations of his faculties. I was obliged to exert myself to stop this daring spirit after encountering much impertinence, and, afterwards, much equivocation & subterfuge, I brought him to terms: he was induced to give me in writing, & acknowledge in open Church, that he, nor any other priest has a right to exercise any spiritual powers without the approbation & consent of the Ecclesiastical Superior. Thus is this matter so far terminated; and, I hope, a stop is put to the scandal, with which we were threatened. I shall return to Baltimore in two days, where I expect to find letters from you.

In this town we have now two very handsome & large Churches, besides the old original chapel,[2] which was the cradle of Catholicity here. This serves for a domestic chapel, being contiguous to the Presbytery house; & there is more consolation in it, than in the more splendid service of the other Churches: for here it is, that every day, & especially on Sundays, that Sacraments are frequented &c. In the presbytery house lately built, live Messrs. Beeston & Graessl (a most amiable German Ex-Jesuit) & Mr. Fleming, an Irish Dominican lately from Dublin, a Gentleman of amiable manners, & temper, & a very excellent scholar. Near to the new Church, lives the above mentioned Capucin.

I have little time to add more at present; & must refer farther communications, till, by returning home, I am relieved from eternal interruptions here. Present my most respectful compliments to the honourable family, in which you live, to Messrs. Stanley, Clinton, your Br. Robt. & all your other Brethren, wherever you may meet them. I am my Dr. Sir   Yr. most affte friend & Servt   J. Carroll   The last part of this letter was written Jan. 8–1790

ALS   St
[1] John Heilbron.
[2] Holy Trinity, St. Mary's, and St. Joseph's (1733).

TO JOHN HEILBRON   29th of Dec. 1789–12 noon

Rev. Sir: I will expect Your Reverence at nine o'clock—nevertheless, I would have rejoiced, if it had pleased you to come more quickly. It will not be postponed,[;] I seek a reply to my proposal, for this reason, that the Custodians of the Church of the Most Holy Trinity are unable to consult together among themselves. If I have what is to be treated about Your

Reverence, they should have begun happily, the remainder will easily be transacted, so that I hope—Paper is lacking to me for persevering in this, nor is he at hand who may seek another—and thus please excuse its scantiness. J.C.

ADfS   AAB

Rde. D.   Cras hora 9a R.V. expectabo—gavisus tamen fuissem, si citius convenire placuisset. Non differatur, quaeso responsum ad meam propositionem, eo quod Eccliae Ssma Trin. Curatores nequeant una inter se verba conferre. Si quae cum Ra Va tractanda habeo, feliciter ceperint, reliqua facile conficientur, uti spero—Charta mihi hoc instandi deficit, neque adest, qui aliam quaerat—Excuset itaque hujus parvitatem.   29 Dec. 1789—ho. 12a—
     J.C.

TO JOHN HEILBRON   Dec. 31, 1789

In his relation of fact, Your Reverence has concealed many things, and has omitted others. 1. You concealed that you thus were assigned by your Regular Superior to America, so that only by their authority, to whom it there pertains, did you undertake the care of souls.[1] 2. You concealed that you, as soon as you had arrived in America, had professed full dependency on the Prefect Apostolic, so that thus you wished to be governed by his most "free" direction, in all things, which pertain to the care of souls, and the place, in which you exercise that care. 3. You concealed that you had received faculties, granted as from the Prefect, just as in truth they were granted. 4. You concealed that in these faculties a clause had been adjoined by the Prefect, in which it was expressed that the faculties had been conceded until they were revoked.

Then, you omitted that you had written to the Prefect, that it had been resolved for you, that a place had been assigned to you, and that you had deserted the souls committed to your care, and against the express will of the Prefect you had set out for Philadelphia, so that you might shepherd them, whose care had not been committed to you, and who had been instructed by others in all helps of Religion, and abundantly so by the pastors assigned to them. You denied that the authority of the Prefect was necessary to you for this; you asserted that a sufficient, general jurisdiction of your Order had been conferred on you; and no jurisdiction, and not even indeed approbation, could be conferred on you by the Prefect of your mission. Since you had known that it was thus decided and settled for you, you have been warned by the Prefect, not to undertake to exercise any faculties in Philadelphia; and in order to reprehend your temerity more strongly, the Prefect has thus tempered the faculties previously conceded to you, so that neither in Philadelphia, nor in its vicinity, within ten miles, has he left the power, validly and licitly, of administering the Sacraments and parochial functions.[2]

Then, you omitted that you had responded to the Prefect in letters which were quite unbecoming, in which you said these things among others, that the Prefect *arrogantly suspended approbation for you,* which you asserted that *you have from another source,*[3] and which, strictly speaking, you are not able to have from him; then, you have added that you will do what you have determined, *not attending* the restriction of faculties, which was altogether *impertinent and against the first principles of Theology.*

You omitted that the Prefect, even though he was thus injured by the dishonest letters [of yours], had attempted, up to that point, to recall you to your sense of obedience and subordination: and with this hope, it was shown to you to what extent his power, conferred by the Roman Pontiff, extended itself, as well for concession, as for restriction and revocation of faculties with respect to Regular and Secular priests. Since the Prefect had employed this condescension toward you, you responded that you did not believe that power was granted to the Prefect, whereby he asserted that he was pleased:[4] and you equivalently repeated this again, after you had been warned about your most unjust imputation of blame to the Prefect.

Certain things aside, as I pass over others, you, having left your own proper station, took up your abode at Philadelphia, and, after those faculties had been removed from you, exercising there whatever pastoral functions you wished. Nonetheless, you exercised them, and thus you utterly denied the Prefect's authority: and then, at length, the faculties, which previously he had granted to you, had been taken away in their entirety.

It is permitted to observe these few things *in the case of fact,* exhibited by Your Reverence. In the [your] appended resolution, almost all things are opposed to correct theology, and they are refuted by the sole inspection of that clausula, annexed to my faculties, a copy of which I already previously communicated. Wherefore, so that I may break off further delays, I refer to those things, which you will find appended to another page.[5]

To Your Reverence, [Your] Servant in Christ   J. Carroll

ACS   AAB

[1] Heilbron sought to justify himself by relying on the adequacy and authenticity of faculties received from his Capuchin superiors in Germany; but had inconsistently sought his authorization from Carroll as well. Carroll points out this contradiction and deviousness.

[2] This implies that Heilbron was still granted faculties at Lancaster, Pa.

[3] I.e., his Capuchin superiors in Germany.

[4] Carroll chose not to openly challenge Heilbron's claim to other sources for his pastoral faculties, which Heilbron represented to others as an acknowledgment.

[5] See following document under this same date.

Dec. 31, 1789   In relatione facti Rv. Va. multa dissimulat, ac alia omittit. Io Dissimulas te ita a Superiore tuo Regulari fuisse in Americam designatum, ut non nisi auctoritate illorum, ad quos ibi spectat, curam animarum ageres—2. dissimulas te, statim atque in Americam advenisses, professum fuisse plenam a Praefecto Apostolico dependentiam, ita ut a liberrima ipsius directione regi cuperes, in omnibus, quae curam animarum spectant, et locum, in quo curam istam exerceres—3o. dissimulas te facultates recepisse, tanquam a Praefecto *concessas,* sicut revera concessae sunt. 4. dissimulas his facultatibus adjunctam fuisse a praefecto clausulam, qua expressum fuit facultates concedi tantum, donec revocarentur.

Deinde omittis scripsisse te Praefecto, tibi animo plane statutum fuisse, ut locum tibi assignatum, et animas tuae curae commissas desereres, et contra expressam praefecti voluntatem Philadelphiam te profecturum, ut eos pasceres, quorum cura tibi non erat commissa, quique aliunde omnibus Religionis adjumentis et assignatis sibi pastoribus erant abunde instructi. Negasti auctoritatem praefecti tibi ad hoc esse necessariam; asseruisti tui Ordinis generalem tibi contulisse jurisdictionem sufficientem; atque nullam jurisdictionem, ac nequidem approbationem tibi a Praefecto missionis conferri posse. Cum ita statuisse & animo te, aestimare dixisses, monitus es a Praefecto, ne aggrederis facultates aliquas Philadelphiae exercere; et ad temeritatem tuam fortius reprimendam, Praefectus facultates tibi ante concessas ita temperavit, ut neque Philadelphiae, neque in ejus ambitu, ad decem millia passuum, potestatem reliquerit Sacramenta et functiones parochiales valide aut licite, administrandi.

Omittis deinde respondisse te Praefecto litteris quam maxime indecoris, in quibus haec inter alia dixisti, praefectum sibi *arrogasse suspendere approbationem, quam aliunde habere* te asseruisti; *et stricte loquendo ab ipso habere te non posse:* deinde adjecisti facturum te, quod statuisti *non attenta* facultatum restrictione, quae omnino *impertinens erat ac contra prima* Theologiae principia.

Omittis praefectum, quamvis lacessitus esset litteris ita inhonestis, conatum tamen adhuc fuisse ad revocandos tuos pristinos sensus, obsequii et Subordinationis: atque hac spe ostendisse tibi, quousque se extenderit ipsius potestas, a Sum: Pont. collata, tam pro concessione, quam pro restrictione et revocatione facultatum, respectu Sacerdotum Regularium et Secularium. Qua erga te condescendentia cum usus esset Praefectus, respondisti te non credere illam potestatem fuisse Praefecto concessam, qua ipse gaudere se asseruit: hocque iterum aequivalenter repetivisti, postquam de injustissima tua Praefecti inculpatione monitus fuisses.

Omittis, ut alia praetermittam, te, propria statione derelicta, Philadelphiae sedem tuam fixisse, et, cum demptae tibi essent facultates illic exercendi functiones quascunque pastorales, nihilominus eas exercuisse, atque ita Praefecti auctoritatem prorsus abnegasse: ac tum demum tibi facultates, quas ante concesserat, fuisse universim sublatas.

Haec pauca observare licuit *in casu facti* a R. V. exhibito. In resolutione adjuncta, omnia fere adversantur Sanae Theologiae, ac refutantur sola inspectione illius clausulae meis facultatibus annexis, cujus copiam jam prius communicavi. Quare ut moras ulteriores abrumpam, refero ad eas, quae paginae alteri adscripta reperiet. Rae Vae.   Servus in Xto   J. Carroll

TO JOHN HEILBRON   On the 31st day of Decre. 1789

Reverend Father John Carol Helbron, Of the Order of Minorite Capuchins, a Peremptory Warning.

The undersigned Superior of the Missions in the provinces of the United States of America, using the power conceded to him by Most Blessed Pope Pius VI himself, utterly takes away and revokes on the second day of December, in the year 1789 all the faculties, which he had previously conceded to you *down to revocation;* which revocation was communicated to you on the seventh day of this same month.[1] Nevertheless by this revocation, and notwithstanding the deprivation of all faculties for exercising, as you wish, parochial functions, you have gone ahead administering the Sacraments, preaching publicly in Church, and performing other ministries, and continued acting, even though you have been warned in writing and in word by the Superior not to do those things, and not to profane the Sacraments, and expose the souls of those coming to you for absolution to the danger of eternal damnation. And you have wanted to defend this manner of acting by most vain and erroneous arguments, after there had been shown to you the faculties conceded to the Superior of the Missions, which take away every excuse for your disobedience. Wherefore so that an end to so great a scandal may in time be imposed, and that the souls of the Faithful may no longer be exposed to so great a danger, I warn you, under penalty of suspension[2] being inflicted upon you, that before the hour appointed after noon on Saturday next, i.e., January 2, 1790, you inform the aforementioned Superior about your coming to your senses, and your future obedience in the matter, about which there is question. Given at Philadelphia, the 31st day of December, 1789. F.A. Fleming, Priest, is a witness.   J.C.

ACS   AAB
  [1] The document was written in Baltimore under the first date and delivered, probably by Beeston, on the 7th.
  [2] This would have the force of excluding Heilbron from exercise of the ministry anywhere in the United States and at Lancaster where Carroll had originally authorized his ministry.

Reverendo Patri Joanni Carolo Helbron, ex Ordine Minoritarum Capuccinorum, Monitio Peremptoria.

Infrascriptus Superior Missionum in Foederatae Americae provinciis, usus potestate sibi a Bmo P.N. Pio Papa VI concessa, facultates omnes, quas tibi *usque ad revocationem* antea concesserat, sustulit prorsus ac revocavit die 2a Decembris, ann. 1789; quae revocatio intimata tibi fuit 7a ejusdem mensis. Hac tamen revocatione, et facultatum omnium ad functiones quasvis parochiales exercendas privatione non obstante, Sacramenta administrare, publice in Ecclesia praedicare, ac caetera ministeria peragere perrexisti, et adhuc peragis, quamvis et scripto et verbo monitus esses a Superiore, ne ista faceres, neve Sacramenta profanationi, et animas ad te pro absolutione accedentium aeternae damnationis periculo exponeres. Hanc agendi rationem defendere vanissimis, ac erroneis argumentationibus voluisti, postquam exhibitae tibi fuissent facultates Superiori missionum concessae, quae omnem inobedientiae tuae excusationem tollunt. Quapropter ut tanto scandalo finis aliquando imponatur, et Fidelium animae tanto periculo non amplius exponantur, moneo te sub poena suspensionis tibi infligendo, ut ante horam sextam post meridiem diei Sabbati proximi, i.e., Januarii 2ae anni 1790, praedictum Superiorem de resipiscentia tua, et futura obedientia in materia, de qua agitur, certum facias. Datum Phila. 2ae die 31m Dec.ris 1789. Testis F. A. Fleming, Sac.   J.C.

THE ESTABLISHMENT OF THE CATHOLIC RELIGION IN THE UNITED STATES[1]   [1790]

Towards the end of the reign of James I. king of England, who died in 1625, the Catholics, oppressed by the penal laws of that kingdom, sought afar an asylum from the persecution which they suffered at home. Lord Baltimore, a Catholic, obtained from the king a grant of all those lands which now form the State of Maryland. This grant was confirmed to him by a charter issued in form immediately after the accession of Charles I. to the throne of his father.* By this same charter, the king granted to all who should emigrate to the new Province, the liberty of exercising their religion, and the rights of citizens. A great number of Catholics, and especially the descendants of ancient families, quitted England, and settled in America, towards the year 1630, under the conduct of Lord Baltimore. With them came Father Peter[2] White, an English Jesuit. This band of emigrants chose for their residence a district of country near the junction of the Potomac and St. Mary's river: the latter afterwards gave its name to the first town that was built there, and which continued to be in the capital of the country, during seventy or eighty years.[3]

Father White, finding himself unequal to the duties which pressed upon him, returned to Europe, in order to procure missionaries: and, from the very imperfect memoirs before me,[4] it appears, that he brought over with him Fathers Copley, Harkey and Perret. Their principal residence was a place which they called St. *Inigo,* a Spanish word which signifies Ignatius. They acquired there a considerable tract of land, a part of which is still in the possession of the Jesuits.

All historians, Protestant as well as Catholic, speak, in favourable terms, of the first Catholic emigrants, who faithfully observed the laws of justice, and by their humane deportment, gained the confidence of the Indians. Not an inch of land did they take by violence from the aboriginal inhabitants: but they purchased a large district,[5] and honourably confined themselves within the limits traced out in the charter, insomuch that neither fraud nor bloodshed disgraced the birth of this rising colony.

In proportion as it increased, (and its progress was rapid,) the heads of the establishment advanced into the country, accompanied by some clergymen; who, for their subsistence, and that of their successors, made several acquisitions of lands.

Towards the year 1640, a design was formed to carry the Gospel to the Indians of the neighbouring parts. In the MS. which was lent me, I find, that the Provincial of the Jesuits wrote, this year, to the young men at Liege, exhorting them to consecrate their services to this difficult and perilous enterprise. In consequence of this invitation, more than twenty requested, in urgent language, to be associated in the new mission: but, from what I can learn from contemporary monuments, it does not appear that they ever crossed the ocean: prevented, in all probability, by the influence of the Protestants who inhabited the district of Virginia; and who saw, with a jealous eye, the incomparably better understanding that existed between the Catholics and the Indians, than between themselves and the tribes around them. Add to this the troubles which arose, the same year, (1640,) in England, and ended in the deposition and decapitation of Charles I. in 1649. The incredible hatred which the dominant party of that kingdom entertained against the Catholics, and the umbrage which was taken by the factious, at any enterprise that could further the promotion of the Catholic Religion, rendered it necessary for the emigrants to break off all communication with the Indians.

As long as Cromwell was in power, the Catholics of Maryland were cruelly harassed: Lord Baltimore was removed from the government, the Catholics were excluded from all offices of trust which they had held before, and the clergy were reduced to the necessity of exercising their functions in secret, and with great circumspection.

From this epoch, I cannot discover any steps taken to diffuse the knowledge of the Gospel among the Indians. Before the death of Cromwell, it is probable that they removed into the interior to a very great distance, and in Maryland, there were hardly clergymen enough to discharge the duties towards the Catholics. The power and influence of the Protestants, supported by the English government, and favoured by the colonies that surrounded them, had greatly increased: and the jealousy, formerly occasioned on the part of the Catholics by their correspondence with the Indians, was still alive.

After the restoration of Charles the Second, Maryland again flourished under the genial government of Lord Baltimore, and his representatives. Pious establishments were formed, and the clergymen were scattered through the different sections of the province. They subsisted not on the contributions of the faithful, but on the products of the lands which they had obtained.

But after the revolution which followed in England, the Catholics were again deprived of public offices, and of the exercise of their religion, contrary to the privileges granted in their charter. In consequence of this intolerance, Lord Baltimore[6] would again have been stript of his authority, had he not unfortunately yielded to the times, and conformed to the Protestant religion. From this era, a tax was levied on all the colonists without distinction, for the support of the ministers of the Anglican Church. Many attempts were made to enforce the penal laws; and if they were not generally carried into execution, but only in certain places, and that, too, at intervals, it was, according to all appearances, less through a spirit of toleration, than through policy. The most distinguished families, impatient of the restrictions, and induced, perhaps, by the example of Lord Baltimore, forsook the Catholic Church.[7] By this means, the Protestant party became strengthened: the seat of government was transferred from St. Mary's to Annapolis, where the Protestants were more numerous: and the Catholics, oppressed and persecuted, were reduced to poverty and contempt.

Notwithstanding these misfortunes, several congregations existed in the province, with resident priests; and others, which were occasionally visited by the missionaries. But they were so removed and dispersed, that a great number of families could not assist at mass, and receive instructions, but once in the month: and though pains were taken by the pious heads of families to instruct their children, it must have been done but imperfectly. Among the poor, many could not read, and those who could, were without books, to procure which it was necessary to send to England: and the laws against printers and sellers of Catholic books were extremely rigorous. It is surprising that, notwithstanding all these difficulties, there were still so many Catholics in Maryland who were regular in their habits, and at peace with all their neighbours. The propriety of their conduct was a subject of edification to all, and continued to be so, until the new emigrants from foreign parts introduced a licentiousness of manners, which exposed the Catholic Religion to the reproach of its enemies.

Near the residences of the clergy, and on the lands belonging to them, small chapels were built, but few elsewhere: so that it was necessary to say mass in private houses. The people contributed nothing towards the expenses of the clergy, who, poor as they were, had to provide for their own support, for the decoration, &c. of the altars, and for their travels from place to place. They demanded nothing, as long as the produce of their lands could suffice for their maintainance.[8]

Towards the year 1730, Father Grayton, a Jesuit, (all the clergymen, it should be remarked, who laboured in the colonies, were Jesuits),[9] went from Maryland to Philadelphia, and laid the foundation of the Catholic religion in that city. He resided there until the year 1750. Long before his death, he built the chapel near the presbytery (St. Joseph's) and formed a numerous congregation, which has continued to increase to the present day. "I remember," said Archbishop Carroll, whose language I here use, "to have seen, in 1748, that venerable man, at the head of his flock."

He was succeeded by Father [Robert] Harding, whose memory is still in benediction in that city: and under whose auspices, and the untiring energies of whose zeal, the beautiful Church of St. Mary's was erected.

In the year 1741, two German Jesuits were sent to Pennsylvania, for the purpose of instructing the German Emigrants who has settled in that province. These were Father [Theodore] Schneider, a Bavarian, and Father [William] Wap[p]eler, a Hollander, men full of zeal and prudence. The former was particulatly gifted with a talent for business, and possessed, says the MS. before me, "consummate prudence and intrepid courage." The latter, after having laboured eight years in America, during which he converted many, was, in consequence of his bad health, constrained to return to Europe. He was the founder of the establishment now called *Conewago.* Father Schnéider formed several congregations in Pennsylvania, built the Church at *Cosenhopen,* and propagated the Catholic religion around that country. Every month, he visited the Germans who lived in Philadelphia, until the time when he judged it expedient to establish a resident German Priest in that city. The gentleman chosen to fill that post, was the Reverend Father Farmer, a distinguished and highly respected personage, who, some years before, had arrived in America, and been stationed at Lancaster, where his life was truly apostolical. It was about the year 1760, that he took possession of his new appointment. "No one can be ignorant," remarks my MS. "of the labours which were undergone by this servant of God." His memory is in veneration among all who knew him, or have heard of his merit. He continued to be a model for all succeeding Pastors, until his death, which occurred in 1786.

In 1776, the American Independence was declared, and a revolution effected, not only in political affairs, but also in those relating to Religion. For while the thirteen provinces of North America rejected the yoke of England, they proclaimed, at the same time, freedom of conscience, and the right of worshipping the Almighty, according to the spirit of the religion to which each one should belong. Before this great event, the Catholic faith had penetrated into two provinces only, viz. Maryland and Pennsylvania. In all the others the laws against the Catholics were in force.[10] Any Priest coming from foreign parts, was subject to the penalty of death; all who professed the Catholic faith, were not merely excluded from offices of government, but could hardly be tolerated in a private capacity. While this state of things continued, it is not surprising that but very few of them settled in those provinces: and they, for the most part, forsook their religion. Even in Maryland and Pennsylvania, as was before mentioned, the Catholics were oppressed: the missionaries were insufficient for the wants of those two provinces, and it was next to impossible to disseminate the faith beyond their boundaries.

By the declaration of independence, every difficulty was removed: the Catholics were placed on a level with their fellow-christians, and every political disqualification was done away.

Several reasons are assigned in the MS. for the immediate adoption of the article, extending to all the members of the States, an unqualified freedom of conscience.

I. The leading characters of the first assembly, or Congress, were, through principle, opposed to every thing like vexation on the score of Religion: and, as they were perfectly acquainted with the maxims of the Catholics, they saw the injustice of persecuting them for adhering to their doctrines.

II. The Catholics evinced a desire, not less ardent than that of the Protestants, to render the provinces independent of the mother country: and, it was manifest, that, if they joined the common cause, and exposed themselves to the common danger, they should be entitled to a participation in the common blessings which crowned their efforts.

III. France was negotiating an alliance with the United Provinces: and nothing could have retarded the progress of that alliance more effectually, than the demonstration of any ill-will against the religion which France professed.

IV. The aid, or at least the neutrality of Canada was judged necessary for the success of the enterprise of the Provinces: and by placing the Catholics on a level with all other christians, the Canadians, it was believed, could not but be favourably disposed towards the revolution.

It was not till after the war, that the good effects of freedom of conscience began to develop themselves. The Priests were few in number, and, almost all superannuated. There was but little communication between the Catholics of America, and their Bishop, the Vicar apostolic of the district of London, on whose spiritual jurisdiction they were dependent. But, whether he did not wish to have any relation to a people whom he regarded in the light of rebels; or whether it was owing, says my old MS., to the natural apathy of his disposition, it is certain, that he had hardly any communication either with the Priests, or the laity, on this side of the Atlantic. Anteriourly to the declaration of Independence, he had appointed the Rev. Mr. Lewis, his vicar; and it was this gentleman who governed the mission of America, during the time that the Bishop remained inactive.

Shortly after the war, the Clergy of Maryland and of Pennsylvania, convinced of the necessity of having a superior on the spot, and knowing, too, that the United States were opposed to any jurisdiction in England, applied to the Holy See, to grant them the privilege of choosing a superior from their own body. The request was acceded to: and their unanimous suffrages centred in the Rev. John Carroll, whose election was approved by the Holy See, and on whom ample power, even that of administering Confirmation, was immediately conferred.

The number of Catholics, at this period, in Maryland, amounted to about sixteen thousand: the greater part of whom were dispersed through the country, and employed in agriculture. In Pennsylvania, there were about seven thousand, and in the other States, as far as it was possible to ascertain, there were about fifteen hundred. In this number, however, were not comprised the Canadians, or French, or their descendants, who inhabited the country to the west of the Ohio, and the banks of the Mississippi.

In Maryland the Priests were nineteen in number: in Pennsylvania but five. of these, five were worn out with infirmities and age, and the rest were advanced in years. None, except those in Baltimore and Philadelphia, subsisted on the contributions of their flocks.[11]

L *Metropolitan: or Catholic Monthly Magazine,* I (March–April, 1830), 91-93, 152-55. Rev. Charles C. Pise ascribed a MS in French to Carroll and translated it for the *Metropolitan.* (See below note 1.) The date is estimated by the fact that when Carroll was superior or beginning his episcopacy, reports to Rome would probably be required about these matters. Pise implies that he did not use all of the MS, apparently the decade before 1790 did not need to be recounted, nor was it in the *Metropolitan.* "Notice of," precedes wording given title here.

*By Charles the name of MARYLAND was given to this new province in honour of his Queen, Henrietta Mary, daughter of Henry IV.[8]

[1] Omitted first paragraph of introduction by Pise: "The following particulars, relating to the establishment of the Catholic Religion in the United States, are selected from an old French MS. preserved in the library of the Archbishop of Baltimore. From certain passages, I am induced to believe, that it was originally written in English by Archbishop Carroll, and translated into the language in which I find it. To all who feel an interest in such details, this notice will be pleasing and valuable."

[2] Should be *Andrew.*
[3] Annapolis became the capital in 1695.
[4] Possibly the *Relationes* by individual missionaries, such as White, as well as the annual reports to the Jesuit General at Rome. "The Religious History of Maryland," by George Hunter, S.J. (c. 1750) is in MPA and may also have been used.
[5] The Indians seemed to have given the land to the Jesuits, the 25,000 acres being possibly envisaged as a Paraguayan style reduction. Lord Baltimore felt that it conflicted with his proprietary right as sole holder of the whole province prior to any other Englishman, who could not receive such without his own mediation with the Indians. Historians do not advert to Protestant hostility as explained in the MS.
[6] Charles Calvert, Third Lord Baltimore, did not yield, but, dying in 1714, his son, Benedict Leonard, did.
[7] Daniel Dulany was such a case, but there do not seem to be many others, as contended.
[8] Before this note of Carroll and concluding the previous sentence is the signature Y.Y. and "(To be continued.)."
[9] Not accurate.
[10] During the provincial period, that is.
[11] Pise has this concluding paragraph: "The MS. here ends: other documents, however, may be had, which will afford a continuation of this interesting subject. Y. Y."

AN ADDRESS FROM THE ROMAN CATHOLICS OF AMERICA
TO GEORGE WASHINGTON, ESQ. PRESIDENT OF THE UNITED STATES
London: M,DCC,XC.

[Preface] THE following Address from the Roman Catholics, which was copied from the American News papers,—whilst it breathes fidelity to the States which protect them, asserts, with decency, the common rights of mankind; and the answer of the President truly merits that esteem, which his liberal sentiments, mild administration, and prudent justice have obtained him.—Under his sanction an Academy is founded and funded.—The wisdom and policy of the measure is resplendent.—At home may be obtained that which our Nation obliges us to seek in foreign climes at a vast expence.—It is governed by a Roman Catholic Bishop, (Dr. John Carroll) a Protestant Divine, and a Dissenting Minister;—they live in harmony;—the discipline, with calm moderation, yet exactness, is duly kept up;—and the students succeed.—A profusion of polite knowledge—Law—Physic, &c. is the prospect of this infant undertaking.—There are to be Schools for Divinity.—Presidents and Professors through the range of Nations are sought;—they must excel, or they will not have the appointment.—Whilst others exclude the Monastic—the Religious life,—America invites to, and throws open her asylum.—The Dominicans and the Capuchins have commenced on that Mission.—And so late as April, 1790, a Colony of Teresian Nuns,[1] under the Abbess of Hoogstreat,—an English Lady superiorly distinguished for accomplishments and piety, has left that Cloister, with permission, and the promise of subjects ready to join her, with protection from the State, and the prospect of establishing another in Philadelphia; where beside the religious observance of her Rule she has been solicited to adopt the tuition of their daughters,—Two Priests,[2] the one was Confessor to the English Dames at Brussels, the other at Antwerp, have accompanied our courageous country women in their perilous voyage and laborious undertaking.

Is this not a lesson?—Britons remain intolerant and inexorable to the claims of sound policy and of nature. Ties of kindred and friends,—whose sacred aspiration—Alas! to NOMINAL LIBERTY, suffers the fettering sanguinary edicts still to blacken her golden aeras,—exile some of her most valuable subjects, and divide their interests, or force their religious compliance to disguise and debase principles, which, if suffered to practise, would constitute and confirm the most lasting affection to their Prince and the country which gives them birth.—Is it true policy, that the Roman Catholics should become voluntary exiles for the free practise of their faith—to educate their children,—to study for their ministry,—or retire to their sacred Cloister?— and this only to serve God in their own way,—not a different God, but adored equally by all! Whilst it is on acknowledged fact, there are laws sufficient to make men, good citizens and good subjects,—where is the boasted liberty which suffers not a disposall of ourselves, but aims so effectually to shackle and annihilate the sould from God.—Britons, view and blush!

THE ADDRESS OF THE ROMAN CATHOLICS
TO GEORGE WASHINGTON, ESQ.
PRESIDENT OF THE UNITED STATES. SIR,

WE have been long impatient to testify our joy, and unbounded confidence on your being called, by an Unanimous Vote, to the first station of a country, in which that unanimity could not have been obtained, without the previous merit of unexampled services, of eminent wisdom, and unblemished virtue. Our congratulations have not reached you sooner, because our scattered situation prevented our communication, and the collecting of those sentiments, which warmed every breast. But the delay has furnished us with the opportunity, not merely of presaging the happiness to be expected under your Administration, but of bearing testimony to that which we experience already. It is your peculiar talent, in war and in peace, to afford security to those who commit their protection into your hands. In war you shield them from the ravages of armed hostility; in peace, you establish public tranquility, by the justice and moderation, not less than by the vigour, of your government. By example, as well as by vigilance, you extend the influence of laws on the manners of our fellow-citizens. You encourage respect for religion; and inculcate, by words and actions, that principle, on which the welfare of nations so much depends, that a superintending providence governs the events of the world, and watches over the conduct of men. Your exalted maxims, and unwearied attention to the moral and physical improvement of our country, have produced already the happiest effects. Under your administration, America is animated with zeal for the attainment and encouragement of useful literature. She improves her agriculture; extends her commerce; and acquires with foreign nations a dignity unknown to her before. From these happy events, in which none can feel a warmer interest than ourselves, we derive additional pleasure, by recollecting that you, Sir, have been the principal instrument to effect so rapid a change in our political situation. This prospect of national prosperity is peculiarly pleasing to us, on another account; because, whilst our country preserves her freedom and independence, we shall have a well founded title to claim from her justice, the equal rights of citizenship, as the price of our blood spilt under your eyes, and of our common exertions for her defence, under your auspicious conduct—rights rendered more dear to us by the remembrance of former hardships. When we pray for the preservation of them, where they have been granted—and expect the full extension of them from the justice of those States, which still restrict them:[3]—when we solicit the protection of Heaven over our common country, we neither omit, nor can omit recommending your preservation to the singular care of Divine Providence; because we conceive that no human means are so available to promote the welfare of the United States, as the prolongation of your health and life, in which are included the energy of your example, the wisdom of your counsels, and the persuasive eloquence of your vitues. John Carroll, In behalf of the Roman Catholic Clergy. Charles Carroll, of Carrollton, Daniel Carroll, Dominick Lynch, Thomas Fitzsimmons. In behalf of the Roman Catholic Laity.[4]

L [Facsimile] London: Printed by J. P. Coghlan, Duke-Street, Grosvenor-Square; and sold by Messrs. Robinsons, Pater-Noster-Row M,DCC,XC.; John Gilmary Shea, ed. (New York, 1857). A fragile copy of the original edition is in NYPL. The Preface may have been by Carroll, or its thoughts suggested by him.
[1] The Carmelites, of Port Tobacco and later Baltimore.
[2] Charles Neale and Robert Plunkett.
[3] In varying degrees, Massachusetts, Connecticut, New York, North Carolina, are examples of requirements in Protestant established churches, immigrant oaths, professions of belief in Protestantism for office holders, etc., which discriminated against Catholics.
[4] Maryland, South Carolina, and Pennsylvania are represented in the names (in that order) of the signers.

RESOLUTIONS ON THE BOSTON CONGREGATION [1790]

The Bishop, being desirous of restoring harmony in the Congregation & promoting the increase of religion, and piety, has resolved as follows. First: That the Rev. Mr. Jn. Thayer be appointed to take charge of the Congregation of Boston, as long as the Bishop or his successors shall judge it to be of general utility to continue him in that employment. Secondly: That all members of the Congregation be earnestly respected to unite together in divine service; the Bishop promising his best endeavours to procure equally to all every reasonable satisfaction. Thirdly: That to promote harmony amongst all, a mode of disposing of the pews shall be proposed, in which all may find equal advantage. But the best pew shall be reserved for the Consul of his most Xtian Majesty. Fourthly: That the Congregation at large ought to contribute & consider themselves as bound to pay the debt, contracted before the late separation, & in consequence of assuming the payment of Abbé La Poterie's debt. The Bishop will think it unjust & dishonourable in the Congregation to let the whole burthen of payment fall on those two persons only, who in this business were agents for the rest. Fifthly:[1] In case of a reunion of both parties, the Bishop will make farther exertions, if they shall be desired, for the welfare & prosperity of the Congn.

Fifthly: The congregation generally will not be under any obligation of contributing to the payment of the debt aforesaid, unless the articles received from the Abbé La Poterie accounted for & restored for the use of the Church under the direction of the Rev. Mr. Thayer. I make us [an] order respecting the things sent by the Archbp.,[2] because, if they are to be p[ai]d for, & the

Trustees are bound for paymt., these last have no other security for their indemnification but the article themselves.[2]

ADf   AAB
[1] This word is deleted and the passage following it was intended to be a sixth resolution, as indicated in the margin by the symbol *S6a.*
[2] This word is a reference to a deleted passage placed after the previous sentence. In substance this passage says that certain goods were sent by the Archbishop of Paris for the congregation, a single entity now determined by the American bishop.

SEMINARIAN'S OATH   [1790]

Formula of the vow to be taken by students [seminarians] of Georgetown College, who receive there gratis education and support.

I N. son of N. of the Diocesis of N. being at age N. although I am altogether unworthy in the divine presence, relying nevertheless on his holiness and infinite mercy, and urged by the desire of serving God, and the care of the salvation of souls, which Our Lord Jesus Christ redeemed by this Precious Blood, I pledge and before the divine Majesty devoutly vow,[1] that I will embrace the ecclesiastical State, and I will give myself to the judgment of the Most Reverend Lordship, Bishop of Baltimore, for the present, to holy orders and also the priesthood.

I likewise pledge and devoutly proffer faith to the above mentioned Bishop of Baltimore and his Successors[2] and, so that I will remain under their authority in caring for the salvation of souls, and without their permission, I will never join myself to any religious order, the Society or congregation whether of regulars [religious orders], or of regular priests. May God so assist me, and this holy bible of God.

AC   AAB   No title. Date is assigned to the period of Georgetown's beginning, when some were brought in for preparation for the priesthood.
[1] The preceding is nearly verbatim from the Jesuit vow formula.
[2] After ordination a commitment to the Select Body of the Clergy was required, which was distinct from this vow.

Formula voti emittandi ab alumnis Collegii Georgiopolitani, qui ibidem gratuitam educationem & alimoniam accipiunt.

Ego N. filius N. Diocesis N. annos habens N. licet undequaque divino conspectu indigni simus, fretus tamen pietate ac misericordia infinita, et impulsus desiderio Deo inserviendi, curandaeque Salutis animarum, quas D. J. Christus pretioso Suo Sanguine redemit, spondeo ac coram divina Majestate Sancte voveo, quod Statum ecclesiasticum amplectar, et ad arbitrium Rvdssmi D. Episcopi Baltimorensis, pro tempore existentis, ad sacros, etiam presbyteratus ordines, promovebor.

Spondeo item et fidem Sancte obligo praedicto Episcopo Baltimorensi ejusque Successoribus me ita sub eorum potestate in curanda animarum salute permansurum, et sine eorundem licentia, nunquam me adstringam alicui ordini religioso, Societati vel Congregationi sive regularium, sive Sacerdotum Regularium. Sic me Deus adjuvet, et haec sancta Dei evangelia.

SPIRITUAL FACULTIES FOR THE CLERGY 1790-98

Faculties Granted to Reverend Misters Delvaux[1] [,Erntzen[2]] until January 1, 1792.

Faculties renewed for Reverend P. Fleming—the 19th of December, 1790, until they are revoked.

Faculties granted to Reverend Mr.—Didier,[3] Benedictine monk at the mouth of the Scioto River, the 27th day of December, 1790 for a period of seven years, unless they are previously revoked. On the 16th day of July, 1791, the faculty was granted to him of celebrating twice a day on feast days and on Sundays down to the 1st of August in the year 1792, unless another priest should come before then.

On the 6th of July, faculties were granted to Reverend Mister William Elling[4] until the 1st of August, 1792, unless previously etc.

On the 1st of August, faculties were granted to Reverend Father Joseph Phelan,[5] a Capuchin, appointed in charge of the congregation at Norfolk, down to the 1st of January, 1792.

In the month of August of the same year, faculties were extended to Reverend Mister Nicholas Delvaux, who had been sent to Coshenhopen, down to the beginning of the year, 1793.

In the month of May, 1793, faculties were given for a period of two years to Reverend Mister Gallagher[6] for Carclopoli, etc.

In the month of March, on the 31st day, in 1794, to Reverend Mr. William Phelan,[7] down to January 1st. On April 20, to Reverend Mr. Eulogio Fromentin[8] down to 1796.

AD   AAB

[1] Nicholas Delvaux. See Dec. 13, 1798.

[2] Paul Erntzen ministered at Goshenhoppen and Lancaster during this period.

[3] Peter Didier. See Sep. 3, 1791.

[4] See Sep. 3, 1791.

[5] In his letter to Carroll, Aug. 20, 1790, Phelan tells of his intention to come to America with the recommendation of Arthur O'Leary and the approbation of Archbishop Troy.

[6] Simon Gallagher. See May 10, 1793.

[7] Possibly the brother of Joseph mentioned above. He intended to go to Halifax by way of Baltimore and may have been persuaded by Carroll to remain in the U.S.

[8] In 1794 he resided at Asylum, Luzern County, Pa., where there were a number of French inhabitants, himself very likely being a French emigré.

Facultates concessae Ris. Domis. Delvaux Erntzen usque ad lam Januam 1792—

Facultates renovatae pro Rev. P. Fleming—19a Decris, 1790, usque ad revocationem.

Facultates concessae Rdo D.—Didier, monacho Benedictino ad oram fluvii Scioto die 27 Dec. 1790 ad septennium, nisi prius revocentur: die 16a, Julii 1791, concessa eidem facultas celebrandi bis in die diebus festis et dominicis usq ad 1am Aug. ann. 1792-, nisi prius accedat alter presbyter.

Die 6 Julii concessae facult. Rdo Dom. Wilhelmo Elling usq ad 1am Aug. 1792, nisi prius etc.

Die 1a Aug. concessae facult. Rev. Patri Jos. Phelan Capucino, Norfolciani praefecto, usq ad 1am Jan. 1792.

Mense Aug. ejusdem anni, extensae sunt facultates Rdo Dom. Nicolao Delvaux, misso ad Coshenhopen, usque ad initium an. 1793.

Mense Maio 1793, datae sunt facultates ad biennium Rev. Dom. Gallagher pro Carclopoli etc.

Mense Martii 31 die, 1794 Rev. Do. Gulielmo Phelan, usq ad 1am Jan.—Aprilis 20—Rd. Do Eulogio Fromentin usq ad 1796.

TO[?]   [1790]

I plan to remain in Europe some weeks, and then return to my diocese before winter. If God should bring me home safely I shall be diligent in carrying out your prescriptions to the best of my ability, but I am not certain that I can ever . . .

ADf   AAB   Fragment. This must have been written early in the year since in the summer he went to England for consecration.

Paucis septimanis in Europa subsistere cogito, et deinde in diocesim meam regredi ante hyemem; cui si Deo visum fuerit me salvum restituere, exequi studiose conabor, in quantum in me fuerit, quae a te praescripta sunt; incertus tamen, an unquam potuerim omnes [. . . .]

LETTER ON ANGLICAN ORDERS   [1790]

Your inquiry is confined to one point, whether the Church of England is possessed of an Apostolical succession of Bishops, Priests, &c; to which, as a Catholic, I answer negatively; for Apostolical succession includes two things essentially to its existence: 1st ordination derived & descending from Christ, & his Apostles: 2ly. Spiritual jurisdiction, regularly transmitted from the same source.

With respect to the first, the Roman Catholic church pretends not to decide the fact, whether the Bishops, commonly called Queen Elizabeth's Bishops, viewed their ordination from other Bishops, ordained in the Church of Rome. This is a point of history, to say the least of it, exceedingly doubtful, & much too complex to be occupied in a loose sheet of paper, after the voluminous works on this subject. Authentic records are alledged, as evidences of the fact contended for by English Protestants: but the authenticity of those records, not produced for nearly, or perhaps more than forty years after the real or pretended period of ordination, has been denied; & with such strength of argument, as to form a very reasonable presumption of their having been fabricated for the very purpose of concealing the deficiency of a legitimate succession. At the beginning of the Reformation, & for many years after, its advocates avowed the utmost abhorrence of the Church of Rome, which they described as the Kingdom of Antichrist; as not only irreformably corrupt for idolatrous. (See the 39 art. of the Church of Engd.), & held her orders too great an abomination, to make her the immediate source of their authority. Whoever looks into the works of Luther, Calvin & their followers; or, those of the most celebrated Protestant Divines of England in the beginning of their defection from the Church of Rome, such as Bishop Jewel,[1] Whitaker[2] &c, will find sufficient evidence of their opprobrious disdain of a succession, coming thro the ministry of a church in communion with the See of Rome. It is therefore not to be thought extraordinary, if, entertaining such opinions, they were easily reconciled to assume the exercise of episcopal & pastoral functions without receiving the imposition of the hands of any Catholic Prelate, as Wesley amongst the Methodists, has since denied the necessity of receiving it from the Church of England; & as Archbishop Cranmer the first & servile instrument of Henry 8th. in the work of reform contended might be done; requiring only the King's authority, as Supreme head, Ecclesiastical, as well as civil, of the Church of England. I have not now with me, in the County [Country?], any books, to which I can refer in proof of the Archbishops doctrine; but am fully confident, that it is not misstated by me.

Many years after the real or fictitious ordination of Archbishop Parker,[3] & his companions, Mr. Mason,[4] a Protestant Divine, produced those Lambeth records, concerning the authenticity of which there has been so much controversy. Independently of other arguments a strong presumption against them is certainly that the first & principal Reformers rejected the necessity of deriving orders from any Roman Catholic Bishops is manifest not only from their own declarations above referred to, but from their example. For the Lutherans in Germany, Sweden & elsewhere do not even pretend to derive their succession from the Prelates of any existing religious Society; & the same is the fact with respect to the Calvinists in France & Geneva: And it is notorious, that the system of Reformation in England, as to doctrine is formed entirely on the principles of those two prevailing sects.

Secondly—There is not the same uncertainty with respect to spiritual Jurisdiction, which is equally necessary to Apostolic succession. Ordination

alone does not convey authority to exercise the pastoral ministry of the
Church of Christ. In the early ages, there was no doubt of the validity of the
ordination of many of those, who then pretended to reform her faith, & were
dispensers [dissenters?] from the great society of Christians, holding communication with the See of Rome. Such were the Montanist, Donatist, Arian,
Pelagian, Bishops &c. But tho' their ordination was unquestionably valid, &
transmitted successively from the Apostles; yet their Apostolical succession,
as Pastors of the Church, was denied; & surely the Church of England herself
will not say, that it was, wrongfully denied. What reason can be as [sic]
assigned for this, which does not equally militate against the present Reformed Churches? Suffering their ordinations to be valid, & descent to them
from Roman Catholic Bishops, these could transmit no other trust, powers,
or commission, as from God, but such as themselves had received. The
commission received at their ordination was, to exercise their ministry agreeably to the profession of faith which they were then requested to make, &
which was committed to their keeping & guardianship: they could only grant
these powers, & this commission to those whom they might ordain; so that
though it should be admitted that the first Protestant Bishops inherited their
ordination from the Church of Rome, yet they would be still far from having
a legitimate claim to Apostolical succession; which essentially includes if not
merely nugatory, implies the transmission of uninterrupted transmission of
the right & duty of preaching the doctrine & administering the Sacraments, as
the same were taught & administered not only by the Apostles, but by their
successors & so perpetuated in the Catholic Church down to the present day.
It is evident that Apostolical succession, so understood, exists not in the
Church of England, any more, than it exists in those Sects above mentioned;
& to acknowledge it in these, would be to reject the unifrom doctrine of all
Christian antiquity & the Fathers of the Church. If it be concluded, that the
first Protestant Bishops received an *extraordinary* mission, like St. Paul,
immediately from God himself, what evidence did they give of such an
extraordinary interposition of Providence? What miraculous events proved it?
& how can it be proved otherwise? They were indeed so far from resorting to
this evidence, that they & their successors, have always contended for a
regular & ordinary mission, pretending that the Church of England is distinguished by this prerogative from other reformed Churches. These few observations, are sufficient to show how little reason she has for this boast: & that
she is left in a dreadful uncertainty as to the validity of her orders &
consequently of at least one of those sacraments which she has retained

T   GU   SC   Date is presumed to have been connected with Carroll's own consecration.
   [1] John Jewel, Bishop of Salisbury, author of *Ecclesiae Anglicanae* (1562) which
under James I became a major guide in the Anglican case for orders as against the English
Catholic position in Thomas Harding's controversy with him.

[2] William Whitaker, Puritan divine, influential in drafting the Lambeth Articles in 1595, a strongly predestinarian, Calvinistic statement, which never found favor with Elizabeth.

[3] Matthew Parker, Archbishop of Canterbury by Elizabeth's appointment in 1559 as a moderate. He probably believed his ordination to be in a Catholic tradition, as against his Puritan critics.

[4] Francis Mason, Arch-deacon of Norfolk, author of *Of the Consecration of the Bishops in the Church of England* (1613), which defended the validity of Parker's consecration.

LETTERS ABOUT PATRICK SMYTH   1790

MPA   Not found. Noted in card catalogue as located in "4 T 1 (6)."

TO SULPICIAN SUPERIOR AT PARIS   1790

There may have been one or more letters before Sep. See Sep., 1790, to Dugnani.

TO SEVERAL CLERGYMEN   Jan., 1790

Not found. See to Carey, Feb. 10, 1790.

COMMENT ON JOHN THAYER LETTER   Jan. 6–1790–

compl[ai]ns of Rouselet—wishes him gone—sollicits the Supr. of the N.E. States—

AM   AAB (8B-H1)

THE STATE OF AFFAIRS [AT FORT VINCENNES]
Baltimore the 10th of January, 1790

1. A piece of property has been granted in the name of his Most Christian Majesty to the Church of Fort Vincennes in perpetuity; and in view of the lack of tithes for the pastor's maintenance, the usufruct of that land was conceded to the priest serving in the parish. The Trustees of the Church are of the sentiment today that this usufruct should be utilized toward the building; and Monsr. Gibault, Pastor among them, believes that it should always be attached to himself as the one serving the parish. First question.

2. The old presbytery land is vacant at present, and of no use to the Church. Several people want to buy it. Is it advisable to sell it? Second question.

Reply to the first question—The usufruct of the land in question, having been granted as a supplement to the tithes, must always remain under the control of the curator of the place, so long as the tithes are insufficient, since such was the intention of the founder. In case the tithes, with a certain portion of the usufruct, are enough to adequately support the pastor he is obliged by the laws of Ecclesiastical discipline to appropriate the other part to the building and to the poor in equal shares: and in case there are no poor to profit by this, all the residue must be given over to building. In the case, that the administration of the land has always been in the hands of the pastor, he should retain it, even if all the usufruct were applicable to the building and to the poor; in this case, his conscience should be the norm for exercising his administration with authority, and the Trustees have the right to see to it that he does so. On the other hand, if the land was always administered by these people, they should stay in possession of it.

Reply to the second [question]. Before anything is decided, I refrain, to be more informed of the matter, particularly by Monsr. Gibault and by the Gentlemen Trustees.   J. Carroll   Ecclesiastical Superior of the United States.

ALS   MoHS   A copy in AAB (9A-H2) has several variations.

Etat du fait

1. Un fond de terre a eté concedé au nom de Sa Majesté tres Christienne à l'eglise du poste Vincennes, à perpetuité: et vu l'insuffisance des dixmes pour l'entretien du pasteur, l'usufruit de cette terre a eté concedé au Prêtre desservant la paroisse. Les Marguilliers de l'Eglise sont de sentiment aujourdui, que l'usufruit doit être destiné à la fabrique; et Monsieur Gibault, Curé du lieu, sense, qu'il doit toujours appartenir à lui même, comme desservant la paroisse. 1ere. Question.

2. Le terrain, ou etoit autrefois le presbytere, est nud á present, & de nul usage pour l'Eglise: plusieurs personnes desirent de l'acheter: faut il le vendre? 2me. question.

Reponse à la premiere. L'Usufruit du terrain en question aiant eté concedé comme supplément au dixmes, doit rester toujours affecté au Curé de l'endroit, tant que les dixmes seront insuffisantes, puisque telle a eté l'intention du fondateur. Au cas que les dixmes, avec une certaine portion de l'usufruit, servient suffisantes à l'entreien honête du Curé, celuiçi est obligé, par les loix de la discipline Ecclesiastique, d'approprier l'autre parti à la fabrique et aux pauvres en portions egales: et dans le cas, que l'administration du terrain ait eté entre les mains du Curé, il doit la retenir, quand même tout l'usufruit seroit applicable à la fabrique et aux pauvres; en çe cas, sa conscience seroit chargée d'exercer son administration avec fidelité, et les Marguilliers ont droit d'y veiller. Au contraire, si le terrain a eté toujours administré par ceuxci, ils doivent en garder la possession.

Reponse à la 2me. Avant que d'y rien decider, je soutraite d'en être plus amplement informé, tant par Monsr. Gibault que par Messrs. les Marguilliers.   J. Carroll.   Supr. Ecclesiastique du les Etats Unis. Baltimore çe 20 Janvier, 1790.

TO FRANCIS NEALE
Balt. Jan. 19, 1790

Rev. Sir.   Your last of Decr. 16 came during my absence at Philada. I found it here the 12th inst. at my return. I am sorry, that my information respecting your Br.[1] proved to be unfounded. I have no alternative left at present than to allow of your remaining some time longer in your present employment, & abandoning the poor Congregns. up the Country to such temporary provision, as can be made for them by the charitable visits of Clergymen, who can find a few days to spare.

I own to you that I cannot reconcile your opinion of the Gentlemen of this district with that candour & charity, which belong to your character.[2] A total conformity of opinions, even in every point respecting the Society, is not to be expected. All of them, as far as I know, esteem it as much as you possibly can; but none of them will dare to say it is necessary, because they know that providence is not tied down to any particular instrument for effecting its purposes, but is able to compass them by a thousand ways unknown to us. While I see the Gentlemen labour for the salvation of souls by teaching, preaching & catechising, & all other functions of the ministry, I shall judge no less from their actions, than their words, that they are full of those sentiments inwardly, which to me they have always professed. When you say, that *all misunderstanding amongst us has arisen from an affection or disaffection to this one point,* you evidently shew, that you have been exceedingly misinformed, since you came into America: for it is notorious, that the only misunderstanding, of which I have any recollection, sprang from a cause totally different & foreign to the Society. If any other misunderstandings have been, excepting the one, to which I allude, they have either been unknown to me, or were of so little account, as to escape my remembrance. My Dr. Mr. Neale, do not you let yourself be diverted from sending for cooperators, or exerting all your endeavours to render every assistance in your power to the spiritual welfare of your Country. You are in possession of my sentiments & earnest intentions in behalf of the Society. I adhere to them most firmly: but if I were even to find, that some of my Brethren were not so warmly affected to it, as myself, it should not make me relent in my endeavours to procure fresh supplies to the Country missions, nor would I lose all esteem for those, who did not think exactly, as I did: nay more; I would consider those to be disturbers of public peace who would prejudice me or my other Brethren against them on that account. Perhaps I might view

matters in the same light as you, had I just come out of a College, after having
lived only with them, who were trained in the same uniform way of thinking,
speaking & acting. But you will find by experience, that men may think very
differently even on subjects interesting to the conduct of Religious affairs,
without therefore deserving to be utterly distrusted. Thus will you think in a
few years more. Pray for me. I am with the utmost regard, Dr. Sir,   Yrs.
afftely & sincerely   J. Carroll

I hope you will still continue to promote subscriptions for the Bible. When
I look at the list of subscribers, I am ashamed for R. Catholics, & particularly
for Charles & St. Mary's Counties. Many in yr Congregns. ought to have their
names in the catalogue. Messrs. Courtney, Reeve, Middleton, Queen, Bowling
&c, &c. Do you tend Matawowman, as directed in my last. You desire to
know how to answer J. H. Ryan. I must leave it to yourself: if his Fr. consent
to his devoting himself to America, I have no doubt of his becoming an
edifying member amongst us. Let him go through the education of Liege,
spiritual & literary, & when he has received orders, it will be time enough to
determine concerning him. If I may judge from his letter he has but a slender
foundation of knowledge in English. Advise him to cultivate his own language.

ALS   MPA
[1] Charles Neale.
[2] The status of the Society of Jesus came into further controversy at this time
because of the use to be made of its property in favor of the proposed college. See July
15, 1788.

TO PIERRE GIBAULT   Baltimore the 20th day of January, 1790

Monsr.   It happened very unfortunately for the affairs of your Church, as
well as for my satisfaction, that the bearers of your letters dated 16th of June
and 28th of July arrived here and left during the time of my absence. You are
wronging Monsr. de la Valiniere in attributing to him alone the accusations,
which I mentioned in my preceding letter.[1] Some travellers who returned to
Philadelphia from Kaskaskias had spoken about them even before his departure; and without knowing, who was the priest that these accusations regarded in particular, I had commissioned him at the time of his departure, to
gather information concerning the matter. Since that time I have received
from different channels the notices, which I let you know about in my
preceding letter. I am even sorry to tell you, that Mgr. Bishop of Quebec, in a
letter which he did the honor of writing me, stressed to me that his
predecessors had thought they ought not to have trusted you so much during
the past few years as they had at the beginning of your Apostolic career. I
fancy, that it was rather on the basis of false reports, that these prelates were

driven to withdraw their first confidence, than on some unworthiness on your part. Because of the uncertainty in which I am, and the fear, on the one hand, of doing you an injustice; or, on the other, of failing in my duty, I wish at present to make no new arrangement. Nevertheless, no one can be more convinced than I of the need for a good Ecclesiastical administration for this whole Western region. Ever since the departure of the Jacobin priest, named Le Dru,[2] I have not received, as his agreement with me stated, any letter from his provincial in France in which he was to certify as to the good conduct of his subject, and authorize his residence in America outside of his Convent. On the contrary, I received from New York details concerning his [*sic.*] conduct of this Religious in Acadia, which overwhelm me with sorrow, and lead me to accuse myself of too great ease in granting him powers, even for a very limited time. I entreat you to gather and send to me at the first opportunity some sound information concerning him, touching upon his conduct at Kaskaskia. I am also worried about Monsr. St. Pierre. He left here without powers to administer Sacraments, which, at the time, I had not the right to give him: and since his departure, I have not been able to bring myself to send him any; because I am in no way convinced that he came to America with the approval of the Superiors of his order, and with the approvals which the rules of Ecclesiastical discipline demand: Monsr. de la Valinere has written to me, it was some time ago, that Monsr. St. Pierre completely disregarded the authority which he first exercised in my name.

Now for some information on this matter, if you so desire it. It was some time ago, that I had some news from Monsr. La Valiniere. A Merchant from New York told me that he had seen him in New Orleans about the month of August, and that he intended to come here by sea.

I am very indebted to you for all the details you gave concerning the possessions of the Fort Vincennes Church. If the opportunity arises, I will do my best to take advantage of it in order to give strength to its claims.

The points on which you agreed with the trustees to abide by according to my decision, are expressed in the enclosed sheet of paper[3] and I added my own way of thinking on each matter. I am sure that my decision will conform to your particular interest and satisfaction as well as to the principles of justice.

Commending myself to your Holy Sacrifices and prayers, I am with respect, Monsr.,[4] your very humble and obedient servant. J. Carroll

You will receive here the formula of prayers, which are to be said for our Ecclesiastical and civil Superiors. You will kindly translate them into French for your own use.

We follow the Roman Ritual here, with the exception of certain days, where we act according to the old customs of the United States for the offices of the English saints. As regards other situations, I advise that you always follow the ritual of Quebec.

ALS   MoHS   An AC (AAB) lacks three paragraphs and has some minor variations elsewhere.
¹ Not found; probably dated Jan., 1789. See above under this date. Gibault's response to the charges by the Bishop of Quebec exonerates him. See Joseph P. Donnelly, *Pierre Gibault, Missionary: 1737-1802* (Chicago: Loyola Univ. Press, 1971), pp. 126, 129. Carroll had judged Gibault on information from the Bishop of Quebec, but was now impressed with Gibault's letter of Jan. 10, 1790 (AAB 2H7) and responded in a respectful spirit, Dec. 27, 1790 (see below).
² F. Le Dru, O.P., in 1796 was reported by James McHenry to Carroll as undermining American interests against the English, who still held forts in the Old Northwest Territory. (See McHenry to Carroll, June 12, 1796 [5D1]).
³ See following entry below.
⁴ An endorsement in another hand appears at this point: "Cath C. Inv[*ind.*]"; the significance and meaning is not clear.

Baltimore ce 20 Janvier 1790   Monsieur   Il est arrivé tres malheureusement pour les affairs de votre Eglise, ainsi que pour ma satisfaction, que les porteurs de vos lettres du 16 Juin, et du 28 de Juillet soient arrivés et repartis d'içi dans le tems de mon absence. Vous faites tort à Monsr. de la Valiniere en imputant à lui seul les accusations, dont j'ai fait mention dans ma lettre preçedente. Des Voyageurs revenus à Philadelphiè de Kaskaskias en avoient parlé même avant son depart, & sans sçavoir, quel etoit le prêtre, que ces accusations regardoient en particulier, je l'avois chargé lors de son depart de philadelphie, de faire des informations à çe suject. Depuis çe tems, j'ai reçu par differentes voyes les notices, dont je vous ai fait part dans ma precedente. Je suis même faché de vous dire, que M̄gr̄ l'Evêque de Quebec, dans une lettre, qu'il me fit l'honneur de m'ecrire, me marqua, que ses precedesseurs avoient cru ne devoir pas se fier si entierement sur vous pendant les dernieres années, qu'ils avoient fait au commencement de votre carriere Apostolique. Je me flatte, que c'etoit plutot sur des faux rapports, que çes prelats ont eté induits à retirer leur premiere confiance, que sur quelque demerite de votre part. Dans l'incertitude, ou je reste, & crainte de vous faire injustice d'une part; ou, de l'autre, de manquer à mon devoir, je ne veux à present faire un nouveau arrangement. Çependant on ne peut être plus persuadé que moi de la necessité d'une bonne administration Ecclesiastique pour toute cette partie de l'ouest. Depuis le depart d'içi du Pere Jacobin, nommé Le Dru, je n'ai point reçu, suivant sa convention avec moi, une lettre de son provincial en France, par laquelle il devoit certifier de la bonne conduite de son sujet, & autoriser sa demeure en Amerique hors de son Couvent. Au contraire, j'ai reçu par la voie de la Nouvelle York des details sur sa conduite de ce Religieux en Acadie, qui m'accablent de tristesse, & me font accuser ma trop grande facilité à lui accorder des pouvoirs, même pour un tems fort limité. Je vous prie de vous procurer, & de me transmettre, par la premiere occasion des bonnes informations à son egard, touçhant sa conduite à Kaskasias. J'ai des inquietudes aussi par rapport à Monsr. St. Pierre. Il est parti d'içi sans pouvoirs pour l'administration des Sacramens, que, dans çe tems, je n'etois pas en droit de lui accorder: et depuis son depart, je n'ai pu me resoudre à lui en envoyer; parceque je ne suis nullement assuré qu'il soit venu en Amerique du grè des superieurs de son ordre, et avec les approbations, qu'exigent les regles de la discipline Ecclesiastique. Mr. de la Valiniere m'a mandé, il y a long tems, que Monsr. de St. Pierre ne tenoit aucun conte de l'autorité, que le premier exercoit de mon part. Des informations encore, si vous voulex bien, à çe sujet. Il y a bien de tems, que je n'ai pas des nouvelles de Monsr. La Valiniere. Un Negociant de la Nouvelle York m' a dit l'avoir vu a la Nouvelle Orléans vers le mois de d'Aoust, & qu'il se proposoit de venir içi par mer.

Je vous suis infiniment obligé de tous les details, dans lesquels vous êtes entre par rapport aus biens de l'Eglise du poste Vincennes; et si l'occasion se presente, je tacherai d'en profiter pour donner solidité à ses titres.

Les points, sur lesquels vous etes convenus avec Mesrs. les Marguillers de remettre à ma decision, sont exprimés dans le papier çi joint; et j'ai ajouté ma façon de penser sur chacun. Je me flatte, qu'elle sera conforme à votre interest & satisfaction particuliere, comme elle est, à çe qu'il me semble, à la justice. En me recommandant à vos Sst Sacrifices et prieres, Je suis avec respect, Monsr. Votre tres humble & obéissant serv. J. Carroll

Çi joint vous reçevrez le formulaire de prieres, qui se disent pour nos Superieurs Ecclesiastiques & civils. Vous aurez la bonté de les traduire en François pour votre usage.

Nous suivons içi le Rituel Romain, à l'exception des certains jours, ou nous faisons, suivant l'ancien usage des Etats Unis, l'office des Saints d'Angleterre. En attendant un autre arrangement, je vous conseille de vous conformer toujours au rituel de Quebec.

TO JOHN HEILBRON   Baltimore, 24 January 1790

On the 22nd of this month I received your letter of the 20th but too late to reply that same day because the post had left several hours earlier. As I read your letter I was struck with amazement and I still am amazed. Of a certainty my letter to Mr. Oellers, which left here on the 18th but was written the previous day,[1] showed how to bring about peace if they who bewail the restriction on your faculties really desire peace. Your reverence knows how unreasonable is the anger and ill temper of the trustees who complain that they were informed so late of the restriction. Although they were repeatedly approached they never evinced a willingness to assent to what I had decided. This they could have learned from me especially after I had stressed it to Messrs. Premir and Oellers[2] in your presence. Moreover, you know full well that I had often expressed my mind to you on this subject. For this reason I cannot persuade myself that you gave a full explanation to the people of Holy Trinity.

What I wrote to Mr. Oellers favors their demands, in other respects neither rational nor restrained, insofar that while the conditions I laid down are not too pleasant they have brought me to the conviction that they do not desire peace except on their own terms. This is readily deduced from your letter. For you say that they are resolved to minister the sacraments to themselves rather than have recourse to St. Mary's Church. What is this but arbitrarily to found a church and appoint a pastor on their own authority. I need not point out to you how this contravenes ecclesiastical practice and discipline. In this whole affair much depends on you; it is within your power to end the disturbance if you wish to forestall a humiliating subjection. If in so serious a matter they refuse to listen to you I pity you, who cannot lead but are subject to the beck and call of others. Under easy and equitable terms you can obtain the faculties for baptizing and marrying, provided that episcopal right and the prevailing ecclesiastical procedure are acknowledged. It is my duty to insist on this. I have already acquainted Mr. Oellers with these conditions. Meanwhile I must emphatically condemn the extreme views of the people of Holy Trinity which you outline. That such as entertain them have lost all true sense of religion is overwhelmingly evident.

ADf   AAB
[1] Not found.
[2] Trustees.

Baltimorae, die 24 Jan. 1790   Rev. D. Helbron, Philadelphiae—   Accepi die 22 hujus literas Rev. Vae. datas 20 ejusdem, nimis quidem sero, quam ut eadem die rescribere possem; quippe multis ante horis rheda postaria discesserat. Miratus sum sane dum illas legerem, neque desino mirari; quippe meae ad Dominum Oellers, quae hinc discessere die 18 (scriptae erant praecedenti die) pacis firmiter stabiliendae viam ostendunt, si pacis ullis omnini conditionibus velint, qui de tuarum facultatum restrictione sunt conquesti. Novit Ra. Va. quam immerito synodales irascantur quod tam sero de illa restrictione fuerint admoniti; cum saepius rogati, mecum tamen convenire nunquam voluerint ut quae statueram, ex me discere possent, praecipue postquam non observare id DD. Premir et Oellers, te praesente, insignaveram. Novisiti praeterea me saepe tibi consilium meum hac de re communicavisse; unde vix mihi possum persuadere omnia a te exposita fuisse Trinitariis, quorum notitiam habuisti.

Quae scripsi Domino Oellers, ita favent vel ipsorum postulatis (quamvis alique neque rationabiliter neque temperate fiant) ut si conditiones a me positae minus placeant in illam me opinionem redacturi sint, ipsos pacem nolle nisi omnia plane suo arbitrio fiant; quod quidem vel ex Rae. Vae. literis non obscure colligitur. Ais enim ipsis statutum esse sibi ipsis potius Sacramenta administrare, quam ullo modo ad Ecclesiam Beatae Virginis recurrere. Quid autem hoc aliud est, quam suo nutu, suaque auctoritate parochiam et parochum constituere; quod quam sit contra omnem Ecclesiae usum et disciplinam, necesse non habes ut Rae. Vae significem. In toto hoc negotio plurimum a te pendent; penesque te est, si indignam subjectionem excutere cupias, animorum motus componere; sin vero te in re adeo gravi audire recusent, me miseret tui, qui non docere sed aliorum nutum sequi debes.

Facillimis et aequissimis conditionibus, baptisandi et matrimonio jungendi facultates obtinere poteris, dummodo jura Episcopalia aut ecclesiasticae superioritatis in tuto posita fuerint, quod munus meum a me exigit. Illas conditiones Domo. Oellers jam exposui. Interim violenta illa Trinitariorum consilia, de quibus memoras, non possum non acriter condemnare. Qui ita secum statuunt, ipsi sane genuina Religionis sensa se in animo non conservare nimis declarant.

TO MATTHEW CAREY   Thursday evening–[Feb., 1790]

Dear Sir   Being just returned from Capn. Barry's, I found your note respecting the passage of Exodus, c: 13.v.9. I have consulted the Latin Vulgate, and the edition of it, to which are annexed the notes of Tirinus; and I find it punctuated as in the London edition. It is therefore advisable to adhere to it, especially as the sense is intelligible, tho' not so easy, as with the punctuation, which you suggest. So many corruptions were formerly introduced into the Scriptures by the liberties taken with the text, that the Council of Trent ordained very wisely the utmost precaution to be used hereafter. I am, Dr. Sir,   Yr m. humble st   J Carroll

ALS   HSP   Date established by reference to Feb. 14, 1790.

TO TRUSTEES IN PHILADELPHIA   [Feb., 1790]

The death of one of my dearest & nearest connections having obliged me to leave Baltimore very suddenly on Easter Sunday, prevented me from answering the next day, your very kind & Christian address by Mr. Bussy. The trouble occasioned by the aforesaid accident, caused me to leave home, without bringing your address with me, so that at present I can only tell you, that nothing could give me more satisfaction, in my uneasiness occasioned by some disturbances at Philada., than receiving, from persons so respectable, such warm & full assurances of subordination to & affection for their lawful & virtuous Pastors. An attachment to the principles, exercised in yr. address & by which you have been always governed in your spiritual concerns, will ever, I hope, distinguish the respectable members of the Philada. Congn. I depend on you in particular, for promoting with your example & influence, respect, & obedience to yr. ministers in the exercise of their functions, & brotherly love for each other. I will do myself the pleasure of communicating my sentiments more fully to you, after I return to Baltre.; In the mean time I have the honour to be with the greatest esteem, Gentn.   Yr. most devoted St. in Xt.   J.C.

ADfS   AAB   Dated by reference to other letters in this controversy. Probably addressed to trustees of Holy Trinity rather than St. Mary's, since disorders were found in the former parish.

TO HOLY TRINITY CHURCH, PHILADELPHIA   Baltre Feb. 4–1790

Whereas a difference of opinion prevails between the subscriber and the Trustees of Trinity Church, Philada, concerning the right of presentation to the said Church, it is hereby declared & made known to all persons, whom it may concern, that the subscriber by granting spiritual powers to the Rev. Mr. J. C. Helbron does not mean to acknowledge the right of presentation claimed by the Trustees aforesaid or others; but that he is actuated only by a desire of preserving peace & unity amongst the Catholics of Philada. He reserves to himself & successors the right of recalling or restraining those powers as he may see cause; at the same time he is ready and desirous to refer the matter in dispute concerning the right of presentation to be finally & amicably determined by persons well versed in Ecclesiastical & beneficiary causes. The subscriber further declares that no use shall be made hereafter of any words, as *pastor, congregation* &c., which have been or may be employed in any instrument of writing between him & said Trustees of Trinity Church, in order to establish thereon the right in this Church to parochial privileges; but that the conferring of that right does & shall depend solely on the Eccles Superior or Bp of the U. S. for the time being.

ADf   AAB

TO JAMES OELLERS   Feb. 4–1790–

Sir   I wrote you a few lines by the last post. I send to day, according to promise, an instrument of writing, declaring my readiness & desire to have our dispute referred to persons competent to decide it, that is to the *Congn. de propaganda fide.* I have acted in this business solely with a view to the preservation of peace; for the writing signed by your Trustees is far from being such as I required. Amongst other things, they say, that both parties, meaning themselves & me are willing that Mr. Helbron should remain *the pastor with full faculties of Trinity Church & Congregation, till the faith is decided &c.* I suppose the word *faith* is a mistake for *cause,* or some equivalent. Besides this, I cannot agree, that the consent of both parties is necessary to discontinue or restrain Mr. Helbron's faculties, even before the cause is determined: on the contrary, I, or my Successors may, at discretion revoke or limit his faculties, as may be done with the pastors of St. Mary's or any other Congregation in these United States. This letter you will be pleased to consider, as an official one and as such to be communicated, with my respectful compliments, to the Trustees.[1] I am   Sir   Yr &c.   J.C.

ADfS   AAB
[1] Oellers was head Trustee of Holy Trinity Church, Philadelphia.

TO LEONARDO ANTONELLI Baltimore, Feb. 6, 1790

I must admit, Most Eminent Cardinal, that I am unduly tardy in replying to your letter of July 11 of last year, and I am all the less worthy of pardon because of the unfailing kindness of yourself and the entire Congregation. In part my conduct was due to the fact that as I was chosen by my fellow priests for the office of bishop I did not wish to do or say anything that might influence the Holy Father or the Sacred Congregation to confirm their choice. On the contrary I prayed that the matter might be taken up anew and one more worthy be made bishop. While I thus reflect on the situation I learn from private correspondence that the matter is settled, and that a papal brief is about to be sent from Rome. I cannot say how sad this makes me for I realize what a great burden is imposed on me, not for a brief period but for a lifetime. In these circumstances my only comfort is that this allotment of anxiety and labor was not my choice but beyond my expectation. And if this has come about through the disposition of divine providence God, I trust, will come to my aid.

You see, most Eminent Cardinal, that I was so taken up with these thoughts that up to the present I have not thanked the Sacred Congregation for their kindness and liberality, despite difficult times, to our Catholic school, a pledge, as one may hope, of profit accruing to religion, and of still greater assistance when the Apostolic See and the Congregation are liberated from current difficulties. We pray earnestly that it happen soon.

A few months I wrote to Rev. Mr. Thorpe[1] whom you mention in your letter, asking him to explain how greatly I have been annoyed by the audacity, misconduct and disregard of every norm of ecclesiastical discipline by a Capuchin priest of whom I expected better things. Eventually he was reduced to order, but I admit that I put so little trust in him that I should dispense with his services but for the fact that I anticipate disturbance and open scandal on the part of some of his compatriots whom he has attached to himself. Recently I discovered that shortly before he came to America he sought release from the obligations of his religious profession, and when this was refused he seized the first occasion to leave monastic enclosure and set out for this country. In all this his superiors lacked prudence, for no regulars are more in need of discipline than those who wish to be freed from it. It would help him and our cause to no small degree if he were ordered back to the monastery by his superior or by the General of his order. His name is John Charles Helbron; he comes from the diocese of Treves in Germany. (see below)[2]

There is good hope of establishing the Catholic cause in Charleston, South Carolina, although many difficulties spring from the poverty of the people, workers for the most part.

In Boston so far our beginnings have not been auspicious because of the imprudence and bad faith of the priest whom I mentioned earlier.[3] He has had two successors, of whom one is Mr. Thayer known undoubtedly to the Congregation at least by reputation. I should wish that both of them stay for I have found that great inconveniences follow when a priest is all alone. I see however that this cannot be because the means of livelihood are inadequate for two, and for other reasons which need not be mentioned.

May it please the Congregation to contribute annually the sum of two hundred gold pieces to Rev. Mr. John Thorpe who, through the hands of merchants in Leghorn and New York, will transmit it safely.

ADf   AAB
[1] Not found.
[2] Documenting enclosure not found.
[3] See Aug. 5-6, 1789.

Baltimori die 6 Feb. 1790   Fateor, Eminentissime Cardinalis, tardiorem me accedere ad respondendum Eme. Tuae literis, scriptis die 11 Julii anni praeteriti in quo minus venia dignus sum, quod summam tuam totiusque Congregationis Sacra me humanitatem ita constanter expertus fuerim. Erat quidem in causa, aliqua ex parte, quod electus a confratribus meis Sacerdotibus ad munus Episcopale, nihil facere aut scribere voluerim quo moveri posset Summus Pontifex Noster vel Sacra Congregatio ut electio confirmaretur, sed continuis ad Deum precibus institi ut res ex integro resumeretur, atque alteri multoque digniori dignitas Episcopalis conferretur. Dum ita mecum delibero, audio ex privatis literis rem jam confectam atque breve pontificium Roma expediendum esse. Quod quanto dolore me afficiat, dicere non possum, qui modo me video, non jam ad breve aliquod tempus, sed dum vita dureverit, gravissimo oneri et periculi pleno alligatum esse video: qua in re nullum mihi solatium adest, praeterquam quod non mea voluntate sed praeter omnem meam expectationem, haec mihi et sollicitudinis et laboris portio acceserit; quod si ex divinae providentiae dispositione evenerit, ipse, uti confido, mihi aderit, qui tam gravi muneri me destinavit.

Vides, Eminentissime Cardinalis, ita me in hac consideratione defixum fuisse, ut Sacrae Congregationi gratias adhuc non reddiderim, quod benigne et liberaliter, praecipue in his rerum difficultatibus, scholae nostrae Catholicae subsidium contulerint, pignus, uti sperare fas est, ut fructus ex ipsa in Religionem derivandi et amplioris subsidii, si aliquando ex his temporum angustiis Sedes Apostolica atque Sacra Congregatio emerserint, uti Deum, ut brevi fiat, enixe precamur.

Paucis adhinc mensibus scripsi Revd. Do. Thorpe, cujus in Eminentiae Vestrae literis fit mentio, ipsum rogans, ut exponere vellet quantam mihi molestiam creaverit, quamque audacter et praeter juris Ecclesiastici normam se hic gesserit sacerdos quidam de quo meliora speraveram, ex Capuccinorum familia. Tandem tamen redactus est in ordinem, sed uti fateor parum ipsi fido neque amplius ejus opera uterer, nisi quorundam ex suis Compatriotis, quos sibi devinxit, turbas et aperta scandala pertimexerem. Nuper cognovi ipsum paulo ante quam in Americam navigasset, a Religiosa sua professione solutionem sollicitavisse, quumque repulsam passus esset, primam occasionem arripuisse ex monasterii septis egrediendi et in has provincias proficiscendi. Quod quidem parum prudenter ipsi permissum fuit a suis superioribus, cum nulli Regulares domestica desciplina magis egeant quam qui illa absolvi desiderant. Unde et ipsi ex communi nostrae causae non parum proderit si ab eisdem superioribus vel a suo Generali monasterium regredi juberetur. Nomen ipsi Joannes Carolus Helbron ex Diocesi Trevirensi in Germania. (v. infra)

Spes bona affulget rei Catholicae firmiter Carolopoli stabiliendae in Carolina Meridionali, quamvis multae se objiciant difficultates propter Catholicorum egestatem qui, ut plurimum, opifices sunt.

In urbe Bostonensi principia Religionis stabiliendae non adhuc fausta fuere, propter imprudentiam et malam fidem illius Sacerdotis cujus antea feci mentionem. Huic duo alii Successere quorum unus est Dom. Thayer, quem Sacrae Congregationi notum esse, fama saltem, minime dubito. Cuperem equidem ut uterque ibidem maneret, cum semper fere expertus fuerim ingentia incommoda ex eo oriri, quod nullus sacerdos solus sit; hoc fieri tamen non posse, satis jam video; tam quia ambobus non suppetit, unde vivant; tum ob alias rationes quas necesse non est commemorare.

Placeat Sacrae Congregationi solvatur annua summa centum aureorum per triennium Rev. Do. Joanni Thorpe, qui interventu mercatoris Liburni et Neo Eboraci illam tuto transmittet.

TO MATTHEW CAREY   Balt. Feb. 10—1790—

Dear Sir   I have a letter from you, without date, recommending a renewal of exertions. Those, I assure, are not wanting. I sent your circular letters, & wrote very pressingly myself to my Brethren below.[1] Mr. Sewall, instead of carrying them himself, unfortunately fell sick on the road, & was obliged to send them by another hand. This was a loss; as he would have done more than twenty letters. I have not reveived their answers—; but some few subscribers have been added to the list, as below, & about four or five pounds received. I expect about eight or ten more will be collected soon.

You may be assured nothing on my part shall be wanting now, or hereafter to promote yr. interest & second the zeal you exhibit for that cause, which it is my more special duty to promote. I am, with great regard & best wishes—Dr. Sir,   Yr. most obedt. st.   J. Carroll.   [*Seven subscribers listed.*]

ALS   HSP
[1] Not found.

TO THOMAS SIM LEE   Baltimore Feb. 10—1790—

Dear Sir   I have been under a repeated necessity of baulking my expectation and desire of doing myself the pleasure of seeing you & your amiable

Lady & family. This has given me real & much concern. I have suffered much likewise from the reflexion of their being so long destitute of a Clergyman to tend them regularly. Just now, when all other difficulties, which in Mr. Francis Neale's way are removed, I find it unadvisable to send him to Frederick on account of very bad health. In his stead, & to supply his place for a time, I have appointed the Rev. Mr. Ryan to reside in Frederick & serve the neighbouring Congregations. He was recommended to me by the Archbishop of Dublin, as a most exemplary Clergyman; & during a residence at Charleston, S. Carolina, of 18 months, he fully answered that character. I presume that all necessaries in the Presbytery house of Frederick are gone much to decay, & that he will be under considerable difficulties at setting out. I recommend him to your & Mrs. Lee's[1] wonted kindness in this respect—; as well, as that you would mention to Mr. Leonard Smith that I request him to speak to the Catholics thereabouts to help to enable him to pay for a horse &c. My respectful & affectionate compliments to Mrs Lee & love to your young family.

I am with the greatest esteem Dr. Sir,   Yrs most afftely   J Carroll

ALS   LP
[1] Mary Digges of Melwood, Md., to whose family Carroll was related by his brother Daniel's marriage. See Apr. 27, 1780.

TO MATTHEW CAREY   Baltre. Feb. 14—1790—

Dear Sir   I sent you a few lines some days ago;[1] since which I have to request you would add the following names to your list of Subscribers to the Doway Bible,—viz: Mr. Oliver Grace—Baltimore—Henry Rozer, Esqr., Notley Hall, Potowmack—George Digges Esqr, Warburton, Do. Col. John Fitzgerald, Alexandria Virga. Mr. Joseph Boarman, near Piscataway, Maryland.

I hear from your correspondent Mr. Rice, that [he—*torn*] is afraid your Customers will make heavy complaints, that they have not yet received their Museum's for December. I mention this out of the sincere regard, which is felt for your interest by, Dr. Sir,   Yr. most obedt. Servt.   J Carroll

ALS   HSP
[1] See Feb., 1790, to Carey.

TO CHARLES PLOWDEN   Rock Creek Feb. 24—1790

My Dear Sir   I have been a few days with my good Mother, & take the opportunity of the leisure, I find here to answer your welcome favours of Sep. 27 & Novr. 1. My last to you was from Philada., and it was at my return to Baltimore, that I found the last of your agreeable favours. I cannot sufficiently acknowledge the most obliging and honourable testimony of Mr

Weld's regard: you will be pleased to express, with all that warmth, which you can communicate to your expressions, my deep sense of his generous politeness. My inclination certainly leads me to accept of an offer not only so flattering, but which will afford an opportunity of seeing some of those friends, whom I shall ever honour & love. But I cannot yet determine, what I shall do. I still flatter myself, that divine providence will provide some worthier subject to be its instrument in founding a church in America. Nothing is yet received from Rome to confirm our proceedings here. Mr Thorpe's letter, which you saw, is my only source of intelligence. I am greatly obliged to you for your anxiety about our proposed Academy, as well as for your generous intentions respecting it. I think we shall get enough of it compleated this summer to make a beginning of teaching; but our great difficulty will be to get a proper President, or Superintendent. The fate of the school will depend much on the first impression made upon the public; & a President of known abilities & reputation would contribute greatly to render that impression, a very favourable one. Many seminaries of education have been raised in the United States within these few years; but, in general they are exceedingly defective in discipline. A college has been lately opened at Annapolis, under the protection of our State legislature, & amply endowed by them. It is erected on principles of perfect equality, as to Religion. The original agents, appointed by act of assembly, to model & encourage it, were three Clergymen & three laymen one of whom were Catholic, Church of England, & Presbyterian. I had the honour of being the former. This matter was broached before we formed a plan for our academy at George-town. I see at present no other advantage to us Catholics in the Annapolis College, than this, that it may be a place for our young lads, who have finished their Grammar education at George town to pursue their higher studies of law, medicine &c. In other respects, it will be hurtful to our Institution.

I have informed Mr. Thorpe[2] of Mr Thayer's arrival & that his reception at Boston as he says, was kind and satisfactory. I have some apprehensions, that his zeal, or, if you please his mind is too aspiring, & too confident of itself. He has made some proposals to me which raise this fear in me; tho, on the whole I believe him to be a virtuous & resolute priest. We have I think, made lately a great acquisition in an Irish Dominican from Lisbon of the name of Fleming: he is a well-informed, decent, & sweet temperd man. He is placed at Philada. & pleases there. By the sample of Capucins, which we have had, they are the least calculated for foreign missions; they have proved turbulent, ambitious, interested, & they unite much ignorance with consummate assurance.

I am glad your V. V. A. A. [Vicars Apostolic] have broken their too long delayed silence. I have not seen the proposed oath: but to me it has always appeared degrading, that Catholics should find it necessary to recommend themselves to Government by renouncing tenets, which form no part of their belief. It is mere pretence in a minister, to suggest such a test, as requisite to convince him of the harmlessness of our Religion. If his mind is not great enough to raise him above the mean & infamous prejudices, which are inspired in the course of national education of England, no tests will satisfy him. I am clearly of opinion that the Catholics ought to speak a manly language &, after giving such proof of their attachment to their country, as any government ought in reason to be satisfied with, to demand equal protection *as a right,* & not suppliantly sue for it, *as a favour.* This would be much more respected, than a thousand attendances & cringings, at a minister's level. Tho I have not seen the proposed oath yet I have met with a declaration in some magazine, which I suppose to be that which was signed so generally.[3] I remember, that, when I read it, I thought it very reprehensible: but not having it by me at present, I cannot refer to the particular passages. With you I entirely coincide in your observations on the quaint, mischievous, & dishonourable appellation of *protesting Catholic dissenters.* I have mentioned to you heretofore (at least I think I did) that in some of our American States, the Roman Catholics, the freely tolerated, were not eligible to the first offices of government. This unjust exclusion has always hurt my feelings. In two or three short publications, I have endeavoured to draw the public attention to this subject: and lately, it becoming necessary for the Roman Catholics to address Genl. Washington as President of the U. States, I have thrown something on this subject into the address itself.[4] If he, in his answer, should take any notice of that part of the address, it will go far towards bringing those states, in which the exclusion prevails, to a repeal of it. My good Mother, with whom I now am & who, in her 85th year enjoys a very competent share of health tho very feeble is much obliged to you for your constant remembrance of her. As her memory & understanding are perfectly sound, she retains the tenderest regard for the memory of her dear friend, yr. honoured Mother, & for all her descendants. Be pleased to offer my most respectful compliments to the Lord & Lady of Lullworth Castle, & to Messrs Stanly & Clinton: & Whenever you have an opportunity, to the most amiable family of Wardour. I am, My Dr. Sr   Ever & afftly Yrs   J. Carroll

ALS   St
   [1] See Dec. 28, 1789.
   [2] Dec., 1789, not found.
   [3] See Oct. 23, 1789.
   [4] Dec., 1789.

TO ANTOINE DUGNANI   Balre—March 16—1790

My Lord   While begging your Excellency to forward my attached letter to his Eminence Cardinal Antonelli, I take advantage at the same time of the opportunity to pay you, my Lord, my most humble respects & gratitude for the confidence with which you have been pleased to honor me in your letter of June 5 of last year. Mr. Jefferson having remained in Virginia for four or five months after his return, I have only had occasion to see him on his passage through this city on his way to New York. He has just married Miss Jefferson in Virginia; I have therefore not been able to take any step to promote the good dispostions she acquired at the Abbey of Panthemont.[1] I ardently desire to begin a Catholic Church in Richmond, the capital of Virginia. Perhaps in that case Providence will revive that young lady's first intentions, & will use her to spread the true faith.

Mr. Thayer, who arrived here toward the end of December, is now in Boston. There are some troubles between him and a very worthy French priest[2] who preceded him there. Religion suffers from this; each one has his adherents; and it is difficult to bring order there without causing a ferment. However I am going to take a survey which becomes necessary.

ADf   AAB
[1] Martha Jefferson, during her father's ambassadorship to France, was educated in this convent and expressed an inclination to become a Catholic. Her father believed that she should wait until she was eighteen years of age before proceeding further. See Dugnani to Carroll Jul. 5, 1787 (AAB).
[2] Rousselet.

Nuncio at Paris—   Balre. March 16–1790—   Mgr—   En priant V. Exc. de faire passer ma lettre çi jointe à son Em. le Cardl. Antonelli, je profite en même tems de l'occasion de vous faire, Mgr mes tres humbles respects & remercimens de la confiance, dont elle a bien voulu m'honorer dans sa lettre du 5 de Juin de l'an passé. Monsr. Jefferson s'etant arreté dans la Virginie pendant quatre ou cinque mois aprés son retour, je n'ai eu l'occasion de le voir qu' à son passage par cette ville pour se rendre à la Nouvelle-York. Il venoit de marier Mademoiselle Jefferson dans la Virginie; je n'ai donc pu jusqu' içi faire aucune de marche pour seconder les bonnes dispositions qu'elle avoit concues à l' abbaye de Panthemont. Je desire àrdemment donner commencement à une Eglise Catholique à Richmond, capitale de la Virginie. Peutêtre qu'alors la providence fera revivre les premiers desseins de cette jeune Dame, & s'en servira pour etendre la vraie foi.

Mr. Thayer, qui arriva içi sur la fin de Decembre, est maintenant à Boston—Il y a quelques inquietudes entre lui, et un tres digne prêtre Francois, nommé Rousselet que l'y a precedé. La Religion en souffre; chacun a des adherans; et il est difficile d'y mettre ordre sans causer une fermentation. Je vais cependant prendre un plan qui devient necessaire.

TO CHARLES PLOWDEN   March 16–1790–

I give you joy for the success of the Patriots in Flanders & Brabant.[1] Vandernoot is a favourite toast in the United States. I have heard, that he bears the character not only of an able but of a very worthy man & an excellent Christian. My Brethren here have been deluding themselves, for a long time, with ideas of a restoration founded on, what appeared to me very shallow support indeed: But at present, I cannot help thinking, that the late convulsions in Europe, when traced to their real sources, must discover to every thinking mind the necessity of a virtuous education, & of encouraging men capable of conducting the rising generation thro all the degrees of moral, religious & literary improvement. On whom then can the governing powers turn their eyes, but on those, who are trained under the discipline of the Society? a few Seminaries or universities may be indeed supplied with excellent instructors without recurring to them; but numerous professors, sufficient to fill the chairs of every considerable town can not be formed, & held to their duty, except it be in a body constituted as the Society. The Emperors character is viewed here, as opprobrious and paltry, in the extreme.[2] I write this after receiving your favour of Nov. 30—by the Decr. packet. From its contents & the purport of Mr. Thorpes, which was inclosed, I dread the arrival of the packet of January.[3] I pity the poor in Europe, who are to eat their bread, till harvest comes in, at a most extravagant rate. The immense demand on us for wheat, flour, & all kinds of grain, from every country of Europe has raised those articles so high here that when the additional charges of freight, commission, insurance &c are added, it will be dear bread indeed to those, who must buy it.

I am afraid, that Mr. Thayer wants that spirit of accommodation, & perhaps of humility, which is so essentially requisite for a labourer in the Lords vineyard. Say nothing of this, till you hear farther from me. I cannot help yet entertaining very favourable sentiments of him; but they are blended with an apprehension, that his success will not be equal to the expectations, which preceded his coming. God bless you & forgive my garrulity. I am as always, My Dr. Sr,   Ever Yrs   J.C.

ALS   St
[1] The Brabancon Revolt against Joseph II and his reforms in Austrian Netherlands. The Catholic lawyer, Henri Van der Noot led the independence movement and the military forces of Col. J. A. Van der Meersch, which were ultimately defeated after initial success.
[2] Under the Erastian theory of Josephenism, he repressed and in some cases suppressed religious bodies.
[3] Reference to his official appointment as bishop, which did not actually come until April.

TO MATTHEW CAREY   [Apr., 1790]

Dear Sir   Mr. Stewart has delivered me your favr. of March 31st. I have a letter now ready for him, to introduce him to & recommend success with my Brethren in Ch[arle]s. & St. Mary's counties.[1] I have forwarded to you, some time ago,[2] the names of some additional subscribers–, to which I now add that of Mrs. Anne Slaughter, near Alexandria, Virga. The Gentlemen, who take in these subscribers, either neglect to require, or to forward the first payment. I had not quite sufficient to pay your draught in favr. of Mr. Rice, but advanced it. I have since been repayed by some receipts coming in. I am constantly attentive to promote encouragement for your useful & necessary undertaking; & think, that in so doing, I am not only rendering justice to you, but discharging a duty belonging to my station. I have had likewise some ideas floating in my mind, which, if I ever find leisure to reduce them into order, may furnish some few articles to your museum. I am with great regard, Dr. Sir   Yr. most obedt. servt.   J Carroll

ALS   HSP   Dated by reference to note 1 below.
[1] See Apr. 3, 1790.
[2] Probably Nov. 14, 1789.

TO CLERGY OF CHARLES AND ST. MARY'S COUNTIES
Baltre. April 3–1790

Rev. Gentlemen[1] –   Mr. Stewart, the bearer of this, is partner with Mr. Carey, & he is going into your neighbourhood to collect the first payments due on the subscription for the Doway Bible. I have furnished him with the names of those, who have desired me to place them in the list of subscribers, without sending the money. I earnestly recommend to you to give him every assistance in your power, not only as to procuring payment, but in enlarging, as much as possible, the encouragement for the useful undertaking, which is the object of it. I am with great respect, Rev. Gentlemen,   Yr. most obedt. & humble st.   J Carroll

ALS   HSP
[1] Letter covering has these names: "Rev. Messrs. Leonard Neale, Joseph Doyne, Francis Neale, & Henry Pile, in Chs. County, & Messrs. Ignatius Matthews, Jn. Boarman, Augstine Jenkins, Newtown, & James Walton, St. Inigo, St. Marys. County."

TO JOHN THAYER
Apr. 9-30, 1790

Not found. See Apr. 30, 1790.

TO JOHN ASHTON
Balt. Ap. 18–1790–

Rev. Sir   I cannot comprehend your meaning, when you say, that you hurried out of my room *for fear of getting angry,* after you had heard part of the popes brief: for certainly *I* could not be the object of your displeasure; & therefore you could give no offence *to me* by freely declaring your sentiments. Mr. Sewall observes, that he told you of the clause, to which you principally object, as soon as you came to Baltimore; I think I did so myself; and he supposed that you regarded it, as Mr. Thorpe says of it, as matter of form for the present, and the subject of future negociation. With respect to myself, my election being compleated in the manner, we requested; and the confirmation being come, my jurisdiction is compleat; the see of Baltimore is filled, & can only be vacated by death, deposition for crimes, or resignation. I do not even know, whether the resignation would be valid without concurrence of the Metropolitan who in the present case is the pope himself. When first I received your letter, I resolved to take no part whatever in the dispute, which might result from it. I have reflected on it more seriously this morning & conceive, that I was restrained only by a false delicacy: and tho' my observations may lay me open to suspicions of ambition or interest, yet I am determined to hazard the incurring of them rather than risk interests, which are so important to the American Church. In the 1st.place I am & ever shall be opposed not only to the popes having the nomination of the Bishop, whilst he is supported by our estates here; but even if the pope himself should be at the sole charge of making provision for him; and one amongst other reasons, is the certainty I have, that the exercise of such power by the pope would draw on our Religion a heavy imputation from the govt. under wch, we live. 2ly. I conceive that future elections will not be conducted as the last: for, if we reflect, we cannot but be sensible, that the greatest inconveniencies will arise from the whole body of the Clergy having a right to vote on such occasions: and therefore it could not be declared in the brief, that elections should be so conducted. The pope, according to the pretensions, which the see of Rome has always supported, says, he will nominate hereafter. But I conceive that the Clergy will have as good right to say, that the election shall be held by members of their own body, & that they never can, with safety, or will admit any Bishop, who is not so constituted. The time for holding this language will be in a Diocesan synod of all the Clergy, & not at a meeting of Chapter only, which is not competent to all the business, which you propose for their deliberation. If the proceeding be made, as I have stated, we shall act conformably to the tenor of our memorial to Rome, in wch. you were one of the agents.[1] The words are as follow. We ask for two things—1um, ut Bonus Pater [first, as a good father] &c. These expressions will justify the American Clergy for objecting to any mode of election being settled, in which they have not been consulted: and with submission to sounder judgments, I think that their representations will command more attention when they send the result of their common delibera[ti]ons in a Diocesan synod with their Bp at their head. Were I to consult my personal feelings, I should have said nothing on this subject. I have made a sacrifice of them to, what I think, a common good.

As to the investing of the Bp with the administra[ti]on &c., I never conceived it as any thing more than the expression of those claims which Rome has always kept up, tho universally disregarded; viz; that the pope is the unvsal administrator, some even have said, *Dominus* of all eclsetl property. Rome cannot give what it never possessed, administra[ti]on of our estates; and I presume that a Bp, who should attempt any thing under such an authority, would be resisted, and deservedly, as the pope would have been, had he attempted it since the dissolu[ti]on. I am &c.

ADf   AAB
[1] See Mar. 22, 1788.

TO JOSÉ IGNACIO VIAR[1]   Baltimore April 20–1790–

Sir   I received on Saturday the honour of your letter of the 12th inst. I cannot express my sensibility on receiving a new proof of his Catholic Majestys zeal for the advantage of true Religion, & for promoting it in the United States. I request, Sir, that you would be pleased to present my most humble respects to his Excellency Don Antonio Porlier; & intreat him to do me the honour of making known to his Majesty, that his princely intentions in favour of the American Church have filled me with a deep sense of gratitude, & attachment to his person & interest; and that similar sentiments will pervade every corner of the United States, in which the Catholic Religion has made any progress.[2]

According to the information sent me from Charleston the number of Catholics is about 200: Every day they become more numerous. Many, whom past discouragements and oppression kept concealed, begin to shew themselves. Our Religion has not been exercised publickly there above two years. The Catholics there are mostly poor. They have no Church; but divine service is performed in a ruinous house, which they have hired. I presume that a Church about 75 feet long by 50 in breadth would be sufficient for some years yet to come. To build & provide such a church with all necessaries for divine service would require at least 15,000 dollars. I have no persons in Charleston with whom I would recommend the money to be lodged. The Clergyman, now there is on the point of leaving the place.[3] Whatever donations it may please his Majesty to bestow, should, I think, be placed in the hands of his Minister in the United States at first or in the bank of New York, or Philada., subject to the Minister's orders. I am soon to leave the United States for Episcopal Consecration. I presume, you will have an answer from your Court about the time of my return; and by that time I shall be able to give farther advices concerning the persons, to whom the execution of his Majesty's beneficent intentions may be committed. I have particular reasons for observing, that it would not be safe to lodge his money in the hands of any of those, who would be very forward to offer their service, if they were informed of the present enquiry directed by Don Antonio Porlier.

May I be allowed to request of you, Sir, to mention me, in your letters to Mr. Gardoqui, with every expression of respect and veneration. I have the honour to remain with the greatest esteem   Sir   Yr. most obedt. & humble servt   J. Carroll

ADf   AAB   Two drafts exist. The one followed here appears to be the one sent, since the second one has a deleted portion omitted from the draft given here.

[1] Spanish Consul General at Philadelphia.

[2] The other draft has the following deleted paragraph at this point: "The Revd. Mr. Ryan, who resided nearly two years in Charleston, returned hither a few months ago, having resigned his station to an Irish Clergyman, the Revd. Mr. Keating. This last Gentleman, discouraged by difficulties & some disappointments, intends likewise to remove himself very soon; I believe, in next month. I have not yet resolved on his Successor, because I desire to procure a very . . ."

[3] John Ryan. Christopher Keating succeeded him, but soon left for Philadelphia, where he was in 1793. After ministering to yellow fever victims, he himself survived an attack.

TO PAPAL NUNCIO IN LISBON   April 23, 1790–Baltre.

My Lord   The Rev. Father Fleming has had the kindness to present to me the letter Your Excellency deigned to honor me with, dated September 4 of last year. It was a true satisfaction for me to be able to place him [Keating] at Philadelphia immediately after his arrival; which I decided not only because of his merit, but also out of respect for the recommendation and endorsement you gave in his favor. Thus far he corresponds perfectly with the picture your Excellency gave of him: and I am not at all surprised that Her Most Christian Majesty[1] honored him with her esteem. The good fortune he had to merit the benevolence of a princess so virtuous will be a very powerful motive for me to serve him in any way I can. To destine virtuous & capable priests for this part of America is one of the greatest benefits one could render to Religion here. I know of only one greater: and that would be the establishment of an institution for the education of Catholic youth which would then become the safeguard of their faith, and the nursery of ministers of the sanctuary, accustomed to the usages, the character, and the climate of those among whom they are to work. Such an establishment now becomes so necessary that His Holiness has just erected an Episcopal See for the United States, and has named as first Bishop of Baltimore the one who now has the honor of writing to Your Excellency. I have been working for several years to form a college, or rather this school; for I dare not dignify it with the name of College; my plans are so limited by our lack of means for the accomplishment of the object of my desires. I would not know how to picture for you, My Lord, all the advantages which would accrue, in a country like this, where

Religion enjoys complete freedom. If I dared to submit the plan for this establishment, which I have the honor of sending you with this letter, to Her Majesty & to accompany it with an account explaining its object and advantages, I flatter myself that she would become the patron of it, & that she would find sweet pleasure in encouraging a design calculated to make reparation for the losses of the faith in so many other countries, by increasing it in this part of the new world where, until now, it has been almost unknown.

I plan to leave for England next month to be consecrated Bishop. Dare I ask Your Excellency to favor me with a letter, and to notify me of his opinion of what I have just written about, & whether it would be imprudent on my part to have sent to Her Most Christian Majesty a plea and account relative to the establishment in question. My address in London will be care of Mr. Strickland, at Messers Wright, Selby & Robinson, Bankers, Henrietta Street, to be held for the one who has the honor to be with greatest respect and devotion to Your Excellt Lordship, J.C.

ADfS   AAB
[1] Queen Marie III, of Braganza.

Nuncio at Lisbon—April 23—1790—Baltimore   Le Rev. Père Fleming a eu la bonté de me présenter la lettre dont V. Exc. m'a daigné honorer, en date du 4 de Septre. de l'an passé. Ce fut pour moi une vraie satisfaction d'avoir pu le placer à Philadelphie immédiatement après son arrivée; à quoi je me suis decidé non seulement à cause de son mérite, mais aussi par respect pour la recommendation & la témoinage, que vous avez rendu en sa faveur. Jusqu'ici il répond parfaitement à l'idée qu'en donne V. Exc: et je ne suis pas de tout surpris que Sa Majesté très fidèle l'ait honorée de son estime. Le bonheur qu'il a eu de mériter la bienveillance d'une princesse aussi vertueuse sera pour moi un motif bien puissant de le servir, en tout ce qui dependra de moi. Destiner dans cette partie de l'Amérique des prêtres vertueux & capables, est un des plus grands biens qu'on puisse faire ici à la Religion. Je ne scais qu'un qui lui soit superieure; et ce seroit l'établissement d'une maison d'éducation pour la jeunesse Catholique, qui deviendroit ensuite la sauvegarde de leur foi, et la pépinière des ministres du sanctuaire habitués aux usages, au génie, et au climat de ceux, parmi lesquels, ils auroient à travailler. Un tel etablissement devient d'autant plus nécessaire, que Sa Sainteté vient d'ériger un Siège Episcopal pour les Etats Unis, et de nommer pour premier Evêque de Baltimore celui, qui à l'honneur d'écrire à V. Excellence. Je travaille depuis quelques années à former ce collège, ou plutot cette ecole; car je n'ose le décorer du nom de Collège; tant mes vues sont bornées par notre insuffisance à accomplir l'objet de tous mes désirs. Je ne scaurois vous peindre, Mgr, tous les avantages, qui en resulteroient, dans un pais comme celuici, ou notre Religion jouit de toute liberté. Si j'osois mettre le projet de cet établissement, que j'ai l'honneur de vous envoyer avec cette lettre, sous les yeux de S.M. &

l'accompagner d'un mémoire, qui en expliqueroit l'objet et les avantages, je me flatte, qu'elle en deviendroit la protectrice & qu'elle trouveroit un doux plaisir à encourager un dessein, qui est calculé à réparer les pertes de la foi en tant d'autres pais par accroissement en cette partie du nouveau monde ou, jusqu'ici, elle a été presque inconnue.

Je me propose de partir pour l'Angleterre au mois prochain pour recevoir la consecration Episcopalle. Oserai-je prier V. Exc. de m'honorer d'une lettre, et de me marquer son sentiment sur ce que je viens d'écrire, & si ce seroit une imprudence de ma part de faire passer à Sa M.T.F. une supplique et mémoire rélatifs à l'établissement, dont il s'agit. Mon adresse à Londres sera à Monsr. Strickland, chez Messrs. Wright, Selby & Robinson, Banquiers, Henrietta Street, pour faire tenir à celui qui a l'honneur d'être avec le plus grand respect et dévouement De V. Exc. Mgr. &   J. C.   Baltre.   ce 23 d'Avril

TO MATTHEW CAREY   Baltre. April 28—1790—

Dear Sir   I am going to leave Baltimore, as soon as possible, I believe in two days—; I shall not however embark before the middle of May.[1] Agreeably to your request, I inclose you a list of those, who have not paid up; which list was made out for Mr. Stewart, before he declined going into the lower Counties. From this, you will see who have paid, at least so far as to the [*blank*—na] mes entered on my list. Since my last,[2] the four new subscribers are to be added—, whose names are the last in the inclosed paper. I find no moment of time to add a line for your museum, hardly enough to thank you for your useful note to the address, & for your good wishes in behalf of, Dr. Sir   Yr. most obedt. & faithful servt.   J Carroll

ALS   HSP
[1] For his consecration to the episcopacy in England.
[2] Apr., 1790.

TO THE CONGREGATION OF BOSTON   Baltimore April 30—1790

Gentlemen   I received last night a letter from Mr. Campbell,[1] informing me, that the whole Congregation was in the greatest disorder, from an apprehension, that Mr. Thayer would leave them; and that they had always considered Mr. Thayer as designed to be their pastor. I have written long ago to Mr. Rousselet to leave Boston, if he finds, that his services are useless; but I have had information, that his removal would be attended with the greatest inconvenience. Superiors generally wish to do the best; but they can not always do so, on account of the contradictory accounts sent them. This is my case. I shall be exceedingly sorry to give displeasure to any individual, & much more, to a great part of the Congregation. But if harmony & subsistance can not be had, without my appointing one Pastor, exclusively of the other, Mr. Rousselet must be nominated on account of prior residence, age, & in having been desired of me in the name of the Congregation to send him to Boston. Before I make the appointment, I must hear once more from Boston.

I must request you, Gentlemen to present my best respect to the Congregation, & to assure them of my sincere desire to serve them, & do every thing for them in the most agreeable manner. I should have gone immediately to visit them & be acquainted with them individually; but I am under the necessity of proceeding abroad for my consecration; & many reasons of general utility to the American Church induce me to prefer Europe for that purpose. If any unforeseen event should determine me for Canada,[2] I should certainly do myself the pleasure of visiting Boston. I earnestly recommend the general welfare of the Catholic Church, & myself in particular to the good prayers of them all, & pray them to be assured of my continual remembrance & sollicitude, earnestly beseeching, that since it has pleased divine providence to unite all parts of the United States under one Episcopacy, all would lay aside national distinctions & attachments, & strive to form not Irish, or English, or French Congregations & Churches, but Catholic-American Congregations & Churches. Yrs J. C.

ADf AAB To "Mason & Campbell" heads the letter, presumably trustees.
[1] Patrick Campbell, a blacksmith and later member of the committee to raise funds for the building of St. Patrick's Cathedral.
[2] Reference to the alternative of consecration at the hands of the Archbishop of Quebec.

TO JOHN THAYER   Baltimore Apr. 30–1790

Revd. Sir   Since my last[1] in answer to yours of the 8th. inst., business has detained me here, & given time for the receipt of a letter from Mr. Rousselet: and as I thought myself bound to write to him concerning those instances of his misconduct, which were alledged by you; I must do the same towards yourself. In the first place he asserts, & says he has witnesses to prove, that in a full committee you asserted, that you were the only pastor of the Boston Congregation, & that you formally declared to the French, that if I appointed another, you would put yourself under the immediate jurisdiction of the Holy See. 2ly that on Easter Sunday you told the Congregation, that it was the last time of your preaching, & was on your departure; but that as you made no preparation to go away, it appeared you did it only to cause a fermentation. 3ly, He relates the manner of his requesting you to begin mass sooner in a very different light from that, in which you placed it. 4ly. that every thing was happy & contented, & our religion respected, till you raised disturbances & uneasiness by your pretensions to Superiority, after your arrival.

Judge, my Dr. Sir, of the situation of a Superior, who has his decision to make with such contradictory information; & who wishes to make a just decision. I must wait an answer to the following matter. Mr. Rousselet having said, that he can make good, by witnesses, the first charge, I have given him notice, that I should advise you of it, that you may disprove his assertion, which is very repugnant to the declaration, which you proposed to be signed, as you wrote, If you really did make such an assertion, as you are accused of, (which is incredible to me) I need not tell you, in how bad & dangerous a light I view it. I beg this matter may be conducted with as much privacy, as it will admit, & with entire charity. I am   Yrs.   J.C.

ADfS   AAB
[1] Not found.

TO JOHN THAYER   Baltimore May 25, 1790

Rv. Sr.   By yr letters of may (dated April by mistake) 11 & 13 I was glad to receive yr. disavowal of yr. expressions of seeking independence wch. were imputed to you & renewed in a certificate dated yr. 9th Inst. of wch. here follows yr. copy. "Nous avons["] &c. The French Gentn. add that so far from professing to proceed to form regulations for ye. Church[1] in consequence of any proposal for yr. acknowledgement of my Authority[,] they have concurred in making yr. Regulations and signed with ye. other Wardens. Ye. 1st articles of wch they send a Copy, wch recognises very fully ye. Jurisdiction of the Bishop of ye. United States. Before I come to yr. point of decision allow me to mention one or two other circumstances of facts mentioned in yr. letters: viz. that Mr. Rousselet spent money in improper unnecessary purposes, yet neglected paying Mr. Campbell who could not afford being out of his money. This Mr. Rousselet absolutely denies & refers to Mr. Campbel for proof. You now inform me tht. ye. Majority of yr. Congt. say tht. they consented to Mr. Rousselets coming on ye. express condition that he should remain only till yr. arrival. To whom did they make this consent known? not certainly to me, to whom yr. name never was mentioned from Boston till yr. arrival that I remember, in any letter except from La Poterie or Mr. Rousselet. After La Poterie's departure, Mr. Campbell wrote to me stating their great distress for want of assistance, without wch. he feared yr. Congregation would be disbanded: but there was no such expression respecting you, as has been told you. And soon after Mr. [Bridry?] requested in behalf of yr. Congt. to have Mr. Rousselet, whom they had seen heared &c approved. You know that I never heared from you after March 17th till yr. arrival in Decr. & had almost dispaired of you: & could not therefore let yr. little beginnings at Boston be defeated, or request Mr. Rousselet to travel from Phila. to hold a place at Boston, perhaps only for a week or the month, if you should arrive soon. Had I conceived that yr. condition wch. is now pretended, was [annexed?] to his call to Boston, I would not have insulted him by a proposal of that place to him. You seem to reproach me for 1rst. [first] inviting you to America &c then exposing you to difficulties wch. do not necessarily arrise from a Missionary life. I surely invited you and still entreat you to share in ye. functions of an Apostolical life: but I never promised to visit you alone or even principally with Jurisdiction in Boston or elsewhere. You were much younger, both in age &c Priesthood than other Clergymen, who live subordinated to their Companions in ye. same house or town. Yr. Conversion however happy to yourself, edifying & advantagious to ye. Publick it might have been[,] could not be a sufficient reason for placing you over the head of such a Man as Mr. Rousselet; and to be candid with you I was not edified with yr. 1rst. letters asking superior authority, and rediculing his pronunciation. I assure you that observation made me perhaps ye more ready to credit his complaint of yr. assuming too much on yourself as soon as you reached Boston. You informed me that Mr. Le Tombes the Consul, wished me to write to him and that he would then give me exact information, but in his answer he says that being in a publick Character it does not become him to interfere. Mr. Rousselet has signified to me that he will with pleasure accept some other appointment; in Conseq[uence], I have made him a proposal which I believe he will accept. It is then in my power now to gratify yr. desire of those, whose petition I received with yr. last letter: And therefore as soon as Mr. Rousselet withdraws, which will be at ye. earliest convenience you will take ye. sole charge of ye. Congren. for the present. I say *for ye. present*, because that sole *final* appointment will depend on ye. talent of Conciliation wch. will manifest hereafter. The French tho' few in number are a very consequential part of yr. Congn. I expect they will be disgusted at Mr. Rousselet's departure. You must use every Condescension consistent with duty to regain their esteem &c affection. *Omnibus Omnia factus,*[1] was ye. Maxim of St. Paul, S. Fr. Sales, S. Fr. Xavier &c all ye. most successful Labourers in His Vineyard; follow their example. I see no cause or propriety in giving you at present any greater degree of Authority than you will possess when Mr. Rousselet withdraws; nor do I see what good you will be able to perform by being Vicar General over the New England States, wch. may not be done either by application when I am in my Diocese or to Mr. Pellentz, my Vicar Genl., in my absence, who will probably have for his Associate ye. Rd. Mr. Fleming. As I am extremely hurried, I hope you will excuse me from further particulars. I earnestly commend myself &c. J. Carroll

LS   AAB   Possibly a fair copy by Sewall.
    [1] "I became all things to all men."

STATEMENT ON JESUIT PROPERTIES   Baltimore May 26–1790

To prevent any disagreement or contention hereafter between the Bishop of Baltimore and his Clergy, or any of them in consequence of any words contained in his Holiness's brief for erecting the See of Baltimore &c; I hereby declare, that I do not conceive myself entitled by the said brief to claim any right of interference in the management of those estates in Maryland & Pennsylvania, which were heretofore applied to the maintenance of the Jesuit missioners; & since their extinction, to the Exjesuits, & other Clergymen admitted to partake of their Labour, in serving the Congregations, which were before served by the Jesuits.   J. Carroll

DS   MPA

TO THE TRUSTEES OF CHARLESTON   June [1790]

Gentlemen: I had the honour to receive with singular satisfaction yr letter dated Charleston Ap. 11. It could not fail of being highly agreeable to me to hear, that a prospect was opened of extending the blessings of true Religion to your flourishing town and state; and that Gentlemen of rank and education warmly and zealously interested themselves in realising so comfortable a prospect. Ever since I received my present appointment, the introduction into and the establishment of a Clergyman at Charleston has been an object very near my heart; but till I was honoured with yr. application a want of information, & multiplicity of other business did not allow me to pay to it that attention I have since given it. You may be assured, Gentlemen, that it shall ever continue to engage my earnest sollicitude; and that, if I live to see a rational ground of success I will do myself the pleasure of paying you my personal respects, both in discharge of my duty & to give consistency to yr. beginnings and every encouragement in my power. And since you have been pleased not only to inform me of your good intentions, but have condescended to sollicit my advice, I will give it freely, and without any other apology, than the occasion of giving it shall suggest.

If either of the Princes, you mention, really intend to support Chaplains for the use of their subjects residing in Charleston, it will be fortunate to have the exercise of our Religion introduced even by these means. But I cannot help expressing a wish that your Clergymen may be entirely independent of and unconnected with any foreign prince. For I conceive that their success & consequently the reputation of Religion will under the blessing of God greatly depend on this personal character, who are to begin the work of the ministry. Now Neither you, Gentlemen, or the Ecclesiastical Superior in these states, can effectually interpose in the appointment of Clergymen protected and supported by foreign Princes; and you know that Ecclesiastics who court the favour of principal or subordinate ministers, are not generally the most respectable of body. But if, as I fear, a sufficient fund cannot be raised to bear the first charges of introducing, nor a sufficient endowment made for the consequent subsistance of two Clergymen; in that case, the French & Spanish settlers with you might very consistently join in solliciting pecuniary help from their respective courts for compleating this purpose: But no consideration shall ever induce me to empower for the exercise of the ministry any Clergyman who shall not bring from their resp. Bishops unexceptionable testimonies of learning & morality & shall afterwards be approved by the Ecclesiastical Superior here. This latter condition is absolutely necessary to insure the honour and respect due to Religion for without it, we may have amongst us disorderly & scandalous Ecclesiastics.

You insinuate that some considerations may render it unadvisable for you to appear in this application, should it be necessary. I easily conceive the delicacy of your situation; and if you find no farther consideration, that your interference would be improper, the Inhabitants, French & Spanish may with propriety state their situation, & request the assistance of their respective princes, in which case it may be in my power to further the success of their request at the C[our]t of France; and by [*illeg.*] & intelligent Prelates in France, to [*illeg.*] You will [*illeg.*] to your preceding favour by informing me [*illeg.*] of the steps, which you will resolve on.

Permit me to make my sincere acknowledgements for your zeal in promoting the interests of Religion. The prejudices of many will, I hope, be overcome by your Christian lives & example; & by the assiduity, zeal, & virtues, of those whom God, I trust, is raising up for your spiritual help & consolation. I recommend to you all to join in your incessant supplications to the throne of mercy, that a proposal originating from so holy a motive may terminate in procuring that blessing to Carolina, which she so greatly wants. Not a Bishop [. . . .]

ADf   AAB   "To the gentlemen at Charleston," presumed to function as trustees. Date assigned is AAB archivist's notation.

TO LEONARDO ANTONELLI [July 1790]

Most Eminent Cardinal Antonelli (private)   In my other letter to you as head of the Congregation I set down what I considered worthy of note;[1] this I write non-officially. In the first place I want to thank you in a very special way not only for giving such attention to whatever pertains to the preserving and spread of the faith, but also for being so well disposed and so ready to grant whatever I wished. Because of your kindness I am touched and inclined to the highest regard, and, may I say, to a reverential affection. This increases my assurance in saying whatever appears to me appropriate for combating the prejudices of the heretics in our regard. But if in your opinion something should not have been said you will keep it to yourself and you will freely admonish me. Here is the first example of this trust, perhaps too a proof of my presumption. You know that hatred of Catholics was aroused in England and Ireland over the wording of the oath to be taken by bishops, and this is the subject of discussion in many parts of the United States.[2] You also know, what I have often observed, what perfect liberty Catholics enjoy almost everywhere in these provinces; and how much they detest there all species [of discord] derived from every kind of vexation because of differences of religion. That is why I am so eager to build a school for Catholic youths, whence those destined to serve in the clerical militia can go to the seminary. With God's help I shall take pains that they are instructed in these essential and fundamental doctrines, and aroused to most earnest endeavor to preserve unity. Meanwhile I grieve that in the past I do not say priests but truly qualified priests have been so few that I have been constrained to accept for the ministry men who have imbibed incongruous doctrines on the authority of the laity, particularly in some German universities. Because of this, when a few months ago, I was informed that the archiepiscopal seminary in Mainz offered to educate gratis for the priesthood some young men from America I decided to decline the offer till I knew more about their theological views. I write this as I sail for England to receive episcopal consecration either there or in one of the provinces of Belgium. [*illegible*] to visit the stations of the diocese in person [*illegible*] are miles apart, and sometimes untold miles from the nearest neighbor.

ADf   AAB
[1] See following item.
[2] See Oct. 23, 1789.

Alteris literis tibi, Eme. Card., tamquam Sacrae Congregationis prefecto, quae dicenda videbantur significavi; has autem privato nomine dandas existimavi, imprimis ut speciali quadam ratione gratias tibi referem, non solum quod operae tantum et studii collocaveris in illis negotiis transigendis quibus fidei apud nos conservationi et incremento consulitur, sed etiam, quod animo ita benevolo illa omnia concesseris, ac paratum denuo concedere te exhibeas, quaecumque fieri desideravi. Hac tua benevolentia accendi me sentio et animari ad summam erga te observantiam, et si dicere liceat, ad amorem reverentialem, et venerationem; unde fiet ut plurimum in me augeatur fiducia libere dicendi quaecunque mihi opportuna occurunt ad tollenda heterodoxorum adversum nos praejudicia quae tamen si tibi Em. Card. videbuntur a me non dicenda fuisse, silentio premes, meque libere commonefacias. En primum hujus meae fiduciae, sive audaciae argumentum! Notum tibi est quantam in Catholicos invidiam conflaverint nuper in Anglia et Hibernia illa verba Juramenti ab episcopis praestandi, et de quibus etiam multus in foederatae Americae provinciis sermo [*ind.*] —Notum tibi est etiam, et a me saepe commemoratum quam perfecta libertate Catholici ferre ubique in his provinciis gaudeant; quamque multum ois generis [*ind.*] ibi abhorreant ab omni generi vexaois propter Religionum discrepantiam. Quod vehementi studio accendar scholae conficiendae pro Catholicae juventutis educatione, ex qua in seminarium instituendum admitti poterint, qui clericali militiae destinantur. Ita enim, favente Deo, illos instrui curabo, ut hac religionis Catholicae summa et capitali doctrina penitus instruantur, atque conservandae unitatis studio vehementer inflammentur. Interim satis nequeo dolere ita hucusque non dicam sacerdotes, idoneos sacerdotes defuisse, ut quosdam in ministerii societatem assiscere compulsus fuerim, qui nescio quid incongrui circa populi auctoritatem ex quibusdam, in Germania maxime, universitatibus hauserint; indeque factum est, ut cum paucis ante mensibus indicatum mihi est, in Moguntino seminario archiepiscopali quibuscum ex America adolescentibus permissum iri, ut gratis ad officia clericalia informarentur, tamen declinandum id prorsus judicavi, donec accuratius de theologicis ipsorum placitis ignovissem. Hoc scribo in navigatione, Angliam versus ut ibi aut in finitimis Belgiae provinciis episcopali characere insignaur. [*illeg.*] dioceseos stationes per me ipsum invisere quippe [*illeg.*] passuum millibus a se invicem distant, atque aliquando ad minimum sexcentis millibus sibi a praemiore esse remotas.

LEONARDO ANTONELLI   July—On the high sea. [1790]

Most Eminent and Reverend Lord   When I received the letter of Your Eminence written November 14 of last year I could not but be greatly moved even though it contained nothing that I did not expect. As I appraise myself, and compare my known defects with the holiness of life and the greatness of the burden which the episcopal character implies, I almost lose heart. And especially when I reflect how religion could be and should be advanced by a vigilant and holy bishop I yearn for the required qualifications, in particular for constancy and courage. Unless I be sustained beyond my merits by divine grace, I should not even begin to hope to answer the expectations and good opinion entertained of me by you, most eminent Cardinal, and the entire Sacred Congregation. To be sure, your benevolence towards me, and that of the Sacred Congregation, as expressed in your letter, will be a spur to the discharge of my office, which I feel binds me to you by the closest bonds of obedience and respect. Will you please inform the reverend fathers of my sentiments, and will you say to the Holy Father that in the new dignity with which he has clothed me despite my unworthiness I shall hold nothing more sacred than the laying of the most solid and enduring foundation not merely of union with the Holy See but also of conformity, obedience and love? For daily experience teaches me that faith and morals are kept intact if there is a close union with Christ's vicar on earth, and that nearly every lapse in either originates in a diminution of respect for the See of Peter. Hence, I am consumed with the desire to complete as soon as possible the school for the education of Catholic youth. From this school those who are called by God to the sanctuary may pass to the seminary to be built. With God's help I shall take pains that they be schooled in the belief that unity of faith cannot endure apart from the authority of the Holy See. Meanwhile I lament that I lack, I do not say priests but suitable priests, in sufficient number, with the consequence that I feel constrained to admit some to the ministry from certain states in Germany who have introduced a new manner of thought and speech among our people. This is why when I was told some months ago that in the archiepiscopal seminary at Mainz a few Americans could be trained for the priesthood I thought it best to do nothing until I could learn more precisely what their theological opinions were.

I write this as I sail for England or the neighboring province of Belgium to receive episcopal consecration. After a stay of about a month in Europe I shall sail again. And if God wills to bring me back safe to my diocese, I shall, as far as in me lies, attempt to carry out whatever you may enjoin, but I know that I cannot in person visit all of the stations in this very extensive diocese, for some of them are at least six hundred miles distant.

I told you of the arrival of Rev. Mr. John Thayer and of his mission in Boston. When I left America there was dissension there because one group of parishioners wished to retain Mr. Thayer while another preferred his predecessor, likewise a very gifted and proper man. Both groups realize that they are unable to support two priests. While I am in Europe I expect to learn the issue of this controversy.

For some time I have wished that the sum of two hundred gold pieces might be delivered to Mr. Thorpe, who will be informed by me how that amount may be applied to its destined use. (Three years ago the Sacred Congregation in its liberality assigned the yearly sum of two hundred gold pieces for a period of three years.) Perhaps it would not be burdensome to pay the full amount now in one installment. This would be most opportune and it would greatly expedite the opening of the school. If Mr. Thorpe does not wish to engage in this transaction perhaps he could indicate how it could be done through the help of a certain merchant in Leghorn.

London July 30   Eight days ago I arrived safely in this place. While I make preparations for the reception of the office of bishop I hear, Eminent Cardinal, that some complaints have been lodged against me with the Sacred Congregation in the name of a certain French priest, La Poterie. Moreover, a booklet teeming with charges, written by him or someone else, pictures me as overly severe on most of the priests, but partial to those who at one time were members of the same institute as I. In public, and in private correspondence, La Poterie has heaped accusations on me and on others as well. Nevertheless nobody ever replied to him nor did I believe that a man so infamous would be so audacious as to bring his calumnies before the Sacred Congregation. Had I foreseen this some official documents left in America would have been sent to you, most eminent Cardinal, and from them it would have been plain that he was a man notorious for his many defects in faith and conduct, one expelled from various French seminaries and other places, one who, abounding in deceit, wandered through many provinces of Europe. These documents signed by a clergyman, Mr. de la Blancherie (unless through lapse of memory I mistake the name) were sent to America by the vicar general of the diocese of Blois. Because of his deceitful conduct La Poterie was unable to settle anywhere in Europe. He came to Boston and contacted me through a letter which seemed to breathe a truly apostolic spirit. Although I had resolved to accept no priest for the ministry who did not submit proper credentials, when he wrote two or three times he finally induced me to grant him certain temporary faculties until I could have more reliable assurances of him. This matter I made known to you, eminent Cardinal, in a letter written two years ago unless I am mistaken.[1] A few months had hardly passed when grave accusations began to be made, and when he knew of them I commended him to Rev. Fr. William O'Brien, of the Order of Preachers, the pastor in New York. But he was found to be guilty of many things that would discredit a man and make him most infamous. For these reasons I withdrew all faculties, but he boldly and sacriligeously continued to exercise the ministry, until, burdened with debts and the object of the contempt of all, he left America.

Should any member of the Sacred Congregation desire further information on this subject after my return to America I shall submit documents which will dispel all doubt. If anything of like tenor should be advanced by anyone (a certain Irish priest[2] upon returning from America broadcast many outrageous falsehoods) and the Sacred Congregation thinks it requires refutation it will not be difficult to do so. Meanwhile I pray the Sacred Congregation not to suffer their good opinion of me to be destroyed by calumny.

To this end in fullest trust and all proper respect   there commends himself to you   Your most obedient and devoted servant   John, Bishop elect of Baltimore.

ALS   PF   Portion under date of July 30 also has ADf   AAB.
[1] Not found.
[2] Patrick Smyth.

Mense Julio, in mari.   Emintissime ac Reverendissime Domine—   Ubi primum redditae mihi sunt literae Emae Domini Tuae scriptae die 14 Novembris anni praeteriti, etsi nihil non expectatum nuntiaverint, tamen non potui non vehementer commoveri. Meipsum enim de novo aestimans, conferensque illos, quos in me sentio defectus cum Epoalis characteris sanctitate et immensa sollicitudine, animo paene deficio; cumque sentio magna pro Religionis incremento fieri et debere et posse a vigili, sanctoque Pontifice, in meipso tamen nearias dotes, ac paecipue constantiam et fortitudinem desidero. Unde spei ac praeconceptae de me opinioni Tuae, Eme. Card:, totiusque Sacrae Congaois responsurum me longissime abest ut audeam sperare, nisi singulari ac praeter omne meum meritum divinae gratiae ope sustenter. Certe magnos mihi stimulos adjiciet ad ministerium meum perficiendum singularis tuae et Sacrae Congaois in me benevolentia, quam illis verbis significasti, ut arctissmo me vobis obsequii et venerationis vinculo constringi sentiam. Dum hae Ementissimis illis Patribus nomine meo notum facere dignatus fueris, ut emssmo D.N. dicere velis, me in hac nova dignitate, qua me immerentem prorsus decorare voluit, nihil habiturum sanctius quam ut fundamenta jaciam solidissimae ac perpetuae, non unionis tantum cum Sede Apostolica, sed etiam observantiae, obsequii et amoris. Doceor enim quotidiana experientia ita maxime fidem et illibatos mores conservari, si cum Christi in terris Vicario arcta fuerit conjuctio: ac omnem fere ab utriusque defectionem inde initium sumere, quod debita erga Petri cathedram observantia subtrahatur. Hinc fit, ut ardenti studio inflammer scholae inceptae quam primum perficiendae pro Catholicae juventutis educatione, ex qua in futurum Seminarium transire valeant, quos Deus ad Sanctuarii ministerium vocaverit. Ita enim in hoc, favente deo, illos instrui curabo, ut plane intelligant fidei unitatem sine Sedia Apostolicae auctoritate consistere non posse. Interim moleste fero, non dicam Sacerdotes, sed idoneos Sacerdotes sufficienti numero deesse, ut quasi compelli me sentiam ad quosdam suscipiendos in ministerii Societatem, qui in hac materia ex quibusdam in Germania provinciis novam sentiendi et loquendi rationem inter Catholicos nostrates invexerunt. Inde factum est, ut cum ante aliquot menses dictum mihi esset in Moguntino Seminario Archiepiscopali gratis adolescentes paucos Americanos ad vitam clericalem institui posse, nihil statim statuendum existimaverim, donec accuratius de Thelogicis placitis cognovissem.

Haec scribo in ipsa navigatione versus Angliam, ut in ea, aut finitissimis Belgii provinciis charactere Episcopali insigniar. Post unius circiter mensis in Europa comoram, rursus me mari committam; et si Deo visum fuerit me salvum Dioecesi meae restituere, quae a te praescripta sunt, quantum fieri poterit, exsequi conabor, incertus tamen de omnibus vastae dioceseos stationibus per me ipsum invisendis; quippe aliquae a sibi proximioribus ad minimum sexcentis passuum milibus distant.

Iam prius significavi de adventu Revdi. Dom. Joannis Thayer, ejusq ad urbem Bostoniae missione. Cum ex America solverem, res in illa statione non erant ita tranquillae; dum una pars Congregationis Dom. Thayer, altera illius praedecessorem, qui etiam optimis moribus praeditus est, retinere cupit; atque utrimque conveniunt non posse duos Sacerdotes a se sustentari. De hujus controversiae exitu in Europa doceri expecto.

Iam pridem desideravi ut summa ducentorum aureorum (nam biennium est, ex quo Sae Congnis liberalitas centum aureos in singulos per triennium annos concessit) Revdo. Dom. Joanni Thorpe solvi posset, qui a me docebitur, qua ratione ad usum destinatum transmitti queant. Fortasse, incommodum modo non esset, ut integra summa trecentorum aureorum simul solvatur, quod valde in praesens opportunum, et ad scholam citius aperiendam multum conferret. Si Dominus Thorpe hujus negotio imminere non dediderat, poterit fortasse indicare, quo ratione transigi possit, ope mercatorii cujusdam Liburnensis.

Londini die 30 Julii. Ante octo dies huc tuto appulsus sum, dum me comparo ad consecrationis Episcopalis suscipiendum characterem, audio, Em. Cardinalis, delatas fuisse ad Sacram Congregationem quasdam adversus me querelas, nomine cujusdam Sacerdotis Galli, cui nomen est La Poterie, et libellum quendam plenum accusationis ab ipso vel alio aliquo conscriptum; in quibus insimulor quasi iniquior in plures Sacerdotes, et quasi unice favere illis, qui ejusdem mecum quondam fuerint instituti. Saepe quidem iste La Poterie literis privatis et publicis multas injurias in me, aliosque congessit; nemo tamen ipsi quidquam respondit, neque credidi virum adeo infamem illuc processurum audaciae, ut calumias suas ad Sacrae Congnis aures deferret. Hoc si praevidissem monumenta quaedam authentica jam in America derelicta, ad te, Eme Cardlis, transmissa fuissent, ex quibus illud constaret virum, omnibus contra fidem et mores notatum, ex pluribus in Gallia Seminariis et alliis locis ejectum, multas Europae provincias, fraudibus plenum, peragravisse. Hae authenticis literis consignata a Revdo viro, Dom. de la Blancherie (nisi per lapsum memoriae nomine fallor) Vicario Generali Episcopi Blesensis in Americam transmissa sunt. Cum nullibi in Europa ob continuas fraudes subsistere posset, Bostoniam appulit, et literis quae spiritum plane Apostolicum praeferre videbantur, me convenit; quibus bis terve repetitis ita tandem me movit, ut, cum antea statuissem nullos ad ministerii Societatem admittere Sacerdotes, qui certa pro se documenta non subministrarent, ipsi tamen ad breve tempus, donec de ipso certius cognoscerem, facultatas aliquas concesserim. Hac de re significavi Tibi, Eme. Cardinalis, literis ante biennium scriptis, ni fallor. Vix elapsi sunt pauci menses, cum graves in eum accusationes insurrexerunt, de quibus et cognosceret, commendavi Revdo. Patri Gulielmo O'Brien, Ordinis Predicatorum, Pastori Neo-Eboracensi. Multa in eo comperta sunt, quae vel infimae sortis virum omni infamia notavissent. Quare omnes ipsi facultates subtraxi; ipse tamen audacter et sacrilege sacra ministeria obire perrexit, donec aere alieno et omnium contemptu gravatus America discessit.

Si quis Emus Cardinalis ex Sacra Congne aliquid de hac re ulterius audire cupit, redux in Americam monumenta subministrabo quae omnem tollent dubitationem. Aut si quid aliud similis tenoris ab allis fuerit collatum (*multa enim insigniter falsa in vulgus jactitavit Sacerdos quidam Hibernus, ex America redux*), quod egere refutatione Sacra Congregao existimaverit, id quidem luculente praestare grave non erit. Interim illam precor, ne bonam suam de me opinionem mihi per calumniam eripi patiatur.

In hunc effectum magna fiducia se tibi cum omni debita veneratione commendat, Eminentissime Cardinalis, Servus obsequentissimus et devotissimus Joannes Epus Baltim. Elec.

TO JOHN TROY London, July 23rd, [1790,]
No. 28 King-street, Bloomsbury.

My Lord, I was favoured with your Grace's most obliging letters of January 25th, about two months ago, and would have sooner acknowledged the honour done to me, had I not been in daily expectation of setting out for Europe, which, however, was not in my power before June 9th. I am now on my voyage to England for consecration. When the subject of an American Bishopric was first started, I received so pressing an invitation from a most respectable Catholic gentleman in England, that I unwarily promised to be consecrated in his chapel if the appointment should fall to my lot. Had it been otherwise, I should have hesitated between Ireland, the land of my forefathers, and Canada, though, on the whole, I flatter myself that my going to England may be attended with some advantages to the cause of religion within my extensive diocese.

It is probable that I shall hear much on the subject of the oath when I am in England—hitherto I have never seen it, though I have heard of the disagreement amongst the VV.AA. [Vicars Apostolic] I shall be very cautious in forming, and more so in uttering, any opinions whilst I am there.

I shall pay every attention to the subject mentioned in your Grace's separate letter.

I am happy to inform you that Messrs. Fleming, whom I have placed in Philadelphia, and Burke,[1] who supplies Mr. O'Brien's absence in New York, give general satisfaction. The former unites all those talents which conciliate esteem and love, and serve for the most useful purposes. The latter is moral, assiduous, and disinterested. Another of your brethren in religion, Mr. Keating, from Lisbon, was just arrived when I left Baltimore. He is much commended by Mr. Fleming, and will be fixed near Philadelphia.

Mr. O'Brien has been to the Havanna, is gone to La Vera Cruz, and in his last letter from the former place, informs me of his intention to cross the Isthmus of Panama, go to Acapulco, Lima, etc., and return to New York in 1793, when he hopes to have collected sufficient to pay off their debts in New York, and finish their church.

I have the honour to be, with the greatest veneration,   My Lord,   Your Grace's most obedient servant,   J. Carroll.

L Moran, III, 507-08.
[1] Nicholas Bourke, who ministered in New York and New Jersey. Probably came from Ireland in the 1780's.

TO ROBERT PETRE   London, August 31, 1790

My Lord: On my return to London last Saturday evening, I was informed that your Lordship had been pleased to honour me, by calling at my lodgings during my absence. I am exceedingly sorry, that your actual residence in the Country puts it out of my power to present my most humble respects, & make my acknowledgments to your Lordship for the honour done me. Perhaps some opportunity may yet be offered, during my short stay in England, of presenting myself before your Lordship. I am anxious to lay open to a Nobleman, who interests himself so warmly in the cause of Religion, its present state in a country, which was once intimately connected with, & still retains a great attachment to this. Your Lordship is sollicitous to see Catholics emancipated from the cruel bondage, under which they have been long held here; and no equitable government, I may add, no Government, which has risen superior to the mean and despicable prejudices of a narrow & interested education, will support the policy of that bondage, after they know the justice and political advantages of not only a free toleration, but of extending equal rights to the professor of all religions. The daily advantages arising to America from this policy should be a lesson to Britain, which in other instances of law, government, trade &c furnishes so many useful instructions to us.

I beg your Lordship to excuse the freedom & length of this, which has been extracted from me by the importance of the subject, as well as by it dwelling almost continually on my mind.

May I presume to offer my humble respects to Lady Petre, & to add, that I have the honour to be with the utmost veneration, My Lord,   Yr. Lordsps. most devoted & obedt. St.   J. Carroll

ADfS   AAB

TO RALPH HOSKINS   [Sep., 1790]

Not found. See Sep. 7, 1790.

TO SIR JOHN WEB   [Sep., 1790]

Not found. See Sep. 13, 1790.

TO CHARLES PLOWDEN   King's Street Sepr. 2—1790

My Dear Sir   Many thanks for yours of Aug. 31st, and for your sollicitude, that I should clear myself to Cardl. Antonelli from the calumnies of Smyth's pamphlet; I rather suspect, that La Poterie has caused his forgeries to fall into the Cardls hands. Coghlan brought me to day some of that vile mans performances; not against me; but some that he foolishly published concerning himself, on his first coming to Boston; and a sort of pastoral instruction which he had the temerity & folly to publish there before the lent of 1788. I shall give Cardl. Antonelli very satisfactory reasons for coming to England. Neither the president of Doway, nor Mr. Wm. Meynell[1] are yet come to town; nor even Mr. Thos. Meynell. There is great inconsistency in the objections, which some make, not to the truth of your doctrine respecting

the Pope's infallibility, but the policy of asserting it in print at this time.
They say, with Mr. Reeve that the English generally understand, that by
infallibility we mean to assert the Popes infallible prerogative in all orders he
issues, or facts, which he asserts. Now if this be true, where is the impolicy of
your asserting that the pope has no such infallibility, but only in doctrinal
points. To obviate this observation which I made yesterday to Mr Chs.
Butler,[2] he said, contrary to your other opponents, that the English not only
object to the popes infallibility in giving orders & stating facts (an infallibility
asserted by no one) but likewise consider his doctrinal infallibility as a
pernicious tenet, & dangerous to civil government.

I have a letter from the Nuncio at Paris, and another from Monsr. Emery,
Superior Genl. of the Seminary of St Sulpice. They both sollicit my passage
to Paris to confer with some Gentlemen of the Seminary, who wish to
employ in the rearing of young Clergymen in America, that experience, which
is now made useless by the revolution in their own Country. They offer to
bestow their services *gratis.* We certainly are not ripe for a Seminary: it will
take some years, before we shall have scholars far enough advanced to profit
by this generous offer. I shall decline therefore going to Paris, till I hear from
them in answer to the letter, I shall send to morrow. On Saturday, I propose
going to Bury for two days. Mr. Talbot says, I must go to secure a handsome
donation to the academy, which will be bestowed on no other condition. This
consideration apart, how much more pleasure would I have in visiting Lullworth?

Our academy, from its situation, will probably be conspicuous. The great
object is, to procure for it an eminent President & good Masters. My letters
from America as well as the public prints, inform me that the district, now
settled for the future capital of the United States, & permanent resident of
Congress, is on Patowmack river. Commissioners under the direction of the
President are to determine the particular spot, in a district of about 50 miles,
lying on that river. The knowledge, I have of the Country, makes me
confident, it will be either at George town, or, what would answer better for
our school within four miles of it. My poor Nephew Danl. Carroll, whom you
knew, is dead; pray for him. I know not, when I shall be able to execute my
promise relative to your book on infallibility.[3] Interruptions of company,
letters, long dinners &c take up my whole time. I cannot yet determine the
time of my repeating my visit to you, or whether I can repeat it at all. Affairs
at Boston demand my return to America. I have received from the two priests
there mutual charges & recriminations.[4] I let Coghlan copy the preamble of
the bull.[5] I have marked a passage or two, which I would have omitted: the
1st is, that a state cannot be safe in which new & various doctrines are
permitted to range (which is contrary to the maxim of our policy & of our
experience in America): the other is, *pro hac vice tantum;*[6] a clause I wish to

keep from the knowledge and notice of our rulers; & which probably will be altered. I think there is in the latter part another clause of the same import.

When I write next to Lullworth I shall presume that Mr. Weld is returned, & shall do myself the pleasure of acknowledging his great politeness & still greater kindness. My affectionate compliments to Mr. Clinton & the young family with you. I am, My Dr. Sir,   Yr. ever affte friend & servt   J Carroll

ALS   St; T   MPA

[1] Thomas Meynell, S.J., was at this time concerned with providing for exiled Catholic priests. William, a secular priest, was Carroll's agent in Rome.

[2] Charles Butler led the Catholic committees after the Relief Act of 1788, but Carroll thought he was inclined to be less firm than desirable with the British government.

[3] *Considerations on the Modern Opinion of the Fallibility of the Holy See in the Decision of Dogmatical Questions with an Appendix on the Appointment of Bishops* (London, 1790).

[4] The Thayer-Rousselet Controversy.

[5] *Ex Hac Apostolicae*

[6] "For this first time only." Carroll feared that this implies that Rome will select the applicant for episcopacy. The early part of this sentence goes beyond the literal expression of the bull on church and state, expressing fear at the implications of passages, which may not have been published. See to Plowden, Sep. 7, 1790.

TO ANTOINE DUGNANI   September [3,] 1790

My Lord   I reproach myself that your Excellency has been apprised of my arrival in England by another voice than my own. Occupied since the moment of my landing by preparations for my consecration, I have neglected an obligation I owed to Your Excellency. I had only returned to London, after having received the episcopal consecration at the chapel of the castle of Lullworth, belonging to one of the most illustrious Catholics of England, when I had the honor to receive your letter of the 24th of August. From the moment there was any question of naming me to the episcopacy, I proposed to go to France to receive consecration there; and it would be from the hands of Your Excellency that I would have wished to request it. But, some months before my departure from America, the troubles of France were described to us as so frightful that I believed Your Excellency would no longer be there and it was then that, only after a long delay, I agreed finally to the pressing invitations which came to me from England. I confess in certain regards to be sorry that I did not keep to my first intention; I would have had the advantage and the honor of presenting to Your Excellency my very humble respects, and of talking of knowledge relating to the duties and usages of my present rank of which I am completely lacking. I am writing to the Superior of St. Sulpice[1] that the arrangements which remain for me to make before my departure (which will be in the course of this month) will not allow me to go to Paris before this time. But I wish so much to profit from my nearness to

Your Excellency that if I should find it possible towards the end of next week, I will not fail to take advantage of a few days [*blank*]. I write with some detail to the Superior General of the Seminary on the principal subject of Your Excellency's letter. If our seminary were already on foot, or even if it had young men educated enough to begin the studies and the practices of the ecclesiastical life, I would regard the offer, generous, disinterested and full of zeal, which the gentlemen of St. Sulpice have made, as one of the great strokes of providence towards my immense diocese. Yet even so, the gentlemen may be able to render to Religion signal services, in embracing the proposition which I have made to the Superior, and of which he will inform Your Excellency.

I shall await with much anxiety his letters in response to my proposition; and in case the purpose seems to merit the attention of the members of his company, I would propose to settle all in the conferences which [. . . .]

ADf   AAB   On exact date see To Plowden, Sep. 2, 1790.
¹ Sep. 3, 1790. There may have been previous letters.

(Le Nonce a Paris—   Bishop of Rhodes)   Mgr   J'ai des reproches à me faire de ce que votre Excellence a eté instruite de mon arrivée en Angleterre par une autre voye, que par moi même. Occupé depuis la moment de mon debarquement des preparatifs pour ma consecration, j'ai negligé un devoir que je devois à V. Exc. Je ne faisois que de retourner à Londres, apres avoir reçu la consecration Episcopale à la chapelle du chateau de Lullworth, appartenant à un des plus illustres Catholiques d'Angleterre, quand j'ai eu l'honneur de recevoir votre lettre du 24d'Aout. Du moment, qu'il s'agissoit de me nommer à l'episcopat, je me suis proposé de passer en France pour y reçevoir la consecration; et c'est fut des mains de V. Exc. que j'aurois voulu la solliciter. Mais, quelques mois avant mon depart de l'Amerique, les troubles de la France nous etoient peints si affreux que j'ai cru, que V. Exc. probablement n'y seroit plus et c'est fut alors qu'apres avoir longtems differé, j'ai consenti enfin aux invitations pressantes, qui me sont venues de l'Angleterre. J'ai lieu à certains egards de regretter, que je ne me suis pas tenu à mon 1er dessein; j'eusse eu l'avantage et l'honneur de presenter à V. Exc. mes tres humbles respects, et de puiser bien des connoissances, relativemt aux devoirs et usages de mon etat actuel qui me manquent absolument. Je viens d'ecrire à Monsr le Supe[rieur] de S. Sulpice, que les arrangemens qui me reste à faire avant mon depart (qui sera dans le cours de ce mois) ne me permettront pas de passer à Paris avant ce terme. Mais je desire tant profiter du mon voisinage à V. Exc. que si je le trouverois possible vers la fin de la semaine prochaine, je ne manqueroi pas de profiter de peu de jours de [*blank*]. J'ecris avec quelque detail à Monsr le Supr. Genl du Seminair per l'objet principal de la lettre de V. Exc. Si notre seminaire etoit deja sur pied, ou même, s'il y avoit une jeunesse assez instruite pour commencer les etudes et les exercices de la vie Ecclesiastique, je regarderois l'offre genereuse, desinteressée et pleine de zele, que font Messrs de St. Sulpice, comme un des grands traits de la providence envers mon immense diocese. Encore même, les messieurs pourroient-ils rendre à la Religion des services signalés, en embrassant la proposition que j'ai fait à Monsr. le Superieur, et de laquelle il instruira V. Exc.

J'attendrai avec bien d'inquietude ses lettres en reponse à ma proposition; et au cas que l'objet paroisse meriter l'attention des membres de sa compagnie, je me proposerai de tout regler dans les conferences que [. . . .]

TO JAMES EMERY[1]   [Sep. 3, 1790]

Having returned to London after an absence of three weeks, I found myself honored by your letter dated August 25th. I saw in it, with the greatest outpouring of goodheartedness, the desire of the respectable Ecclesiastics of your house to extend the kingdom of J.C. in the diocese which is in my trust. I will consider myself extremely happy, if, having considered the state of our present situation, of which I will inform you, you judge that these gentlemen could contribute to the goal which they have in mind.

Up till now we have no seminary. For three or four years I have been applying myself to the founding of an establishment for the education of the Catholic Youth in the dictates and principles of our religion. This literary establishment is just about to be opened for receiving of the young. Their education was not my principal goal, when I conceived the idea for it. I had the intention of training students for an ecclesiastical seminary, which will be under preparation while the youngsters complete their first studies. The fact is that it is in this seminary that the experience and zeal of the gentlemen from St. Sulpice would be of greatest use. But before these future seminarians would be able to profit by their instructions, what will these gentlemen be able to occupy themselves with, since they do not know the language of the country. [?]

Furthermore, will the number of seminarians be considerable enough, for quite a long time to come, in order to occupy more than two or three learned and virtuous Ecclesiastics? Nevertheless, I would very much regret not being able to profit from the good will of the virtuous members of your house. I would hope for the benediction of Heaven upon my diocese for their cooperation, and I would learn from this some matters relative to my duty. Here is something which would perhaps interest them while waiting for the formation of the Seminary. Before the dismembering of the diocese of Quebec etc.

Prior to this review, you will be able to judge, if there is need for a conference. In that case, it would be with great pleasure and interest that I would see a member of your illustrious company. I am planning to go back to America some time this month, and a thousand matters concerning Religion are keeping me in England. When the matter arose of my being made a bishop, my first intention was to be consecrated in France, and to ask Mgr. Nuncio to perform the imposition of hands. But before leaving America, public affairs presented in such awful colors the anarchy in France, that I accepted, after many delays, the pressing invitations, which I received from England. Gratitude for the offer of his house.

ADf   SMS   Dated in reference to Carroll's letter to Dugnani Sep. [3], 1790; and Ruane, p. 26. Considerable amount of crossed-out remarks.
[1] Superior General of the Sulpicians, he resided at Paris at this time.

Etant revenu à Londres depuis une absence de trois semaines, Je me suis trouvé honoré de votre lettre du 25 d'aout. J'y ai vu, avec le plus grand épanchement de coeur [?], le desir des ecclesiastiques respectables de votre maison de contribuer à etendre le regne de J.C. dans le diocese [*illeg.*] qui m'est confié. Je m'estimerai infiniment heureux, si, d'aprés l'état que je vous ferai de notre situation actuelle, vous jugerex que ces messieurs puissent contribuer à l'objet, qu'ils ont en vue.

Jusqu'à ce jour n'y avons point de Seminaire. Depuis trois ou quatre ans je travaille a former un établissement pour l'education de la jeunesse Catholique dans les lettre et les principes de la Religion. Cet établissement litéraire est sur le point de s'ouvrir pour la reception de la jeunesse. Leur instruction ne fut pas mon objet principal, quand j'en ai concu l'idée. Je me suis proposé d'y former des élèves pour un seminaire ecclesiastique, qui se preparera, pendant que la jeunesse, fera ses premieres etudes. Or c'est dans ce seminaire, que seroit sur tout utile l'experience & zele des Messieurs de St. Sulpice. Mais avant que les futurs seminaristes seraient en état de profiter de leur instruction, à quoi ces messieurs, ne sachant pas la langue du pais pourront ils s'occuper?

D'ailleurs, le nombre de Seminaristes sera-t-il assez considerable, pour bien de tems [?] à venir, pour occuper plus de deux ou trois Ecclesiastiques instruits & vertueux? Cependant, j'aurois un très grand regret de ne point profiter de la bonne volonté de membres vertueux de votre maison. J'espererois de leur cooperation la benediction du ciel sur mon diocese, & j'apprend Rois de ça des choses relatives à mon devoir. Voiçi peutêtre un objet qui les interesserait en attendant la formation du Seminaire. Avant le demembrement du diocese de Quebec. &c.

Avant cet exposé, vous serez en état de juger, s'il y a lieu à une conferençe. En ce cas, je verrois içi avec grand plaisir et interest quelque membre de votre illustre compagnie. Je me propose de repasser en Amerique dans le cours de çe mois, & mille affaires concernant la Religion me retiennent en Angleterre. Quand il sagissoit de m'élever à l'episcopat, mon premier dessein étoit de me faire consacrer en France, & de prier Mgr. le Nonce de m'imposer les mains. Mais, avant que de partir de l'Amerique, les relations publiques presentoient en des couleurs si affreuses l'anarchie de la France, que j'ai consenti, après bien des delais, aux invitations pressantes, qu'on me fit en Angleterre. Remercimens pour l'offre de sa maison.

TO CHARLES PLOWDEN London Sep. 7–1790–

My dearest Sir— I returned from Bury this evening by the way of Cambridge (where I staid abt. an hour & half) & found here your agreeable favr. of the 5th. I have no reason to repent & much to exult in the success of my journey. Mr. Gage–£25–Messrs Thomson, Lane, & Beeston ten guineas each; 20 guineas more from a person, who will be *incognita;* & other benefactions to the amount of abt £85–Mr. Hoskins has undertaken Sr. John Lawson, & Mr. Thomson informs me, that he has obtained a generous benefaction; tho I have yet recd. no letter from Mr. Hoskins in answer to mine to him from Wardour.[1] I certainly will give warning to Coghlan tomorrow not to print any account of the transactions of the 15th. Aug. at Lullworth. It would be as disagreeable, as possible to me; and very disrespectful to Mr. Weld. I never knew that Coghlan had any thoughts of it, till yours came to hand. The bull he has mentioned—At your request, I consented to have part of it printed, & allowed him, since my return from you a copy of the preamble to the bull. I noted certain passages, which should not be printed. I heard of the intention of printing your discourse, one day before publication: & supposed you were privy to the design.

I dined with Mr. Chs. Butler the day before I left town. He told me two or three fresh pieces, *sur les affairs du Lewis* were under press. He neither mentioned their authors, or their principles. I presume our friend Mr. Reeve's was one of them.[2]

The letter you inclosed is from Mr. Sewall of Baltimore. The nuns were arrived at N. York.[3] Charles Neale had sailed with them again in a packet for the Chesapeak. Mr. Plunkett went by land from N. York to Baltimore, where he was, when Mr. Sewall wrote. I am sorry to say that Mr. Thayer is one of the two priests at Boston (there are only two) who do not harmonise with each other.

Did I inform you in my last, that I had received from Lord Petre an answer to mine; very polite, wishing me to give him a day at Thorndon; and if that cannot be, promising to see me this week, as business will oblige him to come to town. No answer from Sr. Jn. Webb.[5]

I expect my good friend Mr. Jn. Williams to morrow, & with him my amiable schoolfellow Mr. Horne; & probably little Andrew Robinson. I was disappointed in not finding here a letter from the Capn. of my passage ship with account of her sailing &c. On that will & must depend the greatest pleasure, which Europe can afford, of seeing my most respectable & dear Friends of Lullworth & Wardour.

Sep. 8–This morning I have received a letter from Mr. Thorpe of Aug. 18th. Mr. Cloriviere, Pigot,[6] is a candidate for America. I certainly will admit him. I know his rare virtues: he has been long practiced in the education of young Clergymen—Having failed in all other endeavours to get a president for the academy, I believe I shall write to him to find one for us. I wish Pere le Grou[7] may know English. His superior talents & learning adapt him for that station; and, were it not for the above mentioned defect, I would relieve Mr. Clinton from his burthen. To day likewise I had a letter from Cardl. Antonelli; very affectionate & flattering. In the latter part, he informs me of his having received a letter full of complaints & invectives against me from La Poterie; which he & the Congregation utterly disregarded, & only felt indignation agst. the writer. But then he goes on to inform me, that it having been asserted by him & others, that great heats were raised in America on account of pretended favour to Exjesuits, the congregation intreat me—[to remove all suspicion that I am about to restore the Society of Jesus and urge me to seek out Sulpicians to bring to America.][8]

On the other side, I received a letter last night from our worthy Mr. Francis Neale, who continues in his old stile to urge the reestablishment in spite of every prudential reason against the attempt, till Divine providence opens a better prospect. Adieu, my Dr. Sir—You shall hear from me very soon. Compliments à l'ordinaire—Tell Mr. Clinton, that he sevotere il suo amico di Canford, to whom I wrote lately. God Bless you. I am, Dr. Sr.   Yrs &c   J C

ALS   St
   [1] Ralph Hoskins, S.J., a Marylander, died in 1794. Letter to him has not been found. Wardour was Lord Arndel's castle.
   [2] The discussion of infallibility by Butler and Reeves was criticized by Carroll. Reeve's work was entitled, *A View of the Oath tendered by the Legislature to the Roman Catholics of England* (London, 1790).
   [3] Rev. Mother Bernadine Matthew and the Carmelite nuns from Hoogstraet, Belgium were accompanied by Robert Plunkett, S.J., later the first president of Georgetown College.
   [4] Lord Robert Edward Petre (d. 1801). A member of this family had gone to St. Omer when Carroll was there.
   [5] Sir John Web. Members of this family attended St. Omer about the time Carroll was there.
   [6] Joseph Pierre Picot de Clorivière, later pastor in Charleston, S.C.
   [7] Jean Nicolas Grou (d. 1803), celebrated author of ascetical writings and spiritual director.
   [8] The extended passage from the original Latin letter is given by Carroll. A summary of this by the Editor is given here.

TO CHARLES PLOWDEN   King's street Sept 13 1790.

My dear Sir   I am sorry, very sorry indeed to inform you, that I cannot without the greatest inconvenience, revisit Lullworth, & present once more my respectful thanks to the worthy Master & mistress of the castle. I have ballanced long, in my own mind, the opposite considerations of a farther sojournment in England, & immediate return to America: and I think, after all deliberation that my duty calls me to return immediately to my diocese, &

give the example of residence in it: for, in general, Bishops are so ready to admit pretexts for exempting themselves from that obligation, that I think myself bound to give them no encouragement by my example, even on a plausible pretence. I shall therefore make all necessary preparations for sailing in a fortnight or a little more from this time. I cannot resolve on this without great pain of mind; & indeed without feeling some regret for having come to England, since I must leave it so soon; & in it, leave so many valuable men not only my dearest friends, but the friends of Religion & models of virtue. Long shall I retain the impression made on me at Lullworth, by the goodness, the charity, the loveliness of every branch of that most respectable family; and I am sure, my heart will be full of the gratefullest emotions, when I shall sail abreast of the castle. They will accompany me to America, & will be soothed, tho' revived afresh whenever I shall have the comfort of a letter from you. I would fain persuade myself to run down, if only for three days, to see you once again: but it cannot be; my plans are deranged by maturer reflections. The young Germans from Liege will be here in a few days, & will want my assistance. A Gentleman of St. Sulpice will probably come over to confer with me on the project of some of them passing into America.[1] I must arrange every business relative & preparatory to my departure. I cannot therefore leave London: besides all which, Messrs Williams & Horne are now here having come on purpose to see me, & will probably stay out this week. Cannot you pay your hated London a short visit? Let me have a days notice; if you should so resolve you shall have a lodging got ready for you very near me.

The nomination of President Gibson[2] to the Bishopric of the North is an unexpected event, & gives dissatisfaction to some here. He is in town & I expect to see him this morning. Some suspect that a Bishop for this place is appointed, and that it is either Mr. Southward, or Barnard: but the general, & I fancy, better-founded opinion is, that there is no appointment yet made.

I had a long letter from Mr. Thorpe yesterday of Aug. 21. It chiefly turns on the subject of Cardl. Antonelli being haunted with fears of the revival of the Society in America. I think it is providential, that his alarms have been raised since the issuing of the bull for erecting the See of Baltimore. I suspect that otherwise it would have been refused. I shall now write to the Cardl. in plain language on the subject.[3]

Sir Jn. Lawson has sent me a decent & kind contribution of £10.10. Mr. Hoskins has added something, & more probably will follow. Sr. Jn. Webb has answered my letter,[4] that he shall enquire, whether the little mite, to which he is confined in similar cases, be presentable; and if it be admissible in a subscription, where there are much more munificent names, he shall enter his with sincerity & satisfaction. (Let this be secret). Present my affectionate & most respectful compliments to the Lord & Lady of the Castle, to Messrs Stanley & Clinton, & the amiable young Gentlemen. I am, my Dr. Sir   Yrs afftely   J. Carroll   Did I tell you in my last, that the holy & valuable Mr. Pigot (Cloriviere) is resolved to go to Maryland?

ALS   St
    [1] See Sep. [14-18], 1790.
    [2] William Gibson, President of Douai College, and Bishop of the Northern District, Dec., 1790, was the founder of Upshaw College.
    [3] See Sep. 27, 1790.
    [4] Carroll to Web not found.

ANSWERS TO FRANCIS NAGOT[1]   September [14-18?], 1790

Mr. Nagot takes the liberty of raising the following questions to Bishop Carroll of Baltimore.

1. What would be the cost of a building constructed for the use of a community where one could lodge forty or fifty young men and around which there would be grounds sufficient for walking? House and necessary ground will cost 25,000, or rather 30,000 *livres.* In some situations it will be less.

2. Would it be suitable to construct the building outside the city, on the assumption that land would be less expensive, and dissipation less easy? All things considered, best to be near the Bishop and consequently at Baltimore—where I shall be able to secure a proper piece of ground.

3. How soon could the building be ready? If begun in the spring, 18 months. But the house need not be so large at first, and consequently may be sooner built.

4. Could the priests who will go there to settle easily find a house to rent? Believe they can—If notice be sent beforehand, a house in our own neighborhood shall be ready for them. Two gentlemen to be first sent with a confidential agent.

5. Are living expenses dear there; and how much does boarding cost? Generally very reasonable—Board 450 or 500 *livres.*

6. Would the furnishing precisely needed be expensive, and is it necessary to bring linens? For the passages beds blankets sheets—In general, it will be advisable to carry many articles of furniture—Some may be got as cheap in America.

7. What resources would the priests of the seminary have to live on? I hope to get subsistence for two—in a few years for more—consent of the clergy necessary for this—Will advise with them—Will look out for a proper purchase, and advise the Gentlemen of St. Sulpice.

8. Would it be fitting for them to acquire in the province or elsewhere some lands which they could improve and whose revenue would serve for their subsistence? Proper to purchase an estate for the seminary. I will endeavor to have the Society of priests incorporated—Two thousand *livres*

will procure a tract of back land, which hereafter may be valuable. Consent of Congress unnecessary—Naturalization Act.

9. Could several priests be sent for the Wabash establishment? Only two for Wabash and Illinois.

10. Could the recovery of the lands belonging to the church in that settlement be done without making the new missionaries odious, and would it not be fitting to make the recovery before their entry into the country? No danger of odium on that account. I have taken steps for the Church property—and will take more.

11. St. Sulpice would furnish all the funds of their voyage and of their first days' stay; but who would assure their subsistence afterward if the funds of the country were insufficient or could not be recovered? Ansd. Above.

12. In what season of the year could they leave and with what should they be provided? Last of April—

13. In what form and under what name could they solidly acquire— Climate different in different States. At Baltimore healthy—very cold for two months—very hot for two or three—Generally wholesome. See below.[2]

14. Could they not under the collective name of a society contrive that the house and the properties belong to the society of priests who would then work in the seminary and to those associated with it? Hope it may be obtained.

15. Would it be necessary to obtain the consent of Congress and would the consent be readily granted?[3]

16. What is the temperature of the climate? Is winter rigorous?[4]

17. May priests publicly wear clerical habit. May wear it.

ADf   SMS   On date, see Sep. 13, 1790, and Sep. 19, 1790. Questions were in French.
[1] Francis Nagot, S.S., Vice-Rector of le Grand Séminaire, Paris. James Emery, S.S., General Superior of the Society of St. Sulpice sent Nagot to Carroll, so that the questions are really his. Emery had the alternate plan of a Sulpician mission to the Ohio country (see Emery to Carroll, Aug. 24, 1790 [AAB]).
[2] This phrase is to left of statements in brackets. These remarks belong after question 16, although it is not this way in the MS.
[3] See question 8 above.
[4] See 13 above.

TO ANTONIO DUGNANI   Sep. 19—1790—

My Lord Nuncio   The Reverend Mr. Nagot having sent me the letter which Your Eminence honored me by writing, at first sight I went into conference with him over the purpose of his journey which is infinitely interesting for Religion in my diocese. He will tell you the result of our discussions, My Lord; and I believe Your Eminence will learn of it with pleasure. For myself, I can not help regarding the proposition of the gentlemen of St. Sulpice as a signal mark of providence & a proof that it wishes to dwell upon the faith in the States. I have been happy[1] to have to deal with an Ecclesiastic as informed and worthy in every respect as the Reverend Gentleman. One can not help feeling assured of the success of an entreprise undertaken in a spirit of Religion as purified as that which motivates him.

Your Eminence must realize that I am deeply afflicted by not being able to come to Paris to pay you my respects in person, & to discuss with you the different subjects relating to the preservation and progress of our Holy Religion—but I have had scarcely a moment to myself during my stay in England, and I plan on leaving at the beginning of next week. In returning to America, I will retain sentiments of gratitude & veneration which I feel toward Your Eminence, and I will be delighted to be able to prove it on all occasions.

I take the liberty of sending you a map of the United States of America; which you will be so good as to forward for me on some good occasion to his Eminence Cardinal Antonelli who desired it.

I have the honor to be with most respectful attachment, for Your Eminence My Lord

ADf   AAB

[1] In the French draft, "heureux" was crossed-out, but included in the translation.

Monsr.   l'abbé Nagot m'aiant remis la lettre que V. Em. me fit l'honneur de m'écrire, je suis entré avec lui d'abord en conference sur l'objet de son voyage qui est infiniement interesst. pour la Religion dans mon diocese. Il vous dira, Mgr. le résultat de nos conferences; & je crois, que V. Em l'apprendra avec plaisir. Pour moi, je ne puis m'empêcher de regarder la proposition de Messrs. de St. Sulpice comme un trait signalé de la providce. & une preuve, qu'il veut étendre sur la foi dans les Etats. J'ai été [charmé] d'avoir à traiter avec un Ecclésiastique aussi instruit & respectable en toutes manières que Monsr. l'abbé. On ne peut pas manquer de s'assurer du succès d'une entreprise conduite par un esprit de Religion aussi épuré que celui qui le fait agir.

V. Em. doit être persuadée que je suis sensiblement affligé de n'avoir pu me rendre à Paris pour y rendre personellement mes respects, & m'entretenir avec elle sur les differens objets, qui regardent la conservation & les progrès de notre Ste. Religion—mais je n'ai guère eu un moment à moi pendant mon séjour en Angleterre, et je me propose de la quitter au commencement de la semaine prochaine. En retournant en Amérique, je conserverai les sentiments de reconaissance & de veneration dont je suis remplis pour V.E. et en toutes occasions je serai enchanté de pouvoir en donner des preuves.

Je prends la liberté de vous envoyer une carte des Etats Unis de l'Amérique; que vous aurez la bonté de faire passer de ma part par une bonne occasion à Son Em. le Cardl. Antonelli—qui l'a souhaité.

J'ai l'honneur d'être avec l'attachement le plus réspectueux de V.E.

TO CHARLES PLOWDEN   Sep. 20–1790 London

My very dear Sir   It would certainly give me the highest pleasure to see you once more, but the parting would renew my pain; and I should have so little leisure to enjoy your conversation here, that, all things considered, I am willing to sacrifice the satisfaction of meeting you again to the reasons you assign & both of us feel. I shall write more fully to you in a day or two. Tho I received your letter early this morning I could not get an opportunity of opening it till this moment, when it must go to the post. I can get no certain accounts of Mr. Douglas's nomination.[1] It is a report here, & that Mr. Gibson is negociating an exchange with him. I write this from Mr. Barnards chambers, being just going down to dine with the new Bishop. I received (let it be a secret, if Mr. Weld will not like it) a noble benefaction from him to day of £st.50..0.. I shall write to him soon & beg you to present as usual my best respects & complts. I saw Sr. John Webb to day, but in [*torn*] could do nothing. He promises to see me again [*torn*]

ALS   St
[1] John Douglas was appointed Vicar Apostolic of the London District. Carroll apparently thought that Bishop Charles Berington of the Midland District would have been a better choice, one favored by the Catholic Committee.

TO CHARLES PLOWDEN   London Sep. 25–1790

My dear Sir   I now sit down to give a fuller answer, than in my last, to yours of the 18th. & to supply other deficiencies. I often saw Mr. Gibson, who set out for Doway last wednesday. Great commotions in Lancashire & much discontent here about his nomination. I am not uneasy at Your Brs. delay, especially as far as it concerns our academy. I know & rely on your good intentions. I have taken measures relative to the wreckd goods of Dunkirk. They were shipped, some months ago, to Charleston, S. Carolina. I have got the bill of lading, & will have them brought in one of the packets to Baltimore. Lord Petre did not come to town, as he expected. I wrote to him again yesterday. Sir Jn. Webb, whom I have seen once (I was not at home when he called) has done nothing yet; but I hope he will. Providence seems to favour our views. In consequence of previous correspondence between the Nuncio at Paris & Monsr. Emery, Superior Genl. of S. Sulpice on one hand, & myself on the other, Monsr. Nagot, Superior du petit Seminaire de St. Sulpice has been here. We have settled, that two or three Gentlemen selected by Monsr. Emery, shall come over to Baltimore next spring. They are furnished with the means of purchasing ground for, building & I hope, of endowing a Seminary for young Ecclesiastics. I believe they will bring three or four Seminarians with them who either are English or know it. They will be amply provided with books, apparatus for the altar, Church &c Professors of

Philosophy & Divinity. I propose fixing these very near to my own house & the Cathedral of Baltimore; that they may be, as it were, the Clergy of the Church & contribute to the dignity of divine worship. This is a great & auspicious event for our new Diocese; but it is a melancholy reflection that we owe so great a blessing to the lamentable catastrophe in France. I beg pardon for not having yet written to Chancelllor Villegas,[1] as you desired. It shall not be neglected, & his answer shall be requested *for you.* The young Germans from Liege arrived last night–, with Mr. Thos. Angier,[2] bound to Sir Richd. Bedinfield, where he is to reside. I expect we shall leave town next thursday morning. It is curious, that the newly consecrated Bishop of Virga, Mr. Madison,[3] has taken his passage in the same ship with me. As I shall write to you in a few days, I add no more, than request you to assure Mr. & Mrs. Weld of my respectful & unalterable attachment; the dear young family of my great love for them; & you Cooperators in the ministry of my sincere esteem & affection. I am My dr. friend,   Yr. ever affte   J. Carroll

You must not let it reach France that the Gentlemen of St. Sulpice intend so many things for Religion. They may be bereft of the means by the gripping hand of irreligious despotism.

ALS   St
[1] Not found.
[2] Thomas Angier, S.J., President of Bruges College in 1773, was a companion of Carroll at that time.
[3] Bishop James Madison of the Protestant Episcopal Church of Virginia was returning from his ceremony of consecration.

TO VILLEGAS   [After Sep. 25,] 1790

Not found. See Sep. 25, 1790.

TO CHARLES PLOWDEN   London 27 Sept.–1790

My Dear Sir   You ask an answer to yours of ye. 25th (this day received) by return of post. I wrote to you on Saturday; and now inform you, that the Capn. has not yet given the signal of departure. I expect I shall not leave London before thursday or friday; before that you will hear fully from me. I think all difficulty [is] about leaving out parts of the Bull, either by not publishing it at all, or giving it the title of an Extract from the bull. I have no objection to the printing of clauses from the American constitutions. I only mentioned, that I thought that [passages] from Maryland [law] concerning the acquisition of property was irrelative to the matter of toleration & had as well be kept out of sight.[1] I have received the music & prints this morning from Mr. Weld, & renew my thanks for them & his most kind letter, which I will acknowledge. Sir Jn. Moore died last Saturday morning; I fear as he lived. His Br. now Sr. Thomas,[2] met the news here & will not go down before the burial. Sir Jn. Webb has presented me £30..0..; but it must not be told. I am to be honoured by Lord Petre's visit today, or shall wait on him to morrow morning.

Excuse great haste as I am busy in packing up; and present my respectful & affte compliments as usual. I am, my Dr. Sir,   Yr. ever affte & humble st.   J Carroll

ALS   St
    [1] See Sep. 2, 1790. Probably reference to the situation where Congregation of the Propagation of the Faith might own American church property.
    [2] Baronet of Fawley, County Bershire, his father John had lost the manor, died without issue, thus extinguishing the title.

TO LEONARDO ANTONELLI   London September 27, 1790

I received the letter sent me on August 14th, in which you professed in an even greater degree your own good will and that of the Congregation which I have always experienced. I have already, as you thought, been consecrated bishop. May the most merciful Lord grant that I may always correspond faithfully to the graces He bestows. I am including an authentic testimonial of my consecration. At present, I am preparing to leave, and I think I shall depart next week, when, as I hope, the equinoctial winds will have subsided.

After my return to America, Georgetown College will soon be ready to receive students. This is due to the very generous contribution of the Sacred Congregation which you wish Mr. John Thorpe to pay. Some of the colonists from France arrived in America before my departure. I am glad that a priest has been chosen for them by the Sacred Congregation,[1] but as yet he has not arrived here. They said they want to settle in a territory belonging to the United States.

I see that the Sacred Congregation has in its wisdom taken action concerning that unsavory character, I shall not refer to him as a priest, Claude de la Poterie. I regret however that as a result of his calumny or that of another, any suspicion lingers that I make use of the ministries of such priests to a less degree than those who were members of the extinct Society. Of all the priests who have found their way to us, I believe that there were only two, or at the most, three, who originated this calumny. One of them, La Poterie is altogether untrustworthy; the other is an Irish priest,[2] who on his return from Maryland wrote an infamous pamphlet that was censored by all the archbishops of Ireland. When it appeared, I failed to refute it. This was earnestly requested by the Very Reverend Archbishop of Dublin.[3] The author's letters in his own hand are now in my possession; they would provide an ample refutation. It is impossible to say how great are the errors against truth, and the calumnies against character, which this book disseminates. Most eminent cardinal, if suspicion should arise from such sources as I understood to exist from your letter, it can never be avoided, for there will never be lacking men who, by fair means and foul, will gratify their desires, ambition, or hatred. For it happens not rarely, that priests who come to America fix their eyes on the better positions; and unless they attain these, they take it ill. Their ambition cannot be realized unless the old and well-deserving missionaries, beloved for the most part by their congregations, are removed from their positions. So far are American Catholics from generally disliking the members of the supressed Society, that they greatly desire that those priests be given to them. It is true that some who come from the various provinces of Europe strive to foment discord, but by divine providence, with little success, to the present. When I read your words of recommendation that I extend my care not only to the ex-Jesuit Brethren, but also to other priests, I ran over mentally a list of those whom I had received from the time when this charge of Catholics was laid upon me by the Sacred Congregation. In that time, and especially in these last two years, I find that thirty priests were received, among whom only seven were former Jesuits; and of these four had left Maryland in their early youth, entered the Society, completed their studies, and finally returned to their native country. The other twenty-three are either members of the secular clergy or priests of various orders. But I desire, most eminent cardinal, that you and the Sacred Congregation be thoroughly convinced that the increase of faith and piety are paramount to me; and that I think I should be guilty of a most grievous crime and deserve punishment, if I should strive to promote the restoration of the Society rather than the spread of the Faith. The nature of my office and its responsibility continually demand this of me. And I realize and testify that without the authority of the Holy See the restoration cannot be effected. I am very grateful that you have received the obediential letters for the return of Father John Charles Helbron. However, I shall not use them so long as he acts properly and usefully, and arouses no new dissension. Recently, at the request of the most excellent Apostolic Nuntio, one of the administrators of the Seminary of Saint Sulpice came here from Paris. As a result of our joint consultation, we decided to establish an Episcopal Seminary at Baltimore, from which, as it must be hoped, great fruit to religion will result. In my opinion, it is the supreme indication of the most gracious will of God in our regard that He has aroused excellent priests to come to our aid, especially at a time when the new episcopate established by the Holy See will be most eager to have their assistance.

ALS   PF; ADf   AAB
    [1] Pierre Didier, O.S.B., later vicar general for the trans-Appalachian territory.
    [2] Patrick Smyth.
    [3] Thomas Troy.

To Cardinal Antonelli   Sept. 27, 1790   Accepi Eminentissime Cardinale literas ad me datas 14 Augusti, quibus summam tuam et Sacrae Congregationis in me benevolentiam, quam semper expertus sum, magis magisque confirmasti. Consecrationem Episcopalem, uti credidisti jam accepi; faxitque misericordissimus Dominus ut adjunctis gratiis semper fideliterque respondeam. Consecrationis meae authenticum testimonium hisce includo. Ad reditum jam me comparo, et proxima hebdomada discedere cogito, cum uti spero, procellae aequinoctiales vc. [vacaverint?]

Post meum in Americam reditum Collegium Georgiopolitanum brevi admittendis alumnis erit idoneum; ad quod conferet benevolentissima Sacrae Congregationis collatio, quas Domino Joanni Thorpe solvi voluisti. Pars coloniae ex Galliis profectae in Americam advenerat ante meum discessum. Laetor ipsis a Sacra Congregatione Sacerdotem fuisse designatum, non tamen adhuc huc ipse appulerat. In territorio ad foederatae Americae provincias spectante sedem figere velle dixerunt.

Video de infami homine, ne dicam sacerdote, Claudio de la Poterie, statuisse pro sua sapientia Sacram Congregationem. Doleo tamen, sive ex ejus, sive alterius cujusdam calumnia aliquid adhaerere suspicionis, me illorum sacerdotum opera minus uti, qui ad extinctam Societatem non pertinebant. Ex omnibus qui ad nos commeaverunt Presbyteris, credo qdm duos tantum, vel ad summum tres, ejusdem calumniae auctores extitisse; quorum unus La Poterie omni fide est destitutus; alter Sacerdos Hibernus, qui redux ex Marilandia infamem libellum conscripsit, quem ab omnibus Marilandia archiepiscopis censura notatum, statim atque prodiit, refutare omisi, quod ita a Reverendissimo Archiepiscopo Dubliniensi sollicite rogaret, quamquam auctoris literae propria ipsius manu exaratae, et quae nunc penes me sunt, refutationem abunde suppeditarent. Dici nequit, quantis et contra veritatem erroribis, et contra characterem maledictis scateat ille libellus. Si ex ejusmodi fontibus oriatur suspicio, quam jam existere intellexi ex literis tuis, Eminentissime Cardinale, nunquam illa declinari poterit, cum nunquam defuturi sint, qui per fas et nefas omnia congerent, ut suis vel cupiditatibus vel ambitioni, vel odio satisfaciant. Accidit enim non raro, ut adventantes in Americam presbyteri oculos mox conjiciant in celebriores stationes; et nisi in illis sedem consequantur moleste ferunt; quamvis id fieri nequeat, nisi loco moveantur antiqui et benemeriti missionarii, et suis Congregationibus plurimum dilecti. Tantum enim abest ut praegrandis contra Socios extinctae Societatis, apud Catholicos Americanos existit invidia, ut hos sibi dare Sacerdotes plurimum desiderent; quamquam verum sit aliquos ex variis Europae provinciis advenientes dissidia excitare studeant, ceterum hucusque, bona Dei providentia, parvo successu. Cum illa verba legissem quibus mihi commendasti, ut non solum socios Exjesuitas, verum enim alios Sacerdotes admitterem in partem meae sollicitudinis, ex memoria texui catalogum per me receptorum, ex quo a Sacra Congregatione Catholicae rei cura mihi commissa fuit; atque triginta Sacerdotes intra id tempus, ac praecipue his posterioribus annis duobus cooptatos fuisse reperio, quorum septem solum sunt Exjesuitae, et in his septem, quattuor, qui ex Marilandia profecti, in prima juventute, et Societatem ingressi, confectis studiis, in patriam tandem rediere. Ceteri omnes viginti tres, aut sunt ex clero saeculari, aut variorum ordinum Sacerdotes. Caeterum valde cupio, Eminentissime Cardinale, et tibi et Sacrae Congregationi esse penitus persuasum, fidei et pietatis incrementum mihi prae omnibus cordi esse; meque ita existimare, gravissimo crimini et poenae obnoxium me fore, si restituendae Societati potius, quam Religioni dilatandae labores impenderem; hoc quidem a me perpetuo exiget officii et muneris mei ratio; illus vero, sine Sedis Apostolicae auctoritate fieri non posse, et scio et profiteor.

Gratias habeo maximas, quod literas obedientiales obtinueris pro reditu Patris Joannis Caroli Helbron. Illis tamen non utar, quamdiu ipse recte et utiliter se gesserit, neque nova dissidia excitaverit. His ultimis diebus venit huc Parisiis, rogatu Excellentissimi Nuntii Apostoloci, unus ex Praesidibus Seminarii Sancti Sulpicii, cumquo collatis invicem consiliis, statuimus Seminarium Episcopale mox stabilire Baltimori, ex quo igens, uti sperare fas est, in Religionis negotia fructus redundabit. Maximum, meo quidem judicio indicium est benignissimae in nos divinae voluntatis, quod optimos presbyteros excitaverit ad tantum subsidium nobis conferendum, hoc maxime tempore, quo novus Episcopatus per Sanctam Sedem institutus illorum opera maxime sollicitabit.

TO POPE PIUS VI   London, September 27, 1790

Holy Father—   Two months ago I informed His Eminence Cardinal Antonelli of my arrival in England for episcopal consecration. At the same time I asked him to present me to Your Holiness, and to represent to you that while I undertake the episcopal office with genuine trepidation I also derive no little consolation from the fact that you, Holy Father, did not consider me wholly unworthy of so great an office. Moreover, he was to express my loyalty to you, and to assure you that I shall never fail in that fidelity and obedience to the Holy See, without which, as I have learned from ecclesiastical history and the Holy Fathers, faith totters. May I add further that I shall never fail in my efforts that those who are committed to my care be animated by the same spirit towards the Holy See, and this holds alike for laity and clergy. In order to insure this grace I kneel in all humility before Your Holiness and ask that you impart to us your apostolic blessing.

That God keep Your Holiness safe to the advantage of His Church is my earnest and sincere prayer.   Holy Father,   Your servant and most obedient son,   John, Bishop of Baltimore.

ALS   PF; ADf   AAB

Beatissime Pater   Cum duobus abhinc mensibus Eminentissimum Cardinalem Antonellum de adventu meo in Europam, ut consecrationem Episcopalem susciperem, certiorem facerem, simul rogavi, ut me ad Sanctitatis Tuae pedes sistere dignaretur, meoque nomine profiteretur imprimis me, quamvis hoc onus Episcopale magna formidine suscipiam, tamen non parum consolationis inde derivare quod in te, Bme Patre, non plane tanto munere indignus habitus fuerim; deinde, ut meam Tibi fidem exhiberet, nullo unquam tempore defuturum me illi observantiae et obsequio versus Sam Sedem, sine quibus et ex historia Ecclesiasticia et ex P.P. doctrina didici, fidem mere vacillare. Liceat mihi adjicere ulterius nulli unquam conatui me defuturum, ut eodem ac ego ipse animo erga Sam Sedem sint affecti qui meae curae committentur, tam populus quam Pastores. Ad hanc gratiam certius consequendam provolutus humillime ad pedes Tuae Sanctitatis, rogo ut nobis Apostolicam Benedictionem conferre dignetur.

Ut Sanctitatem Tuam Deus diu incolumem esse velit, suaeque Ecclesiiae utilitati conservet, cum omni devotione et ex animo praecatur.   Beatissime Pater,   Servus ac filius obsequentissimus   Joannes Epus Baltim.

DEBT AGREEMENT[1]   Sepr. 29–1790

When I entered upon office I found Maryland indebted to office in the sum of [£] 1400 p. Since that time Maryland has incurred other Debts.

I propose to forgive in the name of office the debt of fourteen hundred pounds provided Maryland will pay Debt incurred since I entered upon office, & will also provide good Security for the payment of Mrs. White's annuity & quit all Claim of Reversion and all other Claims upon the Province. Maryland[2]

The Subscriber agrees, as far as he has authority, to this proposal, & will urge, with all his power & influence its admission by the Chapter of the American Clergy.   J. Carroll   signed J. Carroll for Maryland Province   3

ADS   St.

[1] Debts were between former Maryland Jesuits and English Jesuits, which carried over to a new and complex jurisdiction following the suppression of the order in 1773. See Hughes, *Documents,* II, 568-69.

[2] Written in large hand in spacing between paragraphs.

[3] Carroll through Ashton took up administration of the defunct province's financial affairs.

TO PETER JENKINS,[1] HOLT, MARKET, HARBOROUGH   London
Octr. 2. 1790

Dear Sir   Mr. Talbot has informed me of the very generous manner, in which you have disposed of £200 in favour of our rising American Seminary. Every acknowledgement is due to you from all, who are concerned in the extension of Religion in the United States: their prayers shall be offerred perpetually for the beneficent promoters of so good a work; & your benefaction, as being so considerable shall entitle you to a greater share in our gratitude, & in our supplications to heaven. I have signed & left in Mr. Talbot's hands an instrument of writing, binding myself to the annual payment required by you.

I expect to embark on monday the 4th. It would have given me great pleasure to have seen you during my residence here. I have been too much hurried to make so distant an excursion: otherwise, I should have been highly entertained with an opportunity of assuring you how much I remain, Dr. Sir, Yr. affectionate & humble st.   J. Carroll

ALS   St
   [1] Prominent Catholic family with a member in the Jesuit order at one time. Others seem to be associates as agents for credit and benefactions, apparently calling for expense charges.

TO JOHN TROY   London, October 3rd, 1790

My Lord,   What excuse shall I offer to your Lordship for my long delay in acknowledging the honour of your most obliging favour of August 5th? I received, with all the pleasure which the subject would admit, your Lordship's congratulations on the event which has lately taken place,[1] and which is to me a matter of so great consequence, and, I may add, of some consequence to the cause of religion. I believe that I told your Lordship before the reasons which determined my choice on England for consecration. I flatter myself that my voyage hither has not been unprofitable to the cause over which it is now our common duty to watch, in preference to everything else.

   Mr. Donnellan has, within these few days, communicated to me the papers you mention. I have read them attentively, and they are such as I humbly conceive would be of benefit if more generally communicated. Since my arrival I have carefully avoided taking any part in the present controversy amongst the Catholics, though I have been urged on all sides. If I had seen any prospect of bringing the principals on each side of the question to a good understanding with each other, most certainly I would have attended much more than I have done to the cause in controversy, and probably should have formed a very decided opinion. At present I can only say, that the oath,[2] in its present form, appears to me inadmissible; that it implies a renunciation of the pastoral powers of the successor of St. Peter; and that its obvious meaning is different from that which the advocates for the oath affix to it. This I have not said to a soul excepting now to your Lordship, and even to you I deliver this opinion, not as one which is founded on much investigation, but as one which forced itself on my mind when I read the oath.

   My baggage has been on board some days: the wind keeps the ship in the river, which I hope to leave very shortly. I was greatly obliged to their Lordships (of your province) who offered me their congratulations through your Lordship. May God pour His blessings plentifully on your and their arduous labours for the extension of the faith! I shall always esteem it a happiness and honour to hear from you. Cardinal Antonelli, in a late letter, recommended me to let your recommendation accompany all priests who go from Ireland to America. In consequence I referred to your Lordship for such recommendation, a Mr. Phelan,[3] a Capuchin friar and postulant for our mission.

I have the honour to be, with the utmost respect, My Lord, Your Lordship's most obedient servant, J. Carroll.

L Moran, III, 508-09.
  [1] Carroll's Consecration at Lullworth Castle Chapel, Aug. 15, 1790.
  [2] Proposed by Sir John Mitford, May 5, 1789, and generally opposed by the English Catholic bishops.
  [3] Lawrence Phelan later served in Philadelphia.

TO HENRY ARUNDELL[1]   London, Oct. 4–1790–

My good and dear Lord— Your Lordship will be surprised to find my letter dated from London: for several days our ship has been prevented by contrary winds from falling down the river; and I wished to defer to the last giving your Lordsp. an answer to yr most kind, affectionate, tho' you must allow me to add, too partial letter from Southampton. I own, that I was greatly affected by it; and could not read it through at once. The pleasure of being so much esteemed by Lord & Lady Arundell was corrected by the confusion, which I felt in knowing, how little I deserved it. I never spent a day at Wardour in my life, which did not fill me with respect for the noble family there: but the last days of my late visit made on me deeper impressions than ever. To add to these your Lordship condescends to request, that you may be allowed to correspond with me: Indeed, my Lord, I shall ever esteem it an honour & a happiness. Letters directed to me at Baltimore, Maryland; & left with Mr. Strickland, Mr. Talbot, or Mr. Joshua Johnson, Mercht. in London will go safe.

A Little before I received your Ldsps last Monsr. Nagot, Superior of the Seminary of St. Sulpice came over hither, in consequence of a previous correspondence between the Nuncio at Paris & me. The object of his voyage was, to concert measures for the erection of an Episcopal Seminary for the Diocese of Baltimore. We arranged all preliminaries; and I expect at Baltimore, early in the summer, some of the Gentlemen of that institution to set hard to work; & I have reason to believe, they will find means to carry their plan into effect. Thus we shall be provided with a house fit for the reception and farther improvement in the higher sciences of the young men whom God may call to an Ecclesiastical state after their classical education is finished in our George-town academy. While I cannot but thank divine providence for opening on us such a prospect, I feel great sorrow in the reflection, that we owe such a benefit to the distressed state of Religion in France.

Relative to the appointment of Bishops here I can only say to your Lordsp., that the opposition, which was intended in the North to be made agst. Bishop Gibson will subside. A remonstrance was to have been signed by the Clergy: but Bishop Talbot[2] having recommended compliance & submission the remonstrance is withdrawn. So says a letter to Mr. Wm. Meynell just returned from Palermo: to whom I have presumed to recommend to see Wardour, as he is under a promise of going to see Mr. Chs. Plowden. Your Lordsp. will find in him a person well informed generally, & particularly in the fine arts.

I cannot presume to answer Your Lordsp's confidential appeal to my judgment, concerning the oath. When I see men of abilities & virtue engaged on both sides, I dare not venture to direct in a matter of so much consequence without studying the question much more than I have had time to do. At present I will only recommend to your Lordsp to consult one or at most two men of whose judgment, in all other matters respecting your spiritual concerns, you have found most reason to rely; and to follow their opinions. But this need not make me so far reserved, as to withold from your Ldsp that at present, and as far as I have considered the subject, my opinion is against the oath: however an opinion formed as mine has been deserves little regard.

I promised to write to Lady Arundell before I leave England: now I propose doing so from Gravesend. Your Lordship knows my sentiments in her regard, & I will, I hope, be the interpreter of them: and I request to have my humble respects made to Messrs Forrester & Nickell. The Dr Booth is here: by him I will send some impressions of the large seal: the small one shall be on this letter. I ought to answer Mr. Nickell's letter, full of kindness & goodness, like himself; but really I have not time. I hope he will excuse me. I depend much on his and Mr. Forrester's[3] prayers; who, I hope, has had advices from Monsr. Picard.

Let Mr. Nickell know that Mrs. Paines vinegar would come too late. I am not less obliged to her for the trouble she has taken. Dr. Madison, the new Protest Bishop of Virginia, is my fellow passenger. I have the honr. to be with the greatest respect, My Lord,   Yr. Lordsps most obliged & humble St.   J. Carroll

ALS   St
[1] Henry, Eighth Lord of Arundell, of Wardour Castle, and very likely a classmate of Carroll at St. Omers.
[2] James Talbot was made Vicar Apostolic in 1781.
[3] Charles Forrester, S.J., assisted at Carroll's consecration. He was chaplain to Arundell.

TO CHARLES PLOWDEN   London Oct. 4–1790

My dear Sir   You will be surprised to find this dated from London. For five or six days, the wind has prevented our ship from falling down the river. Your generous benefaction to George-town academy had best be paid altogether, at your convenience, to Mr. Ths. Wright & Co. for my credit. Mr. Wm. Meynell is here & proposes giving you a visit at Lullworth, which will give you pleasure I am very sure. I think I told you before, that Mr. Nagot, one of the Superiors of St. Sulpice, had been here, & that we have concerted the erection of an Episcopal Seminary at Baltimore. Three of their principal Gentlemen will come over next summer. They will have a fund sufficient for the purchase of ground, building & endowing the Seminary. It will add much consistency to our diocese, and dignity to divine worship in the cathedral. You must not make it very public that the Sulpicians will carry the means of endowment with them. I have expurged some few passages of your account of the establishment of the see of Baltimore. Maryland is so called, not from our Lady, but Henrietta Maria, Queen of Ch[arle]s. the 1st. It was not proper to say, that the Clergy have appropriated a part of their estate to the Bishop: for 1o. it must not appear that our Clergy do any corporate act, before they are a legal corporation. 2ly. no determined part of the estate but only a certain income is assigned him; and if it were this would be saying to the world, that we have, by private authority, made the Bishop, what lawyers call a *corporation sole*. 3ly. not only the Exjesuit missioners, but others called for a Bishop: therefore it ought not to be limited to them alone.

I have left the clauses of the bull for which you contend: but you have been used of late to see so much unjust suspicion entertained against the popes, that your zeal to defend the just prerogatives of the holy See makes you justify expressions, which certainly were introduced for the sake of usurpations on the rights of the civil power, or of the Diocesan clergy. Remember the iniquities and oppression of such popes as Ganganelli, & you will be careful to obey & respect their orders, within the line of their rightful jurisdiction, but not to extend it farther, which sooner or later always does harm.

The protestation against Mr. Gibson, which the Clergy in Lancashire were signing, is laid aside in consequence of a letter from Bishop Talbot, recommending acquiescence & submission.[1]

Adieu, my Dr. Sir. Every moment I expect orders to depart. My baggage has been on board these several days. I only repeat to the family of Lullworth & to Messrs Stanley & Clinton what I have repeated so often & feel so uninterruptedly. I am, my Dr. Sir   Yr. ever affte friend & Servt.   J. Carroll

ALS   St
[1] See Sep. 20, 1790.

TO JOHN THORPE   Dec., 1790

Not found. See Feb. 6, 1790 to Antonelli.

TO FRANCIS BEESTON   [Dec. 2, 1790]

Mr. Beeston—   As I foresee, that I may be detained eight or ten days more by the business before the assembly, I find myself obliged, in the mean time, to take some steps to stop the scandal of Mr. Helbron's proceedings. I therefore commission your Reverence & the Revd. Mssrs Graesl & Fleming; or anyone of you, to deliver, or cause to be delivered to Mr. Helbron, in the presence of witnesses, the inclosed monitories after dating them on the day, in which they shall be delivered; the first, as soon after your receiving it, as can be—; the 2d. after an interval of three entire days; & the 3d. after [an] other three days.

ADf   AAB   There follows in Carroll's letterbook a crossed-out Latin decree, a second that is not crossed-out, and a third and fourth in English.

SERMON ON OCCASION OF POSSESSING HIS PRO-CATHEDRAL[1]
                                                    Baltm Decr [12,] 1790

This day, my Dr. Brethren impresses deeply on my mind a lively sense of the new relation, in which I stand now before you. You have often heard my voice within these walls; and often have I used my feeble endeavours to rouse you from the sleep of sin, & to awake in you the sentiments of virtue & practical piety. But when I thus addressed you I considered it indeed as my obligation to admonish & instruct you; but I did not view it as an indissoluble obligation. My superintendance over your spiritual concerns was of such a nature that I could relinquish it, or be removed from it at pleasure.

But now the hand of providence (Ah! may I hope, that it is not an angry, but a providence merciful to you and me) the hand of providence has formed an indissoluble tie, has bound me by an obligation which I can never renounce; an obligation of ever attending to your eternal interests, of watching perpetually over your conduct; of stemming, to the utmost of my power the torrent of vice & irreligion; of conducting you in the ways of virtue, & leading you to the haven of eternal bliss. The shade of retirement & solitude must no longer be my hope & prospect of consolation. Often have I flattered myself, that my declining years would be indulged in such a state of rest from labour & sollicitude for others, as would leave me the best opportunity of attending to the great concern of my own salvation, & of confining myself to remember my past years in the bitterness of compunction: but it has pleased God to order otherwise; & tho my duty command submission it cannot allay my fears, those fears which I feel for you & for myself.

For, my God! how much reason have I not to fear for myself, when I view the extent of my duties, on one hand; and on the other, my weakness & natural inability to fulfill them. In this my new station if my life be not one continued instruction, & example of virtue to the people committed to my charge, it will become, in the sight of God, a life not only useless, but even pernicious. It is no longer enough for me to be inoffensive in my conduct, & regular in my manners: God now imposes a severer duty upon me: I shall incur the guilt of violating my pastoral office if all my endeavours be not directed to bring your lives & all your actions to a conformity with the laws of God. To exhort, to conjure, to reprove, to enter into all your sentiments, to feel all your infirmities; to be all things to all, that I may gain all to Christ; to be superior to human respects; to have nothing in view but God & your salvation; to sacrifice to these, health, peace, reputation & even life itself; to hate sin & yet love the sinner; to repress the turbulent, to encourage the timid; to watch over the conduct of even the ministers of religion; to be patient & meek; to embrace all kinds of persons; these are now my duties, extensive, pressing & indispensable duties. These are the duties of all my Brethren in the Episcopacy, & surely important enough to fill us with terror: But there are others still more burthensome to be borne by me in this particular portion of Christ's Church, which is committed to my charge, & where every thing is to be raised, as it were from its foundation. To establish Ecclesiastical discipline, to devise means for the religious education of Catholic youth that precious portion of pastoral sollicitude; to educate & provide establishment for training up ministers for the sanctuary, & the services of religion; that we may no longer depend on foreign & uncertain coadjutors not to leave unassisted any of the faithful who are scattered thro this immense continent; to preserve their faith untainted amidst the contagion of error, surrounding them on all sides; to preserve in their hearts a warm charity & forbearance towards every other denomination of Christians; & at the same time to preserve them from that fatal & prevailing indifference, which views all religious as equally acceptable to God & Salutary to men: Ah! when I consider these additional duties, my heart sinks almost under the impression of terror, which comes upon it. In God alone can I find any consolation. He knows, by what steps I have been conducted to this important station; & how much I have always dreaded it. He will not abandon me, unless I first draw down his malediction by my unfaithfulness to my charge, Pray, Dr. Brethren, pray incessantly, that I may not incur so dreadful a punishment. Alas! the punishment would fall on you as well as on myself. My unfaithfulness would redound on you, & deprive you of some of the means of salvation. The fears, which trouble me on my own acct, would receive some abatement, if I could be assured of yr. steady adherence to the duties of yr. holy religion. But how can I be assured of this, when I recollect, what experience has taught me, & that worldly contagion, example, influence, & respects, together with impetuous passions seek perpetually to plunge you into habits of vice, and afterwards into everlasting misery: and when I know, that not one soul will perish from amongst you of which God will not demand of me, as its shepherd a most severe account. Unhappily, at this time, a spirit of infidelity is prevalent,

& dares to attempt the subversion of even the first principles of religion & morality, & to break down all the fences, which guard virtue & purity of body & mind. Licentiousness of discourse & the arts of seduction are practiced without shame &, it would seem without remorse. Ah! will it be in my power to oppose these fatal engines of vice & immorality? Dr. Brethren, allow me to appeal to your consciences. Question them with candor and truth. Can I say more to you to bring you back to the simplicity of faith, to the humble docility of a disciple of Jesus, to the fervent practice of Xtian duties, than I have said to you heretofore? but what reformation followed then my earnest intreaties & exhortations? was prayer more used? were parents more assiduous in the instruction of their children? were their examples more edifying? was swearing & blaspheming diminished? was drunkenness suppressed? was idleness extirpated, was injustice abolished?

May I hope that on this occasion God will shower down more abundant grace? that your hearts will be turned from the love of the world to the love of him?

If I could be so happy as to see prevailing amongst you such exercises of piety, as evidenced your attachment to Religion, & your zeal for your salvation, I should myself [be] relieved from much of my sollicitude.

Prayer—attendance on holy mass; frequentation of the Sacraments; humble docility to the advice & admonitions of your pastors—obey says St. Paul, those who are put over you as having to [render] To God an account for your souls (—Diocese under her patronage—Piety decays, wherever Devotion to the Bd. Lady—)   Thanks for their prayers—   Afternoon.

ADf   MPA.   A second, more polished version used by Shea (pp. 371-72) not found. Dec. 12 was the day sermon was given.

[1] At head of sermon is the following in parentheses: "on taking possession of the Episc. see of Baltm Decr 1790." Carroll arrived in Baltimore on Dec. 7 and the occasion at St. Peter's Church was Sunday the 12th, his first formal preaching as bishop.

TO HENRY ARUNDELL   Baltmre. Dec. 14. 1790

My Lord   I know that your Lordship interests yourself so much in my regard, as not to be indifferent to the prosperous issue of my late voyage across the Atlantic.

I have the pleasure to inform you, that I arrived safely on the 8th Decr., having embarked at Gravesend Octr. 8th We had a blowing and disagreeable passage; but a good ship carried us safely through all difficulties. I hope your Lordship and your incomparable Lady are well convinced that no distance of place or time can efface those impressions of esteem, respect, & allow me to say, of affectionate friendship, with which your virtues, kindness, & condescention have inspired me. God grant, this may find you both, as well as Mrs. Arundell & Clifford, with their respective husbands, in perfect health. Be pleased to present my respectful compliments to Messrs Booth and Forrester & Nichell; and to inform the first that I have conducted his niece thus far in perfect health: that her Br. Charles is arrived to convey her to his house; that she presents her duty respectfully to him.[1] And to Mr. Forrester you will be pleased to say that I retain the greatest sense of his kindness, & shall be glad to know the answers he received from Mr. Picard. Mr. Forrester has so many good qualities to recommend him to esteem & to discover his usefulness, that I am almost ashamed to mention one, which in our present circumstances, would be particularly conducing to the solemnity & propriety of divine worship: his knowledge of the rites and ceremonies of the Church.[2] I request the favor of your Lordship to present my respects to Lady Arundell, and the other branches of your noble and amiable family.

I have not yet seen my Sister,[3] whom her Ladyship honoured with a mark of her regard, & therefore cannot be the interpreter of her sentiments. I have the honour to be with the greatest respect, My Lord,   Your Lordship's most devoted & obedt. Servt.   J. Carroll

C   St
[1] Booth was probably a former Jesuit colleague of Carroll; and Nichell may have been John Nihell, S.J., companion of Carroll at Bruges in 1773.
[2] He assisted at the episcopal consecration of Carroll.
[3] Eleanor and Mary (m. Notley Young) were undoubtedly educated in Europe, where they may have known the Arundells.

TO CHARLES PLOWDEN   [Dec. 14 (c), 1790]

Not found. See to same, Feb. 3, 1791.

TO THOMAS WELD   [Dec. 14 (c), 1790]

Not found. See to Plowden, Feb. 3, 1791.

MEMORANDUM ON WESTERN TERRITORY   Dec. 22. 1790–

1. Kaskasias–Population–at least 300 souls, & increasing rapidly by the return of those, who had removed to the Spanish side of the Mississippi. A handsome well furnished Church. The presbytery burnt down. Vide Mr. Burkes[1] letter.

2. Près du rocher–5 leagues from Kaskasias. About 15 families, of very orderly, well disposed people. A handsome, well furnished church & presbytery.

3 Saint Philippe. 8 leagues from Kaskasias. Five or six families, & a small church.

4 Kaokias. Population about 500 souls—twenty-two leagues from Kaskasias. A church & presbytery or parsonage house. Mr. Gibault now there.

5. Post Vincennes—fifty leagues from Kaskasias, & a fine road. Population—about 200 families—Some land, about four acres front, and forty deep—& a seat for the presbytery. A fine country. No presbytery house at present; but Mr. Vigo[2] invites the Clergyman to reside with him till he shall be provided & if Mr. Vigo should be absent, still orders will be left for his accommodation.

AD   AAB   "Information of Mr. Vigant" appears at top of MS. Joseph Vigo was the name intended. See Dec. 27, 1790, to Churchwardens of St. Vincennes.
    [1] Edmund Burke was Vicar General of the Illinois Territory under the Quebec jurisdiction, eventually going to Nova Scotia.
    [2] Joseph Vigo, Revolutionary War soldier with George Rogers Clark, became a merchant in St. Louis.

TO PIERRE GIBAULT   Balte. Dec. 27, 1790.

I do not know whether you have received the letter which I had the honor of writing you on January 20 of this year. It was entrusted to General Knox,[1] minister of the war department, who promised to have it forwarded with his despatches for Governor St. Clair.[2] In it I told you that I was very relieved about the reports which had been made me against you. At the same time, I thanked you for having had the kindness to go into such great detail relative to the property of the Church at Post Vincennes: and I added my train of thought on the matter which you and the trustees of that place had submitted to my decision. I am sending to the latter by this present occasion a copy of this decision and I request them to give you another copy of it.

Nearly three weeks ago I returned from Europe where I had been for my consecration. On my return, I learned that you were now at Cahokias, where I hope you will find a pleasanter lot than in the place you have just left. For your consolation, I have the pleasure of announcing, Sir, and to the inhabitants of Kaskaskia, Prairie du Rocher, &c., that I have made arrangements with the Superior of the Seminary of St. Sulpice in Paris to receive here, next summer, two Priests of that house who are destined to enter the service of the Christian missions scattered throughout your territories, & one of whom will be assigned to Post Vincennes; the other will go to Illinois to serve either Kaskaskia or Cahokias whichever seems suitable to you and the inhabitants of those places. Thus, Sir, after all the trouble I have had to find virtuous Priests on whom I could rely with confidence, Providence deigns at last to open a way by which I hope that the spiritual needs of the Catholics who inhabit the western lands of the United States will never fail to be supplied. In union with your Holy Sacrifice I have the honor, etc.

ADf   AAB

[1] Henry Knox was a general of the American Revolution who became head of the War Department under the Articles of Confederation in 1785, and was appointed first Secretary of War by President Washington, serving from 1789 to 1795.

[2] Arthur St. Clair had fought with Wolfe at Quebec and against Burgoyne at Ticonderoga. He was badly defeated by the Indians in 1791. At the time of this letter he was governor of the Northwest Territory.

Je ne sçais, si vous avez reçu la lettre, que j'ai eu l'honneur de vous ecrire du 20 Janvier de cette année. Elle fut confiée au General Knox, ministre du departement de la guerre, qui promit de la faire passer avec ses depeches pour Monsr. le Gouverneur St. Clair. Je vous y fis scavoir que j'etois beaucoup tranquillisé sur les rapports, qui m'avoient eté fait à votre desavantage. En même tems, je vous remerciois d'avoir eu la complaisance d'entrer en si grands details relativement aux biens de l'Eglise au poste Vincennes: & j'y ai ajouté ma manière de penser sur la matiere, que vous et les Marguilliers de cet endroit ont bien voulu remettre à ma decision. J'envoie à ceuxçi par la presente occasion une copie de cette decision et je les prie de vous en envoyer une autre.

Je suis revenu de l'Europe il y a pres des trois semaines, ou j'ai eté pour me faire consacrer. À mon retour, j'ai appris que vous etiez maintenant au Cahokias, ou vous trouverez, comme j'espere, un sort plus doux, qu'à l'endroit que vous venir de quitter. Pour votre consolation, j'ai le plaisir de vous annoncer, à vous, Monsr. et aux habitans de Kaskaskias, près du Rocher &c, que j'ai pris des arrangemens avec le Superieur du Seminaire de St. Sulpice à Paris pour recevoir içi, dans l'eté prochain, deux Pretres de cette maison, qui sont destinés à passer au service des Chretientés repandues dans vos contrées; & dont un sera placé au poste Vincennes; l'autre passera à l'Illinois pour desservir ou Kaskaskias, ou Cahokias comme il sera convenu entre vous, et les habitans de ces endroits. Ainsi, Monsr., après toutes les peines que j'ai eu de trouver des Pretres vertueux, et sur lesquels je pouvois me fier avec sureté, la providence daigne ouvrir enfin une voye, par laquelle j'espere, qu'elle ne manquera jamais à supplier aux besoins spirituels des Catholiques, qui habitent les pais occidental des Etats Unis—Dans l'union de vos Sts. S. J'ai l'honneur &c.

TO THE CHURCHWARDENS OF ST. VINCENNES

Baltre.
Dec. 27, 1790

Using the opportunity of Mr. Vigo's departure, I hasten to let you know that, being in Europe, I had the good fortune to make an arrangement with the Superior of the Seminary of St. Sulpice in Paris, through whom you will have the good fortune of seeing arrive in the course of the coming summer a very virtuous clergyman, through whose ministry you will have the happiness of being again aided by the benefits of Religion.

I have no doubt this news will give you very real pleasure, & that you will do everything you can to make his lot happy for him and salutary for yourselves.

I have the honor of attaching to this letter the decision I have reached in a matter which was referred to me by you and by Mr. Gibault, as he has remarked. I sent him my reply in January of last year,[1] but being uncertain whether he has received it I beg you to send him a copy of it. I trust that sooner or later I will have the pleasure of visiting you &c.

ADf   AAB
[1] Not found.

Messrs. Les Marguilliers du poste Vincennes—Baltre. ce 27 Dre. 1790

Je m'empresse, Messieurs, de vous faire sçavoir à l'occasion du depart de Monsr. Vigo, qu'étant en Europe, j'ai eu le bonheur de faire un arrangement avec Monsr. le Superieur du Seminaire de St. Sulpice à Paris, au moyen duquel vous aurez le bonheur, dans le cours de l'été prochain, de voir arriver aupres de vous un tres vertueux Ecclesiastique, par le ministere duquel vous aurez encor le bonheur d'être aidé des secours de la Religion.

Je ne doute que cette nouvelle ne vous fasse un plaisir bien sensible, & que vous ne fassiez tout ce qui dependra de vous pour rendre son sort heureux pour lui & salutaire à vous mèmes.

J'ai l'honneur d'annexer a cette lettre la decision que j'ai fait sur une affaire, qui m'a eté remise par vous & par Monsr. Gibault, comme il m'a marqué. Je lui ai envoyé ma reponse au mois de Janvier de l'an passé; mais etant incertain, s'il l'a reçue, je vous prie de lui en envoyer une copîe. Je me flatte que j'aurai tot ou tard le bonheur de me rendre chezvous &c.

FACULTIES FOR THE CLERGY   [1791]

L   DS   AAB   No date or printer indicated. This is a list of the twenty-one powers granted to clergy of the diocese, which were standard throughout the Church. They touch on marriage questions, confessional absolution, dispensations from vows, the blessing of holy objects, celebration of Mass, etc. Blank space is provided in the beginning for the name of the grantee and at the end for the date. The copy in AAB has been filled in for Apr. 11, 1812. It is assumed that it was printed immediately upon Carroll's return from consecration in Europe and after conclusion of the Synod of 1791, which is quoted in faculty 10. It was accompanied by a letter from E. Fenwick to F. Neale of Apr. 11 [,1812].

GOVERNMENT OF GEORGETOWN COLLEGE   [1791]

a.M.D.G.   It is proper, before the academy is opened, to determine 1o. on its general government. 2o. the particular branches to be taught & the duties of the professors. 3o. the duties & discipline to be observed by all scholars.

4o. the public exercises to be required, & rewards to be conferred on them. 5o. the special duties to be performed by, & the attention to be bestowed on the religious instruction of R. Cath. students. 6o. The salaries of professors, & the means of paying them; and every other matter relating to the temporalities of the academy;

1o. General government. The academy shall be governed by a president, who shall be subject to no controul, excepting that of the superintendents or Visitors,[1] chosen from & by the body of the American Clergy, or such part of it, as may be determined. The President shall have authority over the Masters and Scholars; & require of the former obedience & punctuality in the discharge of their particular duties concerning education. He shall see, that the plan of studies for this academy be carried into execution and that no professor make any deviation from it by his own private authority. If, in defiance of the president, any professor take upon himself to pursue a particular mode of education, he shall refer to the board of Directors,[2] & with their consent shall remove the refractory professor.

The president shall attend personally at all public exercises; shall himself take part in the examination of the Students, shall bestow such public commendation, or reprehension; such rewards or disgrace, as he may judge most conducive to the encouragement of application, and of zeal for literary improvement. He shall visit the different classes frequently; observe the method & attention of the Professors, & the progress of the scholars.

He shall recommend frequently to the Professors to excite their respective scholars to study & a desire of improvement by means of persuasion & motives, which are fitted to act on their understanding & affections, rather than excite their fears. But, as there are some, ungovernable by generous motives, the president shall make general regulations concerning the degrees of punishment to be inflicted in this academy subject however to the approbation of the Board of Directors. (2n. shall this be left to the presidt. or regulated by the visitors?); The predt. to establish a code of penal laws[3] and must provide equally against an excess of severity, or too great remissness in the professors.

The president shall receive from the Supervisors[4] a general regulation concerning the plan of studies, and of discipline to be observed in the academy; to the execution of which it shall be his duty to attend. He must consider himself not only bound to promote literary improvement, but likewise watch over the morals of Teachers & scholars. No immoral Teacher shall be retained; nor any scholar allowed to continue in the schools of the academy, whose habits of immorality shall be found incorrigible & of a tendency dangerous to the virtues of others.

The President must incessantly bend his attention to the points here mentioned: but tho his attention should be unremitted & minute, yet it is advisable for him not to interfere personally, unless circumstances render it absolutely necessary. His authority will be so much the greater, as it is seldomest exerted. Whenever business can be done by the professors themselves, let it be left to them. The president & academy will find great advantage in this; and in general his government will be made easier to him by his testifying a confidence in, &, where it may be done concerting all business relative to the conduct of education with the head professors, who will be flattered by such attention.

The temporalities of the academy shall be under the management of the president; subject however to the inspection and controul of the Visitors.[5]

The hours of school. The days of weekly vacatn General vacation.

2. genl. head. The particular branches of literature to be taught, and the duty of professors in teaching them.[:]

1. The education given in this academy shall begin not earlier, than with those boys, who have already been taught to read. From that period, and at not less than 8 years of age, they may be entered into the academy; and they shall be perfected in their reading, writing, English Grammar, arithmetic, Geography, and, if required, shall receive the first elements of French. A Teacher therefore of English and French shall be provided.

2. There shall be a Teacher of the elements and useful branches of mathematics, whose duty it shall be to instruct his pupils at the hours appointed. If it be found compatible & convenient, the lessons of Geography shall be given by this same professor. (Quaere—may it not be possible to make a lesson of geography a duty of each class? and the particular Master of the class attend to this lesson?)

3. Latin & greek. For each class there shall be a teacher of these languages, especially if the scholars be numerous. The particular authors to be read in each class shall be ascertained in the general regulation of studies. In no class shall the study of English be neglected; but daily exercises shall be performed in it, as well as in Latin & Greek; and, besides an explanation of classical authors in the two last languages, particular English authors shall be read publicly. The Master himself shall explain aloud the lessons for the following day; & accompany the explanation with proper remarks. French shall likewise be constantly attended to, where desired.

4. The masters of the respective classes if Clergymen (excepting the Master of English) shall advance with their scholars, till they commence Poetry. (Quaere—shall they conduct them on to Poetry & Rhetorick? or, shall the professors of those branches always remain the same?)

5. The professors, not Clergymen, shall engage, & they, who are Clergymen shall be directed to submit themselves to the orders of the President in all matters relating to the govt. of the academy & studies: & they must likewise know, that it shall be their duty to preserve in their classes great decorum. They must visit their pupils often at their lodgings, & give them some

employment out of school hours, to prevent idleness & dissipation, as much as possible; they must attend to their morals in and out of schools, as far as it may be directed by the presidt., and must give him notice of any grievous immorality, especially when they are not able themselves to correct it.

6. [*Deleted passage*][6]

3d. general head.—The duties and discipline to be observed by all scholars.[:]

1. Their first duty must be obedience & docility, to the President, their Masters, and all, who are placed over them. Whoever obstinately & perseverantly shall refuse obedience, must be subjected to exemplary punishment; and if he remain incorrigible, shall be expelled from the academy. Their obedience shall be due not only in but likewise out of schools.

2. They shall be punctual in attending at the academy in proper time; & shall perform all exercises required of them, agreeably to the general regulation of studies.

3. They must take great care of their books, pen, ink &c.; & be provided with paper books for writing their exercises.

4. They must keep themselves cleanly & decently clothed, & never come otherwise to school.

5. They must treat each other respectfully & with good manners. If any be notorious for quarrelling, fighting, or for mean abuse of his companions, he will be punished severely.

6. They must all shew extraordinary respect for the President & Professors, wherever they meet them, saluting them with great submission, & uncovering their heads, whenever they go into their presence or to speak to them.

7. Suspended for the present[7] The students of the academy are to be distinguished by some peculiar badge in their dress, without which they are never to appear in publick; and if they neglect wearing it, they shall be liable to punishment.

8. They must avoid carefully all immodest conversation; the frequenting of disorderly company or houses; going to publick houses, or gaming tables; they must never go beyond the limits assigned them; play at games of hazard, or drink intemperately. These vices will be punished with the most exemplary severity.

9. If ever any of the students be concerned in riotous or outrageous abuse either of one another, or of persons not belonging to the academy, they shall be subjected to punishment, or expulsion according to the nature of the case.

10. Students not boarding in the academy, must be & continue all night at their lodgings, six o clock from Novr. 1. till March 1st.; from March 1st. till May 15th. by the half past seven; from May 15th. till Aug. 31. at the half past eight; & from Sepr 1. till Novr. 1st. at the half past seven. They, who board in the academy, must conform to the hours, which will be determined.

11. No student belonging to the academy shall be allowed to bathe, excepting at the place & time to be determined by a subsequent general regulation.

12. On Sundays, none of them are to follow any diversions incompatible with the sanctity of that day; but it is required that all spend it religiously, & with that sobriety, which is required by God's commandment. No playing to be allowed on Sundays—or gaming.[8]

4th. genl. head. Public exercises—Rewards publicly bestowed—Punishment publicly decreed.[:]

1. Daily exercises. Such as may be ordained for each class in the regulation of studies.

2. Weekly exercises. Every saturday a general repetition in each class of all, that has been taught during the week. The last hour, or half hour of school, on each saturday, all the Masters & scholars shall assemble in each school alternately, excepting the English school & two lowest classes of Grammar, & hear the repetition of the class, where they are assembled.

3. Monthly exercises. One day of each month, the President, Professors, and scholars shall attend in the great hall of the academy; where some of each class shall make a public exhibition of their progress, by explaining their authors; by reciting by heart; by reading or delivering their own compositions; by answering historical or geographical questions; shewing their writing, arithmetic, resolving problems &c. The president, on these occasions, will confer at his discretion marks of commendation & rewards; or will testify his disapprobation of idle youths, who have neglected their improvement.

4. Yearly exercises. 1st. A general examination shall be had of each student; by the professors in presence of the president. Their progress shall be noted; those who prove deficient in their examination shall be remanded for farther examination; shall be publicly censured; or, if necessary, shall be sentenced to remain longer in the same class, while their fellow students proceed to a higher.

5. About the same time that this examination is made, exercises for composition shall be given in each class, to be performed in a limited time & for three days successively. At the expiration of the time allotted, these exercises shall be delivered in to the master, who gave the subject, with the name of each person annexed. The progress & literary merit of each student shall be estimated by the compound excellence of composition, & their performance on their examination.

6. On some subsequent day, the best scholars of each class being previously selected shall recite some of their own performances; these exercises shall be introduced by an address from the presidt., and concluded by another from one of the Professors. After which, the names of the students of each class shall be called over, who have signalised them by their merit & pro-

ficience, with some commendation, and, if possible, some reward. If any have deserved by uncommon negligence or irregular conduct to be publicly stigmatised, it must be done on this occasion.

5 genl. head—The special duties of and the attention to be given to Cat. students in their religious instruction.[:] [9]

6. genl. head. Salaries of professors—Temporal concerns of the academy.[:]

1. The salaries of the professors must depend on the funds of the academy: as these will be very scanty, for some time at least, those professors must be preferred, if equally capable who sollicit admission to a clerical state. But as it cannot be expected, that the meer English Teacher will be a candidate for H. orders, it is proposed to give him £80 per ann.

2. The other professors, if candidates for Holy Orders, will give their services, it is hoped, for the same sum. (Quaere. If the president reside in the academy, may it not be advisable to board these professors, who are candidates, & give them £30 per ann. for their exps.?) Professors, already Clergymen to live with President,[10] & have a yearly allowance for their cloathing &c.

3. Each scholar in the English school to pay £5 tuition money. Other scholars to pay eight pounds per ann. half yearly [*fold*] If any scholar die or be removed before the expiration of the half year, a propor [*fold*] part of the payment advd. shall be refunded, if demanded.

4. The president shall keep, or cause to be kept an account with the parents, guardians &c of all scholars: as well as an account of all value received & disbursed; which must be examined half yearly by the board of Visitors;[11] and when the account is approved by them they shall affix to it their approbation & their names.

ADf   AAB   Exact title of MS lacking.

[1] From passage for notes 5 and 11 below, it appears that this is one body and more consistently known by the latter name; it is made up of four members.

[2] Deleted passage at this point has the parenthetical question of whether the president should be empowered to discharge the person. The board appears to include the president and the visitors.

[3] This phrase after the semi-colon appears in the margin of the MS.

[4] The four visitors.

[5] Preceded by "Super[visor]" deleted and followed by this deletion: "If an young clergyman professors or other priests reside with him in the academy, they shall be subject to him for the [. . .]" See note 10 below and its passage reference.

[6] "Catholic Masters must give their Catholic Scholars the example of great respect for Religion; they must attend them to Mass & [. . .]"

[7] Sentence placed in margin of MS.

[8] Sentence placed in margin of MS.

[9] Page is blank below this.

[10] See note 5 above.

[11] See note 1 above.

TO JOHN CAUSSE [1791]

Not found. See to Fromm, Aug. 23, 1791.

TO [?] JUTAU [1791]

Not found. See to Thayer, Sep. 22, 1791

TO THE CONGREGATION OF BOSTON White Marsh Feb. 3. 1791–

Gn–   I was proceeding on a long journey, when I was hon[ored]. with yr. favr. of Jan. 9th &, as you may see by the date of this, have not yet got back to the place of my residence. I am greatly obliged to you & to those, whom you represent, for your congratulations on my return; & you may rest assured, that I feel the greatest concern for the happiness and tranquillity of the Congn. at Boston & a deep sorrow in finding that tranquillity so much disturbed. I forbear saying any thing farther on the subject now, as nothing will be effectual to restore harmony, but my repairing to Boston myself, which I will do as soon as possible tho you must be persuaded, that I wish much for some rest, after my long absence from home. God grant, that my visit to you may produce the happiness we wish for. In the mean time, I earnestly recommend & fervently intreat you not to do, say, write, or publish any thing, which can tend to vilify or irritate Mr. Thayer & his friends, but to waite with patience the result of my visitation, & to pray that it may be attended with the restoration of peace & charity, & the removal of all scandal. I have the honour to be with respect, Gn &c.   J. Balti.

AD   AAB   "Messrs Mass[on] & Campbell" is at the head of the MS. See Apr. 30, 1790, to same and to Thayer for background.

TO JOHN ROUSSELET White Marsh, Feb. 3, 1791–

I duly received at London your letter of July 20th–1790 and a few days ago, being absent from Baltre, I was hond with your favr. of Jan. 2d. of this present year. Before I was honoured with the receipt of the last, I had determined to confirm the appointment made by Mr. Fleming[1] of Mr. Thayer, as I understand that you had announced your resignation, & that Mr. Thayer had been nominated in consequence of it. I had written to Mr. Thayer,[2] that such was my intention: but your last letter, and one received from Messrs Masson & Campbell convince me that my only chance of terminating your dissenssions is to go to Boston, as soon as I possibly can; and in the mean while, my positive injunction on you, as well as on Mr. Thayer is, not to give any hindrance to each other in officiating in your respective places of worship, and to obstain from all publications or addresses to the public in speaking or writing, which have a tendency to vilify or irritate one another, or your respective friends, or to foment divisions. whoever is faulty in this respect, or encourages any of his adherents in such practices, shall forfeit my confidence forever. I did not answer your letter to me at London, because I received at the same time one from Mr. Thayer so contradictory to yours, that it was absolutely necessary to have first more impartial information. Amongst other things, Mr. Thayer inclosed the copy of a letter from you to him written in most uncharitable & insulting language; and since my return, I have seen the copy of another, which he received from you the last of Aug. or beginning of Sepr; for your sake, I hope [it] is not a faithful copy; for it contains so many indecent allusions, & such uncharitable expressions that I should censure you severely if it be written by you.

I am much obliged to you for your congratulations on my return & the very favourable sentiments you are pleased to express in my regard. I am with sincere esteem &c [J. B. of B.?] &c.

ADf AAB
[1] Fancis Fleming, O.P., Vicar General of the Northern District.
[2] See May 25, 1790.

TO JOHN THAYER White marsh, Maryland Feb. 3-1791—

Rev. Sir   I wrote to you some time ago,[1] that I should shortly confirm in regular form your provisional appointment by Mr. Fl[eming]. of pastor of Boston. But immediately after, I was convinced, by letters recd. from your town that no regulation, which I can make, will contribute to the restoration of peace, unless I be there present, & determine, after hearing & seeing all parties. I shall therefore set out on this journey as soon as possible tho it is exceedingly inconvenient, at this time. In the mean while, it is my positive injunction on you and Mr. Rousselet, to let each other officiate without disturbance or molestation in your respective places of worship, and to abstain from all publications or addresses to the public in speaking or writing which tend to vilify or irritate each other, or yr. respective friends, or to foment dissensions. Whoever is faculty in this respect, or encourages any of his adherents in such practices, shall forfeit my confidence for ever. . . . What can be the meaning of a letter I have from Messrs Masson & Campbell, in which it is sd. that you are undr a criml. proscen. [prosecution] by the Atty. Gl. of the . . . [State] & . . . [bound?] over to the Supr. Ct. for trial on the last wednesday in Feby?

ADf AAB
[1] May 25, 1790.

TO CHARLES PLOWDEN   White-Marsh Feb. 3, 1791

My dear Sir   I was obliged to leave Baltimore some weeks ago to make a tour, first to see my good Mother after my return from Europe, & then to Port-Tobo & the Teresian Nuns,[1] whom Charles Neale conducted hither. I came to this house yesterday, & being detained for a few days, I avail myself of the retired situation to pay many epistolary debts, and particularly to answer your last favour of Novr. 29–, which found me two days ago on the road. I gave you information by the first opportunity, of my safe arrival at Baltre Decr. 7th. But having since heard, that the ship, which took my letters for you, Mr. Weld, Ld. Arundell & many other friends[2] was obliged to put back, having sprung a leak, I fear that you have been kept in a state of anxiety longer, than your friendship for me deserved. At my arrival, as my friends in Baltre got notice of the ship being in the bay; I was met by a large body of Catholics & others at the landing, & conducted to our house. On the following sunday, you may believe the concourse of all sorts of people to our Church was very great, tho the day proved unfavourable. Five of my Brethren were with me. They, with the Trustees or wardens of the Church received me, vested in my Pontificals, at the door, & walked into Church processionally; after the *asperges,* & whilst the *Te Deum,* was singing, I was conducted to the foot of the altar, & after it was finished, to the Pontifical seat or throne, where I received the obeisance of the Clergy, & some of the laity, in behalf of the rest, they approaching to kiss the Episcopal ring. The remaining ceremonies were performed, as in the Pontifical, such as giving solemn benediction proclaiming indulgences &c. I have given you this short detail, as I know, that you feel as interest in every thing relative to our Church. It has its successes, and its disappointments here. The Capucin Whelan left his numerous Congregation of Kentucky,[3] composed of emigrants from Maryland, whilst I was in England. They are now without a priest, excepting a rambling Irish one, to whom I refused faculties some years ago. He now sollicits them again; but I shall not grant him any. I am anxious to obtain a good one for the poor souls there who in general are virtuous, & some of them eminently so. At Boston, there has been much offence given to Catholics and Protestants by the disagreement of the two priests & their abettors.[4] I find that I must undertake a journey thither, tho' it be very inconvenient at this time. In other places, we gain ground; and several new settlements for extending religion are in prospect; as in Virginia, N. Carolina & Georgia. In S. Carolina we have one already. Your letter with Coghlan's cartabels is not yet received. Perhaps I shall find it at Baltimore. I trust in God, that our George-town academy will be opened in a few months. Congress having resolved to make that neighbourhood, & perhaps that town their seat, & consequently the capital of the United States, gives a weight to our establishment there which I little thought of, when I recommended that situation for the academy.

I am sorry to learn from your letter, that your internal disputes concerning the oath &c still disturb you. I have always felt, & since my last visit to England feel, yet more than ever, the utmost anxiety for the happiness & respectability of the Catholic body. When I saw Mr. Reeve at Wardour Castle, I found him possessed with an opinion, that the infallibility disclaimed & disavowed by the oath was only, *infallibility* as to facts. I told him, that was impossible no Catholic ever having asserted such a prerogative in the pope. He said, he knew that; but protestants believed & said the contrary, & that this meaning, was clearly ascertained by the bill proposed, of which that oath made a part. As I found him decided in that opinion, & I had not seen the bill, I argued with him no longer; but I was convinced in my mind, that his ground was untenable; & so, you tell me it has proved. I am sorry he has been drawn into that side of the question, as I likewise am for Bp Berington,[5] who is an amiable character, dispassionate & conciliating. I wish, that his being rejected by Rome may not alienate many minds from the centre of Catholicity, & render them easy victims of designing or unsound teachers, such as Goddes &c.

Baltre Feb. 22. I have had yet no opportunity of sending this letter. I resume from the last sentence and conclude that many of your Clergy and Laity will combine to form & insist on modes of election in future which will leave little power to Rome in the Institution of Bishops. Indeed, had the Catholic Clergy required only something of the kind, that is, more powers in the choice of their Bishop, I should have thought them right. But when with that claim, a number of them connected the swallowing down such an oath, they lost with me that interest, which I should have felt otherwise for their success. I shall not fail to attend to the recommendation of our good friend at Rome[6] & convoke a Diocesan synod, as soon as possible; I hope, next summer. But my first object must be to go to Boston, a journey of near 500 miles from this, as soon as our roads & weather will be mended. For we have no turnpikes yet; and at this season of the year travelling on the great thoroughfare roads is dreadful. Mr. Thayer gives me much trouble. I will not say, that he alone is in fault: perhaps I may find his opponent, a French priest, named Rousselet, as much or more so. But Thayer began to write against him in the papers, & some of his friends have answered. I have written to both to desist from their scandalous publications, under pain of suspension. Besides this, Thayer, in the newspaper, gave a sort of general challenge to all adversaries of the Catholic cause to attend his controversial sermons, & to bring their objections. A dissenting minister answered the challenge in the same public manner, & promised to meet Thayer; who replied, that he would stand his ground. I have heard no more yet; but as soon as I heard so much I gave him a good lecture for his rashness, & presumption in undertaking such a step without advising with, or being authorised by his Bishop.

Nothing would induce me to enter into these details, but the knowledge I have of the interest you take in every thing relating to Religion.

It surely is not necessary to request that in assuring Mr. & Mrs Weld of my gratitude, respect, & veneration, you endeavour to convey a most lively impression of those sentiments, & make them fully persuaded, that no one can feel them more intimately, than I do. I have already written a few lines to Mr. Weld; and if I did not esteem that it would be troublesome to him, I should add a few by this occasion. Whenever I call to my remembrance their happy & amiable family, a glow of tenderness spreads over me, and their thousand lovely qualities, their attentions, & sweetness of disposition rush upon my mind. I never saw a more convincing proof, than is exhibited by that family, that nothing is so lovely, as virtue united with a placid temper; & that nothing conveys so forcible an idea of that bliss, which we hope for beyond the grave. I pray most fervently & earnestly, that God may always continue his choicest blessings over every branch of the family: we have the best earnest, that he will do so, in the virtues of their parents & their offspring. It is a reward, due in some manner to the former; and you know it is the promise of the Holy Ghost to the latter. A young man "Walking in his way, even when he is old, shall not depart from it." I have not forgot my promises to Messrs Thomas and Edward. Be so good as to present my respects, as usual, to my dear & excellent friends, Messrs Stanley, Clinton, Porter, Talbot & our other Brethren; those at Wardour particularly. I intend writing to Mr. Forrester; but I may be disappointed in time & therefore for fear of the worse, beg you to mention me to them; & with all respect & gratitude to Lord & Lady Arundell, to Mr. & Mrs Clifford.

I have been obliged to suppress, in great measure the few copies I brought to Coghlan's account of the ceremony of Aug. 15. The clause of the bull, in which the reservation is made to Rome, of future appointments of the Bishop, occasioned such observations amongst a few of our leading men (AntiCatholics) who say it, that it was judged best to disseminate no more copies. You know, how much I objected to that publication. But Coghlan's importunity overcame. I have just read Mr. Burke's pamphlet,[7] &, in general, admire it very much. France is gone. I see, & I wish it may not be, irrecoverably: for Religion, I mean. You have often blamed, & not altogether without reason, the conduct of France for entering into your quarrel with America. However, this may be said; that France aided an injured people in asserting their legal rights. But what can you say now for England, that arbitress of liberty, that scourge of tyranny, for compelling to return to slavery a brave people, who after a series of unparalled oppression, had redressed their grievances without any injury, or the smallest offence of England? Poor Brabant,[8] deserving a better fate! I had the pleasure of finding my Dr. Mother remarkably well in her 80th year; she is ever thankful for your kind remembrance. Our good friend Mr. Digges is not so well. A sore leg at the age of 80, is a serious evil. However he is in good spirits, & takes great delight in hearing yr. letters. They both present their best respects. I am   My Dr. Sir,   Yr. affte friend &c   J.C—

ALS   St   Before the date is written in parentheses: "the residence of Messrs. Ashton, Plunket, & Edenshink."

[1] Carmelites.
[2] Only Dec. 14, 1790, letter to Arundell found.
[3] Charles Whelan served Bardstown, Pottinger's Creek, and Harrod's Town.
[4] Thayer and Rousselet.
[5] Charles Berington, brother of Carroll's correspondent Joseph, coadjutor of Bishop Talbot.
[6] Thorpe.
[7] Edmund Burke, *Reflections on the French Revolution* (1790).
[8] See earlier remarks to Plowden, Mar. 16, 1790.

TO FRANCIS FROMM   Baltre. Feb. 16–1791–

Reverend Sir,   Three weeks ago, I was informed by various sources that the Catholics of Lancaster are much dissatisfied with Your Reverence, and have demanded that someone else be sent there as pastor. Since Your Reverence is not sufficiently versed in English either to preach or even to hear confessions, they especially lament the fact that they and their children are unable to further their knowledge of religion; nor can they derive help from the sacrament of penance, nor, above all, from the Most Holy Eucharist, because they know no language other than our vernacular. Others complain that you are always harsh and morose when you deal with them, and that religious books, which were recommended by your Predecessors and placed in the hands of the faithful to nourish their piety, are considered by yourself as despicable, and condemned as harmful. They further complain that the catechism which was always used is now disdained; and that you are introducing another or are preparing to do so. They say that you hardly ever celebrated daily Mass during your stay in Lancaster, with the result that there has been a lessening of piety and of devotion towards God and the Blessed Virgin. Finally, I do not understand what they mean when they say that, without any reason, you have frequently dealt harshly with a certain widow before the whole congregation.

Therefore, as you have not as yet been admitted officially to the American clergy, but only allowed to engage in certain ministerial works until some decision could be arrived at concerning your position, I have finally come to the conclusion that it would be better for you to return to a monastery in Germany. Whether it be from some weakness of your character or because of the prejudices of others it seems that your labors will bear no fruit for the spreading of the faith here.

ADf   AAB

Baltimore, Feb. 16, 1791   Reverende Domine,   Ante tres hebdomadas, variis ex locis nuntiatum mihi fuit Catholicos Lancastrenses multum conqueri de Reverentia Vestra, atque alium aliquem ibi pastorem postulare. Queruntur imprimis illi, qui praeter nostam linguam vernaculam nesciunt aliam, se suosque filios nihil de religione addiscere posse, neque sacramento paeniten-tiae, adeoque Sanctissimae Eucharistiae umquam adjuvari, quod Reverentia Vestra Anglicam non satis sciat neque ad praedicationis officium neque quidem Confessiones excipiendas. Caeteri lamentantur dure et morose semper secum agis quando te conveniunt; libros religiosos, qui a Praedecessoribus tuis commendati sunt et manibus fidelium traditi ad nutriendam pietatem, nunc a te viles haberi et damnari tanquam noxios; ipsum catechismum, quo semper usi sunt, modo reprobari; teque alium introducere aut saltem prae-parare. Adjiciunt vix unquam per hebdomadam missam a te celebrari, dum ades Lancastriae; unde magna pietatis omnisque erga Deum ac Beatissimam Virginem devotionis diminutio. Demum, nescio quid loquuntur de vidua quadam a te immerito et contumeliose coram frequenti congregatione trac-tata.

Quae cum ita sint; cum clero Americano ascitus huiusque non fueris, sed concessum tibi solummodo, ut quaedam obires ministeria donec, quid de te statuendum foret, perspici posset; meum hoc denuo consilium est, ut Ger-maniam et ad monasterium redeas; siquidem *sive* ex indolis tuae natura, aut ex aliorum praejudiciis fructum nullum ad fidei incrementum videris hic facturum.

TO JOHN THAYER   Balt. Feb. 22–1791–

Tell him he has forfeited all my confidence by publishing his contests in the Newspaper.[1] Nothing can contribute more to vilify us in the eyes of our Protestant Brethren, or give more pleasure to the enemies of our religion &c. I blame not only him, but give to others his opponents their share of blame. I am so affected, that I would instantly withdraw all powers from him & Mr. R., & send a *successor to the pastoral office*, if I had a proper Clergyman &c. Blame him for advertising controversial lectures & undertaking to answer publicly all objections. In a step of so much consequence, he should have advised first with his Bp. Cite Benedict 14th. brief of 1753. Perhaps he carried caution too far. But Mr. Thayers undertaking was too rash & danger-ous, &c. Shall go to Boston, as soon as roads & weather &c. Know not his authority for saying that Indians & all other C[atholics]. in Massachusetts are under him & that no one had any authority to concern with them without his consent. Enjoin, under pain of suspension to publish no more, unless to apologise to the public for bad example &c—

AM   AAB
[1] *Columbian Sentinal,* Sep. 18, 1790, carried Thayer's retort to Rousselet's attack of Sep. 15.

TO JOHN ROUSSELET Feb. 22 [1791]

Have received many of his letters, & extracts from the N.P. [newspaper.] Have seen others not sent by him, particularly publications signed by Messrs Masson & Campbell.[1] If he has had a hand in these, I shall withdraw my confidence from him. If I had another clergyman &c (as to M. Thayer).[2] Under pain of suspension, to publish no more, unless &c (V. supra). Shall go to Boston. But such is the temper of parties, that I hope little success.

AM   AAB
[1] See to same, Feb. 3, 1791.
[2] To Thayer, Feb. 22, 1791.

TO MATTHEW CAREY Balt. Feb. 27–1791

Dear Sir   I am favoured with yours of Decr. 30, with a postscript of Feb. 3rd.; and feel much obliged & indebted to you for the part you are pleased to take in my return. I rejoice with you, that your arduous undertaking is compleated, & shall have great pleasure in hearing, that it will prove beneficial to your interest, as I trust it will be serviceable to my flock. As soon as the bibles can be sent hither, the second part of the subscription money will begin to come in. There is a general impatience prevailing for them. When I was in England, I endeavoured to prevail on Coghlan to take a number of them. He once promised to order 50 copies, but afterwards retracted, on pretence of the difficulty of getting them clear of the custom-house. The Doway bible is quite out of print in England; and if you can, by means of any correspondent, get a number safely landed, Coghlan thinks it probable, they would sell well. Perhaps, in that case, for fear of seisure, your friend should make a new title-page.

I expect to see you at Philada. as soon as it will be convenient for me to move to the northward. It will give me pleasure to find you prosperous in your spirited undertakings, & you may rest assured, that, as far as my abilities extend, they shall be exerted to favour & increase your prosperity. I am, Dr. Sir,   Yr. most obedt. servt.   J Carroll, B. of B.

ALS   HSP

TO [TRUSTEES IN BOSTON] [Mar., 1791]

The Bishop, being desirous of restoring harmony in the Congregation & promoting the increase of religion and piety, has resolved as follows—

First—That the Rev. Mr. Jn. Thayer be appointed to take charge of the Congregation of Boston, as long as the Bishop or his Successors shall judge it to be of general utility to continue him in that employment.

Secondly. That all members of the Congregation be earnestly requested to unite together in divine service; the Bishop promising his best endeavours to procure equally to all every reasonable satisfaction.

Thirdly. That to promote harmony amongst all, a mode of disposing of the pews shall be proposed, in which all may find equal advantage. But the best pew shall be reserved for the Consul of his most Xtian Majesty [of France].

Fourthly—That the Congregation at large ought to contribute & consider themselves as bound to pay a debt, contracted before the late separation, & in consequence of assuming the payment of Abbé La Poterie's debt. The Bishop will think it unjust & dishonourable in the Congregation to let the whole burthen of payment fall on those two persons only, who in this business were agents for the rest.

Fifthly—The Congregation generally will not be under any obligation of contribution to the payment of the debt aforesaid, unless the articles received from Abbé La Poterie be accounted for & restored for the use of the Church, now under the direction of the Rev. Mr. Thayer.[1] I make no order respecting the things sent by the Archbp, because, if they are to be pd. for, & the Trustees are bound for paymt., these last have no other security for their indemnifica[ti]on but the articles themselves.

6o—In case of a reunion of both parties, the Bishop will make farther exertions, if they shall be desired, for the welfare & prosperity of the Congn.[2]

ADf   AAB   Addressee and date established by Mar. 10, 1791. This may have been directed to the whole congregation as well.

[1] Deleted passage: "It is likewise understood by the Bishop, that everything sent by the Archbp [. . . —*double deletion to this point.*] Those sent by the Archbp of Paris were destined for the Congregation of Boston: It is hoped there will now be *one* only; there can be but one acknowledged by the Bishop and consequently [. . .]" It appears that patronage from France gave grounds for the French party in the congregation to claim an ascendancy and a Frenchman for its pastor.

[2] This appears before the fifth point in the MS, "Fifthly" being deleted.

TO JOHN THAYER   Balt March 10—1791

I hereby confirm to you as far as may be necessary, & grant to you spiritual powers for administering the sctnts [sacraments], & exercising parochial duties at Boston. These are to continue in force, till revoked by me or my Successors.[1]

Yesterday I recd. yr. letter of the 23d., the 1st. from you since my return & am rather surprised to find, that you do not acknowledge the rec[eip]t. of any from me[2] nor of many other letters forwarded to you. Rejoiced to hear of his acquittal, tho ignorant of the charge. It is not on acct of yr. acquittal, but for other important reasons, that I have required Mr. Rousselet to resign his pretensions to the pastoral office of Boston. I wished to terminate this matter, when I should be with you myself; but finding it impossible to get away from this [city] before the end of lent, I resolved on this measure without farther dealay. Yr. appointmt. is here inclosed, and it is in the form of all others in this diocese; that is, your faculties are granted *Donec revocentur.*[3] But I beg they may not be published in the newspapers; but kept by you as one of your vouchers; or at most read to the Congregation. As now you will have your authority enlarged, or rather, unrestrained by any opposition, I hope you will use it with such moderation & equal charity, as may engage the hearts & confidence of all. When I left London, Coghlans directories were not come from the press. I left orders for 40 to be sent after me; one was for you. I have heared since that they were sent; but they have not reached my hands. I am R. Sir &c—

P. S. My letter of Feb. 22 did not prepare you to receive the parochial powers, which are now confirmed or granted to you. Indeed my confidence is much diminished by yr. late publications. I trust that you will unite so much self-diffidence hereafter with your confidence in God, as not to undertake things of so much consequence not to yrself only & to Religion at Boston, but every where else without advising with yr Ecc. Supr NB. The faculties granted to you at Phila.   are continued,   *usque ad revocavem.*[4]

ADf   AAB

[1] The addressee and date is stated a second time before the following paragraph.
[2] Of Feb. 3 and 22.
[3] "Until they are withdrawn."
[4] "Until I shall recall them."

TO LOUIS ROUSSELET   Balt. March 10–1791

I write with great concern. You know that I placed gt. confidence in you & felt an affection for you. Judge then, how great was my grief, when yesterday I recd. letters from France & a copy of one from the Bp of Coutance,[1] by which I am informed of matters very prejudicial to yr. character. I know that all these things will be written soon to Boston; and unless all dissensions are composed before they are rcd in that town, your enemies will publish them & scandals will be renewed. For this reason I request & indeed require, that, as soon as you receive this, you make known to your friends, that you have resigned all yr. pretensions to the pastoral office, for the sake of peace & the prevention of farther scandal. This will be the most effectual method of saving your reputation from the discredit into which it will fall, if the accts from France should be divulged. They shall not be made known to any one by me provided you retire peaceably. I shall only write to Messrs. Mass[on]. & Cam[pbell]. that very pressing reasons urge you to resign your pretensions & that I shall only make a temporary provision for a successor, till I can go to Bos. myself. I feel great anxiety for you on every acct &c With a heart full of trouble, I am &c—

NB. As soon as you receive this, you will understand, that I revoke all spl powers & faculties, which were granted by me. I let no one know this besides yrself—

ADf   AAB
[1] In Normandy, France.

TO MASSON AND CAMPBELL   Balt. March 10–1791–

When I wrote my last to you[1] which you honoured with your obliging answer of Feb. 20th, I did not expect that I should have occasion to send you the information, which this will convey. But tho' it gives great pain to me as I am sure it will to you I must send you notice, that reasons of a most urgent nature demand of Mr. Rousselet the resignation of his pretensions to the pastoral office of Boston. He himself will make this known to you. As I cannot, without the greatest inconvenience, set out for Boston before the end of lent, I earnestly request you to use all your endeavours with yr. friends & the friends of Mr Rousselet to acquiese in this necessary & indispensable measure; and to make use of the ministry of Mr. Thayer, notwithstanding all natural reluctance till I can make a permanent establishmt for that Congn In complying with this my request, you will give a fresh proof of yr. attachment to the interests of religion &c—I am &c—

ADf   AAB
[1] Feb. 3, 1791.

TO JAMES EMERY   Baltimore, March 11th, 1791

Since my return, I have taken informations, as exact as the distance of the places permitted, concerning the condition of the French Canadians about the Ohio, Illinois and Mississippi. From the various reports I have received, the situation is as follows:

1) At the post of *Vincennes* or St Vincent, on the Wabash, there are 200 families, all French speaking Catholics, very good people, I am told, sincerely attracted to their religion and its duties. They have no priest at present. There is a fine tract of land attached to the church, and another destined for a presbytery, since the ancient one was destroyed during the late war. The climate and soil are delicious. I have promised the inhabitants that, if possible, they should have a priest within a year. Mr. Vigo, one of the most influential citizens, is anxious to offer him a home with his own family.

2) The village of *Kaskaskias,* on the Illinois, is described to me as one of the finest sites in the U.S. There is a population of at least 300 souls, all Catholics. This population increases every year by the return of those who, during the war, had emigrated to the Spanish dominions beyond the Missis-

sippi. The town has a handsome church, well furnished; but the presbytery was burnt down by accident a short time ago. Kaskaskias is some 50 miles from Vincennes, with which it is connected by good roads. The parish of Kaskaskias and the neighboring localities own extensive tracts of land which, under proper management, promise to become very valuable to religion.

3)Near (Prairie du) Rocher, at 5 leagues from Kaskaskias, there are about 15 families, excellent people and well disposed. They have a church and presbytery, but no priest.

4) At St. Philip–3 leagues from Kaskaskias–5 or 6 families with a small church.

5) Kahokias, 22 leagues from Kaskaskias some 500 souls. They have a priest residing with them since the time they belonged to the Quebec Diocese.

So far I have bestowed little care on these Catholics, because I was in doubt, whether they belonged to my Diocese at all. This point is now settled, and they have been definitely attached to Baltimore.

This is the first position, I can offer to the priests who will come over for Missionary work. They will find in these regions very few attractions, humanly speaking, but can hope to contribute more, perhaps, than is thought at present, to the spread of the Kingdom of Christ.

CS   MPA   "To Sulpician Superior in France" appears at end of this letter.

TO FRANCIS NAGOT   March 11–[1791]

Recd. his letters on the 9th. great joy. Account of affair at Boston. Answer 1o. consent to & rejoice at his & his companys intention to come. 2o. Approve Mr. Emery's design of sending priests & Seminarians. Shall be happy to see Tulloh.[1] Shall write to his Bishop–equally pleased with Mr. Caldwells[2] coming. Shall want masters in the academy who know English; doubt therefore whether the G[entlema]n. from Canada can be employed. 3–give Information concerning the W. settlements–4–will take care of all that shall be sent–desire to have some missals in 4o. & classics–Cor[nelius]. Nepos–Caeser–Sallust–20 copies–Aertius–Ciceronis oranes selectae, de Senectute de amicitia, Somnium Scipionis–de officiis-Virgil. Ovid Tristium–metaphorp[hisis]: all ad usum Debr.–Horatius–Juvenal–by Jouvency[3]–le nouveau testament en grec–histoire fabuleuse de Jouvency–10 copies–l'abbé Batteux–Jouvency de arte docendi &c–2 copies–Join the holy association.

AM   AAB   Notation indicates not sent until Mar. 26.

[1] A young English applicant.

[2] Edward Caldwell was the son of a Presbyterian chaplain killed in the Revolutionary War, adopted by Lafayette and brought to France. Now a Catholic, he applied to the seminary.

[3] Joseph de Jouvancy, S.J., (d. 1719) versatile scholar and literateur of the College of Louis the Great.

TO CHARLES PLOWDEN   Balt. March 21, 1791

Dear Sir   I wrote to you fully the 26th of last month,[1] since which the
packet is arrived with your favr. of Jan. 2d. Before this, you must have heard,
that I arrived here a few days too late to write by the Decr. packet. Your
sollicitude, and that of my most respected & ever esteemed friends on that
account, is a continuation of that generous friendship, which I shall always
esteem as my greatest honour; compared with which, mitres & crosiers are
nothing in my eyes: I abstract from the divine institution of priesthood &
episcopacy, when I say this. God reward you for your donation to the
academy! it will be opened soon; but what to do for a president, I cannot
conceive. I am very glad that Mr. Douglas accepted Mr. Welds invitation to be
consecrated at Lullworth. It will confirm him in his adhesion to the good old
Bishop of Rama,[2] who was himself pleased, I dare say, very much with the
ceremony, tho' it may have fatigued him. He considered, that he was laying
hands on them who would uphold the cause for which he has laboured so
long. Was he as profuse of the oil on their heads, & hands, as on mine? Sacred
as the ceremony, and holy as the unction was, I really was almost sick with
the greasy condition, in which he put me.

I have just received letters from Messrs Emery, Superior Genl. of S. Sulpice
& Mr. Nagot, Superieur du grand Seminaire. Their letters remained so long at
London; and consequently my answer[3] will be so late, that I fear, the colony,
which was to leave France in April under Mr. Nagot, will not set out so soon.
This very day I engaged a house for them. Your first letter, after I left
England, is arrived in Maryland, but not come to my hands. I hear that a
parcel from Coghlan came into Patowmack river some days ago. I have
ordered it here, and expect it soon. In that I expect your favour. As soon as
your new work is finished,[4] order him to send it to Mr. Joshua Johnson's
care. I hope Mr. Thayer will do well now. Having received some unfavourable
accounts of his companion, I have discharged him & left all things at Boston
under Mr. Thayer, till I go there myself after Lent.

I forgot, whether I told you in my last, that the Carmelites have met many
benefactors; that they have begun to receive Novices; & to arrange their
house. The business of a Coadjutor shall be gone on as soon as I return from
Boston.

Your wish, that I might see Mr. Burkes pamphlet, has been gratified. I have
had a hasty reading of it, to which I will return, when I have some leisure. I
applaud him in almost all his sentiments, and admire the extent of his
knowledge, the keenness of his censure & the brilliancy of his wit. His
observations on Dr. Price,[5] applauding in a Christian pulpit the conduct of
the savage wretches, who committed the murders, & insulted their Sovereigns
at Versailles, are a severe, tho just Philippic; and his comparison of their
return to Paris, so pleasing to the Dr., with the Indians of the six nations

coming back to Onondaga from murdering & scalping, is a faithful, tho hideous imagery, & must have brought shame on the patrons of the Old Jewry sermon. However, in many things I cannot agree with Mr. Burke: his principles go almost to persuade mankind to suffer every evil, rather than attempt a change; and surely when he vindicates the parliamentary representation of England, & contends that it is a fair deputation of the sense & interest of the kingdom he flies in the face of common sense. I shall continue anxious to see the work which you were preparing for the press. I have attentively read over your preceding one on infallibility &c.[6] It has given me a great deal of information, & to others likewise. But remember my caution. I fear, there is some mistake in your page 109. If you will consult Lafiteau,[6] *histoire de la Bulle Unigenitus,* you will find, I believe, that the Gallican Bishops, when they adopted the bull, & that which preceded it, Vineam Domini, were very anxious to preserve their character of judges of faith, & before they accepted the Constitutions, examined carefully their conformity with the deposition of faith preserved in their Churches. They would not indeed premise any explanation of the doctrine condemned by the bulls to their acceptation of them, because they knew the art & chicanery of the heretics they had to deal with who would have contended that the Bishops did not receive the Pope's Constitutions absolutely, but only subject to their explanation of them. I shall do myself the honour of writing a few lines to Mr. Weld. Be pleased to tell Messrs Thos. & Edwd, that I have given orders for several days past to buy a ground, and a flying squirrel to send them. I am anxious to avail myself of the opportunity of a person returning to England, who would take good care of them. To morrow is the last market day, in which I shall have a chance of getting them; and shall be exceedingly happy to gratify those amiable, & most estimable young gentlemen. To them & their Brs & Sisters I desire to be most affectionately mentioned. My respects to Mrs Weld will be sent thro her *husband:* I hope English ears are not yet offended with that homely word. To Messrs Stanley and Clinton & Porter, say every thing, that sincere friendship & esteem can suggest to you. I have not seen Mr. Digges or my good Mother since my last; therefore have nothing to say from them. I am my ever dear & respected friend,   Yrs afftely   J. Carroll, B. of Bal.

ALS   St

[1] See letter of Feb. 3-22, 1791, to which Carroll probably refers, there being none for the date he gives.

[2] Bishop Charles Walmesley, O.S.B., consecrated Carroll at Lulworth Castle.

[3] I.e., Mar. 11, 1791.

[4] *Observations on the Oath Proposed to the English Catholics* (1791).

[5] Richard Price, non-conformist minister, delivered the sermon "On Love of Country" Nov. 4, 1789, at a meeting house in Old Jewry (a street in London), which gave occasion for Edmund Bruke's *Reflections on the French Revolution.*

[6] Pierre Lafitan (d. 1764), bishop of Digne in Provence, author of *Histoire de la Constitution Unigenitus* (1737).

TO JAMES FRAMBACH   Balt. March 24–1791–

Rev. Sir—   Having used without effect every peaceable endeavour to prevail on you not to obstruct the service of the Congregations near Frederick, by excluding Mr. R.[1] from his former residence I have advised with many of our Brethren; & they concur in thinking, that compulsory measures must be resorted to, since nothing else will succeed. These therefore will now be adopted unless on cool reflexion, you will finally agree not to give any farther opposition to a measure absolutely necessary for preserving subordn & the salvation of many. I am &c

ADf   AAB
[1] Probably Louis Roels. See to Frambach, Oct. 1, 1787, for source of the problem.

TO FRANCIS FROMM   Ap. 5–1791

Reverend Sir: Only on the first of this month did I receive the letter which you wrote at Lancaster on March 3. From it I understand that you are very much upset, and that certain earlier writings of mine are otherwise interpreted than I intended. For I did not intend to say that affairs were in such a state as you picture them; but actually there are complaints about you from some quarters. It would have been proper, therefore, to read my letter while in a calm frame of mind before you undertook a response. I said indeed that you had by no means been made a member of the American clergy; and this I repeat: for you never promised in writing that you would remain in this vineyard of the Lord as is prescribed by ecclesiastical laws which obtained here before your arrival; nor did it seem expendient to exact this of you for the reason that since you came entirely unexpected you were accepted only conditionally. Nevertheless, granted that leave was given you by your provincial to work here with the permission of the ordinary, your services could be accepted temporarily.

It must certainly be lamented if the state of religion in and about Lancaster is such that among non-Catholics one hears of the bad morals of our people. It is almost three years since I visited them. I have heard about a few that their conduct and manners have deteriorated: but this, in my mind, is not true for the majority; but in this case you are a better judge than I. What you say of the German catechism, namely that it is inadequate and does not contain everything that must be known, I cannot judge because of my limitations in the language. If, however, it be the same catechism used by Mr. Geisler, of pious memory, and a learned theologian, that catechism was held in great esteem. This counsel, however, I give you, that you do not substitute another one before you submit it to the ordinary for examination. I shall provide English catechisms at the first opportunity.

I am not able to indicate if or when you will be given a successor; actually I would not wish to appoint one if you can maintain the station at Lancaster in peace and with benefit to religion. I did indeed suggest a return to Germany, especially because, from the report of many persons, I learned that you, because of the language defect, were of no use to those of our country, and were anything but acceptable to us. I was pained, indeed, that you were reduced to distress for want of the necessities of life: I shall urge Rev. Mr. Ashton to supply what he ought as soon as possible. In the meantime, I am handing over to Mr. Fleming some money so that he may see that you receive it; it is the money which Mr. Sewall entrusted to be sent to you. The sum is eleven pounds and ten shillings; twelve, not eleven pounds were to be sent; Mr. Ashton will correct the error of the account as soon as you chance to meet him.

I learned from Rev. Mr. Fleming that you desire to remain in Pittsburgh. Before a decision can be arrived at, I must know from you what means of livelihood and prospects of fruitful labor you will have there.

A few days after Easter I shall set out for Philadelphia, and there I shall expect further news from you. Did the congregation at Lancaster, and others whom you serve, not contribute anything for the repair of the priest's house?

ADf   AAB

Ap. 5—1791—   Reverende Domine   literas tuas scriptas Lancastriae die 3 Martii, accepi tantum prima hujus mensis; ex quibus commotum te intelligo vehementer, et quaedam a me prius scripta aliter interpretari, quam ego cogitavi. Non enim fuit mihi in animo decere, ita se habere res ac quae de te memorabantur; sed ita se habere quorundam [?] de te querelas. Oportuit igitur animo pacatiore prius legi meas literas, quam te ad respondendum accingeres. Dixi quidem te Clero Americano neutiquam fuisse adscriptum; hocque iterum repeto; non enim unquam scripto promisisti te in hac Domini vinea commoraturum secundum illam formam regiminis Ecclesiastici, quae primo tuo adventu apud nos vim habuit; neque id a te exigere visum fuit, donec plane [*illeg.*] non expectatus advenisti: experimentum tui fieret. Opera tua tamen interea uti licuit, quod permissum tibi esset a tuo Provinciali eam hic impendere, de Ordinarii licentia.

Dolendum sane, si eo loco Lancastriae sint res Religionis, ut tam male apud acatholicos audiat ob perversos nostrorum mores. Sunt fere tres anni ex quo hos visitavi. De paucis accepi, quod vitam minus recte instituerent; at certe de potiore parte longe aliter existimavi. Ita tamen tibi melius, quam mihi perspecta esse debent. Quod ais de catechismo Germanico, scilicet insufficientem esse, neque omnia scitu necessaria complecti, judicare nequeo ob linguae imperitiam: Si tamen idem is sit, quo usus est Dom. Geisler p. m., et Theologus eruditissimus, mirari plane subiret; hoc tamen tibi suggerendum est, ne prius alium aliquem substituere incipias, quam Ordinario, ut examinetur, commitas. Catechismos Anglicos prima data opportunitate submittam.

Indicare nequeo, neque quis neque quo die Successor tibi dandus sit; nullum quidem designare vellem, si tranquille et cum religionis utilitate Lancastriae statio conservari a te queat. Consilium quidem dedi Germaniae repetendae, praecipue quod ex multorum relatione didici te, propter linquae defectum, nihil nostratibus prodesse; neque fere quidquam apud nos gratum esse. Dolui quidem te ad angustias, propter vitae necessaria, redactum fuisse; R. D. Ashton monebo, ut, quae debet, quam primum, subministret. Interim nummos aliquos, quos D. Sewall tibi mittendos commisit, ad D. Fleming transmitto, ut tibi deferendos curet. Summa est undecim lib., & 10 solidorum. Duodecim non undecim lib. mittendae erant; errorem computi corriget D. Ashton, quam primum erit occasio ipsum conveniendi—

Accepi a R. D. Fleming cupere te Pittsburgi commorari. Antequam statui quidquam possit, scire a te oportet, quid ibi commodi ad vivendum et fructuose laborandum sis habiturus.

Paucis post pascha diebus, Philadelphiam proficiscar, ibique ulteriorem ex te notitiam expectabo. Nihilne subsidii conferent ad domus presbyteralis reparationem Lancastrensis congregatio, aliaeque, quibus deservis?

TO LOUIS ROUSSELET   Apr. 12th [1791] Baltre

I received on the 9th your packet of the 25 of March. It did not surprise me to find, that you were much affected by the contents of my last.[1] I could tell you with truth that my own mind was very much distressed when it became necessary for me to act as have done respec[tin]g. you. but, since you & your friends suspect me of acting for particular designs I shall say no more relative my feelings. When we meet, perhaps you & they will do me more justice. You assert positively that my information from France was sent first to Boston & from Boston to me. In this you are entirely mistaken. My advices came to me directly, and the inform[a]n[t] was collected from persons, of whom Mr. Thayer knows nothing. When I am persuaded he will not be made acquainted with the matter of wch, I have [given] notice. I once thought, that some of his acquaintance in Fr. would write to him on this business; But later letters from France assure me that to me alone informaon will be sent. Messrs Masson & Campbell conclude their letter by bidding me farewell: I suppose this was an informaon not to answer them. My intention remains as in my last, to visit Boston immediately after the Easter holidays. I expect to meet trouble there; but I trust, He will give fortitude for whose sake I must encounter it. I am still, Revd. Sir,   Yr affte & most humble St &c—

ADf   AAB
[1] See Mar. 10, 1791.

TO WILLIAM STRICKLAND   Ap. 19—1791—Baltre.

For an organ I will make myself responsible for £st. 120 to be remitted before Aug. 15—1791. If it should require ten or twenty guineas more, & notice sent in time, am confident, the addl sum would be remitted before Xtmass. Mr. Webb was mentioned in London to me as a benevolent & intelligent Gentleman to direct the making of it. Dimensions of church—75 feet long, high in proportion—from organ loft to the highest part of cieling 13 1/2 feet; lateral height 11 feet—9 inch. front breadth of loft, clear for the organ, 12 f. 6. Depth 10 feet—may be made more. Mahogany frame if not too dear, & pipes gilt, or painted gold colour. If mahogany too dear, other wood painted mahogany. Six stops—vox humana & flute—to be sent by fall ships to Balt. & insured to first cost—well packed, pieces marked, & directions sent for setting up. Cases marked R.R.D.J.C.[1] No. 1. No. 2 &c bill of lading sent with it to me or Rev. Mr. Chs. Sewall Balt. Mr. Johnson if needful, will ship it, & shall receive usual commission—Capn. Moore,[2] if finished in time. Organ builder determine whether one or two bellows.

ADf   AAB
[1] Rt. Rev. Dr. John Carroll.
[2] Thomas Moore, master of the ship *Sampson,* on which Carroll returned from his consecration in England.

TO CHARLES PLOWDEN   Boston June 11—1791—

My dear Sir   I have been near three weeks in this town: Mr. Thayer has quarrelled with the French & I wish I may not lose my labour in trying to compose their differences. As it almost constantly happens in these cases, both sides are in fault. It is wonderful to tell, what great civilities have been done to me in this town, where a few years ago a popish priest was thought to be the greatest monster in the creation. Many here, even of their principal people have acknowledged to me, that they would have crossed to the opposite side of the street rather than meet a Rom. Catholic, some time ago. The horror, which was associated with the Idea of a Papist, is incredible; and the scandalous misrepresentations, by their ministers, increased the horror every sunday. If all the Catholics here were united, their number would be about one hundred & twenty. It is probable there are more concealed, & who, in consequence of intermarriages, long disuse and worldly motives, decline making an acknowledgement of profession of their faith. In these circumstances, I am very sorry not to have here a Clergyman of amiable conciliating manners, as well as of real ability.

When I was on my way hither, I did not expect to remain more than ten days, & therefore requested all letters for me to be stopped till my return at

N. York. This has prevented my receiving any from you as I hope to receive, by the April packet just arrived. You may be assured, that I feel an eagerness to hear from you which is very much increased since my visit to Lullworth. So many attachments unite me to the inhabitants of that noble mansion, that I cannot but feel the most anxious desire of being informed of their health and happiness. I expect to meet, at my return to Baltimore the Emigrants of St. Sulpice. A vessel arrived at this port from St. Malo gives me room to believe, that those good gentlemen must be arrived. The public prints inform us of the bill being brought forward in behalf of the Rom. Catholics, and I fear that it is only in favour of the *Protesting* R.C.[1] Your letter would give much light to this transaction. Having written fully to you about the last of March I shall only add, that if I have a moment to spare & an opportunity at New York in my way to Maryland, I shall write to you more fully. Inform our very good friend Mr. Thorpe of my movements.

My best respects to yr. good Ld. & lady of Lullworth their amiable family & our good & respectable Brethren. I am with the utmost affection Dr. Sir,   Yr. most sincere f[rien]d   J. Carroll, B. of B.

ALS   St
[1] Reference to the Catholic Relief Act of 1791 and related discussion of the oath, etc.

ACT OF SUBMISSION FOR JOHN THAYER   Boston June 13. 1791—

The subscriber having been charged with saying, that he would not obey the Bishop, but would place himself under the Jurisdiction of the Pope, in case he should be ordered by the Bishop to leave Boston; hereby declares that he does acknowledge & will submit to the authority of the Bishop, in case his removal should be required by him; & this shall be binding on him, until a general regulation respecting the power of the Bishop in removing Clergymen be settled by common consent of the American Clergy—John Thayer Boston June 13, 1791—

AD   AAB   In Carroll's hand but signed and dated by Thayer.

TO LOUIS ROUSSELET   Boston June 16—1791—

To have seen you would have been much more agreeable, than to receive the polite letter, which you left for me here. On my arrival, I presented your recommendation to me, which was to wait immediately on the Consul. I performed that duty, before your letter was delivered. With him & one or two more of your friends I was obliged to descend to some particulars & shew a part of the information received concerning you. But I have not done this with any others. Even Mr. Thayer knows nothing from me more than that I have received advices from Paris which will not allow me to make any farther use of your services. With all this, I cannot help feeling much regret; for certainly you had gained a considerable share of my affection. But since my arrival in this town I find that you administered the sacrament of penance after your powers were revoked. Did you forget the penalty, which is annexed to such a violation of the laws of the Church? Even now, your visit to the Indians, however charitable & well intended it may be, is irregular, & exposes you to the danger of administering & them of receiving invalidly the sct. of penance.

I have committed this Congregation for the present to Mr. Thayer, & hope you will not disturb its tranquillity.

Mr. Fitzsimmons[1] paid sixty dollars for you at New York; Mr. Fleming claims for Mr. Beeston a much larger sum. I presume that the deposit left at Philada. to answer these demands will be sold. I am &c—

ADf   AAB

[1] Luke Fitzsimmons ministered in New Jersey and New York during this period and later.

PASTORAL APPOINTMENT OF JOHN THAYER   16 June, 1791—

John, through the mercy of God and the approval of the Holy See, Bishop of Baltimore, to the Reverend sir and brother John Thayer, Priest, perpetual greeting in the Lord.

Impelled by my great trust in your religious spirit and zeal for the spread of the glory of God, by these letters I constitute you the pastor of the Catholics in Boston, according to the tenor of the faculties already imparted to you. I authorize you to prevent transient priests from exercising any functions of the sacred ministry before you have examined their documents, and satisfied yourself in respect to their faith and morals. This should be done in a prudent and charitable manner. And if the stay of such men should be extended you will take care that data in regard to them be referred to me or to my successors, or to my Vicar General closest to you.   Given at Boston this 16 of June, 1791—

Joannes, divinae miseratione et Apostolicae Sedis gratia Episcopus Baltimoriensis Rev. D. et Fratri Joanni Thayer, Presbytera, salutem in Domino Sempiternam.

Tua pietate et studio divinae gloriae amplificandae multum fidens, hisce te Catholicorum Bostonensium pastorem constituo secundum tenorem facultatum jam pridem a me concessarum; et auctoritatem concedo cavendi ne peregrini sacerdotes sacrum aliquod ministerium exerceant antequam visis documentis, de fide et moribus secundum prudentiae et charitatis regulas de ipsis statueris. Cavebisque, si fuerit mora illorum diuturnior, ut vel ad me, meosque successores, vel ad Vicarium meum generalem tibi proximiorem de ipsis referatur.   Datum Bost. Hac 16 Junii. 1791.

TESTIMONIAL IN FAVOR OF JOHN THAYER
Boston the 16th day of June 1791

In order to remove all doubt and uncertainty from the mind of any one of the Cath. Congregation of Boston I hereby make known to all concerned, that the Revd Mr John Thayer & no other is now appointed to exercise all pastoral functions for the said congregation.

In witness whereof I have signed & sealed this present instrument at Boston the 16th day of June 1791.   J.C.B. of B.[1]

ADf   AAB
[1] This appears first in the letterbook and was intended as verification for the lay inquirers into Thayer's authority. There was no Latin version of this.

TO JOSE IGNACIO VIAR
New York June 25—1791—

Sir   Having been honoured with your enquiries relative to the state of the Roman Catholic Congregation at Charleston S. Carolina, I take this earliest opportunity, since my return from Boston, to give you the best information in my power. Your first enquiry was, the number of Catholics in that town. This cannot be exactly ascertained, both on account of many being often absent at sea, or on commercial business in the inland Country; & more especially on account of the small & exceedingly inconvenient house, wherein they now meet for divine worship; by which many are prevented from attending. But I have no doubt of the number being at least between four & five hundred, & the certainty of a great increase. The 2d. enquiry was, the expence of building a Church & fitting it with all necessaries for divine service. It is meant, I presume that the Church should not only be sufficient for the actual Congregation, but for such as it will be in a few years. The expence of finishing such a Church with all its appurtenances cannot be less than 15,000 dollars. The furnishing it with necessary ornaments for the altar linen, priestly vestments &c would be an additional expence; but as these can be obtained cheaper in Spain I presume that they, who may be appointed to carry into execution his Majesty's gracious benevolence, will order them to be made there & forwarded to Charleston.

You enquire farther, in whose hands the money destined for the Church of Charleston may be safely lodged. My answer is, that the safest method of disposing of it is, to have it placed with the Ministers of his Catholic Majesty residing in the United States; & in the mean time enquiry shall be made concerning some proper & responsible persons at Charleston who may give security for a right use of the money put into their trust.

Repeating my former request, that you will be pleased to offer to his Majesty the tribute of my most grateful acknowledgment for his religious intentions twoards the Congregation of Charleston I have the honour to assure you of the highest esteem & respect of, Sir,   Yr. most obedt. servt.   J. Bisp. of Baltimore

ALS   ADf   AAB   There is a Spanish notation by the addressee on one MS indicating that it is an ALS.

TO MATTHEW CAREY   Philada. July 12. 1791.

Messrs. Carey & Steuart—   The Revd. Mr. Sewall of Baltimore, & Mr. Stenson of the same place, as well as I myself, are anxious to know whether our directions have been attended to respecting the binding of our bibles; theirs directions respecting the one, for which they subscribed; & my directions for one of the six, I have taken. I am Gentlemen,   Yr. most h. st.   J Carroll.

ALS   HSP

TO PARISHIONERS IN GOSHENHOPPEN, PA.   Philada. July 14th 1791

Dr. Brethren in J.C.   I received a few days ago your address concerning the misconduct of the two persons, you have mentioned, Henry Gibson and John Miller: you likewise have thought proper to bear testimony to the good conduct of the Revd. Mr. Helbron whom I appointed some years ago to take charge of your souls. I have never heared of Gibson & Miller, excepting what you have written. I cannot do otherwise, than condemn very severely their behaviour, as it is stated in your letter: and certainly no Catholic can vindicate their expressions. But, as I have not heared them, and as it is probable, that they would complain of being condemned without a hearing, if I were to pass a censure against them; I can only say at present, if they be guilty that Mr. Helbron will do well to require from them public satisfaction for the scandal they have given, before he admit them to the Sacraments; and that if Miller, as you say, leads a life publicly & notoriously scandalous, he ought not to sing in the Church.

With respect to your commendations of Mr. Helbron I am exceedingly glad, that he acquits himself of his ministerial duties so much to your satisfaction. That he may continue to do so, & that his ministry may be advantagious to your happiness here & hereafter is the fervent prayer of,

Dr. Brethren in J. C.,   Yr. most obedt & humble st   J Bisp of Bal.   For the United States

ADf   AAB

TO MRS. RIDLEY   Baltimore, July 22, [1791]

Bishop Carroll, with two letters and a parcel for Mrs Ridley, sends his most respectful compliments. He informed Mrs Jay that he should be detained a considerable time on the road, & prevented from delivering the letters &c., as soon as she might wish; but she was so kind as to say, that she rather wished them to be delivered safely, than soon. The Bishop hopes, that Mrs. Ridley will receive them agreeably to the desire of her, who honoured him with the commission, & rejoices in the occasion, he has had of being of the smallest service to Mrs Ridley.

AM   HU

TO JOHN HEILBRON   George Town Aug. 14 1791—

Rev. Sir   In compliance with your desire, I consent to your Brothers going immediately to your assitance at Philada.[1] When you are ready to depart for Europe, I will recommend the success of[2] yr. sollicitations in favr. of Trinity Church, by a paper addressed to all.[3]

ADf   AAB   Extensive deletions occur.
    [1] "I have directed his successor to go immediately to Goshenhopen" is deleted at this point.
    [2] The following to "Church" is deleted.
    [3] "[*illeg.*] & able Xtianis" is deleted. Additional deletions say that Heilbron may send for his brother to replace him if he so desires.

TO PETER HEILBRON   [Aug. 14, 1791]

Reverend Sir: While I was in Philadelphia, I learned from your brother that he wishes, and Your Reverence desires eagerly that you be sent to him as soon as possible, as an aid, and you will remain at Philadelphia, while he shall return to Europe to gather help for the Church of the Most Holy Trinity. I freely assent to this desire of yours; and so that the more quickly you may be able to accomplish this plan, I am sending at the same time along with these letters, Reverend Mr. Nicholas Delvaux,[1] to whom all things have been entrusted, even [those things] which pertain to the spiritual aid of souls, whose care you are now engaged in, as well as temporal things to be managed through you by an administrator; and you were considered worthy to prepare the list itself for everything, which they were able to use whether in the cultivation of souls, or in the cultivation of the country, if these are the things which need special mention. I commend myself to your holy S[acrifices of the Mass] & prayers—&c—

ADf   AAB   This letter is on the same page following the previous one in English, which alone has a date. It is assumed the same date covers this Latin letter. "Copies to Messr. Peter & Ch. Helbron Aug. 14 1791" is inscribed on the margin of the concluding page of the Latin letter.
    [1] See Mar. 7, 1793.

Rev. de Domine—   Dum essem Philadae, intellexi ex fratre tuo ipsum cupere, et Ram Vam exoptare ut illi quam primum subsidio mittereris et Phil. subsisteres ipso in Europam redituro causa colligendi subsidia pro Ecclesia Smae Trinais. Huic vestro desiderio, libens assentior; atque ut citius hoc consilium exequi possis, mitto simul cum his literis Rev. Dom. Nicolaum Delvaux, cui omnia committenda sunt, tam quae spectant spirituale animarum subsidium, quarum curam nunc geris, quam res temporales fundi, per Ram Van administrati; dignaberisque ipsum dotem de omnibus instruere, quae usui esse poterunt sive in animarum, sive in ruris cultura, si quae sint, quae speciali commemoratione indigent. Commendo me Ssmis S. et precibus—&c—

TO FRANCIS FROMM   Baltre 23 Aug. 1791—

Although I returned to Baltimore a few days ago, this is the first free moment I have to undertake a reply of Your Reverence's letter from Philadelphia on the seventh of this month. Rev. Mr. Sewall denies that he received any money other than the amount sent to Mr. Ashton; he conjectures that Mr. Ashton referred to the same sum in his letter to you, as you may recall. Ask him about the matter when opportunity arises. What is due to Your Reverence I do not know at all, nor is it my concern. Your predecessors always took care of repairing of the house; and I am certain that Mr. Ashton neither should nor can meet those expenses because of the narrow straits he is in. I am still of the opinion, that the parishioners of Lancaster entrusted to your care were abandoned by you; and without the authorization of Your Ordinary, you went to another parish unlawfully, and there exercised parish duties. This contravenes every law of the Church. In the letter which I wrote on April 5th, I pointed out that I did not want to appoint a successor to you, if the said parish of Lancaster could be handled by you with fruit; nor did I desire that you go to Pittsburgh, until I receive further information on that place. Subsequently, you left Lancaster and went to Greensburg[1] without consulting me, or even mentioning your plans to me. I state the facts as I heard them; whether they are true or not, you know well enough. First: that you desire to alienate the parishoners, and especially the German parishoners, from me, their Bishop, by suggesting that I am not sollicitous for them, and do not care for them: Second: that you ostentatiously presumed to insinuate that I enjoyed no right to the distribution of goods, which Rev. Mr. Browers, of pious memory, applied to sacred uses. Actually, I never interfered in that business, except inasmuch as a Bishop should, by reminding Mr. Cause of his duty:[2] Thirdly: you declared that you could exercise and that you intended to exercise the sacred ministry wherever you wished and without my consent. Before another parish will be assigned you, I await a reply to these charges, one without evasions, and also an explicit acknowledgement of my ordinary jurisdiction, extending throughout all the provinces of the United States. This I do because a story was designedly circulated by Mr. Cause, perhaps by others also, and spread by Germans, to the effect that I am in no way their Bishop. Your letter seems to imply that you took fifty books from the effects of Rev. Mr. Browers. By what right you did so, I do not know. However, that affair must not be transacted with me, but with the Executors of his will, upon whom falls the obligation of accounting for everything to Rev. Mr. Pellentz. What you add about the scandal arising from civil action against Rev. Mr. Cause, is, it seems, indirectly aimed at me, although I had no part in it, I gave no advice, and knew nothing of the affair. But now, since action has been resorted to, I both approve it and judge it necessary. If any scandal results, let it recoil on him who made it necessary. Would that nothing more serious and more unbecoming happen.

ADf   AAB

[1] Westmoreland County, Pa., where Brouwers initiated a parish and supporting property.

[2] Letter not found. On situation see to Antonelli, August 6, 1789. Cause later removed himself from the ministry and there is no evidence that he accepted Carroll's invitation to return.

Mr. From—   Baltimore 23 Aug. 1791.   Reduxi Baltimorem ante paucos dies, hoc primo instanti aliis rebus vacuo, accingo memet ad respondendum litteris Rae Vae datis Philadelphiae septima hujus. R.D. Sewall negat se alios nummos accepisse, quam qui ad Dom. Fleming transmissi fuerant: ex quo conjicit de illis ipsis locutum fuisse Dom. Ashton in suis ad te literis, quarum meministi. Ipse tamen de hac re consuletur, ubi erit occasio. Quid Rae Vae debeatur, ego prorsus ignoro, neque ad meam provinciam spectat. Praedecessores tui de domus reparatione sibi semper providerunt; certumque mihi est Dom. Ashton nec debere, neque propter rerum angustias posse illas expensas solvere. Etiamnum in eaden sum opinione, derelictos a te fuisse Lancastrenses tuae curae commissos, et sine quavis Ordinarii Tui auctoritate, aliam stationem te injussum adiisse, ibique munia parochialia exercuisse; quod est contra omnem regiminis Ecclesiastici rationem. Literis, quas scripsi 5a Aprilis, significavi me nullum tibi successorem designare velle, si eadem Lancastriae statio utiliter a te conservari posset; neque cupere, ut Pittsburgum versus progredere, donec ampliorem de loco illo notitiam haurirem. Posthac, me inconsulto, et nequidem communicato mecum consilio, Lancastria derelicta, Greensburgum adivisti. Hic addo, quae audio, verene an secus, tu optime nosti. Primo: quod Diocesanos meos, ac praecipue Germanos, a me Episcopo suo alienare studeas, suggerendo me nihil de ipsis neque ipsos curare sollicitum esse; Secundo: quod cum quadam affectatione frequenter commemores nil juris mihi competere circa dispositionem bonorum, quae sacris usibus applicuit Rev. Dom Browers p.m.; quasi ego me unquam illi negotio immiscuissem, nisi quatenus Episcopum decet, D. Cause sui officii commonendo; tertio: quod asserueris te posse et velle, ubi libuerit, et absque meo arbitrio, sacra ministeria exercere. Antequam statio aliqua nova tibi assignabitur, tuum ad haec responsum sine ambagibus, expecto, et explicitam declarationem meae jurisdictionis ordinariae, sese extendentis per omnes foederatae Americae provincias. Quod ideo sequitur, quoniam de industria circumfertur fabula a D. Cause, ac forte ab aliis, per ora Germanorum me illorum Episcopum neutiquam esse. Videntur tuae literae significare 50 libros a te desumptos fuisse ex bonis R.D. Browers; quo jure, haud equidem scio; res tamen illa non mecum transigenda est, sed cum Executoribus ejus testamenti, quibus incumbit reddere rationem omnium Rdo D. Pellentz. Quae adjicis de scandalo facto ob actionem civilem adversus R.D. Cause, oblique, ut videtur, in me jactantur; quamquam nil de ea re aut egerim aut suaserim aut sciverim. Sed nunc, ubi intentata est actio, et approbo, et necessariam judico. Si quid scandali resultet in illum recidet, cui imputanda fuit necessitas. Ast utinam nihil ab illo gravius et indignius fiat.

TO JOHN TROY   Aug. 24. 1791

Inform him I want three priests of his recommendation—to live removed; consequently they must be men of unblemished morality, sobriety & of good knowledge. Desire that Mr. Henry Campbell, Curate of Belfast, may be one of the three, if the Arbp find his character to be such as described—Mr. Phelan from Cork not gone to Georgia, but to a smaller distance. Aug. 24—Mr. Hy. Campbell Curate of Belfast—Accept his services, if approved fully by Dr Troy—The sooner he comes the better.

AM   AAB   See ALS version below under this date.

TO JOHN TROY   Baltimore, August 24, 1791.

My Lord,   I recur to your Lordship with the utmost confidence in every concern of religion, where your advice, direction, or co-operation can be obtained. Such is my esteem for your Grace, and the abilities to direct and guide with which God has blessed you, not only for the good of your own country, but also, I trust, of this. I stand now in need of three clergymen for the service of poor abandoned Catholics. They promise faithfully to provide a comfortable support for their pastors. As I know of no country but Ireland which can supply our wants, I presume to make them known to your Grace, not doubting but you will, with your wonted zeal, make known my desire to some virtuous clergymen. Allow me to request, that none may be selected for this service, of whose fitness your Grace has not the fullest conviction, either from personal knowledge or from such testimony as is entirely satisfactory. The stations for which they are destined require men of solid and approved virtue, for they will be left in great measure out of the reach of control or eye of inspection; consequently, unless they be thoroughly established in the habits of a sacerdotal purity of manners, sobriety, and of zeal, they will not be qualified for that destination which is intended. Besides this first requisite of an irreproachable conduct, strength of bodily health is absolutely necessary to undergo the fatigues and constant hardships of labour and diet to which they will be exposed. Finally, they will be placed amongst strangers and bitter enemies to our faith and Church, who will often seek opportunities of engaging in controversy, and not unfrequently with much dexterity. This renders it advisable and indispensable for the clergymen fond of study, of improved understandings, and, above all, skilled in theological science. If your Lordship can find out such, disengaged from more important employment, and zealous to bestow their labours in my diocese, I shall ever esteem it a great favour to receive them from your hands. If your Grace can obtain a character, corresponding to that which I have drawn, of the Rev. Mr. Henry Campbell, curate of Belfast, I shall wish him to be one of the three. I received lately a letter from him, well and sensibly written. He says, that Dr. Karny, President of the Seminary at Paris, the Bishop of Down, in whose diocese he now is, and the Archbishop of Armagh, his native bishop, will bear testimony to his conduct. I shall refer him to your Grace, and if approved of by you, I will receive him.

Our friend Mr. O'Brien was well in Mexico last May, collecting dollars for his church in New York. His vicar, Mr. Michael Burke, of your order, the excellent Mr. Fleming, and his young friend Mr. Keating, are likewise well.

I have the honour to be, with the greatest respect and veneration,   My Lord,   Your Grace's most obedient and humble servant,   J., Bishop of Baltimore.

L   Moran, III, 518-19.

TO JOHN HANCOCK   Baltimore Aug. 28th 1791

Sir   I should have great cause to reproach myself, & would deserve the imputation not only of ingratitude, but absolute insensibility, if I neglected to make my warmest acknowledgments to your Excellency for your innumerable favours, & civilities, during my stay at Boston. They were such as both astonished and confounded me: and I should have paid much sooner the tribute, which I owe your Excellency, if I could have commanded the smallest leisure since my return to Baltimore. I knew that your Excellency was conspicuous for civility & politeness, as well as eminent for patriotism and public services; and I had always heard, that the town of Boston was distinguished for its hospitality: But every thing was far beyond my highest expectations. When my friends here ask me the particulars of my late journey, I feel myself incapable of conveying to them adequate ideas of the friendly, the cordial, the honourable treatment, which I received from the first magistrate of the Commonwealth; & from its respectable citizens: and now that I would testify to your Excellency the grateful feelings of my heart, I experience the same inability of expressing them as strongly, as they are impressed on me.

I must take the liberty of requesting your Excellency to assure Mrs. Hancock, that I retain for her the same sentiments; that her affability & condescension have made a lasting impression on me; & that I shall be anxious for the moment, when I may again renew to both of you every testimony of my respect and veneration. That respect will not allow me to trouble your Excellency with conveying to others my most thankful and respectful compliments. My list would be a long one; for the civilities conferred on me were without number. But I know that your Excellency sees frequently Mr. & Mrs Jaffray, Mr. Sheriff, & his respectable sister Mrs Brown, the Rev. Mr. Thatcher,[1] & Judge Sullivan.[2] Will it be too much presumption to ask, that I may be mentioned to these, as full of gratitude for their civilities & politeness, & as anxious to give every proof of it, which they can command. Desiring once more my very humble respects to your most obliging & polite Lady, I have the honour to be with the utmost esteem,   Sir, Yr. Exy, most obedt & humble Servt   J. Carroll—

ALS   GU
[1] Peter Thatcher, prominent Congregational minister.
[2] James Sullivan, later Governor (1807-08).

TO JOHN THAYER												[Sep. (?), 1791]

Not found. See to same, Sep. 22, 1791.

TO CHARLES PLOWDEN										Baltre. Sep. 3d. 1791

My dear Sir   Since my last, I have received yours of June 12th & July 4th. with the comfortable news from England, & the distressing advices from France. After congratulating most sincerely with you on the happy issue of all your struggles, and giving you full credit for all your zealous endeavours, I shall suppress reflexions on that event, as well as on the unfortunate situation of France and its *late* monarch; for I have no doubt of *his deposition* at least by this time.[1] When I returned from Boston in July, I had the happiness of finding here Mr. Nagot with his company from St. Sulpice; himself, & three other priests belonging to the establishment, viz: a Procurator & two professors; and five seminarians, amongst whom are Messrs Tulloh & Floyd, (English)[,] Caldwell, a native of the United States; and one most amiable Frenchman, already a great proficient in English, & a Canadian. They will be joined soon by one or two natives of this Country. Besides these, came with Mr. Nagot another worthy priest, Mr Delevau, lately Canon of St. Martin de Tours,[2] and a man of handsome private fortune. His attachment to Mr. Nagot, & his excessive sensibility at seeing the devastation of religion in his own Country, drove him from it. These now form the Clergy of my Cathedral (a paltry Cathedral), and attract a great concourse of all denominations by the great decency and exactness, with which they perform all parts of divine service. If in many instances the French revolution has been fatal to religion, this country promises to derive advantage from it. Besides the Seminary, which will be the source of many blessings, I expect some other valuable & useful priests. One, well known to Mr. Nagot, is just arrived in Virginia[3] with a number of French Emigrants, who propose forming a settlement there. You were informed before of those, who arrived last year, and are now well established on the banks of the Ohio under a Benedictine Monk, as their Pastor;[4] a vigorous and active man; but not quite so fervent, I fear as the one just arrived. My only apprehension respecting the Seminary is, a deficiency of means for its support. I believe that my Brethren will join me in appropriating to its use the income of one of our estates here, the annual value of which may be sufficient for the support of the four Directors: in time, the whole of the Clergy here will be pupils of the Seminary, & they will not fail to provide for their *Alma Mater.* In the mean time, I must seek assistance from my friends to pay the boarding & cloathing &c of Mr. Tulloh during his studies; that is, about four years. He has nothing to expect from his family. After all your, and Mr. Welds unexampled liberality to me I should be ashamed to sollicit your farther favours. But good Mr. Stanley, Mr. Clinton, Mr. Porter, and Mr. John Talbot will be kind enought to devote a small annual subscription (for four years) to this good work; that is, to perfect the extraordinary work begun in this youth by divine providence. I beg you, with my affectionate & respectful compliments, to recommend this business to their charitable consideration. I would trouble no person in Europe on this head, were I not obliged here to find means to pay for two other Seminarians. Our George-town academy will be opened next month, but no president yet to be had. This is a terrible inconvenience. The Mr. Elling[5] from Rome is arrived, a good man & promising to be an useful labourer, if his health prove sufficient. We really want some good German priests to make amends for the very indifferent cargoes of Friars & Capucins, we have had from that Quarter. There must be evidently a most deplorable decay of discipline in those orders; the members of them such as I have seen appear destitute of all sense of their own religious duty. Prayer, recollection, fasting, obedience, humility are utterly neglected by them; or little regarded. Some days ago, I received a most earnest letter from a tribe of Indians, whom I knew not to exist in the United States. They are just within the boundaries of Massachusets, & confining to Canada & Nova Scotia. They pray earnestly for a priest; they will have none who is not sent by proper authority. I have already sent for hither two French priests, who are able to support themselves & wish for such employment. If I have time, I will send a copy of their letter, & an account of these good people.

Such have been my continual occupations since my return that I have not yet had leisure enough to convoke a diocesan synod. If possible, one must be held early in November. The business of a Coadjutor, and many regulations to be formed call loudly for the holding of such a meeting. My diocese is yet badly regulated; and it cannot be [*torn*] better, till I can command more time to form regula[tions] [*torn*] alone to answer all letters, to copy them, to attend to a [*torn*] much is of course neglected, & forgotten. If I do not [*torn*—write] often or as fully as you have a right to expect, you must [*torn*—not im]pute the fault to me, but to unavoidable hindrances. I assure you, that there are twenty people in this town to whom I owe, & wish to pay the respect of a civil visit, without having been able to do it for many months; tho' I am busy from five in the morning till between ten & eleven at night. I must however find time to answer Mr. Welds most obliging favr. by the July packet. I have given directions to my market man to get me two ground squirrels & one flying squirrel for my young and amiable friends, to whom as well as to every member of the excellent & honble. family I present my most respectful compliments. My good Mr. is very much pleased with & thinks highly of the honour of yr. constant remembrance. I have not seen Mr. Digges lately. Dr. Sr. Ever Yrs. J. C.

My enquiries hitherto respecting the wife of Michael Brien have been ineffectual. Kentucky is not yet supplied. I am obliged to have recourse to Ireland for it; & expect two priests from thence to go thither. Two wanted in Georgia; one in N. Carolina; four or five in different parts of Maryld. & Pennslvania.

ALS MPA
[1] Louis XVI was not suspended until August, 1792.
[2] Canon Louis de Lavau, S.S.
[3] John Dubois, future bishop of New York, arrived at Norfolk in 1791.
[4] Gallipolis was founded by Peter Didier, O.S.B., in 1790; he later went to Missouri where he served as vicar general.
[5] William Elling, a controversial clergyman at Lancaster, Pa.

TO JOHN ALLEN[1] Baltimore Sepr. 6–1791

Sir Your favour of May 21st., with a postcript of the 23d. was not received before the 27th, of August. I am infinitely obliged to you for your great attention, goodness & charity in forwarding to me the speech of the Indians, of whom you bear so favourable a testimony. My duty & inclination concur in urging me to use my utmost and earliest endeavours to procure them the help which they so earnestly solicit; & letters are gone already for that purpose.[2] I shall be much mistaken as well as disappointed, if those letters produce not the effect desired; but some delay must be looked for. The clergymen destined for this business are now in Europe & cannot come I fear before the spring. But when they do come they will, I am confident, give satisfaction. I say Clergymen; because many reasons have induced me to send for two; This will not increase the charge of the Indians; at least not for some years to come when they will be better able to bear it, as their number probably will be greater. I had not the least knowledge of the tribe of Indians, till, at a late visit to Boston I saw a letter [*torn*–about] them from you to the Rev. Mr Thayer.

Their attachment to the exercises of religion, notwithstanding [*torn*] long deprivation of its public functions, their innocent lives, & their care to instruct their children are strong proofs of the deep impression made on their minds, &, as you justly observe, do great credit to their former French Pastors & Missionaries. My happiness will be great, if Those whom I shall expect next spring, will talk in the footsteps of their predecessors. Conformably to your advice I have sent back the Crucifix, &, in addition to all [*fold*] other kindnesses, request you to be so good as to explain my letter to them. Your services entitle you to all their confidence, & have made it my duty to acknowledge myself, with great esteem & respect, Sir   Yr most obedt & humble st.

ADf   GU
[1] Agent for the U.S. Government for the Maine District.
[2] See March 11, 1791. Francois Ciquard, S.S., went to Maine the following year.

TO THE INDIANS OF MAINE   Baltimore September 6th, 1791

Brethren and beloved Children in Jesus Christ—

I receiv'd with the greatest pleasure the Testimony of your attachment to your holy Religion; and I venerated the sacred Crucifix sent by you, as expressive of your faith—
Brethren and Children,
I embrace you with the affection of a Father, and am exceedingly desirous to procure for you a worthy Teacher and Minister of God's holy sanctuary, who may administer to your young people, your sons and your daughters, the Sacrament of Baptism; may instruct them and you in the law of God, and the exercise of a Christian life; may reconcile you to God your Lord and Maker after all your transgressions; and may perform for your women after Child-bearing the Rites ordained by the Church of Christ.

Brethren and beloved Children—

As soon as I received your request, and was informed of your necessity, I sent for one or two virtuous and worthy Priests to go and remain with you, that you may never more be reduced to the same distressful situation, in which you have lived so long. But as they are far distant, I am afraid they will not be with you before the putting out of the leaves again. This should have been done much sooner, if I had been informed of your situation. You may depend upon it, that you shall be always in my heart and in my mind; and if it please God to give me time, I will certainly visit you myself.

Brethren and beloved Children—

I trust in that good God, who made us all, and in his blessed son Jesus Christ, who Redeemed us, that all the Indians, Northward and Eastward, will be made partakers of the blessing, which my desire is to procure for you; and I rejoice very much, that you and they wish to be united to your Brethren the Americans. You have done very well not to receive amongst you, those ministers who go without being called; or without being sent by that authority, which Jesus Christ has established for the government of his Church. Those, whom I shall send to you, will be such good and virtuous priests, as instructed your Forefathers in the Law of God, and taught them to regard this Life only as a preparation for, and a passage to a better in Heaven.

In token of my Fatherly Love and sincere affection, I send back to you, after embracing it, the Holy Crucifix, which I receiv'd with your letter; and I inclose it in a picture of our holy Father the Pope, the Head on earth, in Christ, of our Divine Religion; and this my answer is likewise accompanied with nine medals representing our Divine Lord Jesus Christ and his most holy Mother. I desire that these may be receiv'd by the Chiefs of the River St. Johns, Passamaquady, the Mickmaes, who signed the address to me. They came from, and have received the Blessing of, our same holy Father, the Vicar of Jesus Christ in the Government of his Church.

That the Blessing of God may come down upon you, your women and Children, and remain for ever, is the earnest prayer of   Your loving Father, Friend and Servant in   Jesus Christ   J. Bishop of Baltimore

ALS   NEHGS; ADfS   GU

TO JOHN THAYER   Baltimore Sepr. 22d. 1791

Rev. & Dr. Sir   I have received your favour of Aug. 21. by Capn. Wailes—, by whom I hope to send this. I sent you a letter by another Boston Capn. (name forgot) about 3 weeks ago,[1] and with it two altar stones of the dimensions, which you desired. By the same vessel, I sent an answer to the Indians,[2] recommended by Mr. Allen; from him and them I received a pressing letter for a clergyman to live with them; a clergyman is sent for, who, I hope, will arrive in the spring. You need have no fears about him, or them;

for probably, there will be two: & as far as human foresight can prevent it, they will give no scandal. The only method wch I can devise to make & perpetuate tranquillity in your Congregation is, to send you a companion. I have written in consequence for Mr. Matignon[3] & hope that he will be at Boston during the course of the winter.[4] I am informed that he will be able to subsist for some years; during which other measures may be concerted. As I know, that he is agreeable to you, I conclude that a good understanding between the Clergy will produce a like effect in the Congregation. I have informed some of the other side that I was labouring for the general happiness of all. To Mr. Jutau who complained much of my treating his letters with contempt, I have written,[5] that besides other reasons of my silence to him, it would appear improper for me to correspond with a person who was deemed unworthy of being continued even amongst the Freemasons.

Did you ever report, that I gave you directions *not to mind the French,* but to attend only to those whom you called your own people? As I never said so, it is not credible that you ever related it. However I have denied the fact to the Consul, to whom, I suppose it was related. They say likewise that you alledged my instructions for removing the pews.[6]

I think, that you have a good prospect of living peaceably in some months: and in the mean time, I earnestly recommend to you to pave the way for that happy event.

I was glad to hear you are resolved to pay your part of the debt. It is honourable & just. The Gentleman who promised me a sum of money for the uses of my diocese, will disappoint me I fear. He had done nothing yet. Depending on this fund, I made the conditional promise to your church of £ st.25. You advise me to forbid all complaints against you: such an order would raise a greater ferment than ever, a cry of injustice; and direct disobedience.

ADf   AAB   A single, light line indicates possible deletion of two passages noted below.
[1] Not found.
[2] See Sep. 6, 1791.
[3] Francis Matignon, S.S., ordained in 1778 and holder of a doctorate from the Sorbonne, jointed Francois Ciquard on the Maine Mission the following year.
[4] The following two sentences appear possibly as deleted.
[5] Letter not found.
[6] The following paragraph appears possibly as deleted.

DIOCESAN CIRCULAR ON SYNOD   Balt. Sep. 27–1791

Venerable Brethren—   In compliance with the decree of the Council of Trent, sep. 24. ch. 2. de Ref. I purpose to hold a diocesan synod on monday the 7th. of next Novr. in St. Peter's Church Baltimore. Many other reasons, besides the obedience due to the above cited decree, have determined the convocation of this synod. The necessity of consulting together on the mode of continuing the Episcopacy of the United States; of providing for the decent ordering of divine worship; of establishing uniformity in the administration of the scmts [sacraments], & discipline of the diocese; & in the exterior government of its Clergy; of concerting means for the extension of our Holy Religion; of devising means, if possible for the decent support of its ministers; these are the principal objects, which will engage your attention.

All Clergymen within the Diocese, secular or regular, employed in the care of souls, are entitled to a seat in the synod: and I should be happy to see you all assembled from every quarter of this extensive diocese, that uniting yourselves together in closer bonds of brotherly charity & encouraged by mutual example, we might devote ourselves with renewed zeal & assiduity to the exercises of an Apostolical life. But I know, that the necessities of the Faithful will make it impossible for all to attend: I desire therefore, that in every district, in which some Clergymen must remain for the sake of the sick & these would communicate their sentiments on the most important points to those Gentlemen, who will come to Baltimore.

In the mean time, between this & the holding of the synod, I beseech you all my Venerable Brethren, to address your fervent supplications to our gracious and merciful God, imploring light and direction from him, that our joint deliberations may contribute in a great degree to preserve, or revive amongst ourselves holiness of life, & exemplary zeal; in the faithful committed to our care, a thorough reformation of life & purity of morals; and generally, an extension of true Religion to promote & increase true faith & religion and holiness throughout the United States. Direct to the obtaining of these important objects all your exercises of piety, & mortification. I humbly recommend myself to your H. S. S. & prayers, & have the honour to be Revd. & Ven. Brethren

ADf   AAB; ADS   AAB   The first version is slightly fuller in content.

TO CHARLES PLOWDEN   Sep. 27, 1791

MPA   Not found.

TO MEMBER OF THE BOSTON CONGREGATION Baltimore Oct. 6—1791

Dr. Sir   As your name stands foremost in the list of subscribers to a paper, which is dated Sepr. 20th, & was received the first instant. To you I address my answer. You and some others of the Congregation have been informed already of my intentions, & of the endeavours, I am using to restore peace amongst you, so necessary for your own improvement in virtue, and for general edification. But if you are not yet content & expect more from me within the short time allowed by your paper I will not deceive you by promising more than I can perform. You give notice that you will send for a priest; who shall not put himself under the jurisdiction of any Bishop. The obvious inference from this is, that you [*illeg.*] to yrselves can never possess, and which schismatics alone pretend, conferr any spiritual [*illeg.*] If unfortunately any priest should be wicked enough to accept his spiritual powers from you that alone will be sufficient proof of his being unworthy of confidence and my duty will command me to interdict him without delay. after wch, you may call him indeed your pastor, & make use of his sacriligious ministry; but I now give you warning, that every pretended act of spiritual jurisdiction exercised by him without Episcopal [*illeg.*] will be null & void; and your consciences will be loaded with a accumulated guilt for resorting to his ministry.

I find it necessary to speak thus plainly to you. I must not leave you ignorant or unmindful of the most certain principles of your faith. The proposed measure is calculated to defeat every hope, and every temperate plan for effecting the so much desired reconciliation. It affords your opponents a plausible opportunity of say, that to gratify your resentment, you are ready to endanger yr. Religion & expose the Sacraments, and even the venerable sacrifice of the altar to a sacrilegious profanation: for these would be the certain consequences of calling an unauthorised priest to officiate amongst you.

You require me to order Mr Thayer to rebuild the pews; & to remove him before the 20th of this month & send you another Clergyman. Were the pews built by the Congregation, or any individuals of it? if so, let either the Congregation or those individuals assert their right to have them restored: I have no objection, if this be done without any breach of charity: To comply with your other requisition of removing Mr. Thayer now would not only be exciting violent opp[ositio]n, but leaving the sick the dying & all generally without assistance even in their greatest need. This I will not do, & am sorry you should demand any thing, which my conscience forbids me to grant.

ADf   AAB

TO CHARLES PLOWDEN   Baltre. Oct. 12–1791.

My dear Sir   The August packet is arrived; but without a letter from you. But I have no reason to complain; you perhaps may have some reason to think *me* remiss in writing; but if you were with me and could see how much I write & then copy for myself, you would not blame me. As far as inclination and friendship are concerned, you have the best right to expect letters from me; but even those claims must give way to duty.

God be praised, the 14th of July[1] has passed away without any violence committed agst. the Rom. Cath. of England; I wish the Dissenters had escaped as well; their sufferings will be a lesson to them not to celebrate with so much parade the memory of a revolution which is connected with principles destructive of the government and constitution of England. I persuade myself, that your Dissenters did not mean to countenance those principles; they must be very blind to your national happiness, if they did; but when once the people are taught to celebrate as great and glorious, what has been done by others; the next step is to follow the example, without discriminating, what was praiseworthy, from that, which was subversive of all order, and licentiously wicked.

The favour shewn lately to Rom. Cath. in England;[2] and the disposition which must now prevail amongst the leading men of the established Church (who are certainly alarmed by the attempts of the Dissenters), would lead me to hope for a happy reunion of England with the Catholic Church, if morals were less corrupt, and the belief of the Christian religion more universal, than, I fear, it is. Men of abilities, temper and moderation might avail themselves of these favourable circumstances; and they would find in the writings of Grotius, of an *essay towards Catholic communion,* and others,[3] many inducements to facilitate so great a work. The Church is likely to lose France; the schism is in its progress to a consummation: the enemies of religion there have had the art to connect pretended political liberty with the subversion of the Catholic faith; and thus the giddy multitude are deluded. When I reflect on this, I say to myself; will not divine goodness repair elsewhere the loss of France? and what country will be so great a reparation as England, the influence of whose example would extend itself over every other protestant Country?

I have already sent you an account of our Seminary.[4] It is now going to begin its functions. The spiritual exercises commence the 16th. inst., which will be followed immediately by the literary. I have entered two American youths into it a few days ago. They will fill the chasm which is likely to happen soon. Mr. Floyd,[5] a young Englishman who came with them from Paris, brought a beginning consumption which has increased so much that he cannot live many days. Mr. Caldwell, whose Fr. was a presbyterian Clergyman in the Jerseys, & was killed during the late War, became one of Mr. La Fayette's family, was carried by him to France, became a Catholic, and entered amongst the Gentlemen of St. Sulpice. Since his arrival here Mr. Nagot, who placed the utmost dependance on him sent him to see his friends, amongst whom I fear he will now remain, at least, there is much reason to apprehend it.

The academy will be opened in a few days; but not so advantagiously, as I hoped. No president *pro dignitate loci.* I can hardly forgive my friends at

Liege. Here was an opportunity for infinite services to the cause of God and his Church. Mr. Molyneux cannot be prevailed on; and indeed he has not the activity of body, nor the *vivida vis animi* [lively spirit] for such an employment. I have recurred to Mr. Plunkett, but cannot get his answer yet. Pray for the success of this establishment, after having concurred to it by your benevolence.

On the 7th day of next month our Clergy are to meet here in a diocesan synod. Then we shall discuss the mode of preserving the succession to the Episcopacy of the United States. Instead of a Coadjutor, I am much inclined to sollicit a division of my diocese, and the creation of another Bishoprick. One only objection of much weight retards my determined resolution in favour of this scheme; and that is, that previous to such a step, an uniform discipline may be established in all parts of this great continent; and every measure so firmly concerted, that as little danger, as possible, may remain of a disunion with the holy See. I am very fearful of this event taking place in succeeding time unless it be guarded against by prudential precaution. Our distance, tho not so great, if geometrically measured, as S. America, Goa, and China yet in a political light is much greater. S. America, & the Portuguese possessions in Africa & Asia have, thro' their metropolitical Countries, an intermediate connexion with Rome; and the missionaries in China are almost all Europeans. But we have no European metropolis, and our Clergy soon will be neither Europeans, nor have European connexions. Then will be the danger of a propension to a schismatical separation from the centre of unity. But the Founder of the Church sees all these things, and can provide the remedy. After doing what we can we must commit the rest to his providence. As I write to Mr Weld, I will send my complimts. to the family of Lullworth thro him. You will be good enough to present them to Messrs. Stanley, Clinton, Porter, Talbot &c. Exhort them not to forget our academy. I have not seen your publications, which Coghlan was to have sent. I am my Dr.Sr., Yr. affte friend &c   J. Bp. of Baltre.

ALS   MPA
    [1] Second anniversary of the storming of the Bastille.
    [2] Catholic Relief Act of 1791.
    [3] Hugo Grotius (1583–1645), *Resolution for Peace in the Church* (1614), *Via ad Pacem Ecclesiasticam* (1642), and *Votum pro Pace Ecclesiastica* (1642).
    [4] See Sep. 3, 1791.
    [5] He died of yellow fever in 1797.

TO JOHN HEILBRON   Balt. Oct. 18th 1791

Rd Sir   I have recd your's of the 13th inst I suppose that Your long journey had some other object besides that of visiting the poor people you mention.[1] However commendable such an undertaking may be in a Clergyman who has no fixed residence, and constant charge; I can not approve of it in them, who without leave of the Bishop or his Vicar, quit their proper station & ramble at so great a distance from the flocks specially under their care. However, I thank you for your information; but wish you to make it more particular. In what part of the country, in what country, or near what town, do those Catholics live, whom you say you found out? are they near to each other, or scattered in thin habitations & at great distances? will a German or an English Clergyman be most useful to them? will they build a house, & stock the land, which they are willing to give for his support? will they afford him subsistance & necessaries, till the land is made fit to give him a living? will they pay for his passage from Europe? These points must be ascertained, before I can venture to send for a Clergyman to assist them: and thus things must remain, till it shall please God to raise up a race of priests, devoted to the salvation of souls, and ready to go, wherever they are directed by their Ecc. Supr with reliance on providence alone for their subsistance. I trust in God, that our new Seminary will furnish Ministers to the American Church endowed with this spirit; and then my Successors will have a glorious opportunity of extending the reign of J. C.

Inclosed is your certificate, such as I promised; but not such as you sollicited in yours, I have many reasons of which you cannot be ignorant for not giving you so ample a commission as you now ask for. the stile of your letter preceding that, wch I now ansr & many other things, you must remember, forbid me to employ you in behalf of my diocese for the purposes;[2] whenever I see proper to make such an application in behalf of my diocese, as you wish to undertake, I shall chuse my own agent. This hinders me not from cordially wishing that you may obtain sufficient to pay the debts of, & finish compleatly Trinity Church & that you may have a safe voyage to Europe. My compliments to your Revd. Brother. &c.

ADf   AAB
[1] Missionary excursions among Pennsylvania Germans described in the following sentences should not be confused with travel to Europe noted in 2 below.
[2] See Certificate of Travel, Oct. 18, 1791. "You mention" is deleted before the semicolon.

CERTIFICATE OF TRAVEL FOR JOHN HEILBRON   18 October, 1791

John, Bishop of Baltimore by the grace of God and good will of the Apostolic See, wishes health in the Lord to the Reverend John Charles Helbron, priest of the order of the Minor Capuchins. You have made known to us, Reverend Father, your longing to return to Europe and awaken the benevolence of the Faithful in behalf of the newly constructed church in Philadelphia dedicated to the Most Holy Trinity. Your wish is to free it from debt, and add to it those touches which contribute to the grandeur of God's house and the completion of a work begun. We willingly accede to your earnest desire, and heartily commend you and your undertaking to our Most Reverend Confreres the Prelates, and to such as God has enriched with kindness and prosperity. To authenticate the foregoing we have affixed our signature and seal to this letter. Baltimore, October 18, 1791

ADfS   AAB

Joannes, Dei et Apostolicae Sedis gratia, Episcopus Baltimori. Reverendo Patri Joanni Carolo Helbron, ex ordine Min: Capuccinorum Saderdoti, salutem in Domino. Significasti nobis, Reverende Pater, desiderium tuum Europam repetendi, ibique Fidelium charitatem sollicitandi pro templo Sanctissimae Trinitati sacro, quod nuper Philadelphiae constructum est; ut nempe ore alieno liberetur, atque iis rebus instruatur, quae ad *decorem domus Dei,* et operis incepti perfectionem pertinent. Huic tuo desiderio libenter acquiescentes, Te, et susceptum a te consilium, Reverendissimis nostris confratribus, Ecclesiarum Praelatis, et aliis, quos Deus et charitate, et rerum temporalium abundantia fecit locupletes, plurimum commendamus, In quorum fidem has literas manu nostra et sigillo munivimus Baltimor 18a Octobris, 1791.

SYNOD REPORT   [November 7-8, 1791]

TO THE GREATER GLORY OF GOD   The Most Reverend Bishop of Baltimore, through letters sent to his clergy September 27, 1791, promulgated his decree that a Diocesan Synod would be held in the Church at Baltimore on November 7th of that year; and he invited to this Synod all the Priests of his Diocese who were officially charged with the salvation of souls and the sacred ministry.

On the day appointed for this assembly the following clerics convened at the Episcopal Church in response to the summons:
James Pellentz, Vicar General of the Bishop for the entire Diocese.   James Frambach[.]   Robert Molyneux, Vicar General for the Southern District.   Francis Anthony Fleming, Vicar General for the Northern District.   Francis Charles Nagot, President of the Episcopal Seminary of St. Sulpice.   John Ashton   Henry Pile   Leonard Neale   Charles Sewall Sylvester Boarman   William Elling   James Van Huffel[1]   Robert Plunkett Stanislaus Cerfoumont   Francis Beeston   Lawrence Grassl   Joseph Eden Louis Caesar Delavan   John Tessier[2]   Anthony Garnier[3]

FIRST SESSION, NOVEMBER 7

All the Priests assembled at the appointed time, vested in surplices, while the Bishop was vested in rochet, amice, alb, cincture, stole and cope, and he bore his precious mitre and his Bishop's staff. At ten o'clock they marched in procession to the Cathedral Church of St. Peter, where all the proceedings were transacted according to the *Roman Pontifical.* After the sermon by the Bishop, all the Priests made a profession of faith; and having named Rev. Leonard Neale and Rev. William Elling as promoters, and Rev. Francis Beeston as secretary, the session was adjourned until three o'clock in the afternoon.

SECOND SESSION

Since nothing in our religion is more sacred or more precious than the Sacraments, we must take special care that they be liturgically administered and worthily received. At the outset, therefore, the Sacrament of Baptism was proposed for discussion, for it is by means of this Sacrament that men are made members of Christian Society. In view of the fact that in our land we must mingle with many Protestant sects, who either do not administer Baptism at all, or administer it only to adults, or, since they deny that it is necessary for salvation, manifest but little care in conferring it, WE DECREE:
1. That conditional Baptism be conferred upon those whose valid Baptism, after diligent inquiry, cannot be morally ascertained. Also on those infants, who, when in danger of death, were baptized by non-Catholic nurses. This should also be done even if they were baptized by Catholic nurses, unless the Catholics were such that there be no room for prudent doubt about the validity of the Baptism administered by them. Pastors must take great care, however, not to re-baptize without any investigation of all who were not first baptized by a Priest, lest they fall under the censure of irregularity decreed by Pope Alexander the Third against repetition of Baptism.[4]
2. We decree that as far as possible, the Pastors of souls write in a book specially set aside for this purpose, the name and age of all whom they baptize, as well as the names of the Parents and Godparents.
3. When adult heretics, who have already been validly baptized, are converted to the faith, there is no need to supply the ceremonies of Baptism that were omitted.

CONCERNING THE SACRAMENT OF CONFIRMATION

4. Generally speaking we decree that for this Diocese the Sacrament of Confirmation be not conferred upon children before they have reached the use of reason, and before they are capable of receiving the Sacrament of Penance. Not infrequently, however, because of particular circumstances, it may be conferred upon younger children.

THIRD SESSION, NOVEMBER 8

CONCERNING THE MOST HOLY EUCHARIST

5. The Sacrifice of the Most Holy Eucharist must be celebrated with all due honor and reverence, and the Faithful should be aroused more and more to the greatest devotion toward this immense pledge of divine mercy in our regard. We wish, therefore, that the people be frequently warned how unbecoming it would be for anything which is used in the Sacrifice to be cheap or dirty, or for the vestments or the linens or the wax candles or the sacred vessels not to be suitable to the offering of such great mysteries. Let them be earnestly reminded how in the Old Testament God commanded that the greatest care be shown for those things which pertained to divine worship. How much more, therefore, does this apply to Christians, who do not, like the Jews, possess the shadow of Goodness, but possess Truth itself and the fulfillment of all prefigurements? Let them likewise be advised of those offerings, which the first Christians always brought forth during the Sacrifice. Let them be further instructed that the divine glory is completely neglected [by those] who provide none of those things, without which the exercises of religion seem to lose their dignity and authority, and the honor paid to the Most Blessed Eucharist is greatly diminished.

6. We decree, therefore, that in each congregation two or three men of especial virtue and authority be chosen as curators of the Church by the pastor or by the congregation itself, and that on Sundays and holy days the curators so chosen, after the reading of the Gospel in the Mass, take up a collection of these offerings.

7. According to the ancient custom of the Church, the offerings should be divided into three parts, if that is necessary; so that one part provide for the support of the Priest, the second be used for relieving the needs of the poor, and the third for furnishing the necessaries of divine worship and for the upkeep of the Church. But if, on the other hand, provision has already been made for the support of the Ministers of the Sanctuary, and for the pressing needs of the poor, let all the offerings be employed in providing for the sacred vessels and for other appropriate articles for divine worship, and for the upkeep of the Church, or even building other Churches in suitable locations.

8. The offerings made by the Faithful to render God propitious to themselves and their families through the most Holy Sacrifice of the Mass should be received by those who serve the altar in such a way as to avoid all appearance either of avarice or of simony. And they should be content with that stipend which will be neither too onerous for those giving it, nor so moderate that the ignorant come to regard the priestly ministry as cheap or of little worth.

9. For the manifestation of greater reverence, Priests must always wear a black cassock when celebrating the Most Holy Sacrifice of the Mass, in so far

as it is possible without inconvenience; and they must wear the cassock also, together with the surplice and stole, in all other public ministrations.

10. It is known from experience that it helps greatly toward the conduct of his entire life, as well as for his eternal salvation, with what preparation a person receive the Holy Sacrament of the Eucharist for the first time. Wherefore all diligence is to be employed by the Pastors of souls, that before First Communion the youth be properly trained in Christian doctrine; and especially that they keep their consciences free from every stain of serious sin. For this purpose the Priest must advise them that before their First Communion, they should make a general confession of their entire past life, after a careful examination of conscience, and with great contrition of heart. The Pastor must also take care that the time of this First Communion be not deferred too long; but on the other hand, they are not to be permitted to receive as soon as they have attained the use of reason. Since the great excellence of the Eucharist demands greater maturity of judgment, it should be postponed until a more perfect use of reason has been attained.

CONCERNING THE SACRAMENT OF PENANCE

11. That ignorant or unworthy Priests may not bring harm to souls by abusing this Sacrament, so wholesomely instituted by Christ to heal the wounds of conscience, under penalty of suspension from all exercise of Orders IPSO FACTO incurred and reserved to us, WE PROHIBIT any Priest, whether secular or religious, who is not approved either by us or by our Vicar General, from hearing confessions. This holds true also for those whose approbation has been revoked, and who presume to engage in its ministry except in a case of necessity. Let the Faithful who have recourse to the ministry of such a Priest, understand that by no means are they absolved from their sins, but they still remain guilty and must present themselves again in the Tribunal of penance to a legitimately approved Priest.

12. WE PROHIBIT also under penalty of incurring a suspension, that any Priest, leave the Congregation committed to his care, go to another without our consent, attach himself to it, and presume to carry on parochial duties.

CONCERNING THE SACRAMENT OF EXTREME UNCTION

13. This Sacrament should be conferred even on boys and girls in danger of death, providing they have attained the use of reason and are capable of committing sin.

CONCERNING THE SACRAMENT OF MATRIMONY

14. Wanderers and travellers are not to be admitted to Matrimony, except after three announcements have been made according to the prescription of the Council of Trent; or unless altogether sufficient testimony be had from

the Pastor of the place whence they came, stating that they are free from previous bonds of marriage.

15. No one may be admitted to Matrimony who is ignorant of Christian doctrine or the principal mysteries of the Faith. But here we must add the following Decree from the Council of Lima, which we feel will be useful and a source of comfort to the pastors of souls, in this diocese, where there are many African slaves, not to mention others, who for various reasons can receive but little instruction in matters of faith. But this decree is concerned with those who are not able to learn Christian doctrine by that method by which others commit it to memory, but who desire to receive the Sacraments and manifestly wish to enter into marriage. Wherefore it is decreed: "They who are burdened with such great impediments that they cannot be instructed in the fullness of the Catechism, must be instructed at least, according to their capacity, in the principle doctrines of the faith; namely that there is one God, the author of all things, who rewards with eternal life those who approach Him, and punishes the wicked and those who rebel with eternal punishment in the afterlife. This God is Himself Father, Son, and Holy Spirit, three persons, to be sure, but one true God. Furthermore, the Son of God, in order to restore man's salvation, became man of the Virgin Mary, suffered for us and died, rose from the dead, and reigns forever in eternity. This is Jesus Christ, our Lord and Savior. And finally, no one can be saved unless he believes in Jesus Christ, and, doing penance for the sins he has committed, receives the Sacrament of Baptism if he be an infidel, or of Penance if he has fallen into sin after Baptism; and furthermore, he determines to observe those things which God and the Holy Church command, the greatest of which is that he should love God above all, and his neighbor as himself."

16. Let the Pastors of souls earnestly see to it that Catholics do not enter into marriage with non-Catholics; but, because of their continual dealings with them in every phase of civil life, it is impossible not to contract marriages of this sort from time to time, especially in those places in which, as yet, there dwell but few Catholics. Therefore, after hearing the opinions of our Brethren present in this Synod, we establish the following regulations according to which Priests, to whom has been committed the care of souls in this Diocese, should proceed when there is question of these mixed-marriages. 1. Let them, with all seriousness and gravity, admonish the Catholic party of the great inconveniences which arise not infrequently from marriages of this sort, and let them exhort the party in question that Christian fortitude should overcome desire, and keep him from so dangerous a marriage. 2. If the Pastors see that their warnings are of no avail in warding off such a marriage, let them diligently consider whether every probable danger of perversion of the Catholic party is absent, in which case he may proceed with the marriage. 3. Let them inquire also whether the non-Catholic party agrees, and is prepared before God and Witnesses, to promise not to put any obstacle to having all

the children from the marriage educated in the true Religion. 4. Let the Pastors further consider what will be the probable outcome if they themselves decline to provide their ministry in the celebration of the wedding; whether this should be broken off, or whether, upon rejection by the Catholic Priest they would have recourse to a Minister not of the true Faith, and contract marriage in this presence without any provision for their children. 5. If the Catholic Priest foresees that this will probably result, he may permit them to contract marriage in his presence, lest they go to a non-Catholic minister. He must be careful, however, to make the necessary inquiries, lest perchance there be other impediments to the marriage, such as a defect by reason of Baptism, or of blood relationship, or something of the sort. 6. These marriages may not be sanctioned with that blessing which is prescribed in the *Roman Ritual* for the Mass for the Bride and Bridegroom.

FOURTH SESSION

(Besides those already mentioned, R. Mr. John Bolton, Pastor of Saint Joseph's and R. Mr. J. Thayer, Pastor of Boston were present.)

CONCERNING ARRANGEMENTS FOR DIVINE SERVICES AND THE OBSERVANCE OF FEASTS.

17. Circumstances demand that Divine Services on Sundays and feast days, in cities or places where there are many clerics, or where the laity have been suitably instructed in singing, and the other ministrations at the altar, should be arranged in one way, while another system is to be followed where there is only one priest, and no instuction has been given in the solemn celebration of Divine Services. In the aforementioned places, when the appointed hour has arrived, let the Litany of Loretto of the Blessed Virgin, who is the Patroness of this Diocese, be chanted. After this, let the first aspersion of holy water be solemnly given as prescribed in the Missal. Then let Mass be solemnly celebrated with chant. On more solemn days, if it be possible, let the Deacon and Subdeacon assist. When the Gospel is finished, let those prayers be read from the pulpit which are prescribed for all classes of men and for the welfare of the Republic. Next the Gospel of the day shall be read in the vernacular. Let the announcements of marriage banns, of the observance of feast days and days of fast be read; if anything else has occurred, the people should be told. Finally, there should be a sermon, such that the hearers shall be instructed to correct their faults, and encouraged to the perfection of the Christian life. In the afternoon service of vespers, after which the antiphons of the Blessed Virgin Mary proper to the season should be sung, and then let Benediction of the Blessed Sacrament be given with solemn singing. Afterwards there should be catechetical instruction. It is desirable that during the services some hymns or prayers be sung in the vernacular.

18. However, where there is only one priest who must do everything himself, let him hear confessions and make all the preparations for the Sacrifice. Unless the people prefer to sing, let him first of all recite in the vernacular the litany of the Most Holy Name of Jesus or of Loretto. After the aspersion of holy water let him begin Mass, and continue to the Gospel. Then let him follow the rest of the prescriptions as mentioned above. After Mass let him lead the whole congregation in a distinct, vernacular recitation of the Our Father, Hail Mary, the Apostles' Creed, and the acts of faith, hope, and charity, then dismiss the congregation, but the children and less educated persons should be kept so that they may be instructed and questioned on the chief points of the faith.

19. 1. At the beginning of our Episcopate, we entreated the Blessed Virgin Mary with Fervent prayers to be the principal patroness of our diocese, so that through her intercession the faith, whole-hearted devotion toward God and holiness of life, might flourish among the people committed to our care, and increase more and more. On the Feast of the Assumption of this same Most Blessed Virgin, we were consecrated the first bishop of Baltimore. Wherefore, while leading with especial devotion the honoring of so great a Patroness, we particularly exhort our Venerable Brethren to venerate with great devotion the Most Blessed Virgin, and to commend the same devotion often and earnestly to their flocks, so that they might realize that by her patronage a shining citadel has been set up in their midst. 2. We decree that the Sunday within the octave of the Feast of the Assumption, or the feast itself if it should happen to fall on a Sunday, should be observed as the titular feast of this Diocese, on which day the people should be exhorted by every means possible to receive piously and reverently the Sacraments of Penance and Holy Eucharist. Moreover, to nourish the piety of the faithful we have asked the Apostolic See to grant generous spiritual benefits on this day. If these should be granted, all of you will be informed.

20. Catholic merchants especially, but also all types of urban laborers, are not able, without serious loss, to abstain from merchandizing and other works on feast days, which non-Catholics are not bound to observe. Wherefore it is greatly to be feared, that, if this observance is rigorously demanded, some people in the future, who will not suffer so great a loss of temporal goods, will endanger their eternal salvation. Therefore, to solve this inconvenience, we decree that each man is to seek out his own pastor and look to his judgment in this matter. We advise our Venerable Brethren that where there is a grave reason, they should dispense these men from the observance of the feasts. Nevertheless, the obligation of hearing Mass remains, if there is more than one Mass celebrated in the place where the dispensation has been granted; if there is only one Mass, the men are urged to attend unless there is a grave inconvenience.

CONCERNING THE PROTECTION OF THE MORALS
OF THE CLERGY.

21. All the Clerics in this diocese, according to the decrees of various canons and especially of the council of Trent, *should dress in a manner befitting their state of life.* Let their dress not only be modest, but such as reminds themselves and others of their profession in life. Consequently, we decree that clerics shall always wear black clothes, or as close to black as possible.

22. Following the decrees of other Bishops, and as far as our condition allows, observing the canons of the Councils, we prohibit clerics to admit to their houses as cohabitants women whose morals are unfavorably suspect, or who have not yet reached forty years of age. We commit to our Vicars General the vigilant care of watching over the observance of this decree.

OF PROVIDING FOR THE LIVELIHOOD OF PASTORS AND OF
CARING FOR THOSE THINGS WHICH PERTAIN TO DIVINE WORSHIP.

23. As the number of Catholics increases and as they have already scattered widely throughout the various, far-distant regions of the American Republic, the problem has arisen in the vineyard of the Lord, much more than before, of a supply of laborers. Moreover, these laborers cannot be obtained or supported unless a subsidy for their upkeep is donated by the Faithful who are bound to do so by Divine precept. For, as the Apostle says, it is only just that "those who have sown among you a spiritual harvest, should reap from you a temporal harvest in return." I Cor. 9/11. Therefore, let the Faithful frequently be reminded of this obligation. Unless they fulfill it, they have only themselves to blame that they do not hear Mass on Sundays and feast days, nor partake of the sacraments in their great trials. Consequently, as long as they refuse to contribute to the support of the pastor in proportion to the amount of temporal goods God has given them, and so through their own fault fail to fulfill Divine and Ecclesiastical precepts, let them know that they are living in the state of sin, and are unworthy to receive absolution in the tribunal of Penance. Besides, let them realize that they shall not only render an account to God for their own sins, but also for the crass ignorance and vice of those poor people who, because of the miserable stinginess of the rich, remain untouched by Christian instruction. Therefore, in order that we might inaugurate here what is being done in other parts of the Christian world, a statute concerning the obligations of the faithful has been determined upon above. What remains to be said on this point we shall add to the instruction which shall be sent out at the same time with these statutes. It should be read to everyone.

CONCERNING THE BURIAL OF THOSE WHO HAVE NOT RECEIVED
THE SACRAMENTS OF PENANCE AND EUCHARIST DURING
THE PASCHAL TIME.

24. Your attention is called to the decree *"Omnis utriusque sexus"* of the Lateran Council. It enjoins upon all Christians annual confession and Communion during the Paschal time, and it declares that those who fail to obey this decree are cut off from the Church during their lifetime, and after death they will not receive ecclesiastical burial. Pastors should not forget to mention this decree each year. If it should ever happen that someone dies without giving any sign of repentance, one who has not obeyed so salutary a precept, a decision is not to be rashly made to give or not give him Christian burial, since the words of the council mean that the penalty is not automatic but must be imposed. If possible the judgment of the bishop or the Vicar General should be sought. However, since this is not always possible because of the great distances of these regions, the pastor should prudently consider the following: 1. Whether the deceased has abstained from the Eucharistic table over the course of many years or only at one or other time. 2. Whether he did this with great obstinacy and, as it were, in contempt of the Church. 3. Whether his morals were notoriously depraved and gave bad example. 4. If these points are established, we empower priests who have the care of souls and are not able to have recourse to ourself or to the vicar general, to give due thought to the aforementioned points with charity and heartfelt mercy toward the living and the dead, and then to proceed according to the tenor of the Lateran Council, if they so judge it to be for the greater glory of God and the future salvation of souls. We warn them, however, that they should never forget that the Church intends by this salutary discipline to hold the living to their obligations, rather than to punish the dead for whom she continually offers prayers by commending the faithful departed to the Divine mercy.

When these statutes had been drawn up by the Reverend Most Holy Bishop, a conference was held with his Venerable Brethren to determine whether the Holy See should be petitioned to erect a new diocese within the boundaries of the present diocese of Baltimore, or to appoint a coajutor for the Bishop of Baltimore. Rev. Mr. John Ashton then preached a sermon on the duties and qualities of the clergy. Finally a *Te Deum* was chanted and the Synod was called to a close.

AC   AAB   There is a letterpress copy published under Marechal (see CUA, Special Coll.).

[1] James Van Huffel, O.F.M., came to the United States in 1789 and returned to England in 1805. See Mar. 6, 1811.

[2] John Tessier, S.S., had taught at Viviers before coming to America.

[3] Anthony Garnier, S.S., scholar and linguist, returned to France in 1803.

[4] Pope Alexander III (d. 1181), *Corpus Juris Canonici* (Leipzig, 1581) II, 644.

AD MAJOREM DEI GLORIAM   Reverendissimus Episcopus Baltimori per litteras ad suum clerum directas die 27 Octobris anni 1791 significavit sibi statutum esse synodum Diocesanam celebrare in Ecclesia Baltimorensi die 7 Novembris ejusdem anni; omnesque suae Dioceseos Sacerdotes, qui animarum saluti et sacris ministeriis legitime vacabant, ad hanc synodum invitavit.

Huic igitur convocationi morem gerentes, die constituta convenire ad aedes Episcopales clerici sequentes [:]

Jacobus Pellentz Vicarius Generalis Episcopi per totam Diocesim   Jacobus Frambach   Robertus Molyneux Vic. Gen. Distr. Meridionalis   Fran. Ant. Fleming Vic Gen. Distr. Septentrionalis   Fran. Car. Nagot Praeses Sem. Epis. Sti Sulpicii   Joannes Ashton   Henricus Pile   Leonardus Neale   Carolus Sewall   Sylvester Boarman   Gulielmus Elling   Jacobus Van Huffel   Robertus Plunkett   Stanislaus Cerfoumont   Franciscus Beeston   Laurentius Grassl   Josephus Eden   Ludovicus Caesar Delavan   Joannes Tessier   Antonius Garnier

Sessio la. die 7a Novris.

Postquam convenissent omnes superpelliceis induti, Episcopus autem indutus rocheto, amictu, alba, cingulo, stola, et pluviali; et mitram pretiosam et baculum pastoralem gerens; hora decima iverunt processionaliter ad Ecclesiam Cathedralem Sancti Petri, in qua omnia parata sunt, ut in Pontificali Romano; et habito sermone ab Episcopo, omnes fidei professionem emiserunt; constitutisque promotoribus Reverendo Domino Leonardo Neale et Reverendo Domino Gulielmo Elling, et Secretario Reverendo Domino Francisco Beeston, sessio prorogata est usque ad horam tertiam pomeridianam.

Ses. 2a

Cum nihil sit in Religione aut sanctius aut pretiosius Sacramentis, praecipuo studio laborandum est, ut illa rite administrentur, et digne suscipiantur. Initium igitur ducendo a Baptismo per quem homimes Christianae Societati aggregantur, considerantesque nos hic terrarum inter plures Heterodoxorum sectas versari, quae baptismum vel omnino non administrant; vel non nisi adultis; vel, quoniam necessarium ad salutem esse negant, sunt parum in eo administrando diligentes; STATUIMUS,

1o. Ut rebaptizentur sub conditione, de quorum valido baptismo post diligentem inquisitionem, certitudo moralis nequit obtineri; ac ut infantes, urgente periculo, baptizati ab obstetricibus haereticis, aut etiam Catholicis, rebaptizentur simili modo, nisi Catholicae tales fuerint, ut nullus sit prudenti dubio locus de baptismo valide ab ipsis administrato. Cavendum tamen est animarum pastoribus, ne, omni omissa inquisitione, rebaptizent quoscunque qui prius a Sacerdote non fuerint baptizati; ne incidant in censuram irregularitatis latae ab Alexandro Papa Tertio contra baptismum iterantes.

2o. Statuimus, ut quantum a Pastoribus animarum fieri poterit, omnium a se batizatorum nomina et aetas, itemque Parentum et Patrinorum nomina in librum specialiter huic usui designatum referantur.

3o. Quando haeretici adulti, prius valide baptizati, ad fidem convertuntur, exigendum non est, ut omissae baptismi caeremoniae suppleantur.

De Sacramento Confirmationis

4o. Generatim loquendo, pro hac Diocesi statuimus Sacramentum Confirmationis non prius conferri pueris, quam rationis usum attigerint, ac Sacramenti Paenitentiae suscipiendi capaces fuerint, quamvis non raro ob circumstantias particulares etiam junioribus conferendum erit.

Sessio 3, habita die 8 Novembris

De Sacrosancta Eucharistia

5o. Ut SSum. Eucharistiae Sacrificium cum omni reverentia ac debito honore celebretur atque ut Fideles magis magisque excitentur ad summam devotionem erga immensum hoc divinae in nos misericordiae pignus, volumus ut frequenter populus moneatur, quam indecorum sit, omnia, quae Sacrificio inserviunt, vilia esse et squallida, non vestes, non pannos, non candelas cereas, non sacra vasa tantis mysteriis conficiendis congruentia. Moneantur de summa diligentia, qua Deus in Veteri Testamento praecepit, ut omnia curarentur ad divinum cultum spectantia. Quanto potius igitur hoc a Christianis fieri convenit, qui non, ut Judaei, umbram bonorum possident, sed ipsam veritatem tenent, atque figurarum omnium complementum? Moneantur item de oblationibus, quas in Sacrificio primi Christiani semper contulerunt; doceanturque ipsos divinae gloriae maxime incurios esse, qui nihil conferunt ad ea suppeditanda, sine quibus, Religionis exercitiis sua dignitas et auctoritas videtur detrahi; et SSaa. Eucharistiae cultus multum imminuitur.

6o. Statuimus igitur, ut in singulis congregationibus duo aut tres praecipuae virtutis ac auctoritatis viri, tamquam Ecclesiae curatores a Pastore, vel ab ipsis congregationibus eligantur, atque ut Dominicis et Festis diebus curatores taliter constituti, post lectum in Missa Evangelium, collectionem oblationum faciant.

7o. Oblationes, juxta antiquum Ecclesiae morem, dividantur in tres partes, si necesse fuerit; ita ut una Sacerdotis sustentationi, una sublevandis pauperum necessitatibus, et altera comparandis quae sunt divino cultui necessaria, et fabricae Ecclesiarum applicetur. Si vero aliunde Sanctuarii Ministris de alimonia, et pauperibus de summa inopia provisum fuerit, omnes oblationes conferantur ad comparanda sacra vasa, caeteraeque divino cultui opportuna, et ad Ecclesias reparandes, vel opportunis locis construendas.

8o. Factae a fidelibus oblationes, ut Deum sibi, suisque per SSum Missae Sacrificium propitium reddant, ita recipiantur ab iis, qui altari deserviunt, ut omnem avaritiae aut simoniacae labis speciem evitent; eoque stipendio contenti sint, quod neque grave erit conferentibus; neque ita modicum, ut Sacerdotale ministerium vile ac nullius valoris ab imperitis existimari possit.

9o. Pro exhibenda majori erga Venerabile Missae Sacrificium reverentia, Sacerdotes in eo celebrando, veste talari nigra semper utantur, quantum sine magno incommodo fieri poterit; ac eadem etiam in caeteris ministeriis publicis, cum superpelliceo et stola, induti appareant.

10o. Experientia notum est multum conferre ad omnem reliquae vitae rationem, atque adeo ad aeternam cujusque salutem, qua animi praeparatione prima vice Sanctum Eucharistiae Sacramentum sumpserit: Quare omnis ab animarum Pastoribus adhibenda est diligentia, ut ante primam communionem juvenes in doctrina Christiana sint probe educati; ac praecipue ut conscientias ab omni gravioris peccati labe integras habeant; ad quem finem eos monere oportebit, ut generalem ante actae vitae confessionem, post sedulum sui examen, et cum magna cordis contritione, communioni praemittant. Cavendum quoque erit Pastoribus, ne hujus primae communionis tempus nimium protrahatur; neque tamen ut ad illam admittantur, statim ac rationis usum adepti fuerint: Sed quoniam summa Eucharistiae excellentia majorem exigit judicii maturitatem, perfectior rationis usus est expectandus.

De Sacramento Paenitentiae

11o. Ut hoc Sacramento, quod sanandis conscientiarum vulneribus tam salubriter a Christo institutum fuit, imperiti aut indigni Presbyteri ad animarum perniciem non abutantur, PROHIBEMUS, sub paena suspensionis ab omni exercitio Ordinis IPSO FACTO incurrendae et nobis reservatae, ne quis Sacerdos, sive saecularis sive regularis, a nobis, aut a Vicario Nostro Generali ad excipiendas Confessiones non approbatus, aut cujus approbatio revocata fuerit, illi ministerio se ingerere praesumat, extra casum necessitatis, Intelligant etiam fideles, qui ad hujusmodi Sacerdotis ministerium recurrerint, sese nullatenus a peccatis suis absolutos fore, sed etiamnum obnoxios remanere oneri illa iterum in Tribunali paenitentiae alteri Sacerdoti legitime approbato exponendi.

12o. PROHIBEMUS etiam sub poena suspensionis infligendae, ne quis Sacerdos, relicta Congregatione ejus curae commissa, ad aliam se transferat, nobis non consentientibus, et in ea sedem figere, et munera parochialia peragere praesumat.

De Sacramento Extremae Unctionis

13o. Conferri debet hoc Sacramentum etiam pueris vel puellis in articulo mortis constitutis, si rationis usum attigerint, ita ut peccati capaces sint.

De Sacramento Matrimonii

14o. Vagi et peregrini ad Matrimonium non sunt admittendi, nisi post tres publicationes factas, juxta praescriptum Concilii Tridentini; aut nisi testimonium omnino sufficiens habuerint a Pastoribus loci, unde discesserunt, ipsos conjugali vinculo liberos esse.

15o. Nullus ad Matrimonium admittitur, qui doctrinam Christianam, aut principalia fidei mysteria ignorat. Hic tamen ex Concilio quodam Limano addendum duximus sequens Decretum quod usui et solamini aliquando erit animarum curatoribus in hac diocesi, ubi multi sunt servi Africani, ut de aliis tacaemus, qui variis de causis parum de rebus fidei instrui possunt. Agitur enim in hoc decreto de illis hominibus, qui doctrinam Christianam juxta methodum, qua ab aliis memoriae mandatur, nullo modo addiscere valent, ad Sacramenta tamen accedere, et signanter matrimonium contrahere cupiunt; atque ita cum iis agendum statuitur: "Qui vero iis tantis impedimentis gravati fuerint, ut copiosiorem Catechesim non admittant, doceantur demum pro suo modo praecipua fidei capita, scilecet unum esse Deum omnium rerum auctorem, qui accedentes ad se vita aeterna remuneret, improbos et rebelles aeternis suppliciis in alio saeculo puniat: Deinde hunc ipsum Deum esse Patrem, et Filium, et Spiritum Sanctum, tres quidem personas, sed unum Deum verum: praeterea filium Dei, propter reparandam salutem hominum, factum hominem ex Virgine Maria, pro nobis passum, et mortuum, ac tandem resurrexisse, et regnare in aeternum. Hunc esse Jesum Christum Dominum, et Salvatorem nostrum: postremo neminem posse esse salvum, nisi credat in Jesum Christum, et paenitens de peccatis commissis, Sacramenta ipsius suscipiat; Baptismatis quidem, si infidelis est; confessionis autem, si lapsus post Baptismum; ac denique statuat ea servare, quae Deus, et Ecclesia Sancta praecipiunt, quorum summa est, ut Deum diligat super omnia, et proximum sicut seipsum."

160. Omnem adhibeant sollicitudinem animarum Pastores, ne Catholici ineant matrimonia cum Heterodoxis: sed quoniam propter continuum eorum inter se, in omni vita civilis ratione, commercium, fieri non potest, ut huiusmodi matrimonia aliquando non contrahantur, praecipue in illis locis, in quibus pauci admodum habitant Catholici; auditis super hac re Confratrum nostrorum in hac Synodo praesentium sententiis, regulas sequentes condidimus, secundum quas circa praedicta matrimonia procedere debent Sacerdotes, quibus in hac Diocesi cura animarum committitur. 1o. Partem Catholicam graviter ac serio moneant de ingentibus incommodis quae ex ejusmodi nuptiis non raro proveniunt, hortenturque, ut Christianae fortitudinis memores sua desideria superent, ac a periculoso matrimonio abstineant. 2o. Si viderint Pastores sua monita ad matrimonium impediendum non profutura, diligenter considerent, num absit omne probabile periculum perversionis partis Catholicae, casu, quo ad matrimonium procedatur. 3o. Inquirant etiam, an pars acatholica consentiat, ac parata sit coram Deo et testibus promittere se nullatenus obstaculo fore, quominus proles omnis ex matrimonio oriunda in vera Religione educetur. 4o. Considerent ulterius pastores, quid probalilius eventurum sit, si ipsi ministerium suum matrimonio celebrando exhibere abnuerint; an hoc abrumpendum; an vero a sacerdote Catholico rejecti ad Ministrum a vera fide alienum sint sese recepturi, coramque ipso contracturi, nulla facta conventione de futura prole. 5o. Si praevideatur postremum hoc probabilius eventurum permittat illis Sacerdos Catholicus, ut coram se contrahant, ne adeant ministrum haereticum; adhibita tamen prius debita inquisitione, ne forte alia impedimenta matrimonio obstent; v.g., defectus baptismi, consanguinitas, aut quid aliud. 6o. Hae nuptiae benedicendae non sunt illa benedictione, quam dandam praescribit Rituale Romanum intra Missam pro Sponso et Sponsa.

Sessio 5a

(cui praeter omnes jam enumeratos astiterunt R. D. Joannes Bolton, Pastor
Sancti Josephi et R. D. E. Thayer, pastor Bostoniae.)

De Ordinandis divinis officiis et festorum observatione

17o. Exigit necessitas, ut aliter ordinentur divina officia Dominicis ac
festis diebus, in civitatibus ac locis, ubi plures sunt Clerici, aut Laici idonei et
instituti ad cantum, et reliqua altaris ministeria; aliter vero, ubi unicus est
Sacerdos nec ulla facultate instructus ad officia divina solemniter peragenda.
In prioribus illis locis, hora competenti, decantentur Litaniae Lauretanae
Beatissimae Virginis, hujus Diocaeseos Patronae principalis, quibus finitis,
solemniter fiat aspersio aquae Benedictae, uti in Missali praescribitur; dein
Missa cum cantu solemniter celebretur; et solemnioribus diebus, si fieri
potest, assistentibus Diacono, et Subdiacono. Finito Evangelio, e suggestu
legantur preces praescriptae pro omnibus hominum ordinibus et felici statu
reipublicae; Evangelium item proprium illius Dei lingua vernacula; fiant
publicationes pro matrimoniis habendis, pro observandis festis diebus, aut
jejuniorum; et si quae alia occurrant de quibus monendus est populus; deinde
sermo habeatur, qui talis sit, ex quo et erudiri auditores, et emendari et ad
vitae Christianae perfectionem animari possint. In officio pomeridiano ves-
perae, iisque finitis, antiphona Beatae Mariae Virginis tempori propria debent
cantari, deinde fiat benedictio cum Sanctissimo Sacramento et solemni cantu
in ejus honorem; ac postea instructio catechistica. Optandum est, ut inter
officia, hymni aliqui aut preces lingua vernacula cantentur.

18o. Ubi vero unicus est Sacerdos, qui solus omnia peragat, expeditis
confessionibus omnibusque ad Sacrificium paratis, recitet primo, nisi assis-
tentes cantari velint, lingua vernacula litanias vel Sacratissimi Nominis Jesu,
vel Lauretanas; quibus finitis, et facta aspersione aquae benedictae, Missam
incipiat, peragatque usque ad Evangelium; deinde caetera prosequatur, uti
superius dictum est; ac post missam, ipso praesente, omni Congregatio dis-
tincte recitet lingua vernacula orationem Dominicam, Salutationem Angeli-
cam, symbolum Apostolorum, atque actus fidei, spei et charitatis, atque ita
conventum dimittat, retentis pueris ac rudioribus personis, ut illos de
praecipuis fidei capitibus interroget ac instruat.

19o. 1o. Initio nostri Episcopatus, Beatam Virginem Mariam in Nostrae
Dioeceseos Patronam principalem ardentibus votis compellavimus, et, ipsa
intercedente, fides atque omnis in Deum pietas, morumque sanctimonia in
populo nobis commisso vigeant, ac magis magisque augeantur. Festo Assump-
tionis ejusdem Beatissimae Virginis die, in primum Baltimori Episcopum
fuimus consecrati; quare singulari cultu tantam Patronam honorandam
ducentes, hortamur imprimis Venerabiles Confratres Nostros, ut et ipsi devotione Beatissimam Virginem venerentur, idemque saepe et serio suis ovibus
commendent, atque ut in ejus patrocinio praeclarum sibi praesidium constitui
existiment. 2o. Statuimus Dominicam quae erit infra octavam Festi Assump-
tionis aut ipsum Festum, si in Dominicam inciderit, tamquam festum princi-
pale hujus Dioeceseos habendum esse, in quo populus omni ratione excitandus
erit ad pie sancteque suscipienda sacramenta Paeniteniae et Eucharistiae. Ad

fovendam autem Fidelium pietatem, nos sedi Apostolicae humiles preces porrigemus pro obtinendis in hoc festum amplissimis gratiis spiritualibus, de quibus, si concessae fuerint, omnes fient certiores.

20o. Catholici, mercatores praesertim ac omnis generis opifices, qui in oppidis degunt, non sine gravi damno a mercibus vendendis, aut ab operibus abstinere possunt, festis illis diebus, quae ab Heterodoxis similiter non servantur; unde merito timendum, si hoc rigorose exigitur, aliquos futuros, qui ne tantam rerum temporalium jacturam faciant, aeternae salutis periculum incurrent. Ut igitur huic incommodo obviam eatur, statuimus unumquemque debere suum pastorem convenire, ejusque hac in re judicium expectare; monemusque Venerabiles Confratres Nostros, ut ubi exigit gravis causa, cum ipsis dispensent in festorum observatione; relicta tamen obligatione missam audiendi, si plures quam una celebrentur in loco ubi dispensatur, vel si illi uni sine gravi detrimento assistere valeant.

De Conservandis Clericorum Moribus

21o. Omnes Clerici in hac diocesi, juxta decreta variorum canonum, et maxime Concilii Tridentini, *vestes gerant suo ordini congruentes;* hoc est quae non solum sint modestae, sed etiam quae ipsum eas gerentem aliosque moneant, cujus conditionis ille sit. quare decernimus, ut Clerici semper vestes gerant, vel nigras, vel nigris proximas.

22o. Inhaerentis decretis aliorum Episcoporum et quantum patitur nostra conditio, Conciliorum canonibus, prohibemus, ne Clerici ad cohabitandum in suis aedibus admittant feminas, de quarum moribus aliqua fuerit sinistra suspicio, aut quae quadragesimum aetatis annum non expleverit; et Vicariis nostris Generalibus committimus, ut hujus decreti custodiae summa diligentia invigilent.

De Providenda Sustentatione Pastorum et Pro Curandis Iis Quae ad Cultum Divinum Requiruntur.

23o. Crescente numero Catholicorum, iisque dispersis per varias longeque dissitas Foederatae Americae plagas, opus est in vinea Domini multo majori quam olim fuerat, operariorum copia, qui tamen obtineri non possunt, aut conservari nisi subsidium pro eorum alimonia a Fidelibus conferatur, uti divino praecepto conferre tenentur, dicente Apostolo aequum esse, ut, *qui spiritualia aliis seminant, de carnalibus ipsorum metant.* I Cor. 9/11. Itaque Fideles de hac obligatione frequenter moneantur, cui nisi satisfaciant, sibi ipsis debent imputare, quod neque Dominicis, et festis diebus missam audiant, neque sacramentorum in summis suis necessitatibus fiant participes. Unde quamdiu pro mensura temporalium bonorum sibi a Deo concessorum ad salutis ministerium conferre renuunt, adeoque praecepta Divina et Ecclesiastica sua culpa non implent; sciant se versari in statu peccati, indignosque esse reconciliationis in Paenitentiae tribunali obtinendae; neque tantum de suis peccatis rationem Deo reddituros, sed etiam de illorum pauperum crassa ignorantia ac vitiis, qui propter ditiorum miseram parcimoniam instructionis

Christianae manent omnino expertes. Ut igitur, quod fit in aliis orbis Xtiani partibus, apud nos quoque initium habeat, jam superius de fidelium oblationibus aliqua statuta fuit; ac caetera quae hac de re dicenda sunt, adjungemus in instructione, quae cum his statutis simul mittetur, et coram omnibus legenda erit.

De Sepeliendis Iis, Qui Tempore Paschali Paenitentiae et Eucharistiae Sacramenta non Suscipiunt.

24o. Notum est decretum Concilii Lateranensis, *Omnis utriusq sexus,* quo praecipitur omnibus Christianis confessio et communio annua circa tempus Paschale, et decernitur contra eos, qui decreto non obtemperant, ut vivi *ab ecclesia arceantur,* mortui vero *sepultura Ecclesiastica careant.* Pastores ne negligant singulis annis, hujus decreti memoriam revocare; et si quando contigerit quempiam e vivis decedere sine ulla paenitentiae significatione, qui tam salutari praecepto morem non gessit, nihil temere statuatur de sepultura Xtiana ipsi danda vel neganda, quoniam verba concilii important, sententiam non latam sed ferendam; verum Episcopi aut Vicarii generalis judicium si fieri potest, expectetur. Quoniam autem propter magnam locorum distantiam id semper dieri non potest, consideret secum prudens pastor: 1o. an mortuus per multos annos, an autem uno tantum vel altero a mensa Eucharistica se abstinuerit; 2o. an id fecerit cum magna contumacia et quasi contemptu Ecclesiae; 3o. an illius mores aliunde fuerint notorie depraevati et mali exempli. 4o. His concurrentibus, potestatem facimus sacerdotibus qui curam animarum agunt, et ad nos vel Vicarium Generalem recurrere non possunt, omnia prius aestimando in charitate et visceribus misericordiae erga vivos et defunctum, procedendi juxta tenorem Conc. Lateran., si ita ad majorem Dei gloriam et animarum salutem profuturum judicaverint. Monemus autem, ut numquam non reminiscantur, velle ecclesiam hac salutari disciplina, viventes potius in officio continere, quam punire mortuos, pro quibus preces continuo offert, omnes Fideles defunctos divinae misericordiae commendando.

His a Rev. Smo. Episcopo constitutis, habita cum Ven. confratibus collocutione de proponenda Sae. Sedi erectione novae Dioeceseos intra fines hujus quae nunc est Baltimorensis, vel de coadjutore Episcopi Baltimorensis designando; concionem habuit Rev. D. Joannes Ashton de clericorum officiis ac virtutibus, et deinde, dicto hymno, *Te Deum,* finis Synodo impositus est.

SPIRITUAL FACULTIES OF THE CLERGY [Nov. 12, 1791]

John, By the Grace of God, and the Favor of the Apostolic See, Bishop of Baltimore, Salvation in the Lord

Confident in your virtue, learning and prudence, we entrust to you the following faculties in our Diocese, and they will be valid until

1. Of dispensing in whatsoever irregularities, except in those which arise either from true bigamy, voluntary homicide, or from the exercise of Order

or jurisdiction, while someone is suspended from it by a judgment rendered by us; and also in the prior cases, if there was a foreseen necessity of workers in some place; however, only with respect to voluntary homicide, scandal is not to arise from this kind of dispensation.

2. Of dispensing and absolving simple vows in favor of other pious works; and dispensing for a reasonable cause from simple vows of Religion.

3. Of absolving and dispensing in whatever case of simony both in fact in benefices in which one has been dismissed and above increment in those incorrectly taken, some work of charity being enjoined and salutary penance, by the free will of the one dispensing, or even if the benefices have been retained, if they were parochial, and are those who as men in charge of parochial matters are not able.

4. Of dispensing among Catholics only in the third and fourth degree of consanguinity: and from simple affinity in the second, third and fourth degrees of mixed marriages; not, however, in the second, only with respect to future marriages: indeed, with respect to the past, of dispensing only in the second degree, only if in no way the first grade is touched, since among those who from heresy or infidelity are converted to the Catholic Faith, and in the stated cases, the offspring brought forth are declared legitimate.

5. Of dispensing with respect to the impediment of Public Honesty, arising from just nuptials.

6. Of dispensing with respect to the impediment of crime, nevertheless with no deception on the part of the spouses, and of restoring the right to the marital act which was lost.

7. Of dispensing in the impediment of spiritual kinship, with respect to the one alleviating, and the one alleviated. However, bear in mind that these matrimonial dispensations are not to be granted, unless under the condition, that the woman has not been raped; and if she has been raped, that she does not continue in the power of the rapist.

8. Of dispensing for Gentiles and Infidels having many wives, so that after conversion and baptism, they may be able to retain the one whom they prefer from them, if only she is faithful, unless the first one wished to be converted.

9. Of administering all the Sacraments, Confirmation and Orders excepted.

10. Of absolving from heresy and Apostasy from Faith, and from Schism, extending even to ecclesiastics, both secular and religious, nevertheless not those, who were from places where a holy office is exercised; unless in places of the missions, in which heresies arose with impunity, they have ceased; nor those who have perjured themselves in a court of law, unless they were born, where heresies arose with impunity; and after the judicial absolution, those who have fallen into heresy again have returned from it, and those only in the forum of conscience. Here, it is to be noted, that in our Diocesan Synod, it has been approved by us in the following words. "We prohibit under pain of suspension from every exercise of Order, incurred 'ipso facto' lest a priest,

either Secular or Religious, not approved by us or by our Vicar General for receiving confessions, or whose approbation was revoked, presumes to enter into that ministry outside a case of necessity."[1]

11. Of absolving from all cases reserved to the Holy See, also contained in the Bull, *Coena Domini:*[2] nonetheless, never of absolving an accomplice in some sin against the sixth commandment.

12. Of bestowing three times in the year a plenary indulgence upon one who is contrite, who has confessed and received Holy Communion: again, of granting a plenary indulgence first to those converted from heresy; and indeed to the faithful whosoever in the hour of death, at least with respect to the contrite, if they are not able to confess.

13. Of applying to himself the same indulgences.

14. Of blessing the altar linens and the other vessels necessary for the sacrifice of the Mass, when the sacred oil is not contained therein; and of reconciling polluted Churches with water blessed by the Bishop, and, in case of necessity, also water not blessed by the Bishop.

15. When individual second weekdays do not impede, in the office, nine lessons, or, if impeded, on the day following, of celebrating Mass of the dead on any altar, even a portable altar, of freeing souls by their intention from the pains of Purgatory through suffrages.

16. Of holding and reading, but those books of heretics or infidels about their religion for the purpose of defending against them in speech or writing.

17. Of bringing Holy Communion secretly to the sick, without lit candles, and of keeping it there for these same sick people, but in a decorous place if there might be danger of sacrilege from heretics and unbelievers.

18. Of putting on secular dress, and otherwise at places where required to travel or where he was not able to remain in them [clergy attire].

19. Of reciting the rosary or other prayers, if he was not able to bring along his breviary with him, or was not able to recite his divine office because of a legitimate impediment.

20. Of dispensing, when it would seem to be expeditious, with respect to the eating of meat, eggs, and products made of milk, in a time of fasting, and in Lent.

21. Of celebrating [Mass] for one hour before dawn, and for three hours after noon, without an assistant, both under the sky and under the earth, nonetheless in a fitting place, even though the altar is broken, or without the relics of the saints, even in the presence of schismatic heretics and infidels. Given [*blank*] on the [*blank*] day [*blank*] in the year

L   AAB   Dated by reference to the First National Synod in this document.

[1] Third Session, Nov. 8, 1791.

[2] "On the Lord's Supper," as titled indicated the accumulation over the years of the excommunications for violations of faith and morals, which were regularly read to the faithful on Maundy Thursday of Holy Week. Although the issue of the bull was suspended by Clement XIV in 1773, the practice of this reference was not abrogated until 1869 by Pius IX.

JOANNES DEI ET APLCAE. SEDIS GRATIA, EPISCOPUS BALTIMORI SALUTEM IN DOMINO.

Tua virtute, doctrina et prudentia fidentes, committimus tibi facultates sequentes in nostra Dioecesi, valituras usque ad

1a. Dispensandi in quibuscumque irregularitatibus, exceptis illis, quae proveniunt vel ex bigamia vera, homicidio voluntario, vel ab exercitio Ordinis aut jurisdictionis, dum quis ex sententia a nobis prolata ab illo suspenditur; et etiam, in duobus prioribus casibus, si praecisa necessitas operariorum in loco aliquo fuerit: modo tamen quoad homicidium voluntarium ex hujusmodi dispensatione scandalum non oriatur.

2a. Dispensandi et absolvendi vota simplicia in alia pia opera; et dispensandi ex rationabili causa in votis simplicibus castitatis, et Religionis.

3a. Absolvendi et dispensandi in quacunque simonia et in reali dimissis beneficiis, et super fructibus male perceptis, injuncta aliqua eleemosyna vel paenitentia salutari, arbitrio dispensantis, vel etiam retentis beneficiis, si fuerint parochialia, et non sint, qui parochiis praefici possint.

4a. Dispensandi *inter Catholicos tantum* in 3o et 4o gradu consang: et affin. simplici, et in 2o, 3o et 4o mixtis; non tamen in 2o solo quoad futura matrimonia: quo vero ad praeterita, dispensandi in 2o solo. dummodo nullo modo attingat primum gradum, cum iis, qui ab haeresi vel infidelitate convertuntur ad fidem Catholicam, et in praefatis casibus prolem susceptam declarandi legitimatam.

5a. Dispensandi super impedimento publicae honestatis justis ex sponsalibus proveniente.

6a. Dispensandi super impedimento criminis, neutro tamen conjugum machinante, et restituendi jus amissum petendi debitum.

7a. Dispensandi in impedimento cognationis spiritualis, praeterquam inter levantem et levatum. —Advertatur autem non concedi has matrimoniales dispensationes, nisi sub conditione, quod mulier rapta non fuerit; et si rapta fuerit, in potestate raptoris non existat.

8a. Dispensandi cum Gentilibus et infidelibus plures uxores habentibus, ut post conversionem et baptismum, quam maluerint ex illis, si etiam fidelis fiat, retinere possint, nisi prima voluerit converti.

9a. Administrandi omnia Sacramenta, confirmatione et Ordine exceptis.

10a. Absolvendi ab haeresi et Apostasia a fide, et a schismate, quoscunque etiam ecclesiasticos, tam saeculares quam regulares, non tamen eos, qui ex locis fuerint, ubi sanctum officium exercetur; nisi in locis missionum, in quibus impune grassantur haereses, deliquerint; nec illos, qui judicialiter abjuraverint, nisi nati sint, ubi impune grassantur haereses; et post judicialem absolutionem illuc reversi in haeresim fuerint relapsi, et hos in foro conscientiae tantum. Notandum hic est, quod in nostra Synodo Dioecesana sancitum a nobis fuit sequentibus verbis. "Prohibemus sub poena suspensionis ab omni exercitio Ordinis, ipso facto incurrendae, ne quis Sacerdos sive Saecularis, sive Regularis, a nobis aut Vicario nostro Generali ad excipiendas confessiones non approbatus, aut cujus approbatio revocata fuerit, illi ministerio ingerere se praesumat extra casum necessitatis."

11a. Absolvendi ab omnibus casibus Sedi Apostolicae reservatis, etiam in Bulla *Coenae Domini* contentis: Nunquam tamen absolvendi complicem in aliquo peccato contra sextum praeceptum.

12a. Largiendi ter in anno indulgentiam plenariam contritis, confessis ac sacra communione refectis: Item concedendi indulgentiam plenariam primo conversis ab haeresi; atque etiam fidelibus quibuscunque in articulo mortis, saltem contritis, si confiteri non valeant.

13a. Lucrandi sibi easdem indulgentias.

14a. Benedicendi paramenta et alia utensilia ad sacrificium Missae necessaria, ubi non intervenit unctio sacra; et reconciliandi Ecclesias pollutas aqua ab Episcopo benedicta, et, in casu necessitatis, etiam aqua ab Episcopo non benedicta.

15a. Singulis secundis feriis non impeditis, officio novem lectionum, vel iis impeditis, die immediate sequenti, celebrandi Missam *de requiem* in quocunque altari etiam portatili liberandi animas secundum eorum intentionem a Purgatorii paenis per modum suffragii.

16a. Tenendi et legendi non tamen aliis concedendi libros haereticorum vel infidelium de eorum religione tractantium, ad effectum eos impugnandi voce vel scriptis.

17a. Deferendi Sanm Scmtum occulte ad infirmos sine lumine, illudque sine eodem retinendi pro iisdem infirmis, in loco tamen decenti, si ab haereticis vel infidelibus sit periculum sacrilegii.

18a. Induendi vestibus saecularibus, si aliter ad loca ipsi commissi transire, vel in iis permanere non poterit.

19a. Recitandi rosarium vel alias preces, si breviarium secum deferre, vel divinum officium ob legitimum impedimentum recitare non poterit.

20a. Dispensandi, quando expedire videbitur, super esu carnium, ovorum, et lacticiniorum tempore jejuniorum et quadragesimae.

21a. Celebrandi per unam horam ante auroram, et per tres horas post meridiem, sine ministro et sub dio et sub terra, in loco tamen decenti, etiamsi altare sit fractum, vel sine reliquuis Sanctorum, vel praesentibus haereticis schismaticis et Infidelibus.

Datum [*blank*] die [*blank*] anno

TO FRANCIS BEESTON[1]   Baltimore Nov. 16. 1791.

When Christ honoured the Institution of marriage by raising it to the dignity and sanctity of a Sacrament, he intended to create in all who were to enter into that state a great respect for it; and to lay on them an obligation of preparing themselves for it by purifying their consciences, & disposing them worthily to receive abundant communications of divine grace. He subjected thereby to the authority and jurisdiction of his church the manner and rites of its celebration, lest any should violate and profane so holy an Institution, by engaging in marriage without due consideration of its sanctity and obligations. It is judged necessary to say this, because lately some of the Congregation have been so regardless of their duty in this respect, as to recur to the ministry of those whom the Catholic Church never honoured with the commission of administering marriage. The persons here spoken of, & others, who have followed their example, hereby rendered themselves guilty of a sacrilegious profanation of a most holy institution, at the very moment of their marriage. It must be left to themselves to consider, whether they can expect much happiness in a state into which they entered by committing an offence so grievous & dangerous to their faith.

To prevent, as much as lies in our powers, a renewal of such profanation and sacrilege, you are desired, Revd. Sir, as well as our other Revd. Brethren, to make known to all that whoever have lately, or hereafter shall be guilty of applying to be married by any other, than the lawful pastors of our Church cannot be admitted to reconciliation & the Sacraments, till they shall agree to make public acknowledgement of their disobedience, before the assembled Congregation & beg pardon for the scandal, they have given. J. Bishop of Baltimore.

ALS   AAB
¹ Lack of a salutation indicates the letter was intended for all of the clergy, which the first sentence of the second paragraph makes clear. This is a semi-official directive related to the recent synod.

MESSRS. ZACHARIE AND LATIL.¹   Balt. Dec. 2d. 1791

Gentlemen,   I have paid very great attention to the subject, which you were pleased to lay before me yesterday evening; and take the liberty of requesting you to communicate this my answer to the Gentlemen, who intended to honour me by their visit, and their request to join next monday in thanksgiving for the royal assent, being given to the new Constitution of France. I wish to bear every testimony of respect to a nation, whose great, as well as amiable qualities have always attracted my esteem and attachment; and to which I owe, as an American, so much gratitude. If the Constitution lately approved by his most Christian Majesty, had done no more, than to assert to a generous people a free government, and political happiness, I would concur with joy and exultation in celebrating so happy an event. But you are not ignorant, Gentlemen, that some parts of this Constitution relate particularly to Ecclesiastical concerns; and you know that the chief pastor of the Church, and almost all the Bishops of France, perhaps the most respectable body of prelates in the world, object to some clauses of the Ecclesiastical constitution, as altering the principles of our faith, and violating those rights of spiritual jurisdiction, which being derived from God, and not from men, are not within the competency of any authority merely human. Such is the judgement, which my respectable Brethren in the Episcopacy have passed on certain arrangements in that Constitution, to which the king has given his sanction: their authority is, and ought to be, great with me.[2] Does it become me, the least of Bishops, to approve, what the great body of the first pastors has so generally disapproved? And would I not be a hypocrite before God by thanking him with my life for that, which I have reason to apprehend may be injurious to his religion?

I have as many reasons for wishing to give you proofs of my utmost respect, that nothing but the imperious voice of duty, could withold me from complying with your desire. I earnestly pray, that your country may derive much increase of happiness, and dignity from the improvements made in its civil constitution; and that its attachment may become still greater to the principles, and duties of that holy religion, which for so many ages has been its glory and happiness. I have the honour to be with great respect &c.

MS   C   AAB   Copy in contemporary hand for Lord Arundell.

[1] Possibly Stephen Zacharie of New Orleans. See from same, Jan. 19, 1803 (8T2).

[2] Reference to the Civil Constitutions of the Clergy and the oath required of the clergy, more than fifty percent of whom declined.

TO CHARLES PLOWDEN   Dec. [?] −22d[1791−92]

[. . . .] will not succeed. You perhaps remember Lucas, who took to profligate courses, & married a rich young widow soon after he came over to Maryland with Mr. Hunter, above twenty years ago. After a negociation of some months with me, he has quitted his woman who on her side is become very penitent; he has retired to live, for a time of probation, with Mr. Walton; has given satisfaction; is very penitent and humble; and has made a public, written acknowledgment of the motives, which influenced him in his defection. I shall be much perplexed, what to do with him: he cannot be employed in Maryland, without offence to many; his former life has been so notoriously profligate; and he will not return to Europe. Chs. Wharton remains, as he was, living on a farm between this town and Philada., unpopular amongst his neighbours, & defeated in two or three attempts to get a living in the Protestant Episcopal, i.e., the Church of England. He is said to be an economist, &, with the produce of his own Estate, & one he got by his nominal wife, he contrives to live in a decent stile. I am told, that he now declines all attempts to obtain ecclesiastical preferment; & I have it from unquestionable authority, that his temper is become insufferable to those, who are always with him. He has lately acted a friendly part with his Brother, which gave me pleasure, & retrieved his character with respect to some instances of his former conduct towards this same Brother.

Dec. 22d. I was disappointed in sending this letter on the day of its first date: and no American Bottom (the only one now to be trusted) has sailed since for England from this port. I am not very safe in committing even to an

American; for, it seems, the Algerines are said to infest the Atlantick; and we much fear, that a misjudged and unwarrantable policy of the combined powers has let loose this enemy upon us; for, most certainly, the temper of this country was not to obstruct their operations.

I owe a letter to Mr. Stone and to my young relation Mr. Carroll:[1] but unless I can retard for one day the departure of the ship, they must excuse me for the present. A report has reached me, that another of our Countrymen at Liege & of a most valuable character, Mr. Matthews,[2] has engaged himself to the service of the Academy by the usual oath. I may be mistaken, as to the nature of this engagement: but, in my apprehension of it, the intervention of his Diocesan Bishop was a necessary preliminary. At all events, I have great cause to regret Mr. Young's[3] actual detention, & the future one of Mr. Matthews, while we are suffering so much for the want of labourers. The former will surely not fail to revisit us as soon, as the present scholastic year has expired.

Will you excuse me, my Dr. Sir, for inclosing to your care a letter for Mr. Connell. I was preparing a packet for Rome by the way of Leghorn, as a vessel was loaded here, & ready to take her departure for that place about a fortnight ago, when the news of Algiers caused an alteration of her voyage. I therefore write now only to Mr. Connell, & beg you to call on Mr. Thos. Wright for the postage extraordinary. I have not yet made up my mind fully concerning a coadjutor; & I wish so to consult my most experienced Brethren, as to render his appointment rather their choice, than my arbitrary will. For, tho I am much opposed, as you or Mr. Milner to *Ecclesiastical democracy*,[4] yet I wish sincerely, that Bishops may be elected, at this distance from Rome, by a select body of Clergy, constituting, as it were, a Cathedral chapter. Otherwise, we never shall be viewed kindly by our government here, and discontents, even amongst our own Clergy, will break out.

Assure your dear young pupils, whom I suppose to be Thomas and my namesake John, of my tender & faithful remembrance. Give my love to Messrs. Young & Carroll, whose parents are well, having seen or heard from them very lately; & to Mr. Matthews. His uncle Leonard Neale is gone lately to Philada. to replace one of our deceased Brethren.

To these, let me add Messrs. Stone, Semmes, Ellerker, Wright, &c, and the Rev. Mother, perhaps the only one alive of my former numerous acquaintance on the Avroi: my young relation Kitty Carroll[5] must not be forgotten. When you can write any thing of poor Aston, which will not give pain, I shall be thankful for it. Here is a long letter with little interesting to relieve the trouble of reading it. My Dr. Mother, & Mr. Digges, she almost 89, he 83 years old, are your humble Sts. as you know   The writer of this is—

ALS   MPA   His mother was 92 in 1796. Date estimated by this and age 89 reference.
[1] Charles Carroll of Homewood, son of Charles Carroll of Carrollton, was at the Academy of Liege.

[2] William Matthews, cousin of Francis and Leonard Neale, came from Liege Academy and later was recorded as at Georgetown 1801–02.

[3] Dominic Young, O.P., accompanied his brother-in-law Edward Dominick Fenwick, O.P., to America in 1804–05.

[4] *Ecclesiastical Democracy Detected* (1792) by John Milner (1752–1826), Vicar-Apostolic of the Midland District in England, considered an extreme Catholic emancipationist and ultramontane.

[5] Catherine Carroll, daughter of Charles Carroll of Carrollton.

Bibliography

[Full titles of printed works referred to as sources for text or editing.]

American Catholic Historical Society of Philadelphia. *Records;* and *American Catholic Historical Researches.*

Brent, John Carroll. *Biographical Sketch of the Most Rev. John Carroll.* Baltimore, 1843.

Guilday, Peter. *The Life and Times of John Carroll, Archbishop of Baltimore.* 2 vols. New York, 1922. Reprinted by Arno Press, New York.

Hanley, Thomas O'Brien. *Charles Carroll of Carrollton: The Making of a Revolutionary Gentleman.* Washington, D.C., 1970.

——— *The American Revolution and Religion: Maryland 1770–1800.* Washington, D.C., 1972.

Hughes, Thomas. *History of the Society of Jesus in North America, Colonial and Federal: Documents;* and *Text.* 4 vols. New York, 1910.

Melville, Annabelle M. *John Carroll of Baltimore: Founder of the American Catholic Hierarchy.* New York, 1955.

Moran, Patrick F. *Spicilegium Ossoriense: Being a Collection of Original Letters and Papers Illustrative of the History of the Irish Church from the Reformation to the Year 1800.* Dublin, 1884.

O'Daniel, Victor F. *The Right Rev. Edward Dominic Fenwick, O.P., Founder of the Dominicans in the United States.* New York, 1920.

Ruane, Joseph W. *The Beginnings of the Society of St. Sulpice in the United States, 1791–1829.* Washington, D.C., 1935.

Shea, John Gilmary. *The Life and Times of the Most Rev. John Carroll, Bishop and First Archbishop of Baltimore.* New York, 1888.

Steiner, Bernard C. *Life and Correspondence of James McHenry.* Cleveland, 1907.